THE ENCYCLOPEDIA OF
FILMMAKERS

JOHN C. TIBBETTS AND JAMES M. WELSH

Contributing Editors
Gene Phillips, Tony Williams, Ron Wilson

Foreword by
Kevin Brownlow

Volume 1

Facts On File, Inc.

The Encyclopedia of Filmmakers

Copyright © 2002 by John C. Tibbetts and James M. Welsh

All rights reserved. No part of this book may be reproduced or utilized in any form or by any means, electronic or mechanical, including photocopying, recording, or by any information storage or retrieval systems, without permission in writing from the publisher. For information contact:

Facts On File, Inc.
132 West 31st Street
New York NY 10001

Library of Congress Cataloging-in-Publication Data
Tibbetts, John C.
The encyclopedia of filmmakers / John C. Tibbetts and James M. Welsh; contributing editors, Gene Phillips, Tony Williams, Ron Wilson; foreword by Kevin Brownlow.
p. cm
Includes filmographies, bibliographical references, and index.
ISBN 0-8160-4384-1 (set)—ISBN 0-8160-4779-0 (v. 1)—ISBN 0-8160-4780-4 (v. 2)
1. Motion picture producers and directors—Biography—Dictionaries. I. Welsh, James Michael. II. Phillips, Gene D. III. Title.

PN1998.2.T53 2002
791.43′0233′0922—dc21   2001033564

Facts On File books are available at special discounts when purchased in bulk quantities for businesses, associations, institutions, or sales promotions. Please call our Special Sales Department in New York at (212) 967-8800 or (800) 322-8755.

You can find Facts On File on the World Wide Web at http://www.factsonfile.com

Text design by Erika K. Arroyo
Cover design by Nora Wertz

Printed in the United States of America

VB Hermitage 10 9 8 7 6 5 4 3 2 1

This book is printed on acid-free paper.

CONTENTS

VOLUME 1

VOLUME 2

FOREWORD

CHASING THE PARADE

By Kevin Brownlow

I have always had a soft spot for film directors. The job is the hardest I have ever tackled, and to succeed (which I didn't) you need qualities of determination, patience, and creativity that very few human beings are born with. Politicians who circle the globe failing to end conflicts should be replaced by film directors, for they are the ideal people to charm both sides, to organize spectacular withdrawals, and then, so as not to disappoint anyone, to stage the battles—harmlessly—to show what might have been. The best of them are miracle workers.

Imagine what it is like, setting up a film, particularly nowadays when so many productions are made for so little. You have to work on the script, find the money (this can take years), track down the locations, supervise the sets, select the crew, persuade the cast, shoot tests, all the time worrying yourself sick about the inadequacies of the budget. Then, when you are near exhaustion, you are ready to go on the floor to make the picture. Critics should be barred from their job until they have done this at least once. Ideally, directors should be trained not in film schools but in the Marine Corps. Making a film is a lot like going to war (business class).

Historically, many directors were treated shabbily by Hollywood. They were well paid, admittedly, but having created the language of cinema, they became mere cogs in the machine. At the height of the studio system, in the 1930s and '40s, scripts were tossed to them along with the morning paper; they were assigned cast and crew and they didn't have the right even to edit their own picture. A few prominent directors kept a degree of creative control, but the fate of the majority was dependent on the feudal power of the producers.

Today, with stars commanding higher salaries than the budget for *Billy Elliott,* directors are often hired hands again. When a new poster goes up, I always look for the name of the director in the batch of credits contractually provided like the small print on the back of a medicine bottle. If you can read the director's name, the chances are it will mean nothing. What happens to all those poor fellows who make one feature and are never heard of again?

The good old days really were exceptional. In the 1920s the director was the whole show; he chose the story, and sometimes wrote it, selected the cast, staged every scene, and often edited the result himself. Producers in those happy days were content to run the studio. Only with the insidious rise of the so-called supervisor was the director's autonomy threatened. The producer put up the money and he wanted to be part of the creative process—at least he wanted people to think he was. I used to wonder what the producer actually did, because he always employed men to do his work for him—the supervisor, the associate producer, the production manager. If you look at the credits of a modern film you will often see as many as seven producers. The job of director has become more difficult than ever. It is tough enough to make a film under perfect conditions. To have to argue with seven producers, not to mention their battalions of yes men, must take all the pleasure out of filmmaking. It would drive me to drink.

Drink is a touchy subject in this context. It is astounding how many directors were alcoholics. Alcohol has always been the curse of the Irish, and most early film directors were Irish, or of Irish descent. Traditionally, Jews didn't drink, so it made sense for Jews to run the business and let the Irish make the pictures. The Irish had a sense of poetry and of theatre, a warmth in dealing with people and a colorful personality. That was, all too often, a euphemism for a drunk. But what drunks they were! Foremost among the great names of early cinema was the incorrigible Marshall (Mickey) Neilan, who made many of Mary Pickford's best pictures. His assistant was an important man, because Mickey would often be overcome by thirst and would leave the set in his charge. John Ford was more disciplined, and drank (to excess) only between pictures. Eddie Sutherland, a delightful fellow who directed many memorable comedies, was known as the Iron Man because he could go out all night and yet be able to direct in the morning. There ought to be a book devoted to the Alcoholic Film Director.

For if directing is hard, directing with a hangover must have been excruciating. George Fitz-maurice used to start the day with something undemanding—like a closeup of a door handle—so he could recover his momentum. To be able to produce so many magnificent pictures under those conditions is indeed astonishing and a tribute to the luck of the Irish. (There were a few Italians who liked the bottle as well, like the brilliant Gregory la Cava.) But there were plenty of sober directors, like King Vidor or Henry King, who made outstanding pictures from a deep love of the medium.

I became aware of these remarkable personalities when I began reading the old fan magazine *Photoplay,* which, under the editorship of James Quirk (Irish), was a fine periodical that took films—and their directors—seriously. It was in these pages that I first read about Rex Ingram, the handsome Dublin-born artist who made Valentino a star in *The Four Horsemen of the Apocalypse* (1921). When Valentino left, he made a star of another young Latin—Ramon Novarro. Deeply disappointed when MGM would not give him *Ben-Hur,* he went to the south of France and set up his own studio. It became a meeting point for artists—George Bernard Shaw, Isadora Duncan, Somerset Maugham. The stills photographer and sometime actor was Michael Powell. He and David Lean, who was profoundly impressed by Ingram's work, expressed their gratitude to Rex Ingram throughout their lives, just as subsequent directors proclaimed their debt to Powell and Lean.

The silent directors seemed to me of exceptional importance because they began it all. There was a generation before Ingram and Neilan and la Cava, however, which consisted mostly of middle-aged men from the theatre, who often took up movies as a last resort. The work was not considered respectable. These little-known names—Otis Turner, William Humphreys, Oscar Apfel—directed the one- and two-reelers that formed the nickelodeon programs. Their names seldom appeared on the films, which were close duplicates of the theatrical experience, filmed in master shot without any use of what we would call "cinema." And yet they could surprise you; Oscar Apfel's *The Passer-By* (1912) opened and closed with a scene of an old man recalling his youth. The camera tracked smoothly in, dissolved from the old to the young man, and reversed the procedure at the end. These early directors were superseded so quickly that many of them ended up as actors in the 1920s, playing bits in films by more talented and ambitious men.

As I watched the silent films I bought from junk shops and other collectors, I acquired a deep admiration for the men who made them. My friend, Bill Everson, a fellow collector and historian, was so impressed with the work of William K. Howard that he altered the order of his first names from Keith William to William K. Everson. I would happily have changed my name, too, but "Clarence," after my idol Clarence Brown—would not have sounded quite right.

It was the acquisition of a Clarence Brown film, *The Goose Woman* (1925), that persuaded me once and for all that the American silent era contained buried treasure. Here was a little-known film so brilliantly thought out and beautifully directed that it was a far more satisfying experience than many of the "classics" promoted by organizations like the British Film Institute. In 1958, when I acquired it, it was superior both in content and technique to most of the films being shown commercially. Yet Universal had destroyed all 35-mm prints of this and their other silent films. (Had the same thing happened to Old Master paintings, the perpetrators would have gone to jail.)

The Goose Woman had been made only about 40 years earlier. It struck me that Clarence Brown, indeed many of the filmmakers of the silent era, might still be alive if one could but know. It was like being fascinated by literature with Scott Fitzgerald still available for interviews! It seemed crazy that pages of critical theory were devoted to a director's intentions, and not one of these writers had the wit to contact the director and find out

what *he* thought. I was an assistant editor, earning £6 10s. a week, living in a bed-sit in Hampstead; I had no hope of traveling to Hollywood. But I felt that someone should do it.

I was pushed into it by a series of extraordinary events. One of the first films I acquired, when I was 11, was a 9.5-mm abridgment of an early Douglas Fairbanks film. It had the title *The First Man*. I went to the local library to see if they had any film books that might mention it—they had one, Bardeche and Brasillach's *History of the Film*. As I took it off the shelf, it fell open at a picture of Fairbanks in a scene from the very film I had just acquired. It was more than a coincidence; it was the start of my career as a film historian. The caption gave the correct title, *American Aristocracy,* produced by Triangle in 1916. When I became a member of the British Film Institute at 13, I discovered their library held an index to the films of Triangle. It listed the cast for *American Aristocracy,* and I can remember it to this day: Jewel Carmen, Albert S. Parker, Charles de Lima, Charles Stevens. . . . When I was 19 and working at a documentary film company, I heard of an actors' agency called Al Parker, Ltd. With my one-track mind, I assumed this referred to *my* Albert Parker, and one day plucked up the courage to ring Mr. Parker up. "Did you ever act with Douglas Fairbanks senior?" I asked. "Act with him?" replied Parker. "I directed him!" Parker invited me to his Park Lane office, and I found myself staring in astonishment at the framed photographs from *The Black Pirate* (1926) lining the walls. Parker loved to talk about Hollywood, although he tended to claim that he discovered Valentino, because he had directed one of his early films (admittedly the one that June Mathis saw and that led to her casting him in *The Four Horsemen*). He was so proud of this film, *The Eyes of Youth* (1919), which starred Clara Kimball Young, that one evening he invited all his top clients—Trevor Howard, Hardy Kruger, James Mason—to his apartment in Mount Street, Mayfair, and I projected it for them.

Parker gave me the untarnished atmosphere of the early days. He was an easterner, had been a stage actor and fellow-roisterer with John Barrymore, whom he directed in *Sherlock Holmes* (1922). I think he based elements of his own persona on that of Barrymore. He was a tough old bird, with an impressive Roman nose (have you noticed how many directors have impressive noses?) and a manner half-aggressive, half-humorous. He terrified the people who worked for him, and he wouldn't have lasted an hour in the politically correct climate of today. He spoke in the vernacular of the time—I was surprised how rude they could be in the age of innocence—and he came up with many silent era jokes. "As Marshall Neilan used to say, There are more horses' asses in the world than there are horses." He and his wife, the actress Margaret Johnston, were very generous to me; they introduced me to Douglas Fairbanks, Jr., who then lived in London, to Clive Brook, another client, and to anyone they thought might be helpful. Curiously, the one thing Parker would not permit was tape recording. I suppose it was the innate suspicion of an agent. So I missed a lot of what he had to say, either because I forgot, or because I was furiously scribbling notes. He relaxed this rule only when it was too late, and his memory had drifted back to his childhood, to the New York of the 1890s—fascinating but frustrating, for all recollection of Hollywood had gone.

I went to America as soon as I could afford it. I had finished work on my first feature (*It Happened Here*) in 1964 and decided to take advantage of TWA's cheap three-week trip to New York. The fact that I had fallen for an American actress provided the impetus. She was busy with rehearsals, so I had plenty of free time. I began to track down veterans who lived in Manhattan. Most were hospitable and helpful, but they were surprised that someone in his twenties should be so fascinated by the past. "Silent pictures look pretty silly today, don't they?" The first part of the encounter was invariably spent restoring their confidence in their

work, explaining that silent films were not jerky, flickery and technically incompetent, despite the damage television might have done. It amazed and saddened me to find that these popular misconceptions had spread even to those who worked in silent pictures. I used to carry a strip of 35-mm film shot in 1915 and a strip shot in 1963; comparing these under the light provided proof of the superb quality of orthochromatic film.

Even when interviewing actors and actresses, I concentrated on my favourite subject: directors. Lillian Gish, as fragile and beautiful as if seen through gauze, talked of her days with the man then regarded as the greatest of all, D. W. Griffith.

"Dedicated? I suppose I was. I knew the financial burden he was carrying. The others didn't. But it was a dedicated life then. You had no social life. You had to have lunch or dinner, but it was always spent talking over work—talking over stories, or cutting or titles. I don't see how any human worked the way he did. Never less than 18 hours a day, seven days a week. They say he saw other people's pictures. He never had the time. If you insisted, he'd borrow a print of *The Last Laugh* and run it at the studio, but that was very rare. He didn't have time to see pictures; he was too busy making them."

Griffith was the subject of universal adulation in those days. *The Birth of a Nation* was regarded as the greatest film of the era. No one seemed aware of the violence of its politics. Said one veteran, "To me, the Klan chasing the Negroes was the same as cowboys chasing Indians." He would have been staggered had he been told that 40 years on, the D. W. Griffith award would be stripped of its name by the Directors Guild because of that very film.

That December, I managed another trip and flew on to Los Angeles. I stayed in a house high in the Hollywood hills, and remember sitting by the telephone with a sense of omnipotence. I could meet practically anyone I wanted—Buster Keaton, Harold Lloyd, or Josef von Sternberg. It was an incredible feeling, marred only by a crippling sense of shyness and the fact that no celebrity worth his salt would have put his name in the phone book. The Screen Directors Guild—"We're sorry, no addresses"—agreed to pass my inquiry to their members by mail. Since I was there for so short a time, this was no help.

One night, I was in the Masquers Club, where I was told several silent stars would be present. In the lobby were photographs of past presidents of the club, and sitting on a couch nearby was an intriguing looking woman in her sixties. I was convinced that she had been in silent pictures, so I began a conversation with a mention of Fred Niblo, whose picture was just above her head.

"Oh yes, he was married to—"
"Enid Bennett."
"Oh yes—but you don't remember. . . ."
"No, but I'm very interested in this period. Particularly in directors."
"Well, my husband was a director."
"Really? What is his name?"
"Oh, you wouldn't have heard of him. Joseph Henabery."
"Joseph Henabery!" I sat down heavily on the arm of a chair. Henabery played Abraham Lincoln in *The Birth of a Nation* and became a director of Douglas Fairbanks and Valentino. "I've not only heard of him. I have a print of one of his pictures."

We arranged to drive out to the Henaberys' Tarzana home at the weekend. California was having its worst flooding for 10 years; torrents of water cascaded down the side streets and cars sent up bow waves. We were late, but Joseph Henabery was warm and welcoming. He was a fervent admirer of D. W. Griffith, whom he somewhat resembled—tall, a striking face dominated by a long nose, with a deep, melodious voice. He had an amazing recall for events that had taken place 50 years before, and he talked solidly and grippingly for four hours, while Mrs. Henabery fed us coffee and toasted cheese sandwiches. This encounter astonished me. We in England all thought that the Feast of Belshazzar scene in *Intolerance,* with the camera apparently moving down from the clouds, had been shot from a captive balloon. Henabery told me it was achieved with a massive tower built on mining rails. It was this that determined me to put all these reminiscences into a book, which became *The Parade's Gone By* (1968) and which is still in print from the University of California Press.

The next director I located was Sidney Franklin, who made *The Good Earth* and *The Barretts of Wimpole Street* in the 1930s. With his brother, Chester, he had also made some remarkably imaginative pictures in the '10s, and become a major director in the '20s with films like *Smilin' Thru* with Norma Talmadge and *Quality Street* with Marion Davies.

When I called him, a deep, dignified, almost English voice answered. "I'm not very keen to do this . . . so many times what is written is inaccurate. I never give interviews or anything like that." When I told him I had been collecting Sidney Franklin pictures since the age of 14, his attitude began to change. Reluctantly, he arranged a date. This reluctance was still noticeable as we began the interview. He was a slightly built, gray-haired man with a moustache; a dark blue jacket and white trousers made him resemble a cricket blue. Franklin had been in love with everything English—many of his pictures, from *The Safety Curtain* (1918), which he directed, to *Mrs. Miniver* (1942), which he produced, had been set in England. But this affection had taken a beating when he finally came to work in London, in 1949, at the height of postwar austerity.

At first he talked with his eyebrows raised, as though full of disdain, but he would unexpectedly break into a mischievous grin. He would begin a tantalizing story, then stop, and say confidingly, "That's for my book." I would try another question. A short pause and he would begin to provide an answer. But just as it became interesting he would break off, "Now, tell me about yourself." I eroded his resistance a little by describing his films to him. "I didn't know I was that darn good," he said. The atmosphere gradually became warmer and the reminiscences livelier. Inevitably, his memory returned to D. W. Griffith.

"On *Intolerance,* there were a thousand idiots on top of the walls of Babylon, throwing down burning oil and big rocks made of plaster of Paris. Well, if one of them hit you, it could kill you. They were dropping so many things that no one could get the extras up to the walls. I was in charge of a group of 500, and Christy Cabanne had a group of another 500. And since I was out in front, I made a speech—'Come on, boys, don't be afraid to approach the walls; follow me!' I charged towards the walls, thinking and hoping they'd all follow. It took a lot of courage. 'Follow me!'—and I'd no sooner got the words out of my mouth than a rock came hurtling from 50 feet up and struck my shield. The shield knocked me cold and my 500 extras went the other way. My mother came across to the studio and said 'Is my son in there?' 'Yes,' they told her. 'His brains are all over the lot.'"

The Franklins became close friends. A few years later, when I was working for the short-lived Oral History department of the American Film Institute, I persuaded him to write his memoirs—I realized that the only way he was ever going to do it was if I sat there, prompting him, letting him drift off into funny stories, making it fun. So this is what we did, and although the result, *We Laughed and We Cried,* was never published, it contained fascinating historical information, which has been used for several books. When he retired, Franklin had brought home all his files from MGM, and in the folder for *Madame Curie* I discovered memos from Scott Fitzgerald in his own handwriting. Franklin told me that he played a lot of golf, and at his favorite course in Palm Desert lived his close friend Clarence Brown.

Oddly enough, this contact did not make it any easier to meet Brown, who was even more suspicious of authors than Franklin. When I returned to London, I dropped him a line mentioning that I had a print of his *The Goose Woman,* and he was intrigued enough to want to see it again. He came to the Motor Show in Paris every year. He had a friend there, a correspondent for the *New York Herald-Tribune,* Thomas Quinn Curtiss, who frequently came to London. One day, Curtiss telephoned me from the Savoy Hotel, and asked me to come round with my projector and show him *The Goose Woman.* I thought this a pretty blatant way of vetting me, but I had no objection . . . so long as eventually I met my idol. Curtiss, very impressed by the film, gave me the okay and I traveled to Paris to the Hôtel Georges V.

Brown was unlike the other directors I had met. He was of Northern Irish Protestant stock, and he was burly, tough, and remote. He and I differed on everything; he had been on the side of the House Un-American Activities Committee during the McCarthy era, and made no secret of his extreme right-wing views. He was reluctant to be recorded, so I had to hold the microphone under the dinner table, for I was determined not to miss a word of what he said. Once he began talking about films, all the toughness fell away and he exposed a deeply sensitive side—the side that appears so strongly in his pictures. When he spoke of the director he first worked for—Maurice Tourneur—he was near to tears. The hard-bitten exterior was a shell to protect a shy and delicate personality. But it didn't make it any easier to converse. He had no small talk. He was primarily interested in cars, airplanes, and real estate. He had made money out of pictures, but he was infinitely richer than his fellow directors, and that was due to real estate. I remember telling him that Lake Arrowhead, location for Murnau's *Sunrise* (1927) as well as for several of his own films, now had houses around the edge. "I know," he said. "I built most of them." When I protested, he snapped: "They've got to live somewhere."

I had the privilege of showing Brown several of his silent pictures, and hearing at first hand the problems he had in making them. At the Cinemathèque in Paris, I arranged with curator Henri Langlois to show him Maurice Tourneur's *Last of the Mohicans* (1920)—and it turned out he had directed most of it after Tourneur was injured. Despite Brown's hard-bitten personality, I became very fond of him, and felt I should write his biography. I hesitated, because I knew all I wanted to know, and I left it to someone else less involved with the man to do a proper job. I am relieved to say that Gwenda Young, a lecturer from University College Cork, is now working on a book about his life and his career.

In the 1960s, I regretted that I was able to record these memories only on audio tape rather than film. One seldom has a second chance in life, but 10 years later I returned for Thames Television, with David Gill, to film no less than 85 interviews for the *Hollywood* series, which was transmitted in 1980, was released on video and laser disc, and

continues to be shown in America to this day. Among the directors who appeared in that documentary were King Vidor, Clarence Brown, Henry King, Al Rogell, Raoul Walsh, William Wellman, Allan Dwan, Henry Hathaway, Lewis Milestone, George Cukor, Frank Capra, and William Wyler. (The British Film Institute will soon release an uncut version on DVD.)

However elusive, however reluctant to talk, most of these great names of Hollywood displayed astonishing friendliness and cooperation once the barriers were overcome. And they all proved to be remarkable people. Some were in their seventies, some well over 80, yet none were senile—none were even old, in the sense that they had retired from life. They were nearly all active, either in the industry, like William Wyler, or in writing or painting. And the sense of exhilaration they communicated made me realize why the '20s was such an astonishing era—when they were young and making pictures.

—Kevin Brownlow
London, November 2001

INTRODUCTION

I'm master in the darkroom, stirring my prints in the magic developing bath.
I shuffle like cards the lives that I deal with. Their faces stare out at me.

—Billy Kwan in Peter Weir's *The Year of Living Dangerously*

"Author! Author!"—Will the Real *Auteur* Please Stand Up?

Second only to the popularity and prestige of today's movie stars is the recognition by critics and public of the presence and stylistic traits of a handful of directors. These days a film like *Erin Brockovich* is not just a vehicle for Julia Roberts but also a work crafted by Stephen Soderbergh. And occasionally, recent films like *Pi* and *The Winslow Boy* are noted not for their casts so much as for, respectively, the emergence of an exciting new directorial talent (Darren Aronofsky) and the ongoing work of a prominent playwright/director (David Mamet). To be sure, remarking the work of specific film directors is nothing new; it has been the special passion of critics and filmgoers since the inception of the commercial cinema at the turn of the 20th century. Indeed, the names of filmmakers were publicly known years before the names of cast members were acknowledged.

In the first two decades of the cinema, Edwin S. Porter, Mack Sennett, Sidney Olcott, Thomas Ince, Oscar Micheaux, and D. W. Griffith in America; Georges Méliès and Louis Feuillade in France; Cecil Hepworth and George Pearson in England; Victor Sjöström and Mauritz Striller in Sweden;

Giovanni Pastrone and Enrico Guazzoni in Italy; Benjamin Christiansen in Denmark—all were singled out for notice in the pages of the trade journals and in the press, and their names were used in the promotion of their pictures. None of them had any prior training in filmmaking or precedents to draw upon; whether they were stage actors or directors, machinists, itinerant salesmen, cowboys, or even explorers (like Robert Flaherty and Ernest Schoedsack), they had to make it up as they went along. If they were not all great, to paraphrase Shakespeare, greatness was at least thrust upon them. In any event, the cult of the director has always been with us, and now that independent cinema is flourishing in so many different directions, and the very apparatus of filmmaking is so accessible and ubiquitous, that fascination and that recognition will continue unabated.

Just as a poet is a maker of poems, a cinema director is a maker of films. Whereas one gives shape, structure, and meaning to verbal images, the director gives shape, structure, and meaning to visual images. This analogy is not new. It was first articulated by the French novelist, critic, and filmmaker Alexandre Astruc in 1948, who claimed that cinema could become "a means of writing just as flexible and subtle as written language." If the cinema was to become a language, the "camera-stylo"—or *camera pen,* as he called it—was the instrument for "writing" it. "By language," Astruc explained, "I mean a form in which and by which an artist can express his thoughts, however abstract they may be, or translate his obsessions exactly as he does in a contemporary essay or novel. That is why I would like to call this new age of cinema the age of the camera-stylo."

Astruc's formulation constituted a major shift in emphasis in accepted theories of film authorship. As John Caughie notes in his *Theories of Authorship,* "traditionally, the reference to the *auteur* in French film criticism had identified either the author who wrote the script, or, in the general sense of the term, the artist who created the film. [Now] the latter sense came to replace the former, and the *auteur* was the artist whose personality was 'written' in the film." Moreover, a film, though produced collectively, "is most likely to be valuable when it is essentially the product of its director . . . and that this personality can be traced in a thematic and/or stylistic consistency over all (or almost all) the director's films." Thus was the so-called *auteur theory* born, to which we will return presently.

The roads to the director's chair have been many. Sometimes forgotten is the fact that many of the silent film directors were formerly actors, chief among them, of course, D. W. Griffith. Charles Chaplin, one of the original "United Artists," quickly emerged from the supervision of Mack Sennett to assume complete charge of every aspect of his films, as Kevin Brownlow's estimable documentary, *The Unknown Chaplin,* amply testifies. And although Chaplin's chief artistic rival, Buster Keaton, credited himself as the nominal director in only a handful of his films, there is no question that his was the presiding genius and controlling force of everything he did (at least in the silent years). The same is true of those other actor-auteurs of the silent period, whose names are con-

spicuously absent from the credits of their films, Mary Pickford, Douglas Fairbanks, and Harold Lloyd.

Although a few actors have essayed the role of director only once—Charles Laughton's *The Night of the Hunter* (1957) remains the best example, an imaginative contribution to the genre of allegorical film; while Marlon Brando's postmodernist western, *One-Eyed Jacks* (1961), wallows in self-indulgence—so numerous are the actresses and actors who have seriously turned to directing that a brief survey will have to suffice. Among the first actresses-turned-director was Lois Weber, who co-starred in films with her husband before assuming the director's chair in 1913, becoming the highest salaried woman director in the world. After Ida Lupino assessed her own actor status as "a poor man's Bette Davis," she turned to directing in the 1950s (she was virtually the only female director working at that time), with *Hard, Fast and Beautiful* (1951) and *The Hitch-Hiker* (1953). More recent examples include Barbra Streisand's sporadic efforts as both actress and director, as the "Yashiva boy" in an adaptation of I. B. Singer's *Yentl* (1983) and as an English professor futilely trying to conduct a platonic relationship in *The Mirror Has Two Faces* (1996); Swedish actress Liv Ullmann's first directorial efforts after leaving the acting ensemble of Ingmar Bergman, in *Sofie* (1993) and an adaptation of Sigrid Undset's epic *Kristin Lavransdatter* (1995); television actress (*Laverne and Shirley*) Penny Marshall's box-office hits *Big* (1988) and *A League of Their Own* (1992); and Anjelica Huston's *Bastard out of Carolina* (1996) and *Agnes Browne* (1999), in which she cast herself as the widow Browne, a Dubliner with no inheritance and seven children to support after the death of her husband.

A brief overview of the numerous male actors-turned-director can likewise provide no more than a hint of a roll call that is vast and varied. Vittorio De Sica's Italian neorealist classics like *The Bicycle Thiefs* (1948) have overshadowed his early fame as a suave leading man in prewar Italian cinema. Similarly, Ernst Lubitsch's celebrated and sophisticated American satires like *Ninotchka* (1939) made him more of a celebrity than his initial stage and screen career as a Jewish comedian. John Cassavetes's experience in improvisational acting helped revolutionize the independent cinema in his first film, *Shadows* (1959). Ron Howard's television acting and apprenticeship under Roger Corman led him to a prestigious movie career that began with his breakthrough film, *Night Shift* (1982). Clint Eastwood's tutelage under Sergio Leone and Don Siegel influenced his signature deliberate pacing and stylized, choreographed violence, particularly evident in *Pale Rider* (1985) and *Unforgiven* (1992). Robert Redford has also exploited his experience as an actor in his character-driven pictures, most notably *Ordinary People* (1980) and *Quiz Show* (1994). More recently, several younger-generation actors have shown promise in their budding directorial careers. Stanley Tucci's directorial debut was the box-office smash, *Big Night* (1996), which was followed by the critically acclaimed *Joe Gould's Secret* (2000). Tim Robbins's *Bob Roberts* (1992), the Oscar-nominated *Dead Man Walking* (1996), and *The Cradle Will Rock* (2000) reveal a thoughtful, probing talent. And Sean Penn's *The Indian Runner* (1991), *The Crossing Guard* (1995), and *The Pledge* (2000) are corrosive dissections of the dark side of human nature.

However, most actors-turned-director have not risen to the artistic level and/or prestige of De Sica, Lubitsch, Eastwood, Redford, and Howard. John Wayne, for example, directed *The Alamo* in 1960 and co-directed *The Green Berets* in 1969, but the results did nothing to dispel his primary credentials as an actor. Fresh from his stint in the *M*A*S*H* television series, Alan Alda has had only moderate success in writing and directing *The Seduction of Joe Tynan* (1979) and *Four Seasons* (1981). Billy Crystal left his *Soap* television series and began his directorial career with the largely forgettable *Mr. Saturday Night* in 1992.

Some of the most important directors had their formative experience as theater playwrights, directors, and producers. Soviet film genius Sergei Eisenstein (*Strike* [1924] and *Potemkin* [1926]) gained his early training from the circus theatres and constructivist techniques of Vsevelod Meyerhold. Before directing his first film, *Ingeborg Holm*, in 1913, the Swedish master Victor Sjöstrom enjoyed a formidable reputation as an actor-director in the theater. In Hollywood, many directors came from Broadway. The first great migration of Broadway directors came on the heels of the coming of sound in 1929. These luminaries included Rouben Mamoulian (*Applause* [1929]) and George Cukor (*The Philadelphia Story* [1940]). The 1940s saw another notable exodus. Orson Welles was not only an actor but also a gifted theater director, whose success with numerous stage and radio dramas for the Federal Theatre and the Mercury Players (*Macbeth, Five Kings, War of the Worlds*) paved the way to a significant but checkered career in Hollywood and abroad with masterpieces (*Citizen Kane* [1941]) and near misses (*The Lady from Shanghai* [1948] and *Mr. Arkadin* [1955]). Elia Kazan left the Group Theatre in 1945 to launch a series of classic dramatic and literary adaptations, like *Streetcar Named Desire* (1951). Vincente Minnelli quit designing sumptuous Broadway revues to inaugurate a series of groundbreaking musicals with *Meet Me in St. Louis* (1944) and *An American in Paris* (1951). Another musical theater maestro, Stanley Donen, teamed up with Broadway dancer Gene Kelly to make movies like *On the Town* (1949) and *Singin' in the Rain* (1952). In the last half-century the list has continued, numbering dance choreographer Bob Fosse (*Cabaret* [1972]), director Josh Logan (*Picnic* [1956]), and playwrights David Mamet (*The Winslow Boy* [1999]) and Tom Stoppard (*Rosencrantz and Guildenstern Are Dead* [1990]).

Preeminent in this galaxy of theatrical notables are Laurence Olivier and Kenneth Branagh. Olivier's early experience in the Birmingham

Repertory Theatre and later in the Old Vic fueled his series of Shakespearean classics, *Henry V* (1944), *Hamlet* (1948), *Richard III* (1955), and *Othello* (1965). Branagh's background in the Royal Shakespeare Company and his Renaissance Theatre Company has led to his own Shakespearean adaptations, beginning with *Henry V* (1989) and continuing through *Much Ado about Nothing* (1993) and *Hamlet* (1996). His *Midwinter's Tale* (1995), a backstage look at a production of *Hamlet* in a rural region of England, remains one of the canniest and wittiest of the screen's meditations on the Bard and the theater in general.

From the ranks of photographers and cameramen have come Stanley Kubrick and Gordon Parks, who worked as photographers for *Look* and *Life* magazines before making their first films, *Killer's Kiss* (1953) and *The Learning Tree* (1967), respectively; Haskell Wexler and Ricky Leacock, with *Medium Cool* (1969) and the *vérité* classic, *Primary* (1960), respectively; Zhang Yimou with *Red Sorghum* (1987); Nicholas Roeg with *Walkabout* (1971); and Jan De Bont (*Speed*).

Indeed, it seems every conceivable background has lent itself in some way to directing. From the editing bench have come such luminaries as Robert Wise (*The Sound of Music* [1965]) and Peter Watkins (*The War Game* [1964]). Beginning in the late 1950s a host of young film critics turned to filmmaking—François Truffaut and Jean-Luc Godard in France (*The 400 Blows* [1959] and *Breathless* [1959]), Tony Richardson (*Look Back in Anger* [1959]) and Lindsay Anderson in England (*This Sporting Life* [1963]), and Peter Bogdanovich in America (*The Last Picture Show* [1964]). Documentary filmmaker Frederick Wiseman was a lawyer before documenting American institutions (*High School* [1962]); and another documentarist, Michael Moore, was a crusading journalist before turning to *Roger and Me* (1985).

Those with backgrounds in drawing and painting include Alfred Hitchcock, whose talents as a graphic artist preceded his first directorial efforts, *The Lodger* (1926) and *Blackmail* (1929); Satyajit Ray, who studied painting and art history at Shintiniketan University before making his breakthrough film, *Pather Panchali* (1955); Kenji Mizoguchi, who left art school and advertising design to make some of the greatest masterpieces in the Japanese cinema (*Life of Oharu* [1951] and *Ugetsu* [1953]); David Lynch, who was trained at the Pennsylvania Academy of Fine Art in Philadelphia before turning to cinema classics like *Eraserhead* (1976) and *The Elephant Man* (1980); Tim Burton, who, before making *Pee-Wee's Big Adventure* (1985), had won a Disney fellowship to study animation at the California Institute of the Arts; Peter Greenaway, who first studied painting at the Walthamstow Art College before turning to film editing and, later, film directing with *The Draughtsman's Contract* (1983); Derek Jarman, whose education at the Slade School of Fine Arts and work as a set designer for the Royal Ballet and the English National Opera enhanced his *Caravaggio* (1986), an idiosyncratic bio-pic of the great Italian baroque painter.

Recently, directors have learned their craft by working in television and by directing commercials and music videos.

Many of these directors were able, by sheer force of personality or controlling vision, to stamp their distinctive personalities and their signatures, as it were, onto their films. Some of them have even been regarded as "auteurs," or authors, by today's critics and moviegoers. However, to what degree they are auteurs constitutes an ongoing debate. Quarrels over such designations came to a head in the 1940s and 1950s when French critics and screenwriters began debating and discussing the issue at length. Critic André Bazin, writing in *Revue du cinéma* in 1946–49, cited the celebrated 1948 essay, "Le camera-stylo," by Alexandre Astruc as a proposition that artists could use the film medium to express their ideas and feelings "as a writer writes with his pen." When Jacques Doniol-Valcroze founded the monthly *Cahiers du cinéma*,

Bazin became its chief critic and began referring to particular films as a "Billy Wilder film," or a "Robert Bresson film," or a "Roberto Rossellini film" in the same breath. To paraphrase a currently popular catchphrase, "It's the *director*, stupid!"

In the January 1954 issue of *Cahiers* an essay entitled "A Certain Tendency in the French Cinema" called for the overthrow of the prestige cinema of literary adaptations that was dominating postwar French cinema. The author, 21-year-old François Truffaut, advocated replacing this "Tradition of Quality" with a cinema that was ruled by the director and not the writer. The "true men of the cinema," Truffaut declared, those deserving the appellation of auteur, included Jean Renoir, Robert Bresson, Jean Cocteau, Jacques Tati, Max Ophuls, and others who wrote their own stories and dialogue. Three years later in *Cahiers,* Bazin defended "the personal factor in artistic creation as a standard of reference," assuming that "it continues and even progresses from one film to the next." As Hilliers writes, Bazin prophetically warned that this attitude could easily degenerate into a "cult of personality" that ignored the contextual realities behind any filmmaker's work: "So there can be no definitive criticism of genius or talent which does not first take into consideration the social determination, the historical combination of circumstances, and the technical background which to a large extent determine it." Bazin's cautionary views would be echoed soon by American critics like Pauline Kael.

From the auteurist position, it was but a short trip to a more extreme view, i.e., that prominent directors in Hollywood deserved auteur status—not just producer-directors like Howard Hawks but also contract directors like Frank Tashlin. In spite of the system in which they worked, or within the burden of their assignment, they were nonetheless able to impose their own stamp or signature upon the finished product. The extent to which a director's "signature" overcame, or peeked through, the cage of the assignment, as it were,

determined the degree to which he or she earned favor as an auteur. This view came to be called the *politique des auteurs.*

An indignant response from French screenwriters was immediate, and *Cahiers* was chastised for abandoning the serenity of film studies for the heat of polemic. Other objections came from England in the autumn 1960 issue of *Sight and Sound,* when Richard Roud and Penelope Houston deplored this "cult of America," which too often placed sensationalist action pictures by Sam Fuller and tawdry melodramas by Douglas Sirk on the same level as more contemplative films by venerated Asian and Indian masters like Satyajit Ray and Yasujiro Ozu. There was no justification, they argued, in taking the bargain-basement brand of American cinema and its directorial auteurs seriously.

Meanwhile, in a shift to American shores, Andrew Sarris began promoting what he called the "auteur theory" as a useful mechanism to understand film criticism and history. Sarris's groundbreaking "Notes on the Auteur Theory in 1962" took up the battle cry of Giraudoux's epigram, "There are no works; there are only authors." A criterion of value in a given director is his "distinguishable personality" and "certain recurring characteristics of style, which serve as his signature." Using Bazin's 1957 article as his springboard, Sarris argued that the auteur theory finds its "decisive battleground" in American cinema; that "film for film, director for director, the American cinema has been consistently superior to that of the rest of the world from 1915 through 1962," as quoted in Harrington. In Hollywood, "because so much of the American cinema is commissioned, a director is forced to express his personality through the *visual* [italics added] treatment of material rather than through the literary content of the material." Directors could be identified and evaluated through three criteria of value, three "concentric circles," as Sarris put it: the outer circle refers to a director's "technical competence";

the middle circle to a director's "signature," i.e., repetitions of certain techniques and themes; and the inner circle to the "interior meaning" that may be derived from the discernible tension between a director's personality and his material. In Sarris's "pantheon" of auteurs were Max Ophüls, Jean Renoir, Kenji Mizoguchi, Alfred Hitchcock, Charles Chaplin, John Ford, Orson Welles, Carl Dreyer, Rossellini, F. W. Murnau, D. W. Griffith, Josef von Sternberg, Sergei Eisenstein, von Stroheim, Luis Buñuel, Robert Bresson, Howard Hawks, Fritz Lang, Robert Flaherty, and Jean Vigo.

This manifesto was later expanded in the Introductions to Sarris's *Interviews with Film Directors* (1967) and the book-length *The American Cinema,* published a year later, two of the most influential film books ever published. Again, the personally expressive qualities of a director, particularly the Hollywood director, were applauded. Indeed, he declared in 1968, "A film history could reasonably limit itself to a history of film directors." It was especially important to rescue from oblivion those directors and those films that had been overshadowed by the unquestioned prestige of the "art" directors of Europe: "Quite often, Hollywood directors have labored in obscurity to evolve an extraordinary economy of expression that escapes so-called highbrow critics in search of the obvious stylistic flourish. Consequently, there has been a tendency to overrate the European directors because of their relative articulateness about their artistic *angst,* and now a reaction has set in against some of the disproportionate pomposity that has ensued." It is possible now, he continued in *Interviews with Film Directors,* "to speak of Alfred Hitchcock and Michelangelo Antonioni in the same breath and with the same critical terminology. Amid the conflicting critical camps, both Rays, Nicholas and Satyajit, have gained a respectful hearing." Sarris then proceeds to rank and categorize hundreds of auteurs, including "Pantheon Directors" (Chaplin, Ford, Renoir, etc.), "The Far Side of Paradise" (Frank Capra, Vincente Minnelli,

Nicholas Ray, etc.), "Expressive Esoterica" (Stanley Donen, Allan Dwan, Frank Tashlin, etc.), and "Less than Meets the Eye" (John Huston, Elia Kazan, Billy Wilder, etc.).

In 1970 appeared Sarris's "Notes on the Auteur Theory in 1970." And seven years later came yet another article, "The Auteur Theory Revisited," which reiterated that auteurist writings from the very beginning had performed a valuable function, if only in that they rescued the film medium and film studies from a frankly exclusionary agenda: "The cinema was no longer a holy temple to which only certain sanctified works were admitted," he wrote. "Cinema was to be found on every movie screen in the world, and Hollywood movies were no less cinematic than anything else." Sarris defended auteurist agendas as more a tendency than a theory, more a mystique than a methodology, "more a critical instrument than a creative inspiration." He also defended it against the structuralists by noting that instead of knowing all the answers before formulating the questions, auteurism knows all the questions before finding the answers.

A rebuke to Sarris's writings was not long in coming. In her famous "Circles and Squares" article in the Spring 1963 issue of *Film Quarterly,* critic Pauline Kael attacked the proposition that a director's distinguishable personality is the prime criterion of value: "Traditionally, in any art, the personalities of all those involved in a production have been a factor in judgment," she wrote, "but that the distinguishability of personality should in itself be a criterion of value completely confuses normal judgment. The smell of a skunk is more distinguishable than the perfume of a rose; does that make it better?" The mere repetition of styles and subjects is hardly anything new, she continues, "In every art form critics traditionally notice and point out the way the artists borrow from themselves (as well as from others) and how the same devices, techniques, and themes reappear in their work." She agreed that the director should have "creative control" of a picture, but not *absolute* power. Moreover, she rejected Sarris's "three circles" of meaning, one by one: The first, "technical competence," was of no value, she said, when it became more important than thematic concerns. Besides, mere technical competence is the province of hacks, not of artists who sometimes must violate it in the service of art. The second, a director's "signature," can only make us more conscious of the director's personality than of the subject. Lastly, "interior meaning" extrapolated from the tension between a director's personality and his material, is nothing more than a thinly veiled affirmation of the studio system, where a director "directs any script that's handed to him, and expresses himself by shoving bits of style up the crevasses of the plots."

The impact of this debate on academic film studies in America has been profound. Ironically, an approach to film studies and criticism that began as a rejection of what Truffaut called the "Tradition of Quality" has catapulted film straight into the groves of academe. As Bordwell and Thompson contend, "the premise of individual artistic expression proved congenial to scholars trained in art, literature, and theater. Moreover, auteurism's emphasis on the interpretation of a film called on skills already cultivated by literary education." Due to the great proliferation in the 1950s of 16-mm film distribution and the subsequent boom in the accessibility of titles on videotape and now DVD, scholars suddenly had a formidable corpus of films and directors to study, not just the "great directors" and the "great films" formerly sanctioned by the establishment. In this way it was possible to trace and analyze the evolution of recurring themes, images, stylistic choices (modes of editing, lighting, camera placement, mise-en-scène arrangements), and plot situations over the course of a director's entire career. Meanwhile, publishers continue to issue a steady stream of individual monographs and biographies of directors as needed to feed the numerous film societies and college classes springing up all over America.

Meanwhile, the auteur theory itself has been subject to reexamination and revision. Beginning in the late 1960s a new generation of critics questioned it as naïve because, in the assessment of Tom Gunning, "it lacked a true understanding of the Hollywood mode of production and the constraints placed on a director's self-expression; suspect because it staked a meaningful interpretation on a 'theological' account of the author-as-creator." In America, historians David Bordwell, Janet Staiger, and Kristin Thompson argued that the impersonal, standardized "group style" of the Hollywood "classical" studio period necessarily subordinated any individual directorial style to only sporadic expression. "[O]vert narration, the presence of a self-conscious 'author' not motivated by realism or genre or story causality, can only be intermittent and fluctuating in the classical film," they wrote in *The Classical Hollywood Cinema*. Otherwise, "for social and economic reasons, no Hollywood film can provide a distinct and coherent alternative to the classical model." In England, a group of writers associated with the British Film Institute attempted to invest the auteurist approach with insights from structuralist linguistics and anthropology, as explicated in Peter Wollen's *Signs and Meaning in the Cinema*.

Meanwhile, thinkers like Michel Foucault and Roland Barthes have reviewed, even questioned, an "author" presence in a given work. In "What Is an Author?" Foucault contends that an author never simply speaks in his own voice; rather, between the actual writer and the reader a series of speakers intervene. Putting it another way, authorship is a process by which "a voluntary obliteration of the self" occurs, where the work murders its author. Putting it in a slightly different way, in "The Death of the Author," Barthes contends that as soon as a fact is narrated, a "disconnection occurs, the voice loses its origin, and the author enters into his own death, writing begins."

No matter how learned or how exotic are these variants and revisions of the auteurist theme, the question—if not the possibility—of directorial authorship has remained central to most film scholarship. In his important new study of Fritz Lang's authorship, *The Films of Fritz Lang: Allegories of Vision and Modernity,* Tom Gunning returns to fundamental issues in the auteur discourse. After acknowledging that a director must struggle to asssert authorship over the "authorless discourse" of the film medium, Gunning argues that the author ultimately becomes a "construction" in those films, a creation as much as any of his films are: "His hand beckons to us to enter his texts and find him, but entices us into a maze rather than setting up a direct encounter. . . . The search for the author takes place in a labyrinth in which at times even the film director himself may have lost his way." In sum, the authorial presence remains "precisely poised on the threshold of the work, evident in the film itself, but also standing outside it, absent except in the imprint left behind."

For a full account of the auteur debates, see John Caughie's anthology, *Theories of Authorship.*

This book by its very nature makes its own presumptions that certain of the many directors examined herein exercised a degree of influence over their finished works. Perhaps they pioneered film form (Porter and Hepworth), benefited from established artistic traditions (Ingmar Bergman and Elia Kazan), worked within a studio system (Mervyn LeRoy and Henry King), belonged to the various "new wave" movements of the 1960s and 1970s (Tony Richardson in England, François Truffaut in France, Peter Weir in Australia, and Robert Altman in America), conducted cinematic experiments (Norman McLaren and Stan Brakhage), existed on the margins of the industry (Edgar Ulmer and Orson Welles), or worked wholly independently (Jim Jarmusch and John Sayles). Certainly our task here is not to categorize directors in any particular order or rank. That sort of evaluation and categorization has already been attempted, with mixed success, as has been outlined earlier. Rather, it is our purpose merely to present a representative cross-section of biographical and critical commentary on each director in the hope that readers may use this information to pursue further investigations of their own pertaining to the particular individuality and merit of a given director.

Some readers may scoff at our presumptive title. We are calling this book an encyclopedia, but in limiting its roster to slightly more than 350 names, it is hardly a comprehensive one. We invited learned scholars to write entries on directors they considered "significant," college professors to write about those filmmakers pertinent to their classroom studies, and buffs to ensure that their favorite directors (no matter how little known) should not escape public notice. We asked only that our contributors make a case for the director's place and/or status within his or her particular professional and cultural contexts. Some entries may seem a bit odd, such as Frank Thompson's comic send-up of "Alan Smithee"—a case study whose relevance to cinema studies we leave our readers to decide. We also insisted that our contributors, whatever their background, ignore the jargon of the specialist and write in a common idiom understandable to the general reader.

—John C. Tibbetts, University of Kansas, Lawrence, Kansas
—James M. Welsh, Salisbury University, Salisbury, Maryland

REFERENCES

Astruc, Alexandre, "The Birth of a New Avant-Garde: La Camera-stylo," in *The New Wave,* ed. Peter Graham (Garden City, N.Y.: Doubleday, 1968), pp. 17–23. It originally appeared in the weekly *L'Écran français* in 1948.

Barthes, Roland, "The Death of the Author," in *Image-Music-Text,* Roland Barthes (New York: Hill and Wang, 1978), pp. 142–148.

Bazin, André, "On the *politique des auteurs,*" in *Cahiers du cinéma: The 1950s: Neo-Realism, Hollywood, New Wave,* ed. Jim Hilliers (Cambridge, Mass.: Harvard University Press, 1985), pp. 248–258. It originally appeared in *Cahiers du cinéma,* no. 70 (April 1957).

Bordwell, David, *Making Meaning* (Cambridge, Mass.: Harvard University Press, 1991).

Bordwell, David, and Kristin Thompson. *Film History: An Introduction* (New York: McGraw-Hill, 1994).

Bordwell, David, Janet Staiger, and Kristin Thompson, *The Classical Hollywood Cinema: Film Style & Mode of Production to 1960* (New York: Columbia University Press, 1985).

Caughie, John, *Theories of Authorship* (London: Routledge and Kegan Paul, 1981).

Eberwein, Robert T., *A Viewer's Guide to Film Theory and Criticism* (Metuchen, N.J.: Scarecrow Press, 1979).

Foucault, Michel, "What Is an Author?" in *Language, Counter-Memory, Practice: Selected Essays and Interviews,* ed. Donald F. Bouchard (Ithaca, N.Y.: Cornell University Press, 1977).

Gunning, Tom, *The Films of Fritz Lang: Allegories of Vision and Modernity* (London: British Film Institute, 2000).

Kael, Pauline, "Circles and Squares: Joys and Sarris," in *I Lost It at the Movies* (New York: Bantam Books), pp. 264–288. Originally in *Film Quarterly* 16, no. 3 (Spring 1963).

Murray, Edward, *Nine American Film Critics: A Study of Theory and Practice* (New York: Frederick Ungar, 1975).

Sarris, Andrew, *Interviews with Film Directors* (New York: Avon Books, 1967).

———, *The American Cinema: Directors and Directions, 1929–1968* (New York: E. P. Dutton, 1968).

———, *Confessions of a Cultist: On the Cinema, 1955–1969* (New York: Simon and Schuster, 1970).

———, "Notes on the Auteur Theory in 1962," in *Film and/as Literature,* ed. John Harrington (Englewood Cliffs, N.J.: Prentice-Hall, 1977), pp. 240–253. Originally in *Film Culture* 27 (Winter 1962–1963): 1–8.

———, "The American Cinema," *Film Culture* 28 (Spring): 1–51.

———, "The Auteur Theory Revisited," *American Film,* July–August 1977: 49–53.

Stam Robert, *Film Theory: An Introduction* (Malden, Mass.: Blackwell Publishers, 2000).

Truffaut, François, "A Certain Tendency of the French Cinema," *Cahiers du cinéma* 31 (January 1954).

Wollen, Peter, *Signs and Meaning in the Cinema* (Bloomington: Indiana University Press, 1972).

·

ENTRIES A to K

Alda, Alan (1936–)   Alan Alda, a tremendously successful and popular actor and sometime writer-director, was born Alphonso D'Abruzzo in New York City on January 28, 1936, the son of an actor whose stage name was Robert Alda. He was educated at Fordham University (B.S., 1956) and attended the Paul Sills Improvisational Workshop. He earned his credentials on stage before moving to film and television, achieving his greatest fame playing the quick-witted army surgeon Hawkeye Pierce in the long-running television series *M*★*A*★*S*★*H* (1972–82). His first film appearance as an actor was in *Gone Are the Days* (1963). He wrote episodes of *M*★*A*★*S*★*H* and also created a television series, *We'll Get By,* in 1975.

In 1979 Alda made his feature film-writing debut with his original screenplay for *The Seduction of Joe Tynan,* in which he also starred as the eponymous hero, a Democratic senator. His film-directing debut was the hit comedy *The Four Seasons,* which he also scripted and in which he starred with Carol Burnett. It was one of the five top-grossing films of 1981. He followed this success with *Sweet Liberty* (1986) and *A New Life* (1988). His next comic hit as writer and director was *Betsy's Wedding* (1990), in which he played Eddie Hopper, who, along with his wife Lola (Madeline Kahn), is determined to stage a fantastic wedding for his daughter Betsy (Molly Ringwald). The comic script offered some humorous surprises when Betsy's older sister, Connie (Ally Sheedy), falls in love with the nephew of a Mafia don (Anthony LaPaglia, who threatened to steal the show as he tried too hard to be a perfect gentleman). He is so crazy for Connie that he finally is willing to break all "family" ties and enroll in the Police Academy. This slapstick comedy offered outstanding performances by Alda, character actor Joe

Alan Alda in *The Four Seasons* (Universal)

Pesci, and comedian Joey Bishop. As director, Alda coordinated the talent perfectly and entertainingly.

References James, Caryn, "A Household Engulfed in Prenuptial Jitters," *New York Times,* June 22, 1990, p. C14; O'Donnell, Monica M., ed., *Contemporary Theatre, Film & Television* (Detroit: Gale Research, 1984).
—J.M.W.

Aldrich, Robert (1918–1983) Robert Burgess Aldrich was born on August 9, 1918, in Cranston, Rhode Island, where his family was prominent in banking and politics. Aldrich attended Moses Brown High School in Providence, Rhode Island, and later studied law and economics for four years at the University of Virginia.

In 1941 he moved to Hollywood where he got a position at RKO as a production clerk. The job as Aldrich recalled was "the lowest human animal on the production scale, the lowest form of life on the set." In early 1942 Aldrich was promoted to second assistant director on the film *Joan of Paris,* and spent the next two years working with such directors as EDWARD DMYTRYK and Leslie Goodwins. In 1944 he was promoted to first assistant director and between 1944 and 1952 he furthered his "apprenticeship" under the tutelage of many distinguished filmmakers, including: Jean Renoir (*The Southerner* [1945]); WILLIAM AUGUSTUS WELLMAN (*The Story of G.I. Joe* [1946]); LEWIS MILESTONE (*The Strange Love of Martha Ivers* [1946]); Abraham Polonsky (*Force of Evil* [1949]); JOSEPH LOSEY (*The Prowler* and *M* [1951]); and CHARLES CHAPLIN (*Limelight* [1952]). Aldrich also began directing for television from 1952 to 1953. Working both in New York and Hollywood he directed episodes of such series as *The Doctor* (NBC-TV); *The Adventures of China Smith* (syndication); *The Schlitz Playhouse* (CBS-TV); and *Four Star Playhouse* (CBS-TV).

In 1953 Aldrich directed his first feature film, the low-budget MGM "B" entry, *The Big Leaguer,* which starred Edward G. Robinson. This was followed by another low-budget film for Monogram, *World for Ransom,* starring Dan Duryea,

which caught the attention of Harold Hecht and Burt Lancaster who had formed Hecht-Lancaster Productions. Aldrich had served as assistant to the producer for two previous Hecht-Lancaster films, *Ten Tall Men* (1951) and *The First Time* (1952), and the duo tapped him to direct *Apache* (1954), an "A" feature that brought international attention to the 36-year-old filmmaker. *Vera Cruz* (1954), another western directed for Hecht-Lancaster Productions, starred Gary Cooper and Burt Lancaster and was shot in SuperScope on location in Cuernavaca, near Mexico City, with a budget of $3 million. It was Aldrich's first big commercial success.

Aldrich's next project was *Kiss Me Deadly,* a *film noir* based on the Mike Hammer novel by Mickey Spillane. According to critics Borde and Chaumeton this film "brought the noir cycle to a dark and fascinating close." Paul Schrader has referred to the film as the "great masterpiece of film noir." The picture was also the first of a dozen films for which Aldrich served as sole producer as well as director. In 1955, spurred by the success of his past work, Aldrich formed his own production company, Aldrich and Associates. The production company made 12 independent films during the next 17 years.

The first film Aldrich made under the newly formed company was a critical indictment of Hollywood, *The Big Knife* (1955), based on the stage play by Clifford Odets. This was followed by *Attack!* a World War II combat film that, according to Arnold and Miller, was an "explicit study of the corruption of authority and the failure of courage in the U.S. Army during the Battle of the Bulge." Much of Aldrich's work thematically resembles that of his contemporary during this period, Stanley Kubrick. In 1956 Aldrich signed a three-picture contract with Columbia. The first film, *Autumn Leaves* (1956), starred Joan Crawford and marked a digression into women's issues. The second film under the contract was *The Garment Jungle,* based on a series of *Reader's Digest* articles by

Lester Velie called "Gangsters in the Dress Business." Aldrich hoped that this film would be an exposé of gangsterism and corruption in the garment industry comparable to Elia Kazan's *On the Waterfront,* but he was replaced by director Vincent Sherman when he refused to "soften" the story into a simple tale of "boy meets girl in dress factory." From 1958 to 1962 Aldrich directed several projects outside of Hollywood, including *Ten Seconds to Hell* (1959), *The Angry Hills* (1959), *The Last Sunset* (1961), and the biblical epic, *Sodom and Gomorrah* (1963).

Aldrich wanted a blockbuster film that would revive his career. That opportunity came with his return to Hollywood in 1962 to direct *Whatever Happened to Baby Jane?* starring Bette Davis and Joan Crawford and released by Warner Bros–Seven Arts. The film was a resounding commercial success and was Aldrich's first box-office hit since *Vera Cruz,* grossing $4 million in the United States alone. It was also the first Aldrich film to be nominated for Academy Awards, five in all, and it prompted a follow-up Gothic horror film, *Hush . . . Hush, Sweet Charlotte* (1964), also starring Bette Davis, along with Olivia de Havilland and Joseph Cotten.

Robert Aldrich's most commercially successful film was the World War II action drama, *The Dirty Dozen* (1967), with Lee Marvin. The screenplay by Nunnally Johnson and Lukas Heller was based on a novel by E. M. Nathanson. In 1967 *The Dirty Dozen* was the 15th highest grossing picture of all time, earning in its initial release $19.5 million.

In 1968, following the success of *The Dirty Dozen,* he formed a new production company called Aldrich Studios. In order to obtain financing Aldrich signed a four-picture contract with Palomar Pictures, the film distributing branch of ABC. Aldrich himself directed two films, *The Killing of Sister George* (1968) and *Too Late the Hero* (1970), as well as the short film, *The Greatest Mother of 'Em All* (1969), and served as the producer for *Whatever Happened to Aunt Alice?* (1969),

a film that echoed his Gothic successes of *Baby Jane* and *Hush . . . Hush Sweet Charlotte.*

Aldrich Studios collapsed in 1973 when ABC-Palomar withdrew its association due to the negative box-office of its films. During the 1970s Aldrich made some of his most interesting and controversial films. *Ulzana's Raid* (1972) with Burt Lancaster was a revisionist western set in the southwest and considered by many to be a metaphor for the Vietnam war. *Twilight's Last Gleaming* (1977), also with Burt Lancaster, was a Cold War thriller concerning the potential for nuclear disaster—and another political comment by Aldrich on the purpose of the Vietnam war. Aldrich's later films include *The Frisco Kid* (1979) and *. . . All the Marbles* (1981). During the 1970s he also served as the president of the Directors Guild of America (1975–79).

Robert Aldrich died on December 5, 1983, from kidney failure.

Other Films As assistant director and assistant producer: *The Big Street* (1942); *The Falcon Takes Over* (1942); *Bombardier* (1943); *Behind the Rising Sun* (1943); *A Lady Takes a Chance* (1943); *Adventures of a Rookie* (1943); *Rookies in Burma* (1944); *Gangway for Tomorrow* (1944). As first assistant director: *Pardon My Past* (1946); *The Private Affairs of Be-Ami* (1947); *Body and Soul* (1947); *Arch of Triumph* (1948); *No Minor Vices* (1948); *The Red Pony* (1949); *The White Tower* (1950); *Of Men and Music* (1951); *New Mexico* (1951); *Abbott and Costello Meet Captain Kidd* (1952). As director: *4 for Texas* (1963); *The Flight of the Phoenix* (1966); *The Legend of Lylah Clare* (1968); *The Emperor of the North Pole* (1973); *The Longest Yard* (1974); *Hustle* (1975); and *The Choirboys* (1977).

References Arnold, Edwin T., and Eugene L. Miller, *The Films and Career of Robert Aldrich* (Knoxville: University of Tennessee Press, 1986); Silver, Alain, and James Ursini, *What Ever Happened to Robert Aldrich?* (New York: Limelight Editions, 1995); Silver, Alain, and Elizabeth Ward, *Robert Aldrich: A Guide to References and Resources* (Boston: G. K. Hall, 1979).

—R. W.

Allen, Woody (1935–) Allan Stewart Konigsberg was born on December 1, 1935, in Brooklyn, New York, to Martin and Nettie Konigsberg. A contentious couple, Allen's parents and their relationship would figure prominently in much of his later work. Marty Konigsberg moved from job to job during Allen's childhood as the family (which included sister Letty) moved from home to home before settling down in the Midwood section of Brooklyn. Allen despised school and later claimed that he learned nothing in his years of New York public schooling or his short stints at New York University and the City College of New York. By the age of 20, he had dropped out of both colleges, gotten engaged to a neighborhood girl named Harlene Rosen (their marriage would last six years, until 1962), and begun writing one-liners and getting them published by local columnists. At around this same time, the young gagwriter adopted "Woody Allen" first as his nom-de-plume and eventually as his permanent name.

Allen's comedy writing career blossomed in the late 1950s, first as a staff writer for NBC's *Colgate Comedy Hour,* then as a writer for Sid Caesar and Garry Moore. He jumped into stand-up comedy as a performer in his own right in the early 1960s, and established a reputation as one of the country's brightest young comics, with Las Vegas bookings and regular guest spots on Johnny Carson's *Tonight Show* and *The Ed Sullivan Show.*

By the mid–1960s, Allen was expanding his comic repertoire with essays in *Playboy* and the *New Yorker* magazines and acting roles in movies such as *What's New, Pussycat?* (1965) and *Casino Royale* (1967). Although he had written a new dialogue track for an old Japanese action picture that became *What's Up, Tiger Lily?* (1966), Allen's true film directorial debut was with *Take the Money and Run* (1969), the story of an inept bank robber played by Allen himself, a practice that set the stage for many future acting/directorial efforts.

In the 1970s, Allen turned almost exclusively to feature film directing and acting, leaving behind

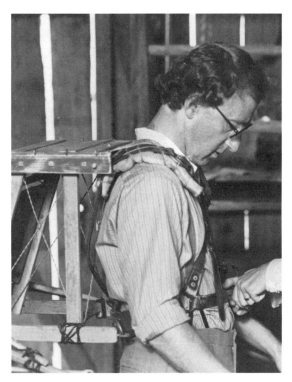

Woody Allen in *A Midsummer Night's Sex Comedy* (Orion)

the television work he despised but continuing to write essays and comic monologues. The early-1970s films directed by Allen are characterized by broad, oftentimes physical, comedy. Included in this period are *Bananas* (1971); *Everything You Wanted to Know About Sex . . .* (1972), a series of vignettes dealing with sexual mores and customs; *Sleeper* (1973), Allen's comic science fiction vision of the future; and *Love and Death* (1975), a spoof on Russian historical romance novels. Throughout this period he continued to play roles in other people's films, including *Play It Again, Sam* (1972) and a rare dramatic role in *The Front* (1976). Allen's two late-1970s masterpieces, *Annie Hall* (1977) and *Manhattan* (1979), represent the peak of his financial and artistic success, with *Annie Hall* garnering the best picture Oscar and a best director Oscar for Allen. These films cemented a new screen persona for Allen, less the frantic slapstick comic of the early 1970s and more the image of the sophisticated if somewhat neurotic New Yorker that he has maintained in the years since.

Through the 1980s and 1990s, Allen has delivered about a film a year in a wide variety of genres and styles. *Stardust Memories* (1980) portrayed Allen as a film director in a Fellini-esque mode; *Zelig* (1983) was a mock documentary about a chameleon-like historical figure; *Broadway Danny Rose* (1984) portrayed Allen as a nightclub comic mixed up with the Mafia; and *The Purple Rose of Cairo* (1985) was a movie fantasy in which a matinee idol comes to life from the screen. Allen hit another artistic high point in 1986 with *Hannah and Her Sisters* (1986), which garnered another best picture nomination.

For much of his career, Allen has been identified with two actresses, both of whom were also his lovers: Diane Keaton, who starred in *Sleeper, Love and Death,* and *Annie Hall* (for which she won the best actress Oscar); and Mia Farrow, who starred in almost all of Allen's 1980s films, including *Broadway Danny Rose, The Purple Rose of Cairo, Hannah and Her Sisters, Radio Days* (1987), and *Alice* (1990). His relationship with Farrow ended, and a scandal exploded onto the front pages of tabloids, in 1991 when it was revealed that Allen was in a relationship with Farrow's adopted daughter, Soon-Yi Previn, who was more than 20 years his junior. He and Previn married in 1997.

The scandal resonated in Allen's first film to be released in its wake, the aptly titled *Husband and Wives* (1992). Allen's other 1990s films include *Manhattan Murder Mystery* (1993), in which Allen reteamed with Keaton; *Bullets Over Broadway* (1994), a lush period piece about a Broadway playwright; *Everyone Says I Love You* (1996), a comic musical; and *Deconstructing Harry* (1997). Allen ended the decade with the mock jazz bio-pic *Sweet and Lowdown* (1999).

Other Films   *Interiors* (1978); *A Midsummer Night's Sex Comedy* (1982); *September* (1987); *Another Woman* (1988); *New York Stories* (1989), "Oedipus Wrecks" segment; *Crimes and Misdemeanors* (1989); *Shadows and Fog* (1992); *Mighty Aphrodite* (1995); *Celebrity* (1998); *Small Time Crooks* (2000).

References   Meade, Marion, *The Unruly Life of Woody Allen: A Biography* (New York: Scribner, 2000); Nichols, Mary P., *Reconstructing Woody* (Lanham, Md.: Rowman & Littlefield, 1998).

—C.M.

Altman, Robert (1925–) Robert Altman was born on February 20, 1925, in Kansas City, Missouri, the son of B. C. and Helen Altman. Altman's father (the B. C. stood for Bernard Clement) was something of a legend in the insurance sales business in Kansas City, while his mother concentrated on homemaking, hobbies, and family

Robert Altman

Robert Altman directing a scene in *Kansas City* (Fine Line Features)

(which included two younger sisters, Joan and Barbara). After stints in Catholic school and military school, Altman enlisted in the Army Air Force at the tail end of World War II, becoming the copilot of a B-24.

From the late 1940s to the mid-1950s, Altman worked at the Calvin Film Company, a local industrial, educational, and commercial filmmaker in Kansas City, an employment punctuated by several failed attempts to break into the Hollywood film industry. *The Delinquents* (1957), an independent feature in the teen exploitation picture mold and written, directed, and produced by Altman in Kansas City, served as his overdue entree into Hollywood; ALFRED HITCHCOCK, reportedly impressed by the film, invited Altman to direct episodes of his television program, *Alfred Hitchcock Presents*.

For the remainder of the 1950s and the first half of the 1960s, Altman worked as a journeyman TV director, logging dozens of credits on such programs as the Hitchcock show, *Bonanza, Combat! The Millionaire,* and *The Roaring Twenties.* In this period, Altman gained a reputation as a maverick that hindered his career in the mid-1960s when he had grown frustrated with TV but had no other viable career options. Finally, Warner Bros. hired him to direct the science-fiction feature *Countdown* (1968). Altman next directed the independent feature *That Cold Day in the Park* (1969) before landing the plum job of helming the 20th Century-Fox adaptation of *M*A*S*H* (1970). *M*A*S*H* was an overwhelming artistic and financial success that allowed Altman to pick and finance his projects for much of the 1970s.

The next few years saw a flurry of projects that represent Altman's artistic apex: *Brewster McCloud* (1970); *McCabe and Mrs. Miller* (1971), with Warren Beatty and Julie Christie; *Images* (1972); *The Long*

Goodbye (1973), with Elliott Gould as a latter-day Philip Marlowe; *California Split* (1974); and *Thieves Like Us* (1974). During the first half of the 1970s, Altman's reputation improved as he became an astute stylist specializing in genre revision (e.g., the detective film with *The Long Goodbye,* the gangster film with *Thieves Like Us*), and he attracted a "repertory company" of sorts composed of actors who would appear in several of his films (including Shelley Duvall, Michael Murphy, Keith Carradine, Bert Remsen, Elliott Gould, Bud Cort, and Henry Gibson). *Nashville* (1975) is arguably Altman's single greatest film, with its incisive examination of the country music industry and of American culture and politics circa the Bicentennial, as well as its innovative techniques of interweaving several storylines and two dozen major characters.

In the late 1970s, Altman's career would falter with some disastrous pictures that included the Paul Newman science fiction film *Quintet* (1979) and the intriguing but financially unsuccessful *3 Women* (1977). After the legendary failure of *Popeye* (1980), Altman retreated almost completely from mainstream filmmaking and spent all of the 1980s making modest filmic adaptations of stage plays. This retreat was physical as well as artistic, as Altman and his creative associates relocated to Paris for much of the decade. *Come Back to the Five and Dime, Jimmy Dean, Jimmy Dean* (1982) and *Secret Honor* (1984) are the high points of this period, while *Beyond Therapy* (1987) is almost certainly the nadir. In the late 1980s, Altman returned to television with projects such as a remake of *The Caine Mutiny Court-Martial* and the multi-part HBO series *Tanner '88* (both 1988).

Altman resumed his position in the Hollywood "mainstream" with the critically acclaimed *The Player* (1992), a biting satire of film industry practices and stereotypes. This was followed by *Short Cuts* (1993), a multi-character, multi-story film similar to *Nashville,* this time focused on the lives and tribulations of a group of Los Angeles residents. Another attempt at the multi-character

form, *Ready to Wear* (1994), was less successful in its examination of the Paris fashion industry. Altman's remaining 1990s films have included an homage to his hometown with *Kansas City* (1996), the neonoir thriller *The Gingerbread Man* (1998), and the tragicomic multi-character *Cookie's Fortune* (1999). Altman's first film of the new century was another multi-character story, *Dr. T and the Women* (2000).

Other Films   *The James Dean Story* (1957); *Buffalo Bill and the Indians* (1976); *A Wedding* (1978); *A Perfect Couple* (1979); *H.E.A.L.T.H.* (1979); *Streamers* (1983); *Fool for Love* (1985); *O.C. and Stiggs* (1987); *Aria* (1988), "Les Boreades" segment; *Vincent and Theo* (1990).

References   McGilligan, Patrick, *Robert Altman: Jumping Off the Cliff* (New York: St. Martin's Press, 1989); O'Brien, Daniel, *Robert Altman: Hollywood Survivor* (New York: Continuum, 1995).

—C.M.

Anders, Allison (1954–   )

Allison Anders first received critical acclaim after the release of her solo feature film debut in 1992 with *Gas Food Lodging.* The film, which tells the story of a single mother raising two teenage daughters in a desert town trailer park, earned Anders the New York Film Critics' Circle Award for best new director and won the Deauville Film Festival Critics' Award as well. The success of the film left Anders poised to support herself and her own two daughters with a career as a film director.

Born November 16, 1954, in Ashland, Kentucky, Anders had a turbulent early life. Her mother was pregnant with her when she and Allison's father married as teenagers. Anders told Graham Fuller, "My dad was wild and handsome, and my mom was a battered housewife; [my mom] says they had a rockabilly marriage." Anders's father abandoned her, her four sisters, and her mother when Anders was only five years old. This abandonment would be merely the beginning of a continuous string of childhood traumas forced upon Anders, who was sexually and physically abused as a young girl by several different men, and raped at the age of 12. Her rough home life, which included a stepfather's violence that peaked when he held a gun to Anders's head, resulted in her running away from home several times.

As a youngster, Anders would often escape her turbulent home life by creating elaborate fantasies. When she was 15 years old, Anders suffered a mental breakdown. After hearing a rumor that her favorite Beatle had died, Anders's fantasy world began to revolve around her relationship with "dead Paul." In a 1994 interview for *Entertainment Weekly,* Anders speaks candidly about her fantasy world not only taking her to the safety of mental hospitals, but also teaching her the craft of "learning to make people who aren't really there stand up and talk." In fact, her fantasy relationship with "dead Paul" would later become the subject of her screenplay *Paul Is Dead.* It would be a few years before she began using these skills as a filmmaker. She first had to make a few detours.

When Anders was 15, her mother left Kentucky with her daughters to escape an abusive husband and stepfather and moved to Los Angeles, where Anders later dropped out of high school at 17. While traveling back to Kentucky to live with relatives, she met the man who would father her first child. Anders moved to London with him and worked as a barmaid until she became pregnant. When her lover made it evident that he did not want her to have the child, Anders moved back to Los Angeles.

After the birth of her daughter, Anders enrolled in junior college while scraping by on welfare and a waitressing job. After the birth of a second daughter, Anders entered the UCLA film school. While there, she landed an internship as a production assistant on Wim Wenders's film *Paris, Texas* (1984). After graduating from film school, Anders and classmate Kurt Voss wrote and directed their first film together. *Border Radio* (1987) took them four years to complete, with production stopping

for months at a time in order to scrape up more money to continue filming. The film, based on the Los Angeles punk scene, gave Anders the hands-on experience she would need to create *Gas Food Lodging* (1992), a tale of a single mother and her two teenage daughters, struggling financially in an isolated gas station–diner.

Anders recalled this phase of her career: "On the first film, *Border Radio,* I didn't know what the hell I was doing. With *Gas Food Lodging,* I was amazed I knew what I was doing." Film critics took notice of the difference as well. The success of *Gas Food Lodging* allowed Anders to get off of welfare and caught the attention of Martin Scorsese, who contacted Anders and invited her to work with him on *Grace of My Heart* (1996). First, though, Anders would write and direct *Mi Vida Loca/My Crazy Life* (1993) and a segment for *Four Rooms* (1995).

Mi Vida Loca is a unique film in that it tells the story of gang life in LA's Echo Park from female gang members' points of view. Anders, a former resident of the Echo Park neighborhood, cast many of the cameo roles in the film with actual Echo Park gang members. This decision, although sometimes criticized as taking away from the clarity of the story due to her inexperienced actors, did lend the film an authenticity it otherwise would not have had. The women Anders cast kept *Mi Vida Loca* true to reality on everything from clothing styles to "funeral scenes where the tears were as real as [the] memories."

Outside issues directly relating to the lives of the women Anders cast in the film added to the impact of their story being told. When filming began, it was merely a year after the LA riots following the Rodney King trial. Also, during filming, one of the women overdosed and left a four-year-old son. Anders raised money for her funeral and adopted the young boy. Anders describes her decision as feeling "absolutely right" on a spiritual level—"I never questioned it." Later, Anders would give the boy's babysitters on-screen credit in *Grace of My Heart* for their assistance during filming.

Anders moved on to write and direct a segment in *Four Rooms* (1995) with fellow directors QUENTIN TARANTINO, Robert Rodriguez, and Alexandre Rockwell. The film, about an ill-fated bellboy's night on the job, was written in four segments with each director writing a segment to take place in four different rooms. Anders's segment titled "The Missing Ingredient" tells the story of a coven of witches who rent the Honeymoon Suite in order to summon a goddess from the dead. Interestingly, Anders's is the only segment with no onscreen violence "I've seen more real violence than [the other directors]," she noted. "I don't want to see it onscreen." Also in 1995 Anders received a MacArthur Award.

Following *Four Rooms* Anders directed *Grace of My Heart* (1996). Martin Scorsese produced the film, which tells the story of a fictitious female singer/songwriter in the '60s. In a 1996 article for *Interview,* Anders says that part of what drew her to the film was the music. She went on to say that music played a role in her life "to the extent that movies were the secondary influence." In 1999, Anders would again return to music as a focal point for the film *Sugar Town.* The film also reunited Anders with Kurt Voss. *Sugar Town* offered a take on the Los Angeles music scene "in what Anders and Voss picture as all its back stabbing, drug-addicted, fame-obsessed, washed up glory." This film won the directors a Fantasporto Directors' Week Award for best screenplay.

Anders's work can additionally be seen as a director on TV's *Sex and the City* and as executive producer of *Lover Girl* (1997). She appeared as herself in the film *Welcome to Hollywood* (1998) and her most recent film, *Things Behind the Sun,* was released in 2001. Without question, Anders has come quite a distance from her tumultuous upbringing and hard-knock life as a young adult. As she continues to etch her career as a director, she works with the conviction that "movies can tell us about our place, or lack of place, in our culture."

References   Allen, Jamie, "Anders, Voss Offer Bittersweet 'Sugar Town'," CNN.com, posted September 13, 1999; Fuller, Graham, "Allison Anders: Shooting Straight: From the Heart," *Interview* (September 1996); Jackson, Devon, "American She," *Mother Jones* 18, no. 2 (March/April 1993), p. 15; Jaworski, Margaret, "Extra Credit," *Family Circle* 110, no. 7 (May 13, 1997), p. 15; Pryor, Kelli, "Her Crazy Life," *Entertainment Weekly* 232 (July 22, 1994), pp. 26–30; Taylor, Ella, "The New Mainstream Hollywood," *Elle* 11, no. 2 (October 1995), pp. 132–134.

—L.H. and T.J.M.

Anderson, Lindsay (1923–1994)   Lindsay Anderson was born in Bangalore, India (April 17, 1923), where his father was stationed with the Royal Engineers. He was educated in England at Cheltenham College and later at Oxford University, where he, along with Gavin Lambert, founded the magazine *Sequence,* which he continued to edit for five years (1947–52), beyond the granting of his M.A. degree in 1948. Between 1948 and 1954 he learned filmmaking by making four industrial documentaries for Richard Sutcliffe, Ltd. In 1953 he made two short personal documentaries. *Saturday's Children,* concerning children at the Royal School for the Deaf in Margate, won an Academy Award in 1955 for best short subject, and *O Dreamland* was a "rather satirical" 12-minute film about an amusement park in Margate. A 40-minute short, *Every Day Except Christmas,* followed in 1957 documenting the workers at London's Covent Garden market, and won the Grand Prix at the Venice Film Festival of 1957. During this period Anderson also made several government-sponsored short films.

In 1957 Anderson directed his first play at the Royal Court Theatre and was appointed artistic director of the Royal Court in 1959. He directed several stage plays for the next five years before returning to work in cinema. When he resumed making pictures, Anderson's first professional feature film, *This Sporting Life* (1963), adapted by David Storey from his own novel of the same title, was one of the defining pictures of the Angry Young Man movement, transferring from stage to screen the story of a coal miner, Frank Machin (Richard Harris), whose brutal strength makes him an excellent rugby player. Though successful as a professional rugby player, he is unable to adjust successfully to his altered station in life. He is exploited for his athletic ability and becomes a pawn in a power struggle between two businessmen who want to control the club. Anderson won widespread praise for his realistic treatment of this angry, inarticulate, working-class character.

The theme of economic and social exploitation was to become central to Anderson's later films, especially the allegorical features he scripted with David Sherwin. These can be viewed as filmed essays in social criticism, excoriating institutions and attempting to show the possible consequences of social privilege and the exploitation of the common man. Anderson took a surreal turn with *If . . .* (1968), the first of a trilogy he made with David Sherwin as scriptwriter, a blistering attack upon the educational system in Britain, exposed as being not only trivial, but also perverse and corrupt. If the circumstances become too extreme and the system is not reformed, Anderson's film suggests, the natural response is likely to be first rebellion, then revolution. The film attacks not only a particular institution but also the very fabric of privileged British society. Although released during the year of student protests and demonstrations in Europe and America, the script, entitled "Crusaders," was completed as early as 1960. Anderson described the film to Elizabeth Sussex as being "deeply anarchistic," involving "a social and political philosophy which puts the highest possible value on responsibility."

If . . . made Malcolm McDowell, who played student rebel Mick Travis, a star. McDowell would later play Alex, the central thug-protagonist of STANLEY KUBRICK's *A Clockwork Orange* (1971), but McDowell would also go on to play Mick Travis, Anderson's allegorical, contemporary Everyman, in *O Lucky Man!* (1973) and in *Britannia Hospital* (1982), with each Travis feature becoming increasingly satirical and bitter. The story line of *O Lucky Man!*—loosely based upon the life of Malcolm McDowell—traces the progress of an innocent young man who sets forth optimistically as a coffee salesman in the north of England, is buffeted by the cynical and corrupt world he encounters, but is rescued by a stroke of good fortune at the end when a film director, played by Lindsay Anderson himself, "discovers" him and makes him famous, lifting him out of poverty and depression. Though he encounters a mad scientist and an evil, unscrupulous capitalist who betrays him, Mick is protected by his innocence and good nature, aided by a little bit of luck.

After perfecting an outrageous satiric style with *O Lucky Man!* Anderson tested its outer limits with *Britannia Hospital* (1982), the eponymous hospital run by the lunatic Dr. Millar (Graham Croden), the same mad scientist who experimented on human beings in *O Lucky Man!* Mick Travis now appears as an investigative journalist out to expose the bizarre goings-on at the hospital, which becomes an emblem for Britain in social, political, and economic disarray, a nation crossing over into madness and anarchy, a diseased nation that is incurably ill. It's a nasty situation, and a nasty—though often humorous—film. "The film took a terrible beating at the time," as Gavin Lambert has written, "partly because its release coincided with the Falklands War, and failed to march to the beat of Thatcher's patriotic drum."

In 1987 Anderson made his first American film, *The Whales of August,* adapted by David Berry from his stage play and starring two movie legends, Lillian Gish and Bette Davis, as two sisters spending their 50th summer together in their coastal Maine cottage. In 1990 Anderson returned to satire with *Glory! Glory!* a blistering attack on hypocritical TV evangelism. In the words of Derek Elley, who reviewed Anderson's last film, *Is That All There Is?* for *Variety* (November 29, 1993), "Lindsay Anderson's typically eclectic contribution to 'The Director's Place,' the BBC Scotland's series of self-portraits, shows the septuagenarian helmer alive and well and feisty," surrounded by friends such as the designer Jocelyn Herbert, writers David Sherwin and David Storey, and composer Alan Price, with whom he had worked on the Mick Travis trilogy. The film proved to be valedictory, however, since Anderson died on August 30, 1994, within a year of its conclusion.

Though he made only a handful of feature films, all of them were distinctive, groundbreaking efforts, informed with political agendas and frequently satirical. His influence was enormous. He organized the first "Free Cinema" program at London's National Film Theatre in 1956, for example, and wrote extensively about directors he admired, such as JOHN FORD, and those he did not, criticizing the Grierson school of documentary filmmaking, for example. He felt that responsible artists should deal with the realities of 20th-century life. His last film, *Is That All There Is?* began with a quotation from his 1956 Free Cinema manifesto: "Perfection is not an aim"—ironic words to live by. His friend Gavin Lambert eulogized Anderson as "the Great Outsider of British films," basically "a romantic at war with reality as he perceived it." He was a great satirist, and like all great satirists, often misunderstood: "His satire is a defence against pain," Lambert explained, "and he scolds because he loves."

References Armes, Roy, *A Critical History of British Cinema* (New York: Oxford University Press, 1978); Graham, Allison, *Lindsay Anderson* (Boston: Twayne, 1981); Lambert, Gavin, "Lindsay Anderson, Unrequited Lover," *Sight and Sound* 4, no. 10 (October 1994): 18–21; Lambert, Gavin, *Mainly About Lindsay Anderson* (New York: Knopf, 2000); Silet, Charles P., *Lindsay Anderson: A Guide to References and Resources* (Boston: G. K. Hall, 1979); Sussex, Elizabeth, *Lindsay Anderson* (New York: Praeger, 1969).

—J.M.W.

Angelopoulos, Theo (1935–) Greece's most important filmmaker actively contributed to a renaissance in Greek literature, music, and art in the 1970s and 1980s. Theodoros Angelopoulos was born in Athens on April 27, 1935, one of four children of Spyros and Katerina Angelopoulos. Although his upper-middle-class family had deep roots in the countryside, it had moved to the city, like many other families at the time. During the Second World War and the subsequent civil war in Greece (1944–49), the Angelopoulos family survived many hardships, including hunger and the political persecution of their father, Spyros. From 1953 to 1957, Theo studied law. After his military service (1959–60) he moved to Paris, France, where he studied film and anthropology. He returned to Greece in 1963, worked for a left-wing newspaper, the *Dimokratiki Allaghi,* and three years later made his first short film, *The Broadcast (I ekpombi).*

At a time when the Greek cinema consisted mostly of melodramas and low comedies, Angelopoulos's first feature-length film, *Reconstruction (Anaparastasis* [1970]), was a revelation. Its subject was taken from a newspaper article about a village woman who murdered her husband after his return from Germany, where he had been a guest worker for several years. The story is retold and restaged several times, so that the motives and even the identity of the killer are thrown into doubt. As the director has remarked, the choice of the title was based on Dostoyevsky's *Crime and Punishment:* "It is rather that her environment is the real murderer, that has murdered her spirit. It's very important that she says, 'I will have no one judge me. I will have no one judge me.' I respect her. She is an amazing person." The movie was filmed in black and white on a tight budget and utilized nonprofessional actors. By preferring to film on location, near the Greek–Albanian border, Angelopoulos set a precedent that he would follow for the remainder of his career. As he has explained, "I believe something special happens on location, in the real place, and I do not mean just the ability to photograph the decor, the landscape. But it is more that when I am in the place I have set the film, all five of my senses are working. I become more completely aware. I therefore feel I am living the experiences I want to film." *Reconstruction* won a major award in Berlin and it was the centerpiece of the Thessaloniki Film Festival.

After his first film, Angelopoulos embarked on a historical tetralogy about Greece in the 1930–70 time period, consisting of *Days of 36* (*Meres tou '36* [1972]), *The Travelling Players* (*O thiasos* [1975]), *The Hunters* (*I kinigi* [1977]), and *Alexander the Great* (*O megalexandros* [1980]). *Days of 36* was Angelopoulos's first film in color. It was made in the last days of the military junta that had governed Greece since 1967, and the rising director felt that he could then challenge it more directly by exposing the cultural climate and historical circumstances from which it had emerged. He submitted a cleansed script to the censors and started shooting. By the time production was completed, observes historian Dan Georgakas, "the junta was out of power but the new government was nearly as hostile to its political perspective as the junta would have been." The second film in the tetralogy is probably the most celebrated by critics. *The Travelling Players* centers on an itinerant theater troupe that performs sentimental melodramas during the years 1939–52, that is, throughout the Second World War and the ensuing civil war. The fates of the actors serve as mirrors of the broader events in the tumultuous history of the country. Moreover, they also parallel the Greek tragedy of the House of Atreus. The interplay between performance, history, and myth is carried out through a dexterous manipulation of time, as in the long take when a man begins a walk in the year 1952 but arrives in 1939. "This shifting in time within one long take

is not meant to be cynical, but economically and unequivocally to nail down the political linkage of a pre-war military regime with a postwar military regime." In a similar scene, a group of Fascists marches away from a 1946 New Year's dance in full-throated song to arrive at their destination in the year 1952. Police start to beat strikers in one time period and finish the task in another. Angelopoulos's manipulations of time are only one of the devices he utilizes with the intent to offer an alternative to the conventional Hollywood narrative paradigm. He prefers the use of the long take to the standard American montage techniques; and in a departure from Hollywood's emphasis on a "star system," he frames his players in long shots, thus diminishing their centrality and imparting more importance to groups than to individuals. Moreover, he breaks the "fourth wall" by having the actors tell their stories directly to the camera; and he stages the action laterally in horizontal compositional configurations, emulating, in effect, the flat, mural-like effect of a frieze. All these strategies form part of what David Bordwell calls the "political modernism" of Angelopoulos, a tendency whose origins Bordwell locates in the work of his predecessors, such as JEAN-LUC GODARD, Jean Marie Straub and Danielle Huillet, Miklos Jancso, and MICHELANGELO ANTONIONI.

With *The Hunters,* Angelopoulos continued his examination of the conflict between left and right, between populists and monarchists in Greek history. In this film, the action transpires on New Year, 1977, when a bourgeois hunting party stumbles upon the corpse of a guerrilla fighter from the civil war of 30 years earlier. The mystery lies in the fact that the body is still warm! Angelopoulos continued this historical exploration in *Alexander the Great,* whose action is set at the beginning of the 20th century. But this time, much of his attention centered on the internecine fights within the left, and this fact caused many who had cheered his earlier films to turn against him. The majority of the critics did applaud the film's courage, however, especially when seen in the context of the earlier work by Angelopoulos.

During the 1980s, the director's films took yet another turn from social drama to an emphasis on more individual characters, though always framing them in the context of broader societal events. In *Voyage to Cythera,* the protagonist, named Spyros, like Angelopoulos's own father, is an old Greek communist who has lived in exile in Tashkent (then part of the USSR) after the civil war, and who returns to his country after an amnesty only to be finally rejected by modern Greece. In 1983, came *The Beekeeper (O melissokomos),* another film about a teacher, also named Spyros, who leaves his wife and daughter to return to the profession of his father and grandfather, beekeeping. In the course of his travel back to the countryside, he finds a young and promiscuous hitchhiker who accompanies him and leaves him at different points in his trip.

Angelopoulos's most accessible film, *Landscape in the Mist* (which won the European "Felix" as best film of 1989), could be subtitled *Children in a Documentary Fairy Tale.* It forms the third part of what Angelopoulos has called a "trilogy of silence," together with *Voyage* and *The Beekeeper.* History (and for that matter, the world of adults) is left behind in this tale, Angelopoulos's only film centered on children. In this film, two children, Voula and her younger brother Alexander, start a journey through Greece in search of their father, a man they don't remember and who might even not exist. This primary focus of the film is myth and fairy tale. As Horton points out, when we see Alexander and Voula walking on a northern Greece highway, "we are left to consider these two figures as simply a young girl and young boy walking in a vast, dark landscape. The minimalism involved—no speech, little action—leads us to dwell upon the scene in our own minds, to open it up to interpretation, meditation, exploration, and thus to consider the mythic dimensions of these to character's lives."

After the resounding success of *Landscape in the Mist,* and throughout the decade of the 1990s, Angelopoulos expanded his scope from Greece to the surrounding Balkan region, with stories that increasingly focused on the plight of this turbulent area of the world, then engulfed in successive conflicts over national borders and identities in Slovenia, Bosnia-Herzegovina, and, lately, Kosovo. In *The Suspended Step of the Stork (To meteoro vima to pelargou* [1991]), he revisits the myth of Telemachus and Odysseus, with the former embodied by a young television journalist (Gregory Karr) who is looking for a famous Greek politician (Marcello Mastroianni) who went off on a journey and has never been seen again. Instead of a conqueror or adventurer, this modern Odysseus has decided to live with the unfortunate refugees of the Balkan wars.

Angelopoulos's next film, *Ulysses' Gaze (To vlemma tou odyssea* [1995]), takes another step out of Greece to explore the disintegration of Yugoslavia in the Republic of Macedonia (called "Skopje" by the Greeks). This time the protagonist is a Greek–American filmmaker (Harvey Keitel) who travels from Greece throughout the Balkans, crossing into Bulgaria, Romania, Serbia, and finally Bosnia, where his journey takes him to war-torn Sarajevo. The film, again taking on the Homeric tradition, also alludes to the Platonic idea that is synthesized in the philosopher's utterance, "And thus, the soul too, if it wishes to know itself, will have to look into the soul." Angelopoulos's first film to be made outside of Greece, predominantly in English and with an international cast, it deepened the concerns he had explored in *Suspended Step,* and it succeeded brilliantly with critics and audiences in Europe, where it won the Grand Prix at the Cannes Film Festival in 1995. Angelopoulos's latest film, *Eternity and a Day (Mia aiwniothta kai mia mera* [1998]), has an aging Bruno Ganz playing an exiled writer called Alexandre, dying from an unspecified illness, when he has a fateful encounter with an eight-year-old Albanian refugee (Achilleas Skevis). As he had done in the past, Angelopoulos glides between past and present in conflating the end of Alexandre's life with his happier years with his wife and daughter in the 1960s.

References   Horton, Andrew, ed., *The Last Modernist, The Films of Theo Angelopoulos* (Westport, Conn.: Greenwood Press, 1997); Horton, Andrew, ed., *The Films of Theo Angelopoulos: A Cinema of Contemplation* (Princeton, N.J.: Princeton University Press, 1997).

—F.A.

Antonioni, Michelangelo   (1912–   )

Michelangelo Antonioni was born September 29, 1912, in Ferrara, Italy. He studied economics at the University of Bologna from 1931 to 1935 and was employed as a bank clerk and journalist from 1935 to 1939. In 1939 he moved to Rome and began to contribute articles to film journals including *Il Corriere Padano.* In 1940 he served as the editorial secretary of *Cinema,* published by the Fascist Entertainment Guild. From 1940 to 1941 he studied at the Centro Sperimentale di Cinematografia in Rome. Like several other students who attended the school founded by the Fascist government, Antonioni would go on to make films whose themes often opposed institutional values. He married Letizia Balboni in 1942 (he has been married to his second wife Enrica since 1986). He collaborated on the script of *Un pilota ritorna,* directed by Rossellini in 1942, and was assigned by the Italian production company to work with Marcel Carné on *Les visiteurs du soir* (1942). Following the end of the war, he continued to collaborate with screenwriters and directors.

In 1943 Antonioni filmed his first documentary short titled *Gente del Po (People of the Po),* which was not released until 1947. He directed six more documentaries between 1943 and 1950. An adulterous love affair was the subject of his first feature: *Cronaca di un amore (Story of a Love Affair* [1950]). This was followed by *La signora senza camelie (Camille without Camelias* [1953]), an account

of a young actress and her film producer husband. North Italy would be the setting for the next two features: *Le amiche (The Girlfriends* [1955]), set among the upper class of Turin and *Il grido (The Cry* [1957]), where Antonioni returns to his native Po valley for a tale of a forlorn artisan named Aldo. Many critics describe Antonioni's work of the 1960s as the Italian version of the French *nouvelle vague.* Although older than his counterparts of the New Wave, his films are marked by the same auteur qualities.

L'avventura (The Adventure [1960]), for which he wrote the story and collaborated on the script, appeared in the same year as *La dolce vita.* Both in their own way would transform Italian cinema. Antonioni's film won the Special Jury Prize at Cannes, although the audience booed and hissed during the screening. Such viewer response prompted strident critical support that guaranteed international release and a chance to attract wider attention. Early audiences may not have known what to think of the film, but by the end of the century *L'avventura* would appear on nearly every list of the most important films ever made. The story involves characters thrust into an unfamiliar landscape who, although arriving at a level of self-knowledge not previously attained, are still bound by the consequences of previous actions. Monica Vitti, the actress who plays Claudia, gave a remarkable, understated performance and Antonioni would rely on her presence for other major projects of the 1960s. She came to define the Antonioni heroine: enigmatic, aloof, and fashionably attired.

La notte (The Night [1961]) starred Jeanne Moreau, Marcello Mastroianni, and Vitti in a story that led to the end of a marriage. The film asked viewers to consider the moral standards they accept or deny as factors in making choices. As in many of Antonioni's films, it is the shift of emotion rather than action that propels the unresolved narrative. The third film in what some have labeled a "trilogy" is *L'eclisse (The Eclipse* [1962]), a tale with Vitti and Alain Delon as lovers whose affair contrasts their individual searches for meaning in the relationships they form. This film also won the Special Jury Prize at Cannes, but by 1962, audiences were more receptive to both the themes and aesthetic of Antonioni's work.

Il deserto rosso (*Red Desert* [1964]) was Antonioni's first color film. Set in the northern industrial town of Ravenna, this work would prove the importance of color as a formal element but also its role in describing the psychological drama of individuals who become increasingly estranged from their environment. The bleak world of factories and technology does not control the action, yet characters are defined by their responses to this environment. Vitti appears as Giuliana and viewers recognize she is an individual at an impasse: Will she choose life in this austere world? The power of the director's vision is that he neither reviles nor celebrates this industrial world. As a modernist, his worldview is not one of nostalgia for the past and he does not bemoan the loss of a traditional culture but does suggest that the waste technology generates is both industrial by-product and human alienation.

Blow-Up (1966) marked the first international project Antonioni filmed outside Italy and in English. It won the best director award from the National Society of Film Critics and the Palme d'Or at Cannes. David Hemmings plays a photographer in "swinging London" who, as a maker of images, comes to question his perception of the images he captures on film. Antonioni traveled to the United States to film *Zabriskie Point* (1969). The film about the American counterculture was the director's examination of a generation foreign in both age and values. Critics in the United States reviled the film. The director witnessed a similar response from Chinese authorities to *Chung-Kuo Cina* (1972). Antonioni documented the China of the Cultural Revolution at the invitation of government leaders. His view of life in the final cut was not the one authorities wished to project to the world, and the film was never shown in China.

The director returned to feature films with *Professione: Reporter* (*The Passenger* [1975]). The story is that of a reporter (Jack Nicholson) who acts impulsively and assumes the identity of a dead gunrunner, only to face a similar violent end. The extraordinary final shot is one frequently examined by film students. Antonioni's films of the 1980s include *Il Mistero di Oberwald* (*The Oberwald Mystery* [1980]) and *Identificazione di una donna* (*Identification of a Woman* [1982]). Antonioni experiments with new video technology but retains familiar themes of individuals searching for identity in their relationships with others and their world.

In the mid-1980s, a stroke and failing health slowed the director's output. With the collaboration of WIM WENDERS, plus a screenplay of his own short stories. Antonioni directed *Par delà les nuages* (*Beyond the clouds*) in 1995. His most recent films are: *Destinazione Verna* (2000) and *Tanto per stare insieme* (*Just to Be Together* [2001]). As a director, Antonioni continues to defy easy labeling. Sometime minimalist, auteur, and neorealist, he can perhaps be understood as adhering to many features of the latter category if the label is used to define what he reacted against rather than what he shared with other directors (beyond the tendency to employ indeterminate endings). Antonioni never limits the reading of his films to a single tradition. He certainly remains the leader among directors of what some term as European "art cinema," an artist with a sophisticated sense of abstract values and a fascination for human emotion, providing viewers with memorable, wordless sequences and indelible images. He has received numerous awards for lifetime achievement in film (Cannes 1982, Venice 1983, and an Oscar in 1995).

Other Films *I vinti* (*The Vanquished* [1952]); *L'amore in città* (*Love in the City* [1953]); *Kumbha Mela* (1989); *Roma '90* (1989).

References Brunette, Peter, *The Films of Michelangelo Antonioni* (Cambridge, U.K.: Cambridge University Press, 1998); Chatman, Seymour, *Antonioni; or, The Surface of the World* (Berkeley: University of California Press,

1985); Perry, Ted, and René Prieto, *Michelangelo Antonioni: A Guide to References and Resources* (Boston: G. K. Hall, 1986); Rohdie, Sam, *Antonioni* (London: BFI, 1990); Wenders, Wim, *My Time with Antonioni: The Diary of an Extraordinary Experience* (London: Faber, 2000).

—J.A.D.

Argento, Dario (1943–)   Dario Argento was born on September 7, 1943, in Rome, the son of producer Salvatore Argento. After working as a film critic in Rome, he began work as a screenwriter and collaborated with Bernardo Bertolucci on writing *Once Upon A Time in the West* (1968). He also worked on a variety of different genre movies in the Italian film industry, usually featuring an international cast. Among these were two other westerns, *Today It's Me, Tomorrow It's You* (1968) featuring Brett Halsey, Kurosawa actor Tatsuya Nakadai, and Bud Spencer; and Don Taylor's *The Five Man Army.* This western version of *Mission Impossible* starred Peter Graves, Bud Spencer, James Daly, and Tetsuro Tamba. As a director he continued this international casting tradition but began working within the particularly stylistic Italian horror film tradition known as "giallo," which emphasized blood and gore.

Argento's first film as director was *The Bird with the Crystal Plumage,* the first of a series of three films whose titles were designed to challenge the viewer in terms of their relationship to solving a particular enigma. These films were scored by Ennio Morricone, a prolific composer well known for his collaboration with SERGIO LEONE, in a significantly aural manner designed to complement both the mystery confronting the characters as well as Argento's flamboyant visual style. Starring American actor Tony Musante and British actress Suzy Kendall, *The Bird with the Crystal Plumage* dealt with a character's attempt to perceive the real nature of a murderous attack in an art gallery, an attempt designed to challenge both the character himself and the audience. Argento has often scripted his films and claims ALFRED HITCHCOCK as his main inspiration, aiming, like Brian DePalma, to carry the director's visual style into new technological directions. DePalma has also expressed his debt to Argento's style in several of his own works.

The film's success led to *The Cat o' Nine Tails* and *Four Flies on Grey Velvet* (both 1971), respectively starring Karl Malden and James Franciscus, and Michael Brandon and Mimsy Farmer. After taking a break from thrillers to direct *Le cinque giornate* (1973), a film about the Italian Risorgimento, Argento returned to the thriller with *Deep Red* (1976). Starring David Hemmings in a deliberate echo of Antonioni's *Blow-Up* (1966), the film saw Argento's first collaboration with the rock group Goblin whose musical score represented Argento's desire to bring the operatic soundtracks of the Italian western into a more hyper-modern dimension.

The following year Argento directed the first of what was designed to be a trilogy dealing with the malign influence of the demonic Three Mothers on human affairs. Set in a German ballet school, *Suspiria* featured young American actress Jessica Harper with cinematic divas Joan Bennett and Alida Valli in a visually stylized exercise in cinematic gore accompanied by Goblin's pounding rock score. Although Argento followed this film with *Inferno,* scored by Keith Emerson of Emerson, Lake, and Palmer, the trilogy remains incomplete. Despite envisaging a final film centered on "Mater Tenebrae," the 1982 *Tenebrae* had nothing to do with the trilogy. It focused on a series of brutal murders somehow associated with a mystery writer played by Anthony Franciosa. Unfortunately, *Phenomena* (1985), starring Jennifer Connelly and Donald Pleasance, was drastically cut for American release and distributed under the title *Creepers.* Like *Deep Red, Inferno,* and *Tenebrae,* it starred Argento's ex-partner Daria Nicolodi, who would usually meet a nasty end in his films. *Phenomena* also saw the first appearance of their daughter Asia Argento, who would later star in her father's films. Argento also continued his interests in operatic style with *Opera* (1987), a film dealing with a fan's sadistic relationship with an opera singer. During the '90s, Argento's films received a mixed reception, but the director began to return to form with *The Stendhal Syndrome* (1996) and *The Phantom of the Opera* (1998). Both starred his daughter Asia Argento, with the last film also featuring Julian Sands as a handsome phantom suffering from the director's favorite brand of sadomasochistic mother fixation.

References McDonagh, Maitland, *Broken Mirrors, Broken Minds: The Dark Dreams of Dario Argento* (London: Sun Tavern Fields, 1991); Knee, Adam, "Gender, Genre, Argento," in *The Dread of Difference,* Barry K. Grant, ed. (Austin: University of Texas Press, 1996), pp. 203–230.

—T.W.

Armstrong, Gillian (1950–) With her strong feminist bent, Gillian Armstrong brought her own distinctive flair to the so-called Australian Renaissance of the 1960s and 1970s. She was born in Melbourne on December 18, 1950, and educated at Swinburne College. After studying filmmaking at the Melbourne and Australian Film and Television School, Sydney, she worked as a production assistant and editor before making a series of documentary films tracking the lives of their female subjects, *Smokes and Lollies* (1975), *14's Good, 18's Better* (1980), and *Bingo, Bridesmaids and Braces* (1988). Feminist historian Gwendolyn Audrey Foster reports that Armstrong tried to capture the everyday paths of average young females, in which "the sorting out process begins—sexual attraction—stereotypes—you start working out what you are considered to be in society. I'm the pretty one; I'm ugly; If only I had this. . . ." Indeed, continues Foster, "The gap between confining socially imposed gender identities and the wish to define ourselves as women is a consistent theme through Armstrong's films."

After directing her first feature, *The Singer and the Dancer* in 1976, the 27-year-old Armstrong went on to direct her "breakthrough" film, *My Brilliant Career* (1979), the first feature film directed by a woman in Australia in more than 45 years. It garnered international acclaim, especially from feminists who regarded it as a celebration of female rebellion against societal codes. Adapted from an autobiographical 1901 novel by the precocious Miles Franklin (a pseudonym for the 19-year-old novelist Stella Maria Miles Franklin), the film depicted the efforts of rebellious young Sybylla Melvyn (Judy Davis), a Bush woman, to escape the life of wife and mother in order to become a writer. As Brian McFarlane has noted, "it uses its narrative set in the 1890s to explore and comment on late 1970s feminist issues. . . . The parallels with Australian women in the 1970s working out the terms of their own lives are as apparent as they are unforced." Critic Molly Haskell reports that some feminists resisted the film's ending: "However vehemently they had argued for new, anti-romantic endings in which women would go off into the sunset alone, would stand tall and strong and solitary without needing men to complete them, when push came to shove they didn't understand why Judy Davis couldn't have a writing career and Sam Neill, too." Indeed, Haskell continues, audiences in general had difficulty accepting the idea that "nuptial bliss might dull the budding writer's acuteness, that companionability might take the edge off the urge to create—particularly for a young woman in that era with the kind of social responsibilities she might anticipate." Three years later Armstrong's *Starstruck* again told the story of an ambitious heroine, only this time it was formatted as a contemporary rock musical.

Her first American film was *Mrs. Soffel* (1984), starring Mel Gibson and Diane Keaton as ill-fated lovers escaping the Allegheny County Prison in Pennsylvania at the turn of the century. Since then, her career has criss-crossed the ocean, mak-

Gillian Armstrong (right) on the set of *Oscar and Lucinda* (Twentieth Century Fox)

ing more films in Australia (*High Tide,* 1987) and America (*Little Women,* 1994). In the former, arguably Armstrong's most beautiful film, a trio of women—Judy Davis as Lilli, a drifter; Claudia Karvan as Aly, the daughter Lilli left behind; and Jan Adele as Bet, Aly's mother-in-law—live out their mundane lives in a poor coastal town in New South Wales. "The transient lifestyles of these women are painted against a backdrop of a society that looks for easily read 'family values,'" writes Foster. "Nothing is obvious or easily read in *High Tide,* most especially the motivations of Lilli, who rejects suitors, family, success, and everything else she is expected to embrace." In the latter a superb cast, including Wynona Ryder as Jo March and Susan Sarandon as "Marmee"

March, is wedded to a script containing more than a liberal dose of feminist rhetoric. The character of Sybylla Mervyn has returned in the incarnation of Jo, who in the end triumphs in the establishment of her own school.

Her most recent film, *Oscar and Lucinda* (1997), is her most ambitious. Adapted from the 1988 book by the Australian novelist Peter Carey, the story begins in 1847 and traces the intersecting lives of Oscar, a boy brought up in the remote countryside of Devon under the stern discipline of his father, a fanatical cleric; and Lucinda, a wayward child in New South Wales. Oscar grows up to be an Anglican cleric, and Lucinda becomes the manager of a glass-works factory. When they meet, these two disparate characters discover their common passion—gambling. Together, they launch the most colossal gamble of their lives, the transportation to a remote village in the outback of a church made entirely of iron and glass. *Oscar and Lucinda* is a miracle of a movie, a luminous, lyric, lovingly detailed sprawl of a story. If at times Ralph Fiennes tends to make his terminally timid character of Oscar seem like a kind of benevolent Uriah Heep, and if the story itself betrays its novelistic origins with some lumpy continuity and shortcomings in the delineation of the secondary characters, this unlikely blend of romance, historical epic, and adventure story is held together by its blazing affirmation of faith and love between the two principals and by the spectacular landscape photography.

"One thing I'm very sensitive about—and have been since film school—is this preconception about women film directors," says Armstrong. "We're always seen as having to be the little mother on the set, which is the last thing I ever was. . . . But it's very hard for any working mother. One advantage female directors have is at least you're not working full time, all the time. . . . Actually, I have wonderful people on my production crew who mother and look after me, and many of them are men."

Other Films *Having a Go* (1983); *Hard to Handle: Bob Dylan with Tom Petty and the Heartbreakers* (1986); *Fires Within* (1991); *The Last Days of Chez Nous* (1992).

References Foster, Gwendolyn Audrey, *Women Film Directors: An International Bio-Critical Dictionary* (Westport, Conn.: Greenwood Press, 1995); Hardesty, Mary, "The Brilliant Career of Gillian Armstrong," *DGA Magazine* 20, no. 4 (September–October 1995): 21–24; Haskell, Molly, "Wildflowers," *Film Comment* 29, no. 2 (March–April 1993): 35–37; McFarlane, Brian, *Australian Cinema, 1970–1985* (London: Secker and Warburg, 1987); Warrick, Steve, "High Tide," *Film Quarterly* 42, no. 4 (Summer 1989): 21–26; Wolf, Jamie, "A Hard Woman Is Good to Find," *American Film,* January–February 1985, pp. 20–26.

—J.C.T.

Arnold, Jack (1916–1992) Jack Arnold, who directed some of the most enduring and beloved science fiction films during the genre's "Golden Age" of the fifties, was born on October 14, 1912, on the kitchen table of his parent's New Haven, Connecticut, home. Originally named Jack Arnold Waks by his Russian immigrant parents, he dropped his last name when he began acting in Broadway plays at the age of 16. During World War II, he learned how to operate a Mitchell camera and shoot documentaries, which led to his co-founding the Promotional Film Company and making industrial films after the war. One documentary, *With These Hands* (1950), was nominated for an Academy Award and prompted Universal to offer him a seven-year contract.

His first directorial feature was *Girls In the Night* (1953), a teenage exploitation drama. Arnold hit his stride with a pair of 3-D fantasy films released in quick succession: *It Came From Outer Space* (1953) and *The Creature From the Black Lagoon* (1954). Both were hugely successful for Universal and demonstrated Arnold's flair for making straightforward, competent B-pictures with a striking sense of locale. *Space* inspired several more desert-based science fiction films; and *Creature* was the forerunner of many monster-from-the-deep imitators. The year 1955 was busy and productive for Arnold, who directed a *Creature* sequel, *Revenge of the Creature,* followed by one of his first color films, *The Man From Bitter Ridge* (1956) and one of his very best films, *Tarantula* (1957). The latter benefited from a surprisingly good script, crisp dialogue, and an able cast. Again using the spooky Arizona desert as more of a character than just a backdrop, Arnold created the quintessential big-bug movie of the fifties with above-average special effects. After shooting an excellent crime drama, *Outside the Law,* in 1956, he returned to fantasy and made an instant classic of a Richard Matheson story, *The Incredible Shrinking Man* (1957). It proved to be Arnold's most accomplished production and a masterpiece of restraint, intelligence, credible effects, and measured suspense. It remains one of the best-loved and most thought-provoking science fiction films of the era. Due to its success he was given larger production budgets, beginning with *The Tattered Dress* and the Orson Welles vehicle, *Man in the Shadow* (both 1957).

Moving briefly to MGM, Arnold shot the cult favorite *High School Confidential* (1958), before going to Paramount for *The Space Children* (1958). Targeted at juveniles, *The Space Children* was hardly the pinnacle of Jack Arnold's career, but it was significant as his last science fiction genre film, coming appropriately at the close of the fifties. In 1959 he directed Peter Sellers in his first starring role for *The Mouse That Roared,* after which Arnold became more interested in television than film, directing only the occasional feature in the sixties and seventies. Arnold battled numerous health problems during his life, including Parkinson's disease, and died on March 17, 1992, in Woodland Hills, California. He remained active in his later years, directing even after having a leg amputated. His television work was vast and included episodes of *Gilligan's Island, The Mod Squad, Rawhide, It Takes A Thief, The Bionic Woman, The Love Boat, Buck Rogers in the 25th Century,* and *The Fall Guy.*

Other Films *The Glass Web* (1953); *Red Sundown* (1956); *The Lady Takes a Flyer* (1958); *Monster on the Campus* (1958); *No Name on the Bullet* (1959); *Bachelor in Paradise* (1961); *A Global Affair* (1964); *The Lively Set* (1964); *Hello Down There* (1969); *Black Eye* (1974); *Boss Nigger* (1975); *Games Girls Play* (1975); *The Swiss Conspiracy* (1977).

Reference Parish, James Robert, and Michael R. Pitts, *The Great Science-Fiction Pictures* (Metuchen, N.J.: Scarecrow Press, 1977).

—W.G.H.

Aronofsky, Darren (1969–) In just two films to date, *Pi* (1998) and *Requiem for a Dream* (2000), Darren Aronofsky has established himself as one of the most technically adroit directors working today. He was born on February 12, 1969. After attending Harvard he turned to filmmaking with his first commercial film, *Protozoa* (1993). He achieved worlwide recognition with his "breakthrough" picture, *Pi,* self-financed for a paltry $60,000. It tells the story of a search by a young mathematician, Max Cohen (Sean Gullette), for the ultimate mathematical truths of the cosmos. He sits alone in his apartment, surrounded by his computer monitors and mainframes, trapped in the entrails of wires and circuits, crunching numbers and popping pills in the service of the Big Pattern. Convinced that numbers are the code to the grand design of the universe, he tracks the infinite progression of "pi" and the Euclidian proportions of the Golden Mean. His paranoid fantasies are well founded. Wall Street thugs are after him to reveal the secrets of Wall Street prediction; and Jewish cabalists pursue what they believe is his discovery of the mystic number 216, the number of letters in the True Name of God. So intense become Max's obsessions and fears that at the moment of revelation, he self-destructs, lobotomizing himself with a hand drill. Max's hyperkinetic mind and his drug-induced hallucinations (are they one and the same?) fill the screen with bizarre images captured with flash-frames, smeary camera movements, and skewed angles—like the stranger he encounters in an otherwise deserted subway car and the living brain in the bowl of his lavatory. The throbbing, metallic *pings* on the soundtrack from composer Clint Mansell aptly buoy up the visuals. The film's message seems to be that whatever pattern or design— Henry James called it "the figure in the carpet"—is out there and within us, it is ultimately unknowable. Even if you start to lisp the Name of God, you won't be around to finish it. The film garnered many awards, including an Independent Spirit Award for best first screenplay and the Sundance Director's Award.

Aronofsky's second film, *Requiem for a Dream,* adapted from a 1978 novel by Hubert Selby, Jr., was no less a harrowing journey into the troubled psyche. It examines addiction in its many forms, to drugs, food, dieting, even to television watching. Harry Goldfarb (Jared Leto) and his mother (Ellen Burstyn) are racing headlong toward their own personal nightmares. She watches television incessantly, eating and dieting by turns, dreaming of appearing on her favorite shopper's program, *Juice*. Harry, on the other hand, is too busy to watch television. He's indulging in drugs and negotiating petty drug deals on the streets. As the months pass both mother and son self-destruct, ravaged by the physical deterioration of drug and diet pill addiction, and caught up in the delusions of their hallucinations. Like *Pi, Requiem for a Dream* employs all manner of visual styles horrific and beautiful by turn—accelerated motion for the "manic" scenes, slow motion for the drug-induced states, extreme wide-angle lenses positioned close to bloated, distorted faces, dolly shots that retreat frantically before the onrushing characters, and split-screen sequences tracking the simultaneous activities of mother and son. A striking visual leitmotif conveys the moment that Harry injects himself with the drug with a stream of flash-cuts of the flash of a match, the down-plunge of the needle, the microscopic image of cell division, the dilation of the pupil of an eye. Again, composer Clint Mansell, assisted by the Kronos String Quartet, punctuates the shots with sound effects and musical fragments. The sheer control and artistry of the film deflects the viewer away somewhat from this catalogue of horrors. And that is its great strength (or its fatal flaw). Either way, the film is compelling, even addictive in its own way. Critics have either dismissed it as what commentator Jeff Gordinier calls "flashy limousine nihilism" or hailed it as what Anthony Lane describes as a landmark in shock cinema: "The cost of drug-taking is in plain view here; nobody dies, but there is loss of limb, liberty, sanity, and honor. On the other hand, the look of drug-taking has never been served up with such panache." Director Aronofsky observes, "This film is like jumping out of an airplane, and halfway down you realize you forgot your parachute. And it ends three minutes after you hit the ground." At this writing, Aronofsky's next project is the fourth "Batman" movie, *Batman: Year One*.

References Gordinier, Jeff, "High Art," *Entertainment Weekly*, November 3, 2000, pp. 43–46; Lane, Anthony, "Actors and Addicts," *New Yorker*, October 9, 2000, pp. 100–101; McCarthy, Todd, "Daring Duo Marks Artistic Excellence at Fest," *Variety*, January 23, 1998, p. 51

—J.C.T.

Arzner, Dorothy (1900–1979)　"There should be more of us directing," said Dorothy Arzner in 1932. "Try as any man may, he will never be able to get the woman's viewpoint in directing certain stories. . . . A great percent of our audience is women. That too is something to think about."

Dorothy Arzner was the only woman director to develop a body of work during the Hollywood studio years from the mid-1920s to the early 1940s. She was the only woman director to make the transition from silent to sound film, and her work includes four silent films and 13 sound pictures from 1927 to 1943. The next woman to direct in Hollywood was IDA LUPINO, whose first film was released in 1949. Unlike other women directors, Arzner had a strong belief in feminism. She was a lesbian and consistently wore masculine attire on the sets of her films as if to make a stand for feminism and lesbianism. If the studio bosses minded, she never heard about it.

Arzner began her film career at the bottom and worked her way up the production ladder. Her first job in the film industry was typing scripts for Famous Players-Lasky, and in 1920 she began editing in addition to her typing chores. She was assigned to the Famous Players-Lasky subsidiary, Realart, where she worked as both script girl and editor. She claimed to have learned more about films in the cutting room than anywhere else. As she became known as a first-rate editor, well-known directors such as Fred Niblo and James

Cruze began asking specifically for her to edit their films. Meanwhile she was continuing to write scripts for other directors at other studios, including Columbia.

When she told Columbia she would like to direct her next script and they agreed, Paramount made her a better offer and her first film was *Fashions for Women* (1927) with Esther Ralston. It was a commercial success, thanks in part to the star, a proven box-office draw; but it also served to get Arzner a long-term contract as a director at Paramount, where she remained until it was reorganized in 1932. She made Paramount's first "talkie," *The Wild Party,* with Clara Bow in 1929 (her second film with Bow). After leaving Paramount she worked freelance and worked with all the major stars of the period, including Katharine Hepburn, Lucille Ball, Clara Bow, Claudette Colbert, Sylvia Sidney, Joan Crawford, and Merle Oberon, at the studios of RKO, Columbia, and MGM. Her best films from a stylistic and popular standpoint include *Merrily We Go To Hell* (1932), *Christopher Strong* (1933), *Craig's Wife* (1936), *The Bride Wore Red* (1937), and *Dance Girl, Dance* (1940).

She stopped making films in 1943, retiring with her domestic partner of 13 years, Marion Morgan, to their home in Santa Monica. Arzner taught film for four years at UCLA in the 1960s where one of her pupils was Francis Ford Coppola. After Morgan died in 1971 Arzner moved to Palm Springs where she died in 1979. She once said of her success, relative to her male cohorts, "I made one box office hit after another, so they knew they could gamble a banker's money on me. If I had a failure in the middle I would have been finished."

Other Films *Manhattan Cocktail* (1928); *Sarah and Son* (1930); *Working Girls* (1931); *First Comes Courage* (1943).

References Acker, Ally, *Reel Women: Pioneers of the Cinema, 1896–Present* (New York: Continuum Press, 1991); Flately, Guy, "At the Movies," *New York Times,* August 20, 1976, p. C-5; Kuhn, Annette, and Susannah Radstone, eds., *The Woman's Companion to International Film* (Berkeley: University of California Press, 1994); *New York Herald-Tribune,* June 26, 1932, sec. vii, p. 6; Slide, Anthony, *The Silent Feminists* (Lanham, Md.: Scarecrow Press, 1996); Smith, Sharon, *Women Who Make Movies* (New York: Hopkinson and Blake, 1975).

—C.L.P.

Ashby, Hal (1929–1988) Hal Ashby was born in Ogden, Utah, in 1929, the youngest of four children. Ashby's father committed suicide in 1941, his son discovering the body himself at the family farm. Ashby eventually left Utah and sought his fortune in California. In 1950 he landed a job at Universal mimeographing scripts. In 1953 he moved to Republic as an assistant film editor. It was at this time that Ashby became an assistant under Robert Swink and worked on such films as William Wyler's *The Big Country* (1958) and George Stevens's *The Diary of Anne Frank* (1960) and *The Greatest Story Ever Told* (1965). He was also assistant editor on Phil Karlson's *The Young Doctors* (1961) and Franklin Scaffner's *The Best Man* (1964).

During the 1960s Ashby became a full editor and assistant director to Norman Jewison, working on such films as *The Russians Are Coming! The Russians Are Coming!* (1965), *The Cincinnati Kid* (1966), *The Thomas Crown Affair* (1968), and *In the Heat of the Night* (1967). Ashby received an Academy Award for his editing of *In the Heat of the Night.*

In 1970 while preparing to direct *The Landlord,* Jewison was unable to carry on the project, and Ashby was asked to step in, making the resulting black comedy the former editor's directorial debut. Ashby's next film, *Harold and Maude* (1971), based on an original script by graduate film student Colin Higgins, is one of his most famous. The black comedy starred Ruth Gordon and Bud Cort and concerns a death-obsessed young man who falls in love with a 79-year-old woman. The music for the film was sung by Cat Stevens. Although a commercial failure upon its initial release, *Harold and Maude* quickly gathered a cult following. Showing up at film revival houses, it was frequently double-billed with another black comedy starring Ruth Gordon, *Where's Poppa?* (1970), directed by Carl Reiner.

The Last Detail (1973), starring Jack Nicholson and Randy Quaid, was Ashby's third feature film. The film concerns a seaman who is being escorted to prison by two MPs. Based on the novel by Darryl Ponsican, the film was a modest success upon its release in 1973. *Shampoo* (1975), starring Warren Beatty and Goldie Hawn, was the director's first major critical and commercial success. The film, concerning a promiscuous Beverly Hills hairdresser (Beatty) and the numerous women in his life, was scripted by Robert Towne and Warren Beatty.

Ashby's next project was a biopic about the life of folksinger Woody Guthrie. *Bound for Glory* (1976) was scripted by Robert Getchell and photographed by Haskell Wexler. The film starred David Carradine as the road-weary folk singer traveling from the dust bowl of Oklahoma to California during the Great Depression. Wexler's subdued photography as well as an exceptional film score by Leonard Rosenman (adapted from Guthrie songs) contributed considerably to this depiction of depression-era America.

Coming Home (1978) was Ashby's biggest critical success. One of the first films to deal with the effects of the Vietnam war, it starred Jon Voight and Jane Fonda. Set during the height of the Vietnam conflict, it showed the psychological effects of the war in its story concerning a disabled vet and the married woman who befriends and falls in love with him. The film received many accolades including the New York Film Critics' Circle Award and an Academy Award nomination for best picture.

Following the success of the film, Ashby again ventured into black comedy (though more satirical) with his film version of Jerzy Kosinki's mod-

ern fable *Being There* (1979). The film starred Peter Sellers in the role of Chauncey "Chance" Gardener, another in Ashby's long line of innocent male protagonists. After *Being There,* and significantly at the end of the seventies, Ashby's career took a downslide. *Second Hand Hearts* (1981) and *Lookin' to Get Out* (1982) both were commercial flops. Ashby made a rockumentary about the Rolling Stones's 1981 tour called *Let's Spend the Night Together* (Ashby was particularly fond of the Stones, using their music extensively in the soundtrack to *Coming Home*), but the film paled in comparison to the Maysles brothers' earlier documentary of the Stones's Altamont concert, *Gimme Shelter* (1970).

In 1985 Hal Ashby hoped for a comeback with *The Slugger's Wife,* based on a story by Neil Simon. The film did not do well at the box office despite a very heavy promotional campaign. Ashby's final film was an action crime drama, *8 Million Ways to Die,* released in 1986. The film starred Jeff Bridges as Scutter, a Los Angeles vice squad detective who accidentally kills a suspect during a drug bust. Scutter becomes an alcoholic who is racked by guilt. He eventually sobers up enough to save a prostitute from a sadistic drug dealer (Andy Garcia).

Some critics suggest that Ashby's eighties films show a shift in the director's world view—from a rebellious view critical of the establishment toward a sympathetic view of surviving life with the possibility of starting over anew. Unfortunately the director was not to realize such a possibility. Hal Ashby died of liver and colon cancer on December 27, 1988, at the age of 59.

Other Films As editor: *The Loved One* (1965). As associate producer: *Gaily, Gaily* (1969). As director: *Second-Hand Hearts* (1981); *Time Is on Our Side* (1982), a documentary.

Reference Biskind, Peter, *Easy Rider, Raging Bulls: How the Sex-Drugs-and-Rock 'n' Roll Generation Saved Hollywood* (New York: Simon and Schuster, 1998).

—R.W.

Attenborough, [Lord] Richard [Samuel]

(1923–) British actor, producer, and director Richard Attenborough was born in Cambridge on August 29, 1923. Frederick L. Attenborough, his father, affectionately known in family circles as the "Governor," was an academic administrator who retired as principal of Leicester University College. The Governor started as a schoolmaster in Liverpool, won a scholarship to Immanuel College, Cambridge, where he taught as a don when Richard was born until 1925, when he was appointed principal of the Borough Road Training College in Isleworth, now known as the West London Institute of Higher Education. The Attenboroughs were social activists who sheltered Basque children from Spain during the Spanish Civil War and Jewish children from Germany during World War II. Richard was educated at Wyggeston Grammar School in Leicester and later earned the highly competitive Leverhulme scholarship to the Royal Academy of Dramatic Art, London, where, in 1942, he was awarded the Bancroft Medal. His stage debut was at the Intimate Theatre, Palmers Green, during the summer of 1941. In June 1943 he joined the Royal Air Force Volunteer Reserve, going into the RAF Film Unit in February 1944, where he served until 1946.

Attenborough's first film role was in DAVID LEAN's *In Which We Serve* (1942), in which he played a sailor suffering from war nerves. He was featured in more than 60 films, continuing to act even after he launched his directing career. Of special notice was his portrayal of Pinkie, the teenaged killer in the film adaptation of Graham Greene's *Brighton Rock* (1947). Other memorable movie roles included two with Steve McQueen, *The Great Escape* (1962) and *The Sand Pebbles* (1966). He worked with director Robert Aldrich in *Flight of the Phoenix* (1965) and with Satyajit Ray in *The Chess Players* (1977). He would return to acting later in his career to play John Hammond, the eccentric founder of Jurassic Park, in the eponymous film by STEVEN SPIELBERG, in 1993, and the English Ambassador in KENNETH BRANAGH's *Hamlet* (1995).

Attenborough formed his own production company, Beaver Films, in 1959, and, with director Bryan Forbes, produced a series of seminal films that helped to launch the British New Wave, notably *The Angry Silence* (1960), *The L-Shaped Room* (1962), and *Séance on a Wet Afternoon* (1964). He later described his first film, *The Angry Silence,* as an attack "on subversion and on the lunatic far left fringe of the trade union and the Labour movements." His breakthrough film as director was *Gandhi* (1984), first suggested to him by Motilal Kothari, a civil servant with the Indian High Commission in London. His casting of a relatively unknown actor, Ben Kingsley, as Gandhi, helped to make this three-hour spectacle, made on location in India, a hit. *Gandhi* won eight Academy Awards, including best film, best director, best screenplay, and best actor (for Kingsley), out of 11 nominations.

Director Richard Attenborough on the set of *In Love and War* (New Line)

Before the tremendous success of *Gandhi,* Attenborough, whose debut picture as director was an adaptation of Joan Littlewood's antiwar musical *Oh! What a Lovely War* (1969), perfected his craft with several pictures: *Young Winston* (1972), starring Simon Ward as Churchill, made for producer Carl Forman, was adapted from Sir Winston Churchill's autobiography *My Early Life: A Roving Commission;* two films written by William Goldman would follow. *A Bridge Too Far* (1977) featured Robert Redford, and *Magic* (1978), an odd but effective picture, starred Anthony Hopkins as a ventriloquist whose personality is being taken over by his evil dummy.

His next film came as something of a surprise, an adaptation of the hit musical *A Chorus Line* (1985), which got three Oscar nominations, followed by *Cry Freedom* (1987) with Denzel Washington playing the antiapartheid activist Steve Biko and Kevin Kline playing journalist Donald Woods, who had written a book about Biko. The film was adapted from Woods's book about Biko, described by Attenborough as "one of the brightest, most charismatic, intelligent and fascinating men ever born in South Africa," murdered "whilst in police custody," and Woods's own autobiography, *Asking for Trouble.* Attenborough had long wanted to make a film about South Africa and had earlier optioned failed projects, one entitled *God Is a Bad Policeman.* He told Frank Price, the head of Columbia Pictures who became head of Universal, "I've got a subject which is bound to be as difficult as *Gandhi.* It's based on two books written by the exiled newspaper editor Donald Woods." Price replied, "I know them well," and offered to make the film at Universal. The director then contacted screenwriter John Briley, who had written the screenplay for *Gandhi,* and the project was in motion.

Other biographical features were to follow. *Chaplin* (1992) starred Robert Downey, Jr., who wanted the role so badly that he worked for a year with mime expert Dan Kamin so that he could play Chaplin convincingly. Downey went on to earn an Oscar nomination for his work and perseverance and won the British Academy Award for best actor. Next was *Shadowlands* (1994), adapted by William Nicholson from his play about the improbable romance between the English writer C. S. Lewis (Anthony Hopkins) and Joy Gresham (Deborah Winger), a much younger divorcée from New York. Debra Winger was nominated for an Oscar, as was William Nicholson for best adapted screenplay. *Shadowlands* won a British Academy Award for best film. In 1996 Attenborough directed *In Love and War,* starring Chris O'Donnell and Sandra Bullock, adapted from the book *Hemingway in Love and War: The Lost Diary of Agnes von Kurowsky,* by Henry S. Villard and James Nagel, published in 1989. Producer Dimitri Villard was the son of Henry Villard, Ernest Hemingway's wartime friend, who, after graduating from Harvard, volunteered as an ambulance driver for the Red Cross in Italy in 1918. Aside from the odd musical, then, Attenborough concentrated on biographical films during his later career. Attenborough later described *A Chorus Line* as "an experience I would not have missed," however. "It was a terrific challenge and technically is probably the best film I've ever made."

Attenborough's record of service was also impressive. For years he served as chairman of Channel Four and of the Royal Academy Dramatic Art (where he was trained as an actor), vice president of British Academy of Film and Television Arts, and Governor of the National Film School; he also served on the British Screen Advisory Council. During the 1990s he became pro-chancellor of Sussex University. In 1976 Attenborough was knighted (CBE), then elevated to a life peerage in 1993 in recognition of his achievements and service, becoming Lord Attenborough of Richmond-on-Thames. He summarized his career for the London *Sunday Times* by saying "I'm not a genius, I'm not an auteur, I'm a craftsman—but not a bad one."

References Attenborough, Richard, *In Search of Gandhi* (Piscataway, N.J.: New Century, 1982); *Richard Attenborough's Cry Freedom* (London: Bodley Head, 1987).
—J.M.W.

Autant-Lara, Claude (1901–2000) Autant-Lara was born Claude Autant in Luzarches (Seine-et-Oize), France, on August 5, 1901 (some sources list 1903), the son of architect Edouard Autant and actress Louise Lara, a pacifist who took her son to London during World War I. Autant-Lara was educated at Lycée Janson-de-Sailly, Paris, and at the Ecole nationale supérieure des arts décoratifs. He also studied in London before returning to France after the war to work as a set painter for Marcel L'Herbier's *Le Carnival des vérités* (1920). Autant-Lara was best known for his post–World War II films in the French "Tradition of Quality." But his earliest work in the industry was more closely related to the avant-garde movements of the 1920s than to the mainstream commercial cinema with which he was later identified. In his youth Autant-Lara was a left-wing atheist, but in 1989 he was elected to the European Parliament as a member of France's far-right National Front party.

Beginning as a set designer in the 1920s, Autant-Lara served as art director for several of Marcel L'Herbier's films, including *The Cruel Woman* (*L'Inhumaine* [1924]), and for JEAN RENOIR's *Nana* (1926); he also assisted René Clair on a number of early shorts. After directing several films, he worked on an early wide-screen experiment, *Construire un feu* (1926, adapted from a Jack London story), using the Hypergonar system designed by Henri Chrétien (and later developed into CinemaScope by 20th Century-Fox). On the basis of his work in this format, he was brought to Hollywood and ended up directing French-language versions of American films for several years. He returned to France and directed his first feature of note, *Ciboulette,* in 1933.

During the war, Autant-Lara exercised greater control in his choice of projects and started working with scenarists Jean Aurenche and Pierre Bost, who would continue to be among his most consistent collaborators. He also started assembling a basic crew that worked with him through the 1960s: composer René Cloerec, designer Max Douy, editor Madeleine Gug, and cameraman Jacques Natteau. (His wife, Ghislaine Auboin, was a screenwriter, assistant director, and actress.) Autant-Lara then rapidly established his reputation as a studio director in the "tradition of quality," setting the standard for "classic" French narrative cinema. For many, the names Aurenche, Bost, and Autant-Lara are synonymous with this movement. Their films are characterized by an emphasis on scripting and dialogue, a high proportion of literary adaptations, a solemn "academic" visual style, and general theatricality, due largely to the emphasis on dialogue and its careful delivery to create a cinematic world determined by psychological realism. They frequently attack or ridicule social groups and institutions, seeming to revel in irreverent depictions of established authority.

Autant-Lara's prominence was effectively eclipsed with the emergence of the French New Wave, although he continued directing films. In the 1950s he, along with Aurenche and Bost, had been subject to frequent critical attacks, most notably by FRANÇOIS TRUFFAUT. In the wake of the success of this new generation of directors, Autant-Lara's work is often seen as no more than "stale" French cinema of the 1950s, which was successfully displaced by the more vibrant and vital films of the New Wave. Yet in spite of, or, indeed, owing to their "armchair" criticisms of authority, bleak representation of human nature, and slow-paced academic style, Autant-Lara's films possess a peculiarly appealing, insolent sensibility.

Autant-Lara's career as filmmaker peaked during the 1950s. *Le Diable au corps* (*Devil in the Flesh* [1947]) was considered scandalous for the way it criticized the war and represented an adulterous affair between an adolescent and a wife whose husband was serving his country. His best-known films include *Le Rouge et le noir* (1954), based on Stendahl's novel *The Red and the Black; La Traversée de Paris* (1956), translated to English as *Four Bags Full,* a black comedy about black marketers during the German occupation; *En Cas de malheur* (*Love Is My Profession* [1958]), with Brigitte Bardot and Jean Gabin; and *Le Comte de Monte Cristo* (1961). His popularity diminished after the cresting of the New Wave, and his last film, *Gloria* (1977), was mainly ignored by critics. In later years his right-wing politics did not set well with many intellectuals, and he was ultimately forced to resign his seat in the European Parliament after being exposed as an anti-Semitic Holocaust denier by the French press. Regrettably, he called into question the existence of Auschwitz and told the monthly magazine *Globe* that a certain French politician who had survived the concentration camps had somehow been "missed" by the Nazis. Autant-Lara died on February 5, 2000, at a clinic in the south of France.

Other Films As director: *My Partner, Mr. Davis* (U.K. [1936]). Three pictures codirected with Maurice Lehmann: *L'Affaire du Courrier de Lyon* (1937), *Le Ruisseau* (1938), and *Fric-Frac* (1939). As director: *Le Mariage de Chiffon* (1942); *Lettres d'amour* (1942); *Douce* (1943); *Sylvie et le Fantôme* (1946); *Occupe-toi d'Amélie* (1949); *L'Auberge rouge* (1951); the "Pride" episode of *Les Sept péchés capitaux* (1952); *Le Bon Dieu sans confession* (1953); *Le Blé en herbe* (1954); *Marguerite de la nuit* (1956); *Le Joueur* (1958); *La Jument verte* (1959); *Les Régates de San Francisco* (1960); *Le Bois des amants* (1960); *Vive Henri IV . . . Vive l'amour* (1961); *Tu ne tueras point* (1962); *Le Meurtrier* (1963); *Le Magot de Joséfa* (1963); *Le Journal d'une femme en blanc* (1965); the "Paris Today" episode of *Le Plus vieux métier du monde* (1967); *Le Franciscain de Bourges* (1968); *Les Patates* (1969); *Le Rouge et le blanc* (1971).

References Cardullo, Bert, "André Bazin on Claude Autant-Lara and Literary Adaptation: Four Original Reviews," *Literature/Film Quarterly* 29, no. 3 (2001); Daley, Suzanne, "Claud Autant-Lara, 98, a Film Director," *New York Times,* February 9, 2000, p. A23.

—B.C. and J.M.W.

Avery, Tex (1908–1980) After WALTER ELIAS DISNEY, Tex Avery, the creator of Bugs Bunny and Daffy Duck, is considered the most important influence on the Golden Age of the Hollywood studio cartoon. At the Warner Bros. animation unit, particularly, he contributed, in the words of commentator Greg Ford, "A new range and complexity, breaking radically with the Disney-established parameters of the Hollywood Cartoon context." He was born Frederick Bean Avery on February 26, 1908, in the small mid-Texas town of Taylor, to Mary A. Bean and George W. Avery, a building contractor. As a boy, he divided his free time between his favorite activities of duck hunting and cartooning. After graduating from North Dallas High School, and convinced he had no future as a cartoonist, he departed for Los Angeles, determined to become an animator. He soon found work as an "in-betweener"—an animator's assistant who drew sequential sketches between a character's main poses—at Universal and, later in 1930, at the Walter Lantz cartoon studio, where he worked on the "Oswald the Lucky Rabbit Series." Now dubbed by his colleagues as "Tex," he quickly took up directorial chores with *The Quail Hunt* and *Towne Hall Follies.*

It was at this time that he began developing his trademark techniques of creating wild visual gags and breaking the "fourth wall" between character and audience. In 1935 the 27-year-old Avery switched to Warner Bros, joining ISADORE ("FRIZ") FRELENG and Hal King in a studio collective soon to be known as "termite terrace," and taking on apprentices CHARLES MARTIN ("CHUCK") JONES and Bob Clampett. "Avery was a genius," Jones recalled in 1980. "I was as ignorant of his genius as I suppose Michelangelo's apprentices were oblivious to the fact that they too were working with genius. In spite of that intellectual weakness on my part,

Avery's brilliance penetrated the husk of my self-assured ignorance. . . ." For the next seven years, beginning with *Gold Diggers of '49* (1936), Avery sacrificed the priorities of story for the faster pace of series gags, each capped by a "topper." Characters were redesigned and reconceptualized, and new ones created: Porky Pig was redrawn (*Porky's Duck Hunt* [1937]) and Bugs Bunny given his definitive personality (*A Wild Hare* [1940]); and Daffy Duck sprang to life in *Daffy Duck and Egg Head* (1937), voiced with a lisping parody of Warner Bros. producer Leon Schlesinger. Biographer John Canemaker notes that "Avery brought brashness, abrasiveness, and an adult sensibility to Warner films. Using parody and satire, he constantly pulled the rug out from under audiences by reversing their expectations regarding the laws of physics or by turning hoary and hallowed fairytales into Rabelaisian sex-and-violence romps." Rejecting the late 1930s Disney style of "realistic" animation, Avery celebrated the surreal aspects of the cartoon *as cartoon,* harking back to the impossible antics of characters like Felix the Cat. Perhaps his most reflexive cartoon was *Porky's Preview* (1941), a cartoon-within-a-cartoon. Porky proudly shows his own homemade cartoon to a barnyard audience. Abruptly, Porky's projector flashes on to the screen a collection of badly drawn, infantile stick figures against a blank white background. "Mainly endearing in attitude," reports Greg Ford, "Avery's *Porky's Preview* may be most properly understood as a short, affectionate greeting card to the Art of Animation, however puerile or sloppily scribbled it may be."

From 1942 to 1954 Avery relocated to MGM where he directed 67 cartoons, including several outrageously updated fairy tales, *Red Hot Riding Hood* (1943), *Swing Shift Cinderella* (1945), and *Uncle Tom's Cabana* (1947). Two more characters evolved from his other work, the deadpan pooch Droopy and Screwy Squirrel, and several classic shorts, *Northwest Hounded Police* (1946), *Slap Happy Lion* (1947), and *Bad Luck Blackie* (1949)—all ded-icated, writes Canemaker, "to paranoia, control, survival, and the film medium itself." When he was not preoccupied with cartoon violence, reports historian Stephen Kanfer, he turned to sex. The alluring female character, Red Hot, appeared during the war years. Kanfer cites *Little Rural Riding Hood* (1943) as a case in point. A country wolf and his cousin visit a nightclub to watch Red's gyrations: "The performance is too calorific for the yokel; his eyes spring from their sockets, his tongue drops to the floor, he ignites his nose instead of his cigarette, all the while babbling 'Wanna kiss the girls, where's the girls, sure do love girls!'" The reflexive nature of the cartoon was pushed to extremes, writes Kanfer: "In Avery's postwar cartoons, animals and people habitually defy natural law and cinematic rules. They race to the edge of the frame only to get caught in the sprockets; telephone to someone on the other side of a split screen—and then reach through the dividing line to touch the character on the other side."

Always a rather tense and enigmatic man (the loss of an eye early in his career allegedly accounted for his remote behavior), at MGM Avery felt tension from several quarters. For one thing, his adult-inflected cartoons, like the Red Hot series, were continually at odds with the censorial Production Code; and there were squabbles with the rival animators of the "Tom and Jerry" cartoons. If not an especially gifted technical artist, Avery nonetheless exerted complete control over his films. He dreamed up the plots and gags, drew the conceptual sketches, timed the action, supervised the voice-track recordings, and arranged for test screenings. "When you're making theatrical cartoons," he explained, "you're using about a half million of somebody's big fat dollars every year. And you feel that you've got to give them something. If you make a weak one, you feel, my gosh, you're letting the studio down."

After the MGM cartoon unit was closed down in 1954, Avery went through a succession of jobs, first reuniting with the Walter Lantz studios (where he did several "Chilly Willy" cartoons), then moving on to producing commercials before ending his career at Hanna-Barbera. Ironically, Avery always wanted to break in to live-action films. That ambition was denied him, however, and he was forced to observe from the sideline while protégées like Frank Tashlin successfully made the jump from cartoons to live-action theatrical features. As Norman Klein points out in his study of Avery, animators at this time were classified in the industry as craftspeople, incapable of making live-action features (no longer true today, with the likes of animator-directors like Tim Burton, Terry Gilliam, and the Brothers Quay).

In his last years at Hanna-Barbera, reports Canemaker, the cancer-stricken Avery was plagued by the feeling that he was "burned out" as an artist, that the industry had passed him by, and that his famed wild humor was not funny anymore. After the suicide of his son, the breakup of his marriage, and an increasing problem with alcohol, Avery found himself lost and neglected. He died a solitary and enigmatic man, acknowledged a film genius but still essentially a "modestly paid worker for hire." Yet, his outrageous humor and madcap pacing have left an indelible mark on today's animation. As Canemaker points out, this is most apparent in *Who Framed Roger Rabbit* (1988), the Genie sequences in *Aladdin* (1992), and Jim Carrey's antics in *The Mask* (1995).

References Canemaker, John, *Tex Avery: The MGM Years, 1942–1955* (North Dighton, Mass.: JG Press, 1998); Ford, Greg, "Tex Avery: Arch-Radicalizer of the Hollywood Cartoon," *Bright Lights* 3, no. 1 (1980): 12–19; Friedwald, Will, and Jerry Beck, *The Warner Bros. Cartoons* (Metuchen, N.J.: Scarecrow Press, 1981); Kanfer, Stefan, *Serious Business: The Art and Commerce of Animation in America from Betty Boop to "Toy Story"* (New York: Scribner's, 1997); Klein, Norman M., "The Mask, Masques, and Tex Avery," in *Reading the Rabbit: Explorations in Warner Bros. Animation,* Kevin S. Sandler, ed. (Piscataway, N.J.: Rutgers University Press, 1998), pp. 209–220.

—J.C.T.

Babenco, Hector (1946–) A Brazilian director from Argentina, Hector Eduardo Babenco was born of Jewish immigrant parents in Buenos Aires on February 7, 1946. In 1963 Babenco left Argentina for Europe, working for Cinecitta in Rome as an extra. When he returned to Latin America in 1971, he settled in São Paolo, Brazil, where he began his career as filmmaker with a documentary in 1972 before turning to feature filmmaking in 1975 with *King of the Night (Rei da noite),* about a man's descent into alcoholism, crime, and prison.

His second feature film, *Lucio Flavio* (1978), told the story of another outsider, a bandit. *Pixote* (1981) concerned delinquents who escape from a juvenile prison and resort to selling drugs. This wrenching story of children marginalized by society was recognized internationally, winning the Silver Leopard at the Locarno Festival and sharing the Grand Prix at the Biarritz Film Festival. The two main characters of his next film, and his first English-language picture, *Kiss of the Spider Woman* (1985), are political prisoners, one of them a homosexual. The film was nominated for an Academy Award for directing, and Babenco was thereafter invited to Hollywood to direct the film adaptation of William Kennedy's

Hector Babenco (right) during the making of *Pixote* (Unifilm/Embrafilme)

Ironweed (1988), populated by bums and losers in Albany, New York, memorably combining the "magic realism" of *Spider Woman* with the unflinching realism of *Pixote.* Jack Nicholson and Meryl Streep were so effective as down-and-outers Francis Phelan and his dying "pal" Helen that they both earned Academy Award nominations for best actor and best actress. Babenco's treatment humanizes without sentimentalizing them. In 1989 Babenco was invited to serve on the jury of the Cannes Film Festival along with Krzysztof Kieslowski, Peter Handke, and jury president Wim Wenders. As John King wrote, "Argentine-born Babenco is one of the few major international successes of Brazilian cinema."

Other Films *The Second Killing of the Dog* (1988); *My Foolish Heart* (1990); *At Play in the Fields of the Lord* (1991).

References Foster, David William, *Contemporary Argentine Cinema* (Columbia: University of Missouri Press, 1992); King, John, *Magical Reels: A History of Cinema in Latin America* (London: Verso, 1990).

—T.L.E. and J.M.W.

Barton, Charles Thomas (1902–1981)

A prolific, energetic, and versatile filmmaker, Charles Barton was the very essence of the working director. Over his three decades as a studio director, he proved himself a master at turning out neatly crafted—if often unexceptional—studio entertainment with assembly-line precision. He was never one of the cinema's great artists and apparently never strove to be. Instead he devoted himself to pure entertainment, sometimes produced against formidable odds.

As a director he turned out brisk, lively B-films for Paramount and Columbia, several highly profitable Abbott and Costello comedies for Universal, and at least two live-action hits for Disney—*The Shaggy Dog* (1959) and *Toby Tyler* (1960). Moving over to television in the early fifties, Barton produced and directed hits like *Dennis the Menace, The Munsters, McHale's Navy, Petticoat Junction,* and *Family Affair.* Further, he directed every single episode, save the pilot, of *Amos 'n' Andy.*

But Barton's film career began years earlier. He entered the industry when he was just a boy, and his career came to encompass virtually every aspect of the business.

Charles Thomas Barton was born in Oakland, California, on May 25, 1902. As an infant, he was carried onstage during a vaudeville turn by actress Edith Chapman. When he was old enough, he became an actor himself, appearing in many popular comedies and melodramas of the day, such as *Alias Jimmy Valentine* and *The Littlest Rebel.*

He recalled appearing in a Bronco Billy Anderson picture in about 1915 (the title is unknown) and was cast as a jockey in Maurice Tourneur's *County Fair* (1920). But because of his short stature (5 feet 2 inches is as tall as he ever got) he decided against pursuing acting as an adult. Instead he began working behind the scenes in the movies, taking a path that led from the mail room to the prop room. From the beginning, he had set his sights on being a director, not because of the money or fame or power, but because of the clothes. "Boy," he said, "seeing these guys coming in there, oh, they were great! Mickey Neilan, De Mille with his riding breeches. I wanted to be a director so I could dress like that!"

As propman and assistant director, Barton worked on many of the classics of the silent and early sound eras: *Peter Pan* (1924), *Old Ironsides* (1926), *Beggars of Life* (1928), and *Monkey Business* (1931), and dozens more. He also worked with—and learned from—most of the greatest directors of the age: James Cruze, Irvin Willat, CECIL B[LOUNT] DEMILLE, HERBERT BRENON, William K. Howard, Edward Sutherland, ROUBEN MAMOULIAN, and WILLIAM AUGUSTUS WELLMAN, among others. It was Wellman who promoted him, during the long and chaotic production of *Wings* (1927), from second assistant prop boy, to first prop boy, to second assistant director, to first assistant director.

Barton became a director in 1934 with the Randolph Scott western *Wagon Wheels.* He remained under contract to Paramount throughout the thirties and made several top-notch B-pictures there, like *Car 99* (1935), a tough cop movie with Fred MacMurray; *The Last Outpost* (1935), codirected with Louis Gasnier, an action adventure starring Cary Grant; and *Murder With Pictures* (1936), a neat, atmospheric mystery starring Lew Ayres.

In 1939, Barton revisited the scenes of his youth by appearing as an actor in William A. Wellman's *Beau Geste,* starring Gary Cooper, and serving as assistant director to Cecil B. DeMille on *Union Pacific,* with Barbara Stanwyck.

Barton spent the first half of the forties at Columbia. Many of the B-pictures he made there are forgettable, but *Island of Doomed Men* (1940) with Peter Lorre is atmospheric; *Reveille With Beverly* (1943) is filled to bursting with great musical acts ranging from Frank Sinatra and Count Basie to Duke Ellington and the Mills brothers; and his series of *Five Little Peppers* films are amusing and bucolic.

But when Barton moved to Universal in 1945, he found his true niche with the Abbott and Costello comedies and forgotten gems such as *Men in Her Diary* (1945). Barton worked well with Abbott and Costello and helmed what are arguably their two best films: *Abbott and Costello Meet Frankenstein* (1948) is a hilarious mix of comedy and horror in which Universal's beloved monsters—Dracula (Bela Lugosi), the Wolf Man (Lon Chaney, Jr.), and the Frankenstein Monster (Glenn Strange)—are treated seriously; and *The Time of Their Lives* (1946) is a genuinely wistful, sweet-natured film in which Lou Costello plays a Revolutionary War–era ghost haunting the estate where he died.

After his stint at Disney, where Barton directed *The Shaggy Dog* and *Toby Tyler,* Barton began to turn his attention to television. Ironically, after turning out dozens of successful films over the previous decades, it was as a TV director and producer that Barton truly made his fortune.

Perhaps Charles Barton never directed a masterpiece, but very few of his films disappoint if taken on their own terms. His direction is economical and functional, but he was always able to coax from them every possible drop of entertainment value they had. If none of his films is remarkable exactly, his career certainly is. It spans virtually the entire history of the Hollywood studio system; and Charles Barton was on hand at the creation of some of the greatest moments in the Cinema.

Other Films   *And Sudden Death* (1936); *The Crime Nobody Saw* (1937); *Behind Prison Gates* (1939); *Nobody's Children* (1940); *Tramp, Tramp, Tramp* (1942); *What's Buzzin' Cousin?* (1943); *Hey Rookie* (1944); *Buck Privates Come Home* (1947); *The Noose Hangs High* (1948); *Africa Screams* (1949); *The Milkman* (1950); *Ma and Pa Kettle at the Fair* (1952); *Swingin' Along* (1962).

References   Charles T. Barton, interviewed by Kevin Brownlow and Frank Thompson, October 23, 1980; Thompson, Frank, "Charles T. Barton," in *Between Action and Cut: Five American Directors* (Metuchen, N.J.: Scarecrow Press, 1985).

—F.T.

Bauer, Evgenii (1865–1917)   A titan of the early Russian cinema, Evgenii Bauer was born in Russia in 1865. His father was a renowned zither player, while his sisters became actresses. Bauer graduated from the Moscow Institute of Painting, Sculpture and Architecture. Over the years, he was an amateur actor, a caricaturist for magazines, a newspaper satirist, a theatrical impresario, and an artistic photographer. He was especially recognized for designing sets for theatrical productions, a talent that eventually brought him into the cinema when he designed the sets for Drankov and Taldykin's commemorative historical film, *Trekhsotletie Tsarstvovaniya Doma Romanovykh* (The tercentenary of the rule of the Romanov dynasty), released in 1913. Encouraged by Drankov and Taldykin, Bauer, then 48 years of age, graduated to directing for their company. After making four films for them, he went over to Pathé's Star Film Factory for whom he made an additional four films. Then in late 1913, he moved to the Khanzhonkov company where he remained for the rest of his career. As an artist, he quickly came to the fore, with his films proving very successful with Russian audiences and critics. He worked in a variety of genres including comedies, patriotic subjects, social dramas, and tragedies of psychological obsession.

Among his comedies were several starring his wife Lina Ancharova, whom he had met when she was a dancer in one of the theater groups that employed him. She demonstrated genuine talent as a comedienne in her films for Bauer. In *Tysiacha v toraia khitrost'* (The 1002nd ruse), filmed in 1915, she plays a flirtatious wife who successfully outwits her husband's attempts to thwart her infidelities by hiding her lover in the closet. Lina Bauer's delightful facial expressions and roguish, knowing manner perfectly matched the mood of this well-crafted bedroom farce.

Bauer's series of patriotic war pictures were made in response to the conflict with Germany and included *Slava Nam, Smert' Vagram* (Glory to us, death to the enemy), produced in 1914 with the great star of the early Russian cinema, Ivan Mosjoukin, in the lead. Perhaps the most outstanding of these topical films is *Revoliutsioner* (The revolutionary), made in 1917 just after the February Revolution overthrew the czarist regime. It deals with a revolutionary who is sent into Siberian exile in 1907 and is liberated a decade later with the fall of the Romanov dynasty. He returns to a hero's welcome but finds himself at odds with his son, a Bolshevik who opposes Russia's involvement in World War I. Eventually, the father is able to persuade him that a successful prosecution of the war will aid the revolution and the two enlist. The film was groundbreaking because it was the first Russian production to dramatize the tyranny of the czarist secret police and the harshness of

Siberian prison life. It also demonstrated Bauer's technical virtuosity, as in the interior scenes between father and son in a darkened room with chiaroscuro lighting illuminating their faces, or the shots of the two in Moscow on a parapet looking out over the city.

However, it is in the field of social dramas and tragedies involving psychological obsessions that Bauer reached his peak. These brooding works seemed to strike deep chords in Russian culture and offer penetrating insights into the mood of late imperial Russia. One of the earliest of these films, *Sumyerki Zhyentsina Dusha* (Twilight of a woman's soul), made in 1913, straddled these genres and is permeated with the melancholy despair of the time. It concerns a noblewoman who tries to break from her idle class by helping the poor and unfortunate. She is attracted to a handsome laborer who rapes her when she visits his slum dwelling. Defending herself, she kills him but is rejected by her fiance, a prince, when she tells him of the incident. Later, she becomes an opera star but refuses to reconcile with the prince. Experimenting with lighting and design to develop his narrative, Bauer uses this film to comment on the gulf between the classes while exploring the psychology of his tormented heroine.

Bauer's dramas of social realism include *Ditya Bol'shogo Goroda* (A child of the big city) (1914), *Nemye Svideteli* (Silent witnesses) (1914), and *Leon Drey* (1915). *Ditya Bol'shogo Goroda's* female protagonist is a young woman whose soul has been tainted by grinding poverty. Orphaned from birth and toiling in a sweatshop, she escapes when a wealthy young man falls in love with her and makes her his mistress. But once his money runs out, she leaves him, spurning his suggestion that they live a modest life together. In the end, she has climbed her way to the top. When her former lover shoots himself on the doorstep of her mansion, she steps over him on her way to a fashionable restaurant, the final shot being a close-up of his body. In *Nemye Svideteli,* it is the callousness of the aristocracy that is exposed. The story relates the seduction of a maid by a wealthy idler in an upper-class household who abandons her when he renews his relationship with a society woman. *Leon Drey* is concerned with an attractive Jewish man who uses his charm to advance in society.

This vein of social comment also appears in Bauer's lavish 1916 drama of high life, *Zhizn' za Zhizn'* (A life for a life). Although based on a French novel by Georges Ohnet, the film, adapted to a Russian setting, perfectly conveys the decadence of the late czarist era. A fortune-hunting prince marries the wealthy daughter of a female industrialist while carrying on an affair with his wife's foster sister who is married to a businessman she does not love. After spending much of his wife's money, he forges promissory notes and is about to be arrested when his mother-in-law shoots him.

Bauer's films on psychological themes brought a new maturity to the cinema and anticipated such later developments as German expressionism. At the same time, they have a uniquely Russian flavor, a brooding attitude linking sex and death. David Robinson, in his article on Bauer for *Sight and Sound,* points out it should not be assumed that these films with themes including necrophilia are projections of Bauer's personal character. But they clearly reflect the Symbolist "decadence" of Russia's "silver age" of literature in the early 20th century, a time when, under the banner of sensualism, Russian artists sought to immerse themselves in describing any kind of thought or activity, no matter how shocking, as a means of liberating the individual from convention. Thus, in Bauer's adaptation of a Symbolist story, *Smert' na Zhizn'* (Life in death), released in 1914, a man (played by Ivan Mosjoukin) is so obsessed with the beauty of his wife that he murders her and keeps her embalmed body in his cellar. *Grezy* (Daydreams, [1915]), one of Bauer's finest works, relates the story of a widower who searches for a substitute for his beloved late wife. He finds an opera singer who resembles

his spouse and marries her. But the singer becomes jealous of his insane worship of his first wife and begins taunting him. When she dares to desecrate his beloved's braids which he reverently keeps in a box, he strangles her with the sacred hair. *Posle Smert* (After death), also produced in 1915, was adapted from Turgenev's story, "Klara Milich." It deals with a man who becomes obsessed with an actress he casually meets several times. When she commits suicide during a performance, he travels to her town to learn from family members the details of what had happened and to obtain her photograph. Returning to his home, he spends a terrifying night repeatedly dreaming of her and seeing her apparition before the shock finally kills him. *Umirdyushchi Lyebyed'* (The dying swan), released in 1917, relates the story of a ballerina and her crazed admirer, an artist who keeps a human skeleton in his studio. He wishes to paint her in the role of the Dying Swan and, to achieve the perfect pose, he ends up strangling her.

Despite Bauer's incorporation of theatrical techniques into his films, his style and those of other pre-Revolutionary Russian filmmakers like Yakov Protazanov were uniquely cinematic in contrast to such stagy early features as Sarah Bernhardt's 1912 *Queen Elizabeth*. At the same time, Bauer's work was distinctly different in tempo from his American contemporaries. In his Biograph years, DAVID WARK GRIFFITH was in the forefront of those who sought to break with the first primitive narrative films by positioning the camera closer to the actors for a new cinematic and naturalistic style of performance. Russia's pre-Revolutionary filmmakers like Bauer built on Griffith's early Biograph experiments to create an alternative cinema of their own with a slower pace of acting and editing as they explored in depth the tortured psychology of their characters and the decadent social milieu. Bauer effectively used cutting within scenes and striking close-ups throughout his career but always within the context of a style that placed primary emphasis on detailed mise-en-scène and measured performance rather than the blending of rhythmic, dramatic editing with dynamic acting characteristic of Griffith's films.

At the beginning of 1917, Bauer was at the top of Russia's film world. He was earning the extraordinary salary of 40,000 rubles and was a major shareholder in the Khanzhonkov company. But on June 9, 1917, by the traditional Russian calendar (June 22 in the West), Evgenii Bauer died of pneumonia at the age of 52.

Upon the news of his passing, the Russian film journals of the period published many tributes to the prolific artist who had directed 82 films in four years, becoming Russia's most renowned director. But a few months after his death, a second, far more radical revolution began sweeping away the remnants of the old society whose agonizing decline Bauer had so powerfully chronicled in his works. The emerging Soviet cinema sought other cinematic models more in keeping with the revolutionary fervor of the new epoch. While Bauer's mastery of cinema left its mark on his coworkers—notably LEV VLADIMIROVICH KULESHOV, an actor and art director on *Za Shchast'em,* and Ivan Perestiani, both of whom continued on as directors in the Soviet era—for the most part, Bauer and the pre-Revolutionary Russian cinema was identified with the czarist era. In the 1920s, with the exciting new Soviet silent montage classics introducing a style that was the diametric opposite of Bauer's, the earlier artist's work was largely forgotten. In the late 1980s, with the collapse of the Soviet system, the surviving works of Bauer, carefully preserved in the Soviet archives, emerged from 70 years of obscurity to be shown internationally, becoming at last a part of world film culture. Few if any of his films had ever reached the West where he was little more than a name. Seen anew, his works embody the spirit of an age, vividly capturing the twilight of imperial Russia. But beyond the manners and mores of his time, Evgenii Bauer, now recognized as one of the early

cinema's most creative directors, continues to speak to the human condition with his uncompromising dissections of social inequities and haunting portrayals of twisted psyches in masterpieces that helped the young medium develop into a mature art.

References Robinson, David, "Evgeni Bauer and the Cinema of Nikolai II," *Sight and Sound,* Winter 1989–90; Tsivian, Yuri, *Silent Witnesses: Russian Films 1908–1919,* British Film Institute, 1990; Stites, Richard, "Dusky Images of Tsarist Russia: Prerevolutionary Cinema," *The Russian Review* 53 (April 1994).

—W.M.D.

Bava, Mario (1914–1980) One of Italy's most accomplished masters of horror, Mario Bava was born on July 31, 1914, in San Remo, Italy. He was the son of Eugenio Bava, an accomplished technician in the days of Italian silent cinema and a set designer for Pathé Frères. Mario Bava, therefore, grew up in an environment of filmmaking and illusion and worked for several years as his father's assistant. He subtitled feature films for export and animated title sequences for various Italian features until the late 1930s, when he began to work as an assistant to some of Italy's finest cinematographers, eventually becoming a director of photography. Over the years, he shot films directed by ROBERTO ROSSELLINI, GEORG WILHELM PABST, RAOUL WALSH, and Robert Z. Leonard, and his stylized lensing was critical in developing the screen personas of such international stars as Gina Lollobrigida and Steve Reeves.

By the 1950s, Bava's innovative lighting techniques and his genius at creating realistic special effects with little or no money had established him as one of Italy's top film technicians. In 1956, Bava collaborated with Riccardo Freda on *I Vampiri* (*The Vampires* [1957]), initially as cameraman and optical effects designer, then directing half of the 12-day schedule in only two days, when Freda abandoned the project after being denied an extension by the producers. Historically significant as the first Italian horror film of the sound era, the film was a commercial flop. Bava was again called on to complete the next Freda film *Caltiki—Il Mostro Immortale* (1959), aka *Caltiki, The Immortal Monster.* For rescuing yet another troubled production, Jacques Tourneur's spectacle *The Giants of Marathon* (1959), the film's producer, Lionello Santi, rewarded Bava by inviting him to select a property for his directorial debut at age 46.

A devotee of Russian literature, Bava chose Nikolai Gogol's story "Vij" as the foundation for *La Maschera del Demonio* (1960), aka *Black Sunday/Mask of Satan,* a gothic horror film that stood as a perfect synthesis of the Germanic expressionism of silent-era horror films, the imitative Universal cycle of the 1930s and 1940s, and the more emboldened expression of violence and sensuality of the Hammer films. This aspect, combined with Bava's peculiar sense of irony and dark imagination, helped to make *La Maschera* into a worldwide success with audiences and critics and made an overnight star of British actress Barbara Steele. Bava's subsequent films encompassed everything from gothic horrors (*La Frusta e il Corpo*) and pop art fantasies (*Diabolik*) to spaghetti westerns (*La Strada Perfort Alamo*), and key themes like the deceptive nature of appearances and the destructive capacity of human nature shone through, and his wholly distinctive visual style endeared him to a generation of film fanatics.

For all of that, his name remains essentially unknown. Based on the testimony of his collaborators, this is perhaps not very surprising. Bava's own view of his talent was colored by a lack of confidence, and his basic shyness prevented him from taking advantage of opportunities that would have made his name more internationally known. Fortunately, directors like Martin Scorsese and Quentin Tarantino have loudly championed his efforts, thereby establishing him as one of the most influential figures in modern cinema. In his film *Sei Donne per L'assassino* (1964), he created and defined the *giallo*—a form of the thriller that concentrates on violent death as opposed to prosaic police procedures. (*Giallo,* Italian for "yellow," refers to the yellow covers of the Italian crime novels of the era.) This film alone has had a tremendous influence on the work of DARIO ARGENTO, Lucio Fulci, and JOHN CARPENTER. Sadly, Bava was not appreciated during his lifetime, and the unfortunate outcome of two pet projects—*Lisa e il Diavolo* (1972) and *Cani Arrabbiati* (1974)—soured his enthusiasm for filmmaking during the latter part of the 1970s. Enlisted by protégée Dario Argento to provide some key effects for his hallucinatory nightmare classic *Inferno* (1980), Bava went uncredited on the final print, though Argento has often spoken of his contribution with much gratitude. The film proved to be the last on which he ever worked. On April 25, 1980, Mario Bava died of a heart attack at the age of 65. Bava's films have had a tremendous influence on the development of the modern horror/thriller film, yet his genius is only just beginning to be recognized.

Other Films *Kill Baby . . . Kill* (1966); *Hatchet for the Honeymoon* (1968); *Bay of Blood* (1971); *Baron of Blood* (1972); *Shock Schlock* (1977); *Venus of Ille* (1978).

References McCarthy, John, *Splatter Movies* (New York: St. Martin's Press, 1984); McCarthy, John, *The Fearmakers* (New York: St. Martin's Press, 1994).

—B.M.

Bay, Michael (1964–) Bay has been hailed by *Newsweek* magazine as the "action-movie heir-apparent to Steven Spielberg and [James] Cameron." He was born in 1964 and grew up in the Westwood section of Los Angeles. He became a film-studies major at Wesleyan College in Connecticut, and, according to his mentor, Jeanine Basinger, his senior thesis film "was about a fraternity boy who was driving his yellow Porsche around town very fast." After college Bay started his career directing commercials and music videos and earned awards that brought him to the attention of blockbuster producers Don Simpson and

Jerry Bruckheimer. Because of his obvious talent for action pictures, Bay was destined for commercial success, if not critical acclaim.

Bad Boys (1995), his first feature film assignment, was a surprise action-comedy hit, starring Will Smith and Martin Lawrence. This was followed by an even bigger hit, *The Rock* (1997), starring Sean Connery, Nicolas Cage, and Ed Harris, another Simpson-Bruckheimer blockbuster that grossed more than $134 million. Harris portrayed General Francis Hummel, a disaffected military man who has taken hostages at Alcatraz Island and is aiming rockets filled with deadly chemicals at San Francisco. Sent in to foil the threat are Stanley Goodspead (Cage), an FBI chemical weapons expert, and Patrick Mason (Connery), a top-secret prisoner of the federal government. The majority of the film is an action-packed cat-and-mouse affair between the good guys and the bad guys, providing delicious contrasts between Harris's pathological hate, Cage's bumbling amateurishness, and Connery's cold-blooded guerrilla expertise. In all, *The Rock,* which was the last collaboration between Bruckheimer and the late Don Simpson, was a kinetically charged, high-performance action vehicle. *Armageddon* (1998) was a noisy, sometimes baffling, always boom-and-doom asteroid-disaster movie—a sort of *Dirty Dozen* of the Spaceways—that earned more than $200 million. Heading an expedition of misfits bound to avert a deadly asteroid headed toward Earth, Harry Stamper (Bruce Willis) blows up the big rock and sacrifices himself in the process. The first half of the film reveals Bay's sure control of spectacle, special effects, and characterization. However, once Stamper's team lands on the asteroid, story and character disappear under an avalanche of frenetic cutting, noise, shouting (lots of shouting), and an interminable series of near-disasters.

By now Bay was positioned as Jerry Bruckheimer's director of choice for massively budgeted summer blockbusters. His bankable track record resulted in *Pearl Harbor,* the biggest picture of 2001,

released on Memorial Day to open the summer season. Rick Lyman of the *New York Times* described this "Disney behemoth" as Bay's "most ambitious project in both length (2 hours 50 minutes) and scope."

Bay described his first three films as "popcorn movies." *Pearl Harbor* would be different, however, "because its subject is more serious and its ambitions are higher." This would be a "gourmet popcorn movie," creating "a false reality, but its purpose is to make it feel more authentic." The challenge for Bay will be to move beyond the Bruckheimer blockbuster formula to more thoughtful, character-driven work. Ultimately, Bay will have to escape the "popcorn" mentality. *Pearl Harbor* was his best opportunity to break through to something more important, but it would have to be something more than a military disaster movie with a love story tucked on to wag the dog.

References Ansen, David, and Corie Brown, "Demolition Man," *Newsweek,* July 6, 1998, pp. 64–65; Dunne, John Gregory, "The American RAJ," *New Yorker,* May 7, 2001, pp. 46–54; Lyman, Rick, "A Connoisseur of Illusions," *New York Times,* May 18, 2001, pp. B1, B19.

—J.M.W.

Beresford, Bruce (1940–) With fellow Australians PETER WEIR and FRED SCHEPISI, Bruce Beresford appeared in the vanguard of the renaissance in Australian filmmaking in the 1970s. One of the most eclectic artists working today, his subjects and style vary greatly from picture to picture. He was born on August 16, 1940, in Sydney, Australia. After graduating from Sydney University, he worked in advertising and television for the Australian Broadcasting Company. In 1961 he relocated to London, where he secured a series of odd jobs, including teaching at a girls' school at Williesden. Ever peripatetic, from 1964 to 1966 he landed a position with the East Nigerian Film Unit in Africa. Back in London he was hired as film officer of the production board of the British Film Institute and as film adviser to the Arts Council of Great Britain, positions he held until 1970. After the passage in Australia of governmental decrees assisting film production, Beresford returned to begin his career in feature films. The time was propitious. The Australian Film Development Corporation (AFDC), the Experimental Film and Television Fund, and a national Film and Television School assisted the financing of feature films and television programs. The AFDC's first major investment was Beresford's *The Adventures of Barry McKenzie* (1972)—based on the satirical comic strip by Barry Humphries—the first of what historian Brian McFarlane refers to as his "ocker" films. It and *Don's Party* (1976), *Barry McKenzie Holds His Own* (1974), and *Money Movers* (1978) presented the cliched image of Australian men as "boorish but good humored, sexually and nationally chauvinistic."

This agenda would change with *The Getting of Wisdom* (1977) and *Breaker Morant* (1979). The first picture was based on an autobiographical 1910 novel by Henry Handel (née Ethel Lindsay) Richardson about the struggles of the free-spirited Laura Ramsbotham (Susannah Fowle), the daughter of an impoverished country postmistress, to survive a moribund educational system and become a writer. Like GILLIAN ARMSTRONG's *My Brilliant Career,* which it slightly resembles, it depicts something of the marginalized position of women in Australian society at the turn of the century. *Breaker Morant* was a fact-based historical drama about Australian guerrilla troops in the Boer War. Three officers of the Bushveldt Carabineers (Edward Woodward, Bryan Brown, Lewis FitzGerald) are court-martialed by a British court on trumped-up charges of atrocities against the Boers, despite their pleas that they were following the British commander's orders as relayed through their commanding officer. The court trial is interrupted by flashbacks reflecting the testimony of

Bruce Beresford directing *Tender Mercies* (Universal)

various witnesses. Historian McFarlane defends the film against charges of its being a simple-minded anti-British tirade: "Certainly, it deplores imperialism and the brutalities practiced in its name; but more complexly it offers a subtle and absorbing examination of a hierarchy of loyalties and orders. . . . If [Lord] Kitchener is discharging responsibilities, as he sees them, to the British government, Morant, Handcock, and Witton justifiably claim loyalty to . . . their commanding officer, through whom, in turn, they receive Kitchener's orders." Not only does the film reflect contemporary issues raised by atrocities in Vietnam, but also, as McFarlane notes, "it reflects that questioning of blind allegiance to a British cause which surfaced tentatively in Australian parliamentary debates of the time." It received international acclaim and was nominated for an Academy Award for best screenplay.

An invitation to come to Hollywood led to his next film, *Tender Mercies* (1983), a Horton Foote script about an alcoholic country singer (Robert Duvall), whose relationship with a young woman and her daughter rejuvenates him spiritually and professionally. Beresford was nominated for an Oscar for best director, and the film went on to receive two Oscars, for best actor and screenplay. His next film, *King David* (1985), thankfully broke from the DeMille tradition of biblical epics, but was less successful with critics and the public, as was *Crimes of the Heart* (1986), based on a play by Beth Henley about a reunion of three sisters—Diane Keaton, Jessica Lange, Sissy Spacek—after the youngest has casually shot her husband. Beresford bounced back with his most successful film to date, *Driving Miss Daisy* (1989), another theatrical adaptation, starring Jessica Tandy and Morgan Freeman as an elderly Southern aristocrat and her black chauffeur. It won four Oscars, including best actress and best picture.

In his recent films Beresford has tackled a wildly varied roster of subjects. *Her Alibi* (1990) was a slapstick adventure starring Tom Selleck as a mystery writer deriving inspiration from a relationship with a wrongfully accused young woman; *Mister Johnson* (1991) was based on a Joyce Cary novel about an English engineer in West Africa during the 1920s; *Black Robe* (1992) was a harrowing depiction of the grim realities awaiting French Jesuit missionaries among the Indian tribes of Canada; and *Paradise Road* (1997) told the fact-based story of the imprisonment and brutalization of female prisoners in a Japanese internment camp in the jungles of Sumatra during World War II.

Black Robe is a remarkable achievement and unlike anything else Beresford has directed. It chronicles the encounters in the early 17th century between French Jesuit missionaries and the Huron, Algonquin, and Iroquois Indian tribes, resulting in privations and death for the former, and the spiritual and physical corruption of the latter. After surviving the hazards of the 1,500-mile trip from New France to Quebec, Father Laforgue (Lothaire Bluteau) finds himself a captive of the fierce Iroquois. No sooner does he escape than he comes across a Catholic mission manned by a dying priest. He learns that the Huron village has been ravaged by fever and the handful of survivors are threatening the mission. Laforgue takes over and mollifies the Indians, who dutifully submit to communion. A concluding title ironically notes that after accepting Christianity, the now-peaceful Hurons were decimated by neighboring tribes. Neither before nor since has Beresford (or anyone else, for that matter) made a picture with such grim and unrelenting realism. The surface textures are absolutely convincing. It was shot on location in Quebec on the banks of the Saguenay River, and near Tadoussac, one of the earliest settlements in North America. All the dialogue with the Indians is in authentic Cree and Mohawk dialects (the Huron language is now extinct). And the savagery of the Huron torture sequences is not for the faint-hearted viewer.

The work of few directors has been as unpredictable—and as uneven—as that of Bruce Beresford. One watches with curiosity, mixed with a certain wary speculation, for each new project.

Other Films   *Side by Side* (1975); *The Club* (1980); *Puberty Blues* (1981); *The Fringe Dwellers* (1984); *Rich in Love* (1993); *Double Jeopardy* (1999).

Reference   McFarlane, Brian, *Australian Cinema, 1970–1985* (London: Secker & Warburg, 1987).

—J.C.T.

Bergman, Ingmar (1918–)   The great themes of this Swedish master are Big Issues of identity and society—birth, death, the psychology of relationships, dreams, legends and superstitions, frauds and miracles, and the breakdown of faith in modern society.

Ingmar Bergman was born on July 14, 1918, in Uppsala, Sweden, the son of a Lutheran pastor who was chaplain to the king in Stockholm. A sensitive child, he developed an early predilection for the performing arts, presenting shows in his own puppet theater and making short films of his own. At age 19, he rebelled against his parents' stringent discipline and left home determined to become a stage director. In 1944 he became director of the Helsingborg City Theatre, relocating later to Malmo, Gothenburg, and Stockholm, and indeed, stage work remained a major part of his artistic life, even after he became a celebrated filmmaker (he continued to direct at the Malmo Theater from 1953 to 1960 and at the Royal Dramatic Theater in Stockholm from 1960 to 1976). His productions of Strindberg, Ibsen, Anouilh, Chekhov, Moliere, and a number of operas have all been reflected in his choice of subjects and attitudes in his films. He once remarked that theatre "is like a loyal wife; film is the great adventure, the costly and demanding mistress."

Signing on with Svenskfilmindustrie as a screenwriter, he debuted with his script for Alf Sjöberg's film, *Torment* (1944), the story of an obsessive relationship between a student and a teacher. After making nine films, including *The Devil's Wanton* (1949), he found his voice with *Summer Interlude* (1951), an account of a doomed teenage love affair against the backdrop of a lyrical summer landscape. Actress Harriet Andersson, one of many performers whose career he would foster, first appeared in *Summer with Monika* (1953). A circus setting dominates the tawdry relationships in *The Naked Night* (1953).

Smiles of a Summer Night (1955) brought Bergman to international attention. Its story of awakening sensuality takes place in Sweden during the belle epoque. A potion with allegedly magical properties triggers an assortment of chance meetings, fervent declamations of love, betrayals, suicide attempts, and a duel of Russian roulette. Amusing, brittle, and bittersweet by turns, it is one of the few Bergman films that harks back directly to the sex comedies of his great Swedish predecessor, MAURITZ STILLER. "[It is] a joy for the moment," Bergman said, "a romantic story, playing with all

the cliches of the comedy of errors—the old castle, the young lovers, the elopement."

The three films that followed consolidated his reputation, *The Seventh Seal* (1957), *Wild Strawberries* (1957), and the Oscar-winning *The Virgin Spring* (1960). In *The Seventh Seal,* set in medieval times, Max von Sydow portrays Antonius Block, a knight returned from a crusade to the Holy Land. A plague is ravaging Sweden and people are mortifying themselves in a mass panic. Block encounters the figure of Death, who has come to claim him. To forestall him, Block talks him into a game of chess, a battle of wits where life and death are the stakes. As a result, although Block loses the game, he does manage to save a family of itinerant jugglers, which symbolizes the survival of universal innocence and good. *Wild Strawberries* was intensely autobiographical, a drama about a man trying to resolve the emotional failures and estrangements of his life. Swedish film master Victor Sjöstrom portrayed Professor Isak Borg, who is on his way to receive an honorary degree in Stockholm. His journey is one of revelation into the sterility of Borg's relationships with his family. Time, reality, and fantasy commingle in a seamless flow as flashbacks and dreams intrude upon his waking hours. At the end, after the doctoral ceremony, Borg goes to sleep, finally at peace with himself and his past.

Bergman's "chamber trilogy" of *Through a Glass Darkly* (1961), *Winter Light* (1963), and *The Silence* (1963) burrows inward to the darker recesses of his characters, to a place where God and understanding are absent. *Persona* (1966), however, marked a turning point in Bergman's work. Metaphysics are abandoned in favor of a psychological study of the symbiotic relationship between a traumatized actress and her nurse. *Cries and Whispers* (1973) continues this examination of mutually lacerating female relationships.

Charges that Bergman's "Nordic gloom"—an early film of his was once described as a story that "moves in a cruel and voluptuous arc from birth to death"—was all encompassing are not entirely accurate. Several of his films ridicule those very pretensions. *The Magician* (1958) is a witty look at the boundaries separating stage illusion from genuine magic in the confrontation between a scientist and an itinerant charlatan. *The Devil's Eye* (1960) is subtitled "a rondo capriccioso with music by Scarlatti." Because Satan is afflicted by a sore eye—a condition that can be cured only by the despoiling of a virgin—he sends Don Juan to seduce the 20-year-old daughter of a pastor. But Satan's plans misfire when Don Juan falls genuinely in love with his intended victim. The stye is cured, however, when the girl's virginity is vanquished on her wedding night. *All These Women* (1964), his first color film, is set in the 1920s and gaily chronicles the affairs of a brilliant cello virtuoso.

Bergman's close-knit "family" of cast and crew unravelled in the 1970s as he lost his home base and was bedevilled with tax problems. He relocated to West Germany, where he was engaged as director at the Residenz Theater in Munich until 1982. The autobiographical *Fanny and Alexander* (1982) marked a return to form, although it is avowedly his last directed film.

All of Bergman's films, in essence, are preoccupied with some aspect of theatrical illusion. As biographer Peter Cowie writes, "The moment of truth is the moment when the mask is torn aside and the real face uncovered. Every Bergman film turns on this process. The mask is shown, examined, and then removed." Thus, the theater, for all its shabby illusions and pasteboard characters, can satisfy our deepest hunger and aspiration to move the commonplace toward the miraculous. It is a process that is like the dream of the juggler Jof, in *The Seventh Seal,* i.e., that his baby son Mikael will one day be a great juggler and perform an impossible trick—make a ball stand still in the air.

Nowhere in Bergman's film output is the interface of theater and film, and the issues of life and death, reality and illusion, experience and innocence, more lucidly and compactly examined than in *The Magic Flute,* his cinematic interpretation of Mozart's last opera. It was made for Swedish television in 1975, and was filmed on the same kind of simple wooden stage on which the opera had been born. Bergman initially wanted to shoot it inside the celebrated Drottningholm Palace, located in a royal park outside Stockholm, but the structure proved to be too fragile to accommodate the performers and crew, so it was reconstructed in the studios of the Swedish Film Institute as it was in Mozart's time. Resisting the temptation to "open out" its stage-bound allegory into a more cinematic realism, Bergman used his camera instead to "expose," even celebrate, the artifice of the crude stage machinery. In this, as in all his films, the great truth is that, like Pamina and Tamino, we are all marionettes dangling from strings plucked by inscrutable gods, surrounded by the illusions of painted backdrops and wind machines.

The film's formal strategy resembles LAURENCE OLIVIER's *Henry V* (1944). It is a perfect arch, beginning on a small stage surrounded by an audience—a typage of huge closeups of shining faces welling out of the darkness—with a curtain rising on a sparely appointed stage. Periodically we hear the creaking of the stage machinery and get glimpses of the backstage activities of the stagehands. After a series of widening dramatic and scenic arcs—in Act Two there is a more cinematic handling of the hallucinations and temptations visited upon the hapless lovers by Sarastro and the Queen—we return at the end to the stark simplicity of the proscenium frame as the Queen's dark forces are banished and love is restored. Close-ups of watchful eyes dominate the film—the gaze of Sarastro, the recurring eyes of the little girl in the audience, the enormous close-ups of the players as they gaze out as *us.* Like Sarastro and the Queen, we, too, are gods for whom these players strut and fret. Who could blame us if, at the end, we glance upward—to see who is up there watching *us.*

Arguably, no other film director has ever dominated a national cinema to the extent that Bergman has. And few have left behind a more personal record of the many demons he has fought throughout his life—disastrous relationships with women, breakdowns, and threats of madness and suicide. "Whether I make a comedy or a farce," he says, "a melodrama or a drama, every film—except for those films made to order—are taken from my private life." In his autobiography, *Images* (1994), he delivers an enlightening comment on the nature of faith and religion in his world: "As long as there was a God in my world, I couldn't even get close to my goals. My humility was not humble enough. My love remained nonetheless far less than the love of Christ or of the saints or even my own mother's love. And my piety was forever poisoned by grave doubts. Now that God is gone, I feel that *all this* is mine; *piety* toward life, *humility* before my meaningless fate and *love* for the other children who are afraid, who are ill, who are cruel."

Other Films   *A Lesson in Love* (1954); *The Virgin Spring* (1960); *Hour of the Wolf* (1968); *Shame* (1968); *The Passion of Anna* (1969); *Scenes from a Marriage* (1973); *The Serpent's Egg* (1977); *Autumn Sonata* (1978); *From the Life of the Marionettes* (1980).

References   Bergman, Ingmar, "My Three Powerfully Effective Commandments," *Film Comment* 6, no. 2 (Summer 1970): 9–12; Bergman, Ingmar, *Images: My Life in Film* (New York: Arcade, 1994); Cowie, Peter, *Ingmar Bergman: A Critical Biography* (New York: Scribner, 1982); McLean, Theodore, "Knocking on Heaven's Door," *American Film,* June 1983, pp. 55–61.

—J.C.T.

Berkeley, Busby (1895–1976)

Hailed as the screen's greatest director of music-and-dance numbers, Busby Berkeley used to boast that he could not read music and never took a dancing lesson in his life. His career flourished in the early to mid-1930s at Warner Bros. and continued sporadically thereafter at Twentieth Century-Fox and MGM. He was born Busby Berkeley William Enos on November 19, 1895, in Los Angeles to a theatrical family. His parents were members of the Tim Frawley Repertory Company. Despite his mother's efforts to keep him out of the theatrical life, Busby grew up in a world of touring stock companies and one-nighters. A sensitive child, he grew up, in the words of biographers Tony Thomas and Jim Terry, "increasingly attached to his mother. . . . Until her death at eighty-five, Gertrude continued to be the strongest influence on Berkeley—he in turn was an attentive and generous son." After his education at Mohegan Military Academy in New York, from 1907 to 1914, he served as an aerial observer in the U.S. Air Corps in World War I. It was at this time that he first organized marching drills and toured stage shows for American and Allied forces. Released from the service, he began his theatrical career as an actor, stage manager, and choreographer between 1919 and 1927 before directing his first Broadway musical, *A Night in Venice,* in 1928, starring Ted Healy and the Three Stooges.

Berkeley was initially unenthusiastic about the film medium. "I had seen a few film musicals," he recalled, "and I hadn't been impressed; they looked terribly static and restricted." However, after coming to the attention of film producer Samuel Goldwyn, who hired him in 1930 to direct the dance numbers for the screen adaptation of Ziegfeld's stage hit *Whoopee* (for which he executed the first of his patented overhead camera shots), Berkeley moved to Warner Bros., where he devised and directed the cinematically inventive musical numbers for *42nd Street* (1933). Critical response to his contributions—which included the numbers "Shuffle Off to Buffalo" and the climactic "42nd Street"—was immediate and enthusiastic. "Busby Berkeley's staging is on a high plane," opined *Variety Bulletin,* "and when the audience in the theatre starts to applaud, there is a reason for it. Not just a flock of chorus girls walking across the stage as a background for the principals, but a suggested story with interesting routines." These prophetic words signaled both the end to the heavy-footed, clumsily executed chorus lines of past screen musicals and the beginning of a new era of precisely executed, wildly imaginative music-and-dance conceptions. Even those few complaints that his production numbers could never realistically occur on a theater stage point up Berkeley's cinematic ingenuity: "Apparently those critics never stopped to think that Berkeley was the first to know that his numbers could not be performed on any 'real' stage," observes Rocco Fumento in his study of *42nd Street*. "It is their very liberation from the stage that makes them exciting. From the real, stage-bound world of the rehearsal hall, he plunges us into a fantasy world with no boundaries." For Berkeley, it was a simple matter of respecting the fact that the motion picture camera has only one eye. "I started planning my numbers with one eye in mind," he recalled. "During my entire career in films I have never used more than one camera on anything. My idea was to plan every shot and edit in the camera."

In the succession of Warner's classics that followed throughout the decade—including *Gold Diggers of 1933, Footlight Parade* (1933), *Dames* (1934), *Gold Diggers of 1935,* and *Gold Diggers of 1937*—Berkeley's musical numbers grew ever more fantastic, obscuring the tepid dramatic stories framing them. "By a Waterfall" featured dozens of women diving and swimming in aquatic formations; "The Shadow Waltz" featured 60 chorines playing electrically illuminated violins; "My Forgotten Man" displayed formations of marching soldiers in its lament for the plight of jobless veterans in depression America; and the Oscar-nominated "Lullaby of Broadway" was a self-contained story in song and dance of 24 hours in the life of a showgirl, culminating in a suicidal fall from a skyscraper balcony. Most spectacular of all was the "I Only Have Eyes for You" number in *Dames,* a wholly surreal rendering of a young man's erotic fantasy, ending in optical mazes and graphic abstractions. Such numbers also subverted the prevailing Production Code's censorial restrictions. The "Pettin' in the Park" routine in *Gold Diggers of 1933* not only displayed images of scantily clad females, but also suggested a "wet dream" quality by sending the girls to the showers after a convenient rainstorm. In the title number of *Dames,* there are implicit lesbian overtones in the images of chorus girls sharing the same bed, coyly grinning when the camera discovers them together. And it seems that Berkeley exploited every opportunity in these and other numbers to send his camera suggestively gliding through the splayed legs of his chorines. In sum, Berkeley expanded the limited confines of theatrical space into a cinematic space characterized by a mobile camera, overhead shots, and a voyeuristic fascination with the female body. In rather more academic terms, historian Rick Altman notes that Berkeley alone of the early musical film directors, "understood the extent to which the audio dissolve liberates the picture plane of all diegetic responsibilities. . . . *Everything—even the image—is now subordinated to the music track* [italics by the author]. . . . It is as if the screen were transformed into an electronically generated visual accompaniment to the music." Meanwhile, indulged in his extravagance by the Warner's bosses (his numbers cost an estimated $10,000 per minute) and relentless in his ruthless perfectionism, "Buzz" became one of the most admired and hated figures in Hollywood.

Upon moving up from the ranks of dance director to director (*Gold Diggers of 1935* was his first directorial effort), he essayed a gangster film, *They Made Me a Criminal* (1939), which brought John Garfield and the Dead End Kids to the screen. That same year he relocated to MGM and returned to his musical métier with *Babes in Arms,* the first of several films pairing Judy Garland and Mickey Rooney. The formula, repeated in *Strike Up the Band* (1940) and *Babes on Broadway* (1941), consisted of Mickey and Judy leading their teenaged friends in amateur musical shows that defy all odds on their way to becoming hits. In 1943, on loan to Twentieth Century-Fox, he directed one of the screen's strangest and most exotic musical films, *The Gang's All Here*. Never mind the wartime story of a soldier and the girl he left behind (Alice Faye), it was Carmen Miranda and the spectacular "Tutti-Frutti Hat" number (with its formations of banana-waving chorines) and the "Polka-Dot Ballet" (with its kaleidoscopic geometric images) that stole the show.

MGM's *Take Me Out to the Ball Game* (1949), a baseball period piece with Frank Sinatra, Gene Kelly, and Esther Williams, was Berkeley's last directorial effort. After working as a choreographer and second-unit director on several more films in the early 1950s, including some Williams vehicles, Berkeley retired from the screen. In 1962 he came out of retirement to devise the circus numbers for the Doris Day vehicle *Jumbo,* and in 1971 he returned to Broadway to supervise a revival of *No, No, Nanette*.

Berkeley's career was plagued by as many problems as triumphs. In 1935 he was charged with drunk driving and second-degree murder after colliding with another car. Defended by famed Hollywood attorney Jerry Giesler, Berkeley was cleared of charges after three trials. Ten years later, after a succession of failed marriages, disastrous financial transactions, and numerous conflicts with producers and stars over his alleged sadistic perfectionism, his beloved mother died, leaving him penniless and in debt. Moreover, the subsequent collapse of his fifth marriage led to a suicide attempt and brief incarcerations in the psychiatric ward of the Los Angeles General Hospital and, later, in a sanitarium.

By the time Berkeley died, on March 14, 1976, his work was being reevaluated and praised by new generations of critics and moviegoers. "Busby Berkeley at his best is incomparable," write Thomas and Terry. "He was a cinematic pioneer who broke new ground by ignoring rules and going his own way. . . . His instinct, his imagina-tion, and his sense of visual effect combined to make him one of the most unique contributors to film history."

Other Films As choreographer: *Kiki* (1931), *Palmy Days* (1931), *Flying High* (1931), *The Kid from Spain* (1932), *Roman Scandals* (1933), *Wonder Bar* (1934), *Fashions of 1934, Twenty Million Sweethearts* (1934), *The Singing Marine* (1937), *Varsity Show* (1937), *Ziegfeld Girl* (1941), *Lady Be Good* (1941), *Born to Sing* (1941), *Girl Crazy* (1943), *Two Weeks with Love* (1950), *Call Me Mister* (1951), *Million Dollar Mermaid* (1952), *Small Town Girl* (1953), *Rose Marie* (1954). As director: *Bright Lights* (1935), *Stage Struck* (1936), *The Go-Getter* (1937), *Hollywood Hotel* (1937), *Men Are Such Fools* (1938), *Garden of the Moon* (1938), *Fast and Furious* (1939), *Blonde Inspiration* (1941), *For Me and My Gal* (1942), *Cinderella Jones* (1946).

References Altman, Rick, *The American Film Musical* (Bloomington: Indiana University Press, 1987); Fumento, Rocco, Introduction to *42nd Street* (University of Wisconsin Press, 1980); Thomas, Tony and Jim Terry, *The Busby Berkeley Book* (Greenwich Conn.: New York Graphic Society, 1973).

—T.W. and J.C.T.

Bertolucci, Bernardo (1940–) Bernardo

Bertolucci was born on March 16, 1940. Influenced by his father, the poet and film critic Attilio Bertolucci, he began writing poetry from a very early age and published it in journals before he reached the age of 12. Eight years later, while attending Rome University, Bertolucci won a poetry prize for his collection *In Search of Mystery*.

Like many formative talents, Bertolucci had shown an interest in cinema by making several nonprofessional 16-mm films. But when his father introduced him to PIER PAOLO PASOLINI (who was also a famous literary talent and critic) in 1961, Bertolucci dropped out of college to become assistant director on Pasolini's first film *Accatone!* Pasolini became impressed with Bertolucci's abilities, leading him to pass on to the young filmmaker the direction and screenwriting of his next project *La Commare Secca* (1962), based on Pasolini's own story. This early film revealed significant traces of the sophisticated visual style and complex narrative techniques Bertolucci would develop in his later films. Focusing on the murder of a prostitute and the ensuing police investigation, the film amalgamated film noir, sophisticated flashback devices, and neorealism.

Bertolucci's next film, *Before the Revolution* (1964), was a visually accomplished adaptation of Stendahl's *The Charterhouse of Parma*. Indebted to French New Wave visual techniques, especially the early style of JEAN-LUC GODARD, *Before the Revolution* began the first exploration of elements Bertolucci would investigate in his later films, such as the relationship between politics and sexuality, freedom and conformity, and the individual's relationship to the contemporary forces of Freud and Marx. These last two elements were featured as competing influences in Bertolucci's films of the 1960s and 1970s. Although they became dormant in his later work, they are not entirely absent from the spiritual dilemmas his protagonists face in the director's more recent films.

Like his mentor, Pasolini, Bertolucci chose to explore the humanistic aspect of personal relationships in his own particular manner. *Before the Revolution* was widely acclaimed in America and France, earning Bertolucci the MAX OPHULS prize in France. After working on a documentary series, contributing to one of the many cinematic compilations peculiar to the sixties, and collaborating on the screenplay of SERGIO LEONE's *Once Upon A Time in the West* (1967), Bertolucci decided to explore his fascination with Godard's political cinema by making an adaptation of Dostoevski's *The Double*. Retitled *Partner* (1968), the adaptation gave Bertolucci the opportunity to explore cinema in his own manner.

After directing *The Spider's Stratagem* (1970) for Italian television, Bertolucci delved further into his fascination with the connection between Freud's Oedipal trajectory and politics in *The Con-*formist* (1970). Shot in a beautifully colored surrealistic style with elaborate camera movements, the film represented his first collaboration with director of photography Vittorio Storaro, who would work on most of his subsequent films. Based on a novel by Alberto Moravia, *The Conformist* represented both Bertolucci's movement toward a more opulent Italian style represented by Luchino Visconti and another contribution to his cinematic philosophy regarding the medium as "the true poetic language."

The acclaim of *The Conformist* led to Bertolucci's most controversial film, *Last Tango in Paris* (1972). Featuring Marlon Brando, newcomer Maria Schneider, and Truffaut actor Jean-Pierre Leaud as a naive, satirical representation of the French New Wave, the film explored the violent conjunction of sexual energy and social constraints. Although these themes occurred in his earlier films, *Last Tango in Paris* developed them in an implosive manner resulting in alienation and death at the climax. As well as representing an older son's rage (Brando's performance is clearly reminiscent of a middle-aged Stanley Kowalski) against patriarchal institutions, the film also represents another Bertolucci movement away from his cinematic legacy, if we see Schneider representing the non-actor approach of Italian neorealism and Leaud as the now burnt-out legacy of the French New Wave. Storaro's cinematography and Gatto Barbieri's musical soundtrack also contributed to the film's stylistic intensity.

Bertolucci then gained the financial resources to make his cherished operatic, Marxist-Freudian epic, *1900* (1976). Shown in two three-hour parts in Europe but edited to three hours for American distribution, *1900* employed American and European stars such as Robert De Niro, Gerard Depardieu, Donald Sutherland, Alida Valli and Stephania Sandrelli (both of whom had worked with Bertolucci before), and Burt Lancaster in a project that also represented Bertolucci's goals of synthesizing American and European cinematic styles as

Bernardo Bertolucci on location during the filming of *The Last Emperor* (Columbia)

well as exploring historical issues against the framework of the then-prevailing contemporary discourses of Marx and Freud. This ambitious work explored many of Bertolucci's key themes, such as the relationship of politics and sexuality, which returned to a state of curious stasis between two opposing political and sexual forces after the Italian partisan victory of 1945. On the other hand, the film was strongly emblematic of the post-1968 stagnation affecting once-dominant historical and political forces.

After finishing this ambitious epic work, Bertolucci directed *La Luna* in 1979. Starring Jill Clayburgh, the film was an intimate chamber drama focusing upon an American opera singer's relationship to her young son and their eventual reunion with his father (Tomas Milian). The film

heralded Bertolucci's movement toward exploring a more intimate world of personal relationships affected by the conflicting worlds of different cultures. After directing *The Tragedy of A Ridiculous Man* (1981), Bertolucci returned to a wider historical canvas by exploring the evolution of a human subject moving from "darkness to light" and continued by depicting the transformation from "a dragon to a butterfly" in *The Last Emperor* (1987), the first film ever shot in Beijing's Forbidden City. Bertolucci then adapted Paul Bowles's novel *The Sheltering Sky* (1990), with John Malkovich and Debra Winger, a box-office failure followed by *Little Buddha* (1994). Emphasizing the spiritual dimensions of human existence linking both East and West, the film contained an outstanding painterly style of camerawork by Vittorio Storaro, especially in the scenes of Siddhartha's transformation. In 1998, Bertolucci decided to return to his low-budget roots with *Besieged,* a subtle chamber drama dealing with the romantic interaction between the worlds of the West (David Thewlis) and Africa (Thandie Newton).

References Bertolucci, Bernardo, *Bertolucci by Bertolucci* (London: Plexus, 1987); Kolker, Robert Phillip, *Bernardo Bertolucci* (Oxford: Oxford University Press, 1985).

—T.W.

Besson, Luc (1959–) Luc Besson was a post–New Wave breakthrough director who had to earn the right to make films through sheer determination and who ultimately managed to break through to Hollywood with spectacular movies, distinctive in the way in which they imagined the future and explored the past. During the 1980s French critics coined a dismissive term to describe the work of Besson and other newcomers such as Leos Carax—*le cinema du look*—suggesting a cinematic style that assaults the eye and overwhelms the viewer with spectacle.

Although born in Paris on March 18, 1959, Luc Besson grew up on the Mediterranean islands of Greece and the former Yugoslavia, where his parents were employed as scuba-diving instructors working for the Club Mediterrannée, and became fascinated with dolphins. Following a period of delinquency, Besson decided to quit school in 1976 and spent the following two years in military service before pursuing a career in cinema; but because he had not earned the *baccalaureat,* he was not able to qualify for the Institut des Hautes Etudes Cinématographiques. Undeterred, he established his own production company, Les Films du Loup, and, later, a second company, Les Films du Dauphin.

From 1978 to 1982 Besson entered an apprenticeship period, during which he worked on short films and commercials. He even went to Hollywood and worked for a time as a "gofer" for Uni-

versal. With a borrowed 35-mm camera he shot an eight-minute film entitled *L'Avant-dernier* with two friends, the actor Jean Reno and singer-songwriter Pierre Jolivet. This film, set in a post-nuclear France, did not compete successfully at the Avoriaz Festival, but it would become the starting point for his first feature-length picture, *Le dernier combat* (1983), shot in Paris and Tunisia and described by Besson as "une balade imaginaire." The "combat" involved in this post-nuclear "imaginary ballad" is between a young hero (Pierre Jolivet) and an evil marauder (Jean Reno). The men in this picture, in the legacy of *Mad Max,* are forced to forage for food, water, and sex, since almost no women have survived.

Besson's second feature, *Subway* (1985), begins with a robbery and a car chase that turns into an extended manhunt. This was followed by *Le Grand bleu* (1988), which focused on the magic of dolphins and the sea and the career of the free-diving champion Jacques Mayol and his rival and friend, Enzo Molinari (Jean Reno), who dies while attempting to beat Mayol's record of 120 meters. Although criticized at the Cannes Film Festival for its length and pretentiousness, the film went on to become a popular success. Besson's interest in the sea continued in *Atlantis* (1991), which Besson began shooting in 1988 as a sort of sequel to *Le Grand bleu.* French critics made comparisons to Jacques Cousteau's *Le Monde du silence,* but Susan Hayward calls the film an "underwater opera" focused upon "marine life threatened with extinction."

La Femme Nikita (1990), starring Anne Parillaud as a programmed assassin, scripted from an original scenario Besson wrote himself, was the film that made Besson an international talent. A tremendous hit with French audiences, it was distributed by Columbia Pictures in America, and later remade by Warner Bros. under the title *Point of No Return* (aka *The Assassin*). Besson wrote the script with Parillaud in mind, transforming her image, in the words of Susan Hayward, "from bimbo-starlette to ferocious androgyne to lethally armed female," and turning her into "*une Mata-Hari irresistible.*" This strategy was successful, and Parillaud won the 1991 Cesar award in France and the Donatello award in Italy for best actress.

La Femme Nikita was released on 100 screens in America, but Besson's next film, *Leon* (1994), under the title *The Professional,* enjoyed a much wider American release, distributed to 1,200 screens. It told the story of Mathilda (Nathalie Portman), a 12-year-old girl orphaned when her parents are brutally killed by a corrupt detective (Gary Oldman), investigating a drug operation in New York's Little Italy. She befriends a neighbor, a professional hit-man, Leon (Jean Reno is brilliant in the role), and wants him to train her to be a professional killer so that she may exact revenge for her parents' deaths. The illiterate, reclusive, and simpleminded Leon then becomes her friend and protector, ultimately sacrificing his life to kill Stansfield, the crooked, drug-dealing detective, who sees Mathilda as a possible witness and potential threat to him. Several American critics were offended by the film's morality—or alleged lack thereof—and criticized the strangely innocent and asexual Leon as a perverse pedophiliac (though he makes no clear advances toward Mathilda) and rejected the film as borderline child pornography. Besson was astonished by the reception. He saw the film as being about "two twelve-year-olds, even though one [Leon] is actually 40." Besson said he "was interested in talking about pure love. Society today confuses love and sex," as he learned from the film's reception.

Besson's next feature, *The Fifth Element* (*Le cinquième element* [1997]), marked a flamboyant return to the genre of science fiction, set in space in the 23rd century and populated by fantastic creatures. It's part apocalypse (the imminent demise of Earth), part spy thriller (Bruce Willis reprising his *Die Hard* role, to a degree), part *La Femme Nikita* (the spectacular Milla Jovovich kick-boxes and karate-chops her way through a slew of villains), part Messiah parable, and part game-show satire (the game show is hosted by Chris Tucker as "Ruby Rhod," the most annoying caricature of a gay black man imaginable). It even throws in an opera aria from *Lucia di Lammermoor,* sung by a blue-tinted diva, who seems to be part octopus. This film is marked by its pushy satire and flip sarcasm, but it is a visual extravaganza, a paradigm for what Besson's French critics called "*le cinema du look.*"

The Messenger (1999) is a retelling of the Joan of Arc story, with Milla Jovovich as the Maid of Orleans, set during the Hundred Years' War. The Crown of France was disputed between the Lancastrian English king Henry VI (as a result of the exploits of King Henry V and the English victory at Agincourt) and the Dauphin, son of the French king Charles VI. By 1428 the English forces, allied with those of Burgundy, occupied much of France. The Dauphin's cause seems hopeless, until Joan the Maid appears on the scene and inspires the French army to drive back the English siege of Orleans, then take the city of Reims. Once the Dauphin is crowned Charles VII, however, he withdraws his support of Joan, who wants to recover Paris, but who is wounded, captured, put on trial as a heretic by the bishop of Beauvais, and burned at the stake. Joan refuses to recant the supernatural "voices" that prompted her heroic exploits. The "messenger" of the film is a personification of those voices in the hooded presence of Dustin Hoffman, as a priest who hears her confession before her execution. Besson's treatment is as overheated as Jovovich's performance as Joan, but the battle sequences are nicely depicted in epic fashion. Jovovich's Joan is as beyond criticism as any other interpretation. If she is played as a fiend incarnate, then the accusations of the court are justified. If she is played as a passive instrument of misguided faith, her own convictions are then honored. If she is played as a dangerous egomaniac, then one understands why the Dauphin first respected, then rejected her. There is a rationale for any of these choices; the role is foolproof. The film attempts to rationalize her visions and fanaticism through a wholly invented childhood flashback and in terms of her own sexual repressions as a result of witnessing the rape and murder by English soldiers of a sister who has protected Joan. The frantic pace of Besson's treatment is the polar opposite of CARL THEODOR DREYER's classic treatment, *La Passion de Jeanne d'Arc* (1928), as can only be expected from this flamboyant new talent.

Reference Hayward, Susan, *Luc Besson* (Manchester, U.K.: Manchester University Press, 1998).

—J.M.W. and J.C.T.

Boetticher, Budd (1916–   ) Oscar Boetticher, Jr., was born in Chicago on July 29, 1916. After suffering an injury at Ohio State University in the early 1930s, he changed his career goals from professional football to becoming a matador. In 1940, he worked on Rouben Mamoulian's *Blood and Sand* as a technical adviser and functioned as a messenger boy at Hal Roach studios and as an assistant to directors such as William Seiter, George Stevens, and Charles Vidor before induction into the military in 1943. During his one-year stint in the service he made propaganda films. After demobilization in 1944, he resumed his Hollywood career, and he directed 11 films as Oscar Boetticher until he changed his first name to Budd. Boetticher has dismissed these films made between 1944 and 1950 as inconsequential, and although Boetticher directed some noteworthy films during 1951 to 1956, such as *The Bullfighter and the Lady* (1951), *Horizons West* (1952), and the gripping film noir *The Killer Is Loose* (1955), his key achievements lie in the cycle of westerns he directed for the Ranown production company between 1956 and 1960.

Beginning with *Seven Men from Now* (1956) and concluding with *Comanche Station* (1960), the best examples of this series utilize the collaborative talents of star Randolph Scott, scenarist Burt Kennedy and supporting heavies such as Lee Marvin, Richard Boone, Lee Van Cleef, and Claude

Akins in both a respectful appropriation of the formal tendencies of the classic western as well as a rigorously minimalist treatment cognizant of the often-fluid boundaries dividing hero from villain and right from wrong. Boetticher's achievement lies in his understanding of the nature of the turbulent emotions within the genre, often treated explicitly by directors such as Anthony Mann, while at the same time keeping them within restraint. It is not difficult to see elements of the controlling technique of a matador evident within Boetticher's directions.

Although Randolph Scott had acted in many westerns before, Boetticher refines his star's image to present him as a lonely figure dominated by fears of aging, sexual loss, and affinity with an outlaw double such as Richard Boone in *The Tall T* (1957), fears he keeps resolutely under control. The spiritual kinship between these two figures also appears in the tensely minimalist interplay between Scott and Lee Marvin in *Seven Men from Now.* In *Ride Lonesome* (1959), tension arises as to whether Brigade's (Scott) stubborn pursuit of the outlaw who murdered his wife years ago will result in his confrontation with the outlaw figure of Pernell Roberts, who wishes to reform. One of the classic and tragic ironies of the film is that Scott's antagonist (played by Lee Van Cleef) has forgotten the original incident and has more feeling for his captured younger brother than Brigade ever shows for his lost wife.

Another virtue of Boetticher's Ranown cycle is the depiction of secondary characters in the various dramas, such as Henry Silva in *The Tall T,* James Coburn in *Ride Lonesome,* and Skip Homeier in *Comanche Station.* The last film begins with Scott's character riding through a desolate landscape in search of his wife kidnapped by the Indians years before. It concludes in the same manner, suggesting that the loner's quest really represents an empty ritual his masculine entrapment requires. Although Boetticher treated the redundancy of the heroic quest earlier, in Scott's more excessive performance in *Decision at Sundown* (1957), it is more rigorously defined and thus more effective in the later film.

Before leaving Hollywood Boetticher directed one of the best versions of the retrospective gangster movie genre that swept Hollywood during the late 1950s and early 1960s. *The Rise and Fall of Legs Diamond* (1961) evoked an excellent performance from Warner Brothers contract player Ray Danton in an intelligent evocation of the tragic rise and fall of the gangster hero as defined by Robert Warshow. The director then left for Mexico and suffered several disastrous personal and professional setbacks documented in his autobiographic study *When in Disgrace.* However, he finally managed to release his bullfighting documentary *Arruza* in 1971, as well as *A Time for Dying* in the same year. Despite good cameo performances from Audie Murphy and Victor Jory, the leading man's inexperience and Boetticher's long absence from Hollywood resulted in a western that reflected none of the qualities featured in the Ranown cycle. Unfortunately, Boetticher was unable to direct his screenplay for *Two Mules for Sister Sara* (1970). His last completed film was *My Kingdom* (1985), which he also scripted.

References   Kitses, Jim, *Horizons West* (Bloomington: Indian University Press, 1969); Sherman, Eric, and Martin Rubin, eds., *The Director's Event* (New York: Athenaeum, 1970).

—T.W.

Bogdanovich, Peter (1939–) Born on July 30, 1939, in Manhattan, Peter Bogdanovich grew up in New York where he attended Collegiate School and studied acting at Stella Adler's Theatre Studio (1954–57). He made his stage directing debut at the Cherry County Playhouse in Michigan. Between 1956 and 1958, Bogdanovich appeared as an actor in several Shakespeare festivals. In 1959 Bogdanovich began directing several off-Broadway theatre productions, and the following year he began writing on the cinema for various journals including *Ivy, Frontier,* and *Village Voice.* Bogdanovich went to California in January 1961, conducting a number of interviews with famous directors, such as ALFRED HITCHCOCK, BILLY WILDER, John Sturges, GEORGE STEVENS, WILLIAM WYLER, and Frank Tashlin. These were published first in the magazine, *Esquire,* and later combined and included in his 1973 book, *Pieces of Time.* Bogdanovich also published several monographs for the Museum of Modern Art on such directors as Alfred Hitchcock, ORSON GEORGE WELLES, and HOWARD WINCHESTER HAWKS.

In 1964, urged by Frank Tashlin, Bogdanovich and his wife, Polly Platt, moved to California. Bogdanovich continued writing for *Esquire* from his new home in Los Angeles, and the next year he was offered a job as second-unit director by Roger Corman. Bogdanovich worked on Corman's biker film, *The Wild Angels,* starring Peter Fonda. In 1967 Corman gave Bogdanovich the opportunity to direct a feature film; the result, *Targets* (1968) starring Boris Karloff, was loosely based on the Charles Whitman shooting at the University of Texas at Austin.

Bogdanovich then turned his attention to a documentary film, *Directed by John Ford* (1971), funded by the American Film Institute and the California Arts Commission. The young director's next film, *The Last Picture Show* (1971), based on the novel by Texas author Larry McMurtry, is considered one of the landmark films of the 1970s. The film, shot in black and white, was, in many ways, an homage to the classic Hollywood cinema. Likewise, Bogdanovich's following films, *What's Up Doc?* (1972) and *Paper Moon* (1973), were nostalgic movies that paid tribute to the director's own cinematic icons, particularly Howard Hawks and John Ford.

When Bogdanovich became determined to make a major star of Cybill Shepherd, the resulting films lost him his connection with the American public. Both *Daisy Miller* (1974), based on the novella by Henry James, and *At Long Last Love*

(1975) were dismal box-office and critical failures. The director's homage to the early days of cinema, *Nickelodeon* (1976), only added to his subsequent disappointments. In 1980 Bogdanovich suffered a personal tragedy when his then-lover Dorothy Stratten was killed by her former boyfriend. In 1985, Bogdanovich directed *Mask,* based on the life of Rocky Dennis, who suffered from a rare disease called craniodiaphyseal dysplasia. The film marked Bogdanovich's return to mainstream filmmaking and was both a critical and commercial success.

Since then the director's work has been sporadic, his sequel to *The Last Picture Show, Texasville* (1990) failed primarily because, like most sequels, it could not live up to the originality of the first film. Likewise his film version of Michael Frayn's *Noises Off* (1992) was pale in comparison to his earlier work. Recently Peter Bogdanovich has been directing primarily for television—*To Sir With Love 2* (1996), *The Price of Heaven* (1997), and *A Saintly Switch* (1999) being the result of some of his efforts in the medium. An observation made by Thomas J. Harris helps assess Bogdanovich's place in cinema history: "What one notices upon a casual scanning of Bogdanovich's 11 features . . . is that his is a rather courageous filmography in terms of genre and subject. Within a relatively brief span of 20 years, one finds a thriller (*Targets* [1968]); a documentary (*John Ford* [1971]); four romantic screwball comedies with occassional dramatic overtones (*What's Up Doc?* [1972], *Nickelodeon* [1976], *They All Laughed* [1981], *Illegally Yours* [1988]); a musical (*At Long Last Love* [1975]); a small-town drama framed by western conventions (*The Last Picture Show* [1971]); a con man/orphan saga (*Paper Moon* [1973]); a period romance (*Daisy Miller* [1974]); a raffish 'star' melodrama with flashes of black comedy (*Saint Jack* [1979]); and a tearjerker—albeit only in theory (*Mask* [1985]). All are genres established in the 1930s, whose spirit Bogdanovich has tried to recapture, with varying degrees of success." If Bogdanovich's cinema is not strictly a personal one, it is one that draws on the rich heritage of American cinematic history.

Other Films *The Great Professional: Howard Hawks* (1967), TV; *Voyage to the Planet of Prehistoric Women* (1968), as "Derek Thomas"; *Fallen Angels* (1993), TV series; *Rescuers: Stories of Courage: Two Women* (1997), TV; *Naked City: A Killer Christmas* (1998), TV.

Further Readings Harris, Thomas J., *Bogdanovich's Picture Shows* (Metuchen, N.J.: Scarecrow Press, 1990); Yule, Andrew, *Picture Shows: The Life and Films of Peter Bogdanovich* (New York: Limelight Editions, 1992).

—R.W.

Boorman, John (1933–)

John Boorman was born in Middlesex on January 18, 1933, and educated in Salesian College. After military service in the British army during 1951–53, he worked as a film editor for Independent Television News between 1955 and 1958 and moved on to become head of documentaries at BBC Television from 1960 to 1964.

His first film as director was *Catch Us If You Can* in 1965. Retitled *Having a Wild Weekend* in the United States, the film featured one-time pop rivals to the Beatles, the Dave Clark Five, in a swinging sixties-influenced work, which also dealt with what would become a common Boorman theme, i.e., the outsider's attempted escape from society. In *Catch Us If You Can,* Barbara Ferris's heroine seeks escape from the commercial rat race aided by Dave Clark (in a surprisingly good performance) and the Five.

The success of the film led to Hollywood offers, with Boorman directing the first of his accomplished masterpieces, *Point Blank* (1967). Featuring Lee Marvin as a hard-boiled criminal who may (or may not) have survived a perilous journey from Alcatraz, the film was an oblique, deliberately modernist study of alienation and uncertainty. Its cinematic style represented a temporary challenge to the classic Hollywood narrative style, which would have depicted the subject matter either within the comfortable generic confines of the gangster film or with film's noir's visual familiarity. *Point Blank* chose no easy options. As a result, it was an individual experiment made possible in a Hollywood influenced by European art cinema—but a type of film impossible to produce today.

Hell in the Pacific (1968) reunited the director with Lee Marvin and teamed him with Akira Kurosawa regular Toshiro Mifune in a film subtly treating the cultural contradictions endemic to the war genre in a manner similar to the French existential alienation of Sartre's *No Exit*. Boorman's last experimental film, *Leo the Last* (1970), attempted to mix the conventions of European art cinema and theatre as well as the emerging radical avant-garde cinema associated with JEAN-LUC GODARD in its casting of Fellini actor Marcello Mastroianni, Samuel Beckett actress Billie Whitelaw, and black actress Glenna Forster-Jones who appeared in Godard's *Sympathy for the Devil* (1969). Sadly, it was a commercial failure.

Despite retreating to a more conventional narrative framework, his next American film, *Deliverance* (1972), was his investigation of an American masculine "heart of darkness" indebted as much to the emergence of a radical Hollywood horror genre as to William Faulkner. Expertly cast and photographed in a disturbingly dark visual style, it elicited strong performances from Jon Voight, Burt Reynolds, and Ned Beatty in a masculinist nightmare about a team of city vacationers who may have killed the wrong man in vengeance for the rape of one of their number. Unfortunately, despite the presence of Sean Connery and Charlotte Rampling and superb photography, Boorman's next film, *Zardoz* (1973), turned out to be an intellectual science fiction wet-dream. However, the unjustly maligned *Exorcist II: The Heretic* (1977) did represent Boorman's attempt to suggest alternative directions within the horror genre format while rejecting the gratuitous sensationalism of the original version.

John Boorman, director of *Excalibur* (Orion)

Excalibur (1981) represented a ponderous, overly visual treatment of the Arthurian legend, while *The Emerald Forest* (1985) combined environmentalist allegory with weak story and acting. *Hope and Glory* (1987) was little better than a sentimentalized feel-good treatment of the war years completely at odds with more compelling documentation in the historical works of Angus Calder. Boorman's major problem has always involved the uneasy amalgamation of artistic influences within generic formats whose parameters need to be understood. He achieves this best in *Catch Us If You Can, Point Blank,* and *Deliverance.*

The General (1999) does little to contradict opinions concerning the decline of Boorman's talent. Shot in a cinematic style tediously copying *Schindler's List* in that film's visual appropriation of Kurosawa's technique in *High and Low* (1963), this postmodernist Irish film noir meanders aimlessly throughout its two-hour narrative length. Its only redeeming value lies in the performance of Jon Voight as an Irish police inspector.

Other Films *Where the Heart Is* (1990); *I Dreamt I Woke Up* (1991); *Two Nudes Bathing* and *Beyond Rangoon* (both 1995).

Reference Ciment, Michel, *John Boorman* (London: Faber, 1986).

—T.W.

Borzage, Frank (1893–1962) Frank Borzage has often been dismissed merely as a sentimentalist who produced gauzy ephemera for an audience that preferred hard-edged clarity. Indeed, his delicate, wistful films of the twenties and thirties seem to exist outside popular taste. While Warner Bros. issued fast, sassy, cynical films like *42nd Street, The Public Enemy,* and *Five Star Final,* Borzage was crafting sweet, sad, deeply romantic dream films such as *Man's Castle* (1933).

But to categorize Borzage as an escapist would be to miss the point. His films were never romantic fantasies but stories in which his protagonists journey toward romance through the treacherous terrain of harsh reality. There is vivid and lyrical beauty in Borzage's work, but there is darkness as well. *Seventh Heaven* (1927), *Street Angel* (1928), *Lucky Star* (1929), *Liliom* (1930), and *Little Man, What Now?* (1934) are tinged with failure, betrayal, and death. *History Is Made at Night* (1937) contrives to run its beleaguered couple over hurdles of disappointment before placing them on a Titanic-like luxury liner, which sinks as its passengers sing "Nearer, My God to Thee." And *A Farewell to Arms* (1932), *Three Comrades* (1938), and *The Mortal Storm* (1938) are set against a world at war; their intense romanticism a comfort against, but not a denial of, the ever-present threat of death and loss.

Frank Borzage was born in Salt Lake City, Utah, on April 23, 1893. He began in show business, as did so many of the directors of his era, as an actor, appearing in many westerns at the Thomas

Ince studios. When he moved to Mutual in 1916, he began directing some of the films in which he acted. For the next decade he made westerns (*The Duke of Chimney Butte* [1921]), melodramas (*Secrets* [1924]), and comedies (*Early to Wed* [1926]).

When he moved to Fox Films in 1927, Borzage melded his own lyrical gifts with a rich, nearly expressionistic studio style, currently flowering with Murnau's *Sunrise*. Borzage teamed Janet Gaynor and Charles Farrell in the bittersweet love story *Seventh Heaven;* the result was an enormous success at the box office, and Borzage received an Academy Award for his direction (he won a second Oscar in 1931 for *Bad Girl,* starring Sally Eilers and James Dunn).

Borzage was never a prolific contract director and seems to have had considerable discretion in which films he chose to make. Hence, his work has a consistency of style and tone that few of his contemporaries could match, even when he addressed very different types of subjects. *Strange Cargo* (1940) is an allegory and *Smilin' Through* (1941), an unabashed tear-jerker, but both are tinged with supernatural elements even as they are suffused with Borzage's natural tenderness and sincerity.

His gesture for the war effort, *Stage Door Canteen* (1943)—a splashy variety show filled to bursting with popular movie stars and musical acts—and his biblical epic *The Big Fisherman* (1959) are the only works in Borzage's filmography that don't seem to have much in common with their director's sensibility. Indeed, *The Big Fisherman,* possibly the most static and tiresome of the CinemaScope epics of its time, has virtually no sensibility at all. It was Borzage's last film and his total disinterest in the subject is evident in every frame.

But the rest of his films offer few such disappointments. His work occupies a unique place in cinema history, and through them Borzage seems to speak a language all his own. True poignance and lyricism have virtually vanished from films today, although they have always been among the rarest of cinematic coins. But in Borzage's hand, they seem natural and effortless. There is not a moment of bathos or saccharine sentimentality in all of his films; his sentimentality is always honest and hard-won; Borzage's intense romanticism is so vibrant, so palpable, that it can exist only in close proximity to pain and heartbreak.

Other Films *The Good Provider* (1922); *They Had to See Paris* (1929); *Young America* (1932); *Flirtation Walk* (1934); *Desire* (1936); *Till We Meet Again* (1944); *Moonrise* (1948); *China Doll* (1958).

References Bodeen, DeWitt, "Frank Borzage," in *The International Dictionary of Films and Filmmakers,* vol. 2, *Directors/Filmmakers* (Chicago: St. James Press, 1984); Katz, Ephraim, *The Film Encyclopedia* (New York: HarperCollins, 1994); Sarris, Andrew, "Frank Borzage," in *Cinema: A Critical Dictionary,* Richard Roud, ed. (New York: Viking Press, 1980).

—F.T.

Brahm, John (1893–1982)

Born in Hamburg, Germany, on August 17, 1893, Brahm was raised in a theatrical family. His father, Ludwig Brahm, was a noted stage actor. John Brahm himself worked as a stage director in Vienna and Berlin prior to working in the film industry. In England Brahm became an editor and production supervisor in London. He supervised such film productions as *Scrooge* (1935) and *The Last Journey* (1935).

In 1936 he directed his first feature film, *Broken Blossoms* (a remake of D. W. Griffith's silent classic). The film was to be Griffith's comeback to the cinema, but he bowed out of its production following several disagreements. As a result of this film, Brahm was brought to Hollywood by Myron Selznick (David O. Selznick's brother) and received a four-year contract from Columbia. His films at Columbia were primarily "programmers" (films meant to be featured as the lower half of a double bill), such as *Counsel for Crime* (1937), *Penitentiary* (1938), *Girl's School* (1938), and *Let Us Live* (1939).

Brahm was signed by 20th Century-Fox in 1941 where he was to direct his best work. His first three projects at Fox teamed him with cinematographer Lucien Ballard, whom he had also worked with on several occasions while at Columbia. Among these films was the "B" feature *The Undying Monster* (1942), an interesting werewolf story that was to foreshadow Brahm's later work. The atmospheric adaptation of Marie Belloc-Lowndes's novel *The Lodger* (1944) is generally regarded as Brahm's greatest achievement. The film boasts fine cinematography (again by Ballard) and a wonderful performance by the portly character actor Laird Cregar. The film is generally considered an offshoot of film noir, in this case "period noir"—as it is set in Victorian London. According to Alain Silver and Elizabeth Ward, "Most of the films of this genre had a quasi-romantic narrative accentuated by a dark and sinister atmosphere. To a certain extent, this may be traced to a European sensibility, latent in the work of directors like Siodmak, Ulmer, Brahm, and even Hitchcock."

Brahm followed the success of this film with an adaptation of a novel by Patrick Hamilton, *Hangover Square* (1945). Laird Cregar once again portrays a demented character, this time a composer/pianist "whose lapses of memory conceal the fact that he is a mentally disturbed murderer." The film boasts a fine musical score by Bernard Herrmann. These wartime films, which also include *Bluebeard* (Edgar G. Ulmer [1944]), *Gaslight* (George Cukor [1944]), and *The Suspect* (Robert Siodmak [1945]), reveal a fascination with Freudian psychology that continued after World War II.

This psychological fixation is also apparent in Brahm's next film, *The Locket* (1946), made for RKO. The story concerns a young kleptomaniac and is distinguished by its innovative use of flashbacks within flashbacks in its narrative structure. Brahm's final feature for Fox was an adaptation of Raymond Chandler's *The High Window* titled *The Brasher Doubloon* (1947). George Montgomery puts in a poor showing as Chandler's detective

Philip Marlowe, and the film itself is distinguished only as another view of Chandler's milieu.

Upon leaving Fox, Brahm's subsequent films are relatively uninteresting. *Singapore* (1947) concerned an amnesiac, played by Ava Gardner, who has forgotten everything about her fiancee, Fred MacMurray. *The Miracle of Our Lady of Fatima* (1952) was an entry in the religious genre, and *The Diamond Queen* (1953) was a historical costumer set in India. Brahm returned to familiar territory with the mediocre 3-D entry, *The Mad Magician* (1954), starring Vincent Price as a murderous turn-of-the-century magician. It was, however, in the late fifties that John Brahm brought his gothic noir sensibilities to bear on another medium—television. In the late fifties and sixties Brahm directed episodes for such distinguished television series as *Alfred Hitchcock Presents* (1955–60), *The Naked City* (1958–59), *Twilight Zone* (1959–64), *Thriller* (1960–62), *The Alfred Hitchcock Hour* (1962–64), and *Voyage to the Bottom of the Sea* (1964). John Brahm died on October 12, 1982.

Other Films *Escape to Glory* (1940); *Wild Geese Calling* (1941); *Tonight We Raid Calais* (1943); *Wintertime* (1943); *Face to Face: "The Secret Sharer"* episode (1952); *The Golden Plague* (1953); *Bengazi* (1955); *Hot Rods to Hell* (1967).

References Coursdon, Jean-Pierre, *American Directors,* vol. 1. (New York: McGraw-Hill, 1983); Silver, Alain, and Elizabeth Ward, eds., *Film Noir: An Encyclopedia of the American Style,* rev. ed. (Woodstock, N.Y.: Overlook Press, 1992).

—R.W.

Brakhage, Stan (1933–)

Stan Brakhage has been called the "foremost living experimental filmmaker" and is credited with radically impacting other filmmakers' perspectives. Working at the margins of avant-garde filmmaking for more than 45 years, he has produced films—*Reflections on Black* (1955); *Anticipation of the Night* (1958); *Dog Star Man* (1961–64); *The Art of Vision* (1965), derived from *Dog Star Man; Mothlight* (1963); and *The Text of Light* (1974)—that are relatively unknown to the general public but are acknowledged as avant-garde classics.

Stan Brakhage was born in Kansas City, Missouri, on January 14, 1933. He began working at age four and trained as a singer and pianist until 1946. Brakhage performed as a boy soprano on live radio and for recordings. In 1951 he began studies at Dartmouth College, but dropped out the next year, still a freshman. Then, at age 19, he began to make films. *Interim* (1952) was his first film. It has narrative elements and is a love story with a very personal expression involving the woman with whom he was in love at the time. He ran a small theater in Central City, Colorado, where he made films and staged theatrical works by Wedekind and Strindberg.

In 1953 he went to San Francisco, to the Institute of Fine Arts, where he met "beat" poets and other artists such as Kenneth Rexroth, Kenneth Patchen, Michael McClure, Robert Duncan, Robert Creeley, and Louis Zukofsky. These were some of the members of the avant-garde who influenced him in the next few years. In 1954 he relocated to New York, met composer John Cage, and studied with Edgard Varese. He became acquainted with avant-garde filmmakers MAYA DEREN, Marie Menken, Willard Maas, Jonas Mekas, and Kenneth Anger. Brakhage's early works include *The Way to Shadow Garden* (1954) and *Reflections on Black* (1955), winner of the Creative Film Foundation Award in 1957. Also in 1955 he shot *Tower House* for Joseph Cornell and another film with Larry Jordan (an untitled film of Geoffrey Holder's wedding). From 1956 to 1964 he lectured on film, and he worked on many commercial film projects, such as television commercials and industrial films. In 1957 he and Jane Collum were married. They eventually had five children before they divorced in 1986. Jane was the inspiration for a shift toward domestic family life in the subject matter of his films. In 1958 Brakhage went to the Brussels film festival and viewed films of Peter Kubelka and Robert Breer. In 1960 he began presenting his own films in public and lecturing. He moved his family to Colorado and made films in the most meager of circumstances while living in the Rockies at Lump Gulch (elevation 9,000 feet.) There he gained an "esthetic distance" from other filmmakers.

After his 16-mm equipment was stolen, Brakhage concentrated on 8-mm filmmaking and completed major works like *Art of Vision* and *Dog Star Man* (1964). He also released *Dog Star Man* with a lengthy manifesto on his theories of vision (published in full by *Film Culture* in 1963) and *Metaphors on Vision*. This film demonstrated his idea of "hypnagogic" (closed-eye) vision. This film and its accompanying text radically influenced the course of avant-garde film. In 1969 Brakhage lectured in film history and esthetics at the University of Colorado, and in 1970 began teaching at the School of the Art Institute in Chicago. In 1974 he completed *The Text of Light,* a major abstract film. In 1981 he left Chicago for a teaching position at the University of Colorado, in Boulder. Brakhage currently resides near Boulder with his second wife Marilyn and their two children.

His early films display narrative elements. Later he moved to abstraction, finding ways to use film as a medium for artistic expression without resorting to narrative elements. Brakhage has concerned himself with the formal elements of cinema as a light-activated, moving medium for artistic expression. Although he has worked virtually alone, many of his techniques, radical esthetics, and philosophy have been absorbed into mainstream cinema (ranging from MTV and Nike commercials to films by Oliver Stone). He has explored film for its inherent rhythm and movement, and he has preferred the esthetic of soundless film. For example, Brakhage has scratched and painted on the film itself to best represent the colors and shapes of the body's sensations that he saw when he viewed images behind his closed eyelids. While viewing one of these films, the shapes and colors

that race across the screen at dizzying speed are enough to trigger a seizure in someone prone to them and to set off headaches in the rest of us. The result is actual physical pain as if one were rubbing one's eyes hard enough to "see stars."

Brakhage's honors and awards include the U.S. Library of Congress selecting his monumental film *Dog Star Man* (1961–64) for inclusion in the National Film Registry; the James Ryan Morris Award (1979); the Telluride Film Festival Medallion (1981); the MacDowell Medal (a prestigious award honoring the most influential American artists in many fields); and the American Film Institute award (the first) for independent film and video artists (the "Maya Deren Award").

References Barrett, Gerald R., *Stan Brakhage: References and Resources* (Boston: G. K. Hall, 1982); Brakhage, Stan, *Film at Wit's End: Eight Avant-garde Filmmakers* (Kingston, N.Y.: McPherson & Company, 1989); Camper, Fred, "Material and Immaterial Light: Brakhage and Anger," in *First Light,* New York Anthology Film Archives, 1998 [an exhibition catalogue edited by Robert Haller]; Dorsky, Nathaniel, "In-situ will present Stan Brakhage. . . .," *In★situ,* Austin, Texas, September 1997 [promotional material for In★situ, a local film society]; Ganguly, Suranjan, "All that is light: Brakhage at 60," interview, *Sight & Sound* 3 (1993): 20–23; Johnson, Jerry, with John Ausbrook, "Film at Wit's End," telephone interview with Stan Brakhage for *The Austin Chronicle,* September 15, 1997; Sitney, P. Adams, *Visionary Film: The American Avant-garde 1943–1978,* 2nd ed. (New York: Oxford University Press, 1979). Note: Connecticut State University's Brakhage information site features a biography and an extensive list of films.

—S.K.W.

Branagh, Kenneth (1960–) Kenneth Charles Branagh was born on December 10, 1960, in Belfast, Northern Ireland, the son of Francis Harper Branagh and William Branagh, who were married in 1954 at St. Anne's Cathedral, Belfast. His father, a joiner by trade, was forced to find work in England in 1967, visiting his family in Belfast every third Friday for three years, until the lot of them moved from Northern Ireland to Reading. Kenneth became interested in school dramatic productions and eventually joined the Progress Youth Theatre. Eventually, he auditioned for the Central School of Speech and Drama and the Royal Academy of Dramatic Art in 1979 and was offered a place at the latter, where he did well, eventually earning the Bancroft Gold Medal.

Leaving RADA in 1982, he made his professional West End debut in Julian Mitchell's *Another Country,* earning two awards as most promising newcomer of 1982. In 1984 he joined the Royal Shakespeare Company and played the lead role in *Henry V.* In 1985 he wrote and directed *Tell Me Honestly,* produced at the Donmar Warehouse in London. In 1986 he directed and starred in the Lyric Theatre, Hammersmith, production of *Romeo and Juliet.* In 1987 he founded the Renaissance Theatre Company with fellow actor David Parfitt and wrote and starred in *Public Enemy,* about a Jimmy Cagney impersonator who imagines himself taking over Belfast as a Chicago-style gangster, produced during the company's first season. In later productions he played the title role of *Hamlet,* directed by Derek Jacobi, and starred with Emma Thompson in a West End production of John Osborne's *Look Back in Anger,* directed by Judi Dench.

Branagh was therefore already a celebrated actor when he directed and starred in the film version of *Henry V* in 1988, which earned him Academy Award nominations for best actor and best director and the Evening Standard Award for best film of 1989. As King Henry he wooed Emma Thompson, a gifted comedienne he also married, until they broke up in 1994. Branagh was soon invited to Hollywood to direct *Dead Again,* in which he also starred in a dual role with Thompson. This was followed by *Peter's Friends* in 1992 and *Much Ado About Nothing,* screened in competition at the 1993 Cannes Film Festival, which was a popular hit as well as a critical success. He directed and starred in *Mary Shelley's Frankenstein* in 1994, a financial success that earned over $100 million worldwide.

The next year he wrote and directed *A Midwinter's Tale,* an amusing comedy about a troupe of actors trying to mount a production of *Hamlet* in a dilapidated church in rural England. The film, which opened the 1996 Sundance Film Festival, was followed by his spectacular four-hour production of *Hamlet,* which had its world premiere on January 21, 1997, at Waterfront Hall in Branagh's native Belfast. It was a remarkable screen adaptation because Branagh was determined to retain the whole combined Folio and Quarto versions of the text, a feat never before attempted. His next Shakespeare film, *Love's Labours Lost* (2000), did not fare as well and was panned by reviewers who did not approve of his updating the play as a postmodern musical that incorporated the music of Cole Porter, Irving Berlin, Jerome Kern, and others.

Regardless of this temporary setback, Branagh has surely become the successor of Laurence Olivier in his ambition to film Shakespeare's plays, but he has also established himself as a viable Hollywood talent, and has had remarkable successes as actor, director, writer, and playwright, all before the age of 40.

Other Film   *The Flight of the Navigator* (1999).

References   Branagh, Kenneth, *Beginning* (London: Chatto & Windus, 1989); Shuttleworth, Ian, *Ken & Em: A Biography of Kenneth Branagh and Emma Thompson* (New York: St. Martin's Press, 1994).

—J.M.W.

Brenon, Herbert (1880–1958)   Herbert Brenon is virtually unknown today, but at the peak of his powers in the 1920s, he was among the most powerful and popular film directors in the world. Known for epics like *A Daughter of the Gods* (1916) and *Beau Geste* (1926), intimate fantasies such as *A Kiss For Cinderella* (1922) and *Peter Pan*

(1924), and compelling dramas like *The Great Gatsby* (1926), Brenon was revered by critics as an artist and admired by studio heads as a proven box-office champion.

Now, more than six decades after he made his final film, *The Flying Squadron* (1940), relatively few of Brenon's films exist. Of those that do, only a couple—*Beau Geste* and *Peter Pan*—are revived with any kind of regularity. Brenon's work has been a victim of failures in film preservation, which in turn have led to his neglect by scholars and historians. With so few of his films available, his place in the history of film is shaky, and his obscurity deepens year by year.

This state of affairs would, no doubt, be shocking to a cinema expert of 1926. Brenon was then considered the equal of CECIL B[LOUNT] DEMILLE, DAVID WARK GRIFFITH, or any of the other filmmaking giants of the era. He was also apparently one of the most temperamental of directors, capable of whipping himself—and his set—into a frenzy when things weren't going right. One of his assistant directors, Charles Barton (later a director himself), reported that Brenon's directorial style was basically an imitative one; he would perform each role for his actors and encourage them to ape his movements and expressions as closely as possible. He could have become quite a good actor—although Barton remembered his style as excessively hammy—and, in fact he did gain substantial experience as an actor early in his career.

Brenon was born in Kingstown, near Dublin, Ireland, on January 13, 1880. It has been claimed that he studied medicine at King's College, London, but if he did, he could not have made much progress, because by the age of 16 he had emigrated to the United States where he began working in the theater, first as an office boy, then as an actor and stage manager in various stock companies. After a brief stint managing a vaudeville and moving picture theater in Pennsylvania, Brenon began writing screenplays in 1911 for Carl Laemmle's Independent Motion Pictures (IMP). The following year he began directing one-reelers.

From the beginning, his work was admired for its quality, with an early version of *Dr. Jekyll and Mr. Hyde* (1912), starring King Baggot, being one of his early triumphs. IMP sent a company to Europe under Brenon's direction later that year, and he made eight films in a very brief span of time in London, Paris, and Berlin. One of the films, *Across the Atlantic,* was an exciting melodrama about aviation in which Brenon not only acted but also performed a dangerously high fall stunt. Also in England, Brenon directed a lavish four-reel version of Sir Walter Scott's *Ivanhoe,* which he gave a genuinely epic treatment.

No sooner had Brenon returned to America than he was off on location again, filming *Neptune's Daughter* (1914) in Bermuda with the swimming star Annette Kellerman. The director gave himself the villain's role in this fantasy—and the part nearly cost him his life. He filmed an underwater fight scene with Kellerman in a large tank. During the struggle, the glass broke and both Kellerman and Brenon were raked across the broken edges, pulled out with 18,000 gallons of water. Despite the painful memory, the director and actress teamed up again in Jamaica to make what must have been one of the most remarkable fantasy epics of the silent era, *A Daughter of the Gods* (1916). Now lost, the film employed over 20,000 extras and utilized fantastic sets that stretched up to a half-mile long. *A Daughter of the Gods* was a Fox production. The studio heads were so outraged at Brenon's disregard of budget and schedule that they removed his name from the credits. According to press reports at the time, he had to sneak into the premiere wearing a false beard.

Brenon's adaptation of Barrie's *Peter Pan* (1924) was a fantasy on a much smaller scale, but it is probably much more charming than the huge *Daughter of the Gods* could have been. Starring Betty Bronson as the boy who wouldn't grow up, Esther Ralston as Mrs. Darling, Mary Brian as

Wendy, and Ernest Torrence as Captain Hook, the film is an excellent adaptation of stage productions of *Peter Pan* of the period. Brenon's respect for Barrie's play is evident throughout, even, at times, to the film's detriment. The director composes most scenes as if within a proscenium arch; the film is never exactly "cinematic" in execution. Nevertheless, the tone is perfect and the performances tuned to perfect whimsical pitch.

Brenon's adaptation of Percival Christopher Wren's epic of the Foreign Legion *Beau Geste* (1926) illustrates both the director's strengths and his weaknesses. As in *Peter Pan,* the performances are first rate. Ronald Colman, Neil Hamilton, and Ralph Forbes play the brothers who join the Foreign Legion to claim responsibility for a crime of which they are all innocent. Alice Joyce plays their aunt, Mary Brian their cousin, and Noah Beery the evil Sgt. Lejaune, who makes life in the desert even nastier than necessary. William Powell plays the weak, cowardly Boldini. Pictorially ravishing (the cinematographer was the great J. Roy Hunt), *Beau Geste* succeeds on nearly every level except the basic one of excitement. WILLIAM AUGUSTUS WELLMAN's 1939 *Beau Geste* starring Gary Cooper has often been called a shot-for-shot remake of Brenon's film, but in fact it moves with an energy that the 1926 version never approaches. When thousands of Arab tribesmen attack the legionnaires in Fort Zinderneuf, Brenon keeps them curiously remote; they resemble bugs swarming over the sand dunes. In the same scenes in 1939, Wellman cuts to close-ups of the marauding Arabs, making their threat more palpably urgent.

In fact, most of Brenon's surviving work shows a style that is staid, subdued, and dignified. His compositions are striking—he is very consciously an "artistic" filmmaker—but he rarely indulges in the kind of kinetic thrills that were second nature to Griffith, DeMille, RAOUL WALSH, Wellman, and other great popular filmmakers.

Still, Brenon's losses are heartbreaking. His *The Great Gatsby* (1926) was hailed as a generally suc-

cessful adaptation of F. Scott Fitzgerald's novel. And *Sorrell and Son* (1927) brought Brenon an Academy Award nomination; one critic wrote of it, "Every man, woman or child should see this engrossing and inspiring entertainment."

Brenon, despite his earlier stage experience, never quite made his peace with talking pictures. *Beau Ideal* (1931), a sequel to *Beau Geste,* is pretty dreadful, despite a cast that includes Ralph Forbes and Loretta Young. But film historian Anthony Slide has called *The Housemaster* (1938) a "minor masterpiece" and "a far more satisfactory study of public school life than, say, *Goodbye Mr. Chips.*"

Brenon made his last films, including *The Housemaster,* in England and quit the business in 1940. He returned to Los Angeles where he lived in apparently contented retirement until June 21, 1958.

Herbert Brenon has not retained the exalted reputation that he bore during the peak years of his career. But the suggestion of quality clings to his name, even though it seems that some of his worst films have survived while some of his best have vanished. But *Beau Geste, Peter Pan,* and *Laugh, Clown, Laugh* (1928) continue to entertain audiences. And with the restoration of some of his earlier work and, perhaps, the discovery of some of those films now thought lost, Herbert Brenon may yet receive the reappraisal that his impressive reputation deserves.

Other Films *Kathleen Mavourneen* (1913); *Absinthe* (1914); *The Heart of Maryland* (1915); *War Brides* (1916); *The Fall of the Romanoffs* (1917); *Shadows of Paris* (1924); *Dancing Mothers* (1926); *God Gave Me 20 Cents* (1926); *Lummox* (1930); *Living Dangerously* (1936); *The Dominant Sex* (1937); *Black Eyes* (1939).

References Gillett, John, "Herbert Brenon," in *Cinema: A Critical Dictionary: Aldrich to King,* vol. 1, ed. Richard Roud (New York: Viking Press, 1980); Lodge, Jack, "Herbert Brenon," *Griffithiana* 57/58 (Gemona, Italy: La Cineteca del Fruili, October 1996); Slide, Anthony, "Herbert Brenon," in *The International Dictionary of Films and Filmmakers,* vol. 2,

Directors/Filmmakers (Chicago: St. James Press, 1984); Thompson, Frank, "Daughter of the Gods," in *Lost Films: Important Movies That Disappeared* (New York: Citadel Press, 1996).

—F.T.

Bresson, Robert (1907–1999)   Robert Bresson, one of France's most distinguished filmmakers, has been both praised and condemned for the apparent austerity of his subject matter and style, which makes few concessions to commercial cinema and popular tastes. Although all of his mature works—he directed only 13 films—were made within the parameters of the New Wave and Second Wave of filmmaking in France, he stands apart from his noisier and more radically expressive brethren. He was always his own man, as it were, on a pilgrimage to create a body of work as insistently personalized as any in the history of cinema.

He was born on September 25, 1907, in the mountainous Auvergne region of France. When he was eight years old his family moved to Paris, where in his teen years he studied to be a painter at the Lycé Lakanal in Sceaux. He worked in the 1930s as a painter and apprentice filmmaker. His first film, a short, *Les Affaires publiques* (1934), was presumed lost until it resurfaced in 1989. It is unlike anything he subsequently made, reports critic Jonathan Rosenbaum in his assessment of the film, a *comique fou* revealing a surreal series of scenes in a slapstick style reminiscent of the Marx Brothers.

After an incarceration by the Germans as a prisoner of war between June 1940 and April 1941, he was released and returned to occupied France in 1943, where he made his feature film debut with *Les Anges du péché* (*Angels of the Streets*). Winner of the Grand Prix du Cinéma Français, it is an astonishing film displaying Bresson's central thematic concerns—the search for spiritual grace and the transformative powers of love. The story involves the strange relationship between Anne-Marie, a novice about to take holy orders and Thérèse, a hardened murderess seeking shelter in Anne-Marie's convent. Near death and too weak to speak as a result of her sacrifices to save Thérèse's soul, Anne-Marie expires as Thérèse speaks her vows for her. Compared to the spareness of Bresson's later work, *Les Anges du péché* has a more flamboyant style, including a "background" musical score, chiaroscuro lighting, and the use of professional actors. Nonetheless, it is a striking debut film and one fully prophetic of the mature style to come.

From the mid-1940s on, Bresson made a succession of noteworthy films, all of which have become acknowledged classics in world cinema: *Les Dames du Bois de Boulogne* (*The Ladies of the Bois de Boulogne* [1945]) depicts the struggle of a young man to find spiritual love with a prostitute; *Le Journal d'un curé de campagne* (*Diary of a Country Priest* [1951]) is based on Georges Bernanos's novel about a young priest who achieves grace through a process of sacrifice and self-starvation; *Un condamné à mort s'est échappé* (*A Man Escaped* [1956]) documents a true story of a prison break; *Pickpocket* (1959) depicts a young thief's willful attempts to be caught and imprisoned; *Procés de Jeanne d'Arc* (*The Trial of Joan of Arc* [1962]) uses transcripts of Joan's trial to chronicle her last days; *Au hasard Balthazar* (1966) is a Christian parable about a series of encounters between a donkey and situations representing the deadly sins of humanity; *Mouchette* (1967) is based on Bernanos's novel about the isolation and hardships endured by a 14-year-old servant girl; *Une femme douce* (*A Gentle Creature* [1969]) derives from a Dostoevsky story about a young woman's fatal inability to be a "faithful wife"; *Quatre nuits d'un rêveur* (*Four Nights of a Dreamer* [1971]), is adapted from another Dostoevsky story, "White Nights," about a young man's doomed love for a suicidal woman; and *Lancelot du Lac* (1974) is an interpretation of the Grail myth. His last two films, *Le Diable, probablement* (*The Devil, Probably* [1977]), and *L'Argent*

(*Money* [1982]) mark a shift from dramas of individual regeneration and redemption to chronicles of, in the words of commentator Kent Jones, "the feelings of defeat and lethargy in the young people around him." They are like nothing else in modern cinema, continues Jones, "as horrifying as they are lucid, as sure of the inherent beauty of the world as they are insistent on the recognition of its manmade horror."

Bresson may be regarded as one of the cinema's true auteurs. His 13 films display a subject and style that are instantly and uniquely his own. As critic Molly Haskell writes, "Bresson has virtually declared himself on a holy mission to turn back the clock, wrest movies from layers of artifice and convention, free our eyes and ears from the glaze of habit and allow us to see and hear with newborn curiosity." His basic theme, says Susan Sontag, is "the meaning of confinement and liberty," wherein the disparity between the spiritual and the immanent is ongoing, and the sense of a release is impending. States of austerity and transcendence—problematic terms that are frequently applied to his work—are approached, not just by the characters in his films, but in the narrative modes of the films themselves.

On the face of it, approaching transcendence on film might seem an impossibility, a "laughable presumption," in Carl Jung's words. Man, avers Jung, can only say something about the "knowable" but nothing about the "unknowable" ("of the latter, nothing can be determined"). Yet, says Bresson, "I would like in my films to be able to render perceptible to an audience a feeling of a man's soul and also the presence of something superior to man which can be called God."

Bresson's method has been examined in detail in the past by such distinguished commentators as Raymond Durgnat, Charles Barr, André Bazin, and Paul Schrader (Schrader's book, *Transcendental Style in Film,* presents a particularly lucid and accessible discussion of four films from Bresson's middle period) and most recently in two symposia of commentators in the May–June 1999 and July–August issues of *Film Comment.* Paradoxically, Bresson begins with the knowable, with the everyday. He has precedents in Byzantine and Chinese art, where a fanatical attention to minute detail renders the surfaces of reality so precisely—without resorting to signifying or connotative suggestions—that a sense of the supernatural is achieved (rather like the hyperclarity of some surrealistic paintings). Whenever possible he films on location—at Fort Montluc for *A Condemned Man,* at the Gare de Lyon for *Pickpocket.* He concentrates on and celebrates the trivial, the small sounds, a creaking door, a chirping bird, static views, blank faces. "He works painstakingly so that his films appear to register and acknowledge all things equally," declares Kent Jones, "—a bouquet of daisies thrown on an asphalt road becomes just as moving as the face of a man behind bars at long last acknowledging his love for the woman on the other side." About the rigorous depiction of the prisoner's cell in *A Condemned Man,* for example, Bresson said, "I was hoping to make a film about objects which would at the same time have a soul. That is to say, to reach the latter through the former." He ruthlessly strips action of its significance and regards a scene in terms of its fewest possibilities. He achieves this in several ways:

1. *Plot.* Bresson dislikes plot. He wants to suppress it. For him, plot establishes a too simple and facile relationship between the viewer and the event. He wants the viewer to have no intercourse with the story. The real drama is an internal one, not an external machination. "Dramatic stories should be thrown out," he has said. "They have nothing whatsoever to do with cinema."

2. *Acting.* Just as the plot is too simple a reduction of life, so does the professional actor traditionally simplify too much his own or his "character's" complexities. He modifies his character's

"unfathomable complexities into relatively simple, demonstrable characteristics," resulting in "too simple an image of a human being, and therefore a false image." Rather, Bresson wants his actors—usually nonprofessionals—to convey a reality that is not limited to any one character. He forces the actor to sublimate his personality and to "act" in an automatic matter. Bresson refuses to give actors interpretive advice on the set; rather, he gives only precise, physical instructions—what angle to hold the head, when and how far to turn the wrist, etc. André Bazin argues that this hieratic tempo of acting, the slow gestures, the "obstinate recurrence of certain behavioral patterns," the dreamlike slow motion confirms that "nothing purely accidental" could ever happen to these people, that each is inexorably committed to his or her own way of life.

3. *Camerawork.* Camera movements and vantage points, particularly the stylization of the track, the high angle, the pan, the close-up, inevitably convey attitudes toward the character and story. Bresson wishes to avoid this. He restricts himself to the relatively shallow depth-of-field of the 50-mm lens and one basic vantage point (usually a medium shot from chest level). He calls the results a "flat" image: "If you take a steam iron to your image," he explains, "flattening it out . . . and you put that image next to an image of the same kind, all of a sudden that image may have a violent effect on another one and both take on another appearance."

4. *Editing.* Bresson prefers the straight, unostentatious cut. Scenes are usually cut short, the shots merely set end to end.

5. *Soundtrack.* Bresson uses asynchronous sound sometimes, but not for editorial purposes. Sound can only reinforce the cold reality. His soundtracks consist mostly of natural sounds, "close-up" sounds that help confirm for us a great concern for the minutiae of life. He avoids using "background" music, reserving

bursts of music only for the climactic moments of his films. When the prisoner in *A Condemned Man* escapes, when Joan is burned, the pickpocket imprisoned, the priest dies, then music on the soundtrack assists in this sense of transformation. At these points, the contrast between the elegantly profound music of Mozart and Monteverdi presents an almost unbearable contrast with the blunt coldness of the images.

6. *Doubling.* Through the use of repeated action and pleonastic dialogue, Bresson makes single events happen several times in different ways. The audiovisual redundancy of Michel's diary entries in *Pickpocket* is an example. Usually an interior narration exactly duplicates the action visible on the screen. Narration does not give the viewer any new information, but only reiterates and emphasizes what he already knows.

7. *Disjunction.* Bresson emphasizes the disparity between characters and environment. Examples include the priest's alienation from his surroundings in *Diary,* the self-incriminating testimony of Joan of Arc, and the inexorable thievery of the eponymous pickpocket. These characters do things quite at odds with their surroundings. The priest renounces the world at the cost of his life; Joan's testimony leads to her immolation at the stake; and the thief steals not through the need for money, but because he must follow the Will to Pickpocket. This disparity grows as the characters behave as if in the grip of something apart from the physical world, an "Other," as he calls it. Nothing on earth can placate their inner passion, says Schrader, "because their passion does not come from earth. . . . They do not respond to their environment, but instead to that sense of the Other which seems much more immediate."

8. *The metaphor of confinement.* The prison cell is the dominant metaphor of Bresson's films, most obviously in *A Condemned Man,* but it needs to be understood in two ways. His characters are

both escaping from a prison of one sort and surrendering to a prison of another. The human body is usually regarded as the most confining prison of all. Suicide frequently occurs in his films. (Indeed, Bresson "killed off" his actors, in the sense that he refused to use an actor in more than one film.)

9. *The human face.* If the prison cell is the dominant metaphor, then the human face is the dominating sign, both iconic and indexical. Bresson used the interrogations of Joan of Arc, not to provide historical information, but, as he explains, "to provoke on Joan's face her profound impressions, to imprint on the film the movements of her soul." Critic André Bazin applauds this technique: "Naturally Bresson, like [CARL THEODOR] DREYER, is only concerned with the countenance as flesh, which, when not involved in playing a role, is a man's true imprint, the most visible mark of his soul. It is then that the countenance takes on the dignity of a sign. He would have us be concerned here not with the psychology but with the physiology of existence."

As a result of the foregoing, Bresson is not so much making the viewer see everyday life in a certain way, but rather preventing him from seeing it in the manner to which he has become accustomed. The everyday is something intractable, and it will not allow the viewer to apply his or her natural interpretive devices. As Paul Schrader says, in Bresson's films "the viewer becomes aware that his feelings are being spurned; he is not called upon, as in most films, to make either intellectual or emotional judgments on what he sees. His feelings have neither place nor purpose in the scheme of the everyday."

In all of Bresson's films there is a final moment, a decisive action that demands commitment from the viewer. Bresson calls this the moment of "transformation." The viewer must, in that moment, face the dilemma of the protagonist,

confront "an explicably spiritual act within a cold environment, an act which now requests his participation and approval. Irony can no longer postpone his decision. It is a 'miracle' which must be accepted or rejected."

To be sure, these final moments do not resolve the disparity of man and environment. Rather, a stasis is achieved, a paradox wherein the spiritual coexists with the physical in a way that no earthly logic can explain. Precedents for this condition may be found in the portrait iconography of Byzantine art—especially the frontal, isolated views of saints. In stasis, says Schrader, "The viewer is able to cross interpret between what seemed to be contradictions: he can read deep emotion into the inexpressive faces and cold environment, and he can read factuality into the inexplicable spiritual actions." However, his characters must remain ultimately inexplicable. They never reveal anything but their mystery—like God.

Characteristically, Bresson always refused to indulge in such metaphysical speculation about his films. Indeed, in a number of interviews he resisted being labeled as a "transcendental" filmmaker. He insisted simply that his films are not *spiritual* experiences so much as *emotional* ones. In a 1962 interview, he tersely noted what he expects viewers to bring to his films: "Not their brains but their capacity for feeling."

Robert Bresson died on December 22, 1999.

References *The Films of Robert Bresson* [essays by Amédée Ayfre, Charles Barr, André Bazin, Raymond Durgnat, Phil Hardy, Daniel Millar, and Leo Murray] (New York: Praeger Books, 1969); Cameron, Ian, "Robert Bresson," in *Interviews with Film Directors,* ed. Andrew Sarris (New York: Avon Books, 1967); Schrader, Paul, *Transcendental Style in Film* (University of California Press, 1972). Two issues of *Film Comment* have been devoted to symposia on Bresson and his work: 35, no. 3 (May/June 1999): 36–62; 35, no. 4 (July/August 1999): 36–54.

—J.C.T.

Brooks, James L. (1940–) If he had never gone into movies, James L. Brooks, born May 9, 1940, in North Bergen, New Jersey, would still hold a noteworthy place in the entertainment world. During the last three decades, he has helped create and/or produce some of television's most influential and critically acclaimed comedies, including *The Mary Tyler Moore Show, Taxi,* and *The Simpsons.* He made the transition to film in 1979 with his script for *Starting Over,* a comedy-drama about the aftermath of divorce, starring Burt Reynolds and Jill Clayburgh.

When he made the leap to directing, the result was the critically acclaimed and financially successful *Terms of Endearment* (1983), the story of a tempestuous mother-daughter relationship and the men in their lives. The movie is alternately funny and sad, and, most of all, true to the unpredictable ups and downs encountered in most families. Shirley MacLaine and Debra Winger shine as the controlling mother and her doomed daughter, respectively, and Jack Nicholson provides smart-alecky comic relief as the womanizing astronaut who romances MacLaine. Brooks expertly blends comic and tragic episodes in one seamless vision of modern life and elicits heartfelt performances from all his actors. The film won Academy Awards for best picture and Brooks's direction and his screenplay adaptation of Larry McMurtry's novel, as well as for best actress (MacLaine) and best supporting actor (Nicholson). Indeed, Brooks's strongest talent, beyond his knack for capturing character through his sharp writing, is his facility with actors. In a four-film career, he has directed 10 Oscar-nominated performances (four of which won).

Brooks's second film, *Broadcast News* (1987), is a savvy satire of network news and its elevation of "flash over substance," as one of his characters puts it. (After graduating from New York University, Brooks himself worked for CBS News as a copy-boy, eventually working his way up to TV newswriter.) The film's social commentary on the trivialization of network news into entertainment now seems timelier than ever, but the film never devolves into preachiness. Instead, it lets its three terrific leads—William Hurt's dim but likable anchorman, Holly Hunter's workaholic producer, and Albert Brooks's brainy but uncharismatic reporter—explore the issues through an old-fashioned romantic comedy format. The film plays like a modern-day *His Girl Friday* but with an ending that offers no traditional romantic resolution. The film also gives a great sense of the day-to-day life of a newsroom—the hustle and bustle and sheer movement of people trying to find their stories and get them on the air.

I'll Do Anything (1994) is Brooks's one flat-out failure. Supposedly a satire of Hollywood, it revolves around a struggling actor, played by Nick Nolte, who must suddenly be a father to his little girl. Brooks originally conceived the film as a modern musical (a risky endeavor, to be sure), but the end result is a shapeless mess with obvious gaps where musical numbers, pulled at the last minute, were originally supposed to be. Even in the midst of failure, some of the performances are decent, with Albert Brooks and Julie Kavner providing the bright spots.

Brooks bounced back three years later with *As Good As It Gets,* a romantic comedy about a writer with obsessive-compulsive disorder, the working-class waitress and single mother who finally falls in love with him, and his gay neighbor. Like *Terms of Endearment,* it balances serious issues of relationships with sophisticated wit and memorable one-liners. Brooks has a natural talent for finding the moment of truth between people, the life-affirming or life-changing incident that reveals the humanity of a character. Brooks directed his two leads (Nicholson and Helen Hunt) to Oscars in what became his biggest box-office success to date.

Brooks does not demonstrate great visual flair as a director—his relationship-based films do not require it—but his true forte is the direction of actors (especially recurring favorites like Nicholson and Brooks) in well-crafted scripts that warmly look at the foibles of everyday people.

Reference Katz, Ephraim, *The Macmillan Film Encyclopedia* (New York: Macmillan, 1994).

—P.N.C.

Brooks, Mel (1926–)

Mel Brooks was born Melvin Kaminsky on June 28, 1926. He began doing impressions as a child and became versatile on the drums and piano before being drafted for World War II. During the Battle of the Bulge, Brooks revealed his flair for comedy when he responded to German loudspeaker propaganda by serenading the opposing side with a rendition of Al Jolson's "Toot-Toot Tootsie." This early satirical attack on a philosophy threatening his own being and race, by using a combination of two minority ethnic signifiers (Blacks and Jews) outside the American culture, would surface in his later films.

Following demobilization, Brooks continued playing the drums at Catskill Mountains resorts and eventually became social director and resident comic at Grossinger's. He changed his name to Brooks to avoid confusion with another performer with the same surname. Brooks used his mother's surname, Brookman, which he changed slightly.

In 1949, he began at 10-year association with television comedian Sid Caesar on *The Admiral Broadway Revue* and *Your Show of Shows*. Brooks both wrote sketches for Caesar and occasionally performed on his shows. In 1960, he came to public attention by recording the comic sketch *The 2,000-Year-Old Man* with Carl Reiner, which became a best-seller on disc. Three years later he won an Academy Award for his satirical short, *The Critic*. Brooks was also responsible for creating the television series *Get Smart* with Buck Henry.

In 1968, he both directed and scripted *The Producers,* featuring Zero Mostel and Gene Wilder as a pair of scheming Broadway producers who deliberately create a Busby Berkeley–type Nazi musical, "Springtime for Hitler," in the hope of cashing in on a box-office flop. To their surprise (and that of the predominantly Jewish audience in the theater), it succeeds. As the basis for a spectacularly successful Broadway musical, it is delighting a new generation of viewers.

After acting in *Putney Swope* (1969), Brooks directed, scripted, and acted in his second film, *The Twelve Chairs,* featuring British comedian Ron Moody (who pioneered the role of Fagin in Lionel Bart's musical *Oliver*) and Frank Langella. Based on a Russian novel and set during the Bolshevik Revolution, the film was not entirely successful. But, like *The Producers,* it revealed Brooks's flair for slapstick, vaudeville humor, satire, and, especially, parody, which he would successfully employ in his following films.

Brooks himself once commented that his humor is based on rage, and Desser and Friedman note that the director "builds all his films on his indignation, attacking serious topics such as bigotry, intolerance, and greed through comedy." For example, although *Blazing Saddles* (1974) is a self-reflexive parodic spoof on the western genre, it also deals with historical issues of racism and intolerance often ignored or marginalized in most representations. Like *The Twelve Chairs, Young Frankenstein* (1974) critiques the mythos of the "old country" and questions who the "monster" really is. *Silent Movie* (1976) critiques Hollywood greed and fashions, while *High Anxiety* (1977) humorously explores Hitchcock's dark humor. As Desser and Friedman show, Brooks's humor certainly belongs to the serious side of his ethnic tradition. *History of the World Part One* (1981) does more to promote Edward Said's critiques of Western civilization than most serious, "politically correct" treatises. But the humor often falls flat in certain points of the film or fails to support the important satirical attacks he wishes to make.

Significantly, Brooks's critique of Lucasfilm marketing strategies in *Spaceballs* (1987) fails both as a

Mel Brooks in *History of the World Part I* (Twentieth Century-Fox)

result of its reliance on stale vaudeville–type humor, leaving the viewer wishing for the stage manager's walking stick to yank off the failed comedian, as well as the fact that the original model was both mediocre and nonserious in the first place. Although Brooks's company, Brooksfilms, has produced significant serious films such as *The Elephant Man* (1980), *The Fly* (1986), and *84 Charing Cross Road* (1987), the director's later films such as *Life Stinks* (1991) and *Robin Hood: Men in Tights* (1993) have failed to live up to the comic and satirical heights of their predecessors.

Other Films   *The 2,000-Year-Old Man* (1974); *To Be or Not to Be* (1983).

References   Yacowar, Maurice, *Method in Madness: The Comic Art of Mel Brooks* (New York: St. Martin's Press, 1981); Desser, David, and Lester D. Friedman, *American-Jewish Filmmakers* (Urbana and Chicago: University of Illinois Press, 1993).

—T.W.

Brown, Clarence (1890–1987)   Clarence Brown was born in Clinton, Massachusetts, on May 10, 1890. He was the son of a cotton manufacturer, Larkin H. Brown. Following the family's move to the South, Brown studied engineering at the University of Tennessee where he received two degrees. In 1913 he founded the Brown Motor Car Company in Massachusetts.

Around 1914, while observing MAURICE TOURNEUR making a film for the Peerless Studios production company in Fort Lee, New Jersey, Brown decided to pursue filmmaking as a career. Brown's association, perhaps a better term being apprenticeship, with Tourneur was to last until 1921. Tourneur's visual style was to be a major influence on Brown's subsequent work as a director. Tourneur's trademark was sophisticated lighting effects and striking compositions, both of which revealed his background as an artist.

Brown shared codirecting credit with Tourneur for *The Great Redeemer* and *The Last of the Mohicans.* In 1921 Brown signed a contract with Universal Pictures, where he directed Lon Chaney in *The Light in the Dark* (1922), which he also coscripted. Two of his major films while at Universal include *Smouldering Fires* (1924) with Pauline Frederick and Laura La Plante and *The Goose Woman* (1925) with Louise Dresser. Both films reveal Brown's accomplished use of mise-en-scène composition and dramatic lighting effects.

Brown made two films for Joseph Schenck and United Artists—*The Eagle* (1925), one of Rudolph Valentino's best films, and *Kiki* (1926), starring Schenck's wife, Norma Talmadge. Brown then signed with MGM, where he was to remain until 1952. His first film for Metro-Goldwyn-Mayer was *Flesh and the Devil* (1926), which starred Greta Garbo and John Gilbert. This was to be the first of seven MGM films Brown directed for Garbo, who considered Brown as her favorite personal director. The films include *A Woman of Affairs* (1928), *Anna Christie* (1930), *Romance* (1930), *Inspiration* (1931), *Anna Karenina* (1935), and *Conquest* (1937). The Garbo films stress Brown's accomplishment and notoriety as a woman's director. As a director of actors, Brown is unexcelled (with the possible exception of George Cukor) and is perhaps the touchstone for the classic Hollywood "studio" style of the 1930s.

Brown also directed five films for Joan Crawford, including *Possessed* (1931), *Letty Lynton* (1932), *Chained* (1934), *Sadie McKee* (1934), and *The Gorgeous Hussy* (1936). At MGM Brown was given the freedom to select his own stories and supervise the editing of his own films. In 1935 a second thematic development occurred in Brown's ouevre. The screen adaptation of Eugene O'Neill's only comedy, *Ah, Wilderness,* starring Wallace Beery and Lionel Barrymore, denotes a shift away from the "woman's film" to films centered on aspects of Americana.

Although there were several silent films in which Brown also covered this terrain, most notably *Last of the Mohicans* (1920) and *The Trail of '98* (1929), which concerns the Klondike gold rush, throughout the rest of his tenure at MGM, the projects selected reflect a nostalgic yearning for a mythic American past. Brown himself contributes to that mythmaking with such films as: *The Gorgeous Hussy* (1936), set in Jacksonian America; *Of Human Hearts* (1938), Civil War America; *Edison, the Man* (1940), the biopic of Thomas Alva Edison starring Spencer Tracy; *The Human Comedy* (1943), William Saroyan's novella concerning the American homefront during World War II; *National Velvet* (1944); *The Yearling* (1946), based on Marjorie Kinnan Rawlings's coming-of-age novel set in the Florida Everglades; and *Intruder in the Dust* (1949), based on William Faulkner's novel concerning a black man accused of murder in the Deep South. Brown's final film for MGM before he retired was *Plymouth Adventure* (1952), which was about the Pilgrim crossing to America on the *Mayflower*. In his career Brown received six Oscar nominations for best director. Clarence Brown died on August 17, 1987.

Other Films   *Wonder of Women* (1929); *Navy Blues* (1929); *Emma* (1932); *Night Flight* (1933); *Wife Versus Secretary* (1936); *Idiot's Delight* (1939); *The Rains Came* (1939); *The White Cliffs of Dover* (1944); *The Song of Love* (1947).

References   Brownlow, Kevin, *The Parade's Gone By* (New York: Knopf, 1968); Estrin, Allen, *The Hollywood Professionals,* vol. 6, *Capra, Cukor, Brown* (New York: A. S. Barnes, 1980).

—R.W.

Brown, Rowland (1900–1963)

Rowland Brown was a director and screenwriter who, except for a handful of films, is largely forgotten today. This is a grievous oversight, for during the decade of the 1930s his was the distinctive voice behind a tough-minded series of Hollywood films. He was born on November 6, 1900, in Akron, Ohio. After completing his education at the University School in Cleveland, Ohio, and the Detroit School of Fine Arts, he tried his hand at fashion illustrating, sports cartooning, and playwrighting. When Universal Studios bought one of his plays, he went to Hollywood to work as a writer and gagman.

His first screen credit was for a Hoot Gibson western, *Points West* (1929). His breakthrough came when his short story, "A Handful of Clouds," came to the screen under the title *Doorway to Hell* (1930), directed by Archie Mayo. It was a prototype for the later, classic gangster films of the thirties in that it implied that success in depression times was available to anyone ruthless and lawless enough to survive. It struck a chord with audiences well aware of the exploits of Al Capone, who was incarnated here in the persona of bootlegger Louis Ricarno (Lew Ayres). James Cagney was featured as Ricarno's friend, Mileaway. Their mob activities are eventually defeated by rival gangsters and by their own mutual betrayals.

A year later the release of Brown's next film, *Quick Millions,* confirmed his growing reputation and gave him his first directorial opportunity. Spencer Tracy stars as "Bugs" Raymond, a young man who rises from petty vandal to a mob boss who conceals his racketeering behind a "respectable" façade of corporate business and high-society connections. Gang warfare breaks out and Bugs is abducted by his rivals, murdered, and deposited lifeless on the steps of a church. Singled out for praise was the film's depiction of the methods gangsters employed to manipulate the working of big business. *Quick Millions* remains one of the best, albeit neglected, gangster classics of the thirties.

After working on the screenplay for *What Price Hollywood!* (1932), Brown resumed directorial control over two films that mark the apogee of his career. *Hell's Highway* (1932) was a grim exposé of chain-gang brutality, but it was quickly overshadowed by a rival release, MERVYN LEROY's *I Am a Fugitive from a Chain Gang. Blood Money* (1933), Brown's masterpiece, was released by Darryl F. Zanuck's newly formed 20th Century Pictures. Part social satire, part racketeering story, part farce, it concerned the slightly nefarious activities of a bail bondsman, Bill Bailey (George Bancroft), whose clientele includes gangland characters (from whom he is in the habit of receiving stolen goods) and little old mothers (from whom he cheerfully demands house deeds in payment for services rendered). A romance with a sexually adventurous socialite (Frances Dee) provides some of the most perversely suggestive dialogue of the pre-Code era. Alas, it was to be Brown's last directorial project, and his career faltered thereafter.

Perpetually at odds with the studio system, Brown found it difficult to get and/or complete directorial assignments, and he had to rely increas-ingly on his screenwriting abilities. In 1934 he exiled himself to England, but when he was removed from the prestigious *Scarlet Pimpernel,* he returned to America and worked on scripts for the noirish thriller, *Nocturne* (1946), and the police procedural, *Kansas City Confidential* (1952), his last film. At the time of his death on May 6, 1963, he was working on a television series based on the life of his old friend, journalist and screenwriter Gene Fowler.

Mere plot synopses fail to convey the true flavor of Brown's films. They look quite "modern" today because he often celebrates the casual, the indirect, and the idiosyncratic at the expense of his nominal subjects. In other words, although his best work is concerned with the ambiguities of law, order, and racketeering, the films are most memorable for their offbeat, subtle, and quirky character revelations. They are full of little camera asides—quirky digressions, anecdotal scenes, and colorful secondary characters. At times, the films seem to wander off somewhere, away from the main plotline, away from our expectations of standard Hollywood formula. As much as Brown might have wanted to be a social commentator, he inevitably becomes before our eyes an artist of the bizarre, a man whose quick eye glitters at the use of a hemorrhoid cushion in the chair of a department store executive, at a female barfly who wears a monocle and men's clothing, at the little mother whose hulking 16-year-old son beats up older women, and at the convict who smiles at the touch of lash or whip. Brown's world is not open to easy definitions or optimistic bromides. As Bill Bailey says in *Blood Money,* "The only difference between a liberal and a conservative man is that the liberal recognizes the existence of vice and controls it; while the conservative turns his back and pretends that it doesn't exist." Whichever, Bill realizes, crime is here to stay—hardly a reassuring commentary for audiences mired down in the Great Depression.

Other Films As writer: *The Devil Is a Sissy* (1936); *Angels with Dirty Faces* (1938); *Johnny Apollo* (1940).

References Miller, Don, "Rowland Brown: Notes on a Blighted Career," *Focus on Film* 17 (1971): 43–52; Tibbetts, John C., "Rowland Brown," in *Between Action and Cut: Five American Directors,* ed. Frank Thompson (Metuchen, N.J.: Scarecrow Press, 1985), pp. 163–182.

—J.C.T.

Browning, Tod (1880–1962) Most memorable among Tod Browning's 62 films are his series of silent Lon Chaney vehicles and his two sound horror classics, *Dracula* (1931) and *Freaks* (1932). Despite an influx of new scholarship on the man, Charles Albert "Tod" Browning remains as strange and enigmatic as many of his films. He is still, as Andrew Sarris classified him, a "subject for further research."

He was born on July 12, 1880, in Louisville, Kentucky. After running away from home as a teenager to join a traveling carnival, he was taken on as a clown by the Ringling Brothers circus. Later, in vaudeville and on the riverboat circuits, he worked in a sideshow act known as "The Hypnotic Living Corpse" and trouped in a "blackface" act called "Lizard and Coon." In 1913, as a result of an appearance in a burlesque show's "live" version of the comic strip, "Mutt and Jeff," he came to the attention of D. W. Griffith at the Biograph Studios in New York City, and for the next two years he appeared in many of Griffith's pictures. In 1915, after following Griffith to Los Angeles, he met his future wife, actress Alice Houghton, and began directing one- and two-reel films.

After completing an assignment as one of seven assistant directors on "The Modern Story Sequence" of Griffith's *Intolerance* (1916), Browning directed his first feature, *Jim Bludso* (1917), a Civil War romance. A series of melodramas for Metro and Universal, including *The Eyes of Mystery* (1918), an "old dark house" picture, and *The Wicked Darling* (1919), one of several vehicles for

actress Priscilla Dean, eventually brought him to the newly formed Metro-Goldwyn-Mayer studio, where Irving Thalberg took him under his wing. By this time, however, Browning was fighting a drinking problem. The assignment to direct Lon Chaney in *The Unholy Three* (1925), an adaptation of Tod Robbins's 1917 novel, proved to be of inestimable personal and professional importance, since it pulled him out of a personal rut and gained him national acclaim. The "threesome" of the title were carnival performers Echo, the cross-dressing ventriloquist (Chaney), the strongman Hercules (Victor McLaglen), and the midget who masquerades as a baby, Tweedledee (Harry Earles). Using a pet shop as a front, they pull a number of cons on wealthy customers. When an innocent man is accused of murder, Echo uses his ventriloqual powers to clear him in court and subsequently determines to lead a "straight" life.

Browning went on to direct Chaney in 10 feature films. It was a mutually satisfying alliance, according to Browning's biographer, David Skal: "The commercial glue that held Browning and Chaney together for the next four years was their mutual interest in themes of boiling sexual frustration and concomitant, visceral revenge. Together they would provide the free-spirited jazz age with a profoundly reactionary shadow-ethos." Inhabiting this nightmare gallery of characters are the contortionist criminal in *The Black Bird* (1926); Singapore Joe, the hideous lecher in *The Road to Mandalay* (1926); Alonzo the Armless, in *The Unknown* (1927); and the nightmarish faux vampire in *London After Midnight* (1927), the most legendary of all "lost" films and the biggest moneymaker of the Browning-Chaney collaborations; "Dead Legs" Flint in *West of Zanzibar* (1928); and "Tiger" Haynes in *Where East Is East* (1929), their last collaboration. The character of Alonzo in *The Unknown* is the most extremely disturbed of these men. His obsessive love for his knife-act partner (Joan Crawford) impels him not only to have his arms amputated but also to attempt the murder of her lover by tying him to the backs of horses and tearing him limb from limb. "The typical Browning protagonist is a man who has been reduced to the state of an animal," according to Stuart Rosenthal. "In almost every instance he displays a physical deformity that reflects the mental mutilation he has suffered at the hands of some element of callous society. . . . Although, in their instinctive behaviour, Browning's heroes are oblivious to the moral contradictions of revenge, they do maintain a latent sense of fairness which influences their dealings with those who have not afflicted them."

Sickened by the repetition of Browning's subject matter, by the time of *West of Zanzibar*'s release, many critics were turning on him. But his best-known work was yet to come. He directed *Dracula* for Universal in 1931, which not only rejuvenated his career but also launched the Universal horror cycle and the career of Hungarian actor Bela Lugosi, who had played the vampire on Broadway and was brought in when Chaney's cancer rendered him unable to perform the role. *Dracula,* despite its reputation, Lugosi's performance, photography by ace cinematographer Karl Freund, and impressive box-office first run, is a static, studio-bound, and airless picture. Certainly it is neither as starkly effective as F. W. Murnau's vampire masterpiece of nine years previously, *Nosferatu,* nor as fluidly cinematic and erotically suggestive as Paul Kohner's Spanish-language version, shot at the same time on the same sets. What is not generally noted is that *Dracula* is the only film Browning directed with authentic supernatural characters and events. Every other film, including the clumsy remake of *London After Midnight, Mark of the Vampire* (1935), is either an examination of the purely psychological states of terror or a variant on the gothic formula where seemingly otherworldly incidents have purely rational explanations. Nonetheless, as biographers David Skal and Elias Savada point out, *Dracula* contains significant autobiographical allusions to Browning's vaudeville career: "What is Dracula, after all, but a 'Living Hypnotic Corpse' who daily lies buried in a coffin box?" Moreover, like Browning, "Dracula presents himself in a highly theatrical and dandified manner, falsifying his true background to advance in society."

Reunited with Thalberg at MGM, Browning directed one of the most remarkable and disturbing films of his or any other generation. *Freaks* (1932) was based on the short story, "Spurs," by Tod Robbins, in which a collection of sideshow performers unite to wreak a horrible revenge on the trapeze artist, Cleopatra (Olga Baclanova), who has betrayed them. No one who has seen it can forget the climactic moment when the freaks creep and crawl around and through the wheels of the circus wagons on a stormy night to launch their horrible retribution on the hapless Cleopatra. Here, Browning reverses his paradigm of the misshapen and the abnormal: As Rosenthal points out, the bulk of *Freaks* is spent dispelling the viewer's initial revulsion to the sideshow characters and arousing hostility toward the so-called normal characters; and the final "chase" scene has the "normal" people the target of violence, and not the reverse. *Freaks* lost $164,000 for MGM and was soon withdrawn due to protests from outraged exhibitors and censors.

After the debacle of *Freaks,* Browning was on the outs with MGM and was assigned weak scripts that turned out to be financial disasters. *Fast Workers* (1933) was a lame attempt at a brittle sex comedy; the aforementioned *Mark of the Vampire* was a laughable piece of gothic hokum (despite fine cinematography by James Wong Howe); *The Devil Doll* (1936) depended more upon special effects than story; and *Miracles for Sale* (1939) marked a tepid return to form. After leaving MGM in 1942 and after the death of his wife in 1944, Browning spent his remaining years in relative seclusion, caring nothing about publicity or posterity, resisting attempts to delve into his private life. He died of a stroke in 1962, just as *Freaks* and other films were undergoing rediscovery at festivals and on college campuses.

"Browning is so aggressive and unrelenting in his pursuit of certain themes that he appears to be neurotically fixated upon them," writes historian Stuart Rosenthal. "He is inevitably attracted to situations of moral and sexual frustration. . . . What sets Browning apart is his abnormal fascination with the deformed creatures who populate his films—a fascination that is not always entirely intellectual, and in which he takes extreme delight."

Other Films *Outside the Law* (1921); *Under Two Flags* (1922); *Man Under Cover* (1922); *Drifting* (1923); *White Tiger* (1923); *Day of Faith* (1923); *The Dangerous Flirt* (1924); *Silk Stocking Girl* (1924); *The Mystic* (1925); *Dollar Down* (1925); *The Big City* (1928); *The Thirteenth Chair* (1929); *Outside the Law* (1930); *The Iron Man* (1931).

References Rosenthal, Stuart, and Judith M. Kass, *The Hollywood Professionals, Tod Browning and Don Siegel* (New York: A.S. Barnes, 1975); Skal, David J., and Elias Savada, *Dark Carnival: The Secret World of Tod Browning, Hollywood's Master of the Macabre* (New York: Anchor Books, 1995).

—J.C.T.

Brownlow, Kevin (1938–) Although best known for his unsparing efforts on behalf of the preservation and restoration of the silent cinema, including the production of many television documentaries about early Hollywood and the European cinema, Kevin Brownlow has also directed a handful of films as an independent filmmaker. He was born on June 2, 1938, in Sussex, about 50 miles outside of London. Among his earliest memories are the V-1 bombings during the war years. He first discovered motion pictures while attending a boarding school in Crowborough, Sussex. These fragments of silent film fired his imagination and soon he was working in a photographic shop in Hampstead. In 1956 at age 18 he began work as a trainee in the

Kevin Brownlow (Lisa Stevens John)

cutting rooms of World Wide Pictures, a documentary film company based in Soho.

While making his first short film, *The Capture,* an adaptation of Guy de Maupassant's story, "Les Prisonniers," he began writing about films for *Amateur Cine World.* His lifelong enthusiasm for the era of the silent cinema bore fruit in 1968 when he published *The Parade's Gone By,* a seminal event in silent film scholarship. It and subsequent books, including *The War, the West, and the Wilderness* (1979) and *Behind the Mask of Innocence* (1992), have established him as the world's leading authority on the subject. Since then he has spearheaded many restorations of silent film classics, most notably ABEL GANCE's 1927 epic, *Napoleon,* which played in the early 1980s at the Kennedy Center and at Radio City Music Hall, among many other venues. This in turn led to his forming Photoplay Productions, which produced several Emmy and Peabody-award-winning documentary television series with his partner, the late David Gill, including *Hollywood: The Pioneers, Buster Keaton: A Hard Act to Follow, D.W. Griffith: Father of Film, The Unknown Chaplin,* and *Cinema Europe: The Other Hollywood.* At this writing, his newest book is *Mary Pickford Rediscovered* (1999).

Meanwhile, with codirector Andrew Mollo, he directed and released two theatrical features, *It Happened Here* (1965) and *Winstanley* (1978). The first is a "counterfactual" history of what might have happened had the Nazis won the Battle of Britain and invaded England. It outraged and baffled many viewers with its controversial subject matter and idiosyncratic, pseudo-documentary techniques, including the simulation of newsreels and combat actuality footage. It was censored and withdrawn from circulation. *Winstanley* is a scrupulously researched and handsomely mounted chronicle of the adventures of Gerrard Winstanley and his "Diggers" in the turbulent times of 17th-century Cromwellian England. Its arcane subject matter, not to mention its catalogue of "inside" cinematic references to the films of CARL THEODOR DREYER, SERGEI EISENSTEIN, VICTOR SJÖSTROM, and others, made so few concessions to the formulas of mainstream entertainment that it quietly faded from public view. Both films were shot on the proverbial shoestring, yet they are impressive achievements in the independent cinema movement in Great Britain in the sixties and seventies. Both are driven by distinctly "presentist" concerns, i.e., both consciously regard their subjects from the perspectives of present-day social, artistic, and autobiographical contexts; and both succeed ultimately in painting imaginative landscapes of their own devising onto the maps of history. (Both films have been recently restored and are now available from Milestone Films in Harrington Park, New Jersey.)

Brownlow attributes their commercial failure, in part, to his decision to abandon theatrical features for the sake of film preservation: "I am sure that must be one of the reasons I ended up as a film historian and not as a film director. At the time I made them I thought that I would continue in feature film making. Certainly I never expected to make my living at film preservation. However, I would not be the film historian I am without having had the experience of making *Winstanley* and *It Happened Here.*" Indeed, Brownlow has devoted his life to a race against the clock to locate, preserve, and present artifacts of the film past before they deteriorate into dust. Otherwise, he warns, "posterity will judge us harshly." Fortunately, as Angela Carter has written in *The Manchester Guardian Weekly,* "His own work will evade such judgment."

References Brownlow, Kevin, *How It Happened Here: The Making of a Film* (Garden City, N.Y.: Doubleday, 1968); Tibbetts, John C., "Life to Those Shadows: Kevin Brownlow Talks about a Career in Films," *Journal of Dramatic Theory and Criticism* 14, no. 1 (Fall 1999): 79–94; Tibbetts, John C., "Kevin Brownlow's Historical Films: *It Happened Here* (1965) and *Winstanley* (1975)," *Historical Journal of Film, Radio, and Television* 20, no. 2 (2000): 227–251.

—J.C.T.

Buñuel, Luis (1900–1983) Luis Buñuel was the most distinctive Spanish filmmaker of the 20th century, even though, paradoxically, he made most of his best-known films while living in self-imposed exile from his native land, in Mexico and in France. A master of surreal satire who was as charming as he was controversial, Buñuel was also an astute social critic and documentarian. His unique, frequently playful tone gave his films an additional aura of baffling mystery.

Luis Buñuel was born on February 22, 1900, in Calanda, Spain. He was educated from an early age in Jesuit schools, and this strict, dogmatic religious training profoundly influenced his life and art. Though Buñuel claimed that "at sixteen I lost my religious belief" and became a self-proclaimed atheist, religious images would always dominate his films, although portrayed in satiric and surreal ways. According to Buñuel, what his Jesuit education taught him was "a profound eroticism, at first sublimated in a great religious faith, and in permanent consciousness of death." Both eroticism and the ubiquity of death permeate many aspects of his films. A childhood fascination with music, theatre, and animals would also later appear in his films.

Buñuel was educated at the University of Madrid and after graduation went to Paris in 1925. Buñuel began to associate with surrealist writers and artists in Paris who would influence his later work. Their ideas helped to shape Buñuel's awareness of the cinema and its potential and suggested how he might incorporate dreams and fantasy to portray the ills of society. His first feature, *Un chien andalou* (1929), done in collaboration with the artist Salvador Dalí, became a touchstone of surrealist cinema. His famous image of an eyeball being sliced by a razor is recognized as quintessentially surreal, an "eye-opener" that continues to shock and discomfit audiences. Although the film has been scrutinized—to no avail—by puzzled critics in search of meaning, its haunting images are not easily forgotten. Asked to explain this enigmatic film, Buñuel simply called it "an incitement to murder." *L'Âge d'or* (1930), Buñuel's next surreal film, blasphemously fused religion with eroticism and was even more controversial. Its release provoked widespread riots and condemnation, which pleased Buñuel because, he explained, the point was *not* to like it.

Las Hurdes (*Land Without Bread* [1932]), an ironic travelogue on the surface, made a political statement concerning a poverty-stricken region of Spain that showed such devastating and desolate people, the Spanish government was eventually forced to establish aid programs. The film was eventually banned by Franco's government. Buñuel's dreamlike, surreal images in this film were all the more disturbing for being reality-based. Critic Anthony Lane was impressed by Buñuel's "tough link between a refined artistic movement and the rawness of political protest."

After *Land Without Bread,* Buñuel would not direct another film for 15 years. During this time, Buñuel worked in the United States in Hollywood as a dubber for Spanish films, and later at the Museum of Modern Art as a film archivist and editor. It was remarkable that a director who made such an auspicious and controversial film debut with *Un chien andalou* could not direct for so many years, but the Second World War disrupted many film careers. Nonetheless, Buñuel seemed content working in the United States during this period, but he eventually wanted and perhaps needed to make more films.

Consequently, Buñuel settled in Mexico, which began a second fertile period in his enigmatic and illustrious creative career. Mexico City would become Buñuel's adopted home city. *Los Olvidados* (1950) brought Buñuel nearly as much attention as his earlier trio of films. The film is an ostensible portrait of Mexico City's lost children—delinquents living on the streets and in the slums. Buñuel accurately depicts the nightmarish world of violence and degradation that plagues the young victims of Mexico's bourgeois capitalist system. The film garnered international attention from critics. Buñuel then filmed surreal adaptations of the novels *Robinson Crusoe* (1952) and *Wuthering Heights* (1953), followed by *El* (1952), also known as *This Strange Passion,* Buñuel's savage attack on the church and the bourgeois class.

Eventually, Buñuel returned to Spain and made *Viridiana* (1961), another antireligious, surrealist parable that Buñuel managed to get by the censors and went on to win the Palme d'Or at the Cannes Film Festival. Viridiana, a novitiate nun, is tricked into marriage and becomes the heiress of a large estate after the uncle who claims to have defiled her dies. Driven by religious motivation, she invites a group of thieves and beggars into her country estate, which they take over. The film became famous for its visual parody of Da Vinci's *Last Supper,* with drunkards and beggars arranged around the table in the positions of Christ and his disciples. As one critic noted, Buñuel was not mocking Christ himself but the "manner in which Christ's image is worshipped." The film was so powerful in its satiric depiction of religion that the Vatican denounced it as "an insult to Christianity." Although the Spanish government tried to destroy the film, it nevertheless was shown at Cannes, where it won the Palme d'Or.

The Exterminating Angel (*El angel exterminador* [1962]) represents a sort of descent into hell and has been compared to Jean-Paul Sartre's play about metaphysical alienation, *No Exit.* In both, the characters are isolated, cut off from the world at large, trapped in a salon where, over time, they are forced to reveal themselves. But the alienation of Buñuel's film is different in that his characters are the helpless victims of a social and religious system. Buñuel's son, Juan, described this as "essentially a comic film, but with a very strong corrosive interior." He claimed there were no "symbolic interpretations" at issue, though the design seems most certainly allegorical.

The Diary of a Chambermaid (Le Journal d'une femme de chambre [1964]) has been considered Buñuel's most political film. According to David Cook, "Buñuel's equation of fascism, decadence, and sexual perversion is perfectly made." The film was shot in France, a country that embraced Buñuel until the end of his career, where he would make his final—often considered his best—films. *Belle de Jour* (1967), for example, a tale of erotic obsession secured Buñuel's reputation as provocateur. In the film, a bored housewife, played by Catherine Deneuve, decides to work afternoons in a brothel. Reality and fantasy mesh as the film pro-

gresses until it is not easy to distinguish one from the other. Critic Andrew Sarris called the film Buñuel's "most surrealistic."

In *The Milky Way* (*La Voie lactée* [1969]) Buñuel presented a symbolic, surreal history of the Roman Catholic Church, told in an episodic narrative about two tramps traveling from Paris to Spain. This attack on religion was only moderately received by critics. Buñuel described the film as "a journey through fanaticism, where each person obstinately clings to his own particle of truth." Among other themes of sex, food, and nature, the film also presents a relaxed, almost giddy portrait of Jesus Christ. This film might be considered as a companion piece to *Simon of the Desert/Simon del Desierto* (1965), a 42-minute parable concerning a saintly medieval anchorite who is tempted by the devil and finally loses his faith when the devil transports him into the hopelessly hedonistic future of the 20th century.

Tristana (1970), set in Spain, tells the story of a virginal girl seduced by her guardian, whom she eventually murders by neglecting to call a doctor after he suffers a heart attack, even though he has nursed her through an illness that brought about the amputation of one of her legs. Joan Mellen interprets the film as a political allegory, with Tristana representing "the generation to be maimed by the [Spanish] Civil War."

The Discreet Charm of the Bourgeoisie (1973), Buñuel's most popular film, satirizes the trivialities of the privileged class; it won an Oscar for best foreign film and was also a critical favorite. It is structured as an extended dream, wherein six friends who try to have an elegant, sophisticated dinner party are continuously interrupted before they can begin. David Cook sees the film as "one long pattern of interrupted episodes, and in this sense Buñuel has created a delightful parody of the mechanisms of narrative cinema." The film is as funny as it is serious about the follies of the privileged class, whose appetites are not entirely dulled by immediate threats of random assassins.

The Phantom of Liberty (*Le Fantôme de la liberté* [1974]) has no discernible trace of a clear narrative plot, or even a fixed set of characters, and has thus been called Buñuel's most surreal film since *Un chien andalou*. Vincent Canby claimed "there is no single correct way to read" the film. Joan Mellen identifies one of the film's major points: "The betrayal of revolutions and the growth of 'revolutionary' societies more repressive than those they replaced have made a mockery of revolution as a quest for liberty." David Cook describes the film as "an authentically surrealist essay on the political violence, necrophilia, and sadism that underlie bourgeois cultural conventions and make an elusive phantom of personal freedom." Through its combination of flashback, dream sequence, and allusion, *The Phantom of Liberty* is a challenging film that breaks the usual conventions of narrative logic and demands repeated viewings to parse out its multiple meanings.

Buñuel's final film, *That Obscure Object of Desire* (1977), is an ironic parable about a young girl who dupes a middle-aged Frenchman out of his money and even his identity. Buñuel cast two actresses with clearly different physical appearances as the lead—the "object" of the title—thus adding to the irony of the film. The film ends with a loud explosion, prompting critic Lane to suggest "Buñuel was back where he had begun," a reference to the immediacy and shock—the explosion—of his first feature, *Un chien andalou*. This final film is a culmination of the themes that have surfaced in many Buñuel films: "In addition to the theme of the impossibility of ever truly possessing a woman's body," Buñuel noted, "the film insists upon maintaining that climate of insecurity and imminent disaster—an atmosphere we all recognize, because it is our own."

Luis Buñuel died in his adopted home of Mexico City in 1983. Throughout his long and distinguished career, Buñuel managed to create a body of work that makes him the definitive auteur and, in the words of David Cook, "the most experimental and anarchistic filmmaker in the history of narrative cinema."

Other Films   *Gran Casino* (1947); *El gran calavera* (1949); *Susana* (1951); *La hija del engaño* (1951); *Una mujer sin amor* (1951); *Subida al cielo* (1951); *El bruto* (1952); *La ilusión viaja en tranvía* (1953); *Cumbres borrascosas* (1953); *El río y la muerte* (1954); *Cela s'appelle l'aurore* (1955); *Ensayo de un crimen/The Criminal Life of Archibald de la Cruz* (1955); *La Mort en ce jardin* (1956); *Nazarín* (1958).

References   Buñuel, Luis, *My Last Sigh* (New York: Knopf, 1983); Cook, David, *A History of Narrative Film* (New York: Norton, 1996); Lane, Anthony, "In Your Dreams," *New Yorker* (Dec. 18, 2000); Mellen, Joan, ed., *The World of Luis Buñuel: Essays in Criticism* (New York: Oxford University Press, 1978).

—W.V. and J.M.W.

Burnett, Charles (1944–)   The internationally respected African-American actor, director, producer, and screenwriter was born in Vicksburg, Mississippi, on April 13, 1944, but he grew up in Watts in south-central Los Angeles. He was educated first at Freemont High School, then at the Los Angeles Community College, where he studied electronics, and then became interested in creative writing before going on to the University of California at Los Angeles to earn his B.A. in theater arts in 1971. Burnett made his first student film as a class project while an undergraduate in 1969, *Several Friends,* in which young black men seemed unable to understand what had gone wrong in their lives. His later films would also explore problems of the poor and the working-class lives of African Americans. As a graduate student he made his first color film, a 14-minute short called *The Horse,* the story of a young boy in the South who witnesses the death of an old horse. This short film won the Hauptpreis at the 15th Westdeutsche Kurzfilmatage Oberhausen in 1977.

Burnett's M.F.A. thesis film, *Killer of Sheep* (started in 1973, but not screened until 1977), was awarded a Louis B. Mayer Grant, given to the most promising thesis project at UCLA. It told the story of Stan (Henry Gayle Sanders), a sensitive black trapped in a dehumanizing job of killing sheep at a slaughterhouse while trying to support his wife and two children and retain his moral values and his sense of dignity. Made on a budget of $10,000, the film won the Critics' Prize at the 1981 Berlin International Film Festival and was proclaimed a "masterpiece" at the 1981 Toronto Festival of Festivals. It later earned a place on the Library of Congress National Film Registry as a "national treasure." As a member of the Los Angeles School of Black Filmmakers, Burnett has reflected the school's preoccupation with history, identity, and family within the African-American community.

In 1980 Burnett was awarded a Guggenheim Foundation fellowship to assist his preproduction work for *My Brother's Wedding* (1983). In 1988 he was awarded one of the so-called genius-grant fellowships by the MacArthur Foundation. Still, industry recognition was a long time coming for an obviously gifted artist. Although Burnett graduated from the UCLA film school in 1974, he had to wait 15 years before breaking into major-league filmmaking, when the Samuel Goldwyn Company took on his first Hollywood-financed film, *To Sleep with Anger* (1990), a low-budget, non-union production made for $1.2 million and shot on location in south-central Los Angeles, starring Danny Glover and Richard Brooks. It told the story of the Gideon household, a middle-class black family, the latest generation of which was becoming increasingly materialistic as the family progressed upward. A mysterious trickster figure named Harry (Danny Glover), drawn from Southern African-American folklore, comes to visit and shakes up the family. "He's a character that comes to steal your soul," Burnett told *The Village Voice,* "and you have to out-trick him. You can bargain with him, but you have to be more clever than he is." On a human scale, the film was "about a man struggling to save

his son and give him a foundation." The film was screened at the Sundance Film Festival in Park City, Utah, in January 1990 and was well received by the National Society of Film Critics and the Los Angeles Film Critics, who awarded it a special citation, but the film was not put into wide distribution by the Goldwyn Company, which decided its drawing power was mainly limited to African-American audiences.

Burnett fared a bit better with his second Hollywood feature, *The Glass Shield* (1995), which grossed $3 million, even though it disappeared from theatres within three weeks of its release. This police story of corruption, focusing on African-American characters within the hostile world of law enforcement, resembled Sidney Lumet's *Prince of the City* (1981) in the way it traced the moral education of a black deputy, J. J. Johnson (Michael Boatman), at a substation of the Los Angeles County Sheriff's Department. Critic Paul Mittelbach called it an American classic and "a masterwork of the highest order." Although Burnett has won numerous awards—fellowships from the Guggenheim Foundation (1981), the MacArthur Foundation (1988), the Rockefeller Foundation (1988), and a grant from the National Endowment for the Arts—he has not really gained the recognition his work deserves, and he has been shamefully neglected by an industry more likely to reward triviality rather than insight and intelligence.

Other Films　*Bless Their Little Hearts* (1984); *Guests of Hotel Astoria* (1989); *When It Rains* (1996).

References　Grant, Nathan, "Innocence and Ambiguity in the Films of Charles Burnett," in *Representing Blackness: Issues in Film and Video,* ed. Valerie Smith (New Brunswick, N.J.: Rutgers University Press, 1997), pp. 137–155; Hachem, Samir, "The House of Spirits," *Village Voice,* August 22, 1989, p. 80; Klotman, Phyllis Rauch, ed., *Screenplays of the African American Experience* (Bloomington: Indiana University Press, 1991); MacDonald, Scott, *Interviews with Independent Filmmakers* (Berkeley: University of California Press, 1998); Mittelbach, Paul, "The Glass Shield," in *Magill's*

Cinema Annual 1996, ed. Beth A. Fhaner (Detroit: Gale/Visible Ink, 1996), pp. 202–204.

—G.B. and J.M.W.

Burns, Ken (1953–) One of the most popular and celebrated documentarians in the last half of the 20th century, Ken Burns has dealt with great subjects that are the history, traditions, and diversity of the American experience. Like those "flaneur" artists and photographers in France in the middle of the 19th century who roamed the streets wresting fistfuls of images from the moving panorama of everyday life, Burns sifts through the desiderata of history with the innocent eye of the casual observer and the practiced gaze of the professional historian. "I will be a translator for people of complex subjects," he said in a 1989 interview; "be the baton in the relay race. I'm trying to take what I can from the scholars who ran the last lap and hand it on to the audience."

Kenneth Lauren Burns was born on July 29, 1953, in Brooklyn, New York. His father was a graduate student in anthropology at Columbia University. His mother died when he was 11. After graduating from high school in Ann Arbor, Michigan, Burns enrolled in Hampshire College in Amherst, Massachusetts, where he studied photography with Jerome Liebling and Elaine Mayes. At this time he met Amy Stechler, his future wife and collaborator. They worked together during his senior year directing a documentary film about Old Sturbridge Village, Massachusetts. After graduating in 1975 with a B.A. degree in film studies and design, he formed his own production company, Florentine Films.

The first Florentine release was a 60-minute documentary about the Brooklyn Bridge, based on David McCullough's book, *The Great Bridge* (1982). McCullough narrated the film, as he would several subsequent Burns projects. *Brooklyn Bridge* took four years to make; and after being entered in several film festivals, was broadcast on PBS in 1982 and nominated for an Academy Award. His second film for PBS, *The Shakers: Hands to Work, Hearts to God,* was inspired by his discovery of Hancock Shaker Village during a trip through rural Massachusetts. As placid as the Shaker film had been, *Huey Long* was charged with the grasping ambition and energetic platform manner of the fire-eating Long. It premiered in 1985 at the Louisiana State Capitol in Baton Rouge, where Long had been assassinated exactly 50 years before. *The Statue of Liberty* was released on the occasion of the centennial of its erection. Ironically, at the time, the Lady of Liberty was surrounded by the restoration scaffolding. Her "confinement," as it were, was regarded by Burns as a metaphor for the threats currently being voiced in America about curbing immigration policies.

Burns devoted the next five years to his most ambitious undertaking yet, *The Civil War.* Working 15-hour days, he shot 150 hours of film and took pictures of 16,000 still photographs acquired from dozens of archives and private collections. The project was smelted down into five parts, 11 hours of film, and 3,000 photos. When it was broadcast on PBS in September 1990, it created a sensation. In addition to garnering an Emmy, a CINE Golden Eagle, a Lincoln Prize, a People's Choice Award, and a Peabody, it spawned a book, *The Civil War: An Illustrated History,* by Geoffrey C. Ward, and a musical documentary, broadcast on PBS in August 1991, called *The Songs of the Civil War.*

Burns's next epic project surpassed even *The Civil War* in ambition and scope. *Baseball* premiered on PBS during the month of September 1994, its nine episodes clocking in at more than 18 hours. Unlike *The Civil War,* whose time-span was restricted to a five-year period, *Baseball* spanned 150 years, from the mythic origins of the game just prior to the Civil War to an open-ended gaze into the future. Indeed, Burns regarded it as a kind of sequel to *The Civil War,* inasmuch as the primary themes of racial conflict and national unity were extended and developed.

His latest projects include more excursions into American history, including *Lewis and Clark: The Journey of the Corps of Discovery* (1998), *Frank Lloyd Wright* (1998), and *Not for Ourselves Alone: The Story of Susan B. Anthony and Elizabeth Cady Stanton*. His recent *Jazz* is described as the third installment of the "trilogy" begun with *The Civil War* and *Baseball*.

His best work relies almost exclusively on his selection and manipulation of still photographs, a technique he admits he learned from the classic *City of Gold* (1958), a Canadian Film Board documentary essay about the Klondike gold rush of 1898. Using a rostrum camera and a frame-by-frame exposure technique, Burns surveys and interrogates the surface of each photograph, bursting through its borders, isolating and seizing details. Exhumed, Frankenstein-like, from the morgues of photographic archives and private collections, the aggregate of images constitutes a collective metaphor, as Burns has said, for the unity-out-of-diversity dynamic of America itself—"the unum out of pluribus." As in the Brothers Grimm tale about "The Juniper Tree," where body parts yearn to conjoin again after being torn asunder, each individual photograph is like an arrow pointing to the secret meaning at the heart of their collective identity. Meanwhile, this visual flow is counterpointed with period music, quotations from letters and diary entries, and a liberal use of "talking heads" of expert historians and informed commentators. Burns's achievement is not without its critics, who regard his work as dangerously contrived, superficial glimpses of history. Burns fiercely objects: "In the last hundred years we have really murdered history. We have allowed the Germanic academic model to overtake our academy and convince historians that they need only speak to one another. History used to be the great pageant of everything that went before this moment, not some dry and stuffy subject in a curriculum. The word 'history' itself gives away its primary organization. It is mostly made up of the word 'story,' and we've forgotten to tell stories."

Other Films *Thomas Hart Benton* (1989); *The Congress* (1989); *Empire of the Air* (1992).

References Edgerton, Gary, "Ken Burns' America: Style, Authorship, and Cultural Memory," *Journal of Popular Film and Television* 21 (Summer 1993): 51–62; Tibbetts, John C., "The Incredible Stillness of Being: Motionless Pictures in the Films of Ken Burns," *American Studies* 37, no. 1 (Spring 1996): 117–133.

—J.C.T.

Burton, Tim (1958–   ) Tim Burton's taste for fantasy and the bizarre has established him as one of America's most successful and imaginative directors. He was born August 25, 1958, and grew up a fan of horror and science fiction. At the California Institute of the Arts he studied animation. Although he is now regarded as an outsider and artistic loner, he began his Hollywood career in the midst of the establishment, when he was hired by Disney studios as an animator in 1980. Burton worked on mainstream films, such as *The Fox and the Hound* (1981), and he also served as animation director on Disney's experiment with science fiction, *Tron* (1982). More important to his artistic development were a pair of short films he made while working at Disney—*Vincent* (1982), a stop-motion animated short in tribute to (and narrated by) his hero, Vincent Price, and *Frankenweenie* (1984), a satiric homage to Frankenstein films, about a boy resurrecting his dead dog. Disney refused to release the latter film nationally, but Paul Reubens saw it, and asked Burton to direct the big-screen debut of his Pee-Wee Herman character in *Pee-Wee's Big Adventure* (1985).

The resulting surrealistic fantasy (and box-office smash) revealed Burton's distinct talent for visual storytelling. After creating the animated "Family Dog" episode of Steven Spielberg's *Amazing Stories* anthology series (followed eight years later by a one-season spinoff cartoon that he produced), Burton created his next hit, the over-the-top ghost story *Beetlejuice* (1988), a vibrant excursion into exotic Grand Guignol. (The following year, Burton developed the film into a Saturday-morning cartoon.) The film also marked the beginning of his collaborations with actors Jeffrey Jones and Michael Keaton and composer Danny Elfman.

In 1989, the back-to-back success of his first two features prompted Warner Bros. to tap the 31-year-old director to helm their big-budget *Batman,* and his Gothic depiction of the comic book character became one of the highest-grossing movies of all time. After turning out three blockbuster hits, in 1990 Burton directed one of his most personal films, the fairy-tale-like *Edward Scissorhands,* starring frequent Burton actors Johnny Depp and Winona Rider, as well as featuring the last live-action feature film performance of Vincent Price, playing the creator of the title character. The film, a fable about acceptance of outsiders, revealed an intimate, personal aspect to his storytelling, all too often overshadowed by blockbusters like *Batman Returns* (1992), his twisted sequel to the original mega-hit, and *Batman Forever* (1995), the Burton-produced third film in the series.

In 1993, he returned to his animation roots when he produced the dazzling stop-motion feature *Nightmare Before Christmas,* directed by Henry Selick from Burton's story and storyboard layouts. The same team created a live-action/stop-motion blend in 1996 with their adaptation of Roald Dahl's *James and the Giant Peach.* Burton's own most recent directorial efforts have focused on tributes to the types of film that first inspired his creative genius. Although a commercial failure, *Ed Wood* (1994) was possibly his greatest critical success to date. This black-and-white biopic of the "worst director of all time" is an affectionate tribute to a man who loved to make movies but who never found true happiness in Hollywood—much like Burton himself, whose desire is to make films that inspire the imagination. *Mars Attacks!* (1996), an attempted parody/homage to "Space Invader" films of the 1950s, suffers from its own excesses; despite its visual punch and quick humor, it attempts too often to be more a true blockbuster than a tongue-in-cheek pastiche of low-budget science fiction films. Burton clearly regained his footing, however, with the release in 1999 of *Sleepy Hollow,* an atmospheric spin on the Washington Irving story, inspired by, and paying reverence to, the ROGER CORMAN/Vincent Price/Edgar Allan Poe films of the 1960s. This American Romantic adaptation (which plays as freely with Irving's text as Corman always did with the works of Poe or Hawthorne) tells its story using the typically proto-Gothic chiaroscuro and *sfumato* of a Burton film. Burton's most recent project is the big-budget remake of *Planet of the Apes* (2001).

Burton's other non-filmic projects include a book of short stories, *Oyster Boy & Other Stories,* released by William Morrow in 1997, which continues his fascination with the macabre.

Other Films *Hansel and Gretel* (1982); *Aladdin and His Wonderful Lamp* (1984); *The Black Cauldron* (1985); *Cabin Boy* (1994).

Reference Hanke, Ken, *Tim Burton: An Unauthorized Biography of the Filmmaker* (New York: Renaissance Books, 2000).

—H.H.D.

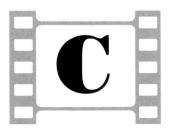

Cameron, James (1954–   ) Among contemporary directors, perhaps none exemplifies big, action-packed filmmaking quite like James Cameron. Born August 16, 1954, in Kapuskasing, Ontario, Canada, Cameron studied physics at California State University, Fullerton, and later drove a truck while writing screenplays. He made a living as an art director and a script doctor, and, when he began making his own films, he thrust himself to the forefront of modern Hollywood's technological wizardry. Every film he has made is a spectacle, the budget of each new film bigger than that of the last, and the results are among the best in blockbuster filmmaking that Hollywood has to offer.

His breakthrough film was *The Terminator* (1984), featuring Arnold Schwarzenegger in what would become his signature role—the heartless killing machine sent from the future to assassinate the woman destined to give birth to a revolutionary leader. Featuring elaborate action sequences, high-tech effects for which Cameron would become famous, and a mythical storyline, *The Terminator* became an instant classic of the science fiction genre and one of the defining films of the 1980s. Cameron cowrote the film with producer Gale Ann Hurd, his first wife, who

also had a hand in producing his next three films. (Cameron has had three subsequent marriages—to director Kathryn Bigelow, and with two actresses who appeared in his films, Linda Hamilton and Suzy Amis.)

Aliens (1986) was a sequel to Ridley Scott's *Alien*. While Scott's original was a suspense film anchored by the director's trademark visual flair, Cameron took the series in an action-adventure direction, with Sigourney Weaver's Ripley, the lone survivor of the first film, turning action heroine and mother figure to protect a little girl. In a rare accomplishment for an action role—and under Cameron's direction—Weaver received an Oscar nomination for best actress.

Cameron followed *Aliens* with *The Abyss* (1989), an underwater thriller that lived up (or down) to its title and was a rare financial and critical disappointment for him. An adventure yarn about the rescue of a sunken research station, *The Abyss* uneasily tried to weave together adventure and domestic drama with a science fiction resolution but ended up slow and muddled.

Terminator 2: Judgment Day (1991) brought Cameron back to familiar ground and was the biggest moneymaker of the year. This time Schwarzenegger played the hero, a terminator on a

Director James Cameron on the set of *Aliens* (Twentieth Century Fox)

mission to protect the heroine's son from another cyborg bent on killing him. Cameron includes dashes of humor, as Schwarzenegger must learn to adapt to the unfamiliar role of caretaker. *T2,* as it is also known, pumped up the chase scenes and effects for a thrilling ride that surprisingly turned sentimental at the end.

True Lies (1994) is an often entertaining action film with Schwarzenegger as a seemingly regular guy living a double life as a secret agent. For Cameron, however, who previously injected some kind of mythological or philosophical element into his films, *True Lies* feels like a standard action film, only more so, with loud, bombastic, over-the-top stunts that crowd out any empathy for the characters. Moreover, for a director known for strong, independent heroines (Sigourney Weaver in *Aliens,* Linda Hamilton in the *Terminator* films,

Mary Elizabeth Mastrantonio in *The Abyss,* Kate Winslet in *Titanic*), the humiliating way Schwarzenegger treats his wife, Jamie Lee Curtis, smacks of an uncharacteristic misogyny. *True Lies* is an often-thrilling action extravaganza that delivers what it sets out to do but lacks the imagination and innovation of Cameron's best work.

Titanic (1997) was a risky proposition from the outset—an old-fashioned love story between Leonardo DiCaprio's poor boy, Jack Dawson, and Winslet's rich girl, Rose DeWitt Bukater, set against the cataclysm of the *Titanic*'s sinking and the naïve, turn-of-the-century belief in unlimited progress. (It is no wonder that Janet Maslin of the *New York Times* compared it to *Gone with the Wind*.) Cameron's mammoth production went over schedule and became the most expensive film ever made, estimated at over $200 million. However, it is clearly his most ambitious film and his greatest achievement. Released in December 1997, *Titanic* went on to break box-office records and was number one for a record-setting 14 weeks in a row. It ultimately became the highest-grossing film ever made, collecting over $600 million domestically and $1.8 billion worldwide. The film also received a record-tying 11 Academy Awards, including three for Cameron himself—picture, director, and film editing. When he declared "I'm the king of the world!" in his acceptance speech for best director, Cameron demonstrated his sense of humor—or egomania—as he quoted the most memorable line from his screenplay.

Titanic is a marvel of storytelling as well as a technical wonder once the ship starts to sink and the film turns into a breathtaking survival yarn. But Cameron did not neglect the human dimension, not only in the love story but also in some of the most deeply moving and beautiful images in any of his films—Jack and Rose "flying" at the bow of the ship, the old couple choosing to die together in their bed, and Jack and Rose reunited in a final scene of transcendence that lifts the story to a whole new level. Cameron's epic undertaking is Hollywood blockbuster filmmaking at its best and a complete experience. It fulfills the promise that he could move audiences with genuine emotions and not just high-tech special effects.

Other Film *Piranha II: The Spawning* (1981).

References Abbott, Joe, "They Came from Beyond the Center: Ideology and Political Textuality in the Radical Science Fiction Films of James Cameron," *Literature/Film Quarterly* 22, no. 1 (1994): 21–27; Arnold, Robert F., "Termination or Transformation? The *Terminator* Films and Recent Changes in the U.S. Auto Industry," *Film Quarterly* 52, no. 1 (Fall 1998): 20–30; Arroyo, José, "Cameron and the Comic," *Sight and Sound,* September 1994: 26–28; Chumo, Peter N., II, "Learning to Make Each Day Count: Time in James Cameron's *Titanic,*" *Journal of Popular Film and Television* 26, no. 4 (Winter 1999): 158–64; French, Sean, *The Terminator* (London: BFI Modern Classics, 1996); Greenberg, Har-vey R., "FEMBO: *Aliens*' Intentions," *Journal of Popular Film and Television* 15, no. 4 (Winter 1998): 164–71; Hermann, Chad, "'Some Horrible Dream About (S)mothering': Sexuality, Gender, and Family in the *Alien* Trilogy," *Post Script* 16, no. 3 (Summer 1997): 36–50; Holliday, Fred A., II, "Hybrid Vigor: Generic Transformation in James Cameron's *Aliens,*" *Creative Screenwriting* 5, no. 4 (July–August 1998): 45–49; Jancovich, Mark, "Modernity and Subjectivity in *The Terminator:* The Machine as Monster in Contemporary American Culture," *The Velvet Light Trap* 30 (Fall 1992): 3–17; Kendrick, James, "Marxist Overtones in Three Films by James Cameron," *Journal of Popular Film and Television* 27, no. 3 (Fall 1999): 36–44; Lubin, David M., *Titanic* (London: BFI Modern Classics, 1999); Mann, Karen B., "Narrative Entanglements: *The Terminator,*" *Film Quarterly* 43, no. 2 (Winter 1989–90): 17–27; Parisi, Paula, *Titanic and the Making of James Cameron: The Inside Story of the Three-Year Adventure That Rewrote Motion Picture History* (New York: Newmarket Press, 1998); Telotte, J. P., "*The Terminator, Terminator 2,* and the Exposed Body,*" *Journal of Popular Film and Television* 20, no. 2 (Summer 1992): 26–34.

—P.N.C.

Campion, Jane (1954–) Jane Campion makes films about strong-willed women who face complicated decisions. She is originally from New Zealand but is often regarded as an Australian filmmaker because she received her film training in Sydney at the prestigious Australian Film, Television, and Radio School from 1981 to 1984. Her talent became clear with one of her first student films, *Peel, An Exercise in Discipline* (1982), which won the 1986 Palme d'Or award for best short film at the Cannes Film Festival. Following on the heels of that success she made three more short films that garnered awards in Australia and abroad, proving that she was a significant member of Australia's Post–New Wave.

The three short films allowed her to move into the independent film market and finance her next film, *Sweetie* (1989), which enjoyed some success in Australia and New Zealand, and won several awards including the Australian Critics Award for best director. *Sweetie* is a dark and intense film about the struggle of an emotionally disturbed young woman to maintain the semblance of a relationship with her family. Her next film, *Angel at My Table* (1990), similarly was a moderate success and added to her growing track record of awards, winning the Silver Lion at the Venice Film Festival. It is a biographical film about one of New Zealand's greatest writers, Janet Frame, who was misdiagnosed as schizophrenic and spent seven years in an asylum before being released after her book won the National Book Award. Her next film, *The Piano* (1993), is a remarkably rich visual masterpiece. It follows the fate of an unwed Scottish woman and her child sent off as a mail-order bride to New Zealand. In New Zealand the mother faces the loss of her beloved piano, which, since she doesn't talk, has become her mode of communication. She embarks on a life-changing and fulfilling, but illicit, romantic engagement in order to stay close to it. *The Piano* won Campion international acclaim as well as another Palme d'Or and an Academy Award for best original screenplay. In 1996 Campion directed *Portrait of a Lady.* Though it starred Nicole Kidman and John Malkovich and gained praise for its visual style, it was not a critical or box-office success. Adapted from the Henry James novel about a woman who loses her freedom when she inherits a fortune, critics wrote that Campion may have lost her vision when she obtained the huge budget and the Hollywood stars.

Campion's latest film, *Holy Smoke* (1999), is about a woman (Kate Winslet) who, having had a spiritual experience with a religious group in India, is lured back to her family in Australia and handed over to a "cult exiter" (Harvey Keitel) in order to be deprogrammed. The woman ends up turning the tables on the "cult exiter" and getting what she wants on her own terms. The trajectory of Campion's films seem to move her further away from the early surrealist twists; but the women continue to be strong-willed, though suffering less for that trait, and come out increasingly victorious.

Other Films *Passionless Moments* (1983); *After Hours* (1984); *A Girl's Own Story* (1984); *2 Friends* (1986).

References Bruzzi, Stella, "Jane Campion: Costume Drama and Reclaiming Women's Past," in *Women and Film: A Sight and Sound Reader,* eds. Pam Cook and Philip Dodd (Philadelphia: Temple University Press, 1993); Pullinger, Kate, "Soul Survivor," *Sight and Sound,* October 1999: 8–11; Baker, Noelle, "The Limits of Sexual Emancipation: Feminism and Jane Campion's Mythology of Love," *Interdisciplinary Literary Studies: A Journal of Criticism and Theory,* Fall 1999: 1–22; Keough, Peter, "Piano Lessons: Jane Campion Composes Herself," *The Boston Phoenix,* January 28–February 4, 1999.

—C.L.P.

Capra, Frank (1897–1991)

A Sicilian immigrant whose tributes to and critiques of the American way of life established him as one of cinema's most influential directors, Frank Capra was born on May 18, 1897, in Palermo, Sicily, to a peasant family. With his parents and three of his six siblings, he came to Los Angeles, California, when he was six years old. Often experiencing the widespread prejudice toward Italians in Anglo-dominated America, Capra would always be conscious of his status as an immigrant and "outsider," a feeling reflected in much of his work. In California, Capra's father found work as a fruit picker while his mother and siblings also held various jobs to support the family. Frank himself sold newspapers on the streets, "stuffed" papers at the *Los Angeles Times,* and played the guitar in a downtown brothel to help pay for his education at Manual Arts High School. Burning with youthful ambition, he later toiled in a steel plant to earn enough to enter the California Institute of Technology in 1916, where his interest in the sciences shifted to literature. Capra was building a distinguished academic record when his father, having just bought a lemon grove with his savings, died in a farm accident, a tragedy that would resonate in several of the director's future films. With his family now in a precarious financial situation, Capra was loaned a tuition fee by Caltech officials to complete his education. After graduating in 1918 with a degree in chemical engineering and after completing a short hitch in the army during the closing days of World War I, Capra began a three-year period of drifting. He performed manual labor, sold books and stocks, worked as a poker player, and had his first jobs in the film industry in 1919–20 as an extra in Hollywood.

His permanent involvement in motion pictures began in San Francisco in 1921 when he was hired by a local producer to direct a one-reel adaptation of a Rudyard Kipling poem, *Fultah Fisher's Boarding House.* In the fall of 1923, Capra, newly married to actress Helen Howell, moved to Hollywood where he worked briefly for the Hal Roach studio as a writer before being hired by Mack Sennett. There, he became part of a writing team collaborating on a series of two-reel comedies featuring Harry Langdon. Langdon soon became Sennett's biggest star and in the fall of 1925, the comedian left the studio to start his own company, taking Capra with him. After assisting Langdon and director Harry Edwards on their first feature, *Tramp, Tramp, Tramp* (1926), Capra directed Langdon in *The Strong Man,* a major critical and popular success upon its release in 1926. Capra's touch was already apparent in the comic story of a Belgian war veteran, a wide-eyed innocent who goes to America in search of a girl, his pen pal during the war, and ends up defeating a corrupt gang of bootleggers that have taken over her small town. Capra's immigrant background clearly found expression in his feature debut, while Langdon's encounter with city slickers and his battle with the forces of corruption foreshadow similar situations in subsequent Capra films.

Frank Capra (Author's collection)

The production history of *Long Pants* (1927), the second film in which Capra directed Langdon, was much more troubled. Beset with problems in his marriage and creative differences with Langdon on the set, Capra was fired by the star after the completion of the film. Capra next went to New York to direct Claudette Colbert in her film debut, *For the Love of Mike* (1927). But the film proved such a flop that Capra briefly returned to his writing job for Sennett before being hired as a director by producer Harry Cohn for his up-and-coming studio, Columbia.

With the release of his first features for the studio in 1928, Capra soon became its preeminent director. The success of *Submarine* (1928), a large-scale action adventure film about navy fliers, inspired two more epics, *Flight* (1929), depicting the actions of Marines in Nicaragua, and *Dirigible* (1931), the story of an expedition to the South

Pole. Meanwhile, his third Columbia film *The Matinee Idol* (1928), starring Bessie Love as the manager of a traveling stage troupe, reveals Capra's appreciation for strong women characters as well as his ability to combine hilarious comedy with poignant drama. Capra's consuming interest in the newspaper world, reflecting his early experiences working at the *Los Angeles Times,* is first evident in his final Columbia silent, *The Power of the Press* (1929), about a reporter (Douglas Fairbanks, Jr.) who discovers that a criminal gang is guilty of the murder for which his fiancee (Jobyna Ralston) has been unfairly accused.

Capra's first experiment with sound, *The Younger Generation* (1929), shifts between silent and talking sequences to depict the experiences of a Jewish immigrant family in New York. The film is a powerful indictment of materialism, relating how a young, upwardly mobile Jew (played by Ricardo Cortez), in his quest for money and status, rejects his own Lower East Side family as obstacles to his social advancement. Too late he discovers the value of human relationships. By then, his father has died and his family has abandoned him. All he has left as the film ends is his lavish but empty and cold mansion.

Capra eagerly met the challenge of sound and was in the forefront of those seeking to liberate early talkies from the confines of the then-prevalent "canned photoplays." Capra's sensitivity in directing players is apparent in Barbara Stanwyck's remarkable performance in *Ladies of Leisure* (1930), a role that made her a major star in only her fourth film and inaugurated her fruitful collaboration with Capra. *Ladies of Leisure* is yet another example of the director's social critique of the upper classes, with the artist rebelling against his father's snobbish values by falling in love with Stanwyck.

Capra became well known for his close association with the screenwriters working on his films, especially Robert Riskin, a New York playwright brought out to Hollywood by Columbia in 1931.

While the director had been developing his personal vision on film since his debut in 1926, Riskin effectively used his ability to draw character on paper. This, together with his flair for witty dialogue, including his uncanny ear for the rhythms of contemporary speech, helped Capra realize a remarkable series of films. Some critics contend that Riskin was Capra's conscience or the source of his vision. Capra made many statements over the years expressing his admiration for, and gratitude to, Riskin.

Riskin first collaborated with Capra by writing dialogue for the 1931 comedy *Platinum Blonde.* A delightful social comedy featuring an engaging cast headed by Robert Williams, Jean Harlow, and Loretta Young, the film concerns a newspaper reporter (Williams) who, while working on a story, meets and falls in love with a beautiful rich girl (Harlow). But after they are married, his easygoing, natural manner fails to adjust to the artificiality of her wealthy family's lifestyle. In the end, he returns to his roots by moving into an ordinary apartment where he begins working on a play with the help of his true love, fellow reporter Loretta Young. Capra's vision in those years also embraced a darker take on the human condition. *Rain or Shine* (1930), a broad comedy set in a circus, concludes with an amazing sequence in which the circus audience, incited by villains trying to steal the enterprise, becomes a raging mob, destroying the circus. In the 1931 drama *The Miracle Woman,* based on a play coauthored by Riskin, Capra indicts phony evangelism. A young minister's daughter (Barbara Stanwyck), embittered by societal hypocrisy, enters into partnership with an unscrupulous promoter to become a charismatic evangelist, offering hope and redemption to the suckers in exchange for their money. In the 1932 drama *Forbidden,* from an original story by Capra himself, an editor (Ralph Bellamy) is obsessed with trying to unmask the private life of a powerful politician (Adolphe Menjou). Menjou is a married man who has for years hidden his illicit affair and the fact that his adopted daughter is actually his own, the result of his liaison with the other woman (Barbara Stanwyck). Far from being a heroic crusader exposing corruption in high places, the editor is portrayed as a vicious pitbull, emblematic of a hypocritical society that insists people deny their true feelings in order to conform to a "respectable" public image.

American Madness (1932), a joint project of Capra and Riskin, was the director's first depiction of the social conflicts of the depression era. In this cinematic masterwork Capra capitalized on the economic unrest and bank failures of the early 1930s by depicting an idealistic bank president (Walter Huston) whose faith in people is in conflict with the bank's conservative board of directors. When mass panic over a robbery leads to a run on the bank, Huston's intervention proves a calming influence and prevents the crowd from degenerating into a violent mob. Capra's next film, *The Bitter Tea of General Yen* (1933), is one of the most unusual films of its time. The story concerns an American missionary (Barbara Stanwyck) trapped in a civil war in China and then rescued by a warlord, General Yen (Nils Asther), whose personality is an extraordinary combination of ruthlessness and tenderness. Finding herself falling in love with the general in spite of herself, her efforts to "reform" him by inducing him to spare the life of his former mistress results only in his betrayal and death. Rich in psychological insight and moral complexity, *The Bitter Tea of General Yen* was a brave attempt to confront controversial subject matter.

Capra's next two films, *Lady for a Day* (1933) and *It Happened One Night* (1934), brought him closer to the formula for which he is best known today. The first was a sentimental comedy, a heartwarming modern fairy tale in which a woman (May Robson) has been reduced to poverty as an apple vendor in order to provide for her daughter's upbringing abroad. When the girl and her aristocratic European fiancé visit New York, the elderly lady, aided by her underworld friends as well as the governor and the mayor, masquerades as a wealthy dowager. Capra remade it in 1962 under the title, *A Pocketful of Miracles. It Happened One Night* had its origins in Samuel Hopkins Adams's "Night Bus," a magazine story that Capra and Riskin refashioned into an exhilarating, witty comedy. Its stars, Clark Gable as the newspaperman pursuing a story about a runaway heiress, and Claudette Colbert as the rich girl, were loaned to Columbia by their studios and gave performances with such brilliance and élan that they helped launch the so-called screwball cycle of the 1930s. Capra insisted on shooting much of the film on location to convey the spirit of America in the depression years, the look and feel of highways, the rural regions, the buses and motels. Again, Capra's critique of materialism emerges when reporter Gable rejects the phony lifestyle of the idle rich and ultimately wins Colbert over to his romantic celebration of a life freed from artificial social constraints. (This perspective reappeared in Capra's second film of 1934, *Broadway Bill,* starring Warner Baxter and Myrna Loy, a tale of a man who rejects the acquisitive monopoly capitalism of his father-in-law to enjoy the simpler pleasure of training a race horse.)

When *It Happened One Night* swept all the major awards at the Motion Picture Academy ceremony in 1935, Capra, who for some years had set his sights on an Oscar, reached the pinnacle of his career. He had triumphed in film beyond his wildest expectations while helping to raise Columbia to the status of a major studio. In his personal life, too, he was now happily married (since 1932) to Lucille Warner and the proud father of a growing family. Yet having to all intents achieved the American dream, Capra was suddenly wracked with self-doubt and a feeling he was somehow unworthy of all this success. These inner torments brought on a severe illness from which he emerged determined to make films that would champion the cause of the common man.

The first film to result from his renewed commitment was the classic comedy-drama, *Mr. Deeds*

Goes to Town (1936), starring Gary Cooper and Jean Arthur. A variant on the country hick besting the city slickers, the story concerns Longfellow Deeds (Cooper), an eccentric, tuba-playing idealist in a small town who suddenly inherits a fortune and migrates to New York where he comes up against the corruption, jaded impersonality, and pseudo-sophistication of the big city. After he is mocked and caricatured by the press, he eventually faces an insanity charge when he attempts to give away his millions to the poor. Ultimately, Deeds's innate goodness wins over his detractors, including the cynical newspaperwoman (Arthur) who, after writing damaging stories about him, finds herself falling in love with him. Cooper's innate sanity and good sense win out, of course, underscoring Capra's belief in individuality resisting the mass conformity of modern life. In another context, the film stands as the first of four films—*Mr. Smith Goes to Washington* (1939), *Meet John Doe* (1941), and *State of the Union* (1948)—in which Capra explicitly depicts a Messiah figure who is first raised by his followers and acolytes to a pitch of power and influence, then betrayed and exposed as a fraud, cast down, and finally resurrected as a true champion of the oppressed.

With *Lost Horizon* (1937) Capra turned to the vein of exotic romance he had tapped in *General Yen*. This spectacular dramatization of James Hilton's novel about the mythical country of Shangri-La, a land hidden in the Himalayas and governed by a High Lama according to the principles of peace and love, featured Ronald Colman as Conway, a visionary Englishman. Made at a time when the world was rapidly moving toward a global conflict, *Lost Horizon* skillfully captures the yearning of the era for a resolution to the problems that were tearing humanity apart. By contrast, *You Can't Take It With You* (1938), based on the George S. Kaufman–Moss Hart play, is a work of optimistic Americana, about a family of endearingly eccentric Americans who do as they please in defiance of the Great Depression.

Capra's work in the 1930s culminated with *Mr. Smith Goes to Washington* (1939), often cited as his greatest film. With a cast headed by James Stewart and Jean Arthur, the film deals with an idealistic, newly appointed junior senator, Jefferson Smith (Stewart), who discovers that a corrupt political machine is running his state. When he learns that his state's senior senator (Claude Rains), whom he had admired all his life as a man of principle, has long since sold out to a corrupt boss (Edward Arnold) with near-dictatorial control over the state, his ideals are shaken. The machine musters all its power to destroy Smith when he tries to expose the level of corruption in his state. He makes a ringing defense of democracy in a speech on the Senate floor—but it is only the confession of the now-penitent senator who had earlier denounced him that finally saves the day. Capra's depiction of high-level corruption and the cynical Washington press corps aroused considerable controversy at the time. But *Mr. Smith Goes to Washington* has long since been recognized as one of the most incisive studies of American political processes ever captured on film.

As the 1940s began and with the rest of the world embroiled in war, Capra, now the president of the Director's Guild, was becoming more and more vocal about social inequities and the threat posed to democracy by fascism. Along with scores of other liberal-minded Hollywood luminaries, Capra's name appeared in ads in the *New York Times* supporting President Roosevelt's 1940 reelection bid and rallying to the defense of the Soviet Union when it was invaded by the Nazis in 1941. Professionally, Capra ended his long, sometimes contentious association with Harry Cohn and Columbia to form a partnership with Riskin to produce independent pictures. The film they created, *Meet John Doe* (1941), reflected Capra's apprehensions about fascism. Gary Cooper plays a drifter, an unemployed bush-league baseball player turned into a headline story by newspaper reporter Barbara Stanwyck, who represents him as a critic of the world's injustices. Newspaper owner Edward Arnold decides to use Cooper's image to create an idealistic movement, the John Doe Clubs, a front for his drive to become an American dictator. When Cooper discovers the media mogul's real agenda, he is prevented from going public by an outraged mob arrayed against their former idol. Because of Capra's indecision about the ending, the film concludes with a draw between the tycoon and those citizens in the clubs who have come to their senses about Cooper and rallied to his defense. It remains one of American cinema's most powerful and prophetic works, an extraordinarily bleak vision of idealism masking a totalitarian, reactionary agenda.

With the increasing likelihood that the United States would soon enter World War II, Capra volunteered his services to the Army Signal Corps. Before leaving Hollywood, he directed a madcap film version of the Broadway hit *Arsenic and Old Lace* (1944) for Warner Bros. an assignment he took on in order to keep his family solvent while he went to work for the military. He completed shooting just after the Pearl Harbor attack. In Washington, D.C., the government assigned him to supervise a series of army training films intended to explain to the troops the history of the war and the reasons why the United States had entered the fray. By skillfully editing film clips, including footage shot by the enemy, and interweaving them with stirring music and narration, Capra and his team of writers and technicians created the *Why We Fight* series, some of the most effective propaganda documentaries ever made. Although he was committed heart and soul to the Allied cause, he was appalled to realize that his own side, the champion of freedom and democracy, was bombing civilians in the enemy countries, atrocities akin to the terrors of the German air raids that he experienced in London. Sickened by the slaughter on both sides, Capra recorded his dismay in his diaries at the time. He emerged from this inner conflict with a strong commitment to

pacifism and a fresh determination to restate on film his belief in a more just and equitable world based on the value of the individual.

Capra returned to Hollywood and civilian life determined to maintain his creative independence. In partnership with fellow directors WILLIAM WYLER and GEORGE STEVENS, he formed a new organization, Liberty Films, to produce their own films. It was for Liberty that Capra created the film which, in a very real sense, distilled all his own life experiences and two decades of filmmaking into a masterpiece that has touched innumerable people over the decades, *It's a Wonderful Life,* first shown during the 1946 Christmas season. The story concerns George Bailey (James Stewart), his life in the New England town of Bedford Falls, the thwarting of his youthful dreams and aspirations by the realities of having to keep the family savings and loan association afloat, his courtship and marriage to Mary (Donna Reed), and the thwarting of his attempts to help the people in his community by the grasping town banker, Mr. Potter (Lionel Barrymore). Pushed over the edge to suicide, George is rescued by an angel named Clarence (Henry Travers), who provides him with a vision of what the town might be like had he never existed. Capra's most extraordinary variation on the immigrant motif, George becomes a stranger in his own community as the townspeople, even his own mother, fail to recognize him. The town, now known as Pottersville, is a dark, corrupt city dominated by the banker, Capra's grim vision of man's existence filled with all the angst of what might yet be the American future. Finally, after one desperate encounter after another and his realization that his life had indeed touched many others for the better, George is released from this nightmarish state. The film ends on a note of affirmation as he is reunited with his family and friends and saved by their financial generosity. Critical and popular reaction to *It's a Wonderful Life* was mixed in 1946–47, but in the 1970s, it reemerged as a television staple and became Capra's most beloved and oft-seen film, enlisting widely varying interpretations but clearly recognized by most as one of the great works of American cinema.

Capra's second film for Liberty, *State of the Union* (1948), starred Spencer Tracy as a liberal Republican candidate for the presidency and Katharine Hepburn as his wife. Tracy sees the White House as a chance to realize his progressive beliefs; however, caught up in the corruption of power politics, he sells out in order to win votes. Chastened by his wife's criticism as well as his own conscience, he publicly renounces his quest in a televised address reproaching his own failings and decrying the state of American politics. With Capra poised to surrender his independence to join the industry as a contract director, the film has obvious autobiographical overtones. It would also be the last of his classic political films. Significantly, the visionary ideals of a world government aroused opposition from the increasingly powerful right wing in an America and Hollywood now being intimidated by the House Un-American Activities Committee.

The years 1936–48 produced films that earned Capra the sobriquet as a "populist" director. Commentator Glenn Alan Phelps notes that most of the pictures from this period depicted "a simple, unassuming young man from small-town America confronting urban industrialists, corporate lawyers, bankers, and crooked politicians. Eventually, through the determined application of the virtues of honesty, goodness, and idealism the 'common man' triumphs over this conspiracy of evil." In a thought-provoking argument, Phelps alleges that what appears to be the pluralist thesis of American democracy—the "triumph of the common man"—is misleading: "Capra's eye discloses a world in which materialism and self-interest seem far more prevalent than the simple virtues his heroes personify. He gives us no confidence in the hero's eventual victory. In fact, we are shown that the forces of privilege, money, and political power have all of the tangible resources

with which to keep the heroic individual in line. Capra draws his portrait of American society too well. The logic of it compels us to perceive no real hope for the champion of right so long as he relies solely upon himself. The deck is too well stacked." Yet, in the final analysis, protagonists Mr. Smith, George Bailey, Long John Willoughby, and Mr. Deeds do affirm that democracy can prevail only when, as Phelps notes, "individuals are politicized by being made aware of their public responsibilities. He seems to be saying that society and the individuals within it will be qualitatively better only when each individual is given a large degree of responsibility for his own actions *and* for the actions of his community."

Capra directed only four more films after the dissolution of Liberty: two Bing Crosby vehicles for Paramount, *Riding High* (1950) (a musical remake of *Broadway Bill*), and *Here Comes the Groom* (1951); *A Hole in the Head* (1957), a comedy starring Frank Sinatra; and his last film, *A Pocketful of Miracles* (1961), a remake of *Lady for a Day*. Between the Crosby and Sinatra films, he returned to his first love, science, directing four informative and entertaining television programs on the subject, a series so skillfully put together that it was shown in classrooms across the country for years.

Unlike contemporaries of his such as ALFRED HITCHCOCK, JOHN FORD, HOWARD HAWKS, and Wyler who did some of their most notable work in the 1950s and 1960s, Capra disappeared from the Hollywood film industry for much of this period. But in a sense, Capra, like Griffith before him, had always stood apart from the industry. At Columbia, he attained an autonomy denied most directors of the time since, once the budget was agreed upon, he was able, with Cohn's blessing, to make whatever film he chose without interference. His most impressive post-Columbia films, *Meet John Doe, It's a Wonderful Life,* and *State of the Union,* were all independently produced. Along with Capra's inability to adapt to the structure of the industry, the changing political and social climate in the post-war years was a further factor in his eclipse in the 1950s. The height of his popularity in the 1930s and early 1940s coincided with the era of Populism and the Popular Front, uniting people of progressive faith to fight the Great Depression. This coalition quickly fell apart after the war. The now-ascendant rightists viewed Capra's films as particularly suspect. Indeed, a 1947 internal report by J. Edgar Hoover's FBI cited *It's a Wonderful Life* and *Mr. Smith Goes to Washington* as subversive, left-wing attacks on capitalism. Moreover, to the beleaguered liberals of the 1950s, Capra's idealism now seemed fuzzy and naively out of touch with postwar realities.

Capra, however, was never a man to fade quietly into obscurity. In 1971, he reemerged with *The Name Above the Title,* a vastly entertaining if notoriously misleading autobiography. Revisionist biographer Joseph McBride—who perhaps had agendas of his own to pursue—calls it a "fairy-tale account of his life" that was convincing to readers at the time because of its "mingling of self-serving episodes with ones that gave the impression of ruthless candor toward his own failings but that actually served to paper over even more damning aspects of his life, the parts he found unspeakable, the parts the book was concocted to conceal." The autobiography also perpetuated the debatable notion that Capra was a true auteur, the sole author of his films. "The book was an attempt to prove he did it all himself," writes McBride. "The 'one man, one film' theory seemed strange indeed to the surviving members of his crew, who read Capra's book with an obvious hurt and embarrassment, though they were reluctant to voice those feelings, directly." It led, moreover, to Capra's new career as a college circuit speaker, "tirelessly fashioning his image for posterity with the help of squads of media acolytes."

In 1982 Capra received the American Film Institute's Lifetime Achievement Award. Following the death of his wife Lucille, with whom he had shared an exceptionally close relationship for over half a century, he suffered a stroke in 1985 and withdrew from the public eye. He died on September 3, 1991, at the age of 94 in his home in La Quinta, California. Survivors included a daughter and two sons, one of whom, Frank Capra, Jr., had become a prominent film producer in his own right.

Capra's work has been the subject of countless analyses by film historians and social commentators, like Jeanine Basinger, Leland Poague, and Raymond Carney. It was Capra who made Barbara Stanwyck and Jean Arthur stars and helped shape the screen images of Gary Cooper, James Stewart, Clark Gable, and Claudette Colbert. Along with John Ford, he was the director most responsible for expressing the American national consciousness on screen in the 1930s and 1940s. However, Capra still has fierce detractors who deride him as the sweetly sentimental purveyor of "Capracorn." Ironically, this view of Capra as a complacent manipulator of mass emotions has also been promulgated by his latter-day conservative admirers who have sought to recast him as the "family values" director in contrast to contemporary Hollywood's supposed ultraliberalism. Even among the critics who most appreciate him as a subtle and powerful artist, there are sharp divisions between those who revere him as an idealist with an affirmative vision of mankind and those who see his point of view as darker, more cynical, more despairing. In truth, Capra resists any attempts at simple categorization because his work is multi-layered. Much like his literary antecedents, Charles Dickens and Mark Twain, Capra was both a popular humorous entertainer and a complex visionary artist. Also like Dickens and Twain, Capra was simultaneously radical and conservative in his outlook, a romantic and a realist in his aesthetics, a man of both tremendous faith and immense doubt. To his stalwart fans, like Justice William O. Douglas, goes the last word. "Frank Capra entertained us; but he also brought tears to our eyes when we revisited with him the shrines of Jefferson and Lincoln and when he made us realize that in spite of all the overreaching and crime and immorality the heart of America was warm and her conscience bright."

Other Films *For the Love of Mike* (1927); *That Certain Thing* (1928); *So This Is Love* (1928); *The Way of the Strong* (1928); *Say It with Sables* (1928); *The Donovan Affair* (1929).

References Capra, Frank, *The Name Above the Title* (New York: Macmillan, 1971); Drew, William M., "Frank Capra: A Lighthouse in a Foggy World" (interview), *American Classic Screen* 3, no. 6 (July–August 1979): 14–16; Maland, Charles J., *Frank Capra* (Boston: Twayne, 1980); McBride, Joseph, *Frank Capra: The Catastrophe of Success* (New York: Simon and Schuster, 1992); Phelps, Glenn Alan, "The 'Populist' Films of Frank Capra," *Journal of American Studies* 13, no. 3 (December 1979): 377–392; Tibbetts, John C., "The Wisdom of the Serpent: Frauds and Miracles in Frank Capra's *The Miracle Woman*," *The Journal of Popular Culture* 7, no. 3 (1979), 293–309; Willis, Donald C., *The Films of Frank Capra* (Metuchen, N.J.: Scarecrow Press, 1974).

—W.M.D.

Carax, Leos (1960–) French filmmaker, born Alexandre Oscar Dupont, the youngest of four children of the scientific journalist George Dupont and Joan Dupont, an American writer; Carax immersed himself in the repertory film theaters of Paris and began writing for *Cahiers du cinéma* while still in his teens. His first films were shorts made in 1978 (*La Fille rêvée*) and 1980 (*Strangulation Blues*). His first feature film, *Boy Meets Girl,* starring Denis Lavant and Mireille Perrier, was completed in 1983 and premiered at the Cannes Film Festival in 1984, earning him critical acclaim. It told a story of two young Parisians born in 1960 (like Carax himself), Mireille and Alex (the director's birth name), offering Carax's first variation on the theme of love without regret. (The name of the character, Alex Oscar, like the Christian names of the director himself, is an anagram for Leos Carax.) The film was enthusiasti-

cally reviewed by David Kehr of the *New York Times* as a "thunderous return to the revolutionary principles and qualities of the French New Wave," recalling both Godard and Jean Vigo.

His second feature, *Mauvais sang* (Bad blood, aka *The Night Is Young* [1986]), again starring Denis Lavant, this time with Juliette Binoche and Michel Piccoli, was his breakthrough picture, earning two awards at the Berlin Film Festival of 1987. It was a stylishly made caper film involving a young thief, Alex (Lavant), who agrees to help an older thief, Mark (Piccoli), steal a serum developed by a pharmaceutical corporation to cure a mysterious virus called STBO, spread by those who make love without true passion. Alex is attracted to Anna (Binoche), who is in turn attached to the older Marc, until the end, when she breaks loose and literally runs away from the relationship. The film was innovative in its technique, even though the plot seemed to lack coherence. This coming-of-age film ends with a car chase and Alex's thwarted escape to Switzerland. The film was clearly imitative of JEAN-LUC GODARD's *Breathless* in its low-life characters and in the way Juliette Binoche was made to resemble Godard's actress, Anna Karina. At the end, moreover, Alex suffers the fate of Belmondo in Godard's *Breathless*. Both films imitated American gangster films in eccentric though inventive ways. Carax's film was considered a postmodern riff on New Wave romanticism that offered surprising twists and focused on images for the sake of images, regardless of narrative logic.

Mauvais sang was criticized, however, for sharing the "postcard aesthetics" of what critics called the self-conscious *cinéma du look*. Carax's work was linked with that of Jean-Jacques Beineix and Luc Besson in the way it was criticized for its flashy but empty *cinéma du look* style. The *cinéma du look* style was also apparent in the next Carax film, *Les Amants du Pont-Neuf* (*Lovers on the Bridge* [1991]), a romantic story of two homeless people (Lavant and Binoche, again) that was extravagantly expensive ($28 million) by French standards and reportedly bankrupted three producers, causing a slump in Carax's career and giving him the reputation of a *cinéaste maudit,* an "accursed filmmaker," to use the phrase coined by the poet-filmmaker JEAN COCTEAU (whom one character believes he has sighted in *Mauvais sang*). With regard to what he now calls the "Alex trilogy," Carax has stated that his first three films were not "original" subjects: "On the contrary, they were three variations on the least original theme possible: *Boy Meets Girl.* Original subjects often make very bad films," he added, films "that are falsely original."

After making a short film entitled *Sans titre* in 1997, Carax staged a comeback in 1999 with *Pola X,* an *hommage* to Herman Melville's *Pierre, or the Ambiguities* (1852), a work Melville began in 1851 after completing his masterpiece, *Moby Dick. Pola X* updates to contemporary France the Melville story of an alienated and spoiled young artist intent upon writing a "great book of truth." In the Carax film, Pierre (Guillaume Depardieu, the son of Gérard Depardieu) is a successful novelist living in Normandy, who discovers he has a half-sister, Isabelle (Katerina Golubeva), whose existence he had never suspected. Isabelle is linked both to Pierre's soulful imagination and to the wars in the Balkans. Pierre runs away with Isabelle to the suburbs of Paris, abandoning both his fiancée (Delphine Chuillot) and his mother (Catherine Deneuve). The film was so titled as to signify that it represented the 10th draft of Carax's attempt to adapt Melville's story. "You don't adapt novels," Carax noted in the film's pressbook, "but rather the enduring sensation that they leave you with."

Surveying the director's first work, Jill Forbes concluded that "the plots are insignificant." What is significant, and what caused Jonathan Rosenbaum to call Carax a "film poet," is the filmmaker's distinctively expressionistic and surrealistic style. "For me," Carax told David Thompson, a screenplay is "more like a musical score, with colors and emotions." His work evokes a sensibility of 19th-century French Romanticism tempered by the elliptical and improvisational style of the French New Wave.

References Forbes, Jill, "Omegaville: *Boy Meets Girl* and *Mauvais Sang*," *Sight and Sound* 56 (Autumn 1987): 292–93; Kehr, Dave, "Leos Carax: A Poet of the Emotions Breaks His Silence," *New York Times,* July 27, 1999; Kenny, Glenn, "*Pola X,*" *Premiere,* September 2000, p. 17; Klawans, Stuart, "Bridge Over Troubled Water: *The Lovers on the Bridge,*" *Nation* 269 (July 19, 1999): 34–36; Rosenbaum, Jonathan, "The Problem with Poetry: Leos Carax," *Film Comment* 30, no. 3 (May–June 1994): 12–19; Thomson, David, "Leos Carax," *Sight and Sound* 64 (September 1992): 6–11.

—J.M.W.

Carné, Marcel (1906–1996) Although not as prolific as his French contemporaries JEAN RENOIR and RENÉ CLAIR, Marcel Carné stands in the front rank of directors working in the 1930s and 1940s. He was born in Batignolles, in Paris, on August 18, 1906, the son of a cabinetmaker. In the mid-1920s he worked as an insurance clerk before moving on to a more desirable profession, cinematographer and director. He began as an assistant with René Clair on his landmark sound film, *Under the Roofs of Paris (Sous les toits de Paris)* in 1929 and, after gaining more experience with the support of another veteran director, Jacques Feyder, directed his first theatrical feature in 1936, *Jenny.* In the meantime, he wrote film criticism for *Cinémagazine* and *Cinémonde* under the pseudonym "Albert Cranche."

His 10-year, fruitful collaboration with the esteemed poet-playwright-scenarist Jacques Prevert produced four of the undisputed masterpieces of the French cinema of the 1930s and early 1940s: *Port of Shadows (Quai des brumes* [1938]), *Daybreak (Le Jour se lève* [1939]), *The Devil's Envoys (Les Visiteurs du soir* [1942]), and *Children of Paradise (Les Enfants du paradis* [1945]). The first two films were exemplars of what has come to be known as "poetic realism," a species of fatalistic romantic melodrama wreathed in a noirish atmosphere of shadows and fog. Actor Jean Gabin starred in both as a doomed figure on the run from a troubled past. *Daybreak* was particularly noted for its intricately realized flashback structure. (It was remade in the 1940s by Anatole Litvak under the title of *The Long Night*.) Critic André Bazin looked back upon these two classics with affection: "Everything came together to make of these two films the most perfect expression of a rather characteristic tendency of French cinema between 1934 and 1939: the *film noir*."

With the German occupation during the war, Carné—who, unlike Renoir and Clair, remained in France—and Prévert abandoned the urban gloom in favor of a more highly theatricalized spectacle for the latter two films. *The Devil's Envoys* was a medieval fable about two agents of the devil (Alain Cuny and Arletty) who attend a baronial banquet and disrupt everyone's lives. When one of the envoys falls in love for real, the devil himself (Jules Berry) intervenes and transforms the lovers into statues. *Children of Paradise*, Carné's masterpiece, was an ambitious, three-hour tribute to the French theater and a thinly disguised evocation of the enduring French spirit that transcends war.

Only 36 years of age at the conclusion of the war, Carné's bright future prospects somehow failed to materialize. His first postwar film, *Gates of the Night* (*Les Portes de la nuit* [1946]), a story about collaborators and black marketeers in postwar Paris, flopped at the box office; and the ill-fated *Fleur de l'age* marked the end of his relationship with Prévert. A dozen more films followed, but Carné never regained the influence and prestige he had hitherto enjoyed. Despite his generosity toward a younger generation of filmmakers, he was dismayed to find he had fallen out of favor with the emerging "New Wave" artists. It was only in 1980 that his foremost detractor, François Truffaut, had occasion to revise his opinion. "I have made 23 pictures," Truffaut said. "I would swap them all for the chance to have made *Les Enfants du paradis*."

Children of Paradise deserves special mention. It was designated in 1979 by the French Academy of Cinema Arts and Techniques as "the best film in the history of talking pictures in France." It is, more to the point, Carné's masterpiece and the one picture in which he most perfectly fused the styles and tone of poetic realism with the artifice of the theater. What Carné himself described as "a tribute to the theater" relies on the conventions of pantomime, farce, melodrama, and Shakespearean tragedy to underscore its story of love's triumphs and frustrations. The setting is Paris during the monarchy of Louis-Philippe in the 1840s, at Carnival time. The action is framed by the rise and fall of a theater curtain, and the story transpires in the Boulevard du Temple, Paris's theater district, which teems with acrobats, clowns, mimes, barkers, peepshows, and animal acts. Two of the story's principal characters are actors based on real-life figures—the elegant mime Jean-Gaspard Deburau (played by Jean-Louis Barrault as "Baptiste Deburau") and the flamboyant Shakespearean actor Frederick Lemaître (Pierre Brasseur). Each performs in his own theater, Baptiste at the Théâtre du Funambules and Lemaître at the Grand Théâtre. What unites them—and links them with the more peripheral characters, the villainous Lacenaire (Marcel Herrand) and the slimy aristocrat Edward de Monteray (Louis Salou)—is their fatal attraction to the enigmatic beauty, Garance (Arletty).

"Jealousy belongs to everyone," observes Lemaître, "even if women belong to no one!" Baptiste and Lemaître must turn to their art to survive. The theater offers them not only solace but also a kind of creative whetstone. As Lemaître says, "When I act, I am desperately in love, desperately, do you understand? But when the curtain falls, the audience goes away, and takes 'my love' with it. You see, I make the audience a present of my love. The audience is very happy, and so am I. And I become wise and free and calm and sensible again, like Baptiste!" Made during the last months of the German occupation of France—it was one of the first films to be released after the liberation—*Children of Paradise* is also about the enduring French spirit during the German occupation. It has been demonstrated that theatrical activities, not political actions, were France's chief bulwark against the Nazi oppression. In the words of Edward Baron Turk, France's theaters were "the 'safe houses' of those collective dreams that take the form of plays and movies [and which] provided a public site for relief from political oppression." Moreover, continues Turk, the film pointed toward the imminent resurgence of the French spirit: "All those who had experienced the outrage, humiliation, and despair of the occupation could perceive in it the infallible sign of assurance that French civilization would reestablish its position of prestige and leadership in the world."

Carné was an officer of the Légion d'honneur and received the Prix Louis Delluc. He resided in an apartment on the rue de l'Abbaye in Paris. In 1977 he completed *La Bible,* a 90-minute documentary on the mosaics of the Monreale Basilica in Sicily, and he continued to experiment with what he called the "spectacle audiovisuel," the multimedia projection of images on a large screen accompanied by a quadrophonic sound system. He was one of the screen's supreme poets of loneliness, writes biographer Turk: "It is perhaps inevitable that a film director who portrays life's essential loneliness will fail to command universal assent. But to overlook Carné's cinema of sadness is to misrepresent the past in conformity with a wish for only positive images of human possibility. Carné's films bear out the Baudelairean view of sorrow and melancholy as fundamental components of art."

Other Films *Bizarre Bizaar* (*Drole de drame* [1937]); *La Marie du port* (1949); *Thérèse Raquin* (1953); *The Cheaters* (*Les Tricheurs* [1958]); *The Young Wolves* (*Les Jeunes loups* [1967]); *The Wonderful Visit* (*La Merveilleuse visite* [1974]).

References Bazin, André, "The Disincarnation of Carné," in *Rediscovering French Film,* ed. Mary Lea Bandy (New York: Museum of Modern Art, 1983), pp. 131–135; Turk, Edward Baron, *Child of Paradise: Marcel Carné and the Golden Age of French Cinema* (Cambridge, Mass.: Harvard University Press, 1989); Turk, Edward Baron, "The Birth of *Children of Paradise,*" *American Film,* July–August 1979, pp. 42–49.

—J.C.T.

Carpenter, John (1948–) John Carpenter was born on January 16, 1948, in Carthage, New York, and spent his formative years being raised in Bowling Green, Kentucky. He was inspired to become a director after seeing such 1950s films as *It Came from Outer Space, Forbidden Planet,* and *Creature from the Black Lagoon.* He studied film at Western Kentucky University and the University of Southern California. In his early twenties he directed *Dark Star* (1974), and after graduation the film was expanded into feature length on a low budget of $60,000. As a student Carpenter made a few short films, one of which, *The Resurrection of Bronco Billy,* won an Academy Award for best short live action film in 1970.

Early in his career Carpenter wrote two film scripts, *The Eyes of Laura Mars* (1978), a successful film starring Faye Dunaway, and a made-for-TV movie, *Zuma Beach* (1978), a film about a rock star down on her luck, played by Suzanne Sommers. Carpenter also had other scripts made into movies, such as *Black Moon Rising* (1986), *El Diablo* (1990), and *Blood River* (1991), all made for TV.

Carpenter's second full-length feature was *Assault on Precinct 13* (1976), his tribute to Howard Hawks's *Rio Bravo.* Though not particularly successful in America, it wowed the audience at the London Film Festival and went on to become a cult hit. The film brought him to the attention of Moustapha Akkad, a producer looking for someone to direct a story idea about a baby-sitter being

John Carpenter behind the scenes of *In the Mouth of Madness* (New Line)

terrorized by a homicidal maniac on the scariest night of the year. *Halloween* (1978) was a huge commercial success, the most successful independent film ever made up to that time. The unrelenting terror and superb pacing marked Carpenter's arrival into the mainstream of Hollywood directors. In the same year Carpenter wrote and directed the TV movie *Someone's Watching Me* (1978), released theatrically in Europe under the title *High Rise*. One of the major reasons cited for the success of *Halloween* was Carpenter's haunting original score, with a percussive ostinato on the piano that evoked the obsessive nature of Michael Myers, the insane killer. (Carpenter has scored most of his own films, with the notable exception of *The Thing* [1981].)

Carpenter's next theatrical project after *Halloween* was *The Fog* (1980), a very atmospheric ghost story set in a coastal town. This was also a big hit and confirmed his reputation as Hollywood's premier master of horror. For his next project, however, Carpenter took a different direction with the big action movie *Escape from New York* (1981), a script written during the early 1970s. Kurt Russell starred as the wisecracking macho hero, Snake Plisskin. *The Thing* (1982) was another box-office success, but it was poorly received by the critics, who felt that the special effects overpowered the story. The haunting score was provided by Ennio Morricone, a premier soundtrack composer. Carpenter then made *Christine* (1983), based on the Stephen King novel about a possessed car, teenage angst, and rock 'n' roll. King admits he was disappointed with the finished project, declaring it seemed lifeless and flat. Carpenter strayed into romantic territory with *Starman* (1984), a science fiction love story. It earned Jeff Bridges an Oscar nomination for his performance in the title role. Two years later saw the release of the big-budget flop *Big Trouble in Little China* (1986), a Chinese martial arts/ghost story set in Chinatown and starring Kurt Russell. The flamboyant and boisterous action of the film took precedence over the horror elements.

After the big-budget failure of *Big Trouble in Little China,* Carpenter returned to smaller-budget films where he had more control. *Prince of Darkness* (1987) was the first entry in a multipicture deal with Universal, and it was an ambitious film that successfully and chillingly explored the metaphysical aspects of pure evil. Next was *They Live* (1988), a great science fiction film starring Roddy Piper, the WWF wrestling star.

More recently Carpenter directed the lackluster *Memoirs of an Invisible Man* (1992), featuring Chevy Chase, but after this, he decided to go low-budget again, returning to TV to direct two segments of *Bodybags* (1993), a trilogy of tales in the *Creepshow* tradition. Carpenter also appeared in the film as the morgue attendant in the "wraparound" story, introducing each tale with some ghoulish puns. Back to the cinema screen again, he made *Village of the Damned* (1995), a remake of another of his favorite films, originally filmed in black and white in the sixties. *In The Mouth of Madness* (1995) received some of the best reviews of Carpenter's career, plus a nomination for best horror picture at the Saturn Awards. It is a superb Lovecraftian tale limned in the best Carpenter style, a moderate success both critically and financially.

In 1996 Carpenter got back together with Debra Hill (producer) and Kurt Russell to bring one of cinema's greatest anti-heroes back to life. Russell reprised his role as Snake Plissken in *Escape from L.A.,* a sequel to *Escape From New York.* It was released to mixed reviews and box office. *Vampires* (1998), an adaptation of a fantastic, action-packed novel by John Steakley, follows a band of vampire hunters who are employed by the Vatican to rid America of some of the meanest blood suckers to ever appear in print. The film was initially released in France to ecstatic critical and commercial response, and the U.S. release saw *Vampires* go to the top of the box-office charts. Carpenter is a consistently successful director, and while some of his films are more well received than others, none of his films has ever lost money. "The extraordinary thing about [Carpenter's] images," writes commentator Morris Dickstein, "is not simply their beauty but their suggestiveness, the unconscious reverberations they have for us. . . . Both Carpenter and De Palma work more by suggestion, like their acknowledged master, Hitchcock, and like some erotic filmmakers who eschew hard-core sex for being too literal and unimaginative." Carpenter himself has declared his fundamental respect for his viewers: "You've got to put them on the edge. And you can't gross them out. Because you'll lose them. . . . Don't show the meat when the knife goes in, don't cut to the blood going everywhere, then all of them will stay with you. If you suggest it, they'll do it right up here, in their heads."

Reference Dickstein, Morris, *The Aesthetics of Fright,* in *Planks of Reason: Essays on the Horror Film,* ed. Barry Grant, (Metuchen, N.J.: Scarecrow Press, 1984), pp. 65–78.

—B.M.

Cassavetes, John (1929–1989)

John Cassavetes's reputation as a director has spanned the spectrum from vilification to glorification, depending upon the willingness of the viewer to learn the language Cassavetes is speaking. His work has been labeled clumsy, poorly and sloppily edited, suffering from bad acting and weakness of plot, as well as bad lighting and atrocious sound. These very same characteristics, however, have been applauded by others as indicators of innovative genius. He was nominated for Oscars as a director, writer, and actor.

John Cassavetes was born December 9, 1929, in New York City. He studied at the Actor's Studio and undoubtedly brought to his directing some of the lessons learned from being trained as a "method" actor. His television acting career started in the early 1950s on well-respected shows such as *Omnibus, Playhouse 90, Studio One,* and *Kraft Theatre.* Beginning in 1953 he appeared in the feature films *Taxi, The Night Holds Terror, Crime in the Streets, Saddle the Wind,* and *Edge of the City.* He made his directorial debut with *Shadows* in 1959, which won five awards at the Venice Film Festival and the Jean George Oriol Award (the French equivalent of the Pulitzer Prize). The success of this film led to his being offered work on two studio films, *Too Late Blues,* starring Bobby Darin and Stella Stevens, and *A Child Is Waiting,* starring Gena Rowlands, Burt Lancaster, and Judy Garland. The ultimate disagreements and arguments over editing of the second film led producer STANLEY KRAMER (whom Cassavetes expert Ray Carney refers to as one of the most powerful men on the West Coast at that time) to label Cassavetes "difficult" and resulted in his virtual blacklisting in Hollywood for nearly a decade.

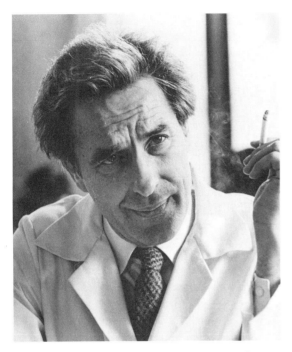

John Cassavetes starring in *Whose Life Is It, Anyway?* (Metro-Goldwyn-Mayer Film Co.)

Cassavetes spent his time in exile furiously writing several scripts for stage plays. One of those scripts was converted into a screenplay for *Faces,* in part reflecting Cassavetes's response to the "casual brutality" of West Coast/Los Angeles shallowness, hypocrisy, and deal making. *Faces* began filming on New Year's Day of 1965, shooting around the cast and crew's "real" jobs, continuing on weekends and evenings until June of that year. The film was shot with primitive equipment (16 mm) and little money. He asked his actors to work for deferred salaries. The principle shooting locations were Cassavetes's own residence and that of his mother-in-law, and the editing and sound mixing was done in the Cassavetes garage. It took three years and five acting jobs by Cassavetes to scrape together the money to complete work for the 1968 debut of what Carney calls "one of the supreme works of genius in all of American film."

Husbands, filmed in 1969 and released in 1970, and *Minnie and Moskowitz,* filmed and released in 1971, followed. *A Woman Under the Influence,* filmed in 1972 and released in 1974, found director Cassavetes, wife and star Gena Rowlands, friends, and other cast members traveling coast to coast to promote and book the film themselves. His next film, *The Killing of a Chinese Bookie,* was filmed and released in 1976 and rereleased in 1978 in a completely reedited print. *Opening Night,* filmed in 1977 and released in 1978, was withdrawn and rereleased in 1991. *Gloria* was filmed and released 1980. His last film, *Love Streams,* was filmed in 1983 and released in 1984. His name appears on *Big Trouble,* but since he was neither the first director nor the editor, he has disavowed this work as his. His son, Nick Cassavetes, shared direction credit with him on *She's So Lovely,* but John Cassavetes's only contribution was the screenplay.

Cassavetes's philosophy of filmmaking was stubbornly individual, and his unwillingness to make things easy for critics and viewers hurt his commercial prospects. His harshest critics said his films went nowhere and took a long time doing it. Narrative and storytelling, however, cannot be said to be the true goals of a Cassavetes film. He felt that plot was confining to his characters. "Don't worry about the words," he would tell his players, "if you get the character right, the plot will take care of itself." He believed in shooting in sequence to help the actors stay in touch with the emotional development of their character. In order to avoid disrupting the flow of the shoot, he relied heavily on medium-distance camera setups and eschewed complicated lighting schemes. As his biographer has stated, "For him, direction was not about control, but responsiveness." Cassavetes felt he learned about these characters from his actors, and said he tackled some of the projects he did to learn more about them. For example, his feelings changed about the characters in *Husbands* from contempt to pity after gaining a deeper understanding of them by making the film. Cassavetes wanted his audience to participate in this act of discovery as well. He wanted to keep the process open and moving. Repeated viewing of his films only enriches the perceptions, since there is no one "right" way of seeing them. He kept his characters liquid and flowing. For example, as Carney described Mabel's costuming in *A Woman Under the Influence.*

> It is significant that in the rare scenes in which props or costumes do figure prominently as conveyors of meaning in *A Woman Under the Influence*—as Mabel's wacky, mismatched clothing does in the school-bus scene—it is not sociologically possible to stereotype her, but to indicate how she eludes categorization. Far from defining her as a representative of a group, the weirdness of her appearance suggest energies that defy economic, ethnic, religious, or ideological categories of understanding. . . . Mabel creates her own identity; it is not created for her by her clothing or ethnic background. If we want to understand her, we must look at her performance, not the furniture of her life.

Actor Peter Falk, who frequently appeared in his films, labeled Cassavetes a man obsessed with making films. His relentless pursuit of getting the shots he was after resulted in his shooting as much as a million feet of film per picture, with retakes running from 10 to 30 or more. He wanted to keep his films fluid and uncongealed, and felt that abstract concepts were a dead end. Any preplanned schema was considered cliché. His films had an improvised feel that he worked hard to achieve, although after *Shadows,* all his films were fully scripted. He has been quoted as saying the *process* was what was important to him, and that after the films were complete, he had little interest in them. The process could take years, however, and Cassavetes sometimes confounded even his supporters. After *Shadows* had won awards, he rewrote, reshot, and reedited much of it.

Cassavetes used film as other artists used clay or paint, or as jazz musicians explore a piece of music: to investigate, analyze, and discover a subject. His was not an art of didacticism in the normal Hollywood sense, and this is what confused his critics and audiences. He wanted to explore the "realness" of language, human emotion, and interaction. He was interested in the bumpiness and raw edges that other filmmakers tried to eliminate from their work. Cassavetes's habit of reshooting and reediting was intended precisely to capture the unguarded moment of body language, the flickering of emotion across a face, or the stumbling, stammering cadence of real language.

He was interested in exploring relationships and the nature of love, but he kept his characters moving in venues that ran the gamut from screwball comedy (*Minnie and Moskowitz*) to film noir (*Killing of a Chinese Bookie*) to tragedy (*A Woman Under the Influence*) to playing with the illusion of reality via a play within a play (*Opening Night*). Even with this diverse body of work to pick through, however, a primary theme emerges: people's inability to express themselves. Characters are inclined to either give too much of themselves away and be defined by the people around them, or they are so uncomfortable in their own skin that they create an artificial persona they can hide behind. The former is best illustrated by Mabel Longhetti in *A Woman Under the Influence.* This character is vulnerable, in pain, and searching for her identity. The other end of this spectrum is illustrated by Cosmo Vitelli, who veils himself in style over substance. This character first emerged as Ben in *Shadows* and repeatedly appears all the way through Cassavetes's work, finally becoming Robert in *Love Streams.* We see people who are disappearing by either turning themselves over to others, or hiding behind illusion and affectation and getting lost behind all the smoke and mirrors.

If one compares film to a mirror reflecting life, Cassavetes would throw that mirror to the ground, retrieve the shards, and glue them together with the sharp edges not quite fitting together. The danger of getting cut and the resulting pain would also be a part of that mosaic. Cassavetes felt that we as a culture were abstracted from reality to such a degree that we were no longer in touch with ways of expressing ourselves. He devoted his life to finding a way through that barrier.

John Cassavetes died on February 3, 1989, from complications of cirrhosis of the liver.

References Carney, R., *The Films of John Cassavetes* (Cambridge, U.K.: Cambridge University Press, 1994); Carney, R., *John Cassavetes: The Adventure of Insecurity* (Boston: Boston University Press, 2000).

—G.M.

Castle, William (1914–1977)   Horror schlockmeister and innovative promoter William Castle was born in New York City on April 24, 1914, as William Schloss, Jr. His surname is German for "Castle." After his parents died, he went to live with his sister. At the age of 13 he visited Bela Lugosi backstage during a performance of *Dracula* and joined his company two years later as assistant stage manager when the production toured America. After working as an actor, dramatist, and producer, he went to Hollywood as an actor in 1937.

He gained a six-month contract at Columbia working as dialogue director, production assistant, editor, and extra before coming to the attention of George Stevens who employed him as dialogue director on *Penny Serenade* (1941). His first director credit was on the Boston Blackie programmer *The Chance of a Lifetime.* After directing further routine assignments, he elicited a strong performance from Robert Mitchum in *When Strangers Marry* (1944), a film influenced by Val Lewton's RKO thrillers. Despite working on many routine assignments, Castle's *Crime Doctor's Man Hunt* (1946), scripted by Leigh Brackett, anticipates certain features of ALFRED HITCHCOCK's *Vertigo* and *Psycho.* Castle also worked as associate producer on

Orson Welles's *The Lady from Shanghai* (1948) before returning to assembly-line directing.

Although Castle worked with many key talents in Hollywood, his abilities never matched those of his peers. However, he immediately saw that his opportunity for fame lay in the self-promotion techniques of directors such as Hitchcock and the showmanship techniques peculiar to Hollywood. As Castle commented, although he was often denigrated as "the poor man's Hitchcock," his real mentor was an earlier entertainment figure: "I have modeled my career on Barnum rather than Hitchcock." Graham Greene's dismissal of Hitchcock as a director relying on gimmicks rather than talent is more relevant to Castle in this regard. His many films have little justification other than for their self-conscious display of gimmicks rather than cinematic achievement.

Castle first recognized this with *Macabre* (1958), the first of a series of horror films he produced and directed in the next six years. Castle distracted audience attention away from plot deficiencies and poor acting by promotional techniques designed to scare and challenge them. These devices were often more effective than the actual films. Audiences attending *Macabre* were given insurance policies awarding their beneficiaries $1,000 if they died of fright. *House on Haunted Hill* (1959) indulged in classic horror film gimmicks such as thunderstorms and disembodied heads as well as a skeleton that floated over the audience in some theaters. *The Tingler* (1959) scared audiences by placing vibrating motors under every 10th seat. These last two films gained enormously from Vincent Price's menacing performances, which led to his enduring identification with the horror genre when ROGER CORMAN put him under contract. Another film, *13 Ghosts* (1960), offered audiences the choice of two different color strips on cellophane "ghost viewers," depending on their belief or disbelief in the supernatural. Castle's *Homicidal* (1961), a film paralleling *Psycho* (1960), is a cult favorite today and probably his finest effort.

Despite his reliance on gimmickry, Castle could also direct some accomplished generic works such as *Strait-Jacket* (1964). Although influenced by Robert Aldrich's *What Ever Happened to Baby Jane?* (1962), the film did contain a good performance by Joan Crawford. However, his reunion of two Hollywood veterans, Robert Taylor and Barbara Stanwyck, in *The Night Walker* (1966) proved disappointing. Castle acquired the rights to Ira Levin's *Rosemary's Baby* when the novel was still in galley form and became producer on Polanski's film version. After making some cameo appearances in films such as *Day of the Locust* and *Shampoo* (both 1975), he produced and coscripted *Bug* (1975) before dying of a heart attack while preparing *2000 Lakeview Drive.*

References Castle, William, *Step Right Up! I'm Gonna Scare the Pants Off America* (New York: Putnam, 1976); Fischer, Dennis, *Horror Film Directors* (Jefferson, N.C.: McFarland, 1991).

—T.W.

Cavalcanti, Alberto (1897–1982) Brazilian-born

Alberto de Almeida Cavalcanti is best remembered today for his documentaries and feature films at the British GPO and Ealing Studios in the 1930s and 1940s and for his tireless efforts to create a Brazilian national cinema in the 1950s. He was born on February 6, 1897, in Rio de Janeiro. Always the international citizen, he studied law and architecture in Switzerland and then moved to Paris in the early 1920s, where be became involved in the artistic avant-garde as an assistant to Marcel L'Herbier. His first documentary essays included *Only the Hours* (*Rien que les heures* [1926]), a "city symphony" that inaugurated a cycle of successors by Walter Ruttmann (*Berlin: Symphony of a Great City*) and Dziga Vertov (*Man With a Movie Camera*).

At the behest of JOHN GRIERSON, Cavalcanti came to Britain's General Post Office, the GPO (later the Crown Film Unit), in 1934. The mission of this government-sponsored film unit, as described by Sir Stephen Tallents, was nothing less than the projection and promotion of English life and institutions to the rest of the world. More specifically, Cavalcanti's expertise in sound recording and editing was exploited as an important part of the GPO product. Thus, his sophisticated sound collages informed three classic GPO films that brought the poetic documentary to its apex: *Song of Ceylon* (1934), *Coal Face* (1935), and *Night Mail* (1936). For the first, directed by Basil Wright, he devised a sound text that supported and counterpointed the scenes of island life with the commercial exploitation of the local industries. *Coal Face* blended the verse of W. H. Auden with the music of Benjamin Britten to indict the grueling, dangerous conditions in the lives of miners. For *Night Mail,* directed by Harry Watt, he again teamed up with Wright, Auden, and Britten to construct a brilliant, rhythmically intense soundtrack that informed a simple story of the night journey of the mail train from London to Edinburgh. Historian Roy Armes declares that *Night Mail* is the culmination of the GPO period, "a collaborative effort which balances Grierson's concern with public information, Watt's naturalistic direction and the more lyrical and experimental approaches of Cavalcanti and Wright."

Cavalcanti turned to feature film directing in 1940 when producer Michael Balcon invited him to join his team of filmmakers at Ealing Studios, a closely knit ensemble of artists—directors Charles Crichton, Alexander Mackendrick, Robert Hamer, Charles Frend, Henry Cornelius, among others—not unlike the group at the GPO. His debut was *Went the Day Well?* (1942), a contemporary fantasy that presumed that despite Hitler's defeat, insurgents were now launching a fifth-column invasion of England. Other features included two films with theatrical and music-hall backgrounds, the Dickensian *Nicholas Nickleby* (1946) and the British mid-19th-century period piece *Champagne Charlie* (1944); and two distinguished contributions to the classic 1946

British ghost-story anthology film, *Dead of Night* (the "Christmas Party" and "Ventriloquist's Dummy" sequences).

He returned to Brazil in 1949 determined to help found the Brazilian Film Institute and create a national cinema identity. "In Brazil I tried to create a conscience of the nationality of films," he recalled. "Films would have not only local colour but a real national, social colour." His leadership of the new Vera Cruz studio in São Paulo was short-lived, however, when he failed to create a studio modeled on Hollywood lines. He moved on to head another São Paulo production company, Kino Filmes, and assumed the chair of the National Cinema Commission, which was developing a plan for an institutionalized national cinema. Before Kino Filmes folded in 1954, Cavalcanti directed two films, *O Canto do Mar* (The song of the sea) and *Mulher de Verdade* (A real woman). The former recounted the tragic consequences besetting a Brazilian family during an epic journey from a drought-stricken village to the seacoast. Cavalcanti's experience in documentary informed this saga with a neorealist quality.

Until the late 1960s he worked in British and French television and taught film studies at UCLA. His book *Film and Reality,* an anthology-history of the documentary film, was published in 1942. He died in Paris on August 23, 1982. "In summary," writes Jack C. Ellis, "it can be said that Cavalcanti seemed always to be the artist, personal creator and, especially, consummate technician. He applied himself to the basic modes of film art—narrative fiction, avant-garde, and documentary—in a full range of capacities—set designer, sound recordist, producer, and director."

Other Films *Half-Way to Heaven* (*À mi-chemin du ciel* [1929]); *Sarah and Son* (*Toute sa vie* [1930]); *Message from Geneva* (1936); *We Live in Two Worlds* (1937); *Four Barriers* (1938); *Watertight* (1943); *The First Gentleman* (1948); *For Them that Trespass* (1949); *Simon the One-Eyed* (*Simão o caolho* [1952]); *The First Night* (*La Prima notte* [1958]); *Thus Spake Theodor Herzl* (1967).

References Barnard, Timothy, and Peter Rist, eds., *South American Cinema: A Critical Filmography, 1915–1994* (Austin: University of Texas Press, 1998); Barr, Charles, *Ealing Studios* (Woodstock, N.Y.: Overlook Press, 1997); Ellis, Jack C., *The Documentary Idea* (Englewood Cliffs, N.J.: Prentice-Hall, 1989).

—J.C.T.

Chabrol, Claude (1930–) The director of over 50 feature films was born June 24, 1930, in Paris, France. The son of a pharmacist, he himself studied pharmacy before turning his energies to the arts. After completing his studies at the University of Paris and the Politiques Ecole Libre des Sciences he worked as a press agent for Fox Studios in Paris. He also wrote film criticism for *Cahiers du cinéma* where, along with FRANÇOIS TRUFFAUT and ERIC ROHMER, he defended film as an art form equal to literature. He helped promote the auteur theory that a film should be marked by the artistry of its "author" or director. He contributed two articles in the 1954 issue of the *Cahiers* devoted to the films of ALFRED HITCHCOCK and collaborated with Rohmer on the 1957 book *Hitchcock*. He played bit parts in some of his own films and those of his contemporaries. He worked as technical adviser on JEAN-LUC GODARD's *À Bout de souffle/Breathless* (1959).

Like several of the *Cahiers* critics, Chabrol soon moved into directing and began a prolific career that was initially supported by government funding for low-budget films. With the inheritance of his first wife Agnes Goule, Chabrol was able to finance his first film. Following the success of his second film he established his own production company that produced films by Rivette, Rohmer, and de Broca. Chabrol and the other directors in his circle would come to be known as the *nouvelle vague* in French cinema. They favored a neorealist style that promoted location shooting, use of available light, and panning/tracking shots.

Chabrol, working as both screenwriter and director, employed open-ended plots and nontraditional narrative. His first feature was *Le Beau Serge* (*Bitter Reunion*) of 1958, followed by *Les Cousins* (*The Cousins* [1959]). *Les Bonnes femmes* (1960), although not well received by audiences and critics at its debut, is now counted among the major films of the French New Wave. This story of four Parisian shop girls is told with the same neutral irony of his earlier films. In the early 1960s he directed *Les Godelureaux* (1960), *L'Oeil du Malin* (*The Third Lover* [1962]), *Ophélia* (1962), and *Landru* (*Bluebeard* [1963]). The latter, a Hitchcock homage, stars Charles Denner in the title role of a mass-murderer.

The mid-1960s period of his career is marked by commercial spy thrillers. Themes such as murder, obsession, and bourgeois criminality appear in his films of the late 1960s, of which *La Femme infidèle* (*Unfaithful Wife* [1968]), *Le Boucher* (*The Butcher* [1969]), and *Les Biches* (*The Does/Girlfriends/Bad Girls* [1968]) were highlights. The latter, starring his second wife Stéphane Audran (Chabrol is currently married to his third wife, Aurore Pajot), was written in collaboration with Paul Gégauff who also worked with Chabrol on a number of projects including *Les Bonnes femmes*. Chabrol writes or collaborates on the writing of most of the scripts for his films.

Marriage and infidelity are subjects that Chabrol regularly addressed in his films including those of the 1970s: *Juste avant la nuit* (*Just Before Nightfall* [1971]), *Le Noces rouge* (*Wedding in Blood* [1973]), *Folies bourgeoises* (*The Twist* [1976]). There is a triad of recurring character names—Hélène, Charles, and Paul—that appear in at least six of Chabrol's films about relationships and infidelity. He employed a similar triad of actors, including Audran, Michel Bouquet, and Jean Yanne.

Chabrol made a number of suspense films in the 1980s: *Poulet au vinaigre* (*Coq au Vin* [1984]), *Inspector Lavardin* (1986), *Masques* (1987). Chabrol ignores conventional thriller plots in favor of emphasizing what he has described as the confrontation between character and story. It is often psychological inquiry that motivates his direction and many of his films are based on factual events, including *Violette Noziere* (1978), which was Chabrol's first film to star Isabelle Huppert as a daughter who poisons her parents. The duo would go on to make *Une affaire des femmes* (*The Story of Women* [1988]), which won the New York Film Critics Circle Award for best foreign film. The grim account of an abortionist in Vichy France, who becomes the last woman to be executed by guillotine, contains an outstanding performance by Huppert as the not entirely sympathetic protagonist. The collaboration continued with *Madame Bovary* (1991), *La Cérémonie* (*A Judgment in Stone* [1995]), *Rien ne va plus* (*The Swindle* [1997]), and *Merci pour le chocolat* (*Nightcap* [2000]).

Chabrol is now often described as a "woman's director" for his later films that focus on a female perspective yet incorporate the recurring themes of class conflict and crime. While his prolific output is often criticized as being of uneven quality, Chabrol's films continually offer a range of ideas, narrative structures, and styles that none of the other New Wave directors equalled.

Other Films *A Double Tour* (*Web of Passion* [1959]); *Le Tigre aime le chair fraîche* (*The Tiger Likes Fresh Blood* [1964]); *Marie-Chantal contre le Docteur Kha* (1965); *La Ligne de demarcation* (*Line of Demarcation* [1966]); *La Rupture* (*The Breakup* [1970]); *Que la bête meure* (*This Man Must Die* [1970]); *La Décade prodigieuse* (*Ten Days' Wonder* [1972]); *Une Partie de plaisir* (*Pleasure Party* [1975]); *The Proud Ones* (1980); *Les Liens de sang* (*Blood Relative* [1983]); *Betty* (1993); *L'Oeil de Vichy* (*The Eye of Vichy* [1993]); *L'Enfer* (*Hell* [1994]); *Au coeur du mensonge* (*Color of Lies* [1999]).

References Austin, Guy, *Claude Chabrol* (New York: St. Martins, 1999); Blanchet, Christian, *Claude Chabrol* (Paris: Rivages, 1989); Magny, Joël, *Claude Chabrol* (Paris: Cahiers du cinéma, 1987); Wood, Robin, et al., *Claude Chabrol* (New York: Praeger, 1970).

—J.A.D.

Chaplin, Charles (1889–1977)   Charles Chaplin was born in London on April 16, 1889. Both of his parents were moderately successful music hall entertainers. When he was still a youngster, his father died of alcoholism, and his mother retired from the stage because of poor physical health and mental illness. Consequently, Chaplin was forced to earn his living in vaudeville before he reached his teens. Mack Sennett, the creator of the Keystone comedies, saw Chaplin perform while the comedian was touring the United States with Fred Karno's vaudeville company and invited Chaplin to go into pictures in 1913. Chaplin left the stage for a career in movies the following year.

Chaplin created the character of Charlie the Tramp and made his first short comedies shortly

Charlie Chaplin (Author's collection)

after joining Sennett. He explained that the Tramp was his conception of the average man. The Tramp is everyman, with whom we can all identify: the well-meaning but inept little fellow whose reach forever exceeds his grasp, but who is always ready to pick himself up, dust himself off, and continue down the road of life, twirling his cane with disarming bravado. Chaplin left Sennett's Keystone studio in 1915 after a year, and transferred first to Essanay, and then to Mutual in 1916–17. With each new contract Chaplin negotiated at each new studio, he received still greater artistic independence. He was now able to make his short films with more care and to explore further the possibilities of integrating a serious dimension into his comedy material. The Tramp character began to be more clearly defined as the pathetic outsider, longing for an acceptance from others that he will never achieve. Perhaps the greatest of his Mutual shorts is *The Immigrant* (1917), which dealt with a subject close to Chaplin's heart, since he had come to America himself as an immigrant in 1913. Moreover, because the immigrant is perhaps the quintessential example of a lonely outsider striving for acceptance in an alien milieu, the role fit the personality of Charlie the Tramp perfectly. When Chaplin left Mutual for First National in 1918, he took yet another step toward total artistic control of his films. Chaplin now became his own producer, as well as writer, director, and star. Moreover, most of the First National comedies were longer than the one- and two-reelers that he had made for other studios, since they averaged three reels apiece; as such, they were to become the prototypes of his later features.

The Kid (1921), running to six reels, was Chaplin's first feature. Prior to his First National films, Chaplin portrayed the Tramp as a rambunctious ragamuffin who felt that he had to cheat to survive in a cold and brutal world. In the First National films, particularly *The Kid,* Charlie emerges as a gentler kind of person, one who receives the kicks that life administers to him with more resignation and less of a will for retaliation than he had exhibited in his earlier comedies. In *The Kid* the Tramp finds an abandoned child (Jackie Coogan) and cares for him until his mother is discovered. The story takes place in an authentically grimy slum setting, reminiscent of the circumstances in which Chaplin himself grew up. In fact, more than any film that Chaplin ever made, *The Kid* is deeply rooted in Chaplin's wretched childhood.

The weaving together of comic and serious elements into a seamless fabric, foreshadowed in earlier films such as *The Immigrant* and *The Kid*, was for the first time fully accomplished in *The Gold Rush* (1925), which he made for United Artists, a production company that he formed in partnership with DAVID WARK GRIFFITH, Douglas Fairbanks, and Mary Pickford, to distribute the feature films each of them made. *The Gold Rush* has scenes that are almost straight drama, in which Chaplin becomes more of an actor and less of a clown, and hence the film is appropriately subtitled *A Dramatic Comedy*. In *The Gold Rush* Charlie the Tramp is called the Lone Prospector, again emphasizing his status as an outsider. He hopes to gain society's acceptance by discovering gold in the Klondike. The ongoing theme in Chaplin's films clearly surfaces in *The Gold Rush*: man's struggle for survival in a tough world, as evidenced in the Lone Prospector's resourcefulness in coping with whatever obstacles life puts in his way. That struggle was never more concretely visualized than in the first appearance of the Tramp in the film: overloaded with gear and shambling along a snowy mountainside, blithely unaware that he is being pursued by a huge bear.

As Chaplin was preparing *City Lights* (1931), talking pictures took Hollywood by storm. Given the faulty sound quality of early talkies, Chaplin decided to make *City Lights* as a silent picture. The only concession that the picture made to the advent of sound was the addition of a musical score, which he composed himself. The film itself, in which the Tramp falls in love with a blind flower girl, combines comedy and drama after the manner of *The Gold Rush*. The film ends with the Tramp meeting the girl after her sight has been restored. While she was blind, Charlie had led her to believe that he was wealthy; and she is surprised to see him for the pathetic Tramp he really is. The final close-up of Charlie that ends the picture is one of the most poignant in cinema history. The Tramp's face reflects several conflicting emotions all at once: he is glad that she recognizes him, but ashamed that he is not the rich man she imagined him to be; he hopes that she will accept him but is afraid that she will not. On this note of uncertainty the movie ends.

The Great Dictator (1940) was his first sound picture to employ spoken dialogue. Made on the eve of World War II, it starred Chaplin in a dual role as a Jewish barber very much akin to the Tramp and as Adenoid Hynkel, the dictator of Tomania—an obvious parody of Adolf Hitler. *Monsieur Verdoux* (1947) had Chaplin playing the title role of a former bank clerk down on his luck who supports his wife and son by marrying and murdering a series of rich widows for their fortunes. When *Verdoux* first appeared, moviegoers were not prepared to see Chaplin in the role of the dapper murderer Verdoux; the Tramp had always wanted to be a lady killer, but this is literally what Verdoux has become. In essence, audiences were not equipped to appreciate black comedy, the genre that finds humor in situations usually reserved for serious treatment. *Verdoux* actually proved that Chaplin was ahead of his time, for only in the wake of later black comedies like Kubrick's *Dr. Strangelove* could audiences appreciate in retrospect the artistry of *Verdoux*. Chaplin's next film was *Limelight* (1952), in which he played Calvero, a has-been music hall performer whose day has long passed.

When Chaplin set sail for Europe in September 1952 for the European premieres of *Limelight*, he was informed in mid-ocean by cable from the U.S. attorney general that he would not be permitted to reenter the country without facing an investigation into his personal character and political beliefs. Chaplin settled down in Switzerland. This incident occurred during the Cold War years that followed the Second World War, in which Senator Joseph McCarthy was conducting his anticommunist witch-hunt. Chaplin was accordingly accused of being a communist sympathizer because he had urged the United States to help Russia in warding off the Nazi invasion. He was further criticized for never becoming an American citizen, although, as he had often said, his patriotism "rests with the whole world, the pity of the whole world and the common people." Chaplin's last film was *A Countess from Hong Kong* (1967), which he wrote, directed, and scored, but in which he did not star.

Chaplin's achievements did not go unrewarded during his lifetime. When the first Academy Awards were presented in 1928, a special award went to Charles Chaplin for "his genius and versatility in writing, acting, directing and producing his films." At the 1972 award ceremonies Chaplin was on hand to be honored again, this time for "the incalculable effect he has had in making motion pictures the art form of this century." In addition, he was knighted in 1975, in recognition of his supreme importance in shaping the motion picture medium as an art form. In the course of *Limelight,* Calvero the clown muses that entertainers are "amateurs— that's all any of us are—amateurs. We don't live long enough to be anything else." Chaplin lived long enough.

Other Films *A Woman of Paris* (1925); *The Circus* (1928); *Modern Times* (1936).

References Chaplin, Charles, *My Autobiography* (New York: Penguin, 1992); Phillips, Gene D., *Major Film Directors of the American and British Cinema* (Cranbury, N.J.: Associated University Presses, 1999).

—G.D.P.

Chen, Joan (1961–) Born on April 26, 1961, in Shanghai, China, Joan Chen majored in English at the Shanghai Foreign Language Institute and achieved fame in China as an actress who had been selected by Jiang Qing, Mao's ruthless wife, to be a model young actress before eventually coming to the United States, where she found a niche on the odd David Lynch television series *Twin Peaks* (1990–91). Her acting assignments included roles in films by major directors, such as WAYNE WANG in *Dim Sum: A Little Bit of Heart* (1984), BERNARDO BERTOLUCCI in *The Last Emperor* (1987), and OLIVER STONE in *Heaven & Earth* (1993). Her debut film as director was made in China in 1999, the award-winning *Xiu Xiu the Sent-Down Girl* (released in Asia under the title *Tian Yu* (Heavenly pond) about a young girl wrenched from her family and "sent down" to the countryside to an isolated outpost on the Tibetan frontier, working with an older man who attempts, unsuccessfully, to protect her from being molested by bureaucrats from the nearest collective farm. The girl is so homesick and miserable that she will do anything to escape her fate and return to her family, even at the expense of disgracing her family by prostituting herself.

According to Asian critic Wena Poon, the bureaucrats, who deported large numbers of such children to the countryside, left them stranded after the Cultural Revolution changed course, and forgot about them, "making them easy prey" for corrupt, "petty village officials" who "harbored little cultural or social empathy for them." The film was banned in China, and Chen had to pay a substantial fine for shooting it on the Tibetan border without government permission. Both Chen and her screenwriter, who wrote the novel upon which *Xiu Xiu* was based, had faced the danger of being "sent down" in Mao's China. Chen escaped this fate by being selected for the acting program in the Shanghai Film Studio in 1975. Chen's first Hollywood feature as director, *Autumn in New York* (2000), was less successful, a three-handkerchief

Joan Chen (Francois Lehr/SIPA Press)

"weepie" starring Richard Gere and Winona Ryder that opened to mixed reviews; but Chen was still praised for her direction, even though she did not have total control of this project, as she had with her first feature, *Xiu Xiu the Sent-Down Girl*, the film upon which her reputation rests and one that showed unusual promise and talent.

References Brady, James, "In Step With Joan Chen," *Parade Magazine*, October 8, 2000, p. 16; Poon, Wena, "Xiu Xiu: The Sent Down Girl," *Film Quarterly* 53, no. 3 (Spring 2000): 49–53.

—J.M.W.

Chen Kaige (1952–   ) Unlike his friend and rival Zhang Yimou, who was born into remote obscurity and under the shadow of his father's political past, Chen Kaige was born in Beijing on August 12, 1952, the son of Chen Huai'ai, a prominent filmmaker and Communist Party member. In 1968, however, Chen's life of privilege

was cut short by the whims of Mao's Great Proletarian Cultural Revolution, and he was sent to work in the countryside. There, it was presumed, this city youth would learn from his rural comrades as he helped them clear the jungle for farm use. After three years of such labor Chen enlisted in the People's Liberation Army. In 1975, after leaving the army, Chen finally returned to Beijing. Three years later, when the Beijing Film Academy reopened its doors after 10 years of Cultural Revolution-mandated silence, Chen was among its first class of new applicants. Though the school had existed almost from the time of the Communist victory in 1949, Chen and his classmates (including such figures as Zhang, TIAN ZHUANGZHUANG, and Hu Mei) were only the fifth class of students to attend. This was due to the fact that school policy admitted only one class of students every four years (as well as to the fact that it had been closed for 10 years). Upon their 1982 graduation Chen and his colleagues were dubbed the "Fifth Generation"—a name that would soon be known throughout the international film industry.

Chen spent his initial post graduation years working in television before he started work on his first theatrical feature, 1984's *Yellow Earth (Huang tudi)*. The film is about a young communist soldier who journeys to China's remote Yellow Earth region during the Revolution to collect folk songs. There he meets and stays with a farmer whose daughter's arranged marriage is sure to come. The young woman is inspired by the soldier and his cause and, at the end, sets off to join the communists in Yan'an, only to drown in a river. Though the ending is bleak, the film caused a sensation when it played the 1985 Hong Kong Film Festival, thus heralding the arrival of a new Chinese cinema. Much of the acclaim centered on the film's look, which draws on classical Chinese traditions in landscape painting. At home, however, the film was greeted with indifference and little box office. Chen's second film, *The Big Parade (Da yuebing*

[1986]), has often been compared (sometimes not favorably) to Stanley Kubrick's *Full Metal Jacket* (1986). *The Big Parade* is about a unit of PLA soldiers preparing for the National Day parade. Like *Yellow Earth, The Big Parade* was shot by Chen's classmate, Zhang Yimou. It marked the last time Zhang would serve as cinematographer on someone else's movie. Zhang soon made his directorial debut, *Red Sorghum* (*Hong gaoliang* [1987]), which achieved the kind of popular success in China that had so far eluded Chen, thus bringing a note of rivalry to a once-strong friendship. The same year, Chen appeared in a small role in Bernardo Bertolucci's *The Last Emperor.* Also in 1987 Chen made *The King of Children (Haizi wang),* the last film he would make in China for four years. The film is about a dedicated teacher who is sent to a poor school in Yunnan Province. He connects with his students but the local officials disapprove of his methods and he is removed.

Again, Chen's film was more popular abroad than at home, and in 1988 he moved to New York City to take up a position as a visiting fellow at New York University. During his stay in America Zhang made a short film, directed a music video for Duran Duran, and watched the 1989 Tiananmen Square massacre unfold on television. Chen returned to China two years later to make *Life on a String* (*Bian zou bian chang* [1991]), the story of a blind musician and his students. In China, again, the film was a failure. Perhaps because of the accumulation of so many failures, Chen decided to try something different with his next film, 1992's *Farewell My Concubine* (*Ba wang bie ji*). For the film, which tells the story of a love triangle between two Beijing Opera performers and a prostitute, Chen borrowed Zhang Yimou's leading lady, Gong Li, as well as Zhang's fondness for lavish historical epics. This nearly three-hour epic raised the ire of China's government and was banned (albeit only temporarily). Overseas, however, it proved to be something of an art house smash, garnering rave reviews and numerous prizes, includ-

ing the Cannes Film Festival's coveted Palme d'Or (which it shared with Jane Campion's *The Piano*). To some Chinese critics, on the other hand, the film was to be criticized for presenting the West with a kind of idealized, pretty-picture view of China and the Chinese. Chen again worked with Gong Li on his 1996 film *Temptress Moon (Feng yue)*. The film deals with the opium-induced destruction of a Republic-era family. This time, however, even many of Chen's Western supporters were left cold by the epically scaled but glacially paced progress of the film.

Chen's next film, *The Emperor and the Assassin* (*Jing ke ci qin wang* [1999]), was an epic in the Kurosawa mold, depicting the ruthless rise of the first emperor of Qin, the man who united the Seven Kingdoms and gave birth to what would someday be called "China." Gong appears in this film as well, as the emperor's lover who betrays him when he attacks her home kingdom. With this film Beijing seemed to forgive Chen his earlier transgressions. The government even granted the producers permission to hold the world-premiere screening in the Great Hall of the People. Since the completion of *The Emperor and the Assassin,* there have been rumors that Chen would soon make his English-language (in which he is fluent) debut with a film entitled *Killing Me Softly.* If true, it would make Chen the first of China's Fifth Generation to try to find popular success in the West.

References Tam, Kwok-kan, and Wimal Dissanayake, *New Chinese Cinema* (Hong Kong: Oxford University Press, 1998); Silbergeld, Jerome, *China into Film* (London: Reaktion Books, 1999); Jiangying, Zha, *China Pop* (New York: New Press, 1995).

—F.H.

Clair, René (1898–1981)

Although indisputably among France's greatest film masters, René Clair shared the curious fate of other great directors like DAVID WARK GRIFFITH, ABEL GANCE, and ORSON GEORGE WELLES, to name just a few, whose greatest successes came early, overshadowing the work of late maturity. He was born René Chomette in Paris on November 11, 1898, to prosperous parents in the grocery store business. After completing his education at the Lycée Montaigne and the Lycée Louis-le-Grand, he served in the Ambulance Corps during World War I. In 1920 under the name René Clair he began acting at the Gaumont Studios. This was a time when the young, ever-restless Clair was in turmoil, smoking opium and secluding himself for a while in a Dominican cloister.

Two years later he directed his first film, *The Crazy Ray,* a fantasy about an invention that suspends all motion. During the shooting he was so poor that he lived in a garret and cut the film with scissors and straight pins. Sometimes he didn't even have enough money to buy tickets to his main location site, the Eiffel Tower. Contemptuous of outworn plot formulas, he chose as his aesthetic model the slapstick of Mack Sennett. "[Sennett] created fantasy-poems in which clowns, bathing beauties, a car, a little dog, a bottle of milk, the sky, the sea, and a firecracker are the interchangeable elements whose every combination creates laughter and astonishment," noted Clair. "Sennett's rapid and fresh lyricism reveals to us a light world in which the law of gravity seems to be replaced by the joy of movement." These precepts are more dazzlingly apparent in the numerous Dadaist visual and editing effects of his next film, a freewheeling experimental short called *Entr'acte.* This landmark in the history of French avant-garde cinema was originally intended as an "intermission" feature for the Francis Picabia–Eric Satie ballet, *Relache.* The first half of the film consists of seemingly disconnected shots in keeping with the anarchic Dadaist spirit. The second takes the viewer to a funeral ceremony led by a camel-driven hearse. A wild chase ensues. Everywhere are bizarre image juxtapositions—a chessboard that contains the Place de la Concorde, an egg that contains a pigeon, a paper boat floating freely over the rooftops, a ballet

dancer with the legs of a girl and the face of a bearded man. Finally, a magician springs out of a coffin and, with a wave of his wand, vanishes himself (and, presumably, the theater audience). Less overtly experimental, but just as visually inventive was Clair's classic 1927 farce comedy, *The Italian Straw Hat,* adapted from a stage work by Labiche. But the best was yet to come.

Clair's finest hour came with the advent of synchronized sound. *Sous les toits de Paris* (Under the roofs of paris), *A nous la liberté* (roughly, We are free), and *Le Million* (The millionaire)—all scripted by Clair, designed by Lazare Meerson, and photographed by Georges Perinal—appeared in rapid succession from 1929 to 1932, and they took ample opportunity to exploit the potentials of the asynchronous union of image and sound. Clair had initially been dubious about the coming of sound. "We were being asked to change our tools and our language in a few months," he recalled in his autobiography, *Cinema Yesterday and Today.* "Hence our hesitation, trouble of mind, and regrets." Contrary to the standard practices of "canned drama" so prevalent at the time, Clair sought to manipulate sound and image independently of one another, creating a kind of counterpoint between the two (he even said that musicians would make better film editors than professional filmmakers). As historian Lucy Fischer has said of this trilogy of films, "The uses of sound had not yet been codified, and the works reflect an aural conception that is far more open and explorative than it would come to be in later years. . . . His explorations were all involved with subverting the illusion of realistic sound in order to liberate the medium and restore to it its poetic powers." *Le Million* is arguably his masterpiece. The whimsical story about a lottery winner and his pursuit of the elusive ticket employs all manner of visual-aural combinations—scenes played out silently with only musical accompaniment, voices declaiming words in rhythmic articulation, lip movements matched to the sounds of musical instruments, song renditions replacing dialogue, choral music that represents a character's internal thoughts, sounds and music that are nonspecific and disconnected from the specific circumstances of a scene, and the "punning" use of sounds, as when a chase for the jacket is accompanied by the sounds of a cheering crowd at a football game. Thus, as Fischer notes, "The film continually alternates between evoking operetta, musical comedy, ballet, and silent scored film."

In response to charges that his pictures lacked social relevance, Clair made *The Last Millionaire* in 1934, but it was such a flop that Clair went into a 14-year exile, traveling to England and America for six English-language features. *The Ghost Goes West* (1936), *I Married a Witch* (1943), and *And Then There Were None* (1945) all had their virtues, chief among them the signature Clair whimsy underscored by darker implications. His return to France and his subsequent postwar films rarely recapture this delicate blend, but their maturity and emotional depth deserve a second look. *Beauty and the Devil* (1950) is a Faustian allegory that contains a vision of atomic holocaust; *Beauties of the Night* (1952) blends eroticism with intimations of suicide; and *Gates of Paris* (1957) ends with a homicide. By the end of the 1950s Clair found himself under attack by New Wave filmmaker François Truffaut for his alleged emotionless, studio-bound artifice. He was regarded, notes biographer R. C. Dale, as "a marionette master whose strings were showing." His reputation never fully recovered from this onslaught, and his last films received only a lukewarm reception. He reserved his last years for directing for the theater and for his 1970 autobiographical commentary on his films, *Cinema Yesterday and Today*. Biographer R. C. Dale sums up his essential greatness: "His has been a career with little waste and excess to it, and is thus all the more substantial. Clair's technical contributions to the cinema are many, still in use today. But it is something else, an elusive quality of grace that animates his characters, and thus his films. . . ."

Other Films *Two Timid Souls* (1928); *July 4th, 1933* (1933); *Break the News* (1937); *The Flame of New Orleans* (1940); *It Happened Tomorrow* (1943); *The Grand Maneuvers* (1945); *Silence Is Golden* (1947); *The Gallant Festivities* (1965).

References Dale, R. C., *The Films of René Clair,* vol. 1, *Exposition and Analysis,* and vol. 2, *Documentation* (Metuchen, N.J.: Scarecrow Press, 1986); Fischer, Lucy, "René Clair, *Le Million,* and the Coming of Sound," *Cinema Journal* 16, no. 2 (spring 1977): 33–50; McGerr, Celia, *Rene Clair* (Boston: Twayne, 1980).

—J.C.T.

Clayton, Jack (1921–1995) Born on March 1, 1921, in Brighton, England, Jack Clayton originally trained as an ice skater before finding work with London Films at the age of 14. From 1935 to 1940, he gained experience as third assistant director, assistant director, and editor before entering the Royal Air Force. During his service, he worked with the RAF film unit and continued his practical education by working as cameraman, editor, and director, before eventually reaching the rank of the unit's commanding officer. In 1944, he directed the wartime documentary, *Naples Is a Battlefield,* which he also scripted and cophotographed in an uncredited capacity. Following demobilization, he worked with ALEXANDER KORDA as production manager on *An Ideal Husband* (1948). He also worked as associate producer with Romulus Films and gained credits in that capacity on British and American productions such as *The Queen of Spades* (1949), *Flesh and Blood* (1950), *Moulin Rouge* (1953), *Beat the Devil* (1954), and *I Am a Camera* (1955).

His first credit as director was on the critically acclaimed and prize-winning *The Bespoke Overcoat* (1956), which he also produced. Winning awards at the Venice Film Festival and from the Academy of Motion Picture Arts and Sciences, this medium-length feature was an adaptation of a short story by Gogol, which scenarist Wolf Mankowitz set in London's East End. It opened with a Jewish tailor played by David Kossoff as the only mourner at the funeral of his impoverished friend played by Alfie Bass who returns as a ghost to fulfill his dream of finally obtaining a bespoke overcoat. Clayton's first film as director revealed two key features of his later career: literary adaptation and the direction of outstanding performances from his actors. Shot in a British "film noir" cinematic style, this haunting tale would also foreshadow the director's later film, *The Innocents* (1961).

However, Clayton's next full-length feature film, *Room at the Top* (1958), brought his name to public attention with his adaptation of a best-selling novel by John Braine dealing with the perennial British obsessions of class and sexuality. Although linked with the then-fashionable "kitchen sink" school of British social cinema, *Room at the Top* had more in common with Clayton's frequent treatment of themes concerning thwarted desires and blocked creativity that would appear throughout his films.

The director clearly distanced himself from any association with the "angry young men" movement dominating British cinema at the time by filming Henry James's novella *The Turn of the Screw* in 1961, which he also produced. *The Innocents* featured Deborah Kerr as James's governess fearing that her two young charges, Miles and Flora, are victims of her predecessor and servant Peter Quint. Since film is a concrete medium, the visual style of the film cannot contain the novel's literary ambiguity concerning questions as to whether the governess is imaging certain events. The ghosts are certainly present. But the key element in the film involves Clayton's fascination with characters suffering from frustration, whether sexual or otherwise, endemic to the social system in which they exist. Superbly shot in CinemaScope with black and white photography by Freddie Francis, the film works within the contexts of both adaptation and creative authorship interpretation.

Clayton's fascination with the frustrated family relationships endemic to British culture appears also in his adaptation of Penelope Mortimer's *The Pumpkin Eater* (1964) and *Our Mother's House* (1967). These two films contain outstanding performances by Anne Bancroft and Dirk Bogarde, respectively. While the Bancroft character struggles with defining her motherhood in an alien world, the children of *Our Mother's House* confront a returned father figure (superbly played by Bogarde in an uncharacteristic role) who embodies a form of paternal reality that their childhood dreams of an ideal family attempt to deny. For Clayton, desires are often blocked or mistaken when confronted with an alienating world of social reality. This may explain his attempt to film *The Great Gatsby* (1974) in an overtly beautiful visual manner whose very artificiality expresses both the naive dreams of its title character and the very illusory nature of his quest to realize his American dream. Gatsby's American desire is really a deceptively beautiful tomb.

The critical and popular failure of *The Great Gatsby* led to Clayton's absence from the screen for nearly a decade. But he returned to direct *Something Wicked This Way Comes* (1983) from a screenplay by author Ray Bradbury. Although compromised by production problems, the film also treated Clayton's typical issue of the dangerous nature of thwarted desires, a theme also evident in his last film, *The Lonely Passion of Judith Hearne* (1987). With outstanding performances by Maggie Smith and Bob Hoskins, the film depicted a repressed Dublin of the 1950s whose victims are both Irish and American and suffering from the same problems affecting all other Clayton characters.

Reference Craston, George M. A., *Jack Clayton: A Guide to References and Resources.* (Boston: G. K. Hall, 1981).

—T.W.

Clouzot, Henri-Georges (1907–1977) Acclaimed for his postwar melodramas, Henri-Georges Clouzot was born in Niort, France, on November 20, 1907. He received his education at the École Navale in Brest and worked for a while as a reporter for *Paris-Midi*. He was offered a job in the film industry while he was interviewing Adolphe Osso in 1930, and between 1930 and 1934 he worked as an assistant to Carmine Gallone, Anatole Litvak, E. A. Dupont, and others. At this same time he contributed dialogue to several films, including: *Le Roi des palaces* (1932), *Caprice de princesse* (1933), and *Tout pour l'amour* (1933). In 1931 Clouzot coscripted and directed the short film, *Le Terreur des Batignolles.* From 1934 to 1938 Clouzot suffered from an extended bout of pleurisy and was confined to several sanitoriums. He returned to the film industry in 1938 and worked as a writer providing dialogue and lyrics to such films as *Le Revolte* (1938), *Le Duel* (1939), *Le Monde tremblera* (*La Revolte des vivants*), *Le Dernier des six* (1941), and *Les Inconnus dans la maison* (1941).

During the Occupation, Clouzot was able (because of the paucity of directors) to move from screenwriting to film directing. His premiere effort, *L'Assassin habite au 21* (The murderer lives at number 21) was a routine police drama. Clouzot's next film, *Le Corbeau* (*The Raven* [1943]), was a suspense thriller concerning poison pen letters being sent to numerous inhabitants of a small village. The film was produced by a German-owned company, Continentale. Although it was deemed "anti-French" at the time, and after the war Clouzot was briefly suspended from the film industry, it is now considered by many critics and historians as being more anti-German in its critique of small-town mores and people under the tyranny of hearsay and scandal.

Clouzot was barred from the film industry for two years by the "purification committee" for having made films during the Occupation that allegedly maligned the French character and demoralized the country. He resumed filmmaking in 1947 with *Quai des Orfèvres* (English title: *Jenny Lamour*) with Louis Jouvet. This film and his next, *Manon* (1948), evoked the film noir style and mood with their lowlife settings and atmosphere. During the fifties Clouzot was able to reach his widest audience and popularity with two films that are considered classic suspense thrillers: *Le Salaire de la peure* (*The Wages of Fear* [1952]) and *Les Diaboliques* (1954). *Le Salaire de la peure* was one of the first postwar French films to obtain wide distribution in English-speaking countries. It concerned the efforts of a group of down-and-out European expatriates in South America to deliver a truck load of nitroglycerin to a burning oil field. It received the Grandes Prix International at the 1953 Cannes Film Festival. *Les Diaboliques* was adapted from a novel by Pierre Boileau and Thomas Narcejac. The film is a brilliant exercise in horror involving a complicated murder plot set in a small boarding school. This particular film helped garner Clouzot a reputation as a master of suspense in the tradition of Hitchcock.

In 1956 the director made an ingenious documentary film about the nature of art. Pablo Picasso is filmed as he paints 15 new works of art before Clouzot's camera. All of these art pieces are destroyed at the end of the film, so that they exist only as part of the film itself. Clouzot shot the film in desaturated color and in CinemaScope. In 1984 the French government declared *Le Mystère Picasso (The Mystery of Picasso)* a national treasure. Ill health plagued many of Clouzot's subsequent film projects. Only three films were completed after *Le Mystère Picasso—Les Espions* (1957), *La Vérité* (1960), and *La Prisonnière* (1968). Henri-Georges Clouzot died in Paris, France, on January 12, 1977. Film historian Roy Armes said of Clouzot's ouevre: "The world of Clouzot's films is one where beauty and tenderness have no place and even love and friendship are rare. It is not at all an unemotional world, but the passions it contains are of the kind which involve dominance and degradation. . . . His natural source material is the thriller and he is at his best in depicting this genre's conventional setting . . . his world is very much a timeless one of human vices."

Other Films *Retour à la vie* (1949); *Miquette et sa mère* (1950); *Karajan: Early Images, Vol. 2* (1965–66) (for French television).

References Armes, Roy, *French Cinema* (London: Secker & Warburg, 1985); Crisp, Colin, *The Classic French Cinema, 1930–1960* (Bloomington: Indiana University Press, 1993); Pilard, Philippe, *H-G. Clouzot* (Paris: Editions Seghers, 1969).

—R.W.

Cocteau, Jean (1889–1963)   A versatile and prolific poet, novelist, playwright, painter, and filmmaker, Jean Cocteau found in the film medium his most personalized expression of mortality and magic. He was born to a middle-class family in Maisons-Laffitte, near Paris, on July 5, 1889. He attended the Lycée Condorcet and was promptly expelled in 1904. As a teenager and protégé of the homosexual actor Edouard de Max, he found his first audiences while declaiming his poems at the Théâtre Femina. During the war years, he began writing for the Ballets Russes (his *Parade* was the "succes de scandale" of 1917), and he volunteered for service at the front with an ambulance unit. He vaulted into public notoriety in the decade of the 1920s with the pantomine ballet *Boeuf sur le toit,* modernistic stage adaptations of Sophocles and Shakespeare, his own play, *Orphée* (1925), volumes of poetry, and numerous paintings and designs.

Blood of the Poet (*Le Sang d'un poète* [1930]) was his first film, "a realistic documentation of unreal events," as he described it. It brought all his diverse talents in poetry and image-making to bear upon an intensely autobiographical document. Cocteau found in the film medium a highly personalized mode of expression. As commentator Arthur B. Evans has observed, "Cocteau was a stubborn

Jean Cocteau

independent who learned the science of film on his own—trial and error. A playwright and poet, Cocteau applied his literary talents to the screen, and many of his films are directly identifiable, in terms of technique, to his poetic works. The balance between his use of word and image on the screen is unmistakable." *Blood of a Poet* begins when a young poet walks through a mirror into a mysterious hotel corridor. After traversing the passage and witnessing a succession of scenes through the keyholes of the rooms, he is forced to commit ritual suicide. Crowned now in laurel leaves, the resurrected poet emerges from the mirror and is transformed into a statue. The cinematic devices include slow motion, skewed camera angles, and non-diegetic aural effects. The imagery is highly personal—the snowball fight is reminiscent of a painful childhood memory (repeated later in *The Terrible Children*), the opium smoker reflects his own drug abuse, the gunshots are a reference to his own father's suicide, and the sexual stigmata suggest his own sexual ambivalence. Bracketing the story are shots of a factory chimney collapsing—its fall interrupted at the beginning and then completed at the end. In other words, the entire film is to be regarded as taking place in but an instant.

For the next 15 years, Cocteau directed no more films but wrote scenarios and adaptations for other directors, the most important of which were the scenario for *The Eternal Return* (*L'Éternel retour* [1943]), directed by Jean Delannoy, and the dialogue for *The Ladies of the Bois de Boulogne* (*Les Dames du Bois de Boulogne* [1945]). His second film as director came in 1946 with *Beauty and the Beast* (*Belle et le bête)*. Perhaps the finest fairy tale ever translated to film, it benefits from the elaborate scenic décor of the Beast's castle and from some gorgeous cinematic trickery, including the sparing but effective use of slow motion. As commentator Michael Popkin observes, in the original tale, the central character is Beauty, but in Cocteau's film, the Beast (Jean Marais) occupies center stage. Like the poet, he must die in one form in order to be reborn in another (echoing Cocteau's dictum, "To live you must die").

Four years later came *Orpheus,* a loose adaptation of his 1925 stage play, *Orphée*—as well as an elaboration of his earlier *Blood of a Poet*—that won the first prize at the International Film Festival in Venice and has come to be regarded as one of the masterworks of the French cinema. The figure of Orpheus is not a great priest, as in the Greek myth, but a famous contemporary poet whose celebrity has annoyed the avant-garde (who stand in for the Bacchantes of the fable). Departures from the original include replacing the horse's sinister oracular messages with radio broadcasts, transforming the glazier Heurtebise into the chauffeur of a fatal Rolls-Royce, and adding the characters of a rival young poet Cegeste and a squad of black-clad motorcyclists as agents of Death (Maria Casares). Like *Blood*, there is a passage through a mirror (the effect accomplished through the use of a vat of mercury), a slow-motion journey through a "Zone," or Underworld of magical visions and encounters, and a confrontation with a black-gowned female representing Death (Casares). Upon reviving the dead Eurydice and bringing her back to the upper world, Orpheus inadvertently breaks his promise never to look at her by inadvertently glimpsing her in the rear-view mirror of the fatal Rolls-Royce. Orpheus is subsequently shot dead and two of Death's motorcyclists bear his body away. Death, meanwhile, who has fallen in love with Orpheus, "kills" him and sends him back to life. For her transgression of the natural laws, she is consigned to a punishment "unimaginable to man." Orpheus and Eurydice, meanwhile, will live happily ever after. Despite the obvious elements of fantasy, Cocteau strove to keep its surface elements relatively commonplace: "The closer one approaches to mystery, the more important it becomes to remain a realist. Automobile radios, code messages, short-wave broadcasts, power failures—such elements, familiar to all, make it possible for me to keep things down to earth."

Cocteau wrote the screenplay and assisted JEAN-PIERRE MELVILLE in a 1952 adaptation of his 1929 novel, *The Terrible Children (Les Enfants terribles)*. It begins with a student named Paul (Edouard Dermit) being wounded during a snowball fight. Invalided at home, Paul is nursed by his sister, Elisabeth (Nicole Stéphane). When their mother dies, brother and sister embark on their respective love affairs, Paul with a model who resembles his sister, and Elisabeth with a wealthy American. They nonetheless remain bonded together in a virtually incestuous embrace. After a series of confused identities and mismatches, Paul dies from poison and Elisabeth is left to mourn. The film is a claustrophobic fable of sibling love, rivalry, and mutual destruction.

The Testament of Orpheus (*Le Testament d'Orphée* [1960]) was Cocteau's last film. Commentator Evans suggests that it must be regarded as "a lasting epitaph of his entire life, works, and self-examinations as a poet." It is the 70-year-old Cocteau himself who at last portrays on screen the role he has assumed all along in his life and work, that of a modern-day Orpheus. Despite its baffling subtitle, "Don't Ask Me Why," he has volunteered the explanation that this film tampers with time and abolishes its narrow limitations; moreover, cinema in general is "the only language suitable for bringing my night into the daylight and putting it on a table in the full sun." Events experienced by the poet within the film seem to transpire with the illogic of a dream, rather in the manner of the earlier *Blood of a Poet*. It begins with a portrait of the poet in 18th-century garb, lost in space-time, who seeks orientation from a professor of science by means of a small box of magical bullets that travel faster than light. After being shot by one of the bullets, the poet falls to the ground and bounces back to his feet in the modern day and wearing a new suit. Thus ensues a series of incidents and encounters with a man wearing a horse's mask, the resurrected figure of Cegeste (late of the earlier *Orpheus*), a dead hibiscus flower, which the poet is enjoined to bring back to life, a tribunal where the characters Heurtebise and Death (also from the earlier *Orpheus*) condemn him to a "life" sentence as a poet, his own "double" (who ignores him), a strange statuelike oracle that spews forth pages of literary works, and, finally, the goddess Minerva, who slays him with the point of her spear. Cocteau expires amid the rubble, his eyes wide open and smoke curling from his mouth. "Pretend that you are crying, my friends," he says, "since poets only pretend they are dead." At which point, the poet rises to his feet and leaves the temple and disappears into the rocky cliffs outside. It is the last

of the many deaths and rebirths that have afflicted the poet.

Cocteau's preoccupation with the mythic, particularly the Orpheus story of art, death, and rebirth, was of primary importance to his work. Orphic allusions surface everywhere, particularly in *The Blood of a Poet,* a seminal document in the surrealistic cinema, and thereafter in *Orpheus* and *The Testament of Orpheus.* Moreover, the concomitant metaphors of mirrors, angels, and acrobats were crucial in exploring that myth. The mirror reflected back to man his own mortality. The figure of the angel shuttled back and forth between the polar states of life and death. Death was not a terminal condition of mortality for Cocteau, but a condition, a speculation, a dream that conveyed him to conditions beyond mere exterior surfaces. Poised precariously between these binary conditions of reality and magic was the third metaphor, the figure of the highwire acrobat, balanced between the circus ring below and the tent roof above. Cocteau himself—and, indeed, the Artist in general—was that angel and that acrobat, either commuting, as it were, between instinct and calculation, between the mundane and the marvelous; or hovering between them. His personal "death journey," as he called it, was frequently achieved by means of opium. In his art—in this case, the film medium—it was gained by the manipulation of plastic materials for the sake of marvelous effects and unlikely juxtapositions of shots that provoked unexpected meanings in the minds of his "enchanted" viewers.

Early in his career Cocteau had received two injunctions, or incantations, that influenced the rest of his life: The ballet impresario Diaghilev had once enjoined him to "astonish me"; and his friend and lover Raymond Radiguet had observed that "elegance consists in *not* astonishing." Perhaps the film medium, which he referred to as a "machine of dreams" and as "the Tenth Muse," was Cocteau's ideal engine in pursuing those dual but contradictory prerogatives. "I search for only the relief and the detail of the images that came forth from the great night of the human body," he said. "I then immediately adopt them as the documentary scenes of another realm."

Jean Cocteau died of an attack of pulmonary edema at Milly-la-Forêt on October 11, 1963. So vivid had been his presence in life that few at the funeral seemed to realize he was dead at all. "Indeed," writes his biographer Frederick Brown, "there were those who half expected him to leap out of the wings and bark stage directions with that resonant, nasal voice of his, persuading the celebrants to do his bidding." The writer François Mauriac noted at the time: "I'm amazed that he could do something as natural, as simple, as undevised as dying."

Other Films *The Two-Headed Eagle* (*L'Aigle à deux têtes* [1947]); *The Terrible Parents* (*Les Parents terribles* [1948]); *La Villa Santo-Sospir* (1952).

References Brown, Frederick, *An Impersonation of Angels: A Biography of Jean Cocteau* (New York: Viking Press, 1968); Evans, Arthur B., *Jean Cocteau and His Films of Orphic Identity* (Philadelphia: Arts Alliance Press, 1977); Popkin, Michael, "Cocteau's *Beauty and the Beast:* the Poet as Monster," *Literature/Film Quarterly* 10, no. 2 (1982): 100–109.

—J.C.T.

Coen, Joel (1954–) and Ethan (1957–)

Joel Coen was born on November 29, 1954, in Minneapolis, Minnesota. His brother and creative partner Ethan was born three years later on September 21, 1957. Both had what they considered banal and ordinary childhoods, characterized by the limitations of the harsh Minnesota winters and the lifestyle of their parents (both college professors). They must have established a powerful bond between them, though, because by all accounts they are a total creative team, with little sign of where the contributions of one begins and the other leaves off. (Although they have maintained the conceit and credit of Joel as director and Ethan as producer since their first feature, both collabo-

rate in both positions, as well as in screenwriting.) The brothers went east for college, Joel to New York University for film school and Ethan to Princeton for philosophy. In New York, they befriended Sam Raimi, another aspiring filmmaker slightly more established (at the time) than the Coens. Raimi hired Joel as an assistant editor for his feature *Evil Dead* (1982), and Raimi, Joel, and Ethan became occasional writing partners (the Coens cowrote Raimi's 1985 film *Crimewave,* and Raimi cowrote the script that would become *The Hudsucker Proxy*). The Coen brothers bootstrapped their own first feature into production by raising $750,000 and selling the film to distributor Circle Releasing Corporation after it was finished.

Blood Simple (1984), a noirish crime story, established many of the Coens's signature stylistic elements: bizarre juxtapositions of narrative and image, violent and bloody confrontations, and quirky, eclectic characters. Impressed with the results of their first feature, Circle Releasing financed the Coens's second film, the comedy *Raising Arizona* (1987). Starring Nicolas Cage, John Goodman, and Holly Hunter, the film was a sort of screwball comedy about kidnapping a baby, and the Coens are reported to have chosen it as their second feature because it was so different from *Blood Simple.*

In the years since, the Coens have oscillated between the two styles, gory noir and screwballish comedy, sometimes combining the two in a single film. They have also established a distinct talent in period stories, which they first exercised in *Miller's Crossing* (1990), a stylized gangster story starring John Turturro and Albert Finney. Their next film, *Barton Fink* (1991), was also a period piece set in 1940s Hollywood, with Turturro as a tormented playwright turned screenwriter. *The Hudsucker Proxy* (1994) was another period piece (late-1950s New York this time) in which Tim Robbins played a hapless businessman who invents the hula hoop. The Coens's greatest artistic success to date is *Fargo* (1996), the story of a faux kidnapping gone bad, set in the Coens's home state of

Ethan (middle) and Joel Coen (right) directing a scene in *Barton Fink* (Twentieth Century-Fox)

Minnesota. Notorious for its caricatured portrayal of the dialect and social customs of the upper midwest, *Fargo* was nominated for the best picture Oscar and Joel for best director, with the brothers winning the Oscar for best original screenplay and Frances McDormand winning the best actress Oscar for her portrayal of a pregnant sheriff in the film. (McDormand also starred in *Blood Simple,* after which she married Joel Coen.) The Coens followed their greatest success with a return to comedy in *The Big Lebowski* (1998), an identity-confusion caper starring Jeff Bridges as the title character. The Coens began the 21st century with *O Brother, Where Art Thou?* (2000), a chain-gang drama inspired by the unmade film mentioned in the Preston Sturges film, *Sullivan's Travels.*

References Bergan, Ronald, *The Coen Brothers* (New York: Thunder's Mouth Press, 2000); Horowitz, Mark, "Coen Brothers A–Z: The Big Two-Headed Picture," *Film Comment,* September/October 1991: 27–32; "Movies of Their Very Own," *New York Times Magazine,* July 8, 1990.

—C.M.

Cohen, Larry (1941–) Larry Cohen was born in New York City's Washington Heights district in 1941. Educated at City College of New York, Cohen had exhibited a precocious interest in comic books and cinema from a very early age. He would combine these two influences later in his career. While working as a page boy at NBC in the late 1950s, he witnessed production in the "Golden Age of television," much of which was shot live. Although well below the minimum age for television writers (some filmographies list his birth date as 1938, which he passed off as his official age), Cohen wrote several accomplished teleplays during 1958–61, which received live transmission. In 1958, he wrote the teleplay for the first "87th Precinct" drama for *Kraft Mystery Theatre.*

The future director was an avid lover of Hollywood cinema and the work of ALFRED HITCH-COCK in particular. He was actually present watching Hitchcock shoot railroad station location scenes in *North by Northwest,* but it would be several years before they officially met. After writing several episodes of *The Defenders,* Cohen relocated to Hollywood and for a time was the most sought-after writer of pilots. Dissatisfied by the way television treated his work, Cohen longed to direct. But he managed to interest Hitchcock in his screenplay, *Daddy's Gone A-Hunting.* For a while, it looked like both would collaborate, but when Universal forced Hitchcock to remove himself from the project, it went to Mark Robson who directed an unsatisfactory version for Warner Bros. in 1969.

Eventually, Cohen wrote, produced, and directed *Bone* in 1972. Known by several titles, such as *Housewife, Beverly Hills Nightmare,* and *Dial Rat for Terror,* the film was a low-budget satirical allegory of affluent Hollywood lifestyles. Poorly distributed by Jack (*The Blob*) Harris, the film has gained a cult reputation over the years. When Sammy Davis, Jr., turned down his *Black Caesar* screenplay, Cohen filmed it with Fred Williamson in the title role. Shot in 1973 on a low-budget with "guerilla cinema" techniques, the film proved a box-office success in the era of so-called "blaxploitation" films. After shooting a hastily conceived sequel, *Hell Up in Harlem* (1973), Cohen then made the first of his outstanding horror films, *It's Alive,* in the same year. Indirectly indebted to the work of Alfred Hitchcock, its

updating of the classic Hollywood horror genre made it a more socially revealing and intelligent film than *The Exorcist.* Cohen denies that his films belong to the horror genre and hopes that viewers recognize the wider allegorical implications contained in his vision.

In 1976, Cohen directed his most ambitious project *God Told Me To,* which merged science fiction themes, religious imagery, and subtle critiques of traditional civilized patterns of behavior together in a highly challenging manner. In 1977, he filmed *The Private Files of J. Edgar Hoover,* featuring many classic Hollywood veterans such as Broderick Crawford, Dan Dailey, Lloyd Nolan, June Havoc, and Howard Da Silva. This film merged elements of horror with an incisive critique of 20th-century American history, stimulating Robin Wood to describe it as the most "intelligent political film" ever made. Distribution problems affected the film but it attracted high respect at film festivals, National Film Theatre screenings in London, and television showings. Despite his high respect for classic Hollywood, Cohen has always been an outsider in the contemporary industry and has lacked the studio backing, respect for his artistry, and wider distribution his work needs.

In the 1980s, he collaborated with Michael Moriarty on four films. The first two—*Q-The Winged Serpent* (1982) and *The Stuff* (1985)—received theatrical distribution, but *It's Alive III* (1986) and *A Return to Salem's Lot* (1987) went direct to video despite being shot as film productions. Although Cohen hoped that his homage to *North by Northwest, The Ambulance* (1990), would receive theatrical distribution, it also went directly to video several years after its production. Cohen's intelligent reworkings of Hitchcock's work and his subversive social critiques, often mediated in comic-strip style, frequently appear too radical for contemporary Hollywood tastes. After reuniting former stars of "blaxploitation" cinema in *Original Gangstas* (1996), which received theatrical release, Cohen is currently developing screenplays for mainstream directors similar to his work for Sidney Lumet in *Guilty As Sin* (1993). However, this resilient talent may soon direct once again.

References Wood, Robin, *Hollywood: From Vietnam to Reagan* (New York: Columbia University Press, 1986); Williams, Tony, *Larry Cohen: Radical Allegories of an American Filmmaker* (Jefferson, N.C.: McFarland, 1997).

—T.W.

Conway, Jack (1887–1952) One of Metro-Goldwyn-Mayer's most reliable contract directors, Jack Conway directed some of the studio's best movies of the thirties. He never established much of a recognizable directorial identity because, like Warner Bros.'s MICHAEL CURTIZ, he was a compelling blend of artist and workhorse in whose work it is difficult to tell where the director's style leaves off and studio style begins. He was a kind of one-man refutation of the auteur theory. His artistic personality never dominated his films; rather, it was an equal but integral element of their style and power. Conway was a team player. This by no means diminishes his achievement. His work was virtually always first-rate in every regard. If he left behind very little in the way of "personal cinema," it must also be said that he put his name to very few films that did not succeed as superior entertainment.

By the time Conway was put under contract to MGM in 1924 he had been working in films for well over a decade. Born in Tacoma, Washington, on July 17, 1887, Conway had early sought a life of adventure, dropping out of high school to work on the railroad. By 1907 he was acting on stage with various stock companies and by 1909 was appearing before the camera in one-reel melodramas and westerns produced by the Nestor Motion Picture Company; he continued acting in his own films into the twenties. Conway served as an assistant director to D. W. Griffith at Triangle, directed many short films at a variety of companies, and directed his first feature in 1915, *The Penitents.*

Conway's skill brought him to the attention of the newly formed MGM; he would remain at the studio for the rest of his career—over 20 more years—and become one of its most dependable filmmakers. MGM's first part-talkie was Conway's *Alias Jimmy Valentine* (1928). And Conway helmed the last film, and only sound film, starring Lon Chaney, *The Unholy Three* (1930), a remake of Tod Browning's atmospheric silent.

Although Conway tended to excel in action pictures—working well with Spencer Tracy, Clark Gable, and Wallace Beery—he was never tied to the two-fisted school as were peers like WILLIAM WELLMAN and RAOUL WALSH. Conway was equally at home with the stylish wit of *Arsene Lupin* (1932), starring John and Lionel Barrymore and the underrated Karen Morley, and the wise-cracking snap of *Red-Headed Woman* (1932), one of Jean Harlow's pre-Code masterpieces. Both *A Tale of Two Cities* (1935) and *Viva Villa* (1934) have a real epic sweep that blends beautifully with the subtle shadings of the films' characters. Ronald Colman's understated role as Sidney Carton in the former is in sharp contrast to Wallace Beery's brash and enthusiastic Pancho Villa in the latter; but Conway's ease and skill with actors is equally evident in both performances.

Similarly, Conway deftly managed the enormous star power of *Libeled Lady* (1936) and guided Jean Harlow, Spencer Tracy, William Powell, and Myrna Loy through what is one of the freshest and fastest of screwball comedies. He also had to make the best of a bad situation when Harlow died during the production of *Saratoga* (1937) and he was forced to complete the film with a double. Because of this, however, the film cannot be listed among his best work. But his action comedies such as *Too Hot to Handle* (1938) and *Honky Tonk* (1941), both starring Clark Gable, are first-rate. *Too Hot to Handle,* particularly, is one of the neglected gems of the thirties—fast, furious, and full of fun.

Jack Conway retired from MGM in 1948 and died four years later. Spencer Tracy gave the eulogy at Conway's funeral stating, "We never would have heard of a place called Hollywood if it were not for the Jack Conways." There is more truth to the statement than might at first appear. Conway was not one of the great artists of the cinema, but he and directors like him kept the studio-era assembly line going, churning out a seemingly inexhaustible supply of entertainment. It was Conway's job to make sure that the product that emerged from that assembly line was of the best possible quality. It's a job he did beautifully from the beginning of his career to the end. He is, and will possibly remain, one of the cinema's unsung figures. But the films he made continue to enthrall and delight audiences and will continue to reward every viewer who seeks them out.

Other Films *Brown of Harvard* (1926); *Bringing Up Father* (1928); *Our Modern Maidens* (1929); *The Gay Bride* (1934); *A Yank at Oxford* (1938); *Boom Town* (1940); *Love Crazy* (1941).

Reference Coursodon, Jean-Pierre, with Pierre Sauvage, "Jack Conway," *American Directors,* vol. 1 (New York: McGraw-Hill, 1983).

—F.T.

Coppola, Francis Ford (1939–)

Francis Ford Coppola was born on April 7, 1939, in Detroit, Michigan, to Carmine and Italia Coppola. Coppola's middle name was a tribute to Henry Ford, as Carmine Coppola served as the musical arranger for the *Ford Sunday Evening Hour* on CBS radio. Carmine Coppola worked as a musician throughout Coppola's childhood, while Coppola's mother served as the family's Italian matriarch and raised Francis, older brother August, and younger sister Talia (who later became an actress not only in Coppola's films but also in Sylvester Stallone's *Rocky* series). Coppola's New York youth was steeped in Italian-American culture, music, new technologies such

as television, and a bout of polio suffered at the age of 10. With his parents' support, Coppola developed an interest in drama, which he studied as an undergraduate at Hofstra University, receiving his degree in 1959. The following year, he enrolled in the UCLA film school, where he made a number of short films and made a contact that would prove crucial to establishing his directing career: Roger Corman.

Coppola became a jack-of-all-trades for Corman in the early 1960s, working on several films and eventually persuading Corman to let him direct his first feature, *Dementia 13* (1963). After working as a screenwriter-for-hire in the mid-1960s, Coppola got another chance to direct when Warner Bros. allowed him to direct a script he wrote while under their employ. The resulting film, *You're a Big Boy Now* (1966), showed the influence of not only the French New Wave but also British cinema of the mid-1960s. The favorable notices for this first Warner Bros. effort led the studio to hire Coppola for a more ambitious directorial project: the big-budget musical *Finian's Rainbow* (1968). When this film ended up as a critical and commercial disaster, Coppola retreated to the maverick, independent type of production he was more used to and directed *The Rain People* (1969), another picture reminiscent of the French New Wave. With this film, Coppola inaugurated American Zoetrope, which would become one of his obsessions throughout the 1970s, as he attempted to turn the vanity label into a full-fledged studio (with little lasting success).

The failures of *Finian's Rainbow* and the first incarnation of American Zoetrope lowered Coppola's stock as a director but did not stop Paramount's Robert Evans from enlisting him for the film adaptation of Mario Puzo's novel *The Godfather* (1972). Coppola directed the picture not as a gangster film but as a family saga, and the film became perhaps the biggest artistic and financial success of Coppola's career, win-

Francis Ford Coppola (left) on the set of *Gardens of Stone* (Tri-Star)

ning the Academy Award for best picture and helping to launch the blockbuster trend of the 1970s. The sequel, *The Godfather, Part II* (1974), nearly matched its success, again winning best picture and establishing Coppola as one of the premier directors of the 1970s. In between the two *Godfather* pictures, Coppola wrote and directed *The Conversation* (1974), which was a critical success but failed to make an impact at the box office. Coppola spent the remainder of the 1970s engaged in the production of his Vietnam epic *Apocalypse Now* (1979), a film that was an astonishing artistic success but had a checkered and infamous production that included several false stops, health problems for various members of the cast and crew, and a number of

problems with the Filipino government, in whose country the filming took place.

In the 1980s, Coppola focused mostly on less-ambitious projects such as the adaptations of the S. E. Hinton novels *The Outsiders* and *Rumble Fish* (both 1983), *Peggy Sue Got Married* (1986), and *Tucker: The Man and His Dreams* (1988). An exception to this was *The Cotton Club* (1984), a film about the 1930s Harlem club scene that had a production almost as storied as that of *Apocalypse Now*. After a delay of many years, Coppola next returned to the *Godfather* saga with *The Godfather, Part III* (1990), in which he concluded the story of the Corleone family. Although he has in recent years resurfaced as a director-for-hire, Coppola's most significant 1990s project was *Bram Stoker's*

Dracula (1992), an ornate, baroque version of the classic vampire story.

Other Films *One from the Heart* (1982); *Gardens of Stone* (1987); *New York Stories* ("Life Without Zoe" segment [1989]); *Jack* (1996); *The Rainmaker* (1997).

References Bergan, Ronald, *Francis Ford Coppola Close Up: The Making of His Movies* (New York: Thunder's Mouth Press, 1997); Cowie, Peter, *Coppola* (New York: Scribner, 1990); Goodwin, Michael, and Naomi Wise, *On the Edge: The Life and Times of Francis Coppola* (New York: William Morrow, 1989).

—C.M.

Corman, Roger (1926–) Roger William Corman was born in Detroit, Michigan, on April 6, 1926, the son of William and Ann Corman. In 1940 the family moved to Beverly Hills, California, where Corman attended Beverly Hills High School and graduated in 1943. He graduated from Stanford University with a degree in engineering in 1947. After spending three years in the U.S. Navy and a semester at Oxford University where he studied English literature, Corman returned to the United States and received a job at 20th Century-Fox as a messenger. Working his way up to story analyst, Corman sold his first story, "House by the River," to Allied Artists. The story was retitled *Highway Dragnet,* in order to capitalize on the popularity of television crime shows, and was released in 1953.

Using the money he made from Allied Artists, Corman formed a low-budget production company, Palo Alto Productions, and made several films with friends who also invested in the company. These include *Monster from the Ocean Floor* (1954), *The Fast and the Furious* (1954), and *Beast with 1,000 Eyes* (1955). In 1954, Corman became a silent partner in the low-budget film company, American Releasing Corporation, which had been formed by James H. Nicholson and Samuel Z. Arkoff with an initial investment of $3,000. Corman directed his first feature, *Five Guns West,* in 1954. Corman quickly began establishing himself as a fast director of genre films for ARC (which became AIP, American International Pictures, in 1956). Corman's early work during this period includes westerns *The Oklahoma Woman* and *Gunslinger,* both 1956, as well as horror/science fiction films such as *The Day the World Ended* (1955), *It Conquered the World* (1956), *The Undead* (1956), *Not of This Earth* (1957), and *Attack of the Crab Monsters* (1957). These films were aimed specifically at the teenage market and distributed primarily to drive-in theatres.

From 1957 to 1959 Corman extended his range of genres to include gangster films (*Machine Gun Kelly, I Mobster*), teen-pics (*Rock All Night, Carnival Rock, Teenage Doll, Sorority Girl*), and exotic adventure films (*She-Gods of Shark Reef, Naked Paradise, Viking Women and the Sea Serpent*). Corman's fast and efficient methods (which included six- to eight-day shooting schedules) guaranteed profits for AIP, as well as for other studios for which he produced and directed. In 1960 Corman convinced Nicholson and Arkoff to allow him to direct a modestly budgeted color horror film based on a short story by Edgar Allan Poe. The resulting film, *The House of Usher,* starring Vincent Price, initiated a cycle of Poe-inspired films that received both critical and box-office acclaim throughout the 1960s.

In 1970 Corman formed New World Pictures, a production and distribution company. This highly successful low-budget film company helped start the careers of such directors as MARTIN SCORSESE, JONATHAN DEMME, JOE DANTE, JOHN SAYLES, and others. In addition to its low-budget bill-of-fare, New World also distributed such foreign art-house films as FEDERICO FELLINI's *Amarcord* and Ingmar Bergman's *Cries and Whispers.* After selling New World Pictures in 1983, Corman formed another production company, Concorde/New Horizon. Much of Corman's subsequent work as a producer includes cable-TV offerings and direct-to-video films.

Other Films *Apache Woman* (1955); *Swamp Woman* (1956); *War of the Satellites* (1958); *Last Woman on Earth*

(1958); *The Wasp Woman* (1959); *Bucket of Blood* (1959); *Ski Troop Attack* (1960); *The Little Shop of Horrors* (1960); *Creature from the Haunted Sea* (1960); *Atlas* (1960); *Pit and the Pendulum* (1961); *The Intruder* (1961); *The Premature Burial* (1962); *Tales of Terror* (1962); *Tower of London* (1962); *The Raven* (1963); *The Young Racers* (1963); *The Haunted Palace* (1963); *The Terror* (1963); *X-The Man with the X-Ray Eyes* (1963); *The Secret Invasion* (1964); *The Masque of the Red Death* (1964); *The Tomb of Ligeia* (1964); *The Wild Angels* (1966); *The St. Valentine's Day Massacre* (1967); *Gass-s-s-s, or It Became Necessary to Destroy the World in Order to Save It* (1970); *Von Richthofen and Brown* (1971); *Frankenstein Unbound* (1989).

References Corman, Roger, *How I Made a Hundred Movies in Hollywood and Never Lost a Dime* (New York: Random House, 1990); Morris, Gary, *Roger Corman* (Boston: Twayne, 1985).

—R.W.

Costa-Gavras, Constantin (1933–) With the release of his picture *Z* (1969), for which he won the Jury Prize at the Cannes Film Festival in 1970, Costa-Gavras became Europe's foremost political filmmaker by revisioning the events of the Lambrakis affair, involving a right-wing assassination in 1963 in Greece, but structuring those events in the manner of detective fiction. Reality-based politics would dominate much of his subsequent work, from *L'Aveu* (*The Confession* [1970]), based on Artur London's autobiography, to *État de siège* (*State of Siege* [1973]), scripted by Franco Solinas and concerning an American "adviser," kidnapped, tried, and executed by the Tupamaros guerrillas in Uruguay, to *Missing* (1982), which won an Academy Award for best screenplay and the Palme d'Or at the 1982 Cannes Film Festival. But the film was controversial, as was its director, as controversial in his way as Oliver Stone was later to become in America.

Konstantinos (Costa) Gavras was born in Kilvia in the Peloponnesus, the son of a Russian father and a Greek mother, in 1933. Because his father was a suspected communist, he was denied entry to Greek universities and unable to get a visa to study in the United States. He was educated in Paris, however, at the Sorbonne and the I.D. Hautes Études Cinématographiques, and in 1956 he became a naturalized French citizen. Before directing his first film, *Compartiment tueurs (The Sleeping Car Murders)* in 1966, he had been working since 1958 as an assistant to Yves Allegret, René Clair, René Clemént, Henri Verneuil, and Jacques Demy.

Z began as a novel by the Greek writer Vassilis Vassilikos, published in 1966 and described by Stanley Kauffmann as a "thinly disguised account of the murder of Gregorios Lambrakis, a leftist deputy and professor of medicine at the University of Athens. After Lambrakis had protested the deployment of Polaris missiles in Greece in 1963 at a political meeting in Salonika, he was struck by a truck and killed, but this was no mere accident." As Kauffmann explained, in Greek "the initial *Z* stands for *zei—he lives*." In the film the murdered deputy was played by Yves Montand, and Jean-Louis Trintignant is the magistrate investigating the death. His quest for justice is the mechanism that drives the film.

Like *Z, State of Siege* derives from and was patterned after an actual political event. In August 1970 a number of political kidnappings took place in the republic of Uruguay, instigated by a terrorist group, the Tupamaros. Among the kidnapped were Daniel Mitrione, a 50-year-old ex-police chief from Richmond, Indiana, and Claude Fly, an agronomist employed by a private firm. Mitrione, once an instructor at the International Police Academy in Washington, D.C., was serving as a "technical adviser" (called an "expert in communications" in the film) to the Uruguayan police, and was believed by the Tupamaros to be an American spy. The Tupamaros demanded the release of some 150 political prisoners, but the government refused to capitulate and ordered some 12,000 soldiers to seek out the terrorists and also round up some 20 suspected urban guerrillas, including former Socialist Party leader Raúl Sendic.

Consequently, the Tupamaros made good their threat: the body of Daniel Mitrione was eventually found in a parked and stolen 1948 Buick convertible. The American Department of State was apparently in agreement and sympathy with the course of action President Jorge Pacheco Areco had followed: "If we pressure governments to accede to such extreme demands," the State Department declared, "it would serve, in our view, only to encourage other terrorist groups to kidnap Americans." The Tupamaros were then placed in the position of having to take the political (and moral) consequences of following through with their threat—either to commit murder or to lose their credibility as a

viable political force. This dilemma is at the heart of the film.

State of Siege made its controversial American premiere in April 1973 not at the Kennedy Center's American Film Institute Theatre, as originally scheduled, but at the Outer Circle Theatre in the city because George Stevens, Jr., national director of the AFI, decided that the film was "an inappropriate choice" for screening at the Kennedy Center because it allegedly "rationalizes an act of political assassination." The Nixon administration was notoriously sensitive to criticism in general, and the Kennedy administration had links to the International Police Academy. According to screenwriter Franco Solinas, the story "was based on an actual chronicle which took place in Latin America a few years ago, a story that tries to

Constantin Costa-Gavras directing a scene in *Music Box* (Tri-Star)

explain some of the ways used by imperialism to penetrate, dominate, and, when it succeeds, alter the reality of Latin America today." Nearly 10 years later, Costa-Gavras would take on another controversial film touching on the State Department's activities in Latin America.

Costa-Gavras crossed over to mainstream Hollywood filmmaking with the film *Missing* (1982), another true story, involving the frustrated attempt of Ed Horman (played by Jack Lemmon in one of his best roles) to locate his son, Charles, who turns up "missing" as a political prisoner in Latin America. The father joins his daughter-in-law, Joyce (Sissy Spacek), in Chile, where he runs into a bureaucratic brick wall, and gets absolutely no help or real cooperation from the United States Embassy. Following a script adapted from Thomas Hauser's book, *The Execution of Charles Horman* (1978), the director's methods in *Missing* are very similar to *Z,* with a comparable level of incremental outrage and disbelief over governmental abuses. The issue was political: "The horror is of a family which hopes the missing person is alive, but does not know. It is a kind of game between hope and death," Costa-Gavras explained to an interviewer. "You go on with hope, which every day becomes bigger—and thinner. It's a permanent torture, and some governments use this as a message of repression. When one man disappears, ten people around him are scared."

Initially, Costa-Gavras was reluctant to offer this project to an American studio "because the subject was too inflammatory, too violently political." But this was an American story, and finally he was convinced to let Universal Studios handle the film. The film proved to be controversial: the State Department issued denials and the battle was joined in the op-ed pages of the *Washington Post,* the *New York Times,* and other papers. Two main contenders were Flora Lewis, foreign affairs correspondent of the *New York Times,* and Alan Berger of the *Boston Globe,* who wrote that Lewis "was no doubt right to suggest that the film *Missing* is not

an exact replica of reality. But if she had consulted the facts she accused Costa-Gavras of distorting, she would have found a reality far more disquieting than any cinematic recreation."

Not all of Costa-Gavras's films have been political thrillers. *The Minor Apocalypse* (1995), for example, in the words of *New York Times* reporter Stephen Holden, was a "comedy satirizing the fall of Communism, aging 1960s radicals, capitalist opportunism and the omnivorous media," starring Czech director Jiri Menzel as an unemployed Polish émigré writer, down and out in Paris. In 1997 Costa-Gavras launched another attack and exposé of media madness and mob psychology in *Mad City,* starring Dustin Hoffman as a hotshot television reporter caught in a museum with a desperate, armed museum guard (John Travolta), who has been laid off and threatens to bomb the museum if he is not given his job back. He takes a group of children hostage and accidentally shoots another guard. The situation escalates from there into an out-of-control media circus. Costa-Gavras, a prime architect of the political thriller as well as a social critic with his camera, was still in excellent form.

Other Films *Un homme de trop (Shock Troops* [1968]); *Section spéciale (Special Section* [1975]); *Clair de femme (A Woman's Glow* [1979]); *Hanna K.* (1983); *Family Business* (1985); *Betrayed (Summer Lightning* [1988]); *Betrayed* (1988); *Music Box* (1990); *Raspoutine* (1995).

References Armes, Roy, *French Cinema* (New York: Oxford University Press, 1985); Kauffmann, Stanley, "On Films: *Z,*" *New Republic,* December 13, 1969, pp. 22, 32; Michalczyk, John J., *Costa-Gavras: The Political Fiction Film* (Philadelphia: Art Alliance Press, 1984); Ray, Michele, "Interview with Franco Solinas and Costa-Gavras," in *State of Siege,* trans. Raymond Rosenthal (New York: Ballantine Books, 1973); Monaco, James, "The Costa-Gavras Syndrome," *Cineaste* 7, no. 2 (Spring 1976): 18–21; Welsh, J. M., "Beyond Melodrama: Art, Politics, and *State of Siege,*" *Film Criticism* 2, no. 1 (Fall 1977): 24–31.

—J.M.W.

Cronenberg, David (1943–) David Cronenberg's reputation has rested largely on his work within the genre of the horror film, where he has explored the sexual dread and postmodern anxieties that surround contemporary themes of biological terror. Because he has worked so often in the horror genre, Cronenberg has often been labeled as an "exploitation" director. While he has employed graphic, even "revolting" special effects, his films also provide a rich offering of complex characters who are forced to make moral choices in a postmodern world devoid of philosophical absolutes.

Cronenberg was born on March 15, 1943, in Toronto, Canada. While a student majoring in English and science at the University of Toronto, he made two experimental science fiction shorts, *Stereo* (1969) and *Crimes of the Future* (1970). Both of these early student films demonstrated what would become Cronenberg's abiding interest in stylistic invention. His first feature, released in 1975, *Shivers* (aka *They Came From Within / The Parasite Murders*), was coproduced with fellow Canadian Ivan Reitman. The film established Cronenberg's reputation as an innovative director of low-budget science fiction and horror. In *Shivers,* an artificially created parasite is unleashed that infects its victims with uncontrollable sexual desire. While *Shivers* is an effective horror film, it is also an irony-laced, prophetic commentary on the dark side of sexual liberation in the 1970s. Even though the film's paranoid view of sexual liberation led many critics to deem its ideology as conservative, even "reactionary," the nature of Cronenberg's material led to critical and political outrage that would mark his early career. In the Canadian parliament, conservative members railed against government funding for what they considered a "disgusting" movie. Canadian critic Robert Fulford titled his review "You Should Know How Bad This Film Is. After All, You Paid for It."

Despite the outcry, Cronenberg's next film, *Rabid,* released in 1977, wryly casts Marilyn Chambers, the former "Ivory Snow Girl" turned porn star, as the unfortunate victim of an operation that leaves her with not only a vampire's lust for blood, but also and conveniently enough, a phallic spike that emerges from under her armpit, making her embrace that of a truly deadly spider-woman. On the basis of *Shivers* and *Rabid,* Robin Wood, in his influential 1979 essay "An Introduction to the American Horror Film," criticized Cronenberg for being a prime example of a director working from the horror genre's "reactionary wing."

Even so, the success of *Shivers* and *Rabid* gave Cronenberg his first opportunity to make a film with more than a minimum budget. That film, *The Brood,* made in 1979, featured Oliver Reed and Samantha Eggar in an offbeat and thoroughly gruesome tale in which genetic experimentation and mutation is identified with emotional rage. *The Dead Zone* (1983) marked Cronenberg's first mainstream hit. The film, his first nonoriginal screenplay, was adapted from a Stephen King novel in which the main character (Christopher Walken) finds that he is able to predict future events in people's lives by simply touching them. He comes to harness his psychic gift not only to solve multiple murders, but also, possibly, to prevent the end of the world. *The Dead Zone* was critically praised for giving precedence to atmosphere and characterization over his earlier dependence on the shock value of special effects.

Cronenberg followed the success of *The Dead Zone* with *Videodrome* (1983), which proved to be one of his most controversial films. *Videodrome* is a self-reflexive, McLuhanesque horror tale about the effects of media violence on society. An opportunistic TV producer, played by James Woods, grows obsessed with an erotic sadomasochistic program emanating from a mysterious pirate TV station. His own sexual fantasies, stimulated by the show, grow increasingly out of control. As the plot unfolds, *Videodrome* becomes postmodern fantasy in which all boundaries between reality and media representation collapse to the point where the viewer of the film, like the protagonist himself, cannot separate the two. The theme that television consumers are being "programmed" by the media is visualized by the image of a newly evolved womblike orifice that opens up in Woods's stomach for receiving video software.

Cronenberg's greatest popular success to date is *The Fly* (1986), a big, glossy remake of the low-budget 1958 classic. The hero (Jeff Goldblum) is a scientist whose atomic structure has been confused with that of a common housefly. While his girlfriend (Geena Davis) stands by hopelessly, the scientist undergoes a gradual but horribly gruesome physical disintegration that was interpreted by many critics at the time as a visual metaphor for AIDS. The film seemed to support Robin Wood's earlier view that Cronenberg's work was motivated by a reactionary fear and loathing of the body and sexuality in the "Age of AIDS."

Cronenberg's next major film, *Dead Ringers* (1988), proved both a resounding critical and, if limited, commercial success. In *Dead Ringers,* considered by many critics his most accomplished work to date, the shock value of biological horror is submerged within a sophisticated psychological exploration of character. Jeremy Irons portrays twins who share the profession of gynecology. The viewer is left horrified, watching the brothers descend into drugs, madness, and, finally, one of the screen's most grisly representations of a homicide/suicide. Cronenberg's tightly controlled use of color, décor, and camera movement offers a chilling and emotionally distant "scientific" examination of masculine sexual dread of the female body, and at the same time, a powerful critique of the patriarchal control of the medical profession, thus seeming to refute Robin Wood's earlier interpretation of Cronenberg as a "reactionary" filmmaker.

This view would seem to be supported by the films Cronenberg made during the 1990s. *Naked Lunch* (1992) was a visually exciting transcription from print medium to film of the life and writings of William S. Burroughs. *M. Butterfly* (1993) was a relatively faithful adaptation of the David Henry Hwang stage play based on the true story of a sexually repressed French diplomat and a transsexual diva from the Beijing Opera. The 1996 film *Crash,* an adaptation of a novel by J. G. Ballard, offered a return visit to *Videodrome*'s theme of modern society's fetishistic cravings for sex, machines, and violence. After a near-fatal auto accident, a film producer (James Spader) becomes involved with a cult whose members are sexually obsessed with the sight of vehicular mayhem. *ExistenZ* (1999) also reflects themes that have resonated in Cronenberg's work since *Videodrome*. In this cyberthriller, the characters, computer programmers played by Jennifer Jason Leigh and Jude Law, find themselves trapped inside a computer game of their own making where the laws of organic nature and cyber reality intermix in ever more perplexing, even inscrutable ways.

While Cronenberg's work has often been condemned as paranoid fantasies that produce reactionary texts, the *BaseLine Encyclopedia of Film* argues that "In retrospect, much of Cronenberg's work can be seen as an ironic critique of the fears and repression that inform our apparently liberated society, rather than a visualization of the director's personal obsessions."

References Rodley, Chris, ed., *Cronenberg On Cronenberg* (Boston: Faber & Faber, 1997); Breskin, David, ed., "David Cronenberg," in *Inner View: Filmmakers in Conversation* (Boston: Faber & Faber, 1992), 201–266; Costello, John, *David Cronenberg* (London: Trafalgar Square Press, 2000); Grant, Michael, *The Modern Fantastic: The Films of David Cronenberg* (New York: Praeger, 2000).

—T.P.

Crosland, Alan (1894–1936)

Alan Crosland seems to have earned an almost accidental place in film history. A competent, if resolutely unremarkable, filmmaker, Crosland directed dozens of features between 1917 and 1936, which, with a few significant exceptions, made no discernible mark in the world of the cinema. Indeed, had it not been for two films that he made in 1926 and 1927, Crosland would be almost totally forgotten today. It was during that period that he directed *Don Juan* (1926), the first feature film released with synchronized musical and sound effects, courtesy of Vitaphone; and *The Jazz Singer* (1927), the film that has, slightly erroneously, become credited as the "first talking motion picture."

It may be that Crosland was chosen for these two landmark projects precisely because he brought little directorial vision to his work. The Warner brothers had gambled everything on Vitaphone; they chose films that would act as a perfect showcase for the technique. The last thing they wanted was a Griffith or von Stroheim who might distract attention away from the studio's true achievement in sound. Alan Crosland was a reliable journeyman whose unpretentious fare proved moderately popular with audiences, and he was guaranteed to do the job with a minimum of fuss. More important, he was guaranteed not to overshadow Vitaphone.

Alan Crosland was born in New York City on August 10, 1894. While still in his teens he worked as both an actor and a journalist, but by 1914 he was directing short films for a variety of studios. He directed his first feature, *Kidnapped,* in 1917 and quickly followed it with a dozen or so films before joining the army in 1919 where he served in the U.S. Signal Corps Photographic Section. However, he was away from filmmaking only for a few months. Beginning in 1920 and throughout the decade, he would typically direct an average of three to seven films per year. Some, like *Bobbed Hair* (1925), a farce starring Marie Prevost, were clever; others, such as *The Beloved Rogue* (1926), a costume picture with John Barrymore and lavish production values courtesy of William Cameron Menzies, were simply lugubrious. But *Old San Francisco* (1927) is visually arresting and dramatically satisfying. Oddly enough, however, the epic climax depicting the 1906 San Francisco earthquake and fire is perfunctory and slightly disappointing. It is the performances and Crosland's staging elsewhere that are imaginative and memorable.

Don Juan, also starring John Barrymore, is an enjoyable, if rather prosaic swashbuckler that profits from lavish production values and an exciting chase climax. It is directed with confidence and energy, but all the personality of the film comes from Barrymore, not Crosland. Similarly, all the power in *The Jazz Singer* emanates from the often overwhelming Al Jolson; otherwise, it looks as if it could have been directed by just about anyone.

The Jazz Singer is widely considered to be the first sound film but it, much like *Don Juan,* is predominantly a silent movie accompanied by recorded music and sound effects. However, in a couple of scenes, Al Jolson actually spoke—"You ain't heard nuthin' yet!" for example—and those moments electrified audiences of 1927. Although sound movies had been around in some form or another since the dawn of the cinema, they had never achieved any kind of mass acceptance. *The Jazz Singer* changed all that. *The Jazz Singer*'s quality as a film has always been debated, but its importance in the history of the cinema is profound. That it swept Alan Crosland along in its bid for immortality seems to have been little more than serendipity for the director.

He directed little of importance after *The Jazz Singer. On With the Show* (1929) was a tediously static two-color Technicolor backstage musical; *Massacre* (1934) is an intriguing western, unusual for its era in that it focused on the injustices done to the American Indian; and *The Case of the Howling Dog* (1934) is notable only as the film that introduced the character of Perry Mason (Warren William) to the screen. His last film isn't even marginally interesting. Original audiences laughed at *The Great Impersonation* (1935), presumably unaware that it was not supposed to be a comedy.

Alan Crosland was by no means a bad director. Had he lived longer—he was killed in an automobile accident in 1936—he might have found a proper place for his talents as a television director. His films are seldom terrible; they usually work well enough on their own terms. But when they even approach greatness or originality, it is normally because of some other element, such as an outstanding performance or script. Nevertheless, Crosland's presence at the helm of two groundbreaking sound films will ensure that his name is never completely forgotten. And discovery of more of his silent work—much of which is lost—may yet serve to elevate his reputation from where it now rests—as one of the luckiest men in show business.

Other Films *The Whirlpool* (1918); *Worlds Apart* (1921); *Shadows of the Sea* (1922); *Sinners in Heaven* (1924); *Glorious Betsy* (1928); *The Scarlet Lady* (1928); *Viennese Nights* (1930); *Midnight Alibi* (1933); *King Solomon of Broadway* (1935).

References Edelman, Rob, "Alan Crosland," *The International Dictionary of Films and Filmmakers,* vol. 2, *Directors/Filmmakers* (Chicago: St. James Press, 1984); Dixon, Wheeler W., *The "B" Directors: A Biographical Dictionary* (Metuchen, N.J.: Scarecrow Press, 1985).

—F.T.

Crowe, Cameron (1957–) Cameron Crowe's film *Almost Famous* (2000) told the story of William Miller (Patrick Fugit), a 15-year-old rock fan from San Diego who was commissioned by *Rolling Stone* to write a piece on a band called "Stillwater." If the film had been a novel, it would have been considered a roman à clef, since the story was, as Crowe admitted, "semi-autobiographical."

Cameron Crowe (left) on the set of *Say Anything* (Twentieth Century-Fox)

Out of high school by the age of 15, Crowe, who was born in Palm Springs, California, on July 13, 1957, was already writing for the *Los Angeles Times* while attending San Diego City College. He then left home to go "on the road" to cover such rock groups as the Allman Brothers and Led Zeppelin for *Rolling Stone,* distressing his mother, a university professor wise enough to know that her teenaged son would be exposed to sex and drugs while covering the rock scene. "It was like a Fellini movie," Crowe told Sharon Waxman of the *Washington Post,* "except I'd never seen a Fellini movie at the time."

Burned-out by the age of 23 after several years of living in the fast lane and churning out cover stories for *Rolling Stone,* Crowe then decided to write a novel called *Fast Times at Ridgemont High,* which he adapted to the screen in 1982, so on-target that it soon became a cult hit, establishing Crowe as a bankable young talent. He went on to write a sort of sequel, *The Wild Life* (1984), before, with the help of JAMES L. BROOKS, becoming the director as well as the screenwriter of *Say Anything* (1989), starring John Cusack, a good picture, followed by a weaker one, *Singles* (1992). In 1996 Crowe really hit his stride as director with *Jerry Maguire,* starring Tom Cruise as an out-of-luck sports agent and Cuba Gooding, Jr., as a cocky football jock. The film earned Oscar nominations, and Gooding won an Academy Award, carrying the director to a new level of achievement.

Always a writer willing to try new projects, Crowe then took time off from directing to work on his interview book *Conversations with Billy Wilder* (Knopf, 1999), whom Crowe considered "the greatest living writer-director," before undertaking his semi-autobiographical film *Almost Famous,* which he began at the age of 43. By that time Crowe had proved himself as an accomplished journalist and writer, as well as a popular filmmaker—rather than merely as a writer who has directed films, as Mark Olsen noted in *Film Comment.*

References Olsen, Mark, "Uncool," *Film Comment* 36, no. 5 (September/October 2000): 61–66; Waxman, Sharon, "The Ultimate High," *Washington Post,* September 10, 2000, pp. G1, G10.

—J.M.W.

Cukor, George (1899–1983) George Cukor, who was born in New York City in 1899, began his professional career as a stage manager in Chicago in 1919, and went to New York thereafter to direct for the Broadway theater during the 1920s. When the movies learned to talk, Cukor, like other stage directors, was summoned to Hollywood in the early 1930s. He became a dialogue director, a position usually filled by someone with theatrical experi-

George Cukor

ence who was hired to help silent-film directors make the transition to talking pictures more smoothly. One of the films he worked on in that capacity was *All Quiet on the Western Front* (1930); later, producers finally decided that he was ready to direct on his own and assigned him to *Tarnished Lady* (1931), starring Tallulah Bankhead.

From the beginning of his career as a director, he always sought to be faithful to his films' literary sources, most of which were novels and plays. He felt that a director can modify the source story to some extent, but he really should not change it in any major fashion; he should rather follow the original work as closely as possible. His films range from classics with Greta Garbo in *Camille* (1937), through his films with Spencer Tracy and Katharine Hepburn such as *Pat and Mike* (1952), to the Judy Garland musical *A Star is Born* (1954). Although many of his pictures are derived from literary works, the sum total of his movies nevertheless reflects the personal vision of the man who made them all, because he always chose material that was consistent with his personal view of reality.

Most often he explored the conflict between illusion and reality in people's lives. The chief characters of his pictures are frequently actors and actresses, for they, more than the rest of us, run the risk of allowing the world of illusion, with which they are constantly involved, to become their reality. This theme is obvious in many of Cukor's best films, including *A Double Life* (1947). Ronald Colman earned an Academy Award for his performance in the film as an actor who becomes so identified with the roles he plays that, while enacting Othello, he develops a murderous streak of jealousy that eventually destroys him. The attempt of individuals to reconcile their cherished dreams with the sober realities of their lives can likewise be found in movies as superficially different as *Holiday* (1938), *Gaslight* (1944), and *Dinner at Eight* (1933). His films also suggest that everyone must seek to sort out fantasy from fact if they are to

George Cukor (Author's collection)

cope realistically with their problems—something Cukor's characters frequently fail to do, as is the case with the central character in *A Double Life*.

In sum, his movies remain firmly rooted in, and committed to, the workaday world of reality. In film after film, Cukor sought to prod the mass audience to reconsider their cherished illusions in order to gain fresh insights into the problems that confront everyone. Film critics have therefore pointed out that his films are both entertaining and thought provoking. It could be said that Cukor was the prototype of the ideal Hollywood director, for he was a skilled craftsman who recognized that a good film is the product of many talents. He was, therefore, able to work successfully within the Hollywood system and at the same time add a personal touch to the motion pictures he directed. Cukor directed his last film, *Rich and Famous,* in 1981, thus earning the distinction of being one of the oldest directors ever to direct a major motion picture. He was likewise marked as enjoying one of the longest continuous careers of any director working in films and television. Cukor received his share of accolades, including the prestigious Life Achievement Award from the Directors Guild of America in 1981. He also won an Academy Award as best director (after five nominations) for *My Fair Lady* (1964), and an Emmy for directing his first television film, *Love Among the Ruins* (1975). Yet some of the satisfaction he derived from his long career, he told this writer, was grounded in the fact that he brought so much enjoyment to so many people. As one critic put it, Cukor's films can be appreciated—or rather, liked—at one level or another by just about everyone.

Other Films   *The Philadelphia Story* (1940); *Adam's Rib* (1949).

References   Phillips, Gene D., *Major Film Directors of the American and British Cinema* (Cranbury, N.J.: Associated University Presses, 1999); Long, Robert Emmett, ed. *George Cukor: Interviews* (Jackson: University Press of Mississippi, 2001).

—G.D.P.

Curtiz, Michael (1888–1962)

Curtiz, Michael (1888–1962)   As "Michael Curtiz," Hungarian-born Mihaly Kertesz became one of Hollywood's most versatile and prolific directors. He was born on December 24, 1888, in Budapest and educated at Markoszy University and the Royal Academy of Theatre and Art. He first entered show business at the age of 14 when he became an extra for a Viennese theater company. His first film was also Hungary's first feature film, *The Last Bohemian* (1912). After two years service in the Hungarian Infantry during World War I, he left Hungary and worked for brief periods in Sweden, France, and Germany. Little is known about this period in his career, and too many historians have written off his pre-Hollywood years. A reassessment is badly needed.

Producer Jack Warner brought him to Hollywood in 1926 where he made a hundred films, culminating in *The Comancheros* in the year of his death, 1962. From the outset, Curtiz established himself as one of Warner Bros.'s top directors. He directed two of their biggest part-talkies, *Tenderloin* and *Noah's Ark* (both 1928), and in 1930 he made no less than six features. Few directors can match Curtiz for his longevity and the diversity of his film output. He was the ultimate Hollywood contract director, comfortably in charge, a consummate craftsman, ready to take on any project, and never fussy about innovative or experimental techniques. "I put all the art in my pictures I think the audience can stand," he said wryly. Nonetheless, most of his films are distinguished by crisp photography, a mobile camera, and a fine eye for detail.

He was notorious for on-set antics—he was nothing short of a tireless and demanding autocrat—and his fractured English ("What are they trying to make from me, a jingle bells?" he once asked a writer). He is best remembered today for his Warner Bros. films from the 1930s and 1940s, including the classic adventure swashbucklers and westerns with Errol Flynn, *Captain Blood* (1935), *Charge of the Light Brigade* (1937), *The Adventures of Robin Hood* (1938), *Dodge City* (1939), *The Sea Hawk* (1940); melodramas with Bette Davis and Joan Crawford, *Private Lives of Elizabeth and Essex* (1939), *Mildred Pierce* (1945); biopics, *Yankee Doodle Dandy* (1942), about George M. Cohan, *Night and Day* (1946), about George Gershwin, *Young Man with a Horn* (1950), about Bix Beiderbecke, *Jim Thorpe—All American* (1951); musicals, *Romance on the High Seas* (1948), *The Jazz Singer* (1953); gangster films, *20,000 Years in Sing Sing* (1933), *Angels with Dirty Faces* (1938); and horror classics, *Doctor X* (1932), *Mystery of the Wax Museum* (1933). He even directed one of Elvis Presley's first (and best) pictures, *King Creole* (1958).

Undoubtedly his best known film is *Casablanca* (1943), the only film for which he received an

Oscar for best director. Humphrey Bogart's breakout performance as Rick, the proprietor of the Café Americaine, symbolized the dilemma of America and its citizens while on the sidelines of the European war, poised between an apolitical, neutral stance and the patriotic call to arms in time of crisis. Its distinguished cast—in addition to Bogart, there was Ingrid Bergman, Claude Rains, Conrad Veidt, and Paul Henried—clever script by Julius and Philip Epstein and Howard Koch, music score by Max Steiner, and, of course, Dooley Wilson's memorable rendition of "As Time Goes By," all blended into one of the most perfect entertainments ever to come out of Hollywood. Scenarist Howard Koch notes that it was perhaps because of the disagreements he and Curtiz had over the story's tone—Koch wanted to emphasize political intrigue and characterization and Curtiz preferred to underscore the romantic elements of the story—that the film achieved a magical balance between the two.

Everywhere in Curtiz's output there are special pleasures—the monumental size and scale of the flood scenes in *Noah's Ark*; the stunning beauty of the two-color Technicolor process in *The Mystery of the Wax Museum*; the loving recreation of the "Give My Regards to Broadway" number in *Yankee Doodle Dandy*; the sea battle between Captain Geoffrey Thorpe's (Errol Flynn) ship and a Spanish galleon in *The Sea Hawk*; the "Begin the Beguine" sequence in *Night and Day*; and the startling execution scene at the end of *Angels with Dirty Faces*. In 1953 Curtiz left Warner Bros. after making 80 pictures. The remainder of his career was spent at other studios, where he continued to make a variety of subjects. He died on April 11, 1962. Curtiz himself summed up his special brand of unpretentious artistry: "To make the best pictures I can that will give audiences their money's worth; to please myself as much as I can without forgetting that the pleasure of my audiences comes first. Thus only do I think I can make any substantial contribution to the art of motion pictures."

Other Films *Sodom and Gomorrah* (1923); *Moon of Israel* (1924); *The Kennel Murder Case* (1933); *Black Fury* (1935); *Virginia City* (1939); *Santa Fe Trail* (1940); *Passage to Marseille* (1944); *Life with Father* (1947); *White Christmas* (1954); *The Adventures of Huckleberry Finn* (1960).

References Kinnard, Roy, and R. J. Vitone, *The American Films of Michael Curtiz* (Metuchen, N.J.: Scarecrow, Press, 1986); Koch, Howard, *Casablanca: Script and Legend* (New York: Overlook Press, 1992).

—J.C.T.

Dahl, John (1956–) John Dahl was born in 1956 in Billings, Montana, and attended the University of Montana, Montana State University, and the American Film Institute in Los Angeles. He got his start as a storyboard artist and assistant director and worked for JONATHAN DEMME on two of Demme's best films, 1986's *Something Wild* and 1988's *Married to the Mob.* When he started making feature films, Dahl explored the rich terrain of neo-noir. Unlike such other filmmakers as DAVID LYNCH and JOEL and ETHAN COEN, Dahl did not achieve widespread recognition for his neo-noir efforts. Admittedly, *Kill Me Again* (1989), his first feature, is not exactly groundbreaking work, but it is a solid throwback to a world of desperate losers, betrayals, and double-crosses. Joanne Whalley-Kilmer is the femme fatale, and Nevada is the backdrop for an entertaining if fairly standard noir plot.

Dahl's next feature, *Red Rock West,* is a special film that defied the normal distribution patterns of modern Hollywood. It played at the Toronto Film Festival in 1993, and, while audiences liked it, nobody was sure how to market it. At the time, cable and video dates were announced, but a small San Francisco-based company called Roxie Releasing believed so strongly in the project that it

contacted the video distributor and made a deal to do a theatrical release. *Red Rock West* debuted on cable in late 1993, and the video release in early 1994 coincided with the theatrical premiere in January. The film had a successful run throughout the year and received terrific reviews.

A kind of cult hit, *Red Rock West* is the story of a decent fellow played by Nicolas Cage (in one of his best roles) mistaken for a hit man hired by J. T. Walsh to kill his wife, the femme fatale played by Lara Flynn Boyle. Complications ensue when she makes Cage a counteroffer to kill her husband, and the real hit man, played by Dennis Hopper, appears. The film is not only very suspenseful but also very funny, with one of the key jokes revolving around Cage's futile attempts to get out of Red Rock West only to find himself constantly being drawn back into the town and its danger. An underappreciated gem of the neo-noir cycle, *Red Rock West* announced Dahl as a major talent.

Dahl's next film, *The Last Seduction* (1994), also debuted on cable before gaining a theatrical run, an unfortunate business decision that robbed star Linda Fiorentino of her shot at an Oscar in the role of Bridget, one of the deadliest of all femme fatales. A woman who robs her drug-dealing husband, hits the road, and finds a new man to exploit, Bridget is one of the sexiest and most memorable of noir creations.

When Dahl finally made a major Hollywood motion picture with big stars, Matt Damon, Edward Norton, and John Malkovich, the results were decidedly mixed. *Rounders* (1998) takes place in the world of high-stakes poker, and, while it has moments of suspense and a great performance by the talented Norton as a low-life card player, it never pulls the audience into its world the way Dahl's smaller films do. Dahl's true forte, it seems, is the low-rent world of noir—the betrayals and surprising twists set against a desolate landscape—but always with a dark, sly sense of humor.

Other Films   *Unforgettable* (1996); *Joy Ride* (2001).

References   Morris, Garry, *"Red Rock West," Bright Lights Film Journal* 12 (Spring 1994): 43; Parker, Jeff, "To Neo Noir and Back: Director John Dahl," *Guerrilla Filmmaker* 2, no. 1 (Fall 2000): 16–17.

—P.N.C.

Daldry, Stephen (1960–)   As artistic director of the Royal Court Theatre (1992–97), the Gate Theatre in Notting Hill (1989–92), and the Metro Theatre Company in Sheffield (1984–86), Stephen Daldry had produced over 100 new plays before making his feature film debut in 2000 with *Billy Elliot.* Specializing mainly in staging well-conceived revivals, his work at the Royal Court included David Hare's *Via Dolorosa,* Ron Hutchinson's *Rat in the Skull,* Caryl Churchill's *This Is a Chair,* and Arnold Wesker's *The Kitchen,* and for Britain's National Theatre two award-winning plays, Sophie Treadwell's *Machinal* and his most impressive theatrical success, the ingeniously staged J. B. Priestley revival, *An Inspector Calls,* which premiered on the Lyttleton stage of the National Theatre in 1992 and was still being produced in London's West End eight years later, long after winning the prestigious Olivier Award. The London *Guardian* called Daldry "The Hit Man."

Born in 1960, the son of a bank manager and a former cabaret performer, Daldry grew up in Somerset in England and earned his degree in English and drama at Sheffield University in 1982. After graduation, Daldry joined Il Circo di Nando Orfei, an Italian circus, as an apprentice clown for 10 months. Back in England in 1984, he co-founded the Metro Theatre Company in Sheffield in 1984, then became a trainee director at Sheffield's Crucible Theater, later serving as associate artist (1987–88). This was followed by his tenure at the Gate, a small, 56-seat theatre located over a pub in Notting Hill Gate, until Daldry joined the Royal Court and directed *Machinal* at the Lyttleton in October of 1993.

By 1999 Daldry was working as a BBC director and producer. His first short film, *Eight,* was nominated for a BAFTA award. The story of *Eight* featured a boy whose father had died in the Hillsborough disaster of 1989, in which 96 spectators were killed when a soccer stadium collapsed. Rumors had Daldry in line to run the National Theatre after the retirement of Trevor Nunn, but by 1997 Daldry had already signed a three-year contract with Working Title Pictures, following the lead of other British theater directors such as Sam Mendes and NICHOLAS HYTNER, who made the transition from stage to screen, and the earlier precedent set by TONY RICHARDSON, who moved from the Royal Court to Woodfall Films during the 1950s. *Billy Elliot,* his breakthrough feature film, set against the backdrop of the 1984 miners' strike in the northeast of England, told the story of a working-class boy who aspires to audition for the Royal National Ballet, "treading a fine line between sentimentality and serious intent," in the words of Edward Lawrenson, and operating from a "Ken Loach-meets-*Flashdance* premise." After an enthusiastic premiere at the Cannes Film Festival 2000, the film grossed over $2 million during its opening weekend in Britain and appeared to be the most substantial British hit since *The Full Monty* (1996). It later opened to rave reviews in the United States and was hailed as the "Fall's Must-See Film" by *Newsweek* reviewer David Ansen, effectively launching Daldry's career as a successful and gifted film director.

References Ansen, David, "Fall's Must-See Film," *Newsweek,* October 16, 2000, pp. 68–69; Kavanagh, Julie, "Sort of Pals in a Kind of Pas de Deux," *New York Times,* October 15, 2000, II, p. 13; Lawrenson, Edward, "Cosmic Dancer," *Sight and Sound* 10, no. 10 (October 2000): 12–13; Lesser, Wendy, *A Director Calls: Stephen Daldry and the Theatre* (Berkeley: University of California Press, 1997).

—J.M.W.

Dante, Joe (1946–) Joe Dante, a "Hollywood maverick" who prefers unearthly subjects like flying saucers, predatory gremlins, and robot armies to the mundane realities of love and war, was born on November 28, 1946, in Morristown, New Jersey. Describing himself as "the kid who liked movies and got to make them," he noted: "It's not a matter of [studio executives] giving you freedom, it's a matter of you finding a way to subvert what they want." He has edited, written, directed, produced, and acted in movies and directed for TV. He loves B movies, horror, science fiction, and cartoons. Dubbed "Son of the Saturday Matinee" and known for his absurdist humor and offbeat creativity, Dante directs films that brim with in-jokes for alert movie buffs.

While attending Philadelphia College of Art he expanded his already encyclopedic knowledge of film and for a student project made *The Movie Orgy* (1968), a pastiche of movie clips, trailers, pieces of TV shows, and commercials. Originally titled, *7 Hour All-Night Once in a Lifetime Atomic Movie Orgy,* there were actually two different versions of the film made, one of which was sponsored on college campuses by Schlitz Beer. He graduated with a degree in motion picture photography in 1968 and worked for a brief time as managing editor of *Film Bulletin,* a trade journal. In the early 1970s ROGER CORMAN hired him as first full-time editor of preview trailers for New World Pictures. In 1976, on a dare, he codirected *Hollywood Boulevard,* a spoof of B movies, with Allen Arkush, produced by Jon Davison for New World—in 10 days for $60,000. In 1977 while with Corman, he edited Ron Howard's first directing effort, *Grand Theft Auto.* In 1979 he was a writer and uncredited codirector for *Rock 'n Roll High School.* He worked with John Sayles as screenwriter, directing *Piranha,* a rip-off of *Jaws,* in 1978 (special effects were shot in a swimming pool at UCLA), and later directed *The Howling,* the popular werewolf movie that he also edited, in 1981.

He directed "It's a *Good* Life" as part of the anthology film, *Twilight Zone—The Movie* (1983), for STEVEN SPIELBERG, followed by the big-budget film, *Gremlins* (1984), also produced by Spielberg. More movies, some more successful than others, followed: *Explorers,* about a kid whose belief in extraterrestrial intelligence leads him to a confrontation with genuine aliens, with Ethan Hawke and River Phoenix in the cast (1985); six sequences of *Amazon Women on the Moon* (1987); *Innerspace,* produced by Spielberg, with Meg Ryan, Dennis Quaid, and Martin Short in the cast (1987); *The 'Burbs,* starring Tom Hanks (1989); *Gremlins 2: The New Batch,* in which he also played the role of Grandpa Fred (1990); *Matinee,* starring John Goodman (1993). *Small Soldiers,* coproduced by Steven Spielberg (uncredited), appeared on the big screen in 1998. He is, in 2001, working on *Everyone Hates the Phone Company.*

In the best Hollywood ensemble cast tradition, Joe Dante likes to use certain actors again and again, and he himself has often acted in his own and others' movies. In 1994 Dante starred in *The Silence of the Hams.* Dante has directed for TV, including such programs as *Eerie, Indiana* (creative consultant and director of five episodes [1991]); *Runaway Daughters,* a kind of B movie from the 1950s, which was made in 10 days and in which Roger Corman appears (1994); *The Second Civil*

War (1997); *Warlord: Battle for the Galaxy,* executive producer (1998); and episodes for *Night Visions* (2000). Joe Dante has directed several other TV shows, including episodes of *Police Squad!* (1982), *Picture Windows* (1995), *Amazing Stories* (1985), and more. Dante has commented, "To try to maintain your own identity in a system that is geared against it is a challenge."

Reference Singer, Michael, *A Cut Above* (Los Angeles: Lone Eagle Press, 1998).

—K.O.

Dash, Julie (1952–) Independent film-maker Julie Dash was born October 22, 1952, in Long Island City, New York, and grew up in the Queensbridge Housing Projects, where her initial interest in filmmaking began. She enrolled in a workshop held at the Studio Museum of Harlem at the age of 17, shooting her first film on Super 8 with the help of photographs from *Jet* magazine that she suspended from pipe cleaners.

The spirit of Dash's work is to capture pivotal events in the lives of black women, focusing on and depicting experiences that have never been shown on screen. Historical events and issues are incorporated into the storylines, with much of her focus on interactions within groups and the dynamics of how relationships work. Dash draws attention away from images of black women who have negative societal influences guiding them, choosing, rather, to promote an inner sanctum of consciousness that envelops black women. She believes that black women are the backbones, griots, and storytellers of the culture, and, most importantly, the viewers she creates for.

Dash entered college first as a psychology major, changing to film production her sophomore year. She received a bachelor of arts in film production from the City College of New York, and in 1973 wrote and produced a documentary, *Working Models of Success.* After graduation she moved to Los Angeles to attend the Center for Advanced Film Studies at the American Film Institute as the youngest fellow ever accepted into the AFI program. During this time Dash also gained experience working on various film crews and, in 1977, adapted the short story, *Diary of an African Nun,* written by Alice Walker. *African Nun* was a winner of the Director's Guild Award in 1977. Dash then created *Four Women,* an experimental film focusing on dance that won the Gold Medal for Women in Film at the 1978 Miami International Film Festival. She conceived and directed the film that was inspired by the Nina Simone song of the same title.

Dash was awarded grants from the National Endowment for the Humanities (NEH) in 1981, 1983, and again in 1985. In 1983, the film short *Illusions* won Dash a nomination for a Cable ACE Award in art direction. Set in 1942, it tells the story of a film executive who is a fair-skinned black woman who passes for white, along with a second character, who is a black singer who dubs the voices of white starlets. Dash argued that both characters are made invisible and voiceless by the film industry and society. The Jury Prize for the Best Film of the Decade by the Black Filmmakers Foundation was given to *Illusions* in 1989. It also won the Black Cinema Society Award in 1983 and is now permanently archived at Clark College in Atlanta and at Indiana University.

Dash moved to Atlanta, Georgia, in 1986, where she formed Geechee Girl Productions and began directing her own film projects. Two notable works for the National Black Women's Health Project were produced in 1987, *Breaking the Silence: On Reproductive Rights* and *Preventing Cancer.* In addition to her company credits were two television productions, *Praise House* in 1991 and *Relatives* in 1990.

In 1981 Dash received a Guggenheim grant to study the Gullah culture of the South Carolina Sea Islands, which resulted in the widely acclaimed film, *Daughters of the Dust* (1992). With this picture Dash became the first African-American woman ever to create a full-length general release film. *Daughters of the Dust* won first prize in cinematography at the 1991 Sundance Film Festival in Utah, and the PBS "American Playhouse" series televised the film nationally in 1992 after its Sundance premiere.

Dash remembers her father's family had roots in the Sea Islands, where the people are called Gullah or Geechee. "For a long time it was an insult to be called Gullah or Geechee, because it was associated with African ties," she says. "It meant you were ignorant, you had a strange accent and you practiced magic." *Daughters of the Dust* is notable for its Afrocentric point of view and a storytelling method that is very different from Hollywood narrative conventions and Euro-American traditions.

Dash also demonstrates a sense of Afrocentrism in the film through her set designs, costumes, makeup, and hairstyles. In addition, she keeps the players' gestures, actions, and motor habits realistic and aesthetically true in order to maintain a sense of West African integrity. These were important considerations for Dash during the film's production. Two examples of Afrocentric motor skills are the way one turns the head slightly to the left to acknowledge an elder who is speaking, and, also, covering the mouth when laughing. Dash used a prototype machine called a speed aperture controller to produce portions of the film. The aperture controller allows a character to speak at 24 frames per second while allowing the camera to move into slow motion in the middle of a scene without starting and stopping. The voice will remain synchronized. The prototype used was the only one that existed in the United States at the time.

Dash produced two film videos in 1992 and 1994, as well as a documentary about author Zora Neale Hurston. Dash received a Fulbright fellowship to create a screenplay about the black British film collective, Sankofa, and moved to London to collaborate with Maureen Blackwood, a member of the Sankofa collective. Dash's future goal is to work on a series of films depicting black women in the United States, from the turn of the 20th century to the year 2000. Each film will display sensitive yet complex portrayals of problems that diverse ensembles of black women must confront.

References *American Visions* 6, no. 1 (February 1991): 46–49; *Black Film Review* 6, no. 1 (1992): 12–20; *Essence* 22, no. 10 (February 1992), p. 38; Chan, V., *Mother Jones* 15, no. 7 (November/December 1990): 60.

—D.W.

Dassin, Jules (1911–)   Jules [Julius] Dassin was born in Middleton, Connecticut, on December 18, 1911, and raised in the Bronx. He first worked as an actor in New York's Yiddish theater, and later in life acted in films he directed in Europe, using the pseudonym Perla Vita. After moving to Hollywood in 1940, he worked on a number of forgettable projects for RKO and MGM before hitting his stride at 20th Century-Fox with *Brute Force* (1947), *The Naked City* (1948), and *Thieves' Highway* (1949). His Hollywood career was curtailed after Edward Dmytryk "named" him while testifying before the House Un-American Activities Committee.

Dassin was true to the character in *Brute Force* who remarks to Hume Cronyn, "Captain, I'm a cheap thief. But I'm not an informer," and expatriated himself to Europe, first to Britain, where he made *Night and the City* (1950), then to France, where he made his most famous film, *Rififi (Du rififi chez les hommes),* selected to represent France at the 1955 Cannes Film Festival, where it won the prize for best direction. *Rififi* made money in Europe and had a limited run in the United States, where it was probably the first film to be seen in America that was credited to a blacklisted artist. Dalton Trumbo wrote that after Dassin took up residence in Paris, he became "an ornament to the world of French cinema, and his films are regarded as representative not of American but of French culture," adding that "the Dassin case is regularly cited in French intellectual circles as a criticism of American democracy."

In 1957 Dassin went to Greece to discuss making *Zorba the Greek,* which was ultimately directed by Michael Cacoyannis in 1964. Dassin settled in Greece and worked with the actress Melina Mercouri, whom he later married in 1966. Their most popular collaboration was *Never on Sunday* (1960), which earned Mercouri an Oscar nomination and the best actress award at the Cannes Festival. Mercouri later became active in politics as a Socialist member of parliament and, finally, as cabinet minister of culture until her death in 1994.

Still "vigorous" at the age of 89, Dassin appeared in New York to introduce the rerelease of his classic caper film *Rififi* in July of 2000. "The title comes from the North African tribe, the Rifs, who were in constant conflict," he told the *New York Times.* "So it's all about melees and conflicts and fighting, out of which the novelist Auguste Le Breton made the word 'rififi.'" Dassin also expressed "surprise" over the way Brian DePalma's *Mission Impossible* (1996) had copied his famous high-wire burglary scene from his film *Topkapi* (1964) "without acknowledgment"—but that is perhaps a tribute to the lasting influence of his work.

Other Films *He Who Must Die* (1957); *Phaedra* (1962); *The Rehearsal* (1974); *A Dream of Passion* (1978).

References Kehr, Dave, "At the Movies," *New York Times,* July 28, 2000, p. B18; McGilligan, Patrick, and Paul Buhle, *Tender Comrades: A Backstory of the Hollywood Blacklist* (New York: St. Martin's Griffin, 1997); Manfull, Helen, ed., *Additional Dialogue: Letters of Dalton Trumbo, 1942–1962* (New York: M. Evans, 1970).

—J.M.W.

Davies, Terence

Davies, Terence (1945–) Terence Davies was born in Liverpool, England, in 1945. The youngest of 10 children, his childhood was passed in a blue-collar world, dominated by an alcoholic, vitriolic, and abusive father. In an attempt to avoid military service, Davies's father drank disinfectants, and there is speculation that this may have accelerated his death from stomach cancer when Terence

was eight. At this same time, Davies's older sisters started to take him to the cinema, where he grew enthralled by movies, most particularly, American musicals and classic Hollywood cinema. Year later, Davies would describe how the movies provided great escape and joy for him. When he was 15 years old, Davies dropped out of school to work as a clerk and, eventually, an accountant in a shipping office. He began writing for radio and the stage, which led to his attending drama school in Coventry (1971–73). After Coventry, Davies secured a grant from the British Film Production Board and completed his first film, *Children* (1974), which he both wrote and directed. This comprised the first film in his Liverpool trilogy, which also includes *Madonna and Child* (1980) and *Death and Transfiguration* (1983). Nonlinear in structure (as nearly all Davies's work is), the films form a growing-into-awareness story, largely autobiographical and centered on the fictional character "Robert Tucker," whom we first meet as an intimidated and bullied school boy. The trilogy follows Tucker through middle-aged expressions of his homosexuality, his transfiguring understanding of his years of sexual and religious (Catholic) guilt, and his death. Made over a stretch of 10 years, financed by three different funding sources, and shot on variant film stock, the trilogy is, nevertheless, lovely, controlled, yet lyrical. While it was highly regarded by critics, it angered a portion of the viewing public, who protested the trilogy's homosexual content.

These first three films were followed by *Distant Voices, Still Lives* (1988), one of Davies's most popular and autobiographical films. Set in working-class Liverpool in the years before and after World War II, the occasion of a wedding brings about the reunion of the members of a dysfunctional family—triggering intimate memories of the family's past, especially of the drunken abuse by the father (Pete Postlethwaite). Davies's drab, almost reticent portrait of these cramped and restricted lives—the color palette of the cinematography desaturates and bleaches out the color—is enlivened by a great emphasis on the popular music of the day. Everybody sings, it seems. Traditional ditties like "Knees Up, Mother Brown," Tin Pan Alley hits like "If You Knew Susie" and "Love Is a Many-Splendored Thing" resound throughout the pubs and parlors. There is a sad beauty to this kind of solace, because it relates so little to these stunted lives—yet it is so *necessary* to them.

Davies's next film was *The Long Day Closes* (1992), a slice-of-life story told through the eyes of a 12-year-old boy, who understands both hardship and hope. Davies's sixth film, *The Neon Bible* (1995), was acclaimed in several newspapers as "one of the year's most beautiful films." Set in the American South of the 1940s, it tells the evocative story of a sensitive, confused young man, who looks to his vibrant and flamboyant aunt (Gena Rowlands) for emotional rescue. "It was close to my heart," says Davies, "but a lot of people said it was just more autobiography, but poorly disguised. . . . I accept that the film was a failure, although I think there are good things in it."

Davies broke fully with his tradition of elliptically structured memory pieces in his seventh film, *The House of Mirth* (2000). Based on Edith Wharton's novel, the film is respectful of Wharton's work, preserving its basic linear narrative scheme. A period piece set among the nouveau riche of New York City in 1905, the story chronicles the tragedy of the gradual fall from social grace of Lily Bart (Gillian Anderson), a beautiful but headstrong young woman whose mounting debts and unconventional behavior prove to be her undoing. "We resist the strong temptations," she tells her friend, the lawyer Seldon (Eric Stoltz), "but we fall victim to the smaller ones." Made on the nominal budget of $8 million, it nonetheless has a handsome look thanks to the cinematography of Remi Adefarasin and the production design of Don Taylor. While a significant departure from his traditional style and subject, *The House of Mirth* displays many of the qualities that have distinguished Davies's work from the start: meticulously beautiful composition, the sparing but effective use of music (excerpts from Mozart's *Cosi fan Tutti* and chamber works by Marcello and Haydn), and the insistence on the prevailing spirit of the human heart against the bleakness and depravity of the outer world. Although there are many opportunities for the use of vivid color schemes, the palette is never garish, but tastefully appointed in the manner of interiors by the painter John Singer Sargent. "Obviously, it doesn't have the same kind of passion you have when you're dealing with things you've actually gone through, or that the people you grew up with and love went through," says Davies. "It's replaced by a different sort of passion, the passion of re-creating the world that you see in the book. If you don't have that passion, then there's no point in putting any film through a camera."

References Fuller, Graham, "Summer's End," *Film Comment* 37, no. 1 (January–February 2001): 54–59; Johnson, Claudia L., "There's Blood on the Walls," *The* [London] *Times Literary Supplement,* October 27, 2000, pp. 18–19.

—J.M.W.

De Antonio, Emile (1919–1989) Emile de Antonio, a political filmmaker who described himself as a "radical scavenger," was born on May 14, 1919, the son of a prosperous doctor, and raised in Scranton, Pennsylvania, comfortably "surrounded by books and servants," as Renee Tajima described him. De Antonio was educated at Harvard University in the same class as John F. Kennedy, but de Antonio struck a very different political stance, joined the John Reed Society at Harvard, and became a Marxist and a member of the Young Communist League. He worked during the 1950s as a longshoreman on the docks of Baltimore, a barge captain, and a professor of philosophy. After serving in World War II, he went to graduate school at Columbia University, then taught at the College of William and Mary in Virginia.

Settling into Greenwich Village, he befriended artists Jasper Johns and Bob Rauschenberg, produced galas for dancer Merce Cunningham, and the 25th anniversary concert for composer John Cage in 1958. Having contacts with the rich and famous in New York society, by the early 1960s he decided, at the suggestion of Dan Talbot, to make a film about the 1954 Senate Army-McCarthy hearings. The first cut was overlong at 12 hours, but after two years of work, the film *Point of Order!* (1964) had been edited down to a 90-minute documentary. Talbot premiered the film at the Beekman Theatre on Manhattan's fashionable East Side. *New York Times* reviewer Bosley Crowther misgauged the film's appeal, dismissing it as "a bewildering look-in on a freakish political event," but Joe McCarthy's shenanigans did not seem "freakish" to young radicals concerned at the time about America's involvement in Vietnam, and de Antonio found his niche as a filmmaker for the New Left. De Antonio specialized in compilation documentaries after his success with *Point of Order! That's Where the Action Is* (1965) covered the mayoral election campaign in New York City, for example, and *America Is Hard to See* (1968) covered Senator Eugene McCarthy's campaign for the American presidency in 1968, focusing upon the senator's success in the primary elections in New Hampshire and in Oregon.

His interest in the Kennedy assassination was inspired by former New York assemblyman Mark Lane, whose critique of the Warren Commission Report became the basis for his documentary *Rush to Judgment* (1967), financed by Woodfall Films, a British company controlled by Oscar Lewenstein and "Free Cinema" filmmaker Tony Richardson. The challenge here was to interview witnesses in Dallas whose testimony the Warren Commission had slighted or ignored, such as William Whaley, the taxi driver "who allegedly drove Oswald away from the assassination scene," as de Antonio told Colin J. Westerbeck, Jr., "dead in an accident soon after he was interviewed" by

CBS. The director found such materials in the CBS film archives in New York, footage destroyed by CBS after network managers discovered what de Antonio was up to. Documentary research in Dallas was complicated by police intimidation, and some witnesses were afraid to cooperate.

De Antonio used similar methods of "radical scavenging" for his Vietnam documentary *In the Year of the Pig* (1969), "scavenging" materials from ABC news and newsreel footage from the French military archives. Backed by Paul Newman, Leonard Bernstein, and Steve Allen, the film was an exposé of Western imperialism in Vietnam. As de Antonio told Colin Westerbeck, "Out-takes are the confessions of the system." Released in America before the Democratic National Convention of 1968, *In the Year of the Pig* was nominated for an Academy Award. It was followed by his Nixon satire, *Milhouse: A White Comedy* (1971). *Painters Painting* (1973) was a documentary about the New York art scene, but other political documentaries were to come, notably *Underground* (1976), a series of interviews with younger antiestablishment radicals codirected with cinematographer Haskell Wexler featuring five members of the Weather Underground movement, and *In the King of Prussia* (1982), which covered the trial of Roman Catholic radicals Daniel and Philip Berrigan in Pennsylvania.

De Antonio's last film, *Mr. Hoover and I* (1990), was an autobiographical self-portrait, recording his life as reflected by the 10,000-page file about his activities gathered by the FBI, which de Antonio obtained through the Freedom of Information Act in 1975. "This film is an attempt at subversion," he claimed. At one point he considered calling the film "A Middle-Aged Radical as Seen Through the Eyes of His Government." As Gary Giddins wrote, "De Antonio's genius was the plowing through public records and splicing together the damning evidence." He was the only filmmaker included on Richard Nixon's "enemies list." He "documented the follies of his own generation—

those who came of age during the Depression, served in the military during World War II—and then remade postwar America," in the words of Renee Tajima, and became "the dean of radical filmmaking." De Antonio died of heart failure on December 15, 1989, in his East Village, New York City, home.

References Giddins, Gary, "Wanted by the FBI," *Village Voice,* August 24, 1990, p. 68; Silberman, Robert, "De Antonio, Emile," in *A Political Companion to American Film,* ed. Gary Crowdus (Chicago: Lakeview Press, 1994), pp. 103–107; Tajima, Renee, "Emile de Antonio, 1919–89," *Village Voice,* January 2, 1990, p. 86.

—J.M.W.

Del Ruth, Roy (1895–1961) One of the most prolific film directors of the 1930s (from 1931 to 1933 alone he directed 13 feature films for Warner Bros.), Del Ruth has received much critical attention recently primarily for his pre-Code work. According to film historian Thomas Doherty, Del Ruth's pre-Code films are like snapshots of depression America in their "straightforward confrontation with everyday problems (hunger, work, money) and the topical subject matter ('ripped straight from today's headlines!')." Pierre Sauvage relates Del Ruth's style to the "fast-paced, low-life Warner Brothers world . . . blending humor and crime." And Andrew Sarris has compared Del Ruth to another Warner Bros. director of the same period, MERVYN LEROY, whom he claims "as long as he is not mistaken for a serious artist . . . can be delightfully entertaining." Perhaps this last comment expresses best Del Ruth's position in film history as a functional studio-era director who made films efficiently and quickly for a depression-era audience hungry for entertainment.

Born in Philadelphia on October 18, 1895, Del Ruth worked as a newspaper reporter and illustrator before moving to California. He began his work in films as both a writer and gagman for Mack Sennett. In 1917 he began directing two-reel comedies for such comedians as Billy Bevan and Harry Langdon. In 1925 he was signed by the fledgling Warner Brothers company where he started to direct feature films.

During the early sound period Del Ruth directed such notable films as *The Terror* (1928), *The Desert Song* (1929), based on the Sigmund Romberg operetta, and *Gold Diggers of Broadway* (1929), which was to initiate the popular Warner Bros. musical series. In 1931 Del Ruth directed the much-neglected first film version of Dashiel Hammett's *The Maltese Falcon,* starring Ricardo Cortez as Sam Spade. That same year he made the first of four films starring the Warner contract actor, James Cagney. *Blonde Crazy* was followed by *Taxi!* (1932), *Winner Take All* (1932), and *Lady Killer* (1933). Also typical of Del Ruth's early thirties work are the films that starred that perennial pre-Code actor, Warren William; among these are *Beauty and the Boss* (1932), *Employees' Entrance* (1933), *The Mind Reader* (1933), and *Upper World* (1934).

Darryl F. Zanuck, whom Del Ruth had worked with closely during his Warner Bros. period, offered him the job of directing *I Was a Fugitive From A Chain Gang,* but Del Ruth turned it down because he felt that the story was too morbid and depressing for the times. In 1934, when Zanuck became production head of Twentieth Century, he gave two directorial assignments to Del Ruth: *Bulldog Drummond Strikes Back* (1934) and *Folies Bergere* (1935). Samuel Goldwyn hired Del Ruth to direct Eddie Cantor in *Kid Millions* (1934). This later film marks a shift in Del Ruth's career toward film musicals. When Twentieth Century merged with Fox studios in 1935, Del Ruth was one of the first directors placed under contract by Darryl Zanuck. *Thanks A Million* (1936) starred Dick Powell as a young singer running for governor.

In the late thirties Del Ruth filmed two musicals starring the former Olympic ice-skater, Sonja Henie, *Happy Landing* and *My Lucky Star* (both 1938). His big musicals for MGM include

Broadway Melody of 1936, Born to Dance (1936), *Broadway Melody of 1938, The Chocolate Soldier* (1941), *Du Barry Was A Lady* (1943), and *Broadway Rhythm* (1944). A return to Warners in the early 1950s saw the director reunited with James Cagney in the musical *The West Point Story* (1950). His other Warners musicals at this time include *Starlift* (1951), *On Moonlight Bay* (1951), based on Booth Tarkington's Penrod stories, and *About Face* (1952), a musical remake of *Brother Rat* (1938). Del Ruth directed the Warner Bros. 3-D horror film *Phantom of the Rue Morgue* (1954); a remake of Universal's 1932 Bela Lugosi vehicle, *Murders in the Rue Morgue,* the film starred Karl Malden.

A brief sojourn into television resulted in Del Ruth's directing episodes for *Richard Diamond, Private Detective* (1957) and *Adventures in Paradise* (1959). A return to film directing resulted in the "B" features *The Alligator People* (1959) and *Why Must I Die?* (1960), an alternate (and weak) treatment of the celebrated Barbara Graham murder trial made famous cinematically as Susan Hayward's *I Want to Live* (1960). Del Ruth worked best under the studio system where he was noted by *Variety* in 1933 as "the fastest of the fast set." Roy Del Ruth died on April 27, 1961, in Sherman Oaks, California, from a heart attack.

Other Films *The Second Floor Mystery* (1930); *My Past* (1931); *Side Show* (1931); *The Little Giant* (1933); *Captured* (1933); *Kid Millions* (1934); *It Had to Happen* (1936); *Private Number* (1936); *Topper Returns* (1941); *Maisie Gets Her Man* (1942); *The Babe Ruth Story* (1947); *Always Leave Them Laughing* (1949); *Three Sailors and a Girl* (1953).

References Barson, Michael, *The Illustrated Who's Who of Hollywood Directors,* vol. 1: *The Sound Era* (New York: Farrar, Straus and Giroux, 1995); Coursodon, Jean-Pierre, *American Directors,* vol. 1 (New York: McGraw-Hill, 1983); Doherty, Thomas, *Pre-Code Hollywood: Sex, Immorality, and Insurrection in American Cinema, 1930–1934* (New York: Columbia University Press, 1999); Sarris, Andrew, *The American Cinema:* *Directors and Directions, 1929–1968* (New York: De Capo Press, 1996).

—R.W.

DeMille, Cecil B[lount] (1881–1959)

The pioneering American director and producer, Cecil B. DeMille, was born on August 12, 1881, in Ashfield, Massachusetts, to Henry Churchill de Mille and the former Mathilda Beatrice Samuel. Both of his parents had theatrical interests. His mother had been an actress before her marriage, and his father, a lay Episcopal preacher and schoolmaster, wrote plays in his spare time. A friend and eventual partner of David Belasco, one of the best-known American playwrights and directors of the late 19th century, Henry de Mille was eventually successful enough in his writing to change his career. When Cecil was 12, his father suddenly died of typhus. The young DeMille, who later changed the structure of his last name, would continue to idolize his father throughout his life.

In 1896 Cecil was sent to the Pennsylvania Military College in Chester, Pennsylvania, and in 1898 he enrolled in the American Academy of Dramatic Arts in New York City to study acting. From 1900 to 1910, DeMille acted in several Broadway plays and for numerous touring road shows. He began writing plays with his brother William in 1906. After Beatrice de Mille founded a theatrical agency, the de Mille Play Company in 1910, DeMille met Jesse Lasky and Samuel Goldfish (later Goldwyn) through his mother's contacts, and with them formed the Jesse L. Lasky Feature Play Company in 1912. Their first film was *The Squaw Man* (1914), directed by DeMille and adapted from an old Broadway play. This six-reel film was the first feature-length motion picture made in the United States. Shot largely around Los Angeles, this enormously successful film helped to establish the city as the center for American motion picture production, and DeMille has therefore often been credited for having "founded" Hollywood.

DeMille directed seven more features in 1914, including *Brewster's Millions* and *The Virginian*, based on Owen Wister's classic western novel. By the end of that year DeMille had established himself as one of the leading film directors in the nation. In his early film career, DeMille preferred shooting stories based on traditional stage melodramas. Over the next two years he directed 22 feature-length films, often writing the screenplays and editing the films himself. The best known of these films was *The Cheat* (1915), a film much admired in France and a film that many critics consider his finest work. *The Cheat* was an audacious melodrama that featured Fannie Ward as an upper-class woman married to a stockbroker who foolishly invests charity funds in a risky stock, loses all, and then turns for help to a nefarious Asian jade dealer (Sessue Hayakawa), who exploits her economically and sexually. The film used experimental lighting, and DeMille developed an editing and visual style that enhanced the psychology of his characters.

DeMille also directed the operatic diva Geraldine Farrar in *Carmen* in 1915, lending motion pictures a new air of respectability. Farrar starred in several other DeMille films, including *Temptation* (1916), *Maria Rosa* (1916), and *Joan the Woman* (1917), DeMille's take on Joan of Arc. *Joan the Woman* was an especially significant film in DeMille's body of work in that it began the long tradition of grand historical epics in which DeMille later specialized. In 1916 the Lasky Company merged with Adolph Zukor's Famous Players to form Paramount Pictures. DeMille was made responsible for all of the films that the studio released.

Later in the decade DeMille's pictures took a new direction, anticipating the changes in public mood that would result from the experience of World War I, and the transforming mores in American society. DeMille's target audience was always the middle class, and his socio-sexual films of the later 1910s and early 1920s reflected a new

Cecil B. DeMille (Author's collection)

morality that was overtaking America. *Old Wives for New* (1918), *We Can't Have Everything* (1918), *Don't Change Your Husband* (1919), *Male and Female* (1919), and *Why Change Your Wife?* (1920) all featured wealthy couples who often changed their partners, only to reunite with their original husbands or wives. The films reflected a staple of DeMille's later films—his combination of sexual titillation and overt moral sermonizing. Several of the films starred Gloria Swanson, who became a major star under DeMille's direction. As his forays into sophisticated salaciousness and amoral decadence progressed in such films as *Saturday Night* (1922) and *Manslaughter* (1922), the once highly respected director found himself under attack by cultural critics. Some historians have argued that DeMille did as much to shape the sexual morality of the 1920s as he did to reflect it.

In 1923 DeMille's career took another sharp turn with *The Ten Commandments.* One of the first of his great biblical epics, the film proved to be one of the greatest moneymakers of the silent era. The biblical story was only half of the film, the latter half being a modern-day Cain and Abel parable. One of the first films with production costs over $1 million, the motion picture recouped its costs several times over. This biblical epic was to be followed by DeMille's $2.5-million production *King of Kings* in 1927, another of his most successful films, and one that played well into the 1950s as a special exhibition. This lavish, reverential, and spectacular film was DeMille's personal favorite.

DeMille remained an eclectic filmmaker throughout the 1920s, although his moralizing became more focused and mindful in the creation of his films. In 1925 DeMille was forced out of Paramount due to various mergers and takeovers and because of his inability to contain the costs of his productions. With the help of bankers, he formed the Cinema Corporation of America and became his own producer. His last film with CCA as an independent producer was *The Godless Girl* (1929), an "exposé" of atheists attempting to take over the public school system. In 1928 CCA came into the hands of Joseph Kennedy, and DeMille's unit was transplanted to MGM. His first sound film was *Dynamite* (1929), but DeMille's initial sound films (which included a third version of *The Squaw Man* [1931]) were commercially unsuccessful, and there was talk that DeMille would simply be another victim of the transition to talking pictures.

In 1931 DeMille returned to Paramount for a mere fraction of his previous salary. The director rebounded, however, with *Sign of the Cross* (1932), which returned to his tried-and-true formula of overt sexuality and debauchery (during Nero's reign, this time), with ample sermonizing over the sinner's eventual downfall. The film, which starred Charles Laughton, Fredric March, and Claudette Colbert, was financially successful but was criticized severely by many in the religious community for DeMille's lascivious scenes, which included Colbert bathing in milk, implied lesbianism, and barbarous torture.

DeMille followed up *Sign of the Cross* with two more historical epics—*Cleopatra* (1934) and *The Crusades* (1935). After the latter film lost over $700,000, DeMille switched to the western genre, filming *The Plainsman* (1937), *The Buccaneer* (1938), *Union Pacific* (1939), and *North West Mounted Police* (1940). All of these films were financially successful.

Meanwhile, in 1936 DeMille entered into radio programming, presenting the *Lux Radio Theatre of the Air,* which recreated shortened versions of Hollywood movies dramatized for radio. As a member of the American Federation of Radio Artists, DeMille was asked in August of 1944 for a one dollar contribution to defeat a proposed California state amendment to end the closed shop. DeMille not only publicly refused to donate to this cause, but also resigned from the radio show and established the DeMille Foundation for Political Freedom. Thereafter, he became one of the most visible and vocal conservatives in postwar Hollywood, and his organization became a rallying point for the later communist witch-hunts.

After several lackluster films, DeMille rebounded again with *Samson and Delilah* (1949), a biblical epic that earned more than $12 million and began a Hollywood trend to cash in on Bible stories. Still another DeMille box-office winner, *The Greatest Show on Earth* (1952), went on to earn an Oscar for best picture (perhaps reflecting the extent of McCarthyism's influence on Hollywood). DeMille's last film, *The Ten Commandments* (1956), was a remake of the 1923 film, mimes the story, and was even more epic in scope than the earlier version. A tremendous blockbuster, the film is still telecast annually. DeMille was scheduled to remake *The Buccaneer,* but was prevented from doing so when he suffered a heart attack while filming *The Ten Commandments.* He let his son-in-law Anthony Quinn have his first directing job on that film, while he served as producer. While on a publicity tour for the film, DeMille suffered another heart attack and died in his home a month later. His autobiography was published posthumously in 1959. DeMille was considered a consummate showman and an expert in self-promotion. He became the symbol of the tyrannical director, wearing a costume that included riding boots and breeches, the figure he portrayed in the Hollywood classic *Sunset Boulevard* (1950), which also featured the star he had created, Gloria Swanson.

References Essoe, Gabe, and Raymond Lee, *DeMille: The Man and His Pictures* (New York: Castle Books, 1970); Higashi, Sumiko, *Cecil B. DeMille and American Culture: The Silent Era* (Berkeley: University of California Press, 1994); Higashi, Sumiko, *Cecil B. DeMille: A Guide to References and Resources* (Boston: G. K. Hall, 1985).

—G.B.

de Mille, William Churchill (1878–1955)

Playwright William de Mille, after devoting his early career to the theater, rather reluctantly followed his younger brother, Cecil, to the picture business. To this day his accomplishments, which were substantial, have been overshadowed by his more illustrious sibling. William was born on July 25, 1878, in Washington, D.C. Following the example of his famous father, Henry de Mille, an established playwright on the New York stage, William determined to seek a career in the theater. He studied playwrighting at Columbia.

Among his stage successes was *The Warrens of Virginia,* which was produced by David Belasco in 1907. When the play was adapted for the screen by his brother, Cecil, William ventured out to California to develop a scenario department for the Famous Players-Lasky Company. In addition to *Warrens,* he assisted his brother in making *Cameo Kirby* (1915) and the Geraldine Farrar vehicle, *Carmen* (1915). These early years instilled in William the urge to direct, to assume the ultimate control over a film that, as a writer, he thought he lacked. His first film was *The Ragamuffin* (1915), which he would remake 10 years later as *The Splendid Crime* with Bebe Daniels. After brother Cecil left Lasky in 1925 to establish his own studio in Culver City, William joined him as director and associate producer. His favorite screenwriter was Clara Beranger, whom he met in 1921 and whom he married in the late 1920s.

William was an early enthusiast of the new talking picture technology. In his book, *Hollywood Saga,* he recounts a meeting in 1928 of the then-fledgling Academy with a large number of prominent Hollywood notables. One by one, they denounced as base and crude the new technology. Only de Mille spoke words of hope. Indeed, in a 1929 lecture at USC, he told his students, "I am awfully glad that the silent picture is passing—as I believe it is. . . . Now the motion picture is really becoming important, it is finding its voice. It now enters the field of dramatic literature and, consequently, it is much more important than it was." He assisted Roy Pomeroy on Paramount's first talkie, *Interference* (1928), and went on to direct his first talkie, *The Doctor's Secret,* a year later. Upon leaving the picture business de Mille turned to teaching at USC. He died in 1955 at the age of 76.

Unlike his more glamorous brother, William was quiet, softspoken, modest, and something of an intellectual. His films in the 1920s, especially *Miss Lulu Bett* (1921), a protofeminist saga of a drudge who acquires riches and an enlightened sense of her femininity, and *Craig's Wife* (1928), an indictment of a woman's materialistic obsession about her house and family, were distinguished for their subtlety and innuendo—characteristics that today are usually credited to directors like Ernst

Lubitsch. He waged a constant battle against screen censorship. "The talking picture must be allowed to grow as an art," he said in 1929, referring to the censorial activities of the Hays Office, "and no art has ever grown in bondage. . . . Freedom of thought and expression means freedom to express the opinion you do not agree with as well as the opinion you do agree with; and in this country we are forced to deliver our birthright of freedom to a little group of narrow-minded, bigoted people who have never read anything but the Bible and do not understand that. . . . The talking picture is going to be one of the greatest instruments in that fight and it has got to be left free."

Other Films   *What Every Woman Knows* (1921); *Clarence* (1921); *Icebound* (1924); *Men and Women* (1925); *Passion Flower* (1930).

References   de Mille, William C., "The Future of the Photoplay," in *Introduction to the Photoplay*, ed. John C. Tibbetts (Los Angeles and Kansas City: National Film Society and Academy of Motion Picture Arts and Sciences, 1977), pp. 312–337; de Mille, William C., *Hollywood Saga* (New York: E. P. Dutton, 1939).

—J.C.T.

Demme, Jonathan (1944–)   Perhaps no contemporary American director has succeeded in such a wide range of film genres as Jonathan Demme. Born February 22, 1944, in Baldwin, New York, Demme's family moved to Florida when he was young. He attended the University of Florida, where he wrote movie reviews, and then, after some time in the air force, worked for producer Joseph E. Levine. He had other jobs on the fringes of show business, including doing publicity work for movie companies and writing for *Film Daily,* before finding himself under the tutelage of ROGER CORMAN. When he struck out on his own, he created a body of work that captured many idiosyncrasies and quirks of the American character. From offbeat comedies to the most highly acclaimed rock concert film to

the only horror film to be awarded the Academy Award for best picture, Demme is fearless in tackling varied subject matter and eliciting often career-defining performances from his actors.

Melvin and Howard (1980) was Demme's breakthrough film—the uniquely American tale of common man Melvin Dummar, whose fabled meeting with Howard Hughes almost makes him rich. Mary Steenburgen, as Dummar's wife, received an Oscar for best supporting actress, the first of four Oscar-winning performances Demme has directed. The film is a bittersweet take on the seeming unattainability of the American Dream, its obsession with success and fame, and a consumer culture full of kitsch. However, like much of Demme's later work, the film maintains a sympathy and generosity of spirit for the lovable losers at the heart of this quintessentially American tale. Demme embraces the eccentricities of his characters and never condescends to them. Melvin is constantly trying to change himself, to become something better, but always seems to fail. Later Demme heroes like Charlie and Audrey in *Something Wild* (1986), Angela in *Married to the Mob* (1988), and Clarice in *The Silence of the Lambs* (1991) will have greater success fulfilling the American notion of self-transformation.

Demme is known for his eclectic taste in music throughout his films, so it is no wonder that he directed the Talking Heads concert film, *Stop Making Sense* (1984), commonly regarded as the greatest concert movie ever made. Employing footage from three nights at a 1983 concert at the Hollywood Pantages Theater, Demme fashioned one of the great musical celebrations on film. A true collaboration with Talking Heads front man, David Byrne, Demme's film captures the energy and urgency of the group's music and the concert experience itself through expert editing and a variety of camera angles. Byrne in his big suit flopping about onstage is one of the most joyous images in a Demme film.

While Demme is one of the most talented film-makers of his generation, his films have not gained the wide audiences they deserve. Two such films are *Something Wild* and *Married to the Mob,* comedies that play with genre expectations. *Something Wild,* possibly Demme's greatest achievement, is a kind of updated 1930s screwball comedy with the sexy free spirit (Melanie Griffith in her best performance ever) liberating the repressed yuppie (Jeff Daniels) from his constraining middle-class existence and hitting the road with him. *Something Wild* is funny, sexy, and, best of all, unpredictable—an energized journey into the heart of Americana that is at once familiar and new all at the same time. When Ray Liotta, as Griffith's estranged husband, shows up in the last act, the film takes an unexpected turn and goes in a whole new direction—one that is both dangerous and thrilling.

Married to the Mob is a gangster comedy with a twist—it focuses on a woman, a mob widow trying to rebuild her life away from the family. Michelle Pfeiffer has never been funnier or more appealing (Demme seems to have a way with female performers), and Dean Stockwell and Mercedes Ruehl are wonderful in support. The details of gangster kitsch, from the way the wives style their hair to the goofy restaurants where the mob guys eat, make the film a wacky delight and yet another underappreciated gem of the 1980s.

Demme's commercial breakthrough came with *The Silence of the Lambs,* which garnered the top five Academy Awards (picture, director, actor [Anthony Hopkins], actress [Jodie Foster], and adapted screenplay). Based on Thomas Harris's novel about an FBI trainee who enlists the help of a brilliant serial killer to help track down another killer, *Silence* is a masterpiece of the horror genre and something completely unexpected from Demme, who before had flirted with the darker elements of American culture but here flings himself headfirst into new territory. The performances are excellent, the confrontations between Hopkins and Foster are tense, and the pacing and editing maintain a level of suspense throughout the film right up to the nerve-racking climax. *Silence* exemplifies a filmmaker commanding all the elements of his craft in service of a taut, thrilling story.

Philadelphia (1993) represents yet another change of pace for Demme. The first mainstream Hollywood movie to deal with AIDS, *Philadelphia* revolves around the struggles of a lawyer (Tom Hanks in an Oscar-winning role) who is fired from his firm because of his disease. Some critics claimed that the film was simplistic and that it played down the homosexuality of the lead character and his lover and gave the hero an unbelievably supportive family to make the project more palatable to a wide audience. And yet *Philadelphia,* while not a radical work, is a worthy entry in the tradition of socially conscious filmmaking. It puts a human face on the AIDS crisis and delivers on an emotional level.

Demme's most recent film, *Beloved* (1998), based on Toni Morrison's novel, is arguably a major misstep in his career. A shapeless, confusing mess about the aftermath of slavery, it features a muted performance by Oprah Winfrey in the pivotal role of a former slave haunted by the daughter she killed to free her from life as a slave. *Beloved* trades the clarity of Demme's best work for an attempt at something grand and epic, but the film is never emotionally moving and often downright puzzling. It is also tedious—one adjective that could never before have applied to Demme's work. Demme ultimately is the one director who can touch the pulse of contemporary America in all its beautiful and frightening oddity, from the wistful dreamers of *Melvin and Howard* to the freewheeling romantics of *Something Wild* to the serial killers of *The Silence of the Lambs.* A portentous stream-of-consciousness period piece about slavery's horrible legacy does not fit the unique sensibility of one of America's greatest living filmmakers.

Other Films *Caged Heat* (1974); *Crazy Mama* (1975); *Fighting Mad* (1976); *Citizens Band/Handle with*

Care (1977); *Last Embrace* (1979); *Swing Shift* (1984); *Swimming to Cambodia* (1987); *Cousin Bobby* (1991).

References Bliss, Michael, and Christina Banks, *What Goes Around Comes Around: The Films of Jonathan Demme* (Carbondale: Southern Illinois University Press, 1996); Conlon, James, "Silencing Lambs and Educating Women," *Post Script* 12, no. 1 (Fall 1992): 3–12; Fawell, John, "The Musicality of the Filmscript," *Literature/Film Quarterly* 17, no. 1 (1989): 44–49; Fischer, Lucy, "Mr. Dummar Goes to Town: An Analysis of *Melvin and Howard*," *Film Quarterly* 36, no. 1 (Fall 1982): 32–40; Murphy, Kathleen, "Communion," *Film Comment* 27, 1 (January–February 1991): 31–32; Negra, Diane, "Coveting the Feminine: Victor Frankenstein, Norman Bates, and Buffalo Bill," *Literature/Film Quarterly* 24, no. 2 (1996): 193–200; Smith, Gavin, "Identity Check," *Film Comment* 27, no. 1 (January–February 1991): 28–30; Sundelson, David, "The Demon Therapist and Other Dangers: Jonathan Demme's *The Silence of the Lambs*," *Journal of Popular Film and Television* 21, no. 1 (Spring 1993): 12–17; Tibbetts, John C., "Oprah's Belabored *Beloved*," *Literature/Film Quarterly* 27, no. 1 (1999): 74–76.

—P.N.C.

Demy, Jacques (1931–1990)

One of the screen's most lyrical directors, Jacques Demy brought music and the spirit of the fairy tale to the French New Wave. He was born in southern Brittany, at Pont-Château (Loire-Atlantique), west of Nantes, on June 5, 1931. Some of his happiest years were spent there, following his bent for photography and teaching himself techniques in animation. Inspired by a viewing of ROBERT BRESSON's 1945 film, *Les Dames du Bois de Boulogne* (which he later called "the first film that made me understand that cinema was a great art"), he pursued cinema studies at the École de Beaux-Arts and the École Technique de Photographie et de Cinématographiques, where he worked as assistant to animator Paul Grimault. His first theatrical feature was *Le Sabotier du Val-de-Loire* (1955), a documentary about a family of clogmakers in the Loire Valley.

In 1961 he directed his "breakout" film, *Lola,* establishing himself as one of the key figures of the French New Wave. Set in his home town of Nantes, it cast Anouk Aimée as the eponymous dance-hall singer who is patiently awaiting the return of Michel, her lover and the father of her child, who had abandoned her seven years earlier. Secondary characters include Roland, a former lover, an American sailor with whom she spends the night, and a mother and daughter whose fate runs parallel to Lola's. This amiable fable blends location realism with tender romance, the whole underscored by a lyrical musical score by Michel Legrand (with whom he would later work on several more films). Aimée's musical number in a top hat is one of the most memorable scenes in all of modern French cinema. Colleague Eric Rohmer pronounced *Lola* "the most original film of the New Wave," and it received the Prix de l'Academie du Cinéma. Demy's next feature, *Bay of Angels* (*La Baie des anges* [1962]), was equally successful. Jeanne Moreau portrayed a woman whose addiction to gambling leads to her abandonment of her husband and children. Like *Lola,* the film was a luminous and lyric evocation of bittersweet love, and it too won the coveted Prix de l'Academie du Cinéma.

Demy's next two films established his international reputation and have remained glowing testimonies to his unique lyrical gifts. *The Umbrellas of Cherbourg* (*Les Parapluies de Cherbourg* [1964]) and *The Young Girls of Rochefort* (*Les Demoiselles de Rochefort* [1967]) were imaginative musicals, the first a true innovation in film—a through-composed opera made in collaboration with composer Michel Legrand. For *Umbrellas* Demy and designer Bernard Evein painted the town, as it were, transforming Cherbourg into a cityscape of brilliant pastels that resembled a Hollywood set. Genevieve (Catherine Deneuve) swears to be faithful to her boyfriend, Guy (Nino Castelnuovo), when he leaves for military service. But as time passes, he fails to return, and both Genevieve and Guy marry someone else. Significantly, Genevieve's husband is Roland, the character who carried an unrequited passion for Lola in Demy's earlier film (an incident recounted here in a flashback). Such interconnections among his films were numerous. Demy's own bittersweet view of the transience of life is perfectly summed up in the conclusion of *Umbrellas:* In an achingly beautiful scene, Genevieve and Guy, now married to others, accidentally meet and renew their enduring affection. But they both realize they must return to the commitments they have made to their respective spouses. Romance and resignation, freedom and commitment intermingle in an indescribable moment. Demy himself insisted the film was not "romantic" but essentially "realistic": "It's a very cruel film and a very realistic one," he declared in a 1971 interview; "when they find themselves at the end there's nothing possible for them any longer, their lives are quite different, they've gone different ways."

The Young Girls of Rochefort was a lavish spectacle in 70 mm, casting GENE KELLY and Catherine Deneuve and her sister, Françoise Dorléac. In a particularly telling moment Deneuve receives a portrait painted of her by an artist who has never seen her before. "He must love a great deal to have imagined me so well," she says. As Peter Hogue has noted about this scene, "Imagination informed with love seems particularly conspicuous in Demy's musicals and fantasy films." It received an Oscar nomination for Demy's direction and Legrand's musical score. Not everyone was wholly enchanted with the results. Critic Carey Harrison opined that Demy "is an habitual offender on the count of sentimentality, and there are embarrassing lapses in this musical, as there have been in his previous films." Yet, continued Harrison, Demy "is capable of a tender, unsentimental euphoria more intoxicating than any other film work in the field of sentimental farce." Both *Umbrellas* and *Young Girls* have been recently restored and distributed for theatrical release.

The Model Shop (1968) was made in America and it was Demy's first film in English. A sequel to *Lola,* Anouk Aimée reprises her role as a sadder, if not wiser woman involved in a romance with an unemployed architect (Gary Lockwod). It was noted at the time that the film's color palette of shriekingly vulgar purples, mauves, bright pinks, and dark blues was more vivid and gaudy than in his earlier films. "It corresponded to my vision of America," he said, "which is a gaudy, baroque vision, where the whole idea of taste . . . doesn't exist. American bad taste took me by storm, I loved it." Back in Paris, Demy directed a musical fairy tale, an adaptation of Charles Perrault's *Donkey Skin* (*Peau d' ane* [1971]), with Catherine Deneuve and Jean Marais. Again, color played an important role: the Blue Kingdom was conceived in lilac, purples, blues, and yellow; and the Red Kingdom in correspondingly hot hues of scarlet, red, and orange. In 1973, while he and his wife, filmmaker AGNÈS VARDA, awaited the birth of their son Mathieu, Demy made one of his most curious features, *The Slightly Pregnant Man* (aka *L'Évènement le plus important depuis que l'homme a marché sur la lune*), about a husband (Marcello Mastroianni) displaying symptoms of morning sickness. Catherine Deneuve portrayed his wife. Demy returned to the all-singing format of *Umbrellas* with *A Room in Town* (*Un chambre en ville* [1982]). Again returning to the setting of Nantes, the film told the story of a striking metal worker (Richard Berry) who is conducting an unhappy love affair with the spoiled daughter (Dominique Sanda) of his landlady. "In the last twenty years, since *The Umbrellas of Cherbourg,*" Demy commented with characteristic irony, "things have changed. My story is more violent, more passionate and has become more funny."

The paradox of Demy's films, not always easily resolved, is the collision between an occasionally cruel realism and the lyric beauty of color and music. "We live, we suffer, and yet music is beautiful, colors are beautiful," he declared. "Even though we are going through the worst troubles and sufferings, red is always lovely, blue is always lovely, and the music of Mozart is always beautiful.

. . . It's a contradiction, not a conflict. So why not use it? Just because my characters may suffer terribly, that's no reason to surround them with hideous, ugly colors or put in grating music."

By the time he finished *Three Places for the 26th* (*Trois places pour le 26* [1988]), with a musical score by Legrand, Demy was suffering from the malady that would eventually kill him. He died of a brain hemorrhage resulting from leukemia on October 27, 1990.

A year after his death his wife released *Jacquot de Nantes,* the first of three films she made in the 1990s about her husband. It is both her tribute to his early years in Nantes and an attempt to link his biography with his subsequent films. Before his death, Demy agreed to allow his wife to photograph him reminiscing about his life. He saw a rough cut of the film before he died. "It's not a documentary about his childhood," said Varda. "It's just him saying, 'Yes, this is true. This is my life.'" Varda's biographer, Alison Smith, declared, "Varda's film stands as the explicitly autobiographical film that Demy himself never made, and the complex transfer of memory which presided over its making is also the subject of the film." Varda's other two Demy-related films are *The Young Girls Turn 25 (Les Demoiselles ont eu 25 ans)* and *The World of Jacques Demy*. The complete trilogy, writes Smith, demonstrates that Varda "envisages memory as an active process; the past is something which has an active role in the present and which can be put to creative use as inspiration, not something to be nostalgically desired."

Other Films *The Pied Piper* (1972); *Lady Oscar* (1978); *Parking* (1985).

References Harrison, Carey, *"Les Demoiselles de Rochefort," Sight and Sound* 36, no. 4 (Autumn 1967): 204; Hogue, Peter, "Playing for Keeps," *Film Comment* 27, no. 4 (July-August 1991): 76–77; Petrie, Graham, "Jacques Demy," *Film Comment* 7, no. 4 (Winter 1971–72): 46–53; Smith, Alison, *Agnès Varda* (Manchester: Manchester University Press, 1998).

—J.C.T.

De Palma, Brian (1940–) Brian De Palma has sustained a career in Hollywood despite numerous setbacks, including outraged protest groups, major flops, and scathing reviews. Yet just when many critics are ready to write him off as a director whose films have never lived up to the promise of his early work, he returns to the limelight with a commercially successful film. Often too easily dismissed as a pale ALFRED HITCHCOCK imitation, De Palma should be judged by the depth and breadth of his work, not simply by his most obvious cinematic fixations.

Born on September 11, 1940, in Newark, New Jersey, De Palma seemed to be transfixed by the technology of the cinema at an early age. There is a story linking his voyeuristic style to a particular childhood trauma. As a young child, his parents split up, his mother accusing his father of infidelity. The young De Palma apparently spent several days stalking his dad with recording equipment, hoping to find evidence to confirm his mother's suspicions. Whether this story is based on hard facts or myth-building fiction, the story reaffirms De Palma's signature approach: the camera as ultimate voyeur, constantly peering at his characters' most personal, intimate moments. His earliest films, largely unseen by American audiences, are considered by many contemporary critics to be ahead of their time. Dark comedy and social satire were not trademarks of early 1960s cinema, yet these films stand up today due largely to De Palma's insightful, humorous social observations.

His first feature-length films, including *Greetings* (1968), *Hi, Mom!* (1970), and *Get to Know Your Rabbit* (1970), were very much in the 1960s counterculture vein, but they received limited distribution. De Palma achieved widespread acclaim in 1973 with *Sisters,* a disturbing thriller dealing with Siamese twins, one aggressive and the other passive. The film, while only a modest box-office success, alerted critics to De Palma's abilities as a talented director of psychological horror stories. His next job, as director of *The Phantom of the Par-*

adise (1974), allowed De Palma to update the classic *Phantom of the Opera* tale as a Faustian rock opera. Deftly satirizing the music business while using split screens and video technology to great effect, many consider *Phantom* to be one of De Palma's strongest movies. While many critics dismissed his next film, 1976's *Obsession,* as more of a Hitchcock rip-off than the *hommage* he intended, he finally achieved breakthrough commercial success with his cinematic version of Stephen King's novel, *Carrie* (1976). Sissy Spacek's portrayal of the film's sympathetic lead character struck a note with the horror crowd, elevating the film above most of the derivative exploitation films of the day.

Perhaps feeling the invincible power that came with success, De Palma followed *Carrie* with *The Fury* (1978), another psychological horror story that exploited his previous film's mental telepathy storyline to excess. The film, though featuring some excellent set pieces, was a commercial failure, due largely to the weak script. De Palma, in turn, retreated from big-budget filmmaking to make *Home Movies* (1979), a flaky farce reminiscent of his first films, which starred his then wife, actress Nancy Allen. *Dressed to Kill* (1980) followed, reviving calls of Hitchcockian plagiarism and offending many women's groups at the same time. While the film's plot at times recalled *Psycho,* the graphic sexuality and violence ensured controversy and led to numerous protests by newly empowered feminist organizations. *Dressed to Kill* does ape some Hitchcock techniques, but the film's stylistic content rarely outweighs De Palma's power to chill the audience. While not a hit in its initial box-office run, De Palma's next film, *Blow Out* (1981), has aged nicely. The story revolves around a Hollywood soundman who may have inadvertently recorded a political assassination while combing a city park for sound effects. Though needlessly violent at its climax, *Blow Out* captures De Palma's strengths as a master of suspenseful action sequences, certainly in debt to Hitchcock, but with a voice and vision of his own.

Brian De Palma (Filmways Pictures)

In 1983, *Scarface* brought renewed charges of racial insensitivity and excessive, graphic violence, and was savaged by critics at the time of its release. Like several other De Palma films, however, *Scarface* found life on the then-emerging technology of home video, spawning legions of dialogue-quoting devotees.

By the time of *Body Double* (1984), his critics were accusing him of needless repetition, perhaps accounting for De Palma's turn away from Hitchcockian-style suspense vehicles. However, his films since that point have turned more workmanlike, and it is more difficult to discern the auteur imprint so prevalent in his earlier films. *Wiseguys* (1986), a misguided attempt at broad genre comedy, led to *The Untouchables* (1987), a commercial success without the trademark flourishes of stylistic suspense he had become known for. A laughable, though technically proficient, reworking of the "Odessa Steps sequence" from

Eisenstein's *Battleship Potemkin* led many critics to wonder if De Palma had grown bored with the filmmaking process. *Casualties of War* (1989) is an honest, highly personalized attempt to critique the futility of the Vietnam war. However, perhaps due to the ham-fisted histrionics of Sean Penn as an angry young soldier, *Casualties* feels at times as though De Palma, belonging to the "film school generation" of the 1960s and early 1970s, is making the film out of some sort of obligation to the liberal values supposedly championed by filmmakers his age.

The year 1990 brought *The Bonfire of the Vanities,* an ill-fated adaptation of Tom Wolfe's popular novel. Wildly inconsistent style, miscast actors, and attempts to soften the book's sarcastic tone are all cited as reasons for the film's failure, one of Hollywood's biggest of recent years. (An excellent account of the film's making can be read in Julie Salamon's book *The Devil's Candy.*) Both *Raising Cain* (1992) and *Carlito's Way* (1993) received modest critical praise, returning De Palma to more familiar ground in the horror and criminal/gangster genres, respectively. The success of 1996's *Mission: Impossible,* from the 1960s television series and starring Tom Cruise as Ethan Hunt, seemed to garner attention for everyone involved, save director De Palma. The film was rescued from a dense, convoluted script by virtuoso action sequences, though De Palma's signature style had seemingly been left out. His latest films, *Snake Eyes* (1998) and *Mission to Mars* (2000), were major critical and commercial disappointments. However, one should not take this as an indication of De Palma's potential future performance, as he has shown a knack for perseverance in such an unforgiving profession as directing.

Other Films *Icarus* (1960); *660124: The Story of an IBM Card* (1961); *Wotan's Wake* (1962); *Jennifer* (1964); *Bridge That Gap* (1965); *Show Me a Strong Town and I'll Show You a Strong Bank* (1966); *The Responsive Eye* (1966); *Murder a la Mod* (1968); *The Wedding Party* (1969); *Dionysus* (1970); *Mr. Hughes* (2000).

References Bliss, Michael, *Brian De Palma* (Metuchen, N.J.: Scarecrow Press, 1983); Bouzereau, Laurent, *The De Palma Cut: The Films of America's Most Controversial Director* (New York: Dembner, dist. by Norton, 1988); Dworkin, Susan, *Double De Palma: A Film Study With Brian De Palma* (New York: Newmarket Press, 1984); MacKinnon, Kenneth, *Misogyny in the Movies: The De Palma Question* (Newark: University of Delaware Press, 1990); Salamon, Julie, *The Devil's Candy: The Bonfire of the Vanities Goes to Hollywood* (Boston: Houghton Mifflin, 1991).

—J.A.

Deren, Maya (1917–1961) Maya Deren is known, perhaps primarily, for her surreal film *Meshes of the Afternoon* (1943), but she also deserves credit for her role in organizing and promoting the avant-garde cinema community in New York City. She was born Elenora Derenowsky to a Jewish family in Kiev, Russia. Shortly after they emigrated in 1922, her father shortened the name to Deren. She received an excellent and advanced education in Geneva, Switzerland, returned home, married, finished college at NYU, and, after separating from her first husband, she got a master's degree in English literature from Smith College in Massachusetts. Her thesis was on the symbolist poets but she also studied perception and gestalt psychology. She wrote furiously and it was a habit she continued throughout her life. One film scholar has noted that in Deren's hands, language and language systems became weapons as they enabled her to rebel against a society that "denied women a voice of power."

In 1941 she took a job as a secretary to the modern dance choreographer Katherine Dunham. It was during this time that she began taking daily amphetamines and sleeping pills prescribed by Dr. Max Jacobson, drug physician to celebrities and politicians from the mid-1940s to the 1970s. It was this addiction that most likely caused the cerebral hemorrhages she died from at age 44. Deren traveled with Dunham to Los Angeles where she met her second husband, Alexander Hamid. They made *Meshes of the Afternoon* together in 1943. This film has been interpreted as significant because it has been constructed as a distinctly woman's discourse. It revises Hollywood's objectification of women by focusing on a female subject who must struggle with her own objectification.

At Land (1944), their second film together, does not critique the Hollywood representation of women and does not divide the action between waking and dreamlike episodes. But it again organizes the narrative action around a female protagonist whose identity is tested by her adventures with the constantly changing objects, people, and various environments surrounding her. The use of multiple selves in her films is a way of interrogating multiple identities as a means toward self-discovery. This theme in her films had been interpreted by some early male critics as an examination of schizophrenia. Deren also disagreed with the majority of (male) critics at the time who consistently tied her films to surrealism and the European avant-garde of the 1920s. She maintained in all her discussion and writing about her films that they were ultimately and rationally ordered and structured. Another film, *Ritual in Transfigured Time* (1946), explores a woman's desire for self-fulfillment through her sociosexual role, albeit in a very abstract manner, and finally concludes that the fulfillment of that role and also fulfilling oneself as a woman are incompatible.

Deren tried always to provide a discursive context within which people viewed her films. She most often traveled with her films to show them at festivals and later to colleges and art museums around the country, and she would very carefully provide an interpretation for them so people would have an understanding of the film as she intended it to be understood. She wanted to make sure that her films were viewed as oppositional to Hollywood's forms and language. In the 1940s and 1950s she lectured on film theory and independent cinema at NYU, Yale University, Smith, Vassar, the Universities of Wisconsin, Chicago and Oregon, Syracuse, Pittsburgh State, Colorado State, Ball State Teacher's College, and the University of Havana. She, more than any other practicing independent filmmaker, brought these new aesthetic ideas and concerns—percolating but focused in New York City—out to the Midwest and the West. She was an accomplished and charismatic speaker and developed a following of young filmmakers such as Stan Brakhage, Kenneth Anger, and Curtis Harrington. In the late 1940s she made the transition from filmmaking to organizing the discourse surrounding films and organizing other independent filmmakers into an art community. She helped organize the Film Artist's Society in 1953, which became the Independent Filmmaker's Association in 1955. And she created the first grant-lending organization for independent filmmakers, the Creative Film Foundation, in 1955. By the time she died in 1961 she, together with others, had created a self-sustaining organizational network for independent filmmaking that ensured the continuation of a vibrant avant-garde cinema in the United States.

Other Film   *A Study in Choreography for the Camera* (1945).

References   Rabinovitz, Lauren, *Points of Resistance: Women, Power and Politics in the New York Avant-garde Cinema, 1943–1971* (Urbana: Illinois University Press, 1991); Acker, Ally, *Reel Women: Pioneers of the Cinema, 1896–Present* (New York: Continuum Press, 1991); Clark, VèVè A., Millicent Hodson, and Catrina Neiman, *The Legend of Maya Deren, A Documentary Biography and Collected Works,* 2 vols. (New York: Anthology Film Archives/Film Culture, 1984).

—C.L.P.

De Sica, Vittorio (1901–1974)   Best known for his contributions to the movement known as "Italian neorealism," Vittorio De Sica was also known in his own country as a fine stage and screen actor. Born in Sora, Italy, on July 7, 1901, he was the son of an Italian businessman. Throughout his childhood Vittorio was on the move, first to Naples (1904–06), then Florence (1907), and finally to Rome (1912). During his adolescence De Sica became involved in theatrical activity—primarily amateur groups. When Vittorio was 21 he fulfilled his military obligation by serving in the Grenadier's Regiment. A few years later he began his professional career as an actor with the theater company of Tatiana Pavlova, a Russian director who was presenting plays in Rome. Between 1923 and 1924 De Sica performed as *secondo brillante* (supporting comic roles) in Pavlova's company. Soon De Sica was playing romantic leads in musical comedies and light and serious dramas. By 1930 De Sica was a full-fledged "star" on the Italian stage, having performed with such companies as the Compagnia Artiste Associati. From 1930 to 1940 De Sica further pursued his acting career in various companies and various successes, and it was during this period that De Sica became known as the "Italian Chevalier." It wasn't until after 1949 that his stage appearances began to decrease, due to his successes as a screen actor and film director.

De Sica appeared in films as early as 1918, when he had a small part as the young Clemenceau in Eduardo Bencivenga's *Il processo Clemenceau*. His first speaking role was in one of Italy's first "talking pictures," Amleto Palermi's *La vecchia signora* (1931). Throughout the thirties De Sica appeared in numerous Italian films, continuing his stage appearances as well. Overall De Sica appeared in 160 films between 1918 and 1974. In 1940, while he was acting in two films and was in between stage appearances, De Sica began his career as a film director. De Sica's first choice was a 1936 stage play, *Twenty Four Red Roses,* which he had performed and was familiar with. The comedy-romance was a success and De Sica followed it with another light comedy, *Maddalena, Zero for Conduct* (1941). De Sica's fifth film, *The Children Are Watching* (*I bambini ci guardano* [1942]) marked a distinct shift in style. This story of the impact of adult folly on a child's mind was the beginning of his collaboration with screenwriter Cesare Zavattini, which would stretch over 23 of his 31 films. Particularly noteworthy are two of the most notable films representative of what came to be called the Italian neorealist movement, *Shoeshine* (*Sciuscia* [1946]) and *The Bicycle Thief* (*Ladri di biciclette* [1948]). With little money available to him, De Sica initiated the use of real locations and nonprofessional actors. Both films bared the truth about conditions in postwar Italy. *Shoeshine* received a Special Academy Award in 1947 and was instrumental in establishing the category of best foreign film.

The Bicycle Thief remains De Sica's most famous film, as well as the most famous of his neorealist pictures. Upon the slim plot, derived from a novel by Luigi Bartolini—the search for a stolen bicycle, which is the sole source of a father's livelihood—hangs a searching examination of postwar conditions in Italy. Among the characters and situations that the bicyclist, Ricci (played by a nonprofessional actor, Lamberto Maggiorani, a factory worker), meets in the course of his search are: striking workers, black marketeers, a drowned child, a gang of toughs, sanitation workers, and poor people praying in a church. After his fruitless search, Ricci is forced to try to steal a bicycle. Apprehended and released, he is as poor as ever, but now aware of the shame he now must bear as a would-be thief. "Its social message is not detached," wrote André Bazin, "it remains immanent in the event, but it is so clear that nobody can overlook it. . . . The thesis implied is wondrously and outrageously simple: in the world where this workman lives, the poor must steal from each other in order to survive." According to John Darretta, De Sica and Zavattini "sought to examine the social and economic problems of postwar Italy and their effects on the ordinary individual. They searched for 'real' characters and filmed them in their everyday landscapes with a camera and editing style that would capture the verisimilitude of a documentary. They had reached the zenith of the neorealistic period."

Miracle in Milan (*Miracolo a Milano* [1951]) and *Umberto D* (1952) confirmed De Sica's international reputation. The former was a break from the severity of the *Bicycle Thief,* a whimsical fantasy about the odyssey of Toto the Good (Francesco Golisano), an orphan who struggles to become an apostle for the beggars of Milan. When they are threatened with violence by a wicked landowner, Toto provides his band of beggars with brooms, with which they fly away to a land "where there is only peace, love, and good." De Sica's use of the fanciful does not obscure the social commentary about the exploitation and dispossession of the innocent by industrial forces. Attacked as being communistic by the Italian right, it was warmly received in the United States, where it was named best foreign film by the New York Film Critics.

Umberto D is considered in some quarters to be De Sica's purest neorealist document. Told in real time, the story of an old man's poverty, loneliness, and alienation from society was called by André Bazin "a truly realist cinema of the time." Further, "It is a matter of making 'life time'—the continuing to be a person to whom nothing in particular happens—that takes on the quality of spectacle. . . ." Umberto D (a nonprofessional actor named Carlo Battisti) is a retired civil servant who is about to be dispossessed of his lodgings and whose only companion is his little dog. Failing to commit suicide, he returns to his hopeless and bleak existence. Although attacked by Italian commentators as an accusation against conditions in contemporary Italy, Bazin predicted rightly that *Umberto D* would prove "a masterpiece to which film history is certainly going to grant a place of honour. . . ."

In the early 1950s De Sica visited the United States where a project with RKO studios was abandoned. De Sica did make an arrangement with producer David O. Selznick to make a film to be shot on location in Italy. The resulting film,

Stazione Termini (1954), released in the United States as *Indiscretion of an American Wife,* starring Jennifer Jones and Montgomery Clift, was a box-office bomb. De Sica's next project was an omnibus film based on several Neapolitan stories by Giuseppe Marotta. *The Gold of Naples* (*L'oro di Napoli* [1954]) was shot on location with a mix of professional and nonprofessional actors. De Sica then made *The Roof* (*Il tetto* [1954]), shot in Rome, also with a cast of non professionals, which is considered by many to be the last neorealist film. In 1959 the director made *Two Women* (*La ciociara*) with Sophia Loren. The film won an Academy Award for best actress, the first time that award had been given to a foreign language film. Many critics lambasted the film as a "sellout" to commercialism. During the 1960s De Sica did indeed make his most commercial films, such as *Boccacio '70* (Act III, "The Raffle" [1962]), *The Condemned of Altona* (1962), *Yesterday, Today, and Tomorrow* (*Ieri, oggi, domani* [1963]), *Marriage Italian Style* (1963), and *After the Fox* (1966). In 1970 De Sica once again won the admiration of the critics with *The Garden of the Finzi-Continis* (*Il giardino dei Finzi-Contini*). The film concerned the effects of the war on a family of wealthy Italian Jews. It received the Academy Award for best foreign film at the 1971 Oscars.

Meanwhile, it should be noted that De Sica returned to acting on the screen in 1959 when he appeared in the title role of Roberto Rossellini's wartime drama, *General della Rovere.* As Bertone, a con man with a gift for impersonation who is forced by the Germans to masquerade as General della Rovere, an important Italian Resistance figure, De Sica lent the role a credibility with audiences already familiar with his acting talents.

In August of 1973, De Sica entered a hospital in Geneva for an operation on a lung cyst. The ailment was to prove fatal, though the severity of it was kept from the director. De Sica's final film, *The Voyage* (1974), starred Sophia Loren and Richard Burton. The evening of its premiere in

Paris, November 13, 1974, Vittorio De Sica died at the age of 72. John Darretta states that, "Despite the prevailing attitudes that the director of *Shoeshine, The Bicycle Thief,* and *Umberto D* had betrayed the ideals of his 'movement' and sold out to commercialism, both *The Garden of the Finzi-Continis* and *A Brief Vacation*—when placed next to *Red Roses* and *Maddalena, Zero for Conduct*—reveal De Sica's long journey from apprentice to expert craftsman."

Other Films *A Garibaldian in the Convent* (1941); *Gate of Heaven* (1946); *Anna of Brooklyn* (1960); *The Witches* (1966); *A New World* (1966); *Woman Times Seven* (1967); *A Place for Lovers* (1969); *Sunflower* (1970); *A Brief Vacation* (1973).

References Bondanella, Peter, *Italian Cinema: From Neorealism to the Present* (New York: Continuum Publishing, 1999); Darretta, John, *Vittorio De Sica: A Guide to References and Resources* (Boston: G. K. Hall, 1983); Bazin, André, "De Sica: Metteur en Scene," in *André Bazin, What Is Cinema?,* ed. Hugh Gray, vol. 2 (Berkeley: University of California Press, 1972), pp. 61–78.

—R.W.

Diegues, Carlos (1940–)

The most controversial and intensely personal of the Cinema Novo directors, Carlos Diegues was born on May 19, 1940, in Maceio, Brazil, the capital of the northeastern state of Alagoas. After moving with his family to Rio de Janeiro, he completed a law degree at the Catholic University, then worked as a journalist before he became active in the film society at the Rio de Janeiro Museum of Modern Art, where he met other participants of the emerging Cinema Novo. His first professional film was *Samba School, Joy of Living* (*Escola de samba, alegria de viver* [1962]), followed a year later by his first feature, *Ganga Zumba,* the first significant work of Cinema Novo to treat Afro-Brazilian history from an insider's perspective. That year Diegues stated his goal for the movement, i.e., "to study in depth the social relations of each city and region as a way of critically exposing, as if in miniature, the socio-cultural structure of the country as a whole."

Diegues's *Xica da Silva* (1976), his most successful film to that date, was based on the life of a legendary slave woman in 18th-century Minas Gerais. Xica (Zeze Motta) is a house slave who seduces an aristocrat and quickly dominates the white society of Arraial do Tijuco. Her outrageous dress and scandalous behavior arouse the anger of the Portuguese authorities, who destroy her palace. She escapes and reunites with her lover, Jose (Stepan Nercessian), and they conspire to continue their subversion of the king and his followers. As historian Peter Rist points out, the film has been the center of controversy due to its focus on the myth of the Afro-Brazilian as a predominantly sexual being.

Bye Bye Brazil (1980) was his eighth feature film and an international success, grossing over $1.3 million in America (making it the third most successful Brazilian film of all time in that country). It is dedicated to Brazilians of the 21st century. As historian Randal Johnson notes, it is "a vast mural of Brazil which is as varied as the country itself." It reveals the country in a process of rapid transformation as an agro-pastoral economy yields to rapid industrialization and the inhabitants of the Amazon jungles retreat before the occupation of multinational corporations. Each of the characters in the Caravana Rolidei, a small-time carioca and circus troupe—a magician/clairvoyant Lord Cigano (Jose Wilker), exotic dancer Salome (Betty Faria), the strongman Andorinha (Principe Nabor), accordianist Cico (Fabio, Jr.) and his pregnant wife Dasdo (Zaira Zambelli)—represents a different aspect of contemporary Brazilian culture. The troupe travels from the sea to the Trans-Amazonian highway to Altamira, presenting their show to small towns not yet "contaminated" by the dreaded television antenna. After a brief separation, the members reunite in Brasilia. The character of Lord Cigano, says Johnson, may be construed as Diegues himself, "an urban artist who has travelled the long roads of Brazil in search of the perfect audience and the optimum form of spectacle." Moreover, continues Johnson, the film's narrative and formal trajectory recall the history of Cinema Novo itself, from its documentary-style opening to the euphoria of the developmentalist period to the disillusionment with the mounting bureaucracy of the government. Just as the troupe has difficulty competing with television and American movies for its audiences and subsequently has to rely on the largess of local mayors, the Cinema Novo movement likewise was forced to turn to state subsidies to survive. The ubiquity of television antennas suggests, notes Johnson, that television is responsible for the destruction of Brazilian indigenous and folk cultures as well as the homogenization of Brazilian cultural expression. Yet, Johnson qualifies this presumption by noting that television "is only part of a larger process of the gradual extinction of indigenous cultures," merely one component of the larger process by which "advanced technology has brought isolated and feudal regions of Brazil into the space age."

The concern of "Caca" Diegues (as he is popularly known) with different forms of cultural communication has led him to experiment with different cinematic styles and genres. As Johnson demonstrates, *Ganga Zumba* contains a sequence wherein slaves act out master/slave relationships. *The Big City* (*A grande cidade* [1965]) is a mixture of western, documentary, melodrama, and thriller genres. *The Heirs* (*Os herdeiros* [1970]) focuses on the role of the National Radio as a consciousness-forming medium in Brazilian history beginning in the 1930s. *When Carnival Comes* (*Quando of carnaval chegar* [1972]) depicts the adventures of a musical troupe in its tribute to the style of the *chanchada* ("light musical comedy"). He has continued to make films, like *Quilombo* (1984) and *Rio's Love Songs* (1994), despite the disarray and virtual collapse of Brazil's film industry in the 1980s.

Other Films *Joanna Francesca* (1973); *Summer Showers* (*Chuvas de verao* [1977]); *Un tren para las estrellas* (1987); *Dias melhores virao* (1994).

References Barnard, Timothy, and Peter Rist, *South American Cinema: A Critical Filmography, 1915–1994* (Austin: University of Texas Press, 1996); Johnson, Randal, "Film Television and Traditional Folk Culture in *Bye Bye Brasil*," *Journal of Popular Culture* 18, no. 1 (Summer 1984): 121–131; Johnson, Randal, *Cinema Novo x 5: Masters of Contemporary Brazilian Film* (Austin: University of Texas Press, 1994).

—J.C.T.

Disney, Walter Elias (1901–1966) Motion picture mogul and amusement park entrepreneur, creative artist, and business visionary, Walt Disney has become synonymous with "family entertainment." Born in Chicago on December 5, 1901, to a midwestern farmer, Elias Disney, he moved with his parents, brothers, and sister to a farm in nearby Marceline, Missouri, five years later. In 1910 the family relocated to Kansas City, Missouri, where the boy Walt went to work delivering newspapers and studying art at the Kansas City Art Institute. After service as an ambulance driver in World War I, he returned to Kansas City and by 1922 was experimenting with cartooning and animation. He served his apprenticeship with the Pesmen-Rubin Commercial Art Studio and the Kansas City Slide Company (later renamed the Kansas City Film Ad Company), where he met another Kansas Citian, the brilliant UBBE ("UB") ERT IWERKS. The two men established their own business that year, Laugh-O-Gram, and made short film advertisements and a handful of fairy tales that were shown in local theaters.

In 1923, bankrupted and seeking new horizons, young Walt took a train westward to Los Angeles, determined to become a movie director. While living with his older brother, Roy, and after failing in his attempts to secure work at the studios, Walt again turned to animation at his own studio on Hyperion Avenue in 1926—a risky move, considering that most animation production at that time was centered on the East Coast. With Iwerks, who in the meantime had followed Walt to Los Angeles—initiating a pattern that would soon be followed by other Kansas Citians, including Isadore ("Friz") Freleng, Hugh Harmon, Rudolph Ising, and composer Carl Stalling—and who assumed most of the drawing chores, Walt produced a series of "Alice in Cartoonland" shorts that combined a live-action little girl with animated backgrounds and situations. The moderate success of these films led to a contract with M. J. Winkler to make "Oswald the Lucky Rabbit" shorts. In 1928 Walt faced disaster when the Winklers and Universal Pictures wrested the character away from him, along with most of his staff. But Iwerks loyally remained, and the two quickly devised a new character, Mickey Mouse.

From his very first released theatrical short, a synchronized-sound cartoon called *Steamboat Willie* (1928), Mickey was a public sensation. By 1932 he was a full-fledged movie star, whose name frequently appeared on theater-house marquees above the rest of the bill. Mickey may rightly be considered the alter-ego, or childlike personification, of Walt himself. Indeed, not only did Walt provide Mickey's falsetto voice until 1947, but also his animators studied Walt's manner and gestures as a model for Mickey. Soon Walt relocated his studio to Burbank.

The 1930s were years of great experimentation and development, closely supervised and guided by Walt. The "Nine Old Men," as they came to be called—including Ollie Johnston, Frank Thomas, Arthur Babbitt, Les Clark, Wolfgang Reitherman, and Fred Moore—were Walt's top staff of young animation directors who revolutionized animation techniques and established standards of quality that were the envy of the rest of the industry. The series of "Silly Symphonies" pioneered technological innovations, like Technicolor (*Flowers and Trees* [1932]) and the three-dimensionality of the multiplane camera (*The Old Mill* [1937]), whose artistic

success was consolidated in the features *Fantasia* (1940) and *Pinocchio* (1941). Other characters joined Mickey in the Disney stable of luminaries, including Donald Duck, whose screen debut was in 1934 with *The Wise Little Hen.* Feature-length animation was launched by the celebrated *Snow White and the Seven Dwarfs* (1938), the riskiest—its expense and its scope caused it to be dubbed "Disney's Folly"—yet the most successful of the Disney product so far.

All the while, Disney was instituting merchandising schemes that expanded his empire into ever-widening enterprises. Newer, larger facilities were demanded, and in 1938 a new studio, located on Buena Vista Street in Burbank, was opened. The war years were times of boom and bust for Walt. On the one hand, the studio threw its energies behind the war effort, producing many training and propaganda films, including Disney's only feature, the animated *Victory Through Air Power* (1944), and the notorious short cartoon *Der Fuehrer's Face* (1943), whose "politically incorrect" rampant stereotyping of the Nazis has occasioned its withdrawal from circulation today. On the other hand, the studio was riven by labor unrest. Walt was outraged when many of his animation staff walked out in 1941. He regarded it not only as a personal betrayal but also as the result of communist conspiracy in Hollywood. He would be bitter about this experience for the rest of his life. That may be a reason why, as the 1950s dawned, he increasingly directed his efforts away from animation to live action features, theme parks, television, and new robotics technologies.

The television series, beginning with *Disneyland* in 1955 and *The Mickey Mouse Club* a year later, cleverly were used not only to recycle existing Disney materials, but also to promote new films like *20,000 Leagues Under the Sea* and *Mary Poppins* and, most especially, the Disneyland theme park. (The television show had several later incarnations, *Walt Disney Presents* in 1959, and *Wonderful World of Color* a year later.) Convinced from his childhood experiences that most amusement parks were sleazy and unsanitary, he was determined to establish a "destination resort"—call it a tidy utopia—that would be more of a family living experience rather than a mere succession of thrill rides. To help build Disneyland, Walt created a separate entity from the studio and called it WED Enterprises (named from his initials), his personal organization for activities outside of filmmaking. Dedicated on July 17, 1955, Disneyland was divided into four regions—Adventureland, Frontierland, Fantasy Land, Tomorrowland—all revolving around the central hub of Main Street U.S.A., through which everyone entering the park must pass (purportedly patterned after the main street of his boyhood home, Marceline, Missouri).

Refusing to rest on his laurels, Walt next turned to an even more ambitious project, Walt Disney World, in Orlando, Florida. Opening in 1971, it was originally intended to include Walt's dream for an "experimental prototype Community of Tomorrow," or EPCOT. Intended as an experiment in urban living, community development, and ecological study, EPCOT was to be a place where the cleanliness and order of Disneyland could be extended to real life. "In its way it is an astonishingly prescient proposal," writes commentator J. Tevere MacFadye, "anticipating the demand for an urban model less dependent on and less dominated by the automobile. At the same time, the plan is as Orwellian as it is utopian, achieving its theoretical perfection only through manipulation of residents and their environment." However, the vision remained unrealized at Walt's death of a circulatory ailment on December 15, 1966.

Since then, under the aegis of Michael Eisner and Roy Disney, Jr., EPCOT has taken a different direction toward a series of international pavilions and, in the case of Spaceship Earth, exhibition spaces devoted to the sciences and transportation, and to man's future on the planet and in outer space. It would no longer have residents; it would have only visitors. Other theme parks include Tokyo Disneyland, which opened in 1983, and Euro Disney in Marne-la-Valle, about 20 miles east of Paris.

In his lifetime Walt Disney won more than 700 awards, including 29 Oscars, four television Emmys, the French Legion of Honor, and Mexico's Order of the Aztec Eagle. Paradoxically, the key to his enormous achievement, and the secret of his universal popularity, was rooted in the humble soil of the Midwest. "It is possible to say that the operative instinct was like the farmer's, which is ever and ever to cut away the underbrush, clear the forest and thus drive out the untamed," writes Richard Schickel. "The drive . . . was . . . a sort of multiple reductionism: wild things and wild behavior were often made comprehensible by converting them into cutenesses, mystery was explained with a joke, and terror was resolved by a musical cue or a discreet averting of the camera's eye from the natural processes."

Walt Disney, more than any other filmmaker in history, embodied what French commentator André Bazin called "The Myth of Total Cinema." From his earliest short films to his later features there is a steady trajectory from crude, two-dimensional, silent cartoons, to works that display an increasing degree of reality: successively, color, wide-screen formats, stereophonic sound, three-dimensionality, and live-action footage; from then on, his live-action films are soon superseded by theme parks, new technologies (ranging from audio-animatronic robotics to digital technologies), and experiments in community living. In sum, he moves from simulated reality to reality itself. Only this "reality" is what Richard Schickel has called "the Disney version," i.e., a view of life and society and art that is packaged and commodified by the cultural manipulations of global corporate capitalism.

Behind it all, the figure of Walt remains rather elusive. The precise nature of his authorship is forever in question. He neither drew, designed, wrote, nor directed; yet he remained at the center of his enterprises, moving like a bee, he said, from flower to flower, from artist to artist and from enterprise to enterprise, pollinating and cross-pollinating them all. Paradoxically, his very omniscience guaranteed his invisibility. "In some respects," writes Jonathan Rosenbaum, "there may be no cultural figure in the West who is as potentially controversial as Walt Disney, even though love and hatred for what he represents are frequently felt by the same people. At the same time, there is certainly no other filmmaker whose aesthetical and ideological preoccupations have permeated so much of modern life."

Other Films   As producer or executive producer: *Dumbo* (1941); *Bambi* (1942); *The Three Caballeros* (1945); *Treasure Island* (1950); *Peter Pan* (1952); *Old Yeller* (1957); *Sleeping Beauty* (1959); *Pollyanna* (1960); *The Absent-Minded Professor* (1961); *Mary Poppins* (1964); *The Jungle Book* (1967).

References   Care, Ross, "Cinesymphony: Music and Animation at the Disney Studio, 1928–1942," *Sight and Sound,* Winter 1976–77: 40–44; MacFadyen, J. Tevere, "The Future: A Walt Disney Production," *Next,* July–August 1980: 5–32; Rosenbaum, Jonathan, "Walt Disney," *Film Comment,* January–February 1975: 64–69; Schickel, Richard, *The Disney Version* (New York: Avon, 1969); Thomas, Frank, and Ollie Johnston, *Disney Animation: The Illusion of Life* (New York: Abbeville Press, 1981).

—J.C.T.

Dmytryk, Edward (1908–1999)   Born on September 4, 1908, in Grand Forks, British Columbia, of Ukrainian parents, Edward Dmytryk started in the film industry at the age of 15 as a messenger and handy boy at Famous Players-Lasky in 1923. He later became a film editor at Paramount in the 1930, when he edited such films as *Million Dollar Legs* (1932), *Ruggles of Red Gap* (1935), and *Zaza* (1939), among others. In 1935 Dmytryk directed his first feature film, Paramount's low-budget *The Hawk,* and by 1939 Paramount made him a full-fledged director of "B" products. In 1940 he moved to Columbia where

he made such "B" entries as *The Devil Commands* (1941), *Under Age* (1941), *Confessions of Boston Blackie* (1942), and *Secrets of the Lone Wolf* (1942). His move to RKO in 1943 resulted in more "B" fodder for the double-feature bills, primarily *Hitler's Children* (1944), a film that focused on the plight of children living in Nazi Germany, *Captive Wild Woman* (1944), an interesting low-budget horror film, and *The Falcon Strikes Back* (1944), a wartime entry in the detective series starring Tom Conway.

In 1943 Dmytryk was given his first "A" feature assignment, the sentimental homefront drama, *Tender Comrade,* which starred Ginger Rogers and Robert Ryan. The film marked his transition from "B" to "A" features. It was followed by what many consider Dmytryk's best film, a faithful adaptation of Raymond Chandler's hard-boiled classic *Farewell, My Lovely,* retitled (due to its star's previous credits as a musical actor) *Murder, My Sweet* (1944). The film starred Dick Powell as detective Philip Marlowe and, according to many scholars, initiated the film noir cycle of the postwar years. The late forties was Dmytryk's most productive phase. Following the success of *Murder, My Sweet* he directed another noir feature with Powell, the underrated *Cornered* (1945). The film concerns the postwar efforts of a Canadian pilot to find the person responsible for his wife's death. *Crossfire* (1947), a film concerning anti-Semitism, garnished six Academy Award nominations, including best picture, best director, and best screenplay (Dalton Trumbo).

In the fall of 1947 Dmytryk was summoned by the House Un-American Activities Committee (HUAC), which was investigating communist influence in the motion picture industry. He was subsequently charged as one of the Hollywood Ten, tried in federal court, and found guilty. Rather than serve his one-year prison term as did the others, Dmytryk fled to England where he made three films. He returned to the United States in 1951, served six months in jail, and publicly recanted (the only member of the Hollywood Ten to do so). Free to work again in Hollywood, Dmytryk was hired by STANLEY KRAMER to direct four films, the most notable of which was *The Caine Mutiny* (1954), based on the Herman Wouk novel and starring Humphrey Bogart. Dmytryk's subsequent work never matched his brilliance in the late 1940s. He taught film at the University of Texas in 1978 and at the University of Southern California in 1981. He also authored several books on filmmaking, as well as the autobiographical *Odd Man Out: Memoirs of the Hollywood Ten*. Edward Dmytryk died on July 1, 1999, at his home in Encino, California, of heart and kidney failure.

Other Films *Television Spy* (1939); *Emergency Squad* (1939); *Counter Espionage* (1942); *Seven Miles from Alcatraz* (1942); *Back to Bataan* (1945); *Til the End of Time* (1946); *So Well Remembered* (1947); *Mutiny* (1952); *The Sniper* (1952); *The Juggler* (1953); *Broken Lance* (1954); *The End of the Affair* (1954); *The Left Hand of God* (1955); *Raintree County* (1957); *The Young Lions* (1958); *Walk on the Wild Side* (1962); *The Carpetbaggers* (1963); *Alvarez Kelly* (1966); *Shalako* (1968); *Bluebeard* (1972); *He Is My Brother* (1974); *The Human Factor* (1975).

Reference Dmytryk, Edward, *Odd Man Out: A Memoir of the Hollywood Ten* (Carbondale: Southern Illinois University Press, 1996).

—R.W.

Donaldson, Roger

Donaldson, Roger (1945–) Born on November 15, 1945, in Ballarat, Australia, a small country town about 60 miles west of Melbourne, Roger Donaldson would become New Zealand's foremost director before going on to a successful career in Hollywood. His father, Frank, was born in England and had migrated to Australia with his family. His mother, the former Dorothy Gumm, helped run a sawmill. Donaldson went to college intending to study metallurgy at the Ballarat School of Mines, switched to geology, then dropped out of school and went to Mt. Isa, a town of 16,000 men and 2,000 women, to become a prospector in the desert.

After becoming interested in photography, Donaldson returned home for another try at college but soon found himself at odds with his father over the issue of Vietnam. Consequently, he struck out for New Zealand and ended up in Auckland, where he first worked as a successful photographer and eventually turned to making commercials. After completing a film called *Sleeping Dogs* in 1977, he moved to England in 1979 with Melvine Clark, a teacher who later became his wife. *Sleeping Dogs,* a spectacular thriller starring Sam Neill as a man on the run from a totalitarian government in a fictional near-future, was successful enough to be the first film from New Zealand to open in the United States and convinced New Zealand politicians that a film commission should be established in that country.

Donaldson then decided to make a film that would draw on his own experience concerning children and separation, which led to *Smash Palace,* his breakthrough picture, which was shown out of competition at Cannes in May 1981 and, as a result, found distributors. "You must understand," Donaldson told Lawrence Van Gelder in 1982, "that in New Zealand there was no way you could go to any film school. There was no way you could learn about filmmaking. The only way was to do it."

Smash Palace (1981) told the story of Al Shaw (Bruno Lawrence), a race driver who owns a wrecking yard in rural New Zealand, the breakup of his marriage to his French-born wife, Jacqui (Anna Jemison), who desperately wants to get back to civilization, and the problems this causes for their eight-year-old daughter. Jacqui teaches French at a local school. Al is mainly interested in tinkering with cars, drinking beer at night, and chasing after other women. The only thing they finally share in common is Georgie (Greer Robson), their daughter, as the marriage is on the rocks. Al, a former Grand Prix driver, goes berserk when Jacqui takes Georgie and leaves him. This film offered a stunning account of a marital smash-up and, in the words of Vincent Canby, made clear that Donaldson was "a filmmaker of potentially worldwide importance."

Other films would follow: *Nutcase* (1983) was a story of children working against terrorists in New Zealand. Donaldson's first Hollywood film was *The Bounty* (1984), a remake of the classic Charles Laughton *Mutiny on the Bounty,* starring Mel Gibson, Anthony Hopkins, Laurence Olivier, Daniel Day-Lewis, and Liam Neeson. The film, which offered more than a simple retelling of the story (in this version Captain Bligh is stubborn, but not mad), was nominated for a Golden Palm award at the Cannes Festival of 1984. *Marie* (1985), adapted from a book by Peter Maas, starred Sissy Spacek as a divorced mother and a whistleblower who exposed corrupt government practices in Tennessee. *No Way Out* (1987), a Kevin Costner thriller that was also a remake of *The Big Clock* (1948), was successful both with critics and at the box office. Although essentially escapist fare, like Donaldson's earlier film *Marie, No Way Out* offered a story of political corruption, but without the same level of moral indignation.

Later films were less successful: *Cocktail* (1988), for example, starring Tom Cruise as a flamboyant bartender, and *Cadillac Man* (1990), a Robin Williams comedy about a salesman under pressure to sell 12 Cadillacs in 12 days or get fired. *White Sands* (1992) starred Willem Dafoe as a sheriff investigating a murder in the American southwest. *The Getaway* (1993) was described as a "halfhearted" remake of the 1972 Sam Peckinpah hit adapted by Walter Hill from a Jim Thompson novel. *Species* (1995) was a revolting exercise in science fiction horror, but effectively done, thanks partly to the work of creature designer H. R. Giger; grossing over $60 million, it was a boxoffice success. *Dante's Peak* (1997) was a rather predictable disaster film starring Pierce Brosnan as volcanologist Harry Dalton, investigating a town in the state of Washington threatened by a volcano. Still, it earned a respectable $67 million at the box office.

Perhaps Donaldson's most successful film after *No Way Out* was *13 Days* (2000), the director's second collaboration with Kevin Costner, offering an artful and convincing reconstruction of the Cuban Missile Crisis of 1962. This film recalled Donaldson's earlier commitment as an antiwar activist. Sergei Khrushchev, the son of Soviet premier Nikita Khrushchev, was particularly impressed by the way the film portrayed "the psychological drama of a president at the very moment when he must make decisions that may determine the fate of his country, as well as others, with no knowledge of what is happening in the opposing camp." John Fitzgerald Kennedy was aware that a naval blockade of Cuba "and announcements of military readiness would serve as signals to the opposing side. And that the future would be determined by how well those signals were understood in the Kremlin." Although the story was slanted rather too much toward the Kennedy aide played by Costner (with a less-than-authentic accent), the drama of the crisis was well captured, as the film offered a brilliant demonstration of how serious the Cuban Missile Crisis was as a turning point in Cold War politics. Hailed as one of the ten best films of 2000, *13 Days* demonstrated that Vincent Canby's recognition 16 years earlier was justifiable.

References   Canby, Vincent, "How 'Smash Palace' Plumbs the Ruins of Love," *New York Times,* May 9, 1982, pp. D15–16; Khrushchev, Sergei, "The Thwarted Promise of *13 Days,*" *New York Times,* February 4, 2001, p. 17; Van Gelder, Lawrence, "Can New Zealand Rival Australia for Movie Honors?" *New York Times,* April 25, 1982, sec. 2, pp. 1, 15.

—J.M.W.

Donen, Stanley (1924–)   Best known for his Hollywood musical films, Stanley Donen has also directed a number of films in a variety of genres. Born on April 13, 1924, in Columbia, South Carolina, Stanley Donen completed his high

school education at age 16 and moved to New York to pursue a career in dance. He made his Broadway debut as a chorus boy in a production of *Pal Joey* at the Ethel Barrymore Theatre, which starred GENE KELLY. A friendship was struck between Donen and Kelly, with Donen becoming Kelly's choreographer. In 1941 Donen appeared in the collegiate musical, *Best Foot Forward,* also directed by Gene Kelly. Moving west to California in 1942, Donen was employed at MGM as a contract dancer and assistant to choreographer Charles Walters. In 1943 he appeared in the chorus of MGM's production of *Best Foot Forward.* When MGM loaned out Gene Kelly to Columbia to star in a Rita Hayworth musical titled *Cover Girl,* Donen assisted on Kelly's dance numbers, particularly the "Alter Ego" dance, in which Kelly dances with himself (a sequence made possible through double exposure). "Years later," noted Donen, "we simply would have used computers, but back then this was something entirely new. We would have to repeat the camera moves by ourselves, with Gene performing the dance twice to the prerecorded sound track. I knew it could be done by having him hit the same spots the second time as he did the first, which Gene could do, and then we could film it by having the camera hit the same marks both times, which I knew I could do." In 1945 Donen conceived, wrote, and directed another classic dance sequence for Gene Kelly in the MGM musical *Anchors Aweigh.* This sequence has Kelly dancing with the cartoon character Jerry the Mouse. Donen originally conceived the dance number with Mickey Mouse in mind, but upon consultation, Disney informed them that Mickey Mouse could not appear in an MGM picture. In 1946 Donen renewed his contract with MGM and cowrote the scenario for *Take Me Out to the Ball Game,* starring Gene Kelly, Frank Sinatra, and Jules Munshin. The 1949 film was directed by Busby Berkeley.

In 1949 Donen codirected, along with Gene Kelly, *On the Town,* a landmark musical film based on the Broadway show with music by Leonard Bernstein and lyrics by Adolph Green and Betty Comden. The story follows three sailors on shore leave in New York. On the plus side, the film boasted extensive location shooting; however, it unfortunately abandoned portions of the Bernstein score, which the producers felt was too "sophisticated" for commercial appeal. "We did try to make it, in a sense, somewhat more realistic than other musicals," recalled Donen in 1992. "It had a freer form to it, and it had the energy and youthfulness of the sailors in New York. What it also might have had was a certain sock of what I'd consider raw, American energy that other musicals at the time might have lacked. . . . What is not true, despite people's saying it all the time, is that *On the Town* was the first picture to be made on location. . . . There may not have been musical numbers done in the streets of New York before, but we didn't break any ground."

Donen received his first opportunity to direct solo when Charles Walters, the assigned director for *Royal Wedding,* refused to direct another picture with Judy Garland. The film, which was to star Donen's childhood idol, Fred Astaire, concerned American entertainers in Britain during the royal wedding of Princess Elizabeth and Prince Philip. Judy Garland was fired during the film's rehearsals and replaced with Jane Powell. The film featured another tour de force dance sequence, "You're All the World to Me," in which Fred Astaire dances on the ceiling in a sequence utilizing a revolving set. In 1952 Donen directed what many consider his finest film, *Singin' in the Rain,* with Gene Kelly and Debbie Reynolds. No less a critic than Pauline Kael refered to it as "perhaps the most enjoyable of all movie musicals, just about the best Hollywood musical of all time." The story by Comden and Green is about Hollywood's transition from silent films to sound, with Kelly playing an arrogant romantic leading actor faced with the challenges of the talking medium and a costar (Jean Hagen) whose Brooklyn accent renders her talking per-

Stanley Donen (left) on the set of *Blame It On Rio* (Sherwood Productions/Twentieth Century-Fox)

formances laughable. Between 1953 and 1955 Donen directed four more musicals for MGM, the most famous of which is *Seven Brides for Seven Brothers* (1954). The film, with a screenplay by Dorothy Kingsley, Frances Goodrich, and Albert Hackett, was based on a short story "The Sobbin' Women" by Stephen Vincent Benet. The production was filmed in the CinemaScope process and starred Howard Keel and Jane Powell. In 1957, Donen, on loan-out from MGM, directed *Funny Face* for Paramount (a VistaVision production), *The Pajama Game* for Warner Bros., and *Kiss Them For Me* for 20th Century-Fox.

When Donen's MGM contract expired, he moved to London to form Grandon Productions with actor Cary Grant. Their first production was the romantic drama *Indiscreet* (1958), based on Norman Krasna's play *Kind Sir* and costarring Cary Grant and Ingrid Bergman. More nonmusicals followed, including domestic comedies *Once More, With Feeling* (1960), *Surprise Package* (1960),

and *The Grass Is Greener* (1960); suspense thrillers *Charade* (1963) and *Arabesque* (1966); a bittersweet romance, *Two for the Road* (1967); two fantasies, *Bedazzled* (1967) and *The Little Prince* (1974); and science fiction, *Saturn 3* (1980). In 1986 Donen produced the Academy Awards presentation and also directed Lionel Ritchie's "Dancing on the Ceiling" music video. Donen then turned his attention to television where he directed several episodes of the TV series *Moonlighting*. In 1998 he received an Honorary Academy Award, "in appreciation of a body of work marked by grace, elegance, wit and visual innovation."

According to biographer Stephen Silverman, "With the arrival of Donen, musicals snapped to and noticeably came of age, integrating in a naturalistic fashion the elements of song, dance, plot, and realistic character motives. Where once danced effete noblemen, who found their romance at courtly balls, now tap-danced Average Joes, who fell head over heels—literally—for the girls next door."

Other Films As assistant choreographer: *Hey Rookie* (1944). As choreographer: *Jam Session* (1944); *Kansas City Kitty* (1944); *Holiday in Mexico* (1946); *No Leave, No Love* (1946); *Living in a Big Way* (1947); *This Time for Keeps* (1947); *Killer McCoy* (1947); *The Big City* (1948); *A Date with Judy* (1948); *The Kissing Bandit* (1948); *Double Dynamite* (1951); *Sombrero* (1953). As director: *Love Is Better Than Ever* (1952, filmed in 1950); *Fearless Fagan* (1952); *Give a Girl A Break* (1953); *Deep in My Heart* (1954); *It's Always Fair Weather* (1955); *The Pajama Game* (1957); *Kiss Them For Me* (1957); *Damn Yankees* (1958); *Staircase* (1969); *Lucky Lady* (1975); *Blame It on Rio* (1984); *Love Letters* (1999), for TV.

References Casper, Joseph Andrew, *Stanley Donen* (Metuchen, N.J.: Scarecrow Press, 1983); Silverman, Stephen M., *Dancing on the Ceiling: Stanley Donen and His Movies* (New York: Alfred A. Knopf, 1996).

—R.W.

Donner, Richard (1930–) One of Hollywood's most commercially bankable producer-directors, Richard Donner has launched several successful film series, the *Superman, Omen,* and *Lethal Weapon* pictures. He was born April 24, 1930. Originally an actor, he broke into directing through television. He directed episodes of *The Rifleman* before taking on his first theatrical feature, titled *X-15* (1961). This quasi science fiction thriller went unnoticed and Donner again turned his directorial attention to television. He directed episodes of popular shows such as *The Fugitive* (1963), *The Man from U.N.C.L.E.* (1964), *Get Smart* (1965), and *The Six Million Dollar Man* (1974), before establishing himself as a feature film director.

In 1976 Donner achieved his first major commercial success with the satanic thriller *The Omen*. This film starred Gregory Peck as Robert Thorn, Lee Remick as Katherine Thorn, and Harvey Stevens as Damien. In the film, Thorn is a highly respected American ambassador to England whose wife, Katherine, gives birth to a stillborn child. Thorn is encouraged by a priest to switch his dead child with a living baby of a mother who died during childbirth. Five years later strange things begin to happen in the Thorn household, all of which can be traced to their son, Damien, who is apparently nothing less than the Antichrist. Although the plot of *Omen* may seem ridiculous, the film was a success after its release. Jerry Goldsmith, who composed the score for the thriller, received an Academy Award nomination for best song and won the Oscar for best original score. Furthermore, the film spawned two sequels, *Damien—Omen II* and *The Final Conflict* (neither was directed by Donner). "*The Omen* was a phenomenal break for me," says Donner, "but while I was making it, I hated it and swore I was going to go back to television. . . . I came out of the first assemblage with the same editor I'm working for now, Stuart Baird, and I said, 'It's a dismal failure.' Then we sat down in the cutting room day in and day out and the picture started to take shape. My confidence began to grow during that editorial process."

Donner used the popularity that he gained from *Omen* to garner the position as director of the big-screen adaptation of *Superman* (1978). There was much anticipation surrounding the film and the choice of an actor who could bring the title character to life. A list of names considered for the part included Robert Redford, Sylvester Stallone, Burt Reynolds, Nick Nolte, and Charles Bronson. Christopher Reeve eventually won the part of Clark Kent/Superman. In addition to Reeve, the film stars Gene Hackman as Lex Luthor, and Margot Kidder as Lois Lane. The film's story begins on the planet Krypton where Superman's father sends his baby son off to Earth, where he eventually disguises himself as Clark Kent, a mild-mannered reporter for a metropolitan newspaper, *The Daily Planet,* to protect his identity. Superman-alias-Clark Kent saves the day (and reporter Lois Lane) a number of times and eventually rescues all mankind from the evil Lex Luthor's plot to take over the world. *Superman* was a major success after its release. An advertisement exclaiming, "You'll believe a man can fly," was on target. While *Superman* boasted some impressive flying effects, they were generally subordinated to the developing romance between Clark/Superman and Lois (including one of the film's highlight sequences, a romantic flight over New York City). *Superman* fared well at the box office and was nominated for Academy Awards for best editing, best score, and best sound. After *Superman,* Donner turned to an intimate chamber drama, *Inside Moves* (1980)—a sort of dry run for the television series, *Cheers.* Although the picture slumped at the box office, it is still Donner's favorite among his films ("*Inside Moves* was an emotional challenge for me, the catharsis of a lot of my thoughts and problems"). Next came *The Toy* (1982) and the sword-and-sorcery epic *Ladyhawke* (1985)—neither of which brought him the same level of success as *Omen* and *Superman.* Other Donner box-office disappointments included a well-intended but failed attempt to make a serious picture about parental abuse, *Radio Flyer* (1992).

Meanwhile, Donner was recapturing his commercial viability with satiric comedies like the Bill Murray Christmas vehicle, *Scrooged* (1988), and the *Lethal Weapon* series. The first entry in the latter series stars Mel Gibson as detective Martin Riggs and Danny Glover as detective Roger Murtaugh. These two police officers are extreme opposites. Riggs is young, suicidal (due to the death of his wife), and lives with his dog in a run-down trailer on the beach, while Murtaugh is an older man, with a wife, four kids, and a home in the suburbs. The film is set in motion when the two officers are forced to partner together. Their personalities collide (which provides many laughs), but the two must learn to work together when they begin investigating and eventually foil a drug-smuggling operation. *Weapon* was well received by fans after its release. It grossed more than $60 million at the box office within the first three months of its

release. The success of *Weapon* and its three sequels is doubtless due to Donner's canny blending of action, comedy, and the "buddy" formula. Other recent successes include *Maverick* (1994), a deconstruction of the popular television series, casting James Garner and Mel Gibson as papa Maverick and son, respectively; and *Conspiracy Theory* (1997), again tapping Gibson's patented neurotic nervousness as a paranoid cab driver.

Other Films   *The Goonies* (1985); *Assassins* (1995).

Reference   Singer, Michael, "Richard Donner," in *A Cut Above: 50 Film Directors Talk about Their Craft* (Los Angeles: Lone Eagle, 1998).

—N.L.

Dörrie, Doris (1955–)   In 1978, as a young graduate from the Hochschule für Film und Fernsehen in Munich, Doris Dörrie wrote the following about the state of the "New German Cinema": "German film has for a long time been aware that it has not been dealt with according to demand, but rather it is a state-supported spectacle, perspective and point of view. And quite carefully one selects what the camera may and may not see. And in general it politely looks past the things that I want to see." Dörrie went on to become an established figure in the German film world. This happened mainly thanks to box-office hits such as *Männer* (*Men* [1985]) and *Keiner liebt mich* (*Nobody Loves Me* [1994]), comedies that spawned scores of imitators and that gave Dörrie at once recognition and trouble. As she said to Klaus Phillips, "I'm quite ambivalent about my influence on the German film market altogether because if it means that nothing can be seen other than German comedies it's a quite disastrous situation."

After studying drama, acting, and film in the United States, Dörrie trained at the HFF, where Wim Wenders also had studied. Unlike Wenders, she felt outside of the old tradition of male filmmakers, such as Hawks, Ford, and Huston, that had so much inspired Wenders and others. She had, in a way, to "invent her own language" to show those things that she was not seeing portrayed on the German screen in the late seventies, when the NGC seemed remote from the problems of the day and more interested in adaptations of venerated literary classics. The young Dörrie worked for the Radio Company of Bavaria, the Bayerischer Rundfunk, where she made documentaries and a children's film. She had started making movies while she studied at the HFF, and her graduation film from the HFF, *Der Letzte Walzer* (*The Last Dancer* [1978]), was shown in festivals in Lübeck and Hof, which latter event she was active in organizing during those years. Also during those last years of the 1970s, she wrote film criticism for the *Süddeutsche Zeitung*. Dörrie's first professional film, *Dazwischen (In Between),* deals with the first love of a 16-year-old girl whose life is troubled by constantly moving between each of her divorced parents' homes. This was followed in 1983 by *Mitten ins Herz (Right in the Heart),* another girl-centered story in which the protagonist's "existential fears make her comfortable surroundings seem like a nightmare," as characterized by Richard and Mary Helt. According to Carole Angier, this film is also where Dörrie first attacked her old enemy: "the coldness and corruption of the consumerist society," to which she was to return later in one of her more controversial films, *Happy Birthday Turk.* As Angier explains, *Heart* established the pattern for the rest of Dörrie's films with this tale of an outsider told in a "pared-down, understated, witty and laconic" style.

Heart was followed by *Im Innern des Wahls* (*In the Belly of the Whale* [1984]), a film about a girl who flees her house to search for her mother after she has had a fight with her father. And then came her international success, with *Männer,* a low-budget comedy ($400,000) at once funny, entertaining, and socially conscious. Since then, Dörrie has not lost her touch and in a prolific career has dealt with the problems of Germany's increasing, yet unrecognized multiculturalism—as in *Happy Birthday Turk,* a detective genre story about a Turkish private eye. In it, the inner struggles of her previous protagonists turn to those of the outsider in society. In this film and since then, she has continued studying the theme of conformity through innovations in storytelling and cinematic style. She has also explored the topic in her more recent box-office hit, *Keiner liebt mich,* made almost a decade after the success of *Männer.* As she told Phillips, this is "a very naturalistic movie; when you walk through the streets of Cologne, it is a very multicultural city, more so than Munich, for instance. That's not something I made up or invented in order to be didactic about German angst of foreigners, it's there." Dörrie's knack for business has also remained unaltered. *Keiner liebt mich* was distributed by Buena Vista in Germany and released theatrically in the United States. Its official debut was made at Hollins College, in Roanoke, Virginia, where Dörrie was a visiting professor. She has also taught screenwriting in Colorado College and in her alma mater, the HFF in Munich.

In 1997, Dörrie married her cameraman from *Men,* Helge Weindler. The couple collaborated in all her subsequent productions until Weindler's death in 1996, when they were working on the shooting of *Bin ich Schön? (Am I Beautiful).* She has also published two collections of short stories in the United States and a third one in Canada.

Other Films *Paradies* (*Paradise* [1986]); *Ich und Er* (*I and Him* [1987]), *Geld* (*Money* [1989]); *Augenblick* (*Glance* [2000]); *Erleuchtung Garantiert* (*Enlightenment Guaranteed* [2000]).

References Angier, Carole, "Monitoring Conformity: the Career of Doris Dörrie," in *Women and Film: A Sight and Sound Reader,* ed. Pam Cook and Phillip Dodd (Philadelphia: Temple University Press, 1993); Phillips, Klaus, "Interview with Dorris Dörrie: Filmmaker, Writer, Teacher," in *Triangulated Visions: Women in Recent German Film,* eds. Ingeborg Majer O'Sickey and Ingeborg Von Zadow, (Albany: State University of New York Press, 1998); Helt, Richard C., and Marie E. Helt, *West German Cinema, 1985–1990: A Reference Handbook*

(Metuchen, N.J.: Scarecrow Press, 1992); Rentschler, Eric, ed., *West German Filmmakers on Film: Visions and Voices* (New York: Holmes & Meier, 1988).

—F.A.

Dos Santos, Nelson Pereira (1928–)

Nelson Pereira dos Santos is considered the "conscience" and progenitor of Cinema Novo, the "new wave" of 1960s Brazil. The movement began in the early 1950s when a group of Brazilian filmmakers, including dos Santos, Glauber Rocha, and Ruy Guerra, came together to discuss establishing a Brazilian cinema independent of foreign models. Brazilian films, particularly those produced at the Vera Cruz Film studios, were accused of slavish imitation of the popular foreign markets, like the United States. "Film as a means of artistic expression should meet Brazilian culture head on," dos Santos declared at the time. "[It] would permit an improved degree of communication and lay the foundations for a genuinely Brazilian cinema as an expression of both a particular culture and a given economy."

He was born in São Paulo on October 22, 1928. His mother, Dona Angelina Binari dos Santos declares that the name "Nelson" derived from her husband's admiration of a character in a silent film by Frank Lloyd. Moviegoing was a family affair for the dos Santos family. From early childhood Nelson, with his parents and siblings, attended the Sunday *matines* of American slapstick comedies and Hollywood romance dramas. "My parents were *cinefilos,* movie aficionadoes," recalls Nelson. "My father knew silent film in its entirety. He knew everything. It was him who gave me my cinema education. . . . That's how I started. The rest came later: the cineclubs, and later the conscious effort of making cinema, the possibility of making cinema in Brazil." At the University of São Paulo, beginning in 1947, Nelson divided his time between studying law and writing movie reviews for *O Hoje,* a Communist Party publication. It was a period of democratic experiments in Brazil, after the *maquis* in France and the *partigiani* in Italy had played a decisive role in the antifascist resistance.

He began his career in cinema as an assistant director, soon graduating to directing two films that came to be regarded as immediate precursors of the Cinema Novo movement, *Rio, 40 Graus* (*Rio, 40 Degrees* [1955]) and *Rio Zona Norte* (*Rio North Zone* [1957]). For the former, he took his camera into the streets "to film a simple story about the people of Rio de Janeiro," as dos Santos put it. It tells the story of five young vendors who, during a Sunday afternoon, try to find the best areas in town for selling their peanuts. Influenced by Italian neorealist tenets, it attempted to portray Brazilian people realistically, says dos Santos, "in their language, gestures, and dress, in order to recognize the existence of underdevelopment." Moreover, he sought to analyze the conditions of social injustice as he found them. The film marked the demise of the Vera Cruz studio. Commentator Peter Rist calls *Rio, 40 Graus* a "landmark film" in the Cinema Novo movement: "In its focus on poor Afro-Brazilians and their interaction with the other levels of society, *Rio, 40 Graus* lay the groundwork for a film movement which would tell the truth about the miserable plight of Brazil's marginals, while championing the richness of their culture."

Vidas Secas (*Barren Lives* [1963]) is considered the high point of Cinema Novo. Based on a 1938 novel by Graciliano Ramos and filmed on location in the northeast *grande sertao* (great desert), it begins with an intertitle, which states that the film is intended to expose "a very dramatic social reality of our days of the extreme poverty that enslaves 27 million of Northeasters, and that no Brazilian with dignity can no longer ignore." The story is set in the early 1940s. Fabiano, his wife Vitoria, and their two young children are on the road, their meager possessions on their backs, looking for work. Many troubles beset the hapless family as Fabiano is unjustly imprisoned, beaten, and forced to forage for food. As they continue to walk through the barren desert, Fabiano's wife asks him, "We cannot continue living like animals, hidden in the wild, can we?" To which Fabiano responds, "No, we can't." Clearly dos Santos is calling for a transformation in Brazilian society, not through violence, but through perseverance, endurance, and improvement of opportunities through education. Unfortunately, it failed to reach a mass audience in Brazil, although it won an award at Cannes in 1964. "In world cinema [*Vidas Secas*] stands as a great example of literary adaptation and as an ideal work of neo-realism," says Rist, "more exemplary than most of its Italian forebears, while its filmic treatment of peasant life has never been surpassed."

After a period spent in making mostly documentaries, dos Santos returned to features with a series of noteworthy films, including *Tent of Miracles* (*Tenda dos milagres* [1977]), an attack on racist hypocrisy; *Road of Life* (*Estrada da vida* [1980]), a light comedy starring two of Brazil's most popular singers; and *How Tasty Was My Little Frenchman* (*Como era gostoso o meu Frances* [1971]), one of dos Santos's most internationally acclaimed films. Based on historical incidents in the 1560s, *Little Frenchman* told the story of a French adventurer who is captured in the Brazilian jungles by Tupinamba Indians. His many attempts to escape are thwarted, and eventually he is killed and eaten by his captors. His last words are a prophecy that his countrymen will avenge him. Despite its high adventure, the film nonetheless contains a biting critique of international colonialism and genocide. In 1984 dos Santos turned to an incident from the recent past to make *Memoirs of Prison (Memorias do carcere),* arguably his masterpiece. It is based on the posthumously published memoirs of Graciliano Ramos, an account of repression and resistance under the dictatorship of Getulio Vargas. Ramos's sufferings for his left-wing allegiance are graphically depicted. "*Memorias* conveys a sense of timeless reflection through the minute examination of a single event," writes Timothy Barnard, "treating it with a wisdom that is neither complacent nor angry, sentimental or strident, but imbued with an awareness of life's complexities and compromises."

Dos Santos has served as director of the Department of Cinematographic Art at the Universidad Federal Fluminense. He continues to make films in the hope that he can, as he puts it, "help create a cinema nourished by popular roots to liberate the people." Glauber Rocha refers to him as the "conscience" of Cinema Novo.

Other Films *Rio Quarenta* (1955); *The Mouth of Gold* (*Boca de ouro* [1962]); *Hunger for Love* (*Fome de amor* [1968]); *The Craziest Asylum* (*Azyllo muito louco* [1970]); *Who Is Beta?* (*Quem e beta?* [1973]).

References Barnard, Timothy, *South American Cinema: A Critical Filmography, 1915–1994* (Austin: University of Texas Press, 1996); Johnson, Randal, *Cinema Novo x 5: Masters of Contemporary Brazilian Film* (Austin: University of Texas Press, 1984); Salem, Helene, *Nelson Pereira dos Santos, O Sonho Possivel do Cinema Brasileiro* (Nelson Pereira dos Santos, the possible dream of Brazilian cinema), ed. Nova Frontiera, 1987; Stam, Robert, "On the Margins: Brazilian Avant-Garde Cinema," in Stam, Robert, and Randal Johnson, *Brazilian Cinema* (New York: Columbia University Press, 1995).

—M.L. and J.C.T.

Dovzhenko, Alexander Petrovich

(1894–1956) Considered a cinematic poet, Dovzhenko was part of the triad of great Soviet filmmakers, along with SERGEI EISENSTEIN and VSEVELOD ILLARIONOVICH PUDOVKIN, but his vision, linked to his native Ukraine, was decidedly different. His loyalty to Ukraine is obvious in the way his films poetically evoke the landscape and folkways, but his films, made in the service of the state, could not be evocative of Ukrainian nationalism, especially during the Stalinist regime, and he had to walk a tightrope politically, lest he fall out of favor.

Alexander Dovzhenko was born of peasant stock in Sosnitsa, in the province of Chernigov in the northeast of Ukraine on September 12, 1894, and he trained to be a primary schoolteacher. He served in the Red Army during the civil war. After the Revolution, he joined the Communist Party and worked as a civil servant for the Ukrainian Commissariat of Education. He then became a career diplomat assigned first to the Soviet Embassy in Warsaw, later becoming secretary of the Berlin consulate. While in Berlin he studied art under Erik Heckel.

In 1923 Dovzhenko returned to the Soviet Union and worked for a while as a book illustrator and political cartoonist, whose work was published in the Ukrainian film magazine, *Kino.* At the age of 32 he decided to take up filmmaking and went to Odessa, where he submitted a film script and was then permitted to direct *Vasya, the Reformer,* a short comedy, for Odessa Studios in 1926. Another comedy, *The Little Fruits of Love,* followed in 1926, then an espionage thriller, *The Diplomatic Pouch* (1927), another popular success that enabled him to take on more ambitious projects.

Zvenigora (1928) was the first film that would define Dovzhenko's poetic and lyrical style, but studio heads in Odessa were puzzled by its metaphorical profusion and would not approve its release until after it had been endorsed by Eisenstein and Pudovkin, both of whom were impressed. "Pudovkin and I had a wonderful task," Eisenstein would later write, "to answer the questioning eyes of the auditorium with a joyful welcome of our new colleague. And to be the first to greet him."

The scope of the film was immense, a symbolic and free-flowing survey of Ukrainian history and folklore spanning centuries, from the Viking invasions to the Revolution. The film offered a symbolic anthology of Ukrainian folk myths, centered upon a grandfather figure who stands for the spirit of the Ukraine. The grandfather tells his grandson, Pavlo, stories about treasures hidden in the mountains of Zvenigora, which proves to be an allegory concerning the true treasures of the Ukrainian people, their intelligence and initiative in harnessing the land's mineral wealth. Dovzhenko later described *Zvenigora* as "a catalog of all my creative capabilities."

Arsenal (1929) was less symbolic and more in keeping with the goals of "socialist realism." It offered a sweeping account of the Ukraine from the World War through the February and October Revolutions, to the suppression of a workers' rebellion in 1918. The style was again symbolic. To demonstrate the brutality of the czarist regime, Dovzhenko filmed Czar Nicholas writing in his diary, "Today I shot a crow," juxtaposed with a shot of an old peasant collapsing in a field from exhaustion. Jay Leyda wrote that this was "the first masterpiece of the Ukrainian cinema [which] broke entirely with traditional film structure and subject, depending solely on a flow of ideas and emotions rather than upon conflicts between individual characters."

Earth (*Zemlya* [1930]) has also been considered a masterpiece of the Soviet silent cinema, but the film was denounced as being "counterrevolutionary," as the Soviet leadership was changing and even Eisenstein was falling out of official favor because of his formalist tendencies. It told the story of young peasants of a Ukrainian village wanting to set up collective farms, in conflict with the *kulaks* (rich landowners), who are attempting to protect their land. The collective farmers are celebrating the arrival of a tractor. One of them, Vasili, walking home down a moonlit path, begins to dance and is murdered by a jealous *kulak* assassin, not because he is an official of the collective farm, but because "he was dancing!" Hope resides in the soil and the regenerative power of the life cycle; apples, seen at both the beginning and the end of the film, are symbolic of the fertility of the land. In the film's final sequence, Vasili's body is carried past apple trees to his burial in the soil. As he is buried, Dovzhenko cuts to shots of a peasant woman giving birth.

Dovzhenko married Yulia Solntseva (1901–89), who was his assistant director on *Earth* and on his first sound film, *Ivan* (1932), about the industrialization of Ukraine, which was not considered a success. She became his most loyal supporter and collaborator, and, after her husband's death, was to become a successful filmmaker on her own, named People's Artist of the USSR in 1981.

In 1935 Dovzhenko directed *Aerograd* (*Air City,* aka *Frontier*), remarkable for its images of the Siberian landscape and its promise of a hopeful future in opening and developing the Soviet Far Eastern frontier. The party was pleased and Dovzhenko was awarded the prestigious Order of Lenin. Stalin then encouraged Dovzhenko to make "a Ukrainian *Chapayev,*" after the model of the civil-war film made by the Vassiliev brothers, under Stalin's scrutiny. What resulted, after three years and at least one false start, was *Shors* (*Shchors* [1939]), a highly personal work, telling the story of Nikolai Shors, the Red commander of the Ukraine from 1917 to 1919. The film eventually won the State Prize in 1941, but it was also admired abroad. Scenes such as "the silver blaze of ripe wheat and sunflowers full of struggling men, crazed horses and black explosions are still able to make any perceptive U.S. filmgoer," *Time* critic James Agee wrote, "wonder, seriously, whether he has ever seen a real moving picture before."

In 1940 Dovzhenko was pressed into service again to make *Liberation* (1940) to celebrate the reunification of Ukraine after the Nazi-Soviet pact, putting a Soviet spin on the reannexation of the Western Ukraine into the USSR. Just after taking over as artistic head of the Kiev Studios in 1941, war broke out, and Dovzhenko spent the next two years in Moscow, where he wrote a novel entitled *Victory* and supervised three documentary features—*Battle for the Ukraine* (1943), *The Kharkov Trial* (1945), and *Victory in the Ukraine* (1945)—that, according to Alexander Birkos, were in fact directed by his wife, Yulia Solntseva.

Back in Kiev after the war, Dovzhenko wrote a stage play about the Russian horticulturalist Ivan Michurin that was then adapted to a film entitled *Love in Bloom,* which was started in 1946 but not completed until 1949 and finally released under the title *Michurin*. The film was made, then remade so as to reflect the theories of T. D. Lysenko, a botanist admired by Stalin. During the final years of Stalinism, creative conditions were not favorable in the Soviet Union. Dovzhenko continued to write screenplays and was about to start filming *Poem of an Inland Sea* when he died of heart failure on November 26, 1956. His wife later made *Poem of an Inland Sea* in 1958, a film about the creation of the Kakhosk hydroelectric station. She also made *The Flaming Years* (1960) from a Dovzhenko screenplay set during the war, and *Ukraine on Fire* (1967), based on Dovzhenko's wartime stories, carrying forward the legacy of her husband's vision.

References   Birkos, Alexander S., *Soviet Cinema: Directors & Films* (Hamden, Conn.: Archon Books, 1976); Kepley, Vance, Jr., *In the Service of the State: The Cinema of Alexander Dovzhenko* (Madison: University of Wisconsin Press, 1986); Leyda, Jay, *Kino: A History of the Russian and Soviet Film* (New York: Collier Books, 1973); Youngblood, Denise J., *Soviet Cinema in the Silent Era, 1918–1935* (Austin: University of Texas Press, 1991).

—J.M.W.

Dreyer, Carl Theodor (1889–1968)

In a 50-year career Carl Dreyer made only 14 feature films, yet he is unquestionably the greatest filmmaker in the Danish cinema and, according to biographer Tom Milne, an artist whose work constitutes "the greatest and most loving voyage of exploration of the human soul the cinema has yet witnessed." He was born in Copenhagen, Denmark, in February 1889. Orphaned as a child, he was adopted and brought up by a strict Lutheran family. He took piano lessons and worked on his first job as a pianist in a Copenhagen café. After a stint as a journalist in Copenhagen from 1909 to 1913, where he covered trials, sports, and the theater, he joined Nordisk Films Kompagni in 1913 as a title writer.

His first film was *The President* (1919), which established the precedent he followed all his life, i.e, adapting his films from either novels or plays. Based on Karl Emil Franzos's novel, it is a melodrama about the past sins of a respected judge coming back to haunt him. *Leaves from Satan's Book* (1920) is a four-part allegory of Satan's incarnations as a Pharisee who tempts Judas to betray Christ, as a Grand Inquisitor in 16th-century Spain, as a revolutionary in 1793 Paris who persuades a young man to betray his lover and the Cause; and as an unfrocked Red monk during the Russo-Finnish war of 1918 trying to entice a young Finnish girl to betray her country. This was followed by an early masterpiece, *The Parson's Widow* (1920), which Dreyer made for the Swedish company, Svensk Filmindustri. A thoroughly enchanting fable rooted in a detailed and picturesque 17th-century village setting, it was about a young parson who upon inheriting his first parish must agree to marry the previous incumbent's widow. He does so only on the condition that his girl friend (introduced to the old lady as his sister) be hired as a maid in the parsonage. The penultimate scene in which the old woman takes leave of her beloved farm before lying down to die is among the most moving scenes in all of cinema.

The Master of the House (1925), drawn from a play by Svend Rindom, was a quiet and sophisticated dissection of a troubled marriage. After his wife leaves him, an overbearing husband comes to realize how cruelly he has exploited her; and the two eventually reconcile. Its detailed examination of everyday life, photographed with a canny sense of the three-dimensionality of the house interior, justifies claims that the film is a precursor to Italian neorealism.

Under the auspices in France of the Société Générale de Films, Dreyer made his last silent film, *The Passion of Joan of Arc* (1928), a landmark in the silent-film era. Despite the exhaustive research into period detail, costume, and ritual—the scenario was drawn from transcripts of Joan's trial—the film consists almost entirely of tight closeups that fragment and limit our vision of the total mise-en-scène of the Palais de Justice at Rouen. Falconetti's performance is likewise a concatenation of facial closeups seen from every conceivable angle. Joan's 29 examinations, lasting 18 months, are telescoped into one trial that lasts just 24 hours.

After a four-year hiatus during which Dreyer returned to journalism, he directed a classic horror film, *Vampyr* (1932), derived from J. Sheridan Le Fanu's vampire story, "Carmilla." Instead of the expected dark chiaroscuro of a standard horror thriller, punctuated with a series of noisy shocks and featuring a vampire with cloak and teeth, *Vampyr* is a "white" film that proceeds deliberately and (mostly) silently, featuring a vampire who is ultimately suffocated by a fall of snowy plaster in a mill. Phantom shadows crawl across the white walls and undulate in the reflections in a lake. The burial sequence, seen from the perspective of the entombed man about to be interred alive, is one of the horror genre's most celebrated sequences. And the vampires are a beautiful young woman and a birdlike little old doctor.

Over the remaining span of years until his death on March 20, 1968, Dreyer completed only a handful of film projects. *Day of Wrath* (1943), based on a play by Hans Wiers-Jenssen, was filmed during the German occupation of Denmark. Despite his protests that it was nonpolitical in nature, it was seized upon by the beleaguered Danes as a symbol of resistance and as a critique of the Jewish persecution by German invaders. It depicts the trial and condemnation to death by burning of two women accused of being witches. The eldest is a relatively harmless soul; her daughter, by contrast, uses her sexual wiles to exact a revenge on her mother's persecutors. Both women are ultimately consigned to the flames. "I am afraid neither of Heaven nor

Hell, I'm only afraid to die," moans the old woman under pain of torture. The pacing is deliberately slow, the action muted, the terror and the torture muffled as the persecutors move quietly about their purpose. *Ordet* (1955) was based on a play by Kaj Munk about a young woman who dies in childbirth but is brought back to life by an act of faith. Naturalistic surface textures blend with quietly miraculous events. Again, the film is marked by restrained acting, simple sets, long uncut sequences, and a deliberately slow pace.

Gertrude (1964), based on a play by Hjalmar Soderberg, was his last film. The title character is an atheist who believes in her freedom to do what she wants with her life; and as a result she rejects all men and retires into solitude out of her conviction that a perfect love is not possible. "The man with whom I live must belong to me entirely," she declares. "I must come first. I don't want to be an object to be played with from time to time." Its technique pares down Dreyer's already notoriously ascetic style. The film's stark indifference to commercial tastes and its garnering of poor reviews guaranteed its disastrous reception at the box office. One critic said it was a film wholly of "photographed sofa conversations."

A project that remained incomplete at Dreyer's death was a proposed script for a life of Christ. Begun during a trip to America in 1949–50, it was to be filmed at last in 1967, but when Dreyer insisted that the film should be made on location in Israel, it was aborted. A year later Dreyer's negotiations with Italian television were abruptly cut short by his death. As Tom Milne points out, ideas, themes, and images recur so persistently throughout Dreyer's work that it is possible to define a typical Dreyer film: "The period is almost invariably the past. The subject is a small, self-enclosed group—a family, a village, a victim and her judges—with the action rarely moving outside an extremely restricted area, and rarely stretching over more than a few hours or days; and within the group, a lonely figure gradually detaches itself, the object of either deliberate or unconscious cruelty." Stylistically, Dreyer has a penchant for close-ups or, at least, closely observed characters, detailed décor, soft-toned lighting, protracted camera takes, the use of inexperienced actors, and a stately tempo moving toward the final catharsis of tragedy. The mystic powers of good and evil are very real in Dreyer, and his characters, especially his women, relentlessly but unsuccessfully pursue their quest for perfect love. Meanwhile, all forms of cruelty, prejudice, superstition, hypocrisy, and rigid religious dogma are denounced.

Notoriously reticent about his private life, fiercely protective of his own artistic integrity, elusive in interviews, rather other-worldly in his attitude, Dreyer has yet to gain the popular acceptance that he deserves. "What I look for in my films," he said, "what I want to do, is to penetrate, by way of their most subtle expressions, to the deepest thoughts of my actors. For it is these expressions which reveal the personality of a character, his unconscious feelings, the secrets hidden deep within his soul." Perhaps an insight into his character and sensibility may be derived from the opening title card of *Vampyr*: "There exist certain predestined beings whose very lives seem bound by invisible threads to the supernatural world. They crave solitude . . . they dream . . . their imagination is so developed that their vision reaches far beyond that of most men."

Other Films *Love One Another* (1921); *Once Upon a Time* (1922); *Michael* (1924); *Two People* (1944); *Thorwaldsen* (1949).

References Bordwell, David, *The Films of Carl-Theodor Dreyer* (Berkeley: University of California Press, 1981); Milne, Tom, *The Cinema of Carl Dreyer* (New York: A. S. Barnes, 1981).

—J.C.T.

Dwan, Allan (1885–1981)

One of Hollywood's most prolific directors, Alan Dwan also demonstrated great versatility and staying power over the course of a career that spanned silent and sound films. Born Joseph Aloysius Dwan on April 3, 1885, in Toronto, Canada, the future director moved to America in 1893. Educated at Chicago's North Division High School and Notre Dame, he obtained his degree in electrical engineering in 1907. After briefly working at his university as instructor of physics and mathematics and as football coach after graduation, he began his career as an illumination engineer developing mercury vapor arc lights for the film industry. Following assignment to his Chicago company's client, Essanay Studios, in 1909, he was offered a position as scenario editor. His work for Essanay's "Flying A" Company in 1910 saw his emergence as director of more than 251 one-reel westerns, comedies, and documentaries. Dwan's list of credits is amazing. He may have directed some 800 films, most of which are lost. According to the director, the list may number 1,850!

After joining Universal in 1913, he signed up with Famous Players the following year and directed several Mary Pickford films. At the same time, he joined the Triangle Company and worked with DAVID WARK GRIFFITH. During these formative years as a director, Dwan's technical education allowed him to introduce several innovations that are now common currency in cinema: He designed the dolly shot to follow an actor in *David Harum*. While working with Griffith on *Intolerance,* he solved the problem of filming the huge Babylonian city ramparts by constructing an elevator on a railroad track, which allowed the camera to move up or down or backward and forward as needed. In 1916 he began a fruitful association with Douglas Fairbanks and the Artcraft company, which resulted in 11 major works, including *Bound in Morocco* (now lost [1917]), *A Modern Musketeer* (1918), *Robin Hood* (1922), and *The Iron Mask* (1929). Now a director of first-rank stature, during the 1920s he directed several lavish Paramount productions starring Gloria Swanson, such as *Zaza* (1923), *Manhandled* (1924), and *Stage Struck* (1925). In 1923, he also directed his favorite

film, *Big Brother,* dealing with underprivileged boys. Although reticent about the arrival of sound, Dwan eventually made a smooth transition to the new medium. His most successful early sound film was *While Paris Sleeps* (1932). He then moved to England to shoot three films during 1932–34. After directing Shirley Temple in the commercially successful *Heidi* (1937) and *Rebecca of Sunnybrook Farm* (1938), he returned to big-budget favor with *Suez* (1938). But apart from *Frontier Marshal* (1939), he returned to the grind of directing routine films.

In 1943, he trained camera units for the army's photographic division. After directing some fast-paced comedies such as *Brewster's Millions* and *Getting Gertie's Garter* (1945), Dwan signed a contract with Republic Studios in 1945. Although most critics describe his Republic work as routine, with the exception of *The Sands of Iwo Jima* (1949), Dwan actually directed some notable films, some of which deserve reevaluation. *Silver Lode* (1954) was a subversive anti-McCarthy western with villain Dan Duryea bearing a similar name to the recently humiliated senator. *Passion* (1954) is an appropriately named vendetta western set in the early days of California, with Cornel Wilde and Raymond Burr. *Tennessee's Partner* (1955) is an underrated western containing sterling performances by John Payne and Ronald Reagan as a dumb cowboy. It is the only project Dwan initiated during his Republic days. *Slightly Scarlet* (1956) is a moody color and Techniscope film noir reminiscent of the pessimistic overtones of James M. Cain and Jim Thompson novels. *The River's Edge* (1957) contains strong performances by Ray Milland and Anthony Quinn in a romantically raw and savage chase drama containing scenes of emotional turbulence. Dwan retired from direction in 1958 after directing an independent production, *The Most Dangerous Man Alive.* It was sold to Columbia and eventually released in 1961. Dwan's final attempt to direct *Marine!,* a biography of "Chesty" Puller for Warner Bros. in 1967, failed when Jack Warner sold the studio. As Peter Bog-danovich described him in 1971, Dwan was really the last surviving pioneer left from the beginnings of the American film industry.

Other Films *An Innocent Magdalene* (1916); *Josette* (1938); *Montana Belle* (1952); The *Woman They Almost Lynched* (1953); *Enchanted Island* (1958).

References Brownlow, Kevin, *The Parade's Gone By* (London: Secker and Warburg, 1968); Bogdanovich, Peter, *Allan Dwan: The Last Pioneer* (London: Studio Vista, 1971).

—T.W.

Eastwood, Clint (1930–) Clint Eastwood became a movie star of the first magnitude, but his reputation as a director has grown over the years to make him more than simply an actor who has also directed films. His films have ranged from the merely silly to the nearly sublime. After spending years on the sets of other directors, notably SERGIO LEONE and DON SIEGEL, he gradually learned the tricks of the trade. His later films go well beyond merely competent craftsmanship. Not all of them have been blockbusters, by any means, but some have. His post-western *Unforgiven* (1992), for example, resurrected an apparently dead genre, reminding viewers of what the western was and what it could accomplish. His adaptation of *The Bridges of Madison County* (1995), based on a wretchedly pretentious and maudlin, sentimental novel, showed viewers what the novel might have become, had it been written by someone more talented than Robert James Waller. Eastwood desentimentalized the character of Waller's sappy photographer, Robert Kincaid, providing him with a sense of dignity, clarity, and muscle, where there had been only flab. Toning up the character and tuning up the novel, Eastwood fixed and rebuilt *The Bridges of Madison County.*

Clinton Eastwood, Jr., was born in San Francisco, California, on May 31, 1930. After graduating from high school, he served with the Army Special Services from 1950 to 1954 before starting his career as an actor in the television series *Rawhide.* He then migrated to Italy to star in Sergio Leone's so-called spaghetti westerns, starting with *A Fistful of Dollars* in 1964. Finally, he translated his laconic western persona into an urban cowboy when he played Harry Callahan for Don Siegel in *Dirty Harry* (1971), a role that made him a superstar and put him in the position of calling his own shots.

Eastwood's first film as director was *Play Misty for Me* (1971), followed by *High Plains Drifter* and *Breezy* (both 1973). *Play Misty for Me,* the story of a jazz disk jockey (Eastwood) who gets involved with a psychotic young woman, has been compared to *Psycho* and the later *Fatal Attraction.* Eastwood claims the critics said "We're not ready for him as an actor, much less a director," but the film was a modest success. Although Eastwood continued to act in films directed by others, his own directing credits continued to build. He directed comedies, mysteries, thrillers, and action-adventures, such as *The Eiger Sanction* (1975), *Firefox* and *Honkytonk Man* (both 1982), *Sudden Impact* (1983),

Clint Eastwood (right) directed and starred in *The Rookie* (Warner Bros.)

Tightrope (1984), credited to Richard Tuggle, but actually directed by Eastwood, *Heartbreak Ridge* (1986), *The Rookie* (1990), *Absolute Power* and *Midnight in the Garden of Good and Evil* (both 1997), *True Crime* (1999), and *Space Cowboys* (2000), a decidedly mixed bag overall, including some critical misfires, but many of them made popular by Eastwood's presence.

The pictures just named do not represent Eastwood's best work, however. Eastwood was at his best when driven by his enthusiasms and his interest in obsessive and self-destructive characters. *White Hunter Black Heart* (1990) was a tribute to the director JOHN HUSTON. *Bird* (1988), a neglected film but one of Eastwood's very best, was a tribute to the jazz musician out of Kansas City, Charlie "Bird" Parker. Eastwood's enthusiasm for jazz also prompted him to make the documentary *Thelonius Monk: Straight, No Chaser* (1989). East-

wood also continued to make westerns. *Pale Rider* (1985) was essentially a remake of the classic *Shane* (1953), with Eastwood himself playing a far more intimidating gunman than Alan Ladd had played for GEORGE STEVENS's classic western, refigured as a story about a big mining operation trying to drive away independent miners panning for gold and staking claims, instead of a big rancher trying to drive away homesteaders.

Pale Rider was an interesting imitation and a distinctive Eastwood western, but *Unforgiven* was wholly original, with Eastwood playing a truly retired gunfighter, Will Munny, who becomes a bounty hunter in order to save the failing family farm. *Unforgiven* was Eastwood's greatest success, winning multiple Academy Awards, including best picture and best director, a masterpiece of genre filmmaking, but also a character-driven picture that went considerably beyond stereotypes. At the age of 62, Eastwood pursued roles of older characters who had seen the world and responded on the basis of their experience. Will Munny, no longer a hard-living hothead, for example, had to relearn his gunfighting skills in order to extract justice from Gene Hackman's lawman, Little Bill Daggett.

Always willing to take chances with risky projects, Eastwood followed the tremendous success of *Unforgiven* with *A Perfect World* (1993), an odd coming-of-age movie about a seven-year-old boy kidnapped by an escaped convict, Butch Haines (Kevin Costner), on the run from a manhunt led by a world-weary Texas Ranger (Clint Eastwood). This film was set in 1963 in Texas, just before the Kennedy assassination, just as the country was "on the brink of a great turning towards the void that will take hold of America," as Eastwood remembered the project.

Eastwood's star power made him a latter-day John Wayne, but Wayne made his best films with the director John Ford and steered clear of directing himself, with two exceptions, *The Alamo* (1960) and his patriotic folly, *The Green Berets*

(1969), which he apparently codirected with Ray Kellogg. Eastwood, in contrast, combined the talents of both John Wayne and John Ford, directing his best pictures himself. Major retrospectives of Eastwood's work were mounted in New York at the Museum of Modern Art in 1980 and in Paris at the Cinématheque Française in 1985, culminating in the French government's naming him Chevalier des Arts et Lettres. Back in California in 1986, this archetypal American was elected mayor of Carmel and served in office until 1988.

"My career in directing started strictly by accident," Eastwood told interviewer Iain Blair in 1997. "The only way I could get to direct was to act in the picture and the only way I could get the picture made was to act in it. So in 1970 I got the job to do both in *Play Misty for Me,* and back then very few actors also directed. Then I'd find a story like *High Plains Drifter,* where I liked the story and also liked the character, so I interspersed them

with films where someone else would direct." That flexibility freed him from his two main acting roles—the Man with No Name in the Leone films, and "Dirty Harry" Callahan in the Don Siegel films. Eastwood was able to take control of his image and his career. As Robert E. Kapsis has written, "No other contemporary dramatic star has directed himself so often."

References Gallafent, Edward, *Clint Eastwood: Filmmaker and Star* (New York: Continuum, 1994); Kapsis, Robert E., and Kathie Coblentz, *Clint Eastwood: Interviews* (Jackson: University Press of Mississippi, 1999); Schickel, Richard, *Clint Eastwood: A Biography* (New York: Knopf, 1996).

—J.M.W.

Edwards, Blake (1922–) One of Hollywood's most enduring, versatile, and productive filmmakers, Blake Edwards has become known primarily for his screen comedies. He was born in

Producer-director-writer Blake Edwards (left) on the set of *Victor/Victoria* (Ladbroke Entertainments Limited/MGM)

Tulsa, Oklahoma, July 26, 1922, to a show-business family. His father was one of the top assistant directors and production managers during Hollywood's heyday, and his grandfather, J. Jordon Edwards, had been a leading director during the silent-film era (he directed several Theda Bara vehicles). Blake began his own show-business career in 1942 as an actor in the film *Ten Gentlemen from West Point*. His debut as a writer came six years later with *Panhandle*. He turned to radio drama in 1949 when he created the enormously popular radio serial, *Yours Truly, Johnny Dollar*. For television, his many writing credits included *Hey, Mulligan* and *Richard Diamond* (1957–59), *Peter Gunn* (1958–61), and *Mr. Lucky* (1961–62). His first movie scripts were *My Sister Eileen* (1955), *Operation Mad Ball* (1957), and *The Notorious Landlady* (1962).

Early directorial efforts embraced a variety of genres, like the comedies *This Happy Feeling* (1958) and *Operation Petticoat* (1959); the bittersweet romance, *Breakfast at Tiffany's* (1961); the social-problem film, *The Days of Wine and Roses* (1962); and the thriller, *Experiment in Terror* (1962). His best-known comedies, the slapstick "Pink Panther" series starring Peter Sellers, began with *The Pink Panther* in 1963, starring Peter Sellers as the inimitable, bumbling Inspector Clouseau, and continued with *A Shot in the Dark* (1964), *The Return of the Pink Panther* (1975), *The Pink Panther Strikes Again* (1976), *Revenge of the Pink Panther* (1978), *Trail of the Pink Panther* (1982), and *Curse of the Pink Panther* (1982). Clouseau is one of the most enduring characters in all of screen comedy. "Clouseau is in largest measure funny because of his sustained faith in himself," comments Myron Meisel in his study of Edwards, "even in the face of the most outrageous challenges to his inner placidity. . . . Clouseau belongs to the tradition of the charmed fool, and his considerable virtues and minor flaws as a comic creation essentially derive from that benighted tradition."

After the failure of the big-budget *The Great Race* (1964), Edwards determined to venture into different directions. "I decided at one point in my career that I would not go on being a director unless I had creative freedom," he recalls. "I was lucky enough to have directed a series of films that made a lot of money, which is what the Hollywood Establishment understands, and I took advantage of it." Subsequent independent efforts included *The Tamarind Seed* (1974), *What Did You Do in the War, Daddy?* (1966), *10* (1979)—his biggest success, *S.O.B.* (1980), *The Man Who Loved Women* (1983), *Victor/Victoria* (1982), *A Fine Mess* (1986), and *Blind Date* (1986). Seven of his films featured Julie Andrews, whom he married in 1969. *That's Life,* released in 1986, about the late mid-life crisis of an architect, was semiautobiographical. Edwards scripted the picture, and Andrews and Jack Lemmon portrayed the Fairchilds, based vaguely on the Edwards clan (Edwards's daughter, Jennifer, and Andrews's daughter, Emma Walton, appeared in the cast). "A lot of the situations that occur in the story have happened in our lives," says Andrews. "All the actors were able to fall back on real-life situations for this improvisational film."

In his study of Edwards, Myron Meisel declares, "Blake Edwards, the most important comic stylist (along with Richard Lester) of the 1960s, and without peer today, parlayed deadpan farce and intricate gag construction into a profound comic metaphysic devoted to whatever possibilities remain for wit and romance in the postwar age."

Other Films *Gunn* (1968); *The Party* (1970); *Wild Rovers* (1971); *The Carey Treatment* (1972); *Micki & Maude* (1984); *Skin Deep* (1989); *Switch* (1991); *Son of the Pink Panther* (1993).

References Meisel, Myron, "Blake Edwards," in Jean-Pierre Cloursodon, *American Directors,* vol. 2 (New York: McGraw-Hill, 1983), pp. 117–132.

—J.C.T.

Egoyan, Atom (1960–)

The most important member of a new generation of Canadian filmmakers, Atom Egoyan's films are quirky, stylized examinations of the darker aspects of the human condition. He was born in Cairo, Egypt, in 1960, in a family of Armenian immigrants. His name came out of the admiration that his father, furniture designer Joseph Egoyan, felt for the then-new nuclear energy technology. When he was three years old, the family moved to Canada, where his was the only Armenian family in Victoria (British Columbia). There, Joseph opened a furniture design and sales business and raised Atom and his younger sister Eve in an artistic atmosphere. Both were educated in music; later Eve would become a professional pianist and Atom would pursue classical guitar. As a young man, Atom Egoyan showed an interest in theater, particularly in the plays of Samuel Beckett and Harold Pinter.

His filmmaking career started when he was 19, as an international relations student at the University of Toronto. At that time he directed three experimental short films and was active in the Armenian student community. Egoyan's first feature film, *Next of Kin* (1984), was financed partially with the sale of his short film *Open House* (1982) to the Canadian Broadcasting Corporation. In this, his only comedy, the action centers around Peter, a Canadian youngster who feels alienated and dissatisfied with his comfortable suburban life and decides to impersonate the long-lost son of an elderly Armenian couple. Filmed with a low budget and on location, *Next of Kin* is clearly different in scale and tone than his subsequent films. However, his interest in examining the dynamics of the family institution, the therapeutic vocation of the protagonist, and the intricate role of ethnicity are far-reaching themes that are already evident in this first film. *Next of Kin* also featured Arsinee Khanjian, a fellow Armenian student and actress who would later become Egoyan's wife, mother to their son Arshile, and a permanent member of his habitual ensemble. The film received the Golden Ducat at the Mannheim film festival and consolidated the fame of its director in independent circles.

Egoyan's next three pictures, *Family Viewing* (1987), *Speaking Parts* (1989), and *The Adjuster* (1991), reaffirmed his place among the new generation of Canadian filmmakers. Based on an original screenplay by Egoyan, *Family Viewing* is the story of another male teenager at odds with paternal authority. The youngster visits his maternal grandmother at the nursing home where the boy's father sent her after the boy's mother left them. When the boy discovers that his father has been erasing their old home-videos in order to videotape his sexual encounters with a second wife, he secretly takes his grandmother out of the nursing home. *Family Viewing* was shown in 12 film festivals around the world and it won prizes in Switzerland and Sweden. In his third feature, *Speaking Parts* (1989), the director's concerns about video technology, memory, family ties, and affective-sexual obsessions were also prominently featured. This time the setting is a hotel where a young aspiring actor works to support himself. A female colleague at the hotel becomes obsessively attracted to the hero. A second storyline involves one of the hotel guests, a film writer who lost her brother to the transplant that saved her own life. Egoyan here coupled his recurrent themes with innovative film style through the use of flashbacks, combinations of film and video images, and the creation of evocative and introspective atmospheres.

The Adjuster (1991), Egoyan's fourth feature film, tells the story of yet another man with philanthropic inclinations, an insurance adjuster who is responsible for checking the claims of fire victims in order to appraise their compensation. Most of the action occurs at a motel and on the grounds of an unfinished suburban development. The characters live in an uncertain world where the impersonality of the exteriors mirrors the anguish and loneliness of their lives. In its formal aspect *The Adjuster* establishes a style that Egoyan had started to define from the start of his career. The emphasis on ambiguous situations, almost expressionistic decors, and austere acting creates an eerie, surrealistic film. *The Adjuster* was exhibited in the Director's Fortnight at the Cannes Film Festival and it won the prize of Best Canadian Feature Film at the Toronto Festival of Festivals.

Egoyan's fifth picture, *Calendar* (1993), was filmed in association with the German television channel ZDF and the Armenian National Television. It is the story of an Armenian-Canadian couple who travel to that former Soviet republic in order to photograph historical monuments for a calendar. The linguistic barriers parallel increasing communication problems between the photographer (Egoyan) and his wife/translator (Khanjian), which is exacerbated as she becomes closer to their driver/guide (Ashot Adamian). The film was shot in Armenia during three days, using film and video cameras. The rest of the shooting took place in Toronto. This film embodies Egoyan's themes of the difficulties in communication, love, and family relationships as it explores also those themes like exile, national identity, and intercultural relations. The complex interplay between monochromatic video sequences and full-color film sequences gives *Calendar* a particular interest. The Toronto sequences in *Calendar* develop a specific narrative pattern like a theme with variations. He receives a number of female visitors in the apartment where he is living alone one year after the trip to Armenia. The film's formal austerity and its attention to detail in every aspect of storytelling and style mark *Calendar* as a distinct contribution to film art and one of the most notable films in Egoyan's career.

In 1994, Atom Egoyan again surprised public and critics with his most popular and widely seen film to that date. *Exotica* combined several space and time levels with compelling visuals and the alluring setting of a nightclub. As he had done before, Egoyan here trained his scalpel-like gaze on the topics of voyeurism, sexual repression, family trauma, and memory, using the Exotica Club as the stage for a powerful story in his personal style. A tax auditor, Francis (Bruce Greenwood), is obsessed by a young club dancer, Christina (Mia Kirschner). Through flashbacks and disjunctions in story order, the film follows their relationship and those of five other characters so that the audience can find the key to what happened to them only by the film's end. Egoyan used all his arsenal of stylistic resources (unusual camera movements, sound bridges, expressionistic use of color and light) in order to create a film that is at once disturbing and tender, hypnotic and memorable. *Exotica* won the International Critic's Prize at the Cannes Film Festival.

The director's next project, *The Sweet Hereafter,* won the Grand Jury Prize at Cannes in 1997 and received nominations for the best director category and for the best nonoriginal screenplay at the 1998 Academy Awards ceremony in Hollywood. In this case, the screenplay was based on a Russell Banks novel of the same title, yet Egoyan's signature is clearly visible. He transferred the action from the United States to a small town in British Columbia where a local schoolbus sinks into an ice-cold lake, killing most of its occupants. The film follows the aftermath of the tragedy in a profound character study that captures as well the breathtaking beauty of the British Columbia scenery. Egoyan's references to the Pied Piper folk tale give a mythical, atemporal dimension to a very contemporary story. The inspired acting and direction are combined with the musical talent of composer Mychael Danna, another of his regular collaborators, and the singing talent of lead actress Sarah Polley to create a film of astonishing, tragic beauty.

After *The Sweet Hereafter,* Egoyan has directed *Felicia's Journey* (1999). Based on the novel by William Trevor. It is the story of two characters. One is an Irish girl (Elaine Cassidy) who travels to England in search of her departed boyfriend. The other is the man who offers her room and board, a middle-aged caterer called Hilditch (Bob Hoskins), who hides a dark secret. As Roger Ebert points out in his review of the film for the *Chicago Sun Times,* "Egoyan is such a devious director, achieving his effects at a level below the surface. He never settles for just telling a story . . . It's as if his films inject materials into our subconscious, and hours later, like a slow reaction in a laboratory retort, they heat up and bubble over. You leave *Felicia's Journey* appreciating it. A week later, you're astounded by it."

In addition to his work in films, Egoyan has also directed the operas *Salome,* by Richard Strauss, and *Elsewhereless,* based on his own play from 1982 and staged in cooperation with composer Rodney Sharman.

Other Films *Howard in Particular* (1979); *After Grad with Dad* (1980); *Peep Show* (1981); *The Twilight Zone* (1985), TV series episode, "The Wall"; *Men, a Passion Playground* (1985); *In This Corner* (1985), TV; *Alfred Hitchcock Presents* (1985), TV series; *Friday the 13th,* TV series; *Looking for Nothing* (1988), TV; *Montréal vu par. . . .* (1991), segment "En passant," aka *Montreal Sextet; Gross Misconduct* (1993), TV; *A Portrait of Arshile* (1995); *Bach Cello Suite # 4: Sarabande* (1997); *Yo-Yo Ma Inspired by Bach* (1997), TV series.

References Harcourt, Peter, "Imaginary Images: An Examination of Atom Egoyan's Films," *Film Quarterly* 48, no. 3 (Spring 1995): 2; Pevere, Geoff, *Exotica* (Toronto, Canada: Coach House Press, 1995); Desbarats, Carole, *Atom Egoyan* (Paris: Editions Dis Voir, 1993).

—F.A.

Eisenstein, Sergei (1898–1948) Leading architect of a revolution in Soviet cinema in the 1920s, Sergei Eisenstein was an important theorist as well as a celebrated filmmaker. Sergei Mikhailovich Eisenstein was born on January 23, 1898, to assimilated and baptized Jewish parents in Riga, Latvia, in czarist Russia. His father was an architect and civil engineer for the city of Riga. When his parents separated in 1905, Eisenstein divided his boyhood years between Riga and St. Petersburg. Fluent in French, German, and English, he bowed to pressure from his father to study

civil engineering. However, his real interests lay with the theater and the cinema, and his first cinematic encounter was a viewing in Paris of the films of Georges Méliès.

Even the Bolshevik Revolution couldn't deter Eisenstein from his love of the arts. After serving in the civil war in the Red Army as a civil engineer, he abandoned his career in engineering and attached himself to the swirl of theatrical activity surrounding the great Russian theater visionary, Vsevelod Meyerhold. This radical experimentalist had broken from the traditional "naturalist" theater and pursued in his classes and productions the modernist movements of "constructivism" and "biomechanics." Like every other student, Eisenstein participated in every aspect of production, including writing and acting. Indeed, in some measure the October Revolution not only broke down the old social, economic, and political order, as historian Richard Taylor suggests, "it also overthrew the traditional notions of art and of the arts. If one thing characterizes the revolutionary Soviet artists of the 1920s it is the relative ease with which they moved from one art form to another, from literature to scriptwriting, from painting to set design—in Eisenstein's case from sketching through set design and stage direction to film-making—and this in turn helps to explain the ease with which they drew upon the techniques of those various art forms to enhance the effectiveness of their own activity in one particular form." And one finds in Eisenstein's first published article, "The Eighth Art" (1922), a wildly eclectic discussion of the techniques of the circus, the detective story, and the films of Charlie Chaplin. Later writings would pinwheel out into the realms of Charles Dickens, Kabuki theater, and the Japanese ideogram.

In 1924, the Proletkult Theater offered him the job of directing the first of eight episodes of the film series, *Towards the Dictatorship.* He completed only one episode, but it was enough to alter the course of Soviet cinema. *Strike* (1925), which premiered on April 28, 1925, depicted the brutal czarist crushing of a worker's strike. Its episodes depicted the working conditions of the workers, the preparations for a strike, the infiltration of the workers by capitalist-hired spies and provocateurs, the daily activities of the workers during the strike, and the slaughter of the strikers by mounted troops. With *Strike* Eisenstein found in the concepts of montage, which he had first studied in the legendary workshops of his mentor, Lev Kuleshov, the formal artistic equivalent to the Marxist revolution and Hegelian evolutionary theory. Moreover, he adopted the concept of the multiple protagonist, or collective hero, as an ideological and structural element.

Eisenstein's theories of montage—which he called the "cinema of attractions"—have often compared the juxtapositions, or "collisions," of shots to the explosions in an internal combustion engine that drive an automobile forward. The result is the creation of a synthesis in the mind of the viewer, a third element that is greater than the sum of the two shots. Nowhere is this strategy more fully worked out than in his next film *Battleship Potemkin,* made in 1925 to celebrate the anniversary of the 1905 Revolution. The 28-year-old Eisenstein had left the Proletkult Theatre after abandoning plans to make the remaining films in the planned prerevolutionary cycle. Coscripted by Nina Agadzhanova, it again is a story of revolution, in this case the mutiny of sailors against ship's officers in June and July of 1905 aboard the *Battleship Potemkin.* When the sympathetic people of Odessa are crushed by mounted czarist troops, the mutineers turn their ship's guns on the town. The sequence depicting the Cossacks' slaughter of the townspeople, the celebrated "Odessa Steps" sequence, is a veritable catalogue of Eisenstein's methods, including flash frames, extreme close-ups, jarring jump cuts, skewed angles, dynamic compositions, and the compression and expansion of time. Crowds surge, boots stomp, rifle barrels level toward targets, sabers pierce flesh, and a baby carriage trundles down the steps. After more than 75 years, the cumulative impact of this sequence is still overwhelming. Ironically, this scene was not included in the original script. Eisenstein himself related the inspiration for the scene: "No scene of shooting on the Odessa Steps appeared in any of the preliminary versions or in any of the montage lists that were prepared [before filming began]. It was born in the instant of immediate contact." The film's reception alone deserves an extended volume. Its international career began with its enthusiastic reception in Berlin (thanks to the entrepreneurship of Russian intellectual Vladimir Mayakovsky) and quickly extended to the United States and beyond. Interestingly, it was Douglas Fairbanks, Sr., who saw the film in July 1926 during his tour of Russia, and whose favorable pronouncements hastened the film's release in New York, where it premiered on December 5, 1926 (in a version reedited for the American market by none other than John Grierson).

Battleship Potemkin was the last film over which Eisenstein would exercise total control. In 1927 he was called upon by the Soviet film agency, Sovkino, to make a film commemorating the 10th anniversary of the Bolshevik Revolution of October 1917. This was mostly in response to the assignment by the film trust, Mezhrapom, that Eisenstein's colleague and rival, VSEVELOD ILLARIONOVICH PUDOVKIN, would chronicle similar events in his *The End of St. Petersburg* (1927). Both directors worked simultaneously on their respective projects. *October* (released internationally as *Ten Days that Shook the World,* a title borrowed from the book by John Reed), coscripted by his assistant, Alexandrov, was originally intended to be shot in two parts. The first part would cover events from February to October 1917; and the second, the subsequent civil war. Only the first part was realized. It featured extensive use of what Eisenstein called "intellectual montage," i.e., the selection of juxtaposed images to create metaphors in the service of political ideology. In his article,

"Beyond the Shot" (1929), he declared, "Each [shot] taken separately corresponds to an object but their combination corresponds to a *concept*. The combination of two 'representable' objects achieves the representation of something that cannot be graphically represented." Because the film was made at a peak in the fight against leftist opposition, before its release Eisenstein was instructed to edit out nearly one-third of the film, including scenes of many of the leading participants in the revolution, notably Leon Trotsky. It was premiered to the general public on March 14, 1928. Composer Edmund Meisel, who had written the music score for *Potemkin,* came aboard to write the score. What survives, notably the recreation of the storming of the Winter Palace in Leningrad and Kerensky's assumption of power, reveals Eisenstein at the height of his powers.

In August 1929, Eisenstein set off for a trip to Europe and North America. After lecturing and attending film congresses throughout Europe, he arrived in the United States in 1930 to work and to study modern film techniques. He was already armed with a contract signed by Jesse Lasky, production head of Paramount, when he arrived in Hollywood. Among the numerous projects Eisenstein suggested, but which were aborted in various stages of conception and/or production, was a screen dramatization of *An American Tragedy.* Historian Marie Seton reports that Eisenstein's script ran afoul of the Paramount brass: "They wished to be rid of him, and his refusal to compromise over *An American Tragedy* opened the way."

In December 1930 Eisenstein left Hollywood after signing a contract with Upton Sinclair, a muckraking novelist and socialist reformer who wanted to produce a film about Mexico. Immediately charmed and fascinated by Mexico, its people, and its folkways, he determined to make *¡Que viva México!,* a six-episode chronicle of a large portion of Mexican history. However, due to conflicts with Sinclair—Eisenstein had been pursuing a perfectionist course that overran Sinclair's

budget—the collaboration deteriorated and Eisenstein was forced to halt shooting in January 1932. When he tried to return to Hollywood to edit his footage, he was refused entrance into the United States. Sinclair, moreover, reneged in an agreement to ship the film to the Soviet Union. Although a version of *¡Que Viva México!* was eventually edited by Eisenstein's biographer and friend, Marie Seton, it proved to be but a poor shadow of what the film could have been.

After returning to the Soviet Union in 1933 he retreated to the Caucasus in extreme depression. He led a reclusive life, devoting himself to his theoretical work, eventually deciding to return to Moscow to teach at the Film Institute. Moscow had changed since his trip to America. Under Stalin, the left opposition had been exiled, imprisoned, or killed, and any opposition to the bureaucracy in the party had been stifled. The bureaucracy had declared war upon dialectical materialism, and this could be seen in the realm not only of politics but also of the sciences and arts. Eisenstein's contemporaries and colleagues, LEV VLADIMIROVICH KULESHOV, DZIGA (DENIS KAUFMAN) VERTOV, Pudovkin, and others had all fallen under the shadow of accusations of being "formalists" who had betrayed the Soviet ideology. Only one filmmaker, Lev Kuleshov, came to his defense. Under this pressure, Eisenstein, who had long carried on a fight against the conventions of plot and story, changed his technique to the new aesthetic, socialist realism.

In the middle of 1935, he began work on his first film in over three years, *Bezhin Meadow.* This story of the martyrdom of young peasants to the Soviet cause was commissioned by the Communist Youth League to commemorate the contribution of the Young Pioneers to collective farm work. Several problems conspired to abort the project, including Eisenstein's own succumbing to smallpox and, later, influenza.

In 1937, after the installation of a new film administration more favorable to him, Eisenstein was given the task of making a film that would not only provoke the patriotic spirit of Russian citizens against the perceived German threat but would also serve as a warning to the Germans that war against the Soviet Union would be fatal. To do this he would reach back to the 13th century to retell the saga of Prince Alexander Nevsky, who raised up an army from the Russian peasantry to beat back the Teutonic knights. *Alexander Nevsky,* coscripted by Pyotr Pavlenko, was completed in 1938 and earned Eisenstein the Order of Lenin as well as the title of Doctor of the Science of Art Studies. It was his first sound film, and it benefited from an effective music score by Sergei Prokofiev. The spectacular Battle on the Ice, its most famous sequence, was, amazingly, not shot on ice at all, but during a summer heat wave in a field that had been leveled and covered with a solution of sodium silicate to "duplicate" the appearance of ice. So closely did Eisenstein work with composer Prokofiev, that, as Jay Leyda reports, "the music was to determine the filming or cutting as often as the filming was to determine the music." *Alexander Nevsky* premiered on December 1, 1938. In the meantime, the finished film revealed that Eisenstein's formalistic insistence on strategies of montage had been replaced by the more politically approved camera and editing techniques— extended takes and composition-in-depth shots— that were closer to the mise-en-scène school of the French.

Eisenstein's next film was projected to be a three-part historical spectacle about Ivan the Terrible, the Russian czar who unified the country into one nation in the 16th century. Ivan had resorted to the most ruthless measures to destroy the rule of the boyar nobility, thus earning him the "terrible" sobriquet. The film was to be another epic about a great national hero that would win Eisenstein favor from the party. Reuniting with composer Prokofiev and the actor Nikolai Cherkassov (who had played Nevsky), Eisenstein commenced shooting in 1942. Every facility was placed at his disposal. Its spectacle, pacing, and mise-en-scène resembled more a grand opera than a motion picture. When *Ivan the Terrible, Part One,* was released in 1945, it won the Stalin Prize, first class, for Eisenstein, Cherkassov, Prokofiev, and several others who worked on the film. In 1946, *Ivan the Terrible, Part Two,* was completed. It had the same cast and production crew as Part One, and it continued the story of the fight for Russian nationhood. The character of Ivan by this time had undergone a major change. In a paranoid rage, he relied increasingly on his handpicked band of fanatical young security guards, the *Oprichniki,* to carry out his vendettas against the boyars. Before the film could be released, however, Eisenstein was stricken with a heart attack at a dinner celebrating the completion of the editing of Part Two. Moreover, and unfortunately for Eisenstein, the film was considered by many to be a thinly disguised attack on Stalin, and it was later condemned by the Central Committee of the Communist Party. In February 1946 Stalin declared he would approve its release only after extensive reshooting and reediting. Eisenstein's health by then had deteriorated to the point that further work on the film was impossible, and he spent his last months at his flat in Potylika, happy in the knowledge that colleague and friend Jay Leyda had arranged for the publication of his aesthetic writings, *The Film Form* and *The Film Sense,* and putting in order his voluminous collection of notes, correspondence, and scenarios. He died on February 9, 1948.

Not long before his death he published a statement concerning his long struggles with his art and with the Soviet state, touching specifically upon the controversies surrounding his *Ivan.* "Some of us forgot the incessant struggle against our Soviet ideals and ideology which goes on in the whole world," he wrote in a generally conciliatory tone. "We lost for the time comprehension of the honourable, militant educational task which lies on our art during the years of hard work to construct the Communist Society in which all people are involved. The Central Committee justly pointed out to us that the Soviet artist cannot treat his duties in a light-minded and irresponsible way. Workers of the cinema should study deeply whatever they undertake. Our chief mistake is that we did not fulfil these demands in our creative work."

It is impossible to overestimate Eisenstein's significance to the history of cinema. In his invaluable volume of collected writings by Eisenstein, Richard Taylor declares: "If there was one person who could properly lay claim to the title of 'cinema Shakespeare' it would have to be Eisenstein. His position in the development of cinema as an art form was in many ways similar to that of Shakespeare in the development of modern drama and it was certainly as seminal. But, unlike Shakespeare, Eisenstein was more than the leading practitioner of his art: he was also its principal theorist. He was therefore not only cinema's Shakespeare: he was also in some sense its Stanislavsky, its Brecht—or perhaps most appropriately, its Meyerhold."

References   Eisenstein, Sergei, *Film Form* (Meridian Books, 1957), p. 37; Bergen, Ronald, *Sergei Eisenstein: A Life in Conflict* (New York: Overlook Press, 1997); Bordwell, David, *The Cinema of Eisenstein* (Cambridge, Mass.: Harvard University Press, 1993); Marshall, Herbert, *Sergei Eisenstein: Nonindifferent Nature* (Cambridge, U.K.: Cambridge University Press, 1987); Seton, Marie, *Sergei M. Eisenstein* (New York: A. A. Wyn, n.d.); Taylor, Richard, ed., *Eisenstein: Writings 1922–1934* (Bloomington: Indiana University Press, 1988).

—B.M. and J.C.T.

Ephron, Nora (1941–   )   Nora Ephron began her career as a journalist, first as a newspaper reporter for the *New York Post,* then as a feature writer for *Esquire, The New York Times Magazine,* and *New York Magazine.* After publishing two best-selling collections of essays, *Crazy Salad* and *Scribble, Scribble,* she wrote the best-selling novel *Heartburn* (1983), which she later adapted for the screen, the story of Rachel Samstat, a cookbook writer, and her husband Mark Feldman, a syndi-

cated columnist, as their marriage is breaking up, an odd book that also included "fabulous" recipes. The novel is a roman à clef and partly reflects the breakup of her second marriage to *Washington Post* Watergate reporter Carl Bernstein after she discovered he was having an affair when she was seven months pregnant with her second son, Max. It represents an attempt to laugh at male vanity and heartbreak. Mike Nichols directed the novel from her screenplay in 1986.

Ephron was born on the Upper West Side of Manhattan into a literary family that moved to Southern California when she was three years old. Henry and Phoebe Ephron were successful writers, famous for *Carousel* and *Daddy Long Legs,* both of which were adapted to the screen. Nora was educated at Wellesley College, and, given her interests and background, naturally attracted to other writers. Her first husband was the writer Dan Greenburg. Her third husband, whom she married in 1987, was Nicholas Pileggi, the author of *Wiseguy,* the source of Martin Scorsese's *Good-Fellas* (1990) and *Casino* (1995), which was also filmed by Scorsese.

Ephron demonstrated a real talent for romantic comedy, as shown by the popular hits *When Harry Met Sally* (1989), which she scripted for Rob Reiner, and *Sleepless in Seattle* (1993), which she directed herself and scripted with Jeff Arch and David Ward and which won an Academy Award nomination for best original screenplay. This success saved her career as director, since her debut film as director, *This Is My Life* (1992), fell far short of covering its expenses. After another marginal film, *Mixed Nuts* (1994), which she wrote with her sister Delia (with whom she collaborated on several screenplays), Ephron scored again with *Michael* (1996), starring an angelic John Travolta. Her next film was even more popular, *You've Got Mail* (1998), another romantic comedy with Tom Hanks and Meg Ryan that was a remake of an earlier classic, *The Shop Around the Corner* (1940), a wonderful Lubitsch comedy that had been adapted to the screen from Nikolaus Laszlo's play *Parfumerie,* updated by Ephron to cyberspace. Ephron's best films recall classic Hollywood and effectively exploit the nostalgia for well-loved but half-forgotten earlier hits. The ghost of *An Affair to Remember* (1957) hovers above *Sleepless in Seattle,* for example, but no one has done a better job of recalling such echoes of Hollywood's Golden Age. Ephron has written and directed with extraordinary wit and skill.

References   Milvy, Erika, "For New-Fashioned Romance, Click Here," *New York Times,* November 15, 1998, sec. II, pp. 2, 32; Hunter, Stephen, "What Got Lost in Nora Ephron's 'Mail,'" *Washington Post,* January 1, 1999, pp. G1, G5; Smith, Dinitia, "She's a Director with an Edge: She's a Writer," *New York Times,* December 13, 1998, sec. II, pp. 17, 20.

—J.M.W.

Etaix, Pierre (1928–   )   With his better-known mentor, Jacques Tati, Pierre Etaix emerged from the post–World War II years as France's most distinguished film comedian. The paucity of materials in English about Etaix, however, is puzzling. One looks in vain in the standard film reference books for biographical information. This may be due in part to the relatively small number of shorts and features he has made and to their limited distribution outside France.

Etaix (pronounced eh-TEX) was born on December 23, 1928, in Rouanne, France. Although he was trained as a painter—he also was a talented cartoonist and stained-glass designer—he yearned to make films. In 1954 he went to Paris in response to an invitation to join comedy filmmaker Jacques Tati at Tati's Spectra Studios. This began a fruitful association between the two men, although, as documented by biographer David Bellos, their relationship would end in ill feelings. At first Etaix worked as an office junior and general errand boy. At one point early in their association he intended to produce a cartoon strip of the adventures of Tati's beloved screen character,

Monsieur Hulot, but nothing came of it. In any event, Etaix's talents in gag construction soon made him invaluable to Tati, and for Tati's classic *Mon oncle* (*My Uncle* [1958]), he worked as an assistant director, scouting locations and contributing gag ideas (for which he received little recognition). With patience and forbearance, he put up with Tati's exacting, at times unreasonable, demands, quietly working for little compensation. By the late 1950s, however, he felt exploited and underpaid, and he announced plans to strike out on his own. Tati felt betrayed. "He made Etaix feel as if the parting had been worse than a divorce," writes Bellos. "The bad blood was never properly purged, and there was never a reconciliation between two men whose interests and talents were remarkably close."

With longtime writing collaborator Jean-Claude Carrière, Etaix struck out on his own in 1961–62, directing and starring in two comedy shorts, the Oscar-winning *Heureux anniversaire* (*Happy Anniversary*) and *Rupture*. His first feature was the masterfull *Le Soupiran* (*The Suitor* [1962]), winner of the Prix Delluc, followed by a sentimental circus comedy, *Yo Yo* (1965), which won the OCIC at Cannes. In *Le Grand amour* (1969) he portrayed a married man wistfully yearning after the love of a young secretary (Annie Fratellini). Information is scant regarding his more recent films, including *Tant qu'on a la sante* (*As Long As You're Healthy* [1966]), *Le Grand amour* (*The Great Love* [1970]), *Pays de Cocagne* (1970), *L'Âge de Monsieur est avancé* (1987), and a documentary, *J'ecris dans l'espace* (*I Write in Space* [1989]).

His other activities have included frequent stints as a supporting actor in films, most notably in ROBERT BRESSON's *Pickpocket* (1959), Claude de Bivray's *Une grosse tête* (1962), FEDERICO FELLINI's *The Clowns* (1970), and *Max, mon amour* (1986) and a collaboration with the clown Nino in cabaret and television shows.

Etaix's work has been rightly compared to that of his hero, BUSTER KEATON. Indeed, Etaix's dapper, smallish figure and rather melancholy aspect and demeanor, not to mention his mastery of subtle gag construction, confirm the comparison. As a result of several meetings between them, they became good friends. Indeed, inasmuch as Etaix's early films are virtually silent, with minimal use of dialogue and sound, they seem to be homages to silent comedy in general. It is unfortunate that so little information is available on this fine French filmmaker. Much needs to be done to bring him to today's audiences.

Reference Bellos, David, *Jacques Tati: His Life and Art* (London: The Harville Press, 1999).

—J.C.T.

Farrow, John Villiers (1904–1963) John Villiers Farrow was among the most intriguing, versatile, and enigmatic film directors ever to work in Hollywood. In addition to his work as a film-maker, he was a poet and novelist, a prolific author on Catholic subjects, a decorated naval hero in World War II, and an Academy Award-winning screenwriter. Critic David Thomson wrote, "[Farrow] seems one of the more engaging, enterprising and critically neglected of entertainment directors," and film historian Wheeler Dixon described him as "one of the cinema's more overlooked artists . . . always worthy of attention in even his most minor works."

An unsung stylist, Farrow's work is marked with a fluidity and technical assurance reminiscent of MAX OPHULS. But unlike those of the bittersweet Ophuls, Farrow's themes were almost invariably dark, concerned with death, betrayal, and paranoia. It is entirely fitting that the main characters in two of Farrow's films are Adolf Hitler (*The Hitler Gang* [1944]) and Satan himself (*Alias Nick Beal* [1949]).

Some of his films have a reputation today—notably *The Big Clock* (1948), *His Kind of Woman* (1951), and *Hondo* (1953)—but Farrow has never achieved the kind of cult status claimed by other top directors of his era like John Ford, Howard Hawks, Alfred Hitchcock, Frank Capra, and others. Nor has his work ever received the reappraisal that is now long overdue.

Farrow's films are astonishingly complex, composed of stunning, baroque camera work, sharp, incisive performances, and dark, sometimes twisted, narratives. *His Kind of Woman* (1951), starring Robert Mitchum, Jane Russell, and Vincent Price, is a violent and comic romance. *Hondo* (1953), starring John Wayne and Geraldine Page, is a classic western (filmed in 3-D) that balances the sinister aspects of its hero's character with a surprisingly positive portrayal of Indians. *The Hitler Gang* (1944) is a bloody, no-holds-barred propaganda piece, as hysterical as it is heartfelt; and *Wake Island* (1942) is the precise opposite of a typical World War II flag-waver—the story of a massacre of American troops and engineers by the Japanese in the opening days of the war. In what is possibly his best film, *The Big Clock* (1948) with Ray Milland and Charles Laughton, Farrow contrives to have his hero—an "innocent" man—forced to track *himself* down in a murder investigation.

More than any American director of his time, Farrow seems obsessed with cinematic virtuosity. Crucial scenes in *China* (1943), *Two Years Before the*

Mast (1946), and many others are designed around elaborate, seemingly endless camera tracking shots, which follow characters in and out of buildings, up and down stairs, all in a single take. Farrow began his movie career as a scriptwriter, but no other writer/director ever treated his own words so ruthlessly. His precise compositions, serpentine camera movement, and expressive and foreboding lighting were Farrow's preferred method of story-telling; he never used a word when an image would do as well.

However brilliant he was as a director, Farrow made few friends on the set. He tended to be cold and unsympathetic, preferring to solve technical problems rather than help actors hone their per-formances. Glenn Ford, having worked—and clashed—with Farrow on *Plunder of the Sun* (1953), refused to make *Hondo,* forcing producer John Wayne to take the starring role. Barbara Stan-wyck was so outraged by Farrow's behavior on the set of *California* (1947) that, at the end of produc-tion, she forced him to apologize to the entire cast and crew. Farrow may have been more thoroughly disliked by his casts and crews than any other Hol-lywood director—a rather breathtaking idea when one considers the endless line of martinets who have aspired to that throne. Ironically, it was during this same period that Farrow was made a Knight of the Holy Sepulcher by Pope Pius XI, was awarded the Grand Cross of the Holy Sepulcher by Pope Pius XII, and was given the Lateran Medal from the Vatican.

Born in Australia in 1904, Farrow served in the Merchant Marine and two years in the U.S. Marines. He came to Hollywood as an illegal alien in the mid-1920s, was nearly deported for having improper papers, and slowly began making a career for himself as a writer for silent films, notably WILLIAM WELLMAN's *Ladies of the Mob* (1928) and VICTOR FLEMING's *Wolf Song* (1928). He married Maureen O'Sullivan in 1936 and, after helming a few scenes in the chaotic production *Tarzan Escapes* (1936), directed his first film, *Men in*

Exile, the following year. After directing about 15 more competent if generally unexceptional movies, he left pictures to join the Royal Canadian Navy in 1939. He contracted typhus and was sent back to the United States where he directed the stirring *Wake Island* (1942) from a wheelchair. Far-row returned to active duty and was in Europe when hostilities ceased. He received the 1939–45 Star, the Atlantic Battle Star, the Canadian Decora-tion, the Defense Medal, the Canadian Volunteer Medal with Silver Maple Leaf, the World War II medal, and a Letter of Commendation from the Naval Ministry. He was also decorated by the gov-ernments of Belgium, the Netherlands, Romania, and France.

Farrow converted to Catholicism when he married O'Sullivan and soon became immersed in, and nearly obsessed by, the Faith. His biography of Father Damien, the Leper Priest, was published in 1937 and has never gone out of print. He wrote several other important books on Catholicism and was decorated several times by the Vatican and var-ious Jesuit groups.

Farrow's prewar films were generally efficient, unpretentious entertainments—light-hearted mys-teries like *The Saint Strikes Back* (1939) starring George Sanders, thrillers like *Five Came Back* (1939), remade by Farrow in 1956 as *Back From Eternity,* and domestic melodramas such as *My Bill* (1938), *Sorority House* (1939), *Reno* (1939), and *A Bill of Divorcement* (1940), a remake of George Cukor's 1932 version, starring Maureen O'Hara. But after the war, Farrow found his identity as an artist. *Two Years Before the Mast* (1946), *Submarine Command* (1951), *Botany Bay* (1953), and *John Paul Jones* (1959) reflected Farrow's love of the sea. And *The Big Clock, Alias Nick Beal,* and *The Night Has a Thousand Eyes* (1948) illustrated his interest in and understanding of the more sinister aspects of human nature.

Farrow was removed by producer Mike Todd as director of *Around the World in 80 Days* but shared an Academy Award for the script with

James Poe and S. J. Perelman. His last film was the CinemaScope epic *John Paul Jones* (1959), starring Robert Stack and, in her film debut, the director's daughter Mia Farrow. He spent the last years of his life working on an epic film about the life of Christ to be called *The Son of Man*. It was never produced.

Admired by the more perceptive critics of his own era—writers like Manny Farber, who called Farrow "an urbane vaudevillian"—Farrow is virtually unknown today, usually remembered only as the husband of Maureen O'Sullivan or the father of Mia Farrow. But his best work is marked by such an individual point of view and by such breathtaking bursts of invention and virtuosity that rediscovery and reappraisal is inevitable.

Other Films   *West of Shanghai* (1937); *Blaze of Noon* (1947); *Red, Hot and Blue* (1949); *Where Danger Lives* (1950); *Copper Canyon* (1950); *Ride, Vacquero!* (1953); *A Bullet Is Waiting* (1954); *The Sea Chase* (1955); *The Unholy Wife* (1957).

References   Dixon, Wheeler W., *The "B" Directors: A Biographical Dictionary* (Metuchen, N.J.: Scarecrow Press, 1985); Farber, Manny, "Underground Films" (1957), reprinted in *Movies (Negative Space)* (New York: Hillstone, 1971).

—F.T.

Fassbinder, Rainer Werner (1945–1982)

The leading figure and guiding spirit of the "New German Cinema," Rainer Werner Fassbinder is often considered the most original and important European filmmaker of the 1970s. When the scowling wunderkind of German cinema died at the age of 36 after a night of ingesting an excessive amount of alcohol, valium, and cocaine, he left the world 41 feature films made in a period of 13 years. Many of Fassbinder's films are now considered landmarks in world cinema, leading Vincent Canby to call Fassbinder "the most dazzling, talented, provocative, original, puzzling, prolific and exhilarating filmmaker of his generation."

Rainer Werner Fassbinder was born on May 31, 1946, in the Bavarian town of Bad Wörishofen. His family was financially secure and they were highly respected members of the community, his father being a doctor and his mother a translator. The young Fassbinder rebelled early on, shocking his parents when he declared his homosexuality at age 15. While still a teenager he made himself at home in the gay bars, where he took up the profession of pimp for the local drag queens, including Udo Kier, who would act in a number of his later films. During this period, Fassbinder became obsessed with both the aura of American movie stars and the melodramatic excesses of Hollywood films, particularly the work of Douglas Sirk and Samuel Fuller. Fassbinder claimed that as a teenager, he would watch as many as 15 movies a week.

Even though Fassbinder hated school, he was so determined to become a filmmaker that he applied to the Berlin School of Film. When his application was rejected, he moved to Munich and started a theater company he named the "Anti-Theater." He not only wrote original scripts for the company, but also staged the productions and performed on stage. Many of the actors employed in the Anti-Theater would stay a part of Fassbinder's extended family, becoming principal players in his films, including Hanna Schygulla, Ulli Lommel, Kurt Raab, and Harry Baer.

The fame of the Anti-Theater gave Fassbinder the opportunity to make a series of films for German television. In 1969, he made his first theatrical film, *Love Is Colder than Death (Liebe ist kälter als der Tod),* a gritty gangster film indebted to the American B-films of SAMUEL FULLER. Hanna Schygulla played the femme fatale, with Fassbinder himself taking on the role of the film's anti-hero, an ex-con and pimp. It was hardly a success and was booed when it was shown at the Berlin Film Festival. Fassbinder's next film fared better with both critics and festival audiences. *Katzelmacher* (1969), an attack on bourgeois fascism and German xenophobia, won numerous awards including one from the German Academy for outstanding artistic achievement. His early films, including *Why Does Herr R. Run Amok?* (*Warum läuft Herr R. Amok?* [1970]) and *Beware a Holy Whore* (*Warnung vor einer heiligen Nutte* [1970]), followed in the tracks of *Love Is Colder than Death* and *Katzelmacher,* a mixture of Hollywood film noir and European neorealism, depending largely on improvisational acting.

With *The Bitter Tears of Petra von Kant* (*Die bitteren tränen der Petra von Kant* [1972]) a new impulse begins to emerge, one indebted more to the over-the-top melodramas of Douglas Sirk than the gritty work of Samuel Fuller. *The Bitter Tears of Petra von Kant* is a lurid, highly stylized view of the jealousies and sadomasochistic passions that engulf three lesbians. The film is set in the opulent apartment of high-fashion designer Petra von Kant (Margit Carsensen) where she and the object of her desire, a fashion model played by Hanna Schygulla, engage in an increasingly destructive rondelet of mind games.

Ali: Fear Eats the Soul (*Angst essen Seele auf* [1974]) is even more indebted to the Hollywood melodramas of Douglas Sirk. A radical revisioning of Sirk's *All that Heaven Allows* (1955), it's a bittersweet, melodramatic love story between a lonely 60-year-old German cleaning lady and an attractive 30-year-old Moroccan auto mechanic. As they seek to find comfort in each other's arms, family objections, social rejection, and racial prejudice increasingly invade the private world they have tried to create. The theme of class difference is also at the center of *Fox and His Friends* (*Faustrecht der Freiheit* [1975]), Fassbinder's first film to explore gay male relationships. Fox, a subproletarian carnival worker (played by Fassbinder), wins a lottery worth 500,000 DM. His new wealth leads him into a romance with a bourgeois lover who tries to turn Fox into a model of middle-class respectability while swindling him out of his money and his self-respect. The film won praise for its nonstereotypical, if not always flattering,

portrayal of its gay characters. The *New York Times* declared it "the first serious, explicit but non-sensational movie about homosexuality to be shown in this country."

The Marriage of Maria Braun (1978) proved to be Fassbinder's greatest international success and is often considered to be his masterpiece. In the ribald comedy, Hanna Schygulla plays Maria Braun, an ambition-driven woman who manages to use the marriage vow to raise herself from the ashes of post–World War II Germany to become a titan of industry.

Fassbinder returned to the world of gay culture for *In a Year of Thirteen Moons* (*In einem Jahr mit 13 Monden* [1979]), a sad depiction of the last days of a transsexual who impulsively undergoes a sex change operation only to please a rich lover, who then rejects her. Broke and alone, Elvira turns to her family and friends, only to experience further rejection and betrayal. In the *New York Times,* Vincent Canby declared the film to be "grotesque, arbitrary, sentimental and cold as ice. It's only redeeming feature is genius."

In 1980, Fassbinder produced one of his most audacious projects, *Berlin Alexanderplatz,* a 15-hour epic made for German television that follows a dim-witted transit worker, living in Berlin between the wars, who becomes involved with the criminal underworld as the country falls increasingly under the spell of Nazism. The next year, Fassbinder turned again toward Hollywood to make *Veronika Voss* (1981), a hypnotic, quite mad tribute to Billy Wilder's *Sunset Boulevard* (1950). The film's ceaseless camera movements chronicle a faded movie star's descent into morphine addiction and emotional collapse.

By the completion of *Veronika Voss,* Fassbinder's own life, never stable, seemed to be imitating Veronika's descent into addiction and increasingly obsessive-compulsive behavior. As his fame grew, his personal life, always self-publicized, became increasingly complicated by gossip and public scandal. Actors in his films recounted to an ever-eager press his violent outbursts. Some, like Irm Hermann, claimed physical abuse. Two of his lovers committed suicide, one hanging himself after a murderous rampage, another found dead in Fassbinder's apartment.

By the time Fassbinder made his last film, *Querelle,* the enfant terrible of German cinema seemed increasingly out of control. In *Querelle,* based on the novel by Jean Genet, American actor Brad Davis plays the title role of a cocky, amoral sailor, a stud who flaunts his sensuality in any and all directions. After killing a fellow sailor, Querelle takes refuge in a brothel, where he begins to come to terms with the depths of his homosexual lusts. Franco Nero is the officer who succumbs to Querelle's advances and Jeanne Moreau is the chanteuse who likewise comes under his sway.

Beyond the already sensational nature of the story, Fassbinder played out the drama on a stylized, purposefully artificial set depicting the French port of Brest as a landscape of kitschy phallus-shaped towers complete with archetypal gay iconography, from leather men to bare-chested Tom of Finland–like sailors, to a tortured Jeanne Moreau, all shot against a backdrop, described by Gary Morris as "a kind of permanent orange sunset, as if the world were at its end."

Those connected with the production of *Querelle* report that it was a tortured period for the director, and indeed the filmmaker seemed to be working at the end of his own world. Shortly after completion of *Querelle,* Fassbinder was found dead, apparently from an overdose of whiskey, valium, and cocaine. As Morris notes, "Fassbinder left this world in the same way as many of his cinematic creations: overworked, overwrought, and finally overdosed on life." Even so, "This prodigiously inventive artist distilled the best elements of his sources, Brechtian theatrics, Artaud, the Hollywood studio look, classical narrative, and a gay sensibility . . . into a body of work that continues to enlighten and disturb."

Other Films *Gods of the Plague* (*Götter der Pest* [1969]); *The American Soldier* (*Der Amerikanische Soldat* [1970]); *The Merchant of Four Seasons* (*Händler der vier Jahreszeiten* [1971]); *Effi Briest* (*Fontane Effie Briest* [1974]); *Mother Küster's Journey to Heaven* (*Mutter Küsters Fahrt zum Himmel* [1975]); *Satan's Brew* (*Satansbraten* [1976]); *Lili Marleen* (1980); *Lola* (1981).

References Elsaesser, Thomas, *New German Cinema: A History* (New Brunswick, N.J.: Rutgers University Press, 1989); Hayman, Ronald, *Fassbinder: Filmmaker* (New York: Simon and Schuster, 1985); Morris, Gary, "Profile: Fassbinder," *Bright Lights Film Journal* 12 (May 1998).

—T.P.

Fellini, Federico (1920–1993) Federico Fellini is one of the most celebrated directors in the history of cinema, whose oeuvre spans the years from Italian neorealism to his own maturity as one of cinema's most idiosyncratic and visually extravagant directors. He was born on January 20, 1920, at the viale Dardanelli 10, in the resort city of Rimini, on the Adriatic coast of northeastern Italy. Although he rarely returned to his native city in later life, its social milieu and its geographical location would influence his work, surfacing, for example, in his fascination with itinerant entertainers and the cinema, his erotic preoccupation with women, his ambivalence toward the Catholic religion, and his tendency to use the sea as a symbolic setting in many of his pictures. Of his childhood, Fellini said, "As a child, I was very timid, solitary, vulnerable to the point of fainting. . . . I liked to be pitied, to appear unreadable, mysterious. I liked to be misunderstood, to feel myself a victim, unknowable." A particular form of escape and pleasure for the young man were the carnivals and circuses that passed through Rimini each year. Because of his use of these character types— often outcasts—his later films are often considered grotesque theatrical spectacles. "The cinema is also circus," he has said, "carnival, fun-fair, a game for acrobats."

Fellini's father was a wholesaler in groceries who traveled frequently while his mother remained at home. Federico was educated in Catholic schools in Rimini until 1938 when he left for Florence, where his early aptitude for drawing, especially in caricature and cartoon, was put to work for local comics and newspapers. Commentator Edward Murray has noted that Fellini's training in drawing and writing for the comics "not only supplied him with part of his future subject matter but may have also taught him some valuable lessons in cinematic form." Fellini himself remarked regarding his storyboards, "Any ideas I have immediately become concrete in sketches and drawings." Meanwhile, his writing skills eventually led to assignments for papers in Rome, a city that became for Fellini a new home and place of protection and creative freedom. It was there in 1943 that he met and married the actress Giulietta Masina, who would appear in seven of Fellini's films.

It was his work with director ROBERTO ROSSELLINI that essentially led him to directing his own films. Fellini coscripted Rossellini's *Open City* (1945); *Paisan* (1946), for which he also served as assistant director; and the controversial *The Miracle* (1948), in which he also acted the part of a wandering shepherd who seduces a peasant woman (Anna Magnani). *Variety Lights* (*Luci del varieta* [1950]) and *The White Sheik* (*Lo Sceicco bianco* [1952]), Fellini's first directorial efforts, both reveal vestiges of neorealism in their gritty surface details, although they deal with theatrical performers and the treacherous fantasy of illusions. In *Variety Lights,* codirected by Alberto Lattuada, the leader of a fading vaudeville troupe abandons his lover and troupe for another girl. *The White Sheik* alludes to the world of the *fumetti,* those popular Italian comic strips whose illustrations were composed of photographs, not drawings. The story is about a young bride who is lured away from her commonplace life by the charms of the comic strip character, "The White Sheik," her romantic

dream hero (Alberto Sordi). *I Vitelloni* (*The Young Ones* [1953]), Fellini's first masterpiece, is a semi-autobiographical tale about five adolescents in Rimini caught up in the transition from carefree youth to responsible adulthood. Through the course of the picture, as commentator Peter Bondanella has observed, "Each of the *vitelloni* experiences a crisis as his illusions collide with reality." One of them, Moraldo, suffers a moment of truth that impels him to leave the provinces. "Moraldo realizes that childhood illusions," continues Bondanella, "such as the ones his fellow *vitelloni* never abandon, are unworthy of a mature individual in the adult world. And so, Moraldo sets out, as Fellini did years earlier."

Fellini's next two films, *La Strada* (*The Road* [1954]) and *Nights of Cabiria* (*Le notti di Cabiria* [1958]), constituted his "breakthrough" into international renown. The first is a variant of the Beauty and the Beast fable, a tale of a pair of itinerant performers, the waif-like Gelsomina (Giulietta Masina) and the brutish strongman Zampano (Anthony Quinn), that is heartbreaking in its poignancy and pathos. The abuse of the woman and the tragedy of the strongman demonstrate the power of redemption through suffering. *La Strada* won the Oscar for best foreign film in 1954. *Nights of Cabiria* also won best foreign film Oscar, and again reiterates the theme of spiritual redemption. In the film, a young prostitute (Masina in the title role) survives the hazards of a cruel world and opportunistic men by clinging to her romantic ideals of love and innocence. It remains one of Fellini's most sensitive and compassionate pictures and later inspired the Bob Fosse musical, *Sweet Charity.* These two films, notes biographer John Baxter, present a characteristically Felliniesque image of the female: "Equally common in his early work is a beaming androgyne, clown-like and sexless, famously embodied by Giulietta Masina in *La Strada* and *Le notti di Cabiria.* Just as much as the fertility figures of the later films, Gelsomina and Cabiria are a child's vision of sexuality: half playmate, half puppet, sexually neutral."

On the other hand, there is a lack of spiritual redemption and purity evident in Fellini's most well-known and popular film, *La Dolce Vita* (1960), which also won an Oscar for best foreign film, as well as the Palme D'Or at Cannes. The film depicts an almost infernal journey through the high life of Rome, a soulless, empty universe where the paparazzi and spoiled bourgeois aristocrats play out the endless round of their sterile lives. This decadent world of the upper class is regarded through the eyes of a journalist, played by Marcello Mastroianni (who would become Fellini's onscreen alter ego), who, despite loathing the degradation around him, is himself caught up in it. At the same time, it is also a love letter to the city of Rome. Fellini said, "The star of my film is Rome, the Babylon of my dreams." He also commented on the tragedy of spiritual collapse, suggesting, "There is a vertical line in spirituality that goes from the beast to the angel, and on which we oscillate. Every day, every minute, carries the possibility of losing ground, of falling down again toward the beast." Commentator David Cook says of the film, "Its superficially realistic milieu is corruption and decadence, and its visual extravagance borders on the fantastic." *La Dolce Vita* solidified Fellini's international reputation as an auteur.

His next picture, *8½* (1963), also a best foreign film winner, is often regarded by critics as Fellini's masterpiece. Though not as popular among general audiences as *La Dolce Vita, 8½* is an astonishing achievement, not just for its story and theme, but also for its distinctive style and seamless blend of reality and dream, life and art. The film is a self-reflective meditation on the cinema itself, on filmmaking and illusion. It is both autobiographical and allegorical, depicting conflicting feelings of art and reality, of spectacle and normalcy. The film is also an existential examination about the meaning—and meaninglessness—of life. Fellini said, "*8½* is meant to be an attempt to reach an agree-

ment with life . . . an attempt and not a completed result. I think for now it might indicate a solution: to make friends with yourself completely, without hesitations, without false modesty, without fears and without hopes." *8½* is ultimately about its own making—the central character is a film director (Mastroianni)—and about the wellsprings of the creative urge. It remains, for most critics, Fellini's crowning achievement.

Juliet of the Spirits (*Giulietta degli spiriti* [1965]) was Fellini's first foray into color, and in some ways it was a feminine counterpart to *8½*. It also uses dream sequences and surreal settings to depict the nature of the female psyche. The female mystique has always been important to Fellini's films. He believed that women represent to man his darker impulses, the mysterious side of him that he cannot comprehend. The female characters often dominate the men and show how they (the men) remain helpless and confused.

Fellini Satyricon (1969) is another vision of decadent Roman society transplanted to the time of Petronius. Perhaps because its bizarre, extravagant visuals—Fellini's obsessive fascination with the ugly, the misshapen, the crippled is nowhere more in evidence than here—swamped the thin storyline, it was attacked by critics and ignored at the box office. Somewhat more moderate in tone, *The Clowns* (1970) is a made-for-television documentary about the history of the circus clown and his role in art and society. The film is also a nostalgic look at the clownish pleasures Fellini enjoyed as a boy. Clowns are representative of society, he said: "Clowns are the first and most ancient anti-establishment figures and it's a pity that they are destined to disappear under the feet of technological progress. It's not just a fascinating human microcosm that is vanishing, but also a view of life and the world."

After *Fellini's Roma* (1972), an examination of his adopted city, Fellini made *Amarcord* (1973), another best foreign film Oscar winner (the title is relatively meaningless, a mere cipher). The film is one of Fellini's testaments, a semiautobiographical story of provincial Italian life in Rimini. Because the town no longer existed as he remembered, he seized the opportunity to remake the place and its people according to his own memory and imagination. "My cinema has always been about the provinces," Fellini said, "therefore childhood, and a whole lifetime that one dreams one is seeing again." Biographer Baxter notes that the picture also brought out Fellini's attitudes about the fascist politics of his youth: "Fascism dominated Fellini's public pronouncements about *Amarcord*. The Fascists, he said, conspired with the Church to keep his generation in a sort of moral and emotional slavery. 'Fascism is always waiting within us,' he warned, taking a high moral tone at odds with his usual indifference to politics. 'There is always the danger of an upbringing, a Catholic upbringing, that knows only one goal: to place a person in a situation of intellectual dependence, to limit his integrity, to take from him any sense of responsibility in order to keep him in a never-ending state of immaturity.'" For most critics, *Amarcord* marks the end of Fellini's most creative output.

The last 20 years of Fellini's film career produced only intermittent moments of brilliance. Still, Fellini made several more features that are as engaging and interesting as his earlier, more successful work, though he never regained the notoriety he once held. *City of Women* (*La Città delle donne* [1980]), as Baxter notes, is "a parade of sexually charged images from childhood" and from the brothels of Rome. At the same time, continues Baxter, "Women in Fellini's films . . . are infantile symbols of idealized motherhood." The protagonist's (Mastroianni again) lack of understanding of women is ultimately tested when he finds himself trapped at a large feminist convention. He is forced to relive his childhood sexual confusions, a subsequent unhappy marriage, and his many later conquests. *Ginger and Fred* (1985) is a satire on the intrusion and ubiquity of television and the media. It is also an elegy to a time when art and extrava-

gance could flourish, as contrasted with a modern world where style and beauty no longer have a place. *Intervista* (1988) is a homage to Cinecitta, the studio where Fellini made almost all of his films. It is also an excellent documentary on filmmaking and Fellini himself, who makes it clear that the only reality he knows is that which he can create on screen. Fellini's final film, *The Voice of the Moon* (*La Voce della luna* [1990]), marks a last return to the provincial countryside. It is a comic attempt to show how true communication can be achieved without the aid or influence of multifaceted communication vessels such as television.

Fellini died on October 31, 1993. As David Cook suggests, "Fellini was first and foremost a great ringmaster whose circus was the human comedy as it existed both inside and outside himself; his theme was the mystery of identity."

Other Films *The Swindle* (*Il bidone* [1955]); *Spirits of the Dead,* third episode (1967); *Fellini's Casanova* (1976); *Orchestra Rehearsal* (1978); *And the Ship Sails On* (1983).

References Baxter, John, *Fellini: The Biography* (New York: St. Martin's Press, 1993); Burke, Frank, *Federico Fellini: "Variety Lights" to "La Dolce Vita"* (Boston: Twayne Publishers, 1984); Cook, David, *A History of Narrative Film* (New York: Norton, 1996); Murray, Edward, *Fellini The Artist* (New York: Frederick Ungar, 1985); Costantini, Costanzo, *Conversations with Fellini* (New York: Harcourt Brace, 1995).

—W.V. and J.C.T.

Feuillade, Louis (1873–1925)   The screen's first master of the crime thriller, Louis Feuillade has influenced the work of subsequent directors like LUIS BUÑUEL and ALFRED HITCHCOCK. He was born in Lunel in the south of France on February 19, 1873, the son of a merchant, and grew up in a very religious family. Afer a four-year stint in a cavalry regiment, a brief time with the family wine business, and a brief career in journalism, he drifted into the movies in 1905, crafting brief farcical and vaudeville pieces with anecdotal titles like "Papa Takes the Purge" and "Don't Go Out with Nothing On." A more ambitious series of dramatic vignettes appeared after 1910, which finally led to the serial films on which his reputation rests today.

He began his celebrated cycle of crime serials in 1913 with the five-part *Fantômas,* based on the pulp hero created two years before by the prolific hack novelists Marcel Allain and Pierre Souvestre. Fantomas was a masked criminal dressed in black tights and a hood who eluded the efforts of the pursuing detective, Juve. Historian Richard Roud claims that the spectacular success of the stories and the film is accounted for by the fact that working-class readers and audiences found enjoyment in stories that reflected the real-life contemporary attacks by terrorist gangs and anarchists upon the more privileged classes. The most celebrated sequence in the serial depicts Juve's pursuit of Fantomas on the Quai de Bercy, as both dart in and out of huge wine barrels.

Les Vampires, unlike *Fantômas,* was Feuillade's original invention. The first and second parts premiered on November 13, 1915, and the last appeared on June 30, 1916. The entire serial clocks in at approximately seven hours. The basic plot outlines are simple: A band of criminals led by the Grand Vampire (Ayme) and Irma Vep ("Musidora," stage name of Jeanne Roques) commit a series of brilliant crimes, for which they are pursued by a journalist, Philippe Guerande (Mathe), and his assistant (Marcel Levesque). After many adventures, the miscreants are discovered during an orgy in their hideout and are killed. Of the Vampires we know little, save that they have a predilection for pilfering exotic jewels and are masters of disguise and sabotage, an underground cabal lurking underneath all aspects of society. As for Irma Vep, who created a sensation with her first appearance in the third episode, we know only that her name is an anagram of "vampire." The titles of the episodes admirably convey a sense of events and atmosphere: as, "The Gem That Kills," "The Eyes That Fascinate," "The Master of the Thunder," "The Bloody Wedding." Feuillade improvised the story during the production, and the episodes appeared at intervals of two to five weeks. Feuillade deftly blends elements of realism, fantasy, and comedy in depicting a landscape of crime and paranoia.

The contemporary surrealists Louis Aragon and André Breton, among others, rhapsodized over the results in their book, *The Treasure of the Jesuits:* "One day it will be understood," they wrote, "that there was nothing more realistic or poetic than the serial films. . . . They are beyond fashion, beyond taste." Actress Musidora they dubbed "The Tenth Muse." During the recent revival of the entire serial (1998), critic Geoffrey O'Brien described its peculiar pleasures: "Severed heads turned up in hatboxes; householders were lassoed out of windows and then rolled down stairways in baskets; motorcars raced on dark errands along deserted country roads; conspirators caroused in low dives; masked assasins slipped across the roofs of Paris. . . ."

Later serials included *Judex* and *Tih Minh* (a sequel to *Les Vampires*). *Judex* (1915) was Feuillade's most popular film, due in part to the fame of the actor in the title role, Rene Creste. A sequel, *The New Mission of Judex,* appeared in 1917. *Tih Minh* depicts the Vampire gang's revenge for the death of Irma Vep. Later films like *Vendemiaire* offer a contrast to what went before. They are infused with a sentimental, moralizing tone that had been relatively absent from the earlier work.

After Feuillade's death on February 25, 1925, of complications following peritonitis, he slipped into an obscurity that has only occasionally been lifted, beginning with a revival of *Fantômas* in 1944 and continuing with *Les Vampires* in 1963 and 1998. "Please believe me," said Feuillade, "when I tell you that it's not the experimenters who will finally obtain for film its rightful recognition, but rather the makers of melodramas—and I count myself among the most devoted of their number . . . I believe I come closer to the truth than they do."

Feuillade's achievement was nothing less than the forging of a genre that flourishes in today's caper melodramas and crime thrillers, from the James Bond series to the Batman pictures. At the same time, his films possessed a unique, disarming ease and matter-of-factness of manner and presentation. As commentator Geoffrey O'Brien writes, Feuillade's "downright cheerful manipulation of the frightful" was his special province and would not be seen again until the advent of Alfred Hitchcock. Moreover, the use of real locations, the docks, massive stone buildings, avenues and squares, country estates, impart a substantial realism to the otherwise bizarre proceedings. "Contemporary audiences got . . . the thrill of seeing all these extraordinary and terrifying things happening in the streets they knew," writes historian Richard Roud, "that they walked down every day. For them (and in some measure for us, too) there was a conjugation of a naturalistic rendering of Paris with the evocation of strange and frightening happenings." If the films lacked the intricate editing strategies and camera mobility of Feuillade's contemporaries DAVID WARK GRIFFITH and FRITZ LANG—typically, they stage the action in theatrical fashion in extended camera takes from a fixed vantage point—they achieve a stark kind of poetry and a ritual deliberateness of pacing all their own. "Every shot is not just a composition," writes O'Brien, "but an event."

New Wave filmmaker ALAIN RESNAIS places Feuillade midway between the dual currents of the French silent cinema, GEORGES MÉLIÈS and LOUIS and AUGUSTE LUMIÈRE: "I believe there is also a Feuillade current, one which marvelously links the fantastic side of Méliès with the realism of Lumière, a current which creates mystery and evokes dreams by the use of the most banal elements of daily life."

Other Films Feuillade wrote and directed an estimated 800 films, of which the following is necessarily only a brief listing: *Benvenuto Cellini* (1910); *Androcles* (1912); the "Detective Dervieux" series (1912); the "La vie drole" series (1913–16); *Barabbas* (1919); *Les deux Gamines* (1920); *L'Orpheline* (1921); "Belle humour" series (1921–22); *Le stigmate* (1924).

References O'Brien, Geoffrey, "Silent Screams," *New York Review of Books,* December 17, 1998, pp. 8–12; Roud, Richard, "Maker of Melodrama," *Film Comment* 12, no. 6 (November–December 1976): 8–11; Roud, Richard, "Louis Feuillade and the Serial," in *Rediscovering French Film,* ed. Mary Lea Bandy (New York: Museum of Modern Art, 1983).

—J.C.T.

Fincher, David (1962–) David Fincher's films walk a tightrope between hard surfaces and dreamlike narratives. He was born in Denver, Colorado, in 1962. Involved with making movies since the age of eight, Fincher has quite a productive and varied résumé. He has worked extensively in commercials and music videos, belonging to a generation of filmmakers not content to relegate themselves solely to motion picture directing, and without the cultural stigma of "selling out" to commercial interests.

At the age of 18, Fincher went to work for GEORGE LUCAS's Industrial Light and Magic. Over the next four years he worked on such films as *Return of the Jedi* (1983) and *Indiana Jones and the Temple of Doom* (1984), finally leaving ILM to direct television commercials. Some of his work includes spots for the American Cancer Society, Nike, and Levi's. Fincher has also directed a number of music videos for artists as varied as Madonna, Aerosmith, Paula Abdul, and the Rolling Stones. His directorial debut came in 1992, as he was selected to helm *Alien³*, the third installment of the popular 20th Century Fox franchise. Difficulties with Fox, a poorly written script, and a lack of direction have all been blamed for the poor reception of *Alien³*. While visually stunning, the film was a critical and box-office failure, and forced Fincher back into the world of television commercials. He filled his time with steady work in music videos and commercials while waiting for another opportunity to direct a feature film. That opportunity came when he read the script for *Se7en,* a dark thriller that pits two homicide detectives against a serial killer who has taken the seven deadly sins as inspiration for his murders. With the box-office power of its star, Brad Pitt, the film was a commercial sensation, grossing over $100 million in its initial run. *Se7en* was a critical success, as well, with many critics noting the film's ominous and eerie style as crucial to the story.

Fincher's follow-up, 1997's *The Game,* stars Michael Douglas as a ruthless executive who has all the accoutrements of success, but is unable to find any meaning behind the mansions, automobiles, and fancy restaurants that his success brings. His life changes when his younger brother gives him a birthday gift that literally changes his life. While the film found success with critics, it was considered a disappointment, given the film's modest box-office take and the high expectations after the success of *Se7en.*

Most recently Fincher directed the adaptation of Chuck Pahlaniuk's novel, *Fight Club.* Starring Edward Norton and Brad Pitt, the film tells the story of a jaded 20-something (credited as the Narrator) who has become desensitized to his late 20th century surroundings. He regains some stimulation when he meets Tyler Durden. Carefree, unbridled, and raw, Durden represents everything that emasculated men in the last part of the 20th century have seemingly lost. Durden unleashes the pent-up frustration in the Narrator, who recaptures his life by starting Fight Club, where men, devoid of all feeling, literally beat each other senseless to regain their senses. Things begin to unravel when Fight Club grows bigger than anyone imagined, ultimately leading the characters in the film to question their entire existence. Like *The Game,* the ending turns the viewer topsy-turvy with an unexpected revelation of the tenuousness of what was presumed to be reality.

Perhaps what thematically characterizes all of Fincher's films is an unflinching glimpse into the brutal, violent soul of humanity. A recurrent Fincher scenario, suggests commentator Gavin Smith, "is repressed straight white masculinity thrown into crisis by the irruption of an anarchic, implacable force that destabilizes a carefully regulated but precarious psychosocial order." Never one to pander to an audience's squeamishness, Fincher ably captures the darkness and decay of modern urban life. While his detractors have criticized his films as all style and no substance, his fans eagerly await his next project, hoping to find more commentary on contemporary cultural discontent.

References Dyer, Richard, *Seven,* BFI Modern Classics (London: BFI, 1999); Smith, Gavin, "Inside Out," *Film Comment* 35, no. 5 (September–October 1999): 58, 60–62, 65, 67–68.

—J.A.

Fisher, Terence (1904–1980) Born in Maida Vale, London, on February 23, 1904, Terence Fisher was raised by his grandmother in a strict Christian Science household. He left school, Christ's Hospital, Horsham, Sussex, while a teenager and joined the Merchant Marine, serving an apprenticeship aboard HMS *Conway,* between 1926 and 1928. He was a junior officer for the P & O Lines in 1929. Upon leaving the naval service he worked briefly as a department store window dresser before his employment by Shepherd's Bush Studios as a clapper boy in 1930. Fisher worked himself up through the ranks as a runner, then as an assistant film editor, and finally as an editor in 1936.

He directed his first feature film, *Colonel Bogey,* a supernatural comedy, for the Arthur Rank organization in 1947. Much of Fisher's early work is characterized by an emphasis on composition and a balanced style. During this period Fisher directed primarily romantic dramas and some period pieces such as: *To the Public Danger* (1948),

Song for Tomorrow (1948), *Portrait from Life* (U.S. title: *The Girl in the Painting* [1948]), *Marry Me!* (1949), *The Astonished Heart* (1949), *So Long at the Fair* (1950), and *Home to Danger* (1951). Fisher was employed primarily as a director-for-hire and not associated with a particular studio until 1952, when he began directing films for Hammer Film Productions, Ltd.

Much of Fisher's early work at Hammer was mediocre low-budget fare at best—*Mantrap* (1953), *Face the Music* (1954), *Murder by Proxy* (1955), and others—although two films stand out among them. *The Four-Sided Triangle* (1953) and *Spaceways* (1953) are early British science fiction films that atypically emphasize character over plot. In 1956 Fisher obtained his big break when at the age of 52 he was asked to direct the Hammer remake of *Frankenstein*. The film, titled *The Curse of Frankenstein,* was shot in lush Eastmancolor (originally it was to be shot in black and white) and starred Peter Cushing and Christopher Lee. It was the touchstone for all of Hammer's subsequent horror product, which, because of box-office impetus, became the studio's specialty.

Hammer studios became Fisher's home throughout the remainder of his career, and it was there that he directed his best work. Lest we adhere too much to auteurism, it must be said that Hammer supplied Fisher with the means and support that affected his creativity. According to Peter Hutchings, "It is fair to say that when Fisher did eventually emerge as a director with an identifiable signature in 1957 (with *Curse of Frankenstein*), it was just one part, albeit an important one, of the creative team at Hammer." In 1958 Fisher directed *Horror of Dracula,* which many consider to be the masterpiece of English Gothic cinema, as well as *The Revenge of Frankenstein,* in which the doctor (aristocratically portrayed by Peter Cushing) was resurrected rather than the monster.

Two significant factors stand out in establishing Fisher's style at Hammer: the orderliness of his mise-en-scène, which was ideally suited to recreat-ing the Victorian and Edwardian world in which the majority of these films are set, and the use of a paternal figure of authority around which many of the films revolve. Fisher was at the helm of many of Hammer's remakes from the Universal Pictures pantheon of cinematic terrors: *The Mummy* (1959), *The Curse of the Werewolf* (1961), and *The Phantom of the Opera* (1962). In addition he also directed three science fiction thrillers for independent production companies: *The Earth Dies Screaming* (1964), *Island of Terror* (1966), and *Island of the Burning Doomed* (1967). Fisher also continued to direct series films for Hammer concerning Frankenstein and Dracula: *The Brides of Dracula* (1960), *Dracula—Prince of Darkness* (1965), *Frankenstein Created Woman* (1966), *Frankenstein Must Be Destroyed* (1969), and Fisher's final film *Frankenstein and the Monster from Hell* (1973). According to Peter Hutchings these final films, including what some consider his best work, *The Devil Rides Out* (1968), based on the classic thriller by Dennis Wheatley, reveal a "further maturing of his directorial skills. . . . They show a depth of response which perhaps had not been there before, and Fisher's *mise-en-scene* has become even more precise and magisterial." Fisher died on June 18, 1980, in Twickenham, Middlesex, England.

Other Films   *The Last Page* (1952); *Wings of Danger* (1952); *Stolen Face* (1952); *Distant Trumpet* (1952); *Blood Orange* (1953); *Three's Company* (1953); *The Stranger Came Home* (1954); *Mask of Dust* (1954); *Children Galore* (1954); *The Flaw* (1955); *Stolen Assignment* (1955); *The Gelignite Gang* (1956); *The Last Man to Hang?* (1956); *Kill Me Tomorrow* (1957); *The Hound of the Baskervilles* (1959); *The Man Who Could Cheat Death* (1959); *Stranglers of Bombay* (1959); *The Two Faces of Dr. Jekyll* (1960); *The Sword of Sherwood Forest* (1960); *Sherlock Holmes and the Deadly Necklace* (1962); *The Horror of It All* (1964); *The Gorgon* (1964).

References   Dixon, Wheeler W., *The Charm of Evil: The Life and Films of Terence Fisher* (Metuchen, N.J.: Scarecrow Press, 1991); Hutchings, Peter, *Hammer and Beyond: The British Horror Film* (Manchester, U.K.: Manchester University Press, 1993); Meikle, Denis, *A History of Horrors: The Rise and Fall of the House of Hammer* (Lanham, Md.: Scarecrow Press, 1996); Pirie, David, *Heritage of Horror: The English Gothic Cinema 1946–1972* (New York: Avon Books, 1974).

—S.D.

Flaherty, Robert Joseph (1884–1951) Frequently described as the "father of the American documentary film," Robert Flaherty was a fiercely independent figure in the documentary movement in the first half of the 20th century. He was born in Iron Mountain, Michigan, on February 16, 1884, and educated at Upper Canada College, Toronto. During the first decade of the new century, he worked as an explorer, surveyor, and prospector for the Canadian Grand Trunk Railway. In the mid-teens he surveyed for William MacKenzie, an industrial entrepreneur, searching for iron ore deposits along Hudson Bay. It was at this time that he took a camera with him while traveling through the land of the Inuit. However, his footage was destroyed in a fire. Five years later a determined Flaherty returned to the Hudson Bay area to shoot more film of Eskimo life. Released as an experiment by Pathé Exchange, the resulting documentary feature was *Nanook of the North* (1922), a popular sensation and a landmark in the documentary film. Its success encouraged Flaherty to devote the rest of his life to making documentaries about faraway and exotic cultures whose way of life was threatened by industrialization.

He traveled to Samoa in 1923–25 and produced *Moana* for Paramount. Again, as in *Nanook,* he captured on film a "primitive" and "natural" way of life that was rapidly disappearing. Two more films about the South Seas followed in the late 1920s, *White Shadows in the South Seas* and *Tabu* (for both of which he received coproduction credit). As the box-office cachet of these films began to wane, Flaherty was forced to look elsewhere for financing. In 1931 he went to work for John Grierson of the Empire Marketing Board in

Great Britain. *Industrial Britain* was the result, although Grierson himself made the final edit. A year later Flaherty moved on to the Aran Islands, off the coast of Ireland, to begin shooting *Man of Aran* (1934). It was a gritty picture of the rugged life of the local fishermen. His next project was *Louisiana Story* (1946), a lyric and poetic tribute to Cajun life in the bayous.

For all the respect, even the veneration, accorded Flaherty in his lifetime—the term "documentary" was coined to describe his film, *Moana*—he remains a controversial figure. In his zeal to document the disappearing traditions of "primitive" ways of life, he frequently staged and even falsified the conditions he found. For example, the Eskimos he photographed in *Nanook* had long abandoned activities like igloo-building. Yet, he asked them to relearn the procedure for the camera. Some of the fishing and hunting sequences were also staged. In *Moana* he photographed an initiation ceremony wherein young males were painfully tattooed—even though that particular ritual had not been practiced by the tribe for years. For *Man of Aran* he staged a shark hunt in a lashing storm, against the better judgment of the fishermen. And in *Louisiana Story* he faked a tug-of-war between a young boy and a ferocious alligator.

While Flaherty's visual style was rather pedestrian, he had a canny sense of the medium's technological possibilities. He pioneered the use of long lenses for closeup work, utilized the new panchromatic film (for *Moana*), deployed the new 35-mm Arriflex camera (for *Louisiana Story*), initiated the practice of shooting and printing film on site, and encouraged the subjects of his films to assist in the filmmaking process. Other methods were unpredictable, even erratic. He usually worked without a plot or a script in an attitude characterized by his wife and associate, Frances, as "nonpreconception." He camped out with his subjects, and he watched and waited. He shot miles of film, seemingly without any preplanned purpose, and eventually used only a small percentage of the footage. In this way he allowed the film to assume its own shape, as it were. Only later did he begin to impose his own vision and organization onto the product. "What he seeks out among his peoples are their consistent patterns of physical behavior," writes commentator Jack C. Ellis, "rather than aberrations of human psyches and antisocial actions which are the basis for western drama from the Greeks on. Flaherty may ultimately have been most concerned with the human spirit, but what he chose to show were its basic material manifestations. . . . What it means to survive, to exist in the culture and in the environment one is born into, are the stuff of which his films are made." Flaherty's example has been followed by other American filmmakers, notably by Merian C. Cooper and Ernest B. Schoedsack in *Grass* (1925), which recorded the migration of 50,000 Bakhtiari tribesmen in central Persia (Iran) to find pasturelands for their herds; and in the popular travel-expedition pictures of the 1930s by the husband-and-wife team of MARTIN and OSA JOHNSON, *Wonders of the Congo* (1931) and *Baboona* (1935).

Other Films   *Elephant Boy* (1937); *The Land* (1942).

References   Ellis, Jack C., *The Documentary Idea* (Englewood Cliffs, N.J.: Prentice-Hall, 1989); Griffith, Richard, *The World of Robert Flaherty* (London: Victor Gollancz, 1953).

—J.C.T.

Fleischer, Max (1883–1972) and David (1894–1979)

In its heyday of the 1920s through the early 1940s, the Fleischer Brothers studio produced, next to the Disney studio, the most creative and influential work in American animation, introducing to the screen the characters "Koko the Clown," "Betty Boop," "Popeye," and "Superman." Max was born in Vienna, Austria, on July 19, 1883, the son of a Jewish tailor, and came to America at age four with his parents. He and his five siblings (Dave was born on July 14, 1894) grew up in a home at the present site of Radio City Music Hall. After studying at the Art Students League and the Cooper Union in New York, he worked as a staff cartoonist for the *Brooklyn Daily Eagle,* where he became acquainted with cartoonist John R. Bray, who would later play an important part in his career. Max's penchant for mechanics and inventions landed him a job as art editor of *Popular Science Monthly.* By 1915 he was applying his talents to animation and to the patent of the rotoscope, a machine by which photographed live action movements could be transferred to the drawing board. A year later he joined forces with John Bray to supply Paramount with animated short subjects using brother Dave as the human model for the "Out of the Inkwell" series, featuring the adventures of the animated character, "Koko the Clown," amidst live-action backgrounds.

Acclaimed for the smooth movements produced by the rotoscope process, Max and Dave left Bray and established their own studio in Long Island City to make more "Out of the Inkwell" cartoons. The Koko films of the mid-1920s—at a time when Walt Disney was still struggling in Los Angeles to establish a style and a studio—like "Modeling," "Bedtime," and "Koko's Catch," all followed the same pattern: Koko would materialize out of the inkwell of the cartoonist (Max in live-action), interact with a "live" setting (still photographs), and then dive back into the inkwell. Without the aid of mattes or process screens the Fleischers were able to create an amazing variety of special effects.

By the mid-1920s the brothers had developed a working partnership not unlike that enjoyed by Walt and Roy Disney. Max, like Roy, devoted his full time to running the business while Dave, like Walt, was the more artistically creative partner, writing and directing the "Inkwell" series with a tiny staff of 17 animators. Other experiments followed in this amazingly fertile period, including two hour-long, quasi-animated films, *Einstein's*

Theory of Relativity and *Darwin's Theory of Evolution,* in cooperation with the American Museum of Natural History; the "Bouncing Ball" device for theater sing-alongs (the "ball" was not animated at all, but a luminescent white ball on the tip of a stick photographed in synch to music while a drumlike cylinder on which the lyrics were printed was turned by hand); and several synchronized-sound song cartoons produced in 1925 in collaboration with a recording process devised by inventor Lee DeForest (four years before Disney's first sound cartoon, *Steamboat Willie!*).

In 1929 in their new studios at 1600 Broadway in Manhattan, the Fleischers began making a series of talking cartoons for Paramount called "Talkertoons," beginning with *Noah's Lark.* Another Fleischer brother, Lou, was called in to handle the musical aspects of these films. These early-1930s products abounded with weirdly stylized forms and vulgar humor. "These were East Side Jewish kids or people like me, raised in very broad ethnic surroundings," recalled Fleischer animator Shamus Culhane in Leonard Maltin's *Of Mice and Magic.* "So they had this very vigorous style . . . kind of earthy, certainly very crude, but honest." Maltin himself adds, "The Fleischer crew not only grew up in New York, but lived and worked there; its gray canyons, seamy characters, and unique sensibilities permeated their work. There was no mistaking the gritty appearance of a Fleischer film." New characters replaced the semiretired Koko, including "Bimbo," a kind of humanized dog, and "Betty Boop," who appeared in 1930 in *Dizzy Dishes.* The Boopster was originally a nameless hybrid of a dog and a sexy girl, conceived and drawn by Grim Natwick (a later Disney animation director); but by the time of *Boop-Oop-A-Doop* and *Any Rags* in 1932 she emerged a wholly human female, whose voicing by Mae Questel imitated the singer Helen Kane, and whose curvaceous splendors (accessorized by a garter, short skirt, and décolletage) immediately drew the ire of the Hollywood censors. Two of the best Betty

Boop cartoons featured bandleader Cab Calloway, *Minnie the Moocher* and *Snow White.* Maltin hails the latter as a surrealistic masterpiece, made years before the Disney version, achieving a bizarre and dark, nightmarish quality unsurpassed by subsequent Boops.

It was in a Boop cartoon that "Popeye" made his screen debut in 1933. The Elzie Segar comic strip character had debuted in 1929, and in the Fleischers' hands created a sensation in titles like *I Yam What I Yam* and *Blow Me Down, I Eats My Spinach.* Animator Jack Mercer supplied the voice. Popeye reached his artistic and commercial peak in 1936–37 with *Popeye the Sailor Meets Sinbad the Sailor* and *Popeye Meets Ali Baba and His 40 Thieves,* elaborate two-reel Technicolor films utilizing a "3-D" effect achieved by blending animated figures with miniature sets on a revolving turntable. Compared to the Boop cartoons, the Popeyes had more plot and more scenic detail. They also added more substantial amounts of spinach than had been deployed in the original comic strip. By 1938 Popeye had surpassed Mickey Mouse as America's most popular cartoon character.

The Fleischers' most ambitious project was not as disastrous at the box office as has been frequently alleged, but it marked an unfortunate change in the Fleischer modus operandi. *Gulliver's Travels,* a feature-length animated film released in 1939, had been inspired by Disney's spectacularly successful *Snow White and the Seven Dwarfs.* A staff expanded to nearly 700 left New York to relocate in the Fleischers' new studios in Miami, Florida. Despite the impressive rotoscoping of Gulliver himself, it was at best a mixed success. The script left Jonathan Swift far behind, adapted only the "Lilliput" episode, added a gallery of Fleischer characters and incidents, and featured a lackluster musical score. Moreover, the foreign markets, so crucial to any film's success, were closed due to the outbreak of war in Europe. In the final analysis, as historian Leslie Cabarga contends in his definitive *The Fleischer Story,* the Fleischers' decision to abandon their own idiosyncratic visual and comical style in favor of the smoother, more realistic Disney model, "made their later cartoons almost indistinguishable from the cutesy pap Disney's other imitators turned out." Another historian, Mike Barrier, agrees: "Almost everything amusingly peculiar had disappeared from the cartoons, leaving behind labored, badly drawn imitations of the Disney films."

As things turned out, Max should have listened to his own theories about the essential qualities of animation, voiced previously: "It was, and still is, my opinion that a cartoon should represent, in simple form, the cartoonist's mental expression," he is quoted in Stefan Kanfer's history of commercial animation, *Serious Business.* "In other words, the 'animated oil painting' has taken the place of the flashiness and delightfulness of the simple cartoon. It must stay in its own backyard." Somewhat more successful was a second feature, *Mr. Bug Goes to Town* (1941), about a colony of bugs that lives in the garden of a home in a big city. The early 1940s saw other productions of variable quality, including the charming two-reeler, *Raggedy Ann and Raggedy Andy* (1940), and the highly successful "Superman" series. Backed by a Paramount media blitz, bolstered by a new, more angular, noirish look, these shorts—launched with *Superman* in 1940 and continuing for the next two years with titles like *The Bulleteers, The Magnetic Telescope,* and *Mechanical Monsters*—were exciting and dramatic and certainly were the most visually sophisticated works the Fleischers ever produced. Among the Fleischers' contributions to the history of the Man of Steel were the famous tag lines, "Look! Up in the sky—it's a bird! It's a plane! It's Superman!" and "Faster than a speeding bullet."

Nonetheless, by 1942 Paramount had grown dissatisfied with the expenses of the new Miami studios and decided to bail out on the Fleischers. The whole story behind this move is unclear and smacks of conspiratorial obfuscation, declares Cabarga darkly. At any rate the renamed studio

(Famous Studios) was sent back to New York without Max and Dave. After more than 20 years the brothers found themselves out of work, outclassed by Disney, and eclipsed by the popularity of the MGM "Tom and Jerry" series and the zany anarchism of the Warner Bros. "Looney Tunes." The brothers' personal squabbles, always simmering beneath the surface of their work, now erupted into a complete break between them. Max, now nothing more than a figurehead, ended his days working for the Jam Handy Company in Detroit making educational films. His "last hurrah" was supervising a new series of "Inkwell" cartoons in 1961. He died on September 11, 1972. Brother Dave worked as a gag man for Universal live-action films before his death in 1979. Max was survived by his son, Richard, who became a successful live-action director (*20,000 Leagues Under the Sea* [1954]; *The Vikings* [1958]; *Soylent Green* [1973]).

Never the visionary and astute businessman like Walt Disney, Max Fleischer focused on mechanical innovation in favor of economic feasibility. As Maltin writes, "He took great pride in the many inventions he fathered and boasted of his fifteen separate patents in the animation field. But like so many other inventors, once he developed the machines he didn't know how best to implement and exploit them."

References Barrier, Michael, *Hollywood Cartoons: American Animation in Its Golden Age* (New York: Oxford University Press, 1999); Cabarga, Leslie, *The Fleischer Story* (New York: Nostalgia Press, 1976); Kanfer, Stefan, *Serious Business* (New York: Scribner, 1997); Maltin, Leonard, *Of Mice and Magic: A History of American Animated Cartoons* (New York: New American Library, 1980).

—J.C.T.

Fleming, Victor (1883–1949) One of the most powerful directors in Hollywood during the 1930s and 1940s, Victor Fleming is remembered today primarily for his work on two blockbusters from 1939, *The Wizard of Oz* and *Gone with the Wind.* This is a grievous oversight, inasmuch as Fleming was a filmmaker of great range and integrity, and he played a decisive role in nurturing the careers of such luminaries as Gary Cooper, Clara Bow, Jean Harlow, Spencer Tracy, Judy Garland, and Clark Gable. He was born on February 23, 1883, in Pasadena, California. After the death of his father, the four-year-old Victor moved into the household of his uncle, a San Dimas citrus farmer. When his mother remarried, he relocated with her to Los Angeles. At age 14 he quit school and went to work in a machine and bicycle shop, but his enthusiasm for automobiles soon led to his work in the "pit" for race drivers and, eventually, his own participation in racing. Soon, he was flying airplanes. Inevitably, perhaps, his passion for machines led to motion pictures.

A chance acquaintance with film director ALLAN DWAN led to his first job in the business as a cameraman for Dwan's American Film Company. After photographing (and doubling as a stunt extra) several two-reel westerns, Fleming followed Dwan to DAVID WARK GRIFFITH's film unit at Triangle in 1915. At this time he met the young Douglas Fairbanks, newly arrived in Los Angeles from Broadway. The two remained personally and professionally close until Fairbanks's death in 1939, with Fleming acting as, variously, cinematographer and director on many Fairbanks films, including *The Good Bad Man* (1916), *Wild and Wooly* (1917), *When the Clouds Roll By* (1919), and *Around the World in Eighty Minutes* (1931).

During wartime, Fleming made training films and supervised camera development for the U.S. Army and Signal Corps. Back on the job at war's end, Fleming made three lightly satiric films from screenplays by the redoubtable team of Anita Loos and John Emerson: *Mamma's Affair* (1921), *A Woman's Place* (1921), and *Red Hot Romance* (1922). Throughout the rest of the 1920s, he made pictures for Famous Players-Lasky, establishing

himself as a director of great versatility. *Dark Secrets* (1923) was an exotic melodrama, *To the Last Man* (1923) was the first of several Zane Grey westerns, *Mantrap* (1926) helped establish screen "flapper" Clara Bow as a major star, and *Rough Riders* (1927) romanticized the exploits of Col. Theodore Roosevelt in the Spanish American War of 1898. (Alas, many of these and other titles from the 1920s are now "lost" films.)

After directing a talking sequence in *Wolf Song* (1929), Fleming turned to sound films with a vengeance in the classic *The Virginian* (1929), which not only demonstrated fully the potentials of the new sound technology, but also boosted Gary Cooper and Walter Huston to screen star status (as the Virginian and Trampas, respectively). Shot on location in the High Sierras, near Sonora, California, the film achieved a camera mobility and naturalness of sound recording hitherto rare in the development of the talking picture.

As the 1930s dawned, Fleming switched to the MGM studio, where he soon became one of its top directors. Working with his favorite screenwriter, John Lee Mahin, he continued to work in a diversity of subjects, including sex comedies like the classic pre-Code *Red Dust* (1931) and *Bombshell* (1933); action pictures, like *Treasure Island* (1934) and *Captains Courageous* (1936); and the spectacles, *The Wizard of Oz* and *Gone with the Wind.* The relationship with Clark Gable proved to be especially fruitful, producing, in addition to *Red Dust,* titles like *Test Pilot* (1938), *Boom Town* (1940), and *Adventure* (1946). As commentator John A. Gallegher has noted, Gable was Fleming's ideal actor, a man who both shared in and imitated Fleming's manner and attitudes. They would work together with the same empathy as other director-actor teams, JOHN FORD and John Wayne, RAOUL WALSH and James Cagney, FRANK CAPRA and James Stewart, and MARTIN SCORSESE and Robert De Niro.

So reliable was Fleming in the eyes of studio executives that more than once he was brought on to a set crippled by delays and artistic and personal differences. Such was the case with both *The Wizard of Oz,* where he replaced Richard Thorpe and GEORGE CUKOR (and proved adept at the new three-strip Technicolor technology), and *Gone with the Wind,* where he joined a long line of directors, including Sam Wood, KING VIDOR, and George Cukor. Although the issue of which director did exactly what on *GWTW* is very complicated, even controversial, it was Fleming who received the Oscar for best direction.

Less celebrated than the aforementioned titles, Fleming's remake of *Dr. Jekyll and Mr. Hyde* (1940) ranks as one of Hollywood's finest, most thoughtful, and disturbing horror films. With less emphasis on the silly makeup that had marred the Fredric March version in 1931, Mahin's script emphasized more the psychological aspects of the story, particularly the Freudian implications of Hyde's relationship with a prostitute (Ingrid Bergman). Indeed, the grim scenes of violence between the two constitute one of Hollywood's strongest and most probing indictments of the destructive consequences of physical and sexual abuse. It was at Fleming's insistence, by the way, that Ingrid Bergman and Lana Turner were cast against type—Bergman as the floozy and Turner as the virtuous Victorian maiden. Bergman, purportedly one of the great—if unrequited—loves of Fleming's life, reappeared in Fleming's last film, *Joan of Arc* (1948). One of his biggest and most expensively mounted pictures, *Joan* nonetheless did only mild box office and was savaged by critics who found it something of an antique in its conservative techniques and attitudes.

Soon after its release, Fleming died of a massive heart attack on January 6, 1949. He was just a month shy of his 66th birthday. Aside from a predilection for action pictures and a reputation as a "man's director," one looks in vain for any stylistic or thematic consistencies in Fleming's work. He was, notes John Gallegher, an unpretentious and self-taught craftsman who became one of the true professionals in a business all too often marred by self-indulgent ego and temperament. "Fleming mastered his medium with an expert control of acting, narrative, action, and cinematography, always with first-rate production values and maximum entertainment appeal."

Other Films *The Mollycoddle* (1920); *Abie's Irish Rose* (1929); *The White Sister* (1933); *Tortilla Flat* (1942); *A Guy Named Joe* (1943).

References Gallegher, John A., "Victor Fleming," in *Between Action and Cut,* ed. Frank Thompson (Metuchen, N.J.: Scarecrow Press, 1985); Sauvage, Pierre, "Victor Fleming," in *American Directors,* ed. Jean-Pierre Coursodon, vol. 1 (New York: McGraw-Hill, 1983), pp. 116–118.

—J.C.T.

Ford, John (1894–1973) Once, when he was asked which film directors he most admired, ORSON GEORGE WELLES is said to have replied, "The old masters, by which I mean John Ford, John Ford, and John Ford." Similarly, the great Japanese director AKIRA KUROSAWA habitually wore sunglasses on the set of his films, not because he was bothered by sunlight, but because he had once seen a photograph of his idol, John Ford, wearing the same dark glasses. Over the course of his near-59-year career as a filmmaker, Ford would win four Academy Awards for direction, and was the first recipient of the AFI's lifetime achievement award. Yet, for all of this, the man himself remained deceptively simple and self-effacing, often introducing himself by saying "My name's John Ford. I make westerns."

Born John Martin Feeney on February 1, 1894, the eventual John Ford was the 10th child of John A. Feeney and Barbara Curran, Irish immigrants. As a boy, Ford spent a great deal of time at the local nickelodeon. But Ford first felt the pull of a career in the movies through the influence of his older brother, Frank T. Feeney, who was over 12 years Ford's senior. Frank, who had literally run away to join the circus, had not been heard from in

10 years before young John saw him in a western at the local nickelodeon.

John soon joined his brother in California in 1914, where he entered into a kind of apprenticeship under his elder brother, who was now called Francis Ford and was a highly successful director/actor. Young John, then called Jack, quickly adopted the new surname as well. For the next three years he worked as an actor, stuntman, extra, assistant director, and any number of other jobs under Francis and others. Ford even made his way into Griffith's *Birth of a Nation* (1915) as one of the heroic Klansmen. Then, in 1917, he was given a chance to direct his first picture, *The Tornado,* in which he also starred. Two more two-reel action pictures followed, and Ford's reputation began to grow. The year 1917 also introduced John Ford to one of the most important figures of his life: actor and western star Harry Carey. Carey and Ford would collaborate on 25 silent films over the next four years. Ford's relationship with Carey would be echoed throughout the rest of Ford's career through his relationships with such performers as Victor McLaglen, Will Rogers, Henry Fonda, James Stewart, Ward Bond, and John Wayne.

Between 1917 and 1927 (and the coming of sound) Ford directed over 60 films, many of them westerns, including such titles as *Straight Shooting* (1917), *The Outcasts of Poker Flat* (1919), *The Iron Horse* (1924), and *3 Bad Men* (1926). Prior to his 1939 landmark, *Stagecoach,* however, Ford's early sound career was relatively free of cowpokes and gunfights. Instead he produced a string of action pictures (*Seas Beneath* [1931]), war films (*The Lost Patrol* [1934]), prestige period dramas (*Mary of Scotland* [1936]), a Shirley Temple adventure (*Wee Willie Winkie* [1937]), and three Will Rogers comedies (*Doctor Bull* [1933], *Judge Priest* [1934], and *Steamboat 'Round the Bend* [1935]). His most important pre-1939 film, however, was 1935's *The Informer,* a moody, atmospheric drama about an IRA soldier (Victor McLaglen) tortured by guilt after he becomes an informant. The film's

John Ford

black and white photography showed the influence of German expressionism, and the Irish setting was one to which Ford would return in subsequent films, most importantly in 1952's *The Quiet Man*. Indeed, characters and motifs from Ford's ancestral homeland would become one of the strongest thematic threads linking nearly all of Ford's films.

The year 1939 was seminal in Ford's career. Over the course of those 12 months he released three films that would, along with a number of other 1939 releases, come to symbolize the Hollywood studio system at its best. The first of these was *Stagecoach,* an exciting western whose box-office success is credited with rescuing the career of John Wayne, a dear friend of Ford, from

B-movie doldrums and restoring the prominence of the western genre. *Young Mr. Lincoln,* which features Henry Fonda in the title role, was similarly successful at the box office. The film is a moving and amusing depiction of the future president as a young, idealistic lawyer. Ford's final 1939 film, *Drums Along the Mohawk,* a Revolutionary War adventure also starring Fonda, is remarkable primarily because it was Ford's first color film. The next two years saw Ford produce such classics as *The Grapes of Wrath* (1940); *The Long Voyage Home* (1940), an adaptation of several Eugene O'Neill plays and reportedly the author's favorite of all the film adaptations of his work; and *How Green Was My Valley* (1941), the film that took home the best picture Oscar over *Citizen Kane. Valley* would also prove to be Ford's last feature film for four years.

The onset of World War II brought Ford into active duty as a lieutenant commander in the U.S. Navy. Ford went to work for the Office of War Information and began producing a series of short docudramas on the U.S. war effort. The most notable of these is probably 1942's *The Battle of Midway,* which featured some of the most incredible combat footage of the war. Ford took up the camera himself on a number of sequences, including one in which several U.S. sailors risk their lives to raise the American flag while under heavy Japanese bombardment. Ford was wounded in the eye during the battle and was awarded the Purple Heart and took to wearing those dark glasses so admired by Kurosawa.

Near the end of the war Ford returned to feature filmmaking to produce *They Were Expendable* (1945), a substantially true story about the men who piloted the U.S. Navy's PT Boats in the Philippines at the beginning of World War II. The year 1946 saw Ford return to the western with *My Darling Clementine,* a mythic retelling of the legend of Wyatt Earp, whom Ford had actually met during the silent era. In 1948 Ford directed *Fort Apache,* the first in his so-called cavalry trilogy, which has often been viewed as lionizing the U.S.

Cavalry while demonizing the Native American combatants. However, a close viewing of *Fort Apache* reveals a more evenhanded approach to both subjects. The cavalry is depicted as being riddled with class warfare, drunkards, and ineffectual commanding officers while the Apache are briefly seen as an honorable people at the end of their rope—victimized by unfair treaties and corrupt government officials. *Apache* is also notable as Ford's only screen pairing of his two favorite leading men, John Wayne and Henry Fonda. The other films in the trilogy, 1949's *She Wore a Yellow Ribbon* and 1950's *Rio Grande,* are both exciting and entertaining, though somewhat less interesting than *Fort Apache.* In 1955 Ford again teamed with Fonda for what would prove to be the final film in their long collaboration, *Mister Roberts.* Fonda, who had played the title role on Broadway for a number of years, disagreed with some of the choices Ford made, and the two eventually came to blows over the film. Not long after, Ford took ill and was replaced by Mervin Leroy.

In 1956 Ford released what was arguably his last epic masterpiece, *The Searchers.* A morality tale in the guise of a western, the film used its Monument Valley locations, seen in many earlier Ford films, as a kind of stage upon which unfolded a near-Shakespearean drama of hatred, murder, and vengeance. Ethan Edwards (Wayne in perhaps his best role) is a Southern Civil War vet and virulent racist, who spends years questing after revenge for the murder of his brother's family and the kidnapping and probable rape of his nieces by a band of Comanche. Stark, violent, and centered around a thoroughly unsympathetic protagonist, *The Searchers* is perhaps the strongest film of Ford's long career. Its imprint can be seen in such disparate films as Kurosawa's *Hidden Fortress* (1958), Scorsese's *Taxi Driver* (1976), and Spielberg's *Saving Private Ryan* (1998).

The 1960s would prove to be Ford's last productive decade, and one in which he seemed to try to redress some of the "sins" of his past.

Sergeant Rutledge (1960) is a well-meaning but flawed depiction of the African-American "Buffalo Soldiers" of the U.S. Cavalry. Woody Strode played the title character, a brave soldier accused of the rape and murder of a white woman. Though the courtroom sequences are stilted and too on-the-nose, the film's action sequences are quite good, and one of them, in which Rutledge rescues his pursuers from attacking Indians and then makes his escape across a river, can be seen as historic. As Strode himself said, "You never seen a Negro come off a mountain like John Wayne before. I had the greatest Glory Hallelujah ride across the Pecos River that any black man ever had on the screen. And I did it myself. I carried the whole black race across that river." In 1963 Ford bid farewell to Wayne when the two teamed a final time for *Donovan's Reef,* an amusing but forgettable comedy set in Hawaii. *Cheyenne Autumn* (1964) would prove to be Ford's farewell to both the western and Monument Valley. The film was an attempt to redress the negative image of Native Americans in earlier Ford works like *Stagecoach.* In 1966 Ford released what would prove to be his final feature film, *7 Women.* Ironically, a filmmaker who had built his career on tough films about macho soldiers, cowboys, and boxers, bowed out with a film about a group of women missionaries fighting off a horde of Mongolian bandits. Though Ford continued to plan projects over the remaining seven years of his life, none of them ever came together. On August 31, 1973, Ford died of cancer, ending a film career that had stretched from the silent era through the fall of the studio system.

Ford was, by anyone's estimation, a central figure in the history of American cinema. Stories about him quickly attained the status of legend, such as the time a studio executive once complained to him that he was four pages behind schedule on his latest film. Without a word, Ford picked up the script, ripped out four pages at random and said, "Now we're back on schedule." He was also a man of contradictions. A political conservative who once declared, "God bless Richard Nixon," Ford was instrumental in heading off Cecil B. DeMille's attempted right-wing takeover of the Director's Guild during the height of 1950s McCarthyism. Though he could often be cruel and insulting on the set, he nevertheless was deeply loyal to actors he liked and always made sure they had work, thus giving rise to his famous "stock company." A happily married man for over 50 years, to the former Barbara Smith, he was occasionally thought to have affairs (most notably with Katharine Hepburn during the production of *Mary of Scotland*). And finally, though often in the employ of the major studios, Ford was able to create a body of personal, artistic work that has been compared to that of such foreign film artists as Jean Renoir and Kurosawa. He may have modestly said, "I make westerns," but he clearly did much more than that.

Other Films   *The Fugitive* (1947); *3 Godfathers* (1948); *Wagonmaster* (1950); *The Last Hurrah* (1958); *The Man Who Shot Liberty Valance* (1962).

References   Doherty, Thomas, *Projections of War* (New York: Columbia University Press, 1993); Gallagher, Tag, *John Ford: The Man and His Films* (Berkeley: University of California Press, 1986); Hardy, Phil, ed., *The Overlook Film Encyclopedia: The Western* (Woodstock, N.Y.: Overlook Press, 1991); Place, J. A., *The Western Films of John Ford* (Secaucus, N.J.: Citadel Press, 1974).

—F.A.H.

Forman, Miloš (1932–)   "I was born in the town of Čáslav in central Bohemia," Miloš Forman wrote in his memoir, *Turnaround* (1994), "a town of about ten thousand people, whose history went back to the thirteenth century." The year was 1932, on February 18. His father, Rudolf Formanova, was a professor at the Teachers' Institute in Čáslav. His parents built a summer hotel in 1927 on a lake in northern Bohemia, which his mother, Anna, managed. In 1940, after the

Germans arrived in Čáslav, Forman's father was arrested by the Gestapo because he belonged to Pribina, an underground resistance group. Then, in 1942, his mother was also arrested and sent to Auschwitz, where she died in March of 1943. Her son was left in the care of his grandfather.

In 1945 Forman attended a school for war ophans in the town of Poděbrady, where he first met Ivan Passer, with whom he would much later collaborate on Czech films. Another classmate was Václav Havel from Prague, later destined to become a dissident writer and, finally, president of the Czech Republic. Thereafter, Forman was accepted into the screenwriting program at the Prague Film Academy, where he studied with the poet and writer Milan Kundera. After graduating from the Film Academy in 1954, Forman moved quickly into a career in television and film.

In 1958 Forman collaborated with Alfred Radok on two projects: *Grandpa Automobile* (*Dědeček automobil*) and *Laterna magika* (*Magic Lantern*), shown at the Brussels Exposition of 1958. *Latern magika II* followed in 1960. In 1963 he made two short films in collaboration with his friends Ivan Passer and cinematographer Miroslav Ondříček, *Audition/Talent Competition* and *If There Were No Music* (*Kdyby ty muziky nebyly*), that were combined to make a feature entitled *Konkurs* (Talent competition). This documentary, "hitherto unequalled in Czechoslovakian cinema," was criticized by Josef Škvorecký as "a cruel record of female self-love, conceit and dreams of fame," but Forman replied, "The cruelty which glares at you from the screen is present in the very nature of the audition," and to "deprive it of that cruelty would mean depriving it of its essence."

Forman's next film, *Black Peter* (*Černý Petr* [1964]), was adapted from a short story by Jaroslav Papoušek, set in 1947 and transformed into a study of teen apathy that escaped government notice because, as Forman calculated, "People don't take comedies seriously." The film won first prize at the Locarno Film Festival, and Forman continued his analysis of Czech family life in *Loves of a Blonde* (*Lásky jedné plavovlásky* [1965]). According to Peter Hames, both films not only focused upon "the impermanence of young love, the confusion and despair of middle age, and the gulf between the generations," but were also critical of "some of the obvious absurdities" within Czech society. Forman's last Czech film, *The Fireman's Ball* (*Hoří, má panenko* [1967]) pushed the envelope of satire too far in its criticism of governmental bureaucracy. "The Czech ideology was that film had to reflect life as it should be. We wanted to show life as it is. That required some fancy strutting around the censors, and subjects which on the surface were innocent. But between the lines, the audiences could read something more." After the Soviet invasion of Prague in 1968, a tougher government banned the film for 20 years after Forman's escape from communism. When the Soviets invaded, Forman was in Paris, and he did not return home.

Taking Off (1971), Forman's first American film, was a continuation of themes Forman had first explored in Czechoslovakia. Nothing much seems to happen. A girl (Linnea Heacock) runs away from home, auditions for a singing lead (she literally can't sing), meets and presumably falls in love with a young rock musician, and returns home. (One of the auditioning singers is Carly Simon.) The young lovers are not the well-scrubbed models of youthful perfection found in Erich Segal's *Love Story* (1970), but the focus of the film falls not on the youngsters, but on their parents (Buck Henry and Lynn Carlin). The father blunders into a situation of his own making: Thinking that his daughter has run off, he overreacts, gets roaring drunk, then brutalizes the girl when he returns home to find her there. Consequently, she *does* run off. Desperate to find her, the parents join a group called SPFC (Society for the Parents of Fugitive Children), which turns out to be simply a group of pot-smoking ninnies. Significantly, the daughter seems not at all interested in dope, whereas the parents, in an idiotic attempt to "understand" her, get presumably stoned, shedding their inhibitions—ultimately to their own chagrin. Though *Taking Off* won the Special Jury Prize at the Cannes Film Festival of 1971, it was not a commercial success.

Taking Off was a less than brilliant debut effort, but respectable enough, and certainly typical of Forman's concerns at the time. Forman's next project was the decathlon episode of the Munich Olympics film, *Visions of Eight* (1972), another respectable effort, but his next film, *One Flew Over the Cuckoo's Nest* (1975), adapted from Ken Kesey's novel (1962) and Dale Wasserman's play adaptation (1971), was to establish Forman as one of Hollywood's major talents. The casting was brilliant, with Jack Nicholson playing troublemaker Randall Patrick McMurphy, a patient at the Oregon State Hospital in Salem, and Louise Fletcher as his nemesis at the mental hospital, Nurse Ratched, a control freak. A strong supporting cast included Danny DeVito, Christopher Lloyd, and Will Samson as Chief Bromden. The film won five Academy Awards, including best picture and best director. In 1977 Forman became an American citizen.

Forman's Academy Award sweep was followed by a film adaptation of a defining musical of the protest generation, *Hair* (1979), but the problem was that by the time Forman had arranged funding and organized the project, the Age of Aquarius had long since passed. Working with choreographer Twyla Tharp and playwright Michael Weller, Forman opened up the play to location shooting in New York's Central Park and the Lincoln Memorial in Washington, D.C., and developed a new story line that Forman claimed "was hidden in the original one," but the film, involving a tribe of hippies protesting conscription in the Vietnam War, did not appear until four years after the evacuation of Saigon. The approach was highly imaginative and visionary, but the subject was dated.

Miloš Forman (Dino De Laurentiis Corporation/Paramount)

Two more outstanding adaptations were to follow, both of which would earn critical acclaim, keeping Forman at the top of his game. The first was *Ragtime* (1981), beautifully adapted by Michael Weller from the 1975 novel by E. L. Doctorow, involving more plots and characters (historical and fictional) from the turn of the century than any film could possibly digest. The central plot concerns a ragtime piano player named Coalhouse Walker (Howard E. Rollins, Jr.), whose automobile, a prized possession, is trashed by some racist volunteer firemen in New Rochelle, New York, where his wife, Sarah, works for a prosperous middle-class family; in the aftermath, Sarah is killed, and Coalhouse becomes the leader of a group of black terrorists who take over the J. P. Morgan library. The film featured a fine cast that included Mandy Patinkin, novelist Norman Mailer (as the architect Stanford White), and Jimmy Cagney, in his last film appearance, as the New York police commissioner.

Forman told Doctorow that the story was "too sprawling. It must be focused. I decided we will concentrate on three characters, Coalhouse Walker, Younger Brother and Evelyn Nesbit. We will build them up, strengthen their mutual relationship, make it into a *story*." The final cut came in at just under three hours. Producer Dino De Laurentiis pressured Forman into cutting an additional 20 minutes, the Emma Goldman subplot, which caused the director to consider the film "an amputee." Even so, the film got eight Oscar nominations.

His next film, *Amadeus* (1984), not only adapted but also rewritten and restructured by Peter Shaffer from his hit play, would fare far better. It grossed nearly $55 million and swept seven Academy Awards, including best picture and Forman's second best director award. With F. Murray Abraham in the lead as the poisonous Antonio Salieri leading another brilliant cast, Forman was able to make the film in Prague, with its picturesque streets that made the picture wonderfully atmospheric, but the miracle of this adaptation was the way in which Shaffer restructured the play so that the music of Mozart could be perfectly incorporated, in ways not possible on the stage.

Forman's next fim, *Valmont* (1989), was a superior adaptation of the novel *Les Liaisons dangereuses,* but it was overlooked and neglected because it had been eclipsed by the tremendous success of the Stephen Frears adaptation of Christopher Hampton's play version. *Dangerous Liaisons,* made the year before and involving the same characters. Forman's next film, *The People vs. Larry Flint* (1996), earned Forman another Oscar nomination for best director and Woody Harrelson for best actor, but this film was attacked by feminists and excoriated because it dealt sympathetically with the smut merchant who built an empire publishing *Hustler* magazine. "The film just died," Forman told *Entertainment Weekly* in 1999. "That pains me because I think it was very unjust. The film never committed the crimes for which it was accused. In general, I believe in the arguments supporting what Flynt does. But I've never bought a *Hustler* magazine, and I'm not planning to." Forman's following film was another biopic, *Man on the Moon* (1999), starring Jim Carrey as the eccentric comedian Andy Kaufman. The film got much media attention but was not a box-office success. Forman's main talent has been for satire and, especially, for his extraordinary ability to adapt literary and dramatic works successfully to the screen, not for biography.

Other Films   *Dob e placená procházka* (*A Well-Paid Stroll,* TV [1966]); *The Little Black Book* (1999).

References   Buckley, Tom, "The Forman Formula," *New York Times Magazine,* March 1, 1981, pp. 28–31, 42–44, 50; Forman, Miloš, and Jan Novak, *Turnaround: A Memoir* (New York: Villard Books, 1994); Hames, Peter, *The Czechoslovak New Wave* (Berkeley: University of California Press, 1985); Jensen, Jeff, "Moon Landing," *Entertainment Weekly,* December 10, 1999, pp. 51–54; McCreadie, Marsha, "*One Flew Over the Cuckoo's Nest:* Some Reasons for One Happy Adaptation," *Literature/Film Quarterly* 2 (Spring 1977): 125–131; Safer, Elaine B., "'It's the Truth Even If It Didn't Happen': Ken Kesey's *One Flew Over the Cuckoo's Nest,*" *Literature/Film Quarterly* 2 (Spring 1977): 132–141.

—J.M.W.

Forsyth, Bill (1946–) Bill Forsyth was born in Glasgow, Scotland, the country that defines his most successful and beloved films. The son of working-class parents, Forsyth had little interest in film as a child and young teen; his chief artistic obsessions were fiction and poetry. It was only when he answered a classified advertisement and found work as an apprentice at a small film production company that he began to watch movies seriously. Like the directors of the French New Wave, his first cinematic heroes, Forsyth sought to extend the formal and stylistic boundaries of cinema. One early Forsyth experiment, a 45-minute film entitled *Waterloo* (1970), featured very long takes (two of them 10 minutes long) and a fragmented narrative built from a "psychological monologue."

Waterloo's screening at the Edinburgh Film Festival cleared the theater—but within a few years Forsyth packed the house at that same festival with his first feature film, *That Sinking Feeling* (1979), a story of out-of-work youths who rob a sink factory. Forsyth was the first Scot to make a narrative feature film while living in Scotland, and he was hailed as a pioneer in what everyone hoped would be a revitalized U.K. cinematic tradition. *That Sinking Feeling* bears the characteristic Forsyth touches: a gentle absurdity, a strong sense of physical location, detailed and suggestive characterizations, and a lyrical sense of the ineffable in life. Written and directed by Forsyth, shot in 16 mm with a cast rounded up from the Scottish Youth Theatre, and made on a minuscule budget of £6,000, *That Sinking Feeling* was the critical success that helped generate funding for Forsyth's breakthrough film in the U.K., *Gregory's Girl*. This 1981 film of a young soccer player (John Gordon-Sinclair) who falls in love with the new woman on his team (Dee Hepburn) was a surprise hit all over the U.K.

When its honors were capped with a major screenwriting award, producer David Puttnam, fresh from his Oscar triumph with *Chariots of Fire*, gave Forsyth the go-ahead to write and direct *Local Hero*, which in many respects would become Forsyth's signature film. Starring Burt Lancaster, Peter Riegert, and Denis Lawson, and with a wonderful supporting cast who brought Forsyth's passionately strange characters to life, *Local Hero* (1983) portrays an American corporate officer sent to buy up a beautiful seaside village in northern Scotland. When he gets there, he finds himself outwitted by the savvy natives and by love and the aurora borealis as well. The movie charmed audiences everywhere and brought Forsyth his first real fame in America.

For his next film, however, Forsyth made no concessions to the American market he had just cracked, or to his growing image as a quirky Scot making funny movies about eccentrics. Instead, he returned to his native Glasgow to write and direct 1984's *Comfort and Joy*, a film whose script he had been working on for a decade. *Comfort and Joy* is an ambitious and fascinating psychological study of love, family, and war as seen through the life of radio disc jockey Alan "Dickie" Bird, a man who loses his longtime lover, then has a midlife meltdown, and soon thereafter finds himself in the middle of a business and family feud over ice cream. The film's conclusion reaches toward a paradoxical union of opposites as the solution to its human dilemmas, but the narrative lacks the clarity and drive of *Local Hero*, and the film was not nearly as successful as its predecessor.

In 1987 Forsyth made his first movie in America, an adaptation of Marilynne Robinson's novel *Housekeeping*. Forsyth's love for the book is evident throughout, and Christine Lahti shines in the lead as Sylvie; by the end, however, the very deliberate pace and sometimes wooden voice-over narration overwhelm the film's strong sense of character and setting. The ensuing decade was not a successful one for Forsyth. His next film was 1989's *Breaking In*, written by John Sayles. Working for the first time from a script he did not write, Forsyth tried to make an existential film about an old safecracker who takes few risks (Burt Reynolds) and a young thief whose oddities make him almost impossible to work with. The studio wanted a buddy movie instead, and Forsyth was disappointed in the final version of the film.

By 1990 Forsyth was hard at work on *Being Human* (1994), his most ambitious project and most conspicuous failure. Trying to demonstrate the essential isolation of human beings in every era of civilization, Forsyth ended up with a star (Robin Williams), a large budget by Forsyth's standards (over $20 million), massive studio interference, and a movie that took nearly a year of editing and other postproduction fiddling to be deemed releasable in the United States. Depressed and discouraged, Forsyth made no films for the next five years.

He finally broke his artistic silence with 1999's *Gregory's Two Girls,* a return to his Glasgow roots and a sequel to his most conspicuous early success. Forsyth has repeatedly complained that his movies are misunderstood, that moviegoers' expectations limit the cinema's growth and maturation, and that he gets most of his pleasure from writing, not directing. Yet these dour sentiments cannot erase the magic and human depth in Forsyth's work. One can only hope that Forsyth, once the young hero of an emerging national cinema, will find the comfort and joy he needs to resume his career.

Other Film *Andrina,* made for BBC Scotland (1981).

References Dick, Eddie, ed., *From Limelight to Satellite: A Scottish Film Book* (London: BFI, 1990); Hacker, Jonathan, and David Price, *Take Ten: Contemporary British Film Directors* (Oxford: Clarendon Press, 1991).

—W.G.C.

Fosse, Bob (1927–1987) Robert Louis Fosse was born on June 23, 1927, in Chicago, the son of Cyril and Sarah Alice Fosse, both of whom had an interest in show business. Although he attended Ravenswood Grammar School and graduated from Roald Amundsen High School in 1945, he obtained his real education at Frederick Weaver's Chicago Academy of Theatre Arts, where he learned tap, toe, and acrobatic dancing. When Fosse's father could no longer afford to pay for the lessons, Weaver waived the fees and teamed him with Charles Gross in exchange for 15% of his earnings. The Riff Brothers (Fosse and Gross) played the burlesque houses featured in Fosse's autobiographical film *All That Jazz* (1979). He enlisted in the U.S. Navy in 1945 and spent two years touring the Pacific with the navy's Special Services division. After he was discharged in New York in 1947, he got a job as a dancer in *Call Me Mister.* During the show's run he met and married Mary Ann Miles, with whom he danced

professionally after the show closed. However, their marriage ended in 1951 after he fell in love with Joan McCracken, when they both appeared in *Dance Me a Song,* in which he made his Broadway debut. McCracken urged Fosse to study acting and dance, and his work at the American Theatre Wing resulted in a successful screen test with MGM. After small roles in *Give a Girl a Break* and *The Affairs of Dobie Gillis,* Fosse danced in and did some choreographing for MGM's *Kiss Me Kate* (1953). That led George Abbott and Jerome Robbins to hire him to choreograph *The Pajama Game* (1954), which was a smash hit on Broadway.

In 1955 Fosse returned to Hollywood to choreograph and star opposite Janet Leigh in *My Sister Eileen* for Columbia. Fosse then teamed again with Robbins and Abbott for the show *Damn Yankees,* which starred Gwen Verdon, who would become his third wife in 1960. Fosse's developing sexual relationship with Verdon perhaps contributed to the torrid sexual choreography in the musical, which was criticized by some as salacious and immoral. When *Pajama Game* and *Damn Yankees* were subsequently adapted to film in 1957 and 1958, Fosse did the choreography. From 1956 to 1968, however, Fosse concentrated on choreographing and directing musicals, and his collaboration with Verdon was mutually beneficial. She won three Tony awards for her work in his musicals, and he won nine Tony awards during his lifetime. After choreographing *Bells are Ringing* (1956) and *New Girl in Town* (1957), Fosse was named, at Verdon's insistence, director/choreographer of *Redhead* (1959); he became one of the few choreographers who had also directed a musical. After being dismissed as director of *The Conquering Hero* (1961), Fosse made a comeback by staging the dance numbers for *How to Succeed in Business Without Really Trying* (1962) and for *Little Me* (1962). After failing with *Pleasures and Palaces* (1965), which he directed and choreographed, he made his best musical show with Verdon, *Sweet*

Bob Fosse (left) directing a scene on the set of *Star 80* (The Ladd Company)

Charity (1966), which was loosely based on Fellini's film *Nights of Cabiria* (1956).

When *Sweet Charity* was filmed in 1968, it was Fosse's first film as a director, and it made his career in film; even without Verdon—Shirley MacLaine played Charity—it demonstrated Fosse's mastery of two disparate media, although the film was a financial disappointment. *Cabaret* (1972), however, was both a critical and a financial success. Fosse opened up the show, insisted on grimy realism, and stressed the Nazi theme in a film far removed from previous "backstage" musicals. It won him an Oscar for best director. After *Cabaret,* Fosse directed and choreographed *Pippin* (1972), a rock musical for Broadway. During the rehearsals Fosse met Ann Reinking, who became his lover; Fosse's marriage to Verdon, which had deterio-

rated because of his infidelities, ended in a legal separation in 1971. Fosse's Tony for *Pippin,* his Oscar for *Cabaret,* and his Emmy for *Liza with a Z,* a television variety show starring Liza Minnelli, all occurred in 1973; no one else has ever won these awards the same year. Uncomfortable with such honors, however, the insecure Fosse thought that it was all a sham, claiming to his friends: "I fooled everybody."

After 1973 all of Fosse's projects were at least partly autobiographical. In *Lenny* (1974), Fosse's only nonmusical film, Fosse dealt with Lenny Bruce's attempt to liberate language, much as Fosse liberated dance; in the stage musicals *Chicago* (1975) and *Dancin'* (1978), Fosse focused on marginal performers attempting to make it big and to reconcile performance with reality; and in *All That*

Jazz (1979), he filmed the life of Joe Gideon, his alter ego, in flashback against a present in which Joe attempts, despite a heart attack, to stage a play like *Chicago* and a film like *Lenny*. Like Fellini's *8½* (1963), *All That Jazz* is a recapitulation of an artist's life and work. Fosse's last film musical, it is remarkable for its unorthodox subject matter and for its technical virtuosity in staging musical numbers. Joe Gideon, like Fosse, was hugely talented but still insecure, both as an artist and as a man, as he hears what Falstaff called "the chimes at midnight" and is embraced in a dance of death. The film was distinctively surreal, as close to Fellini's style as the American cinema has ever come.

Star 80 (1983), Fosse's last film, also had ties to Fosse's life, for it concerned the Pygmalion transformation of women into stars, something Fosse was noted for; but the film was a box-office failure. The story, about the murder of Playboy playmate Dorothy Stratten, was simply repulsive, but in her incisive profile of the director, Joan Acocella considered *Star 80* even more autobiographical than *All That Jazz* in its insecurity and its morbid fascination with sex. Fosse returned to the stage with *Big Deal* (1986), which he totally controlled and which was considered disappointing. Before he died in 1987, however, Fosse mounted what has been considered the definitive production of *Sweet Charity*. His lasting contributions to the stage and to film musicals were combined in *Fosse: A Celebration in Song and Dance* (1999), a musical revue developed in part by Ann Reinking, the woman who replaced Verdon in his affections, and directed by Reinking and Richard Maltby, Jr. Meanwhile, his 1975 musical *Chicago* was successfully revived in 1995 and enjoyed. His work could be revived and replicated, but never quite imitated successfully. "His work was tacky, pushy, obsessive," Joan Acocella wrote, yet "he was a moralist of a generation that had little hope of innocence. He was clearly drawn to innocence; its presence, or its mourned loss, is at the center of his best work."

References Acocella, Joan, "Dancing in the Dark," *New Yorker,* December 21, 1998, pp. 100–108; Gottfried, Martin, *All His Jazz: The Life and Death of Bob Fosse* (New York: Bantam, 1990); Grubb, Kevin, *Razzle Dazzle* (New York: St. Martin's Press, 1989).

—T.L.E.

Francis, Freddie (1917–) Freddie Francis has had two careers in the motion picture industry, running concurrently. He is considered one of the best cinematographers in the business; and he has also directed some of the most interesting and unusual of England's Hammer studios horror film repertoire. Unlike the creature features or slasher films made by others in the genre, Francis's movies avoid excessive sensationalism. His films stress form, suggestion, and complex emotional overtones. Francis was born in Islington, London, on December 22, 1917. His education ended in 1934 when he became a stills photographer apprentice at a movie studio. He would hold this position for two years. He progressed through the system, first as a clapper, then a camera loader, and finally a focus puller. When war broke out, he served in the army making films as both a cameraman and editor for the next seven years.

At the conclusion of the war, Francis returned to the film industry as an assistant cameraman and worked on films directed by Michael Powell, including *The Macomber Affair* (1946), *The Elusive Pimpernel* (1950), and *The Tales of Hoffman* (1951). The cinematographer on these films was Christopher Challis. John Huston was so impressed by Francis's camera work that he had him assist the veteran Oswald Morris on three films: *Moulin Rouge* (1953), *Beat the Devil* (1955), and *Moby Dick* (1956). He became a cinematographer shortly after that. Francis's experience with a camera and viewfinder gave him a unique perspective as a cinematographer. His reputation grew with each picture, including *A Hill in Korea* (1956), *Room at the Top* (1959), *Saturday Night and Sunday Morning* (1960), *Sons and Lovers* (1960), and *The Innocents*

(1961). He won his first Oscar for *Sons and Lovers* (1960), which was directed by Jack Cardiff.

His directing career began with *The Day of the Triffids* (1963), for which he directed an uncredited 25 minutes. That same year he directed two other films for which he received credit, *Vengeance* (1962) and *Paranoiac* (1963). The latter film was made for Hammer studios. Most of the films Francis directed were based on the Hammer model: low budget, tight schedule, and use of experienced but inexpensive performers. Francis had a contempt for monsters such as Dracula and Frankenstein. This is clearly demonstrated in two films he made involving these creatures. In *The Evil of Frankenstein* (1966), the monster has absolutely no personality and is seldom on the screen. Most of the evildoing is committed by the good doctor himself and a vengeful hypnotist. Romance between an agnostic and a committed Roman Catholic is the emphasis in *Dracula Has Risen from the Grave* (1968), while the title character (played by Christopher Lee) is merely a hurdle in the path of true love. Peter Cushing and Christopher Lee were teamed up in Francis's *The Skull* (1965). They play rivals attempting to acquire a skull of the Marquis de Sade. The skull is thought to have extraordinary power, and its possession leads to tragic results. Most of the horror in the film comes from viewing murder and mayhem through the eyes of the skull itself. Francis would work with Cushing and Lee in two other films, *Dr. Terror's House of Horrors* (1965) and *The Creeping Flesh* (1973). Francis's success with these films led to other assignments in the horror genre for Hammer and other studios, including *Nightmare* (1964), *Hysteria* (1965), *The Psychopath* (1965), *The Deadly Bees* (1966), *They Came from Beyond Space* (1967), *Torture Garden* (1968), and *Tales That Witness Madness* (1973). Monsters in all of these films were on screen for a minimum amount of time, if at all. *Mumsy, Nanny, Sonny, and Girly* (1970) was concerned with a dysfunctional and murderous family. It was a critical and box-office dud. However, it

was and remains a visually stunning film and Francis's own favorite among his pictures. That same year he directed Joan Crawford in the critical and commercial failure *Trog* (1970). The film was about a caveman who was unearthed, comes to life, and goes on a rampage.

Nonhorror projects never got beyond the planning stage, and before he returned to cinematography, Francis made two more horror films in 1975, *The Ghoul* and *Legend of the Werewolf.* Bored with directing low-budget horror features, for the next 10 years Francis returned to photography with several features, including *The Elephant Man* (1980), *The French Lieutenant's Woman* (1981), *The Executioner's Song* (1982), and *Dune* (1984). Upon his return to directing in 1985 he made *The Doctor and the Devils.* The film was a period piece dealing with graverobbing in the 19th century. It was largely unsuccessful. His final directorial piece was *The Dark Tower* (1987), a haunted house–type story set in a skyscraper. The film was so poor that Francis used a pseudonym, Ken Barnett. Critical accolades followed his next efforts as a cinematographer, especially *Cape Fear* (1991) and *Glory* (1989), for which he won his second Oscar.

While he is best known for his cinematography, many of Francis's horror films were critically acclaimed. He summed up his insecurity as a director when he said, "I consider myself a successful cameraman, but I'm still a struggling director."

Other Films   As director: *The Intrepid Mr. Twigg* (1969); *Tales from the Crypt* (1972); *Demon Master* (1973).

References   Gifford, Denis, *A Pictorial History of Horror Movies* (London: Hamlyn Publishing, 1973); Jensen, Paul M., *The Men Who Made the Monsters* (New York: Twayne Publishers, 1996).

—S.D.

Franju, Georges (1912–1987)   An enigmatic figure whose work is an occasionally baffling compound of closely observed reality and poetically realized fantasy, Georges Franju occupies a special place in postwar French cinema. He

was born in Fougères, in Brittany, on April 12, 1912, the son of a public works contractor. A brilliant but desultory student, he left school and drifted through an assortment of activities, including a stint in the military in Algeria and a job preparing sets for the Folies-Bergère in Paris. A passion for the cinema resulted in his cofounding (with Henri Langlois) the Cinémathèque Française in 1936, whose initial agenda to save endangered silent films was transformed during the war into a mission to rescue French films from the occupying Nazis. After more archival activities for the International Federation of Film Archives, Franju launched in 1949 a series of documentary shorts that established his reputation as a documentary filmmaker. Already apparent was his signature sensitivity to the strangeness of the world and the sense that terrors may lie behind the most mundane events. The series included *The Blood of the Beasts* (*Le Sang des bêtes* [1949]), a dispassionate depiction of the daily cruelty and horror of a slaughterhouse, whose workers do their grisly business with dispatch, even humor; *Hôtel des Invalides* (1952), which undercut patriotic sentiments with shots of orphaned children and disabled and disfigured war veterans; and *The First Night* (*La Première nuit* [1958]), about a poor boy whose search in the subway for the girl he loves results in his inadvertent incarceration under ground during the night.

His first feature, *The Keepers* (*La Tête contre les murs* [1959]), concerned a rebellious youth, Gerane (Jean-Pierre Mocky), who has been committed to an asylum by his tyrannical father. He escapes with the aid of a strange girl (Anouk Aimée), but he is recaptured and returned to the institution. Franju's next film, *Eyes Without a Face* (*Les Yeux sans visage* [1959]), is a Faustian tale of a surgeon (Pierre Brasseur) who kidnaps and murders young women in the hope of grafting their facial skin onto the disfigured visage of his daughter (Edith Scob). Driven mad by the ordeal (the surgical procedures are excruciatingly graphic), the daughter murders

her father and wanders off into the night. *Thérèse Desqueyroux* (1962) was an adaptation of François Mauriac's classic novel about a sensitive young wife who tries to escape her suffocating marriage by attempting to poison her husband. Failing in that endeavor, she suffers a cruel punishment at the hands of her bourgeois family and is held virtual prisoner in the family mansion.

Judex (1963) and *Thomas the Impostor* (*Thomas l'imposteur* [1964]) find Franju at his most eerily poetic. *Judex* harked back to the celebrated pre–World War I serial crime thrillers of Louis Feuillade, with their costumed heroes and villains, bizarre crimes and conspiracies, and surreal atmospheres. Like its predecessors, Franju's film is set in Paris in 1914. The black-clad figure of Judex (Channing Pollock)—the name is Latin for "judge" or "judger"—is dedicated to avenging the death of his father at the hands of the corrupt banker, Favraux, and the villainous Diane (Francine Berge). He is aided by the comic private detective Cocantin (Jacques Jouaneau) and a glamorous acrobat Daisy (Sylva Koscina). Judex's seeming god-like status is immediately apparent in his first appearance, when the camera tilts up from his shoes to the hawks-head helmet he is wearing. His power over life and death is suggested when he restores a dead dove to life by issuing sparks from his hand. His hideout is a parody of the standard "superhero" lair, with secret entrances and exotic appurtenances, such as a television machine, which enables him to monitor Favraux's activities. These supernatural gifts are revealed to be mere illusions, however, when Judex's disguise is broached and he is unveiled as a mere mortal. In Franju's hands, what we might expect to be a slam-bang aggregation of comic-book adventures is actually a deliberately paced, elegant, and cool meditation on reality and illusion. "People say that a mask is mysterious," Franju has cryptically observed. "Not at all, it *recovers* a mystery, but it is not mysterious. What is mysterious is the face *dis*covered." Meanwhile, Franju is characteristically dismissive about any alleged tributes to the work of Feuillade himself, admitting, "In point of fact I don't give a damn about Feuillade, and personally I don't think I have been influenced by him."

Thomas the Impostor, arguably Franju's masterpiece, was scripted by Jean Cocteau after his own novel. The strongly autobiographical story depicts the efforts of a Polish-French princess who, with the aid of a 16-year-old youth (Thomas) impersonating a great general, organizes a private ambulance service to reach the front and aid stricken soldiers. Faced with the cruel reality of war, the idealistic princess recoils in horror, but the equally romantic Thomas is unfazed. When he is finally and fatally wounded, his view of life as a great charade remains intact: "I'm lost if I don't pretend to be dead," he murmurs before expiring. A surreal beauty masking the brutal horrors of war hovers over the battle scenes. For example, in the midst of a bombardment of Rheims, Thomas dances excitedly among the explosions, watching raptly as the great cathedral disappears behind a column of black smoke. And in another scene, Thomas blithely plays with his revolver, firing at his image in a mirror, while the princess gazes horrified at a medic who prods mutilated bodies with a pitchfork to determine who is alive enough to be worth saving. Between Cocteau's script and Franju's direction, a perfect harmony of fragile fantasy and brute reality is achieved.

Franju's later films maintained his ambivalent stance toward love and violence, fantasy and reality. *The Sin of Abbe Mouret* (*La Faute de l'Abbé Mouret* [1970]), is adapted from Emile Zola's story of a young country priest, Serge Mouret (Francis Huster), whose purity fails before a sexual involvement with a beautiful country girl, Albine (Gillian Hills). When the two lovers are separated by a fanatical priest, the girl languishes and dies. Her death is morbidly poetic: She is asphyxiated by the heavily perfumed flowers that fill her bedchamber. Franju's last major theatrical film, *The Last Melodrama* (*Le Dernier melodrame* [1978]), depicted a curious and deadly interface between the fantasy of the theater stage and the mundane reality of its spectators. A touring theatrical company arrives in a small provincial town, triggering the violent jealousy of a barman who fears his wife will leave him for the glamor of the stage. As a result of his being killed while trying to sabotage the theater tent, the wife sets it ablaze. "Franju delights in showing the interplay that creates a living theater of contact between performer and spectator," writes commentator Robert Brown. "The barman's wife is seen as she sees herself, caught in the void between imagination and reality, between her dream—the theatre—that she has destroyed on account of her imprisoning background, and her existence—provincial domesticity—that she has ruined on behalf of her imaginative desires."

Most of Franju's subsequent works were made for television, including an adaptation of Joseph Conrad's *The Shadow Line* (1971) and an eight-part serial, *The Man Without a Face* (*L'Homme sans visage* [1974]). Franju lived as an invalid for several years before his death in Paris on November 5, 1987.

Robert Brown observes that most of Franju's characters seek and find a liberation from their confining circumstances, although it is an escape that is bitterly ironic. In *La Premiere nuit,* after being trapped overnight in the Metro, a boy emerges into a park that seems like a baffling maze. Christiane in *Eyes Without a Face* kills her father and escapes the hospital of horror, only to fall victim to her own madness. The eponymous heroine of *Thérèse Desqueyroux* leaves the provincial prison of her family only to find herself leading a solitary life in the city. The impostor Thomas insulates himself from the brutalities of war by slipping into his own, ultimately fatal fantasy. The barman's wife in *The Last Melodrama* sets fire to the very theatrical dream that had represented her escape from a dull provincial life. Brown notes: "Freedom clearly does not mean freedom from anguish for a filmmaker who describes himself as an 'active pessimist.'" Franju's films have won the devotion of the cognoscenti but the indifference of mainstream critics and viewers. He is criticized, justifiably in some instances, for a deliberate pacing, austere style, and slack narrative drive. And yet the images intrigue and tantalize, sometimes long after the film has ended. Characteristically, Franju was fond of quoting Baudelaire's maxim, "The person who looks outside through an open window sees much less than somebody who looks at a closed window." Franju explains: "Of course, if you look through an open window you see what is there. But looking through a closed window you imagine everything."

His honors included Chevalier of the Légion d'Honneur, Chevalier of the Ordre des Arts et des Lettres, and Officier of the Ordre National du Mérite.

Other Film *Spotlight on Murder (Pleins feux sur l'assassin* [1961]).

References Brown, Robert, "Georges Franju: Behind Closed Windows," *Sight and Sound* 52, no. 4 (Autumn 1983): 266–271; Milne, Tom, "Georges Franju: The Haunted Void," *Sight and Sound* 44, no. 2 (Spring 1975): 68–72; Milne, Tom, "Thomas l'imposteur," *Sight and Sound* 25, no. 2 (Spring 1966): 87–89.

—J.C.T.

Frankenheimer, John (1930–) John Frankenheimer is an illustrious member of that cadre of American film directors—including Arthur Penn, Sidney Lumet, and Delbert Mann—who gained their apprenticeship in the Golden Age of "live" television. He was born in Malba, New York, on February 19, 1930, and grew up in the borough of Queens. He attended La Salle Military Academy during his high school years. His first experience in making movies came in the U.S. Air Force's Film Squadron unit, when he directed documentaries while stationed in Burbank, California. After military service, he went to CBS in the early 1950s to pursue a career in television. Quick, versatile, and techni-

Director John Frankenheimer on the set of *The Island of Dr. Moreau* (New Line Productions)

cally adept in the new medium, his first projects were varied, to say the least—a religious series, *Lamp Unto My Feet;* an interview show with Edward R. Murrow, *Person to Person;* a variety show, *The Gary Moore Show;* and 152 "live" dramatic presentations for anthology programs, like *Climax!* and *Playhouse 90,* between 1954 and 1960. Examples of the highly literate nature of many of these programs are *The Turn of the Screw,* based on Henry James's novella and starring Ingrid Bergman, and *The Last Tycoon,* adapted from F. Scott Fitzgerald's novel.

Moving into theatrical features, his first film was *The Young Stranger* (1956). His best-known films include the political assassination thriller, *The Manchurian Candidate* (1962); a fable about the military takeover of the American government, *Seven Days in May* (1963); and *Grand Prix,* a Cinerama racing epic. Less familiar, but no less full of quirky surprises, are *The Train* (1965), a World War II thriller about Nazi theft of art masterpieces; *French Connection II* (1975), an offbeat sequel to the William Friedkin original, and *The Fourth War* (1990), one of the first spy melodramas to reflect the thaw in cold-war tensions between East and West. Arguably his masterpiece is *Seconds* (1966), a lamentably undervalued modernization of the

Faust allegory, starring Rock Hudson in his finest role. As an exercise in Kafkaesque horror, it occupies a special niche in the American horror cinema.

Frankenheimer's television experience has contributed to his visual style. He is known for glaring closeups and staging in depth, rather than width, which necessitates working with a preproduction storyboard artist; and he consistently employs hard lighting, wide-angle lenses, and hand-held cameras to impart a restless, edgy quality to his dramas. Thematically speaking, he is preoccupied with the conflicts between individuals and society. In *The Train,* the "enemy" is the Nazi regime; in *Birdman of Alcatraz,* the prison government; in *52 Pick-Up,* the corruption of ruthless people; in *Manchurian Candidate,* political greed.

In recent years, aside from a few theatrical releases, like *Ronin* (1997) and *Reindeer Games* (2000), he has returned to television, directing a series of films for Turner and HBO Television, including *Against the Wall,* about the Attica prison revolt; *The Burning Season,* the story of Chico Mendes; and *Andersonville,* about the Civil War prison camp. Because they are not mainstream subjects, Frankenheimer is convinced they could not have been financed as theatrical feature films. "There shouldn't be any stigma attached to a director who says he wants to do a cable movie, or a movie of the week. Why not do a wonderful subject for TV that will be seen by millions of people rather than the nonsense they're doing now and have it do no business." Frankenheimer was honored in 1996 by a double retrospective at the Museum of Modern Art and the Museum of Television and Radio.

Other Films   *The Young Savages* (1961); *The Fixer* (1968); *The Gypsy Moths* (1969); *Black Sunday* (1976); *The Island of Dr. Moreau* (1996).

References   "Dialogue on Film: John Frankenheimer," *American Film,* March 1989, pp. 20–24; Pratley, Gerald, *The Cinema of John Frankenheimer* (New York: 1969).

—J.C.T.

Freleng, Isadore ("Friz")   (1906–1995)

During a career in the commercial animation business spanning almost 60 years, "Friz" Freleng became, with TEX AVERY and CHARLES MARTIN ("CHUCK") JONES, the top cartoon director-producer at Warner Bros., responsible for developing the characters of Porky Pig, Bugs Bunny, Elmer Fudd, Yosemite Sam, and many others. His nickname "Friz" was derived from a fictional politician named "Frisby." Freleng was born in Kansas City, Missouri, on August 21, 1906. He knew WALTER ELIAS DISNEY, a fellow Kansas City resident, during Walt's apprentice years in the early 1920s, but he didn't work for him until 1927, when he left Kansas City to join Walt's Los Angeles operation to work on the "Alice in Cartoonland" and "Oswald the Lucky Rabbit" shorts. Soon after, he went over to the Winkler Picture Corporation in New York to work on the popular "Krazy Kat" cartoon series.

He found his true niche at Warner Bros. in 1930, where he remained as a mainstay director/producer for three decades (excepting a brief period in 1937–38 when he worked at MGM), directing more cartoons than anyone else (about 266). The Warner animation unit on Sunset Boulevard (housed in a rickety building affectionately dubbed "termite terrace" for obvious reasons), under the supervision of Disney's former Kansas City animators Hugh Harmon and Rudolph Ising, was developing a mouselike character called "Bosco," and to Freleng went the assignment of animating him in his first "Looney Tunes" adventure, *Sinkin' in the Bathtub* (1930). In many more "Looney Tunes" and "Merrie Melodies" cartoons Freleng either created, supervised, or directed with fellow animators Bob Clampett, Chuck Jones, Tex Avery, and Robert McKimson a new group of zany, iconoclastic characters, including the stuttering Porky Pig (who debuted in Freleng's *I Haven't Got a Hat* [1935]), the manic Daffy Duck (who first appeared in *Porky's Duck Hunt* [1937]), the befuddled Elmer Fudd (*Elmer's Candid Camera* [1940]), and wiseacre

Bugs Bunny (*A Wild Hare* [1940]), the tussling Sylvester the Cat and Tweetie Bird (the Oscar-winning *Tweetie Pie* [1947]), and Speedy Gonzales (the Oscar-winning *Speedy Gonzales* [1955]). Another character, Yosemite Sam, remained one of Freleng's favorites. The gun-totin' blowhard debuted in Freleng's *Hare Trigger* (1945). "I was looking for a character strong enough to work against Bugs Bunny," recalled Freleng. "For me, Elmer Fudd wasn't it—he was so dumb a chicken could outsmart him. So I thought to use the smallest guy I could think of along with the biggest voice [Warner's voice ace, Mel Blanc] I could get." Yosemite reached his pinnacle with the Oscar-winning *Knighty-Night Bugs* (1958). Freleng's special passion and sensitivity for music led to many happy associations with Warner composer, Carl Stallings (another of Disney's former Kansas City colleagues), including a special favorite, *Rhapsody Rabbit* (1947), in which a tuxedo-attired Bugs Bunny performs Franz Liszt's "Second Hungarian Rhapsody" to a boogie-woogie beat.

In 1960 he turned to television and worked with Chuck Jones on the *Bugs Bunny Show,* aired on the ABC network. By means of transitional moments and new animation, Freleng and Jones assembled existing six-minute cartoons into half-hour formats for the two-season series of weekly shows. In 1963 he launched his last major creative venture with former Warner Bros. executive David H. DePatie. Still working from within the Warner plant, the independent DePatie-Freleng Enterprises created several successful television cartoon projects, including more Warner Bros. "Road Runner" and "Speedy Gonzales" cartoons and the popular "Pink Panther" series (both the celebrated pre-title sequences for Blake Edwards's "Panther" movies and the short cartoons). The first Pink Panther short, *The Pink Phink* (1964), won an Oscar (the only one of his five Oscars that Freleng accepted personally). A feature-length compilation of his work appeared in 1981, *Friz Freleng's Looney Looney Looney Bugs Bunny Movie.*

Freleng was modest about his work and always credited his associations with other gifted directors as a mutually creative enterprise: "We didn't actually steal from each other, but everybody did learn things from each other, little nuances that one director does, like Chuck Jones. Chuck would see things in my cartoons that he applied to his. And I saw things in his that would apply to me. I took some from him, he took some from Tex Avery, and so on. We all learned from the other person. That's the way it went."

In his history of Warner Bros. animation, *That's All, Folks!,* Steve Schneider praises Freleng's accomplishments: "Freleng made crucial contributions to every phase of Warner Bros.' development. . . . As a director, his impeccable timing and ability to fashion fully rounded, credible characters gave his cartoons a kind of classicism—a wholeness and balance through which humor and beauty became one. . . . Freleng was alone in animation in his ability to make cartoons that were both charming and rowdily funny."

References Beck, Jerry, and Will Friedwald, *Looney Tunes and Merrie Melodies: A Complete Guide to the Warner Bros. Cartoons* (New York: Henry Holt, 1989); Catsos, Gregory J. M., "An Animated Conversation with Friz Freleng: Hare-Raising Tales from a Life in 'Toons,'" *Outre* 19: 54–61, 78, 80–81; Merritt, Russell, and J. B. Kaufman, *Walt in Wonderland: The Silent Films of Walt Disney* (Baltimore: Johns Hopkins University Press, 1993); Schneider, Steve, *The Art of Warner Bros. Animation* (New York: Henry Holt, 1988).

—J.C.T.

Freund, Karl (1890–1969) Karl Freund was born on January 16, 1890, in Königinhof, Bohemia (now Dvur Kralove, Czech Republic). Hailed for his cinematographic expertise as "the Giotto of the screen," he began his long, distinguished career in motion pictures at the age of 15 as an assistant projectionist in Berlin. He recalled later in life that a film showing a locomotive, apparently charging straight at the audience, inspired him to want to make pictures. By age 17 he was an apprentice cameraman and at 18 he was shooting newsreels and shorts for Pathe News.

As Germany's "Golden Age" of cinema dawned around the 1920s, Freund's prowess in fluid camera movement and expressive lighting in such notable silent films as Paul Wegener's *Der Golem* (1920) and F. W. Murnau's *The Last Laugh* (1924) made him popular with Germany's best directors. His innovative techniques in the *entfesselte Kamera* (the mobile camera), such as attaching a camera to a swing or strapping it to his chest for a dramatic subjective view, earned him a reputation as a pioneer in liberating the camera from its tripod. Equally adept at lighting, his painterly use of deep shadows in E. A. Dupont's *Variety* (1925) moved one contemporary critic to comment that "even Renoir would have envied such blacks." Working with the largest budget of his career, Freund shot the UFA super-production *Metropolis* in 1926 for Fritz Lang. For this visual tour de force, he developed new equipment such as a motorized dolly and a double-lens camera that could simultaneously film actors and model miniatures. "Freund helped make *Metropolis* a filmmaking landmark," writes historian Leonard Maltin. "This futuristic film, made on a tremendous scale, involved more special effects than any of Freund's previous endeavors; needless to say, they were carried off beautifully." In 1927 he collaborated with Walter Ruttman to produce and cowrite the highly regarded documentary *Berlin: Symphony of a Great City*. The entire picture was shot through hidden cameras, made possible with a high-speed film stock developed by Freund.

In 1929, he emigrated to America to work with the still-experimental Technicolor process. His notoriety in the film industry as a "giant," both physically at 360 pounds and by reputation as a master cinematographer, was international and he was soon under contract with Universal Studios. After assisting Lewis Milestone with *All Quiet on the Western Front* (1930) by devising the now-famous "butterfly" ending, the studio gave him major shooting assignments on several classic features, such as *Dracula* (1931), directed by Tod Browning, and *Murders in the Rue Morgue* (1932), by Robert Florey.

Beginning with *The Mummy* in 1932, Freund moved into the director's chair. His trademark moody lighting and mobile camera work made this one of Universal's most stylish productions from the early thirties. Though he was said to be a domineering, if not overbearing, director on the set, the rotund Freund somehow acquired the affectionate nickname of "Papa." He directed only a single feature in 1933, the musical drama *Moonlight and Pretzels,* but the following year he was quite busy directing the mystery *Madame Spy* and the comedic *The Countess of Monte Cristo,* both starring Fay Wray, as well as the drama *I Give My Love* and the comedies *Uncertain Lady* and *Gift of Gab.* His contract expired, he left Universal and went to MGM in 1935 to direct the bizarre horror film *Mad Love,* starring Peter Lorre in his Hollywood debut. The old master's penchant for using dramatic angles and shadows for artistic expression no doubt had a lasting effect on his young cameraman, Gregg Toland, when the latter went to work with Orson Welles on *Citizen Kane* (1941).

After *Mad Love,* Karl Freund returned to cinematography and never directed again. He claimed to find directing chores routine and dull, saying "the camera at least gives some latitude for special creativeness." His photographic talents would enrich a vast range of memorable pictures from *Camille* (1936), to *Pride and Prejudice* (1940), to *Key Largo* (1948). He received the Academy Award in 1937 for his cinematography on *The Good Earth.* In 1944 he founded the Photo Research Corporation of Burbank, which initially manufactured light-measuring equipment. Freund turned to television in the 1950s, pioneering the use of three cameras to film live programs while working on the *I Love Lucy* show. He eventually became chief cinematographer for

Desilu Productions. In 1954 the Academy of Motion Pictures Arts and Sciences gave him a technical award for his design and development of a direct-reading brightness meter. Having spent his last years experimenting with new photographic techniques, Freund passed away on May 3, 1969, after a short but comfortable retirement from his Photo Research Corporation, which had grown into a multimillion-dollar concern serving the television and film industry.

Reference Maltin, Leonard, *Behind the Camera: The Cinematographer's Art* (New York: Signet Books, 1971).

—W.G.H.

Friedkin, William (1935–)

William "Hurricane Billy" Friedkin was born on August 29, 1935, in Chicago, Illinois, the son of Raechael (Rae) Friedkin and Louis Friedkin. His mother was an operating room nurse, his father a semiprofessional softball player, a merchant seaman, and a discount clothing salesman. Friedkin's parents were unable to send him to college, so he began working in the mailroom of WGN-TV in Chicago, a position he sought after reading an ad promising "opportunities for young men to succeed in television." He started in 1953 and was in the mailroom for six months before being promoted to floor manager, then to director, in short order. He was barely 18 years old.

From 1953 to 1961 Friedkin directed some 2,000 television programs, ranging from classic drama to baseball games. Eventually he became interested in documentary film, an interest that led to his production *The People versus Paul Crump,* which won the Golden Gate Award at the San Francisco Film Festival in 1962 and was also cited for several other international awards. This success enabled him to work on his first feature film, *Good Times* (1967), starring Sonny and Cher, a production Friedkin now considers "not viewable." In 1968, *The Night They Raided Minsky's* was released, starring Jason Robards, Britt Eklund, and several other talented actors, an

William Friedkin (left) on the set of *Rules of Engagement* (Paramount)

enjoyable and promising film, although flawed. In the same year *The Birthday Party* was released starring Robert Shaw, an adaptation of the play by Harold Pinter, and a production Friedkin is still proud of. *The Boys in the Band,* adapted from Mart Crowley's play and released in 1970, was reputed to be the first mainstream film about gay life in the United States. After completing these projects, Friedkin later claimed that no one should film a play. Even so, in 1998, Friedkin successfully took on another adaptation, *12 Angry Men,* structured like a stageplay but originally written as a teleplay by Reginald Rose and made into a feature film by Sidney Lumet in 1957. Friedkin's television remake was nominated for the Director's Guild of America award.

In 1971, Friedkin's first great success, *The French Connection,* was released and gained him international acclaim. It is a brilliant, gritty film starring Gene Hackman, Fernando Rey, Roy Scheider, and Tony Lo Bianco. The plot involves two New York policemen who assist in breaking up a heroin ring in the late 1960s. It featured one of the most famous and exciting car chase sequences ever filmed and won an Academy Award for Friedkin as best director. His brilliant directing continued with *The Exorcist,* released in 1973, which earned another Oscar nomination for best director. Friedkin has said that "*The Exorcist* is the 'only' film I've ever made that I think is pretty good." *The Exorcist* starred Ellen Burstyn, Max von Sydow, and, in her film debut, Linda Blair.

In 1977 *Sorcerer* was released, a remake of the 1953 Henri-Georges Clouzot film *The Wages of Fear.* Friedkin still believes *Sorcerer* is very watchable, but, unfortunately, it flopped at the box office, as did *Cruising* (1980), starring Al Pacino, Paul Sorvino, and Karen Allen. *To Live and Die in L.A.* (1985), starring William L. Peterson and Willem Dafoe, was a moderately successful film about the drug trade from the point of view of secret service agents. Nine years later, *Blue Chips* was released, in 1994. The director was drawn to this script because as a high-school student he was a smallish (5 feet 11 inches) but talented basketball player. The film starred Nick Nolte, Mary McDonnell, and J. T. Walsh, and also included Bob Cousy and Shaquille O'Neal in smaller roles. This film was a moderate success because of its game sequence realism. *Jade* followed in 1995, starring David Caruso, Linda Fiorentino, and Chazz Palminteri, scripted by Joe Esterhaus. Again, this film flopped.

Rules of Engagement, released in 2000, fared better, though reviews were mixed. The film starred Tommy Lee Jones as Col. Childers, a highly decorated Marine who leads a rescue mission to the American Embassy in Yemen and orders his men to fire upon an angry group of armed street demonstrators. The cowardly ambassador who was rescued refuses to support Childers's account of the incident when Childers finds himself the target of an investigation and trial for murder. Samuel L. Jackson played Col. Hodges, whom Childers asks to serve as his defense attorney, who convinces the jury that the Marines fired upon the crowd out of self defense. Civilian and military prosecutors alike are all cardboard martinets, while Childers and Hodges are the grizzled patriots who know better than anybody else what the proper "rules of engagement" are. The film's right-wing, militaristic spin alienated some reviewers. His next project, *Night Train,* starring Ving Rhames, was still in production in 2000. New projects under consideration in 2000 were *The Diary of Jack The Ripper* and *The Sonny Liston Story.*

Friedkin has enjoyed a long but checkered directing career in film and television. Many of his best sequences derive from the handheld camera, especially in *The French Connection.* His definition of the director's job is to keep in his head the shape of the entire film, from setup to completed shots. He has yet to equal the early successes of *The French Connection* or *The Exorcist.* His first and best Hollywood lesson was "success has many fathers, but failure is an orphan."

Other Films *Deal of the Century* (1983); *The Twilight Zone,* TV series (1985); *Cat Squad,* TV (1986).

References Biskind, Peter, *Easy Riders, Raging Bulls* (New York: Simon and Schuster, 1998); Emery, Robert J., "William Friedkin," in *The Directors / Take Two* (New York: TV Books, 2000); Segaloff, Nat, *Hurricane Billy: The Stormy Life and Times of William Friedkin* (New York: Morrow, 1990).

—J.B.

Fulci, Lucio (1927–1996)   Notorious for his graphic excesses in violence and gore, Lucio Fulci was one of Italy's foremost directors of horror thrillers. Born into an impoverished family in Rome on July 17, 1927, Fulci was a studious youth who studied medicine until the expense of medical school forced him into a different direction. A lover of classic Italian cinema, Fulci switched to film school and studied under several of Italy's great film theorists and worked for filmmakers such as MAX OPHULS and Marcel L'Herbier.

In the early 1950s, Fulci worked as a screenwriter and assistant director on many popular Italian comedies, including *Un Americano a Roma,* featuring the comic genius, Toto. In 1959 Fulci made his directorial debut with *The Thieves.* Following this and an unsuccessful release of his next film *I Ladri,* a discouraged Fulci left the world of film to work with the well-known writer Ugo Pierro Vivarelli, collaborating on Italian rock-and-roll songs. His talent for composing eventually led him back into film directing with musical comedy, and over the next seven years, Fulci directed numerous films including *I Ragazzi del Juke Box* (*The Jukebox Kids*), *Urlatori alla Sbarra* (*Howlers of the Dock*), and *Agenti Segretissimi* (*The Worst Secret Agents*).

In 1966, with the film *Tempo di Massacro* (*The Brute and the Beast*), Fulci broke away from comedy, first making westerns and then, with *Una Sull'altra* (*Perversion Story*), a succession of successful thrillers. The thriller was new to Italian audiences and Fulci cashed in on their curiosity. Coming off his first major success, Fulci directed a medieval film entitled *Beatrice Cenci,* which flopped at the box office and had the audience shouting, "Kill the director," during one of its screenings. Lucio regarded *Beatrice Cenci* as one of his best, and a film too sophisticated for Italian audiences. Over the next eight years, Fulci directed 10 more films, most falling within the thriller genre. *Una Lucertola con la Pelle di Donna* (*Lizard in a Woman's Skin*) was one of the most notable; it featured the wizard Carlo Rambaldi, and represents Fulci's first foray into effects-based filmmaking. In 1972, Fulci released *Non si Sevizia un Paperino* (*Don't Torture the Duckling*), a biting political and religious satire; it won numerous awards and was very successful with the Italian public. Unfortunately for Fulci, a politician assumed the film was poking fun at him and had the director blacklisted for over two years. In 1977, Fulci directed his last thriller, *7 Notes in Nero* (aka *The Psychic*), which received a limited theatrical release in the United States and proved to be a major hit in Italy.

In 1979, Dario Argento's reedited edition of George Romero's *Dawn of the Dead* forever changed the face of Italian cinema. It was a film that ignited Italy's passion for producing low-budget horror and subsequently sparked Fulci's long-time career with the "walking dead." Based upon the financial success of *7 Notes in Nero,* Fulci teamed up with legendary film producer Fabrizio De Angelis to make *Zombie,* cashing in on Italy's zombie craze. Infused with a theme, the film grossed over $30 million and Fulci was established as a premier horror director. As a filmmaker, the ceaselessly imitative Fulci quickly learned what the genre was all about and came to be relied upon to dish out the gore with eye-popping virtuosity. Fulci's films were often weak on plot, but delivered some of the most graphic special effects ever experienced by a viewing audience, all choreographed in front of the camera (his films did not utilize computer-generated special effects). The typical Fulci fare included numerous throat slittings, decapitations, disembowelments, eye gouging, and cannibalism so intense that many of his films were not rated, causing problems with distribution and screening. The success of Fulci's *Zombie* forged a five-picture collaboration with De Angelis that led to such films as *Gatto* (*The Black Cat*), *Paura nela Citta dei Morti Viventi* (aka *The Gates of Hell*), and most notably *The Beyond,* a film that many consider to be Fulci's best. After the success of *The Beyond,* Fulci directed one more picture in collaboration with De Angelis, the notorious *Squartatore, di New York* (*The New York Ripper*). The film was a total disaster for both director and producer. Banned in many countries, Fulci had made a slasher film that both lost money and failed critically. Its unsatisfactory release and production nightmares put an end to the relationship with his best producer. Fulci went on to make 15 more horror films within a nine-year span, none of which had the impact of *The Beyond*.

Fulci died on March 3, 1996. The Italian film community and horror fans in general were shocked by the sudden loss. Fulci was three weeks away from going into production on *Wax House,* a collaboration with DARIO ARGENTO. Many considered the film to be the start of a new era for Fulci. But fans around the world were left to discover Fulci's talent within his previous body of work.

References McCarthy, John, *Splatter Movies* (New York: St. Martin's Press, 1984); McCarthy, John, *The Fearmakers* (New York: St. Martin's Press, 1994).

—B.M.

Fuller, Samuel (1911–1997) In his book on underground filmmakers and writers in postwar America, *American Noir,* author David Cochran writes, "In a series of low-budget movies made between 1949 and the mid-sixties, Sam Fuller staked out his vision of America, a world populated with pickpockets, prostitutes, safecrackers, infantry soldiers, assassins, and lunatics. In Fuller's view such figures represent the hope of America's redemption, constantly finding themselves pitted against hypocritical pillars of respectability, communist agents, and the internal contradictions of postwar American ideology. Throughout Fuller's oeuvre, the Cold War ethic of pluralism runs amok as a wide range of characters debate what it means to be an American and member of a viable community." Samuel Fuller was one of the true "mavericks" of American cinema, whose tabloid style of filmmaking exerted a tremendous influence on such filmmakers as MARTIN SCORSESE, QUENTIN TARANTINO, and JIM JARMUSCH.

Samuel Michael Fuller was born in Worcester, Massachusetts, on August 12, 1911. At the age of 13 he quit school and worked as a copyboy for the New York *Journal,* and within two years he became the personal copyboy of the tabloid's editor, Arthur Brisbane. Fuller accepted a position on the San Diego *Sun,* where he became one of the youngest crime reporters in the country. During the Great Depression his wanderlust took him across the country, and he wrote and published several pulp novels under various pseudonyms. In 1936 he moved to Los Angeles and sold his first script to the Boris Petroff film *Hats Off.* Fuller garnered his first screen credit for writing in 1938 for *Gangs of New York,* directed by James Cruze. Several other screenwriting efforts followed, with Fuller receiving coscript credit. In 1942 Fuller enlisted in the U.S. Army, serving as a corporal in the 16th Company of the U.S. Army Division First, commonly known as "the Big Red One," because of its distinctive shoulder insignia. During his term of service Fuller was wounded twice, receiving not only a Purple Heart, but also a Bronze Star and a Silver Star for his bravery in combat.

Fuller returned to Hollywood after his discharge. His novel *The Dark Page* had been purchased by HOWARD HAWKS, but was not filmed until 1952 under the title *Scandal Sheet.* Otherwise, although he was receiving steady work as a scriptwriter, Fuller felt that he was stagnating, primarily because none of his screenplays were reaching the production stage. In 1948 the independent Lippert Productions asked him to write a number of low-budget westerns. Fuller offered to work for scale in order to write and direct, thus ensuring production control over his own material. The company agreed and in 1949, Fuller began his career as a director with *I Shot Jesse James.* The film presented a unique twist on the outlaw legend from the perspective of Bob Ford (John Ireland), Jesse James's killer. In 1950 Fuller made the first fictional film concerning the Korean War, *The Steel Helmet;* made for under $100,000, it grossed over $6 million. The combat film starring Gene Evans (soon to be a Fuller regular) earned the director a contract with 20th Century-Fox. His first film at Fox was another combat feature, *Fixed Bayonets* (1951), not as successful as *The Steel Helmet.* Fuller set up his own production company, Samuel Fuller

Productions, in 1952. His first independent film was *Park Row* (1952), a story concerning the newspaper industry at the turn of the century. The film was a financial disaster, costing Fuller all his earnings from *The Steel Helmet*. In 1953 Fuller directed *Pickup on South Street*, starring Richard Widmark, at Fox. This classic film noir won the Bronze Lion Award at the Venice Film Festival.

In 1955 Fuller founded his second production company, Globe Enterprises. Fuller made six films for Globe, which were released through other distributors: *Run of the Arrow* (1957), for RKO; *China Gate* (1957), for 20th Century-Fox; *Forty Guns* (1957), for 20th Century-Fox; *Verboten!* (1958), for Globe; *The Crimson Kimono* (1959), for Columbia; and *Underworld U.S.A.* (1960), for Columbia. It was during this period of activity that the director gained the attention of the French journal, *Cahiers du cinéma*. In 1963 Fuller made two films, which, though generally regarded as his best work, led to his expulsion from the Hollywood studio system and his self-imposed exile in Europe. *Shock Corridor* is about a reporter who goes undercover in a mental institution in order to solve a murder case. Eventually the reporter himself goes mad. Beneath the surface of this melodramatic plotline was an indictment of American society in the postwar era. Likewise, *The Naked Kiss,* about a former prostitute who attempts to go straight in a small town, uncovered the hypocrisy of postwar America. According to David Cochran, "Fuller most fully stood in contrast to the dominant midcult sensibilities of cold-war America in his insistence on portraying the ugliness of life." Such a vision was completely opposite to mid-sixties Hollywood style. The public and critics alike vehemently attacked both of these films, and Fuller found himself shut out from Hollywood with no offers coming to direct further films.

In 1966 Fuller directed several television episodes for *The Iron Horse* (ABC), an hour-long western starring Dale Robertson and produced by Screen Gems. In 1968, after a sojourn to France where he appeared in Jean-Luc Godard's *Pierrot le fou* (1965), Fuller returned to the United States and directed the film *Shark!* The production was plagued by bad luck, including a Mexican stuntman who was killed during production. Fuller returned to Europe, where his film career was limited to acting in several projects. In 1980 Fuller made the *The Big Red One,* an autobiographical account of his experiences in World War II. The film starred Lee Marvin, Mark Hamill, and Robert Carradine and was shot primarily in Israel.

Throughout the rest of the decade Fuller's sporadic directorial projects were supplemented by his appearances in other director's films. In 1995 a documentary was released concerning the maverick director titled, *The Typewriter, The Rifle, and the Movie Camera.* After recovering from a stroke, Fuller returned to Hollywood, where his last film appearance was in Wim Wenders's *The End of Violence* (1997). Samuel Fuller died on October 30, 1997, in Hollywood, California.

Other Films *The Baron of Arizona* (1949); *Hell and High Water* (1953); *Merrill's Marauders* (1961).

References Cochran, David, *American Noir: Underground Writers and Filmmakers of the Postwar Era* (Washington, D.C.: Smithsonian Institution Press, 2000); Garnham, Nicholas, *Samuel Fuller* (London: Secker and Warburg, 1971); Hardy, Phil, *Samuel Fuller* (London: Studio Vista Limited, 1970); Server, Lee, *Sam Fuller: Film Is a Battleground.* (Jefferson, N.C.: McFarland, 1994); Tracey, Grant, "*Film Noir* and Samuel Fuller's Tabloid Cinema: Red (Action), White (Exposition), and Blue (Romance)," in *Film Noir Reader 2,* eds. Alain Silver and James Ursini (New York: Limelight Editions, 1999).

—R.W.

Gance, Abel (1889–1981) One of the most important figures in the development of cinema as an art, Abel Gance was born on October 25, 1889, in Paris, France. Until his death in Paris on November 10, 1981, at the age of 92, the director's account of his background as a child of the well-to-do French bourgeoisie was accepted as accurate. Subsequent research revealed that Gance was the illegitimate son of Abel Flamant, a prosperous Jewish physician, and Françoise Pèrethon, who was of the working class. The stigma of being both Jewish and illegitimate in a France where anti-Semitic and class prejudices still persisted, despite a revolutionary heritage, may help explain the rebellious, anti-aristocratic sentiments that would color much of his film work. Abel was raised by his maternal grandparents in the village of Commentry until he was eight. When his mother married Adolphe Gance, a chauffeur and mechanic who later became a taxi driver, Abel moved to Paris to live with them. Although he adopted his stepfather's surname, his natural father continued to provide for him and gave him the benefit of an excellent education. Given this stimulus, the youth began reading omnivorously and developed literary and theatrical ambitions at odds with his father's desire that he should take up the law.

Although he worked for a time in a law office, by the time he was 19, Gance had become an actor on the stage and in 1909 began working in the new medium of cinema as an actor and scriptwriter. In 1911, with the help of friends, Gance formed a production company and directed his first film, *La Digue (ou Pour sauver la Hollande),* a one-reel costume drama. He followed this with several other successful short narrative films noted for their rich lighting and décor. As with all of his silent features and a majority of his sound films, Gance also wrote the scripts. Yet he had not lost sight of his theatrical ambitions and authored *Victoire de Samothrace,* a play intended to star Sarah Bernhardt. But the outbreak of the First World War prevented its production, and Gance returned to filmmaking with the startling short, *La Folie du Docteur Tube* (1915). Working for the first time with cameraman Léonce-Henry Burel, Gance employed mirrors for the distorted effects in this avant-garde comedy about a mad doctor who is able to transform people's appearances through a special powder he has invented. In embryonic form, the film, however playfully, marks Gance's first excursion into the conception of a visionary able to transform reality and can also be read as an allegory of the cinema's special, magical properties.

Gance's next films were feature-length thrillers for Film d'Art in 1916, in which he introduced into French cinema the kind of editing style that had been developed in America by DAVID WARK GRIFFITH. And in some of them, like *Barberousse* (1916), he began devising his own technical innovations, including huge close-ups, low-angled close-ups, tracking shots, wipes, and the triptych effect.

In 1917, inspired by the French success of CECIL B[LOUNT] DEMILLE's *The Cheat,* Gance turned to society dramas in which the narrative centered on human emotions and psychological conflicts. The first of these was *Le Droit à la vie,* followed by *Mater Dolorosa,* the story of a woman's troubled marriage to a doctor. With its striking chiaroscuro photography, *Mater Dolorosa* scored a major box-office success, both in France and in other countries, including the United States. The series of society dramas culminated with a masterpiece, *La Dixième Symphonie* (1918), in which a composer's marital problems inspire him to write a symphony expressing his sufferings. Establishing the director as the new artistic leader of the French cinema, the narrative enabled him to comment on the nature of genius. The shots of enraptured listeners during the first performance of the composer's new symphony illustrate Gance's belief in the transformative power of art.

Gance's next work, *J'accuse* (1919), was his first epic film, a massive, deeply moving indictment of war. Profoundly affected by the horrors of the First World War, which had devastated France and taken the lives of many of his friends, Gance created a film that, upon its release soon after the Armistice, became the screen's first cry of revolt against the organized slaughter that had ravaged modern civilization from 1914 to 1918. In the film's famous climax, the hero, a poet, develops the mystic power to call back the ghosts of the war dead (played by real soldiers from the front, many of whom died in battle shortly after appearing in the sequence) to accuse the living and demand to know the reason for their sacrifice. Gance's use of rapid cutting, superimposition, masking, and a wildly tracking camera accentuates the intensely emotional blending of camera actuality and poetic drama. The film was a spectacular hit throughout Europe, and Gance, hoping for an American success, took it across the Atlantic, where he presented it at a special screening in New York in 1921 for an appreciative audience that included D. W. Griffith and the Gish sisters. But the U. S. distributors mutilated *J'accuse* for its subsequent general release, even distorting its antiwar message into an endorsement of conventional militaristic attitudes.

Gance's American journey was sandwiched in between his work on his second epic, *La Roue,* which he filmed during 1919–20 and completed final editing in preparation for its 1922 release upon his return from the United States. A monumental production 32 reels long and requiring three evenings for its original presentation, *La Roue* is a powerful drama of life among railroad workers, rich in psychological characterization and symbolic imagery. To dramatize his story of a railroad mechanic's tortured love for his adopted daughter, Gance elaborated his use of masking and superimposition and perfected his fast cutting into the rapid montage that would soon be adopted by Russian and Japanese silent filmmakers for whom *La Roue* was a seminal influence. Complex in its thematics, the film's images animate machines and the forces of nature with a life and spirit of their own while the wheel (*roue*) of the film's title becomes a metaphor for life itself. Gance's extraordinary symbolism is exemplified in the film's conclusion: as the old railway mechanic dies quietly and painlessly in his mountain chalet, his daughter joins the local villagers outside in the snow in a circular farandole dance, a dance in which nature itself, in the form of clouds, participates. Shot entirely on location at the railroad yards in Nice and in the Alps, *La Roue* remains a work of extraordinary beauty and depth. Jean Cocteau said of the film, "There is the cinema before and after *La Roue* as there is painting before and after Picasso," while

Akira Kurosawa stated, "The first film that really impressed me was *La Roue.*"

Gance climaxed his work in the silent era with *Napoléon,* an epic historical re-creation of Napoleon Bonaparte's early career during the French Revolution. A superspectacle, the film advanced the technique of cinematic language far beyond any single production of the decade. The definitive version originally ran over six hours in length, and its amazing innovations accomplished Gance's intent of making the spectator part of the action. To create this effect, Gance utilizes rapid montage and the handheld camera extensively. An example of his technique is the "double tempest" sequence in which shots of Bonaparte—on a small boat tossing in a stormy sea as huge waves splash across the screen—are intercut with a stormy session of the revolutionary Convention, at which the camera, attached to a pendulum, swings back and forth across the seething crowd. For the climax, Gance devised a special wide-screen process employing three screens and three projectors. He called this invention Polyvision, using the greatly expanded screen for both vast panoramas and parallel triptych images. As with *La Roue,* the film's unusual length enables Gance to develop his narrative fully, peopled with numerous characters, both historical and fictional, who bring to life the epoch of the late 1700s. The director began filming *Napoléon* in 1925 and finally unveiled his masterpiece to the world at a gala premiere at the Paris Opera in 1927. Although many of those who saw Gance's original cuts (both the six-hour version and a shorter one he supervised) recognized *Napoléon* as an unequaled artistic triumph, the film ultimately proved too technically advanced for the industry of its period. MGM, which bought international distribution rights, presented the film in Europe in various mangled and mutilated versions. Their American release, shown as sound was sweeping the industry in 1929, ran only 72 minutes and eliminated all of Gance's pyrotechnics. Although film historian KEVIN BROWNLOW's later

restoration would eventually establish for many *Napoléon*'s artistic preeminence, the film remains one of the cinema's controversial masterworks—due not only to a technique and scope that broke all the rules of filmmaking but also to Gance's admiring depiction of the young Bonaparte.

Gance portrayed Bonaparte as an idealistic, visionary leader championing the French Revolution, an interpretation characterized by some critics as "fascistic," but a conception that belies an informed consideration of Gance's personal history and beliefs, and one that ignores the fact that his 1927 film was only the first of a planned series of films on Napoleon's life. In the succeeding films, he had intended to depict Napoleon drifting more and more away from his revolutionary beginnings as he became an emperor. The heroic portrayal of the young Bonaparte in the film he did make is very much in the democratic Romantic tradition of great writers like Byron, Hugo, and Heine, who had exalted the Man of Destiny as the very embodiment of revolutionary energy. That Gance should view with sympathy a leader who did much to liberate European society from aristocratic and feudal privileges should come as no surprise, given the director's own "outsider" background. Gance's radical technique is thus wedded to a radical vision of history at odds with the classical restraint that had long held both social organization and aesthetics in check. Further underscoring the director's philosophy is his own memorable performance in the film as the "Archangel of the Revolution," the left-wing Jacobin leader, St. Just.

Gance pioneered the coming of sound in France in 1930 with another ambitious epic, *La Fin du monde,* an imaginative science fiction film with pacifist overtones in which a conflict-ridden world narrowly escapes destruction by an oncoming comet, with Gance himself playing the lead role of a scientist who foresees the catastrophe. After the film was slashed and reedited by the producers for its 1931 release, a discouraged Gance had to settle for directing and supervising less-ambitious projects over the next few years. In 1934, he attempted to bring back past glories by dubbing dialogue onto a revamped version of his silent *Napoléon,* adding another innovation, stereophonic sound. Within a year, his cinematic fortunes began to turn around and he directed a series of films that demonstrated once again his mastery of cinema. Although Gance's work in the sound era spanned over three decades, his talkies have often been dismissed as a long decline from the heights of his career in the silent era. While it is true he never again created works as ambitious as *La Roue* or *Napoléon,* it is clear, as François Truffaut pointed out, that he continued to explore characteristic themes in highly accomplished works revealing him to be as great a master of film form as he had been in the 1920s.

The first of his major sound films, *Lucrèce Borgia* (1935), is an astonishing drama of the political intrigues of the Borgia family in Renaissance Italy, with scenes of full-frontal female nudity that were a striking departure from the prevailing cinematic codes of the time. In his depiction of Cesare Borgia's brutal rule, Gance created a historical film whose figures stand in striking contrast to those in *Napoléon.* Whereas Bonaparte and the other French Revolutionary leaders pursue power in order to realize ideals, Cesare Borgia's ruthless drive for domination reflects no more exalted idea than the satisfaction of his own lust and self-aggrandizement. The people's aspirations for freedom, voiced by another farsighted leader, Savonarola, are also thwarted by the dictatorship of Cesare's corrupt father, Pope Alexander VI. In reflecting Gance's deeply rooted aversion to aristocratic rule, this portrayal of the Borgias' intrigues may represent a cinematic response to the French rightists of the 1930s who still yearned for a restoration of monarchy and aristocracy.

The following year, Gance directed one of his two greatest sound films, *Un grande amour de Beethoven,* a fictionalized biography of the composer (memorably portrayed by Harry Baur), in which Gance returned to his theme of creative genius and his conviction that artists are forever misunderstood by their contemporaries. By far his most technically innovative film since *Napoléon,* Gance blended rapid montage with sound, creating striking effects new to the medium. In the scenes culminating in Beethoven's composition of the *Pastoral* Symphony during a stormy night, Gance conveys the sense of Beethoven's oncoming deafness when the sound track is suddenly completely silent. Gance manifests his antipathy to aristocracy once again, contrasting Beethoven's artistic dedication and purity of spirit amidst poverty and neglect with the unworthy dilettante nobleman, Count Gallenberg, who marries the woman the composer loves. Released in 1937 to widespread international critical acclaim, *Beethoven* established Gance as just as great a leader in the creation of sound films as he had been in the silents.

Gance's next film, a new version of *J'accuse,* was his other monumental artistic triumph of the sound era. Although he included some battle-scene footage from the 1919 silent version and based several of the characters on those in the earlier production, the new *J'accuse* was essentially a different film, a reworking with new plot elements, rather than simply a remake. Released in 1938, the film's hero is yet another seer, a World War I veteran who develops an invention intended to prevent war. His plans are sabotaged by an unscrupulous politician and manufacturer, allied with the corrupt ruling establishment, who steals his invention and uses it not for peace but to foment war instead. In the awe-inspiring climax, Gance passionately denounces the coming Second World War, with his hero once again summoning forth the spirits of the war dead (played this time by mutilated veterans of the first conflagration) to indict the living at a time of renewed war hysteria.

In striking contrast, Gance's two 1939 films, *Louise* and *Le Paradis perdu,* mark a nostalgic return to the pre–World War I Paris of the director's youth. *Louise,* adapted from Gustave Charpentier's opera, with Grace Moore in the lead, allowed the director to incorporate cinematic techniques during the operatic sequences, such as images of a singing working class superimposed over awakening Paris streets, or the subtle play of light and shadow when Louise's father, gently swaying her back and forth, sings his aria. *Le Paradis perdu* includes both romantic lyricism and high comedy as it chronicles several generations. The story of a man whose happiness is destroyed by the First World War is especially poignant in its resemblance to Gance's own life and career and that of his country, both soon to be affected by yet another war.

Gance directed two films during the war, *La Vénus aveugle* (1941), a drama with feminist overtones, and *Le Capitaine Fracasse* (1942), an exhilarating swashbuckler, before the unsettled climate of a France menaced by the Germans forced him into a temporary sojourn in Spain, then ostensibly neutral. But there he encountered further difficulties, failing in his efforts to direct a film. Beset with hardships in postwar France, Gance struggled in vain to direct an epic film about the life of Christ, to be entitled *La Divine Tragédie.* After over a decade of absence from directing, he made *La Tour de Nesle,* a costume film released in 1954. He followed this with *Magirama,* a 1956 program featuring several shorts in which he revived his three-screen technique of Polyvision. For these experiments, he worked for the first time with Nelly Kaplan, a young admirer of his from Argentina, who later became a prominent director in her own right. Kaplan also assisted Gance on his last two theatrical features, *Austerlitz* (1960) and *Cyrano et d'Artagnan* (1963). Although a return to the Napoleonic saga, *Austerlitz* fell victim to studio interference so that, despite characteristic Gance touches, the finished product was far below his expectations. But the visually striking *Cyrano et d'Artagnan* proved to be an outstanding late work. This stylish swashbuckler with dialogue in Alexan-

drine verse, philosophical and psychological insights, and another heroic dreamer in the person of the poet and inventor Cyrano de Bergerac, was by far the best of Gance's postwar films.

In the years immediately succeeding *Cyrano et d'Artagnan,* Gance directed two films for French television, *Marie Tudor* (1965) and *Valmy* (1967), and in 1971 released a final revision of *Napoléon* retitled *Bonaparte and the Revolution,* for which he shot new footage to be added to the original silent work, creating a film less coherent than the original. Even so, his opportunities in his old age were sharply diminished. While his period of greatest productivity had ended in the early 1940s, all through the lean years he continued to be caught up in plans for new cinematic innovations and dreams for fresh epic projects. The unrealized *Le Divine Tragédie* had itself derived from a series of films on the founders of the world's great religions, *Les Grands Initiés,* which he had conceived decades before as a means to promote peace and brotherhood. In 1939 he did extensive research for an epic film about Christopher Columbus, but the outbreak of World War II scuttled his immediate plans for the film. Nevertheless, he returned to the idea, writing an elaborate screenplay for the Columbus film. Indeed, in his last years, his attempts to raise funds to direct the film became his consuming passion. These later years of unfulfilled dreams were marked by persistent poverty. He continued to share his life with his third wife, Odette (Sylvie?) Vérité, whom he married in 1933 and who died in 1978. His first marriage was to Mathilde Thizeau in the 1910s, and his second, in the 1920s, to Marguerite Danis, who also acted in films, including *Napoléon* and Jean Epstein's *The Fall of the House of Usher* (1928).

The adversities of his last years were somewhat alleviated by the work of film historians, especially Kevin Brownlow, who brought him to the attention of a new generation with his documentary on the director, *The Charm of Dynamite,* and his history of the silent film, *The Parade's Gone By* (1968).

In a final twist of irony worthy of his films, Gance received his greatest recognition at the very end of his life, when Brownlow's restoration of the silent *Napoléon* was theatrically revived around the world with live orchestras in 1980–81. The *Napoléon* revival of the early 1980s, besides heralding a new-found interest in silent films as a whole, seemed to augur a full though belated critical and popular recognition of Gance, particularly in the United States, where the mutilation of his work by commercial interests in earlier decades had hindered his reputation.

Yet, despite initial rhapsodic reviews of *Napoléon* in the popular press, some critics, instead of expressing regret that Gance had not received his due during his lifetime, sought to justify his treatment at the hands of the industry and earlier critics. They recycled the argument that his techniques were overblown self-indulgence, that he had little of real importance to say, and this his long career in the sound era was an unmitigated decline. Perhaps worst of all, these critics soon turned to the kind of ideological axe-grinding that had also damaged Griffith's reputation. Although Gance was far from being a highly political artist and, as Steven Kramer maintained, was "only consistent within his own semi-mystical framework," the director's critics began inferring that his admiration for visionary heroes like Bonaparte reflected some sort of protofascist agenda. The line of attack apparently succeeded in dampening enthusiasm for any sustained revival of Gance's work in the United States. Although more of his films are now available on video, there has been no full retrospective of Gance's work outside France in the two decades since his death and the *Napoléon* revival. The restored versions of his three silent epics—*J'accuse, La Roue,* and the even more complete *Napoléon* (expanded beyond the shortened Coppola version)—never became accessible to American film devotees. Despite this comparative neglect, Gance remains one of the greatest directors in film history, a genius whose artistic courage and romantic, humanist vision created major works of cinema while inspiring many other directors, from his silent-film contemporaries to the French *nouvelle vague* of the 1950s and later. This pioneer invented Polyvision, a precursor of Cinerama (*Écran panoramique triple de l'écran ordinaire, polyvision et écran variable,* patented in 1926), Perspective Sound (*Perspective sonore,* patented in 1929, improved in 1932), and the *Pictographe* (1938). The failure of the critical establishment to recognize or fully appreciate Gance's artistry has been a shameful oversight that succeeding generations will surely rectify.

Other Films *Mater Dolorosa/Le Serment* (1934); *Le Maître de forges* (1933); *Poliche* (1934); *La Dame aux Camélias* (1934); *Le Roman d'un jeune homme pauvre* (1935); *Jérôme Perreau, héro des barricades* (1936); *Le Voleur de femmes* (1936); *Quatorze Juillet* (1953).

References Brownlow, Kevin, *The Parade's Gone By* (New York: Alfred A. Knopf, 1968); Brownlow, Kevin, *Napoleon: Abel Gance's Classic Film* (New York: Alfred A. Knopf, 1983); Welsh, James M., and Steven Philip Kramer, *Abel Gance* (Boston: Twayne, 1978).

—W.M.D.

Godard, Jean-Luc (1930–) Jean-Luc Godard, the guiding spirit of the French *nouvelle vague* of the 1960s, is the cinema's most famous revolutionary. The international impact of Godard's *Breathless* (aka *A Bout de souffle* [1960]) offered a challenge to the tenets of the "classic Hollywood film" that had a lasting impact on the history of world cinema. As critic, theorist, and filmmaker, Godard's personal project, spanning four decades, has been nothing less than to redefine the very nature of the cinema's content and form.

Jean-Luc Godard was born in Paris into an upper-middle-class Protestant family on December 3, 1930. While a student at the Sorbonne, he attended the *Ciné-Club du Quartier Latin* more regularly than his university classes. While attending film programs at the *Ciné-Club,* the young

Godard met Jacques Rivette and ERIC ROHMER. In 1950, the three would found *La Gazette du Cinéma,* a monthly film journal that lasted five issues. Two years later Godard started writing film criticism for *Cahiers du cinéma* and *Amis du Cinéma.* In addition to film criticism, he wrote also theoretical essays on the nature of the cinema, one titled "Towards a Political Cinema" extolling the political engagement of the Soviet cinema in which he declared, "No doubt only Russia feels at this moment that the images moving across its screens are those of its own destiny." In another essay, Godard decries that, in the modern world, "we have forgotten how to see." The quest for a cinema that will allow us to see again will inform all of Godard's own films.

Between October 1952 and August 1956, Godard took a respite from his writing to travel and, for a while, labor as a construction worker in Switzerland. Meanwhile, he used the money he made as a worker to make his first short, 20-minute film, *Operation Beton.* In 1957, he returned to Paris and became a regular contributor to both *Arts* magazine and *Cahiers du cinéma.* As Godard later said, "All of us at *Cahiers* thought of ourselves as future directors." Between August 17 and September 15, 1959, Godard took leave of his writing to shoot his first feature film, from a screenplay by fellow *Cahiers* critic François Truffaut, *Breathless.*

In making *Breathless,* Godard said, "what I wanted was to take a conventional story and remake, but differently, everything the cinema had done. I also wanted to give the feeling that the techniques of film-making had just been discovered or experienced for the first time." The "conventional" story involves a petty thief become cop killer, Michel Poiccard (Jean-Paul Belmondo), who fancies himself a Bogart-like romantic hero. Michel has a brief affair with an American expatriate (Jean Seberg). They talk; they make love; they talk some more; she betrays him to the police. But Godard tells his "conventional" story "differently" as a fragmented and elliptical narrative, with an

iconoclastic camera and editing style employing a handheld camera, jump-cutting, flash-shots, and a disregard for continuity.

Godard's second film, *The Little Soldier (Le Petit soldat* [1960]), generated political controversy due to its criticism of the French-Algerian war. The film was scheduled for release in the fall of 1960, but was banned for two years by the French Censorship Board. In 1961, Godard made his third film, *A Woman Is a Woman (Une Femme est une femme),* starring Jean-Paul Belmondo and Anna Karina (whom Godard married that year). The wife wants to have a baby; the husband does not. When the husband accuses his wife of using trickery to get her way, accusing her of being "dishonorable," she counters, "No, I am a woman." During the period of Godard's marriage to Karina, a number of his films would explore the difficulties of married love and the impossibility of men and women communicating with each other, as in *The Little Soldier, My Life to Live (Vivre sa vie* [1962]), *Band of Outsiders (Bande à part* [1964]), *Pierrot le fou* (1965), and *Alphaville* (1965). After a tempestuous marriage, Godard and Karina were divorced in 1965. Two years later, he married actress Anne Wiazemsky.

Masculin féminin (1966) continued to meld charming moments with hard-edged cultural analyses of the new generation coming to age in the 1960s, the children of "Marx and Coca-Cola." As Godard's work progressed through the second half of the 1960s, his films became less narrative and increasingly took on the form of filmed philosophical and political essays. In *Made in USA* (1966), *La Chinoise* (1967), and *Weekend* (1967), traditional narrative takes second place to lengthy monologues on a wide range of political subjects. *Made in USA* (1966) employs a fictional story of a woman's attempt to discover the identity of her lover's murderer as a pretext for an exploration of the Ben Barka murder and the assassination of John F. Kennedy. In *La Chinoise,* Godard declares his sole allegiance to an "agit-prop" aesthetic. The film depicts five middle-class Parisian Maoists as they plot their first terrorist attack. At one point, the hero, Guillaume (Jean-Pierre Léaud), stands at a blackboard that lists the names of influential writers and artists, which he erases one at a time until only the name "Brecht" is left.

As the political crisis in France intensified during the spring of 1968, Godard all but abolished narrative altogether in an attempt to reinvent a revolutionary cinema capable of inciting revolutionary action. In *Joyful Wisdom* (*Le Gai savoir* [1968]), two filmmakers, played by Jean-Pierre Leaud and Juliet Berto, sit in a television studio and try to reinvent a language of images and sound. As the film director played by Yves Montand says in *Tout va bien* (1972), the cinema must search for "new forms for new contents."

In the midst of the May Uprising, Godard left France for London to begin filming *One Plus One,* also titled *Sympathy for the Devil* (1969). In the film, the Rolling Stones are shown recording their album *Beggar's Banquet;* a figure representing liberal democracy, named Eve Democracy (Anne Wiazemsky), wanders through the streets of London writing political slogans on walls. These scenes are intercut with the revolutionary activities of a Black Power group juxtaposed with a bookseller who publishes pornography and reads *Mein Kampf* while inciting his customers to harass Jews.

In 1971, Godard was involved in a serious motorcycle accident, which marked a turning point in his life and work. During his rehabilitation, Godard divorced Wiazemsky and married the woman who had been his working partner for the past 30 years, Anne-Marie Miéville. He also grew disillusioned by his earlier hortatory embrace of Maoism. *Tout va bien* (1972) was seen as something of an apology for the Marxist reductionism of his earlier films. The film concerns a disillusioned film director (Yves Montand) who stops making films after the Paris Uprising of 1968 only to end up making TV commercials for a living.

Between 1974 and 1978, Godard and Miéville moved to Rolle, Switzerland, and worked together on three experimental films and two video series. In the late 1970s, Miéville urged Godard to return to more mainstream filmmaking. *Every Man for Himself* (*Sauve qui peut la vie* [1980]) continued Godard's experimentation with cinematic form; however, it once again relied on characters and story. Much of the film is autobiographical. A filmmaker named Paul Godard follows his girlfriend, also a filmmaker, to a new life in the Swiss country. Godard has refered to it as his "second first film." It was also his most commercially successful film besides *Breathless.*

During the 1980s, Godard reestablished his reputation as a director of innovative feature-length films. *First Name: Carmen* (*Prénom: Carmen* [1983]) won the Golden Lion at the Venice Film Festival, and Godard's 1985 *Hail, Mary* (*Je vous salue, Marie*) generated controversy (and publicity) when religious groups protested the filmmaker's modern retelling of the Immaculate Conception. Mary is a basketball-playing teenager who pumps gas at her father's filling station, Joseph is a cab driver, and the archangel Gabriel is an unshaven bum. As critic Jack Ellis observed, "To many it was 'shocking and profoundly blasphemous'; to others it was a continuation of Godard's recurrent meditations on the alluring mystery of woman and her ultimate strangeness, which he began with *Breathless* and *A Woman Is a Woman* twenty-five years earlier."

In 1985 Godard began a film collaboration with novelist Norman Mailer for a film based on *King Lear.* A character named William Shakespeare, Jr. (Burgess Meredith), seeks to recover the works of his ancestor, which have been lost in the technological holocaust of Chernobyl. Writing in the *New Yorker,* Richard Brody noted that "True to Godard's later style, the film's real story is precisely how to tell the story, or whether it is in fact possible to do so."

Godard continues to seek new ways to tell a story and, if "it is in fact possible to do so," releasing three films in 2001—*After the Reconciliation, The Old Place,* and *In Praise of Love*—as well as five hours of an eight-part series of meditations on filmmaking titled *Histoire(s) du Cinéma.*

Other Films *The Riflemen* (*Les Carabiniers* [1963]); *Contempt* (*Le Mépris* [1963]); *Letter to Jane* (1972); *Passion* (1982).

References Brody, Richard, "Profiles: An Exile in Paradise," *New Yorker,* November 20, 2000, pp. 62–76; MacCabe, Colin, *Godard: Images, Sounds, Politics* (Bloomington: Indiana University Press, 1980); Narboni, Jean, and Tom Milne, eds., *Godard on Godard* (New York: Viking Press, 1972); Sterritt, David, *The Films of Jean-luc Godard* (Cambridge, U.K.: Cambridge University Press, 1999).

—T.P.

Greenaway, Peter (1942–) One of cinema's most relentlessly formalistic directors, Peter Greenaway reduces sex, violence, and politics to the grids of numbers, letters, and patterns. "I want to regard my public as infinitely intelligent," he has said, "as understanding notions of the suspension of disbelief and as realizing all the time that this is not a slice of life, this is openly a film." For the films of Peter Greenaway, this statement may be of assistance in understanding this highly artistic director whose list of films includes *A Walk Through H* (1978), *The Draughtsman's Contract* (1982), *The Belly of an Architect* (1987), and *The Cook, the Thief, His Wife, and Her Lover* (1989).

Born in 1942 in Newport, Wales, Greenaway informed his parents at the age of 12 that he intended to be a painter. He bypassed a university education and went to the Walthamstow College of Art, which considerably disappointed his family who believed his artistic endeavors were worthless. In 1965, he began work as a film editor for the Central Office of Information, where he spent 11 years cutting films that were designed to portray the intricacies of the British way of life through numbers and statistics. It has been argued that this was Greenaway's greatest stylistic influence, though Greenaway himself states that one of his

primary influences is his desire to "dump" narrative considerations. According to Greenaway, if you want to tell a story, you should be a writer; the vocabulary of the cinema should no longer be used for the sole purpose of telling stories. In sum, the cinema has much to offer *outside* the slavery of the narrative. However, Greenaway has also stated that he wants to make mainstream movies: "I don't want to be an underground filmmaker; I want to make movies for the largest possible audience, but arrogantly, I want to make them on my terms."

Listing, organizing, counting, and tabling are primary themes in many of Peter Greenaway's films. The director feels that when you name a thing, you possess it. He is fascinated by the lists present in 19th-century science and 20th-century literature and the seriousness with which they were created. Greenaway acknowledges that such list-making is ephemeral, in that it is an attempt at an ownership and a comprehension that cannot be obtained. Moreover, his films are often rife with full frontal nudity, referencing painterly traditions of the nude in art history. Greenaway states that the loss of physicality would preface the loss of perspective over all the other senses.

Peter Greenaway has been significantly influenced by television and has described his film approach as influenced by the language of television. He often employs the use of the smaller frame within the larger frame along with the shifting of color schemes, as evident in some of his best-known films, like *Prospero's Books* (1991—an astonishing attempt to adapt Shakespeare's *The Tempest* to the screen, word for word, and to visualize the text itself in boxlike inserts—and *The Draughtsman's Contract,* wherein the world is viewed through the device of the artist's optical grid. Indeed, *Prospero's Books* is one of his most densely layered visual experiences. In his article about the film, "Anatomy of a Wizard," Howard A. Rodman takes inventory: "Actors vie for screen space with superimposed calligraphy, Muybridge-like animatics and all manner of body parts. Greenaway's trademark long lateral tracking shots—now a seminaked woman skipping rope, now a tableau from Hals or Vermeer, now a very young boy urinating with gleeful (artificially enhanced?) abandon into a swimming pool where Sir John [Gielgud] is bathing—compete for attention with cadenced drops of water, rhythmically pulsing balls of fire and, above all, the lovingly rendered scrape of pen against parchment." As with many Greenaway films, reaction to each of these supposedly accessible films was mixed upon their release.

His most commercially successful film, *The Cook, the Thief, His Wife, and Her Lover,* centers around the lives of the Thief (played by Michael Gambon), an abusive, violent, and perverse man whose Wife (Helen Mirren) endures the brunt of his abuses until she happens upon a quiet and unassuming man (her Lover) and begins an affair with him in a restaurant with the aid of the Cook, the owner of the restaurant and a perfectionist, forever seeking a new culinary challenge. The film is visually stunning, to the point of extravagance, as costume, set, and character are lit with the lush color of each room: red for the dining room, white for the bathroom, and green for the kitchen. According to Greenaway, the restaurant is a microcosm of our modern, consumerist society. People like the Thief and the Wife go to restaurants to see and be seen as much as to eat. The setting and characters underline the gluttony and excess of this consumerist society. This theme of consumption is the focal point of the film—firstly as the Thief gorges like a pig at the table, secondly as he force-feeds the Lover to his death, and finally, as the Thief himself is forced to consume his own evil doings. As empathetic a character as the Wife is, she is not the passive and victimized character the viewer assumes, for by the conclusion of the film, it is she who takes action to put an end to all the torment by providing the crucial solution to her own suffering.

The Pillow Book (1996) is a story of a fetish and the hold it maintains on a young woman. Nagiko, the female protagonist in this film, is presented

each birthday with a passage from the Pillow Book, the diary of Sei Sho-Nagon, lady in waiting to the imperial court during the Heian Dynasty. The characters of the text are painted on her face and neck by her father, a calligrapher. The smell of the ink and the act of the painting are intertwined, for Nagiko, with the blackmailing of her father, who is forced by his publisher to be the man's sexual slave. Eventually, Nagiko is forced to marry the publisher's son, who burns her books and diaries, resulting in Nagiko's move to Hong Kong. There, she becomes a model and is obsessed with inscribing calligraphy on her body, first executed by herself and then by a series of lovers. Finally she meets the young Englishman, Jerome (Ewan McGregor), with whom she falls in love. He opens a new world for Nagiko by asking that she decorate him, in effect making the woman who would be paper into a pen. In a tragic twist, Jerome is also the lover of a man, the same publisher of her father now operating out of Hong Kong. Nagiko sends her explicit poetry to the publisher by way of Jerome's skin, and the poetry is rejected. Jerome dies in what was to be a suicide attempt, his body exhumed by the publisher, and the poems published in an elegant book. The stated purpose of the film, in Greenaway's ever-artistic and experimental style, is to mesh flesh with text, sex with literature. Style and story are fused expertly in the film as Japanese characters scroll down the movie screen and frames beget frames, within which human skin becomes paper and flesh becomes literature.

The intersections of looking and seeing, observation and comprehension stand at the core of Greenaway's wickedly melodramatic *The Draughtsman's Contract* (1982). The action is set in the 17th century in an English manor where sex, betrayal, and murder run rampant. Dissatisfied with his marriage, a landowner (Dave Hill) leaves his estate to take a two-week vacation alone. In an attempt to save the relationship, his wife asks a draughtsman (Anthony Higgins) to paint 12 pictures of their estate from 12 different vantage points as a surprise gift. The draughtsman consents but only if the wife agrees to another contract, i.e., to provide him with daily sexual favors. The daughter of the family becomes sexually involved with the draughtsman as well, and the debauchery carries on until one day the lord of the manor is found dead in the moat. The draughtsman is suspected, and he tries to defend himself by noting that the clues to the real murderer's identity may be found in his paintings (executed by Greenaway himself). The draughtsman has scrupulously painted everything within the frame of his optical grid during his daily sittings, including tell-tale details of a murderous conspiracy, i.e., a ladder balanced against a window, a garment flung over a hedge, etc. But he records only what is *seen* and not what is *known* (the difference between observation and knowledge). He perishes at the hands of assassins. "The draughtsman comes to grief," notes commentator Alan Woods, "because, well aware of the relations between property and image, he remains satisfied with drawings in which objects are represented as if in an inventory. . . . Within the spaces which he records, are, however, objects as symbols, clues regarding murder or adultery. He is drawing stage sets, filled not with property, but with properties, but he will not or cannot recognize this. . . ." This offbeat film is a witty and baroque exercise in color, décor, and costume. The film was praised not only for its mesmerizing photography and costume but also for the elegantly rambunctious musical score by Michael Nyman.

The less-accessible films of Greenaway are said to require a doctorate in semiotics to be understood. Of these, perhaps the most widely known is the early film, *A Walk Through H* (1978), financed by the British Film Institute. It details, in a nonlinear manner, the deciphering of the connection between various books, birds, and objets d'art. The film journeys through a series of 92 maps and 1,418 species of birds presented by Tulse Luper (Greenaway's alter ego appearing or referenced in numerous films), who states that the time to decide what H stands for is at the end of the journey, at which time its meaning will scarcely matter. Order and chaos are held in an equipoise. "Order, in Greenaway's work," writes Alan Woods, "—his films, his writings, his pictures, his exhibitions—is always linked to absurdity and human vanity." However, continues Woods, "Order, in the world, is mocked by disorder and decay, counting is helpless in the face of the countless things to count; this is what we are reminded of by Greenaway's organizing principles and counting games, because their arbitrary and whimsical nature is foregrounded." Less adulatory is critic Julian Bell's assessment that much of Greenaway's work is much ado about nothing, that beneath his fascinating and intricate surfaces are the "banal" propositions that humans are "bodies driven by biology" and that "any representation (by men, maps, films, etc.) always traduces or is inadequate to the reality (of women, nature, the body, etc.)." Thus, his "intricate conceits" are hollow; "the hollowness lies in his wishing to push them forward as if they were urgent, unacknowledged truths."

Greenaway's latest film, *8½ Women* (1999), details the experiences of a father, distraught over the recent death of his wife, whose son encourages him to rediscover his sexual being by opening a bordello. The idea is taken directly from Fellini's 1963 film, *8½*. Among the members of the "harem" are Kito, the strong but repressed business woman; Palmira, the spiritual woman who is more attracted to the aging widower than his young son; and Giulietta, the simple but mysterious woman with amputated legs, which factor into the title along with the homage to Fellini and the significance that this is Greenaway's eighth-and-a-half feature film. The themes of *8½ Women* include sexual power, miscommunication between men and women, the inevitability of chance, and art as a metaphor for both human form and human existence.

Greenaway is about to embark on the most ambitious project of his life, *The Tulse Luper Suitcase,* in which the director will use the full battery of techniques that can be brought to the screen. This alter ego was created by Greenaway himself years ago—Tulse to rhyme with pulse and Luper, the Latin word for wolf, meaning the wolf on your pulse. This life work is an 18-hour-long project that starts by discussing American fascism in 1933 Utah and finishes at the end of the Cultural Revolution in China. It is also a project about the history of the 92nd element, uranium, which Greenaway calls the ultimate American treasure, and which is being buried again now, at the end of the cold war. There are 92 suitcases that have to be packed and unpacked in the film, and a great many games are played with the letter "U" in USA and the "u" in uranium. *The Tulse Luper Suitcase* project has involved the production of a film a year over a span of four years, a 52-part television series, two back-to-back CD-ROMs, a book, and possibly an exhibition at the Guggenheim Museum. Another aspect involves the rewriting of the *Arabian Nights.* The 1,001 tales will be posted on the internet, one every night, just as Scheherezade related them to the Sultan.

Greenaway has long been merging art with the cinema, cinema with technology, technology with ritual and obsession. His works move beyond cinema into the other arts with his various painting exhibitions and, recently, the production of an opera. According to the director himself, "Creation to me, is to try to orchestrate the universe to understand what surrounds us. Even if, to accomplish that, we use all sorts of stratagems which in the end prove completely incapable of staving off chaos."

Other Films *Train* (1966); *Tree* (1966); *5 Postcards from Capital Cities* (1967); *Revolution* (1967); *Love Love Love* (1968); *Intervals* (1969); *Erosion* (1971); *Coastline* (1971); *H Is for House* (1973); *Windows* (1974); *Water* (1975); *Water Wrackets* (1975); *Dear Phone* (1976); *Goole by Numbers* (1976); *One to One Hundred* (1978); *Eddie Kid* (1978); *Vertical Features Remake* (1978); *Zandra Rhoades* (1979); *The Falls* (1980); *Terrence Conran* (1981); *A Zed and Two Noughts* (1985); *The Belly of an Architect* (1987); *Drowning by Numbers* (1988); *Fear of Drowning* (1988); *Hubert Bals Handshake* (1988); *A Walk Through Prospero's Library* (1991); *Rosa* (1992); *The Baby of Macon* (1993); *Death of a Composer* (1999).

References Bell, Julian, "Lights, action, Darwin," *Times Literary Supplement,* February 27, 1998, p. 36; Corliss, Richard, "I Paint the Body Erotic, Peter Greenaway's Latest Film Transforms Creative Writing into a Living Art," *Time International,* March 10, 1997, p. 46; Howe, Desson, "The Greenaway Effect," *Washington Post,* May 26, 2000, p. 52; Rodman, Howard, A., "Anatomy of a Wizard," *American Film,* November–December 1991, pp. 35–39; Simon, John, "Movie Reviews," *National Review* 49 (July 14, 1997): 53; Woods, Alan, *Being Naked and Playing Dead: The Art of Peter Greenaway* (New York: St. Martin's Press, 1997), pp. 35–42.

—K.L.R.

Grierson, John (1898–1972)

John Grierson is a towering figure in the development of the motion picture documentary in Britain, America, and Canada. He was born on April 18, 1898, in Deanston, Scotland, the son of a Scots schoolmaster. He studied at Glasgow University, where he took a degree in philosophy in 1923. After military service in the Royal Navy during World War I, he came to Chicago in 1924 on a research grant in social sciences. Dismayed at the apathy he saw all around him, disturbed at what he regarded as the failure of the American "melting pot," yet encouraged by the role the American popular press was playing in the education and assimilation of foreign immigrants, he formulated a mission in life—nothing less than the moral and political education of the citizenry by means of the motion picture. "I look on cinema as a pulpit," he declared.

His meeting with documentary pioneer ROBERT JOSEPH FLAHERTY was a turning point in his life. Hailing his films—he coined the term "documentary" in reaction to Flaherty's *Moana*—

he developed a love-hate relationship with the man. He acknowledged Flaherty's position as the "father of the documentary," yet he deplored his seeming obsession with filming the remote and the primitive to the exclusion of contemporary life, what Grierson described as "the drama of the doorstep." Another major influence came Grierson's way while in New York, when he helped prepare SERGEI EISENSTEIN's *Potemkin* (1926) for its New York debut. The editing techniques by the visionary Russian would quickly become a part of Grierson's cinematic vocabulary.

In 1927 he was back in England and associated with the Empire Marketing Board, whose mission was to promote trade and unity among the various parts of the British Empire. Convinced that the motion picture could play a key role in this mission, he made his first film, *Drifters* (1929), a gritty depiction of life among the herring fishermen of the North Sea. Apart from the Flaherty model, *Drifters* had no interest in picturesque traditions and quaint fishing villages. Rather, it declared that the modern fishing industry had become "an epic of steam and steel," and its final scenes depicted the quayside auctioning of the catch and its injection into international trade.

After the success of *Drifters*, Grierson increasingly assumed the role of creative organizer of his pictures, rather than of hands-on director. Entering into his most fertile and productive period, he formed his own EMB Film Unit. His organizational skills and sympathy for the working class enabled him to find finances for his projects while, at the same time, shield his workers from bureaucratic interference. By the mid-1930s the Film Unit had collected an outstanding team of talented young filmmakers, including Stuart Legg, Paul Rotha, ALBERTO CAVALCANTI, and Basil Wright. Even Robert Flaherty worked at the unit for a short time (on *Industrial Britain*).

A committed leftist, Grierson avoided pretentious aestheticism in favor of working-class propaganda and exposés of inadequate educational systems and poor slum conditions. Art is a hammer, not a mirror, he insisted. Films like *Housing Problems* and *Coal Face* (1935–36) urged reform of working and living conditions. The British government, on the other hand, grew suspicious of these "communist" leanings, preferring that EMB deliver a more supportive picture of working-class conditions.

The EMB Unit was dissolved in 1934, and Grierson moved on with his team to the General Post Office. This bureau was not just a post office, but a kind of communication ministry trying to develop the mediums of wireless, radio, and television. Important GPO productions (released through the Gaumont-British studio) included *Song of Ceylon* (1935), a poetic examination of the impact of the tea trade on the country of Ceylon, and *Night Mail* (1936), director Harry Watt's classic chronicle of the mail-train routes between Edinburgh and London. *Housing Problems* and *Workers and Jobs* (1935) were innovative in that they took microphones to the workers so that they could talk directly into the camera about the problems of their daily lives and rat-infested environment.

After resigning from the GPO in 1937, Grierson set up the Film Centre, which did not produce films but developed nontheatrical distribution outlets for documentary movies. A year later he went to Canada to help coordinate legislative support for that country's film production. Accordingly, the National Film Act was passed in 1939, and Grierson was elected as Canada's film commissioner. The result of his activities was the National Film Board of Canada, which was fully operating by the end of World War II. Grierson's ambition was to use films to reach the scattered population of Canada, particularly the territories to the west. At one time, 30 mobile film units took to the road and screened films for local citizens. Friends and colleagues were called in to support the mission, including Stuart Legg, Joris Ivens, Boris Kaufman, and NORMAN MCLAREN. The

NFB stands as the most impressive and active monument to Grierson's vision of the use of film by governments in communicating with their citizens.

After the war, Grierson left the board and went to New York City. He was increasingly assailed by attacks from the right against films that allegedly favored communist-dominated unions. In 1947 he went to Paris as director of mass communications and public information for UNESCO. In the years after 1955, he returned to Scotland, where he worked for television and the Films of Scotland Committee. He died on February 19, 1972.

In the assessment of historian Jack C. Ellis, Grierson's great value lies in his "multi-faceted, innovative leadership in film and in education." Moreover, "As a theoretician he articulated the basis of the documentary film, its form and function, its aesthetic and its ethic. As a teacher he trained and, through his writing and speaking, influenced many documentary filmmakers, not only in Britain and Canada, but throughout the world."

Other Films As producer: *The New Generation* (1932); *Cargo from Jamaica* (1933); *Granton Trawler* (1934); *Children at School* (1937); *The Face of Scotland* (1938); *Judgment Deferred* (1951); *Man of Africa* (1953).

References Ellis, Jack C., *The Documentary Idea* (Englewood Cliffs, N.J.: Prentice-Hall, 1989); Hardy, Forsyth, ed., *Grierson on Documentary* (New York: Harcourt, Brace, 1947); MacCann, Richard Dyer, *The People's Films* (New York: Hastings House, 1973).

—J.C.T.

Griffith, David Wark (1875–1948)

Recognized throughout the world as the single most important individual in the development of film as an art, D. W. Griffith was born on January 22, 1875, in Crestwood, Kentucky, to a middle-aged couple, Jacob Wark Griffith and Mary Perkins Oglesby, whose fortunes had suffered in the aftermath of the South's defeat. The elder Griffith was a Confederate Civil War veteran and Kentucky legislator, but he died when David was 10 years old, leaving a legacy of debt and poverty. By the time Griffith was 14 years old, his family was forced to abandon their unproductive farm for a new life in Louisville, where his mother opened a boarding house, an undertaking that soon failed. Griffith left high school to help provide for the family, taking a job in a dry-goods store, and, later, in a bookstore, which became his "university," exposing him to the world of ideas.

Fired with an ambition to become a playwright, Griffith began working on the stage in Louisville at the age of 20 and was soon touring in stock companies. For a decade he alternated work on the stage with manual labor, holding a variety of jobs as he continued to write. Griffith and his young actress wife, whom he had married in 1906, then turned to the new motion picture industry for their livelihood. Griffith began his work in motion pictures near the end of 1907 by playing the lead in *Rescued from an Eagle's Nest,* directed by EDWIN S. PORTER for the Edison Company and released in early 1908. Griffith soon moved to the Biograph Company in New York City, where he both acted in films and provided stories.

When Biograph's chief director became ill, Griffith was hired as a replacement. With the release of his first film, *The Adventures of Dollie,* in the summer of 1908, a new, decisive chapter in cinema history began. For the next five years, Griffith, working in anonymity as the studio refused to publicize the names of its talents, directed hundreds of mostly one-reel films for Biograph that reshaped the very language of film. In film after film, Griffith broke with the stagy, unimaginative approach to screen narrative still prevailing in the industry. Working in partnership with his brilliant cameraman, G. W. "Billy" Bitzer, Griffith demonstrated a singular genius in developing camera effects and movement, lighting, close-ups, and editing into a coordinated cinematic technique that gave motion pictures their basic grammar and transformed film into an art form. But Griffith's genius went far beyond technical tricks. His use of close-ups and medium shots enabled the spectator to empathize with the emotions expressed by the characters; his rhythmic editing style intensified the drama; his panoramic long shots created an impression of epic grandeur; and his innovations in lighting, with the help of Bitzer, added mood and aesthetic quality to the images. Placing great value on the use of locations for the realism he sought to heighten the drama, Griffith was one of the first filmmakers to work in Hollywood, when in 1910 he began annually taking his company from New York to California for seasonal filming.

Griffith built a stock company of young actors and actresses that included Mary Pickford, Blanche Sweet, Mae Marsh, Lillian and Dorothy Gish, Robert Harron, Henry B. Walthall, and Lionel Barrymore. Griffith drew from his players a new, more restrained acting style wholly different from that of the stage. In many of his films his actresses, for example, projected more assertive heroines, in keeping with the aspirations of the suffragette era.

His rhythmic editing style in chase films like *The Lonely Villa* (1909) and *The Lonedale Operator* (1912) created a sense of excitement by intercutting action between the chaser and the pursued, employing shorter and shorter shots to add to the suspense. Again, in *A Beast at Bay* (1912), he used the technique to film a race between the heroine's car and a train commandeered by her rescuing boyfriend. Extending this technique to such films as *The Battle at Elderbush Gulch* (1913), Griffith played a pivotal role in the development of the western genre.

Griffith also was dealing with many subjects in his films, reflective of his progressive social vision. In such films as *The Redman's View* (1909) and *Ramona* (1910), he denounced the white man's oppression of the American Indian. He excoriated capitalism's injustice toward the poor in such films as *A Corner in Wheat* (1909) and focused his camera on scenes of urban poverty in

D. W. Griffith (Author's collection)

The Musketeers of Pig Alley (1912) and many other works. Griffith climaxed his years at Biograph with his first feature-length film, *Judith of Bethulia* (1913), an epic dramatization of the apocryphal story of the ancient Jewish heroine who saved her community from invading Assyrians. Like many of his subsequent works, *Judith of Bethulia* demonstrated his abhorrence of imperialism through its depiction of the ravages of war and its effect on civilians.

Confronted with a Biograph still unwilling to tackle longer, more ambitious features, Griffith left the studio in 1914 and entered into a partnership with Harry Aitken of Mutual to set up his own independent company in Hollywood. He took Billy Bitzer and many of his players with him, including Lillian and Dorothy Gish, Blanche Sweet, Mae Marsh, Henry B. Walthall, and Robert

Harron. That same year he directed several feature films of which the most noted was *The Avenging Conscience,* a psychological thriller adapted from Edgar Allan Poe's "The Tell-Tale Heart." This was followed by the film that would make Griffith's name a household word and establish the motion picture as the dominant narrative medium in 20th-century America. At the same time, this film would create a controversy that has clouded Griffith's reputation over time. With the assistance of Frank E. Woods, he adapted *The Clansman,* a best-selling melodrama about the Reconstruction era by Thomas Dixon, expanding the story and its staged dramatization into a large-scale depiction of the Civil War and its aftermath, alternating spectacular scenes with poignant, intimate scenes of families caught up in the vortex of events. The director perfected techniques that he had been adapting and improving over a six-year period.

Released early in 1915, *The Birth of a Nation,* with an unprecedented running-time of three hours, electrified audiences across the country and became the American cinema's biggest box-office hit before the 1920s. It premiered in Los Angeles on February 8, in New York on March 3, and after a special White House screening, President Woodrow Wilson purportedly said it was like "writing history with lightning." Praised by many reviewers as the first great achievement of a new art, its presentation in legitimate theaters with orchestral accompaniment finally signaled that the motion picture had come of age.

But along with the plaudits came controversy, which has only increased over the decades. Griffith's portrayal of a Reconstruction era in which Southern whites were rescued by the Ku Klux Klan from vengeful carpetbaggers and unruly blacks reflected the prevailing historical view of Reconstruction put forth by the Dunning School. Led by the National Association for the Advancement of Colored People, pressure groups repeatedly tried to ban the film as racist propaganda and an incitement to violence, claiming that *The Birth of a Nation* was the principal source of American racial violence from 1915 on and that its continued distribution was the leading factor in the Klan's revival during the 1920s. In considering the case brought to the courts by Mutual in defence of film's free speech, the Supreme Court issued a verdict denying the film medium First Amendment protection. This would stand until the early 1950s, when the decision was reversed in the landmark "Miracle" case.

While the NAACP failed in its efforts to have the film banned outright, its strategy did serve to diminish appreciation of Griffith's overall achievement. Forgotten amidst all the emotional invective was the film's passionate indictment of the horrors of war and its effect on ordinary individuals, a point of view that added to its initial popularity at a time when public opinion was strongly opposed to U.S. involvement in World War I. Griffith himself believed he had presented an antiwar film and an accurate picture of the Civil War and Reconstruction and was shocked at the charges of racism and angered by attempts to suppress his film.

Griffith's next endeavor surpassed *The Birth of a Nation* in its scale and sweep. Intended in part as a response to the attacks on *Birth* (he published a broadside defending free speech in America), *Intolerance* (1916) introduced a revolutionary new narrative structure that broke with preceding conventions while further perfecting his use of dramatic close-ups, camera movement, and parallel editing to create what is perhaps the cinema's foremost masterpiece and surely the most ambitious film produced before the 1920s. In 1914, prior to the release of *The Birth of a Nation,* he had begun making what would become the "Modern Story" of *Intolerance,* a dramatic indictment of societal injustice toward the poor in the United States. With the working title of *The Mother and the Law,* this film included a powerful depiction of capitalism's brutal suppression of labor, an attack on capital punishment, and a forecast of the evils resulting from Prohibition. But seeking to outdo both *The Birth of a Nation* and spectacular European imports such as *Cabiria,* as well as responding to critics of his earlier film, Griffith decided to expand this narrative to encompass four stories from different periods in history, illustrating the persistence of intolerance and inhumanity throughout the ages.

Instead of telling these stories sequentially, Griffith intercut his "Modern Story" with the Judean Story portraying the events leading to the crucifixion of Christ, the French Story dramatizing the massacre of the Huguenots, and, most spectacular of all, the Babylonian Story depicting, with massive sets and thousands of extras, the destruction of ancient Babylon and its civilization by the imperialist forces of Cyrus of Persia in league with the city's reactionary clergy opposed to the reforms introduced by Prince Belshazzar. In the climax, "History itself," in the words of archivist Iris Barry, "seems to pour like a cataract across the screen" during the rapid intercutting between the four parallel stories. In scope, ambition, film form, and thematic complexity, *Intolerance* was a towering achievement.

The pacifist message of *Intolerance* was consistent with America's antiwar mood in 1915 and 1916. The film was quite popular upon its release, but as the United States moved toward full-scale war with Germany in 1917, attendance began to fall off, and, ultimately, *Intolerance* failed at the box office. Overseas, however, *Intolerance* enjoyed a far more sustained success. The film ran for 10 years in the USSR and became the single most important influence on the emerging Soviet filmmakers of the 1920s. In France, Germany, and Scandinavia, Griffith's epic also paved the way for a generation of filmmakers, while at home it was to influence such directors as CECIL B[LOUNT] DEMILLE, REX INGRAM, Erich von Stroheim, and KING VIDOR. Called by film historian Theodore Huff "the only film fugue," Griffith's masterpiece remains a timeless landmark of cinematic art.

Griffith followed *Intolerance* with *Hearts of the World* (1918), the most notable of several films he directed on behalf of the Allied cause in World War I. Though he later regretted the film's heavy propaganda as incompatible with his antiwar sentiments, Griffith provided another poignant portrayal of the devastating effects of war on ordinary citizens as a French village is overrun by Imperial German forces. After the war Griffith returned to the more tranquil world of his rural past through a series of films that included *True Heart Susie* (1919), an idyll starring Lillian Gish, acclaimed decades later as one of the world's greatest films by French New Wave directors Jacques Rivette and Eric Rohmer. Even more impressive was *Broken Blossoms* (1919), a poetic masterwork and the most influential of his intimate films. The story concerns a Chinese Buddhist (Richard Barthelmess) transplanted to London and the tragic outcome of his love for an innocent young white girl (Lillian Gish) whom he vainly attempts to shelter from her abusive, pugilist father. In this attack upon racism, Griffith's narrative fusing of realism and romanticism is accomplished through strikingly new and innovative soft-focus photography, bold close-ups, and an atmosphere created entirely through sets replicated at his studio. The film was an immediate critical and popular success. Griffith's ability to reproduce and transcend reality foreshadowed the German *Kammerspiel* films, while his sensitive direction of Lillian Gish and Richard Barthelmess in the leads set new standards for cinematic performances.

Meanwhile, Griffith had sought to maintain his independence and creative control in the Hollywood-based film industry. Initially releasing his features through Mutual, he had left that organization in 1915 to form Triangle in partnership with Mack Sennett and THOMAS HARPER INCE. He then left Triangle in 1917 and released his films, first through Paramount-Artcraft, and then through First National. In 1919 he joined with Mary Pickford, Douglas Fairbanks, Sr., and CHARLES CHAPLIN to form United Artists, and, in a further effort to remain free of industry control, moved his production company from Hollywood to a new studio in Mamaroneck, New York. He scored his greatest popular triumph since *The Birth of a Nation* with *Way Down East* (1920), the most acclaimed of his bucolic pictures. To intensify the drama, Griffith filmed on location in New England, including the famous climax on the ice floes in which Lillian Gish is rescued by Richard Barthelmess. Adapting a venerable turn-of-the-century melodrama about a country maiden betrayed by a callous playboy, Griffith transformed the story into a potent attack on Puritanism and the sexual double standard toward adultery. Although the film evoked nostalgia for agrarian America, its simultaneous indictment of provincial bigotry and sexism was very compatible with the emerging 1920s, which would grant women the right to vote, promising a new era of greater gender equality.

Griffith's next great film, *Orphans of the Storm* (1921), was a spectacular recreation of the French Revolution. As in his previous epics, Griffith presented events in human terms, showing his feminine protagonists, two sisters played by Lillian and Dorothy Gish, as separated by the *ancien régime* and caught up in the storm of revolution. Griffith's political hero is Danton, who leads the people in their struggle to overthrow the regime. The film's historical villain, Robespierre, is portrayed as a puritan who uses the license of the frenzied mob as a means to construct a new tyranny on the ruins of the old, an incipient moralistic orthodoxy that simply perpetuates despotism in a new guise. Once again, Griffith's narrative underscores his belief in the individual and his opposition to the historical oppression of women by the ruling elite.

Contrary to legend, most of Griffith's Mamaroneck films made money, but because of the debts incurred by the director in managing his studio and his ineptitude in business matters, he failed to realize the profits from the films made after *Way Down East*. The Hollywood establishment grew increasingly resentful of Griffith's Eastern-based defiance of the West Coast industry. Moreover, it was claimed that Griffith was wedded to an old-fashioned, Victorian outlook and out of touch with the times. Nevertheless, he continued to produce solid achievements like the last of his rural films, *The White Rose* (1923), shot on location in the South, with Mae Marsh in the role of an unwed mother deceived by a minister, and *America* (1924), another large-scale epic, this time depicting the American Revolution. In between was *Dream Street* (1922), an impressionistic melodrama that featured some synchronized-sound sequences. Griffith's work at Mamaroneck climaxed with *Isn't Life Wonderful?* (1924), his most extraordinary experiment since *Broken Blossoms*. Distinguished for its social commentary, the film was made largely on location in Germany and depicted the harrowing conditions of postwar Europe. Centering his narrative upon the experiences of a refugee family struggling to survive in the chaos and deprivation that followed the German defeat, Griffith conveyed, with relative restraint, the poverty of the time in his scenes of listless, undernourished people with their meager savings crowding in line for meat as they watch the prices steadily climb (recalling similar scenes in his early one-reeler, *A Corner in Wheat*). An artistic triumph that anticipated Italian neorealism and influenced directors from King Vidor and FRANK BORZAGE to AKIRA KUROSAWA, whose *Wonderful Sunday* (1947) was a remake of Griffith's film, *Isn't Life Wonderful?* proved a risky commercial gamble. In the age of Coolidge prosperity, American audiences were less interested in films of social commentary that expected them to empathize with problems experienced by people abroad. Therefore, *Isn't Life Wonderful?* failed at the box office and Griffith was forced to become a contract director for Paramount.

Griffith's later films of the 1920s, made for Paramount on the East Coast and for producer Joseph Schenck at United Artists in Hollywood, have been dismissed as largely commercial imitations of other Hollywood productions of the time, but they do not necessarily represent a creative decline. The last of his Mamaroneck films, *Sally of the Sawdust* (1925) was intended for Paramount distribution but was released by United Artists. With W. C. Fields reprising his stage hit *Poppy, Sally of the Sawdust* combined Fields's comic genius with Griffith's own vision, as he drew on his youthful memories of working in the theater when actors were still shunned by respectable people. *The Sorrows of Satan* (1926), adapted from Marie Corelli's gothic romance about a critic who sacrifices his integrity in pursuit of the worldly success offered him by Satan, recalled the director's early years with Linda Arvidson, when he was attempting to establish himself as a writer. *The Battle of the Sexes* (1928), in its wryly comic depiction of a middle-aged businessman who allows himself to be seduced by an attractive gold-digger, arguably reflected the director's own mid-life crisis.

Griffith successfully met the challenge posed by the coming of sound with his 1930 biopic *Abraham Lincoln.* Walter Huston was memorable as the 16th president in a film that chronicled Lincoln's birth in a log cabin to his assassination at Ford's Theatre. The scenes of Lincoln's courtship of Ann Rutledge against a pastoral backdrop are in the classic vein of Griffith's rural films, while the Civil War scenes serve as another of the director's compelling commentaries on the suffering engendered by war, though Griffith's political sympathies are fully with Lincoln in his efforts to preserve the Union and abolish slavery. The film's box-office appeal did not match its critical success, however, and Griffith, unhappy with changes made in the final-release print requested by his producers, sundered his ties with Schenck to make one more try for independence.

His next film, *The Struggle,* made on the East Coast in 1931, would prove to be his last. Having suffered for several years from a drinking problem, Griffith conceived a film that reflected his own torments while opposing Prohibition. *The Strug-* *gle* relates the story of a good-natured but weak-willed working man who succumbs to the allure of the speakeasy, causing a personal decline that nearly destroys his family. Griffith took his cameras out into the streets of the Bronx to record the unvarnished reality of tenement life, an approach consistent with his earlier films but at odds with Hollywood's preference for studio work. The combination of Griffith's unpolished realism and an unheroic leading man in the throes of alcoholism (Broadway star Hal Skelly in an outstanding performance) held no appeal for depression-era audiences of 1931. The film was a commercial and critical disaster that ended Griffith's directorial career, although later critics would recognize it as one of his finest works.

Griffith's remaining years were marked by unfulfilled attempts to realize his literary ambitions and intermittent efforts to resume directing. He assisted Hal Roach on *One Million B.C.* (1940), for example, a project with which Griffith became quickly dissatisfied. Although frustrated by intermittent bouts of alcoholism, Griffith did make a belated effort to adjust to domestic life. Separated from Linda Arvidson for 25 years, he finally divorced her in 1936 and married Evelyn Baldwin, a young woman who had played a supporting role in *The Struggle,* but that marriage also ended in divorce. There were no children from either marriage. Although toward the end Griffith was not destitute, he was far from wealthy. The highlights of his later years were a special Oscar presented to him by the Academy of Motion Picture Arts and Sciences in 1936 for his contributions to film art, and a 1940 retrospective of his work by the Museum of Modern Art, which had begun the task of preserving and disseminating his films. On July 23, 1948, at the age of 73, Griffith died in Hollywood of a cerebral hemorrhage and was buried in Kentucky, near his birthplace.

After his death, Griffith's reputation rose, then fell. The high point came during the 1960s and

1970s, as the cinema-studies movement grew, culminating in a commemorative postage stamp issued in 1975, his centenary year. The ultimate decline of his reputation in his own country was symbolized by the Directors Guild of America's decision in 1999 to retire their prestigious D. W. Griffith Award, demonstrating the guild's tardy disapproval of the racist implications of *The Birth of a Nation*. Although political correctness ultimately tarnished his reputation in America, the art of D. W. Griffith transformed creative expression throughout the world, establishing motion pictures as the dominant narrative form of the 20th century, if not beyond.

Other Films *Home, Sweet Home* (1913); *The Great Love* (1918); *Romance of Happy Valley* (1919); *Scarlet Days* (1919); *The Greatest Question* (1919); *The Idol Dancer* (1920); *The Love Flower* (1920); *One Exciting Night* (1922); *That Royle Girl* (1925); *Lady of the Pavements* (1929).

References Barry, Iris, *D. W. Griffith: American Film Master* (New York: Museum of Modern Art, 1965); Bitzer, Billy, *Billy Bitzer, His Story* (New York: Farrar, Straus, Giroux, 1973); Brown, Karl, *Adventures with D. W. Griffith* (New York: Farrar, Straus, Giroux, 1973); Drew, William M., *D. W. Griffith's Intolerance: Its Genesis and Its Vision* (Jefferson, N.C.: McFarland, 1986); Gish, Lillian, *The Movies, Mr. Griffith, and Me* (Englewood Cliffs, N.J.: Prentice-Hall, 1969); Henderson, Robert M., *D. W. Griffith: His Life and Work* (New York: Oxford University Press, 1972); Schickel, Richard, *D. W. Griffith: An American Life* (New York: Simon and Schuster, 1984).

—W.M.D.

Guest, Christopher (1948–) Christopher

Guest's biography reads like one of his improvised comedy routines. He was born in New York City in 1948, the son of an American mother, Jean Pauline Hindes, an actress and CBS executive, and Peter Haden-Guest, an English baron in the county of Essex, whose title has since passed to the director-writer and actor, making him the Fifth Baron Haden-Guest of Saling. His younger brother, Nicholas, also an actor, was cast with Christopher in WALTER HILL's western, *The Long Riders* (1980). His half-brother, Anthony Haden-Guest, is a British journalist. "I attended Parliament for two years running," Guest told the *Washington Times*, "but I don't get to do that now. They kicked us out of the House of Lords—all the hereditary peers. We have titles but no votes. You know the English job description of 'minister without portfolio'? I'm a peer without portfolio." But, as Guest told another interviewer in typical deadpan manner, "Don't feel sorry. I still have the fancy stationery."

After being raised in London, Guest worked on the *National Lampoon* radio show and appeared onstage in the *National Lampoon* satirical review *Lemmings* in 1973. By the middle 1980s Guest was teamed with Billy Crystal on *Saturday Night Live*. In 1984 he married the actress Jamie Lee Curtis, with whom he fathered two children, Annie and Thomas. When they married, they agreed never to work together, in order to keep their personal lives "separate from the business." Guest's debut film as director was the Hollywood spoof *The Big Show* (1989), which in retrospect seems a bit of a clinker in comparison to his later improvisational comic method that drives his cult classics, *Waiting for Guffman* (1997) and *Best in Show* (2000). He worked out the method first in shaping his character, Nigel Tufnel, in the Rob Reiner-directed "rockumentary" spoof *This Is Spinal Tap* (1984), the first cult film with which he was associated, a send-up of a fictional band of heavy-metal losers, consisting of Guest, his friend Michael McKean as David St. Hubbins, and Harry Shearer as Derek Smalls. These misguided rockers are described by Reiner's fictional director as "treading water in a sea of retarded sexuality and bad poetry." Guest's Nigel dismisses this criticism as merely "nitpicking."

In 1992 ROB REINER directed a sequel scripted by Guest, *The Return of Spinal Tap*, "documenting" a so-called reunion concert that featured cameos by Paul Anka, Jeff Beck, Jamie Lee Curtis, Kenny Rogers, Martin Short, and Mel Torme, just as the original *Spinal Tap* had cameos by Billy Crystal, Paul Shaffer, and Angelica Huston, and a cast that included Dana Carvey. This was followed in 1993 by *The Attack of the 50-foot Woman,* a campy remake of the 1958 science fiction "classic." Better work would follow.

Guest perfected his improv methods in an ensemble that included longtime friends—Michael McKean, whom he had known since 1967, co-writer Eugene Levy, and SCTV colleague Catherine O'Hara—when he made *Waiting for Guffman,* with Guest himself playing closeted-gay drama teacher Corky St. Claire, directing a sesquicentennial pageant drama in small-town Blaine, Missouri. The temperamental Corky believes that a New York producer named Guffman is coming to see their work and may be interested in taking it to Broadway, but waiting for Guffman is rather like waiting for Godot, in the hayseed Midwest. The musical numbers, built upon Levy's lyrics, are purely inspired lunacy, driven by the "and so, on with the show" ethic of Ethel Merman.

After *Guffman* became a cult sensation, Guest and Levy collaborated again on *Best in Show* (2000), a "mockumentary" send-up of dog shows and the people who frequent them. The plot was simply constructed, following five dogs and their owners to the Mayflower Dog Show in Philadelphia. Guest himself played the most apparently "normal" owner, Harlan Pepper of Pine Nut, North Carolina, whose forlorn bloodhound, Hubert, competes admirably. Eugene Levy played a geek with literally two left feet, accompanied by Catherine O'Hara as his nymphomaniac wife. Guest and Levy used the same formula for *Best in Show* that had worked so well for them in *Guffman,* constructing scenarios that would permit the actors to improvise their characters, but the satire was rather more nasty, and the film lacked the freshness of *Guffman.* Even so, the film had favorable reviews and probably reached a larger audience than *Guff-*

man had done, partly because of heightened expectations for Guest, and partly because it was competing against a very weak field.

"Red, White, and Blaine," the pageant drama of *Waiting for Guffman,* was truly wretched, though sincerely klutzy and awkward, but, as Anita Gates noted, "It still has a little of theatre's magic, the power to transport." However, in *Best in Show* there is nothing of the residual nostalgia for community theatre that saved *Guffman* from being merely a brutal parody. "I don't make movies that make fun of anything," Guest claimed, not too convincingly, since the film came awfully close to the "one-dimensional parody" that Guest had hoped to avoid. The danger of satire is that it can alienate, but Guest has developed a distinctive satiric method that can charm sophisticated viewers.

References   Arnold, Gary, "Christopher Guest at His 'Best,'" *Washington Times,* October 15, 2000, p. C5; Gates, Anita, "Handling Stars Who Respond to Affection," *New York Times,* September 24, 2000, sec. II, pp. 13–14; Wloszczyna, Susan, "This Is Christopher Guest," *USA Today,* September 27, 2000, pp. D1–2.

—J.M.W.

Guy-Blaché, Alice (1873–1968)   "There is nothing connected with the staging of a motion picture that a woman cannot do as easily as a man, and there is no reason why she cannot completely master every technicality of the art," said Alice Guy-Blaché in 1914. Guy-Blaché was the first woman film director and the first director of fiction films, and it is said that she spent the first half of her life making films and the second half trying to convince the film world to give her credit for it.

She was born to a comfortable middle-class family in 1873. Her parents encouraged her to learn typing and stenography, and in 1895 she got a job as a secretary for Léon Gaumont. At that time Gaumont was more interested in producing photographic and film equipment than finished films, and when he began selling Lumiere's new film cameras, Guy-Blaché asked whether she could experiment with recording short plays on film. Her film, *La Fée aux choux* (The cabbage fairy [1896]), said to be the first fiction film, was exhibited at the International Exhibition in Paris in 1896 and was so popular that Gaumont promoted her to head a new film production unit of the company.

The early years of film production were years of experimentation and offered women like Guy-Blaché far greater possibilities than at any time since. She directed over 400 films, including nearly 70 two-reelers and 14 four-reelers, and she was involved in the production and writing of over 300 others. However, only 50 of her oeuvre survive. Her greatest success in France was *The Passion of Christ* (1906), which was a very popular subject of films in the early period. Scholars agree that what sets Guy-Blaché's *Passion* apart from the others is its exceptionally sophisticated staging, which utilized all levels and depths of the frame to depict ongoing action. She made over 300 films in France before she met and married Herbert Blaché-Bolton who worked for Gaumont in London.

Gaumont sent the couple to America in 1907 to promote a new sound technology for films, Chronophone. Sound did not catch on in motion pictures at this point and Guy-Blaché started her own film production company called Solax in 1910. Her films were so popular that by 1912 she was making over $25,000 a year and was the only woman in the United States to do so.

On the strength of that wealth she and her husband built their own studio in the center of the U.S. film industry, Fort Lee, New Jersey. It was the largest studio in the United States at the time and allowed her a very large scope for further experimentation with split screen and special effects, as well as improving the general quality of directing for the camera. She had large signs hung around her studio on which was painted "Be Natural," and

as a result, she got realistic performances from her actors and actresses, which were enhanced by the use of close-ups. This allowed a more subtle filmic storytelling than was evident in the work of many of her cohorts, like DAVID WARK GRIFFITH, who still relied on the exaggerated style of acting for the theater. Though she was a Victorian woman in her personal life, the female protagonists of her films were usually the ones who controlled narrative direction and flow, putting them at least on equal footing with their male counterparts. One short film, *Matrimony's Speed Limit* (1913), depicts a young woman who controls events so that her fiancé will marry her even after he has lost his money and called off the engagement. Another is *House Divided* (1913), in which a husband and wife suspect each other of cheating. Though she made films in many genres, including westerns, epics, and melodramas, her favorites were love stories with happy endings.

In this respect it is a wonder that she was not able to continue directing following the reorganization of the film industry after World War I. After Herbert Blaché left Gaumont in 1913 he started Blaché Features and convinced his wife to go in on it with him. According to reviews, she enjoyed great success as opposed to the mediocre performance of her husband. After the war the larger film studios started buying up the independents; and rather than sell out, Guy Blaché and her husband tried to make a go of it. They could not. Her husband left her and went to California with a younger actress, and she sold off her studio equipment at auction in 1921. She moved back to France and tried to get work in the film industry there for many years, to no avail. To support herself and her two children she began writing stories for adolescents. Later in her life she tried to retrieve her early films in France and the United States but was unsuccessful. In 1953 she was awarded the French Legion of Honor, although throughout the 1970s film historians on both sides of the Atlantic continued to credit her films to other, male directors. In 1964 she returned to the United States and lived with her daughter until her death on March 24, 1968, in Mahwah, New Jersey. Today she is widely recognized as the pioneer she was, not only as a woman filmmaker but also as an innovator and creator of the film industry itself. A documentary film, *The Lost Garden: The Life and Cinema of Alice Guy-Blaché,* was released in 1995 through the National Film Board of Canada.

Other Films *Beasts of the Jungle* (1913); *The Sea Wolf* (1915); *The Ocean Waif* (1916); *The Divorcée* (1919), et al.

References Acker, Ally, *Reel Women: Pioneers of the Cinema, 1896–Present* (New York: Continuum Press, 1991); Guy-Blaché, Alice, "Woman's Place in Photoplay Production," *Moving Picture World* 21, no. 3 (July 11, 1914), p. 195; Kuhn, Annette, and Susannah Radstone, eds., *The Woman's Companion to International Film* (Berkeley: University of California Press, 1994); Slide, Anthony, *The Silent Feminists* (Lanham, Md.: Scarecrow Press, 1996).

—C.L.P.

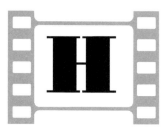

Hall, Sir Peter (1930–   )   Sir Peter was born on November 22, 1930, in Bury St. Edmunds. He attended the Perse School, then St. Catherine's College at Cambridge University, where he began directing plays as an undergraduate. After a number of years directing in Britain, with occasional trips to the United States, he became one of the founders and the managing director (1961–68) of the Royal Shakespeare Company. He continued as a codirector at the RSC until 1973 while also directing for the Royal Opera House at Covent Garden. He took over from LAURENCE OLIVIER as director of the National Theatre in 1973, remaining until 1988; he was also artistic director of the Glyndebourne Festival Opera, 1984–90.

He is only incidentally a filmmaker; his body of work consists of seven films and seven television specials; four of the television specials were opera, and two were broadcast versions of stage plays. His first film was a comedy, *Work Is a Four-Letter Word* (1967). His second was *A Midsummer Night's Dream* (1968), shot quickly using actors from the Royal Shakespeare Company, including David Warner, Diana Rigg, Helen Mirren, Judy Dench, Ian Holm, and Ian Richardson; it is a nervous, somewhat sexy reading of Shakespeare's play. *Three Into Two Won't Go* (1969) is a ponderous melo-drama in which Rod Steiger falls for a young hitchhiker (Judy Geeson) and leaves his wife (Claire Bloom); Universal shot extra footage to lengthen the film for television. *Perfect Friday* (1970) is a comic caper film in which a London deputy bank manager plans to rob a branch bank; it features Stanley Baker, Ursula Andress, and David Warner.

Hall then abandoned film for two decades, concentrating on theater and opera. He returned with *She's Been Away* (1989) and after another hiatus, *Never Talk to Strangers* (1995), a pedestrian thriller with Rebecca DeMornay and Antonio Banderas. During the intervals he directed *Le Nozze di Figaro* (1973), *The Homecoming* (1973), *Fidelio* (1977), *L'Incoronazione di Poppea* (1984), *Albert Herring* (1985), *La Traviata* (1987), and *Orpheus Descending* (1990) for television. He also did a miniseries, *The Camomile Lawn* (1992), and a television movie, *Jacob* (1994).

References   *Peter Hall's Diaries* (London: Oberon, 2000); Hall, Peter *Making an Exhibition of Myself* (London: Sinclair-Stevenson, 1993).

—W.K.

Hallström, Lasse (1946–   )   The award-winning Swedish director Lasse Hallström was born in Stockholm, June 2, 1946. While in high school, he made a short film about a band formed by his fellow classmates; he then went on to a career in television, directing *The Love Seekers,* which was selected as the Swedish entry for the Montreaux Television Festival. His feature film debut was a romantic drama entitled *A Guy and a Gal* (*En kille och en tjej* [1975]), followed by a concert film, *ABBA—The Movie* (1977), *Father-to-Be* (1979), *The Rooster* (1981), and *Happy We* (1983). His international breakthrough picture was made in 1985, *Mitt Luv Som Hund* (*My Life as a Dog*), though the film was not exported until two years after its completion.

The film, adapted from a semiautobiographical novel by Reidar Jonsson, offered a touching coming-of-age story of a 12-year-old boy, Ingemar Johansson (Anton Glanzelius), who lived during the 1950s with his brother Erik (Manfred Serner) and his mother (Anki Liden), who is dying of tuberculosis. The boy is accident-prone and frequently bickers with his brother, upsetting his mother, so he is sent away to spend the summer with an aunt and uncle, where he continues to get into trouble, but makes a new circle of friends. After he returns home, his mother dies and the boy is devastated by grief when he returns to live with the aunt and uncle. Eventually, he comes to terms with the hand fate has dealt him.

Although the plot takes a tragic trajectory, the film is distinguished by many comic moments as Ingemar becomes involved in a budding romance with an athletic tomboy who at first humiliates him on the soccer field, then teaches him how to box. In many ways a sentimental crowd-pleaser marked by Hallström's signature charm, *My Life as a Dog* earned Academy Award nominations for best director and best adapted screenplay for 1987 and was named best foreign film by the New York Film Critics Circle, as well as earning a Golden Globe in 1988 for best foreign-language film.

His first American feature film was entitled *Once Around* (1991), a bittersweet romantic comedy starring Holly Hunter and Richard Dreyfuss. This was followed by *What's Eating Gilbert Grape?* (1993), another coming-of-age film that starred Johnny Depp as Gilbert Grape and Leonardo DiCaprio as his retarded younger brother. This film, distinguished by brilliant performances and outstanding cinematography by Sven Nykvist, earned broad critical praise, as well as Academy Award and Golden Globe attention for DiCaprio. *Something to Talk About* (1995), another romantic comedy, starring Julia Roberts and Dennis Quaid, warranted far less critical acclaim, but the director's next two pictures would fare much better.

In 1999 Hallström's adaptation of John Irving's *The Cider House Rules,* starring Tobey Maguire, Charlize Theron, and Michael Caine, put Hallström back into Oscar contention. The film was nominated for best picture and won Academy Awards for best adapted screenplay (for John Irving) and for best supporting actor (Michael Caine as Dr. Wilbur Larch). "I love Lasse Hallström's film of *The Cider House Rules,*" John Irving later wrote, "but all of the novel's crude moments are missing from the movie. And don't you suppose that any story about life in a Maine orphanage earlier in this century, especially a story that focuses on the life of an illegal abortionist's apprentice, there would be more than a few *very* crude moments?" Still, the author was not displeased and praises Hallström repeatedly in his memoir, *My Movie Business.*

Hallström's next film, *Chocolat* (2000), another "bittersweet" crowd-pleaser, was still another Oscar contender for Juliette Binoche and supporting actress Judi Dench. It was a sort of fairy tale about a woman, an independent-minded pagan outsider (Binoche), who moves into a French village controlled by a very conservative, uptight Roman Catholic mayor and dares to open a chocolate shop during Lent, tempting the villagers with her confections. Johnny Depp makes another appearance, this time as the gypsy leader of a group of boat people. Juliette Binoche was nominated for an Academy Award for best actress, and the film also earned nominations for best supporting actress (Judi Dench), best original score, best adapted screenplay (Robert Nelson Jacobs), and best picture. Arguably, Lasse Hallström could be considered the most successful Swedish film director to cross over to the Hollywood mainstream. He has shown a special talent for mixing nostalgia, pathos, and comedy while telling serious stories about social misfits who somehow manage to defy conventionality and adapt to their surroundings.

References Howe, Dessin, "My Life as a Dog," *Washington Post Weekend,* May 8, 1987; Irving, John, *My Movie Business: A Memoir* (New York: Random House, 1999).

—J.M.W.

Handke, Peter (1942–)

Peter Handke, the Austrian-born novelist, essayist, and playwright, is best known for his writing, but, as a friend of the German director WIM WENDERS, he has also had screenwriting experience, first on *Die Angst des Tormanns beim Elfmeter* (*The Goalkeeper's Fear of the Penalty Kick* [1972]), which he adapted for Wenders from his own novel, then on *Falsche Bewegung* (*Wrong Move* [1974]), which he freely adapted and updated for Wenders from Goethe's *Wilhelm Meister's Apprenticeship.* Handke was encouraged by Wenders not only to adapt his own novel *Die Linkshändige Frau* (*The Left-Handed Woman*) but to direct it as well, as he in fact did, with Wenders's support in 1977. Wenders produced the film, his regular cameraman Robie Müller was the cinematographer, and the film was edited by another Wenders colleague, Peter Przygodda. The film premiered at the Hof Film Festival on October 30, 1977, and was later praised in America as "a genuinely poetic film."

Handke was born in Griffin, Austria, in December of 1942. Aside from the four years he spent as a child in postwar Berlin, he was raised and educated in Austria, graduating with a law degree from the University of Graz. After publishing his first novel, *The Hornets* (*Die Hornissen*) in 1966, he caused a scandal by attacking established German novelists at a "Gruppe 47" meeting in Princeton, New Jersey, challenging their "realistic" achievements and criticizing their complacency. In 1967 his plays won the Gerhart Hauptmann Prize. After living in Germany for several years, Handke moved to a suburb of Paris, residing in the house where his novel *Die Linkshändige Frau* was set. After separating from his wife, he moved to Salzburg, Austria.

Handke acquired a reputation for arrogance with the release of his first play, entitled *Offending the Audience* (*Publikumsbeschimpfung* [1966]), in which he renounced all conventional modes of communication, and he became a fierce critic of postwar German literature. His plays were antitheatrical *"Sprechstücke"* that assailed time-honored conventions of drama. He was later hailed by the British novelist and critic Malcolm Bradbury as "unmistakably one of the best writers we have in that self-discovering tendency in contemporary writing we have chosen to call post-modernism."

Handke's first film, *Chronik der laufenden Ereignisse* (Chronicle of current events), was made in 1970 for Westdeutsche Rundfunk television. The title was lifted from a Soviet underground newspaper. Handke described the film as follows: "*Chronik der laufenden Ereignisse* insofar as it tried to be an allegory of two years of West German history, might also be seen as an allegory of the mythical struggle between cinema and television images, in which at the end, the cinema images are suppressed by the television images. The symbol of this victory would then be the television clock, which, after it suddenly kept going [and didn't gong] once in the middle of the film, gongs routinely at the end of the film." The "gong" refers to the clock that keeps ticking during CBS's *60 Minutes,* since many of the shows on German television are American imports. Kathe Geist explains: "Just as *Goalie* had been an anti-thriller [its protagonist was a murderer, after all] and *Wrong Move* an anti-*Bildungsroman, Chronik* was an anti-television television film."

Handke made provocative qualitative remarks through intertitles, such as "Nothing has definitive value any longer; there is no accepted order anymore. All concepts of good and evil, right and wrong, true and false have been jettisoned." The questions are discussed by fictional characters, and a panel representing prominent Americans such as Robert McNamara and film director Delbert Mann. At the end the clock chimes, and, as Geist describes it, "Order is restored in the name of mediocrity and hypocrisy, i.e., television."

In his next film, *Die linkshändige Frau,* Handke forgoes the role of impish provocateur to direct the film, since Wenders did not want to direct and encouraged the novelist to helm the picture. In fact, Handke had first imagined the story as a film and had actually written a screenplay, but was unable to get the project funded. Consequently, he rewrote the story in novella form and it was published in 1976. The novella then generated interest in the making of a film, but by then Handke had lost his original screenplay and had to rewrite it from scratch.

The story of *The Left-Handed Woman* is simply and utterly straightforward. The "woman," Marianne, a translator, and her son meet her husband, who has been abroad on a business trip. He is happy to return to his family, but out of the blue, she tells him: "I suddenly had an illumination that you were going away, that you were leaving me. Yes, that's it. Go away, Bruno. Leave me." This "illumination" comes as a surprise to the husband, the reader, and the viewer, and is never explained psychologically. In the written story the action is described as one might see it on a movie screen. The point of view is utterly "objective." Nothing is explained; things just happen. Marianne finds work translating a French novel, and life goes on. A feminist friend offers to help, and an actor wants to court her, but she is happiest alone, with her son Stefan.

The narrative is totally lacking in sentiment. Marianne's "strange idea" of liberating herself from a domineering husband, her "illumination," as she calls it, causes her to redefine her other relationships as well. She is not entirely antisocial, however, as can be seen at the party in the novel's closing section; but she is determined that the people who gather at her home be on an equal footing. For that reason, her publisher's chauffeur is invited in as an equal. As he says to his employer at the party, "Tomorrow you won't speak to me anyway." Marianne gives the man a taste of liberation.

Marianne has a talent for breaking down barriers among other people, but she will not give herself away, and she will accept people only on her own terms. At the end of the story, after her visitors have left, she articulates this point, adding, "No one will ever humiliate you again." The film, starring Edith Clever as "Die Frau," Bruno Ganz as Bruno, the husband, and Rüdiger Vogler as "The Actor," closes with a motto quoted from the poet Vlado Kristl: *"Ja, habt ihr nicht bemerkt, das eigentlich nur Platz ist für den, der selbst den Platz mitbringt"* ("Have you noticed: there's only room for those who make room for themselves.").

The novel, which differs in some particulars of setting and action from the film, was written as a challenge. As Handke has explained in his notes for the film production, "I wanted to try a kind of prose in which the thinking and feeling of the individual characters would never be described—in which, instead of 'she was afraid,' the reader would find: 'she left,' 'she walked over to the window,' 'she lay down next to the child's bed,' etc.—and I felt this form of limitation actually acted as a liberating force on my literary work."

This method is perfectly realized in as meticulous an adaptation as the cinema has ever seen. The minimalist approach creates its own ambiguous charm. Since the author first imagined the story in screenplay form before writing the novella, and since the novelist directed the film himself, after rewriting it as a screenplay, it is impossible to say which version carries the more authority and is the substantive text, the novella or the film. It has become a touchstone and a paradigm for a particular kind of filmmaking, regardless of whether the director is a regular practicing filmmaker.

Other Films   *Das Mal des Todes* (1986); *Die Abwesenheit* (1992).

References   Corrigan, Timothy, *New German Film: The Displaced Image* (Bloomington: Indiana University Press, 1994); Geist, Kathe, *The Cinema of Wim Wenders: From Paris, France, to Paris, Texas* (Ann Arbor, Mich.: UMI Research Press, 1988); Linville, Susan, and Kent Casper, "Reclaiming the Self: Handke's *The Left-Handed Woman*," *Literature/Film Quarterly* 12, no. 1 (1984): 13–21.

—J.M.W.

Hare, David (1947–)   David Hare, a committed socialist playwright, has extended his talents to screenwriting for television and film, but has remained very much a man of the theater. His concerns are predominantly moral and often satiric, reflecting the stance of the "angry" playwrights of the 1950s, carried forward into a second generation of "furious" playwrights, as critic Jack Kroll aptly described them. Like TONY RICHARDSON, Hare went on to carry those concerns into cinema.

Hare was born on June 5, 1947, in Sussex, England, the son of Clifford Theodore Rippon and Alice Gillmour Rippon. First educated at Lancing College, he went on to Jesus College, Cambridge, earning an M.A. in 1968, and began writing plays at the age of 22. He cofounded the Portable Theatre Company with Howard Brenton and Snoo Wilson, an experimental troupe that toured Britain. He became literary manager of the Royal Court Theatre in 1969 and was appointed resident dramatist in 1970, the year his play *Slag* won him the *Evening Standard* most promising playwright award. After the Royal Court, Hare was resident playwright at the Nottingham Playhouse, where his play *Brassneck,* written in collab-

oration with Howard Brenton, premiered in 1973. In 1974 Hare cofounded another fringe company, Joint Stock, which produced his play about the Chinese Revolution, *Fanshen,* in Sheffield.

After establishing himself as a successful playwright, Hare began writing for television. His teleplay *Saigon: Year of the Cat* was directed by Stephen Frears for Thames Television in 1983, following the award-winning teleplay, *Licking Hitler,* that Hare wrote and directed himself for BBC television in 1978. "Writers don't have careers," Hare once remarked. "Directors do." In 1980 Hare wrote and directed *Dreams for Leaving,* starring Kate Nelligan, also for BBC television. Hare later wrote the screenplay adaptation of his most successful play to date, *Plenty,* for the film directed by Fred Schepisi and released by 20th Century-Fox in 1985, starring Meryl Streep as the deeply troubled Susan Traherne, Charles Dance as her bureaucrat husband, and Sir John Gielgud as his superior at the Foreign Office, a man betrayed by his government during the Suez Crisis.

In 1985 Hare also wrote and directed the feature film *Wetherby,* which earned the Golden Bear Award at the Berlin Film festival and a large measure of critical acclaim internationally. Jean Travers (Vanessa Redgrave), a schoolteacher in the Yorkshire town of Wetherby, near Leeds, invites friends to dinner at her country cottage. A mysterious, uninvited guest, John Morgan (Tim McInnerny) shows up, but Jean assumes her friends have invited him. The next day Morgan returns and commits suicide. The film then concentrates on what happened before and during the dinner party, and what happens after the suicide. Jean's past is explored in flashback, and, to a degree, Morgan's as well, but his motives are never explained.

Washington Post reviewer Megan Rosenfeld dismissed *Wetherby* as a "pretentious movie" with "Pinteresque dialogue." Reviewers were perplexed that so much was left unanswered. Stanley Kauffmann of the *New Republic* asked many of the same questions about Jean that others had asked about Susan Traherne in *Plenty:* "What are we supposed to think of her? Admirable? Solipsistic? Rightly strong? Gently ruthless?" And, more important, "What does Hare think of her?" Although Kauffmann found the film ultimately "unsatisfying," he made favorable comparisons to Ingmar Bergman and devoted a long column to exploring it. Vanessa Redgrave led a strong cast that also included Ian Holm, Judi Dench, Joely Richardson, and Suzanna Hamilton. *Film Comment* thought enough of the film to publish a substantial interview with Hare.

Hare's next film, *Paris by Night* (1988), an unconventional thriller, starred Michael Gambon and Charlotte Rampling as a 40-year-old, overworked, ambitious, and successful politician who has nothing but contempt for undisciplined behavior, until her own life starts to spin out of control. "I'd describe it as a character study of a new kind of British woman," Hare told Christine Pittel: "She is a character who believes a lot of quite stupid and half-thought things, apparently very intolerant of other people, who in the film commits a terrible action, and yet, we wanted to make you feel for her." In other words, a character type Hare had also created in many of his plays: "You can see she's doing terrible things, but you can't bring yourself to dislike her, nor can you actually like her. It's profoundly disorienting to an audience, which of course is exactly what I want."

Strapless (1989) starred Blair Brown as another 40-year-old woman, Lillian Hempel, an American doctor working for the British National Health Service, who gets involved with European gigolo Raymond Forbes (Bruno Ganz), a fraud and bigamist addicted to high romance, who courts her with oblique dialogue, then abandons her. Thereafter Lillian has a breakdown, but recovers herself after getting a sentimental trinket that somehow restores her faith so that she can participate in her sister's fashion show. American reviewers dismissed the film as a "muffled, romantic art movie, enervating and preposterously rarefied," in

the words of Hal Hinson of *The Washington Post.* Gary Giddins of *The Village Voice* found it merely "revolting." In 1991 Hare returned to BBC to direct *Heading Home,* starring Joely Richardson, Gary Oldman, and Stephen Dillane.

Hare returned to feature filmmaking in 1997 to direct the film version of Wallace Shawn's *The Designated Mourner,* which Hare had also directed at London's Royal National Theatre. The film starred Mike Nichols, Miranda Richardson, and David de Keyser and was highly praised for its acting. For the most part, however, Hare has preferred to write successful political plays for the London stage, such as *The Secret Rapture* (1988), *Racing Demon* (1990), *Murmuring Judges* (1991), *The Absence of War* (1993), *Skylight* (1995), *Amy's View* (1997), and his one-man-show, *Via Dolorosa* (1999). In general, his films have eclipsed audiences.

"To me film's completely unreal. The whole idea that movies represent reality—excuse me? For a start, they're two-dimensional images," Hare remarked to Christine Pittel: "There is no reality in movies at all. What there is, in any period of time, is a dominant style, which is accepted as the orthodox thing. What you're always doing as a film maker is trying to stylize in a way which sharpens things up, which is painterly without being distracting. Hitting that middle between what the audience expects and just opening their eyes about that much wider without alienating them is the trick."

References   Hare, David, *Writing Left-Handed* (London: Faber & Faber, 1991); Hinson, Hal, "Fuzzy Foundations," *Washington Post,* May 19, 1990, p. C3; Kauffmann, Stanley, "Against the Darkness," *New Republic,* August 12 & 19, 1985, pp. 24–26; Lawson, Steve, "Hare Apparent," *Film Comment* 21, no. 5 (October 1985): 18–22; Pittel, Christine, "Torn Between Hare and Hitchcock," *New York Times,* July 31, 1988, sec. II, pp. 19, 22.

—J.M.W.

Hark, Tsui (1951–   )   Tsui Hark was born in Vietnam on January 2, 1951, and lived in the

Cholon district of Saigon. His father was a pharmacist with 16 daughters and sons from three marriages. Artistic interests ran through the entire family, despite the hopes of Hark's father that at least one of his sons would become a doctor. Stimulated by the photographs his father brought back from his frequent trips to Hong Kong movie studios, young Tsui made his first film on 8 mm at the age of 10. He was sent to Hong Kong when he was 14 for his high school education and three years later applied to study pharmacy overseas at Southern Methodist University in Dallas, Texas. He transferred to the University of Austin to study film, unbeknownst to his father. After writing a student paper about the work of director King Hu, Hark became bored with Texas and moved to New York in 1974. While there he co-directed a 45-minute documentary with Christine Choy, *From Spikes to Spindles,* developed a community theater group, and worked on Chinatown cable television.

He returned to Hong Kong in 1977 and immediately found employment at TVB, which also gained talents such as Ann Hui, RINGO LAM, and Chow Yun-fat—invaluable training they would later use in their own films. In his nine-month tenure at TVB, he directed one of the episodes in a popular television melodrama, *The Family,* which featured Chow Yun-fat in a supporting role. After moving to another television station, CTV, he gained the attention of the movie industry when he filmed a costume drama, *Golden Dagger Romance,* in a cinematic way using a portable camera. After six months at CTV, he directed his first film, *The Butterfly Murders,* in 1979. This merger of detective story, martial arts, and science fiction flopped at the box office. The following year he directed *We're Going to Eat You* and *Dangerous Encounters of the First Kind.* The latter's social criticisms of Hong Kong society evoked storms of protest, resulting in the film's reediting.

After joining Cinema City and directing the comedy *All the Right Clues . . . For the Right Solution* (1981), Hark came to prominence by directing the classic *Zu: Warriors from the Magic Mountain* for Golden Harvest in 1983. This special-effects extravaganza literally changed the face of Hong Kong cinema since it merged Eastern and Western values, the latter of which appeared in Hark's employment of many Lucasfilm technicians for this film. He then founded the famous Film Workshop, which employed many key talents of Hong Kong's New Wave cinema. Tsui Hark was instrumental in launching John Woo toward his present status by employing him to direct *A Better Tomorrow* (1986), which Hark also produced. The two talents also cooperated on *A Better Tomorrow 2* (1987), *Just Heroes* (1987), and *The Killer* (1989) before their relationship deteriorated. In 1989, Hark directed the Vietnam-related *A Better Tomorrow 3* (aka *Love and Death in Saigon*), which Woo had expressed interest in. While Woo later made his Vietnam film, *A Bullet in the Head* (1990), Hark's version changed Woo's male emphasis toward the role of the female, inasmuch as Anita Mui's Kit is the person who educates Chow Yun-fat's Mark in gunplay techniques.

Tsui Hark has been described as the ROGER CORMAN of Hong Kong cinema, referring to the American director's role in his production company New World Cinema. Hark has frequently played a behind-the-scenes role as line producer, screenplay consultant, and often unofficial director in terms of the extent of his involvement. He plays an active collaborative function in many of his films. Although his fast-paced style is evident in films such as *Peking Opera Blues* (1986) and *The Blade* (1995), traces of his involvement also appear in his films as producer, such as *A Chinese Ghost Story* (1987), directed by Ching Siu-tung, and *Dragon Inn* (1992), directed by Raymond Lee.

Like many Hong Kong talents, Hark is interested in films that deal with the relationship of the present to the past, especially issues concerning the 1997 reunification. Hark's *Once Upon a Time in*

China series revived the old Cantonese folk hero, Wong Fei-hong, and updated him in films dealing with China's relationship with national traditions and the encroachment of the modern world. The first three films starred Jet Li in the role originally played by veteran actor Kwan Tak-hing and dealt with the character's development from a traditional hero to one more fully aware of issues raised by a complicated, changing world. Hark's American-based films such as *Double Team* (1997), starring Jean-Claude Van Damme and Dennis Rodman, are seriously compromised and bear little relationship to his Hong Kong films.

Reference   Teo, Stephen, *Hong Kong Cinema: The Extra Dimensions* (London: British Film Institute, 1997).

—T.W.

Hartley, Hal (1960–)   Once called the "JEAN-LUC GODARD of Long Island," Hal Hartley grew up in the Irish-Catholic enclave of Lindenhurst, settled by Newfoundlanders who moved there during the 1950s. His father, Hal, Sr., was an ironworker, crane operator, and building foreman in Manhattan. He studied art for a year after completing high school, then enrolled in the film program of the State University of New York at Purchase. Hartley's first feature film was financed by Jerome Brownstein, the owner of a production company where Hartley worked as an assistant, making industrial films and commercials. That film, *The Unbelievable Truth,* shot on a budget of $60,000, premiered to rave reviews at the Toronto Film Festival of 1989. In his *New York Times Magazine* profile of Hartley, Peter de Jonge noted that the young director could have then taken the film to the Sundance Festival to parlay a Hollywood production deal, but he chose, instead, to begin work on another low-budget production, *Trust* (1990), which also debuted at the 1990 Toronto Film Festival, then went on to win the first annual Waldo Salt Screenwriting Award at the 1991 Sundance Festival, the Critic's Prize at the Sydney Film Festival, two prizes at the Hous-

ton Film Festival, the Audience Award at the São Paulo Film Festival, and the Jury Critics' Prize at the Deauville Film Festival. No doubt Hartley knew which of his early films would dazzle the film festival clientele.

Hartley has been loyal to his production crew. Cinematographer Michael Spiller has worked with Hartley since they first met at Purchase. Actresses Karen Sillas, Elina Löwensohn, and Parker Posey all met Hartley at SUNY Purchase. Production designer Steve Rosenzweig worked on all of Hartley's early short films and on such features as *Amateur* (1994) and *Flirt* (1996). Editor Steve Hamilton met Hartley through Michael Spiller. Producer Ted Hope was Hartley's assistant director and line producer on his first two feature films. Hartley completed his first short film in 1985 and by 1988 had made three shorts: *Kid, The Cartographer's Girlfriend,* and *Dogs.* In 1991 Hartley made three short films for PBS—*Theory of Achievement, Ambition,* and *Surviving Desire,* all for American Playhouse. In 1993 Hartley directed several music videos, followed by a short video *NYC 3/94,* exhibited at the 1994 New York Film Festival, and a short film for Comedy Central, *Opera No. 1* (1994).

Hartley's films have focused on eccentric, intelligent misfits: a convicted murderer and a young girl obsessed with the idea of a nuclear Armageddon in *The Unbelievable Truth,* for example; a brilliant 30-year-old misfit who carries a live hand grenade in *Trust;* two brothers searching for their father in *Simple Men* (1992); a virginal, nymphomaniac nun (Isabelle Huppert, the first celebrity to work for Hartley) and an amnesiac pornographer pursued by professional assassins for reasons he cannot remember in *Amateur* (1994). The latter film is oddly balanced between a Roman Catholic awareness of evil in the world inscrutably perceived, and Catholic morality in conflict with repressed lust. Hartley's plots, far removed from the concerns of traditional Hollywood, have earned him a substantial cult following, especially among women. *New York Times* reviewer Janet Maslin was one of Hartley's strongest supporters, for example. She called *Henry Fool* (1998), Hartley's take on a mysterious, unpublished writer, "a great American film that's no more likely than [Robert Altman's] *Nashville* to turn up on the American Film Institute's Top 100 hit parade," but one that will linger "in the hearts and minds of viewers receptive to its epic vision." *Henry Fool* was followed by *The Book of Life* (1999), a whimsical treatment of the Book of Revelation as "a hip religious fable that begins facetiously and becomes steadily more reflective," in the words of *New York Times* reviewer Stephen Holden.

Washington Post reviewer Rita Kempley, on the other hand, was not swept away by Hartley's "arty romance," *Flirt* (1996): "In a peacockish display, the writer-director tells the same story three times with three different characters in three different locales. With every change of scene, the actors grow less important and Hartley's heavy-handed auteurship more intrusive," she complained. "This isn't a flirtation, it's art-house date rape." *Flirt* consisted of three short films, all based on the same situation but shot in New York, Berlin, and Tokyo, with different actors and crews. Hartley has been called no ordinary filmmaker: "His timing is offbeat, his narratives off center," Ellen Pall wrote. Hartley himself claims "characters are interesting when they have their own agendas." Geoff Brown of the London *Times* described the characters as being stuck "in a muddle of desires, ambitions, and self-doubts that make up relationships." *Amateur,* for example, "presents women as sex objects, but then punctures the presentation. An action film cliché is offered for real, only to disintegrate into jest. The rug is always pulled from under our feet." Hartley may not be an American Godard, but he is an American original, whose method of working with a tight group of actors and colleagues and writing his own scripts does resemble Ingmar Bergman's method and is far, far from Hollywood's.

References Brown, Geoff, "Elegantly Turning Prose," *The* (London) *Times,* January 5, 1995, p. 34; de Jonge, Peter, "The Jean-Luc Godard of Long Island," *New York Times Magazine,* August 5, 1996, pp. 18–21; Pall, Ellen, "The Elusive Women Who Inhabit the Quirky Films of Hal Hartley," *New York Times,* April 9, 1995, sec. II, pp. 15, 22.

—J.M.W.

Hathaway, Henry (1898–1985)

One of Hollywood's most prolific and enduring contract directors, Henry Hathaway excelled at virtually every genre and mode of filmmaking. He was born on March 13, 1898, in Sacramento, California, the only child of acting parents Rhoady de Fiennes and Jean Hathaway. At age 10 he turned his back on formal education and worked as a child actor for ALLAN DWAN's American Film Company. "I was doing everything," Hathaway recalled in a 1974 interview. "Whenever they needed a kid, I was it. If the Indians had to steal a child . . . it was me." After serving as a gunnery instructor in World War I, he returned to Hollywood as a prop man for director Frank Lloyd. Stints as assistant director for JOSEF VON STERNBERG and VICTOR FLEMING convinced him that the only security in the picture business lay in directing. His own debut as a director came with Zane Grey's *Heritage of the Desert* in 1932. During the next two years Hathaway did eight more low-budget Grey adaptations, most of them starring a young Randolph Scott.

His "breakthrough" picture, *Lives of a Bengal Lancer* (1935), featured Gary Cooper in a swashbuckling saga of life in India under the Raj. Having gained something of a reputation as an action director, Hathaway immediately switched gears with another Cooper vehicle, *Peter Ibbetson* (1935), a fantasy romance about a convicted murderer who enjoys a dream romance with the woman he loves. *The Trail of the Lonesome Pine* (1936), a Technicolor melodrama about feuding mountain families, revealed yet another Hathaway penchant, the ability to craft a piece of rural Americana. These three aspects of Hathaway's talents were to surface repeatedly in his subsequent career. For example, his action pictures included the combat drama *The Desert Fox* (1951) and more swashbucklers, such as *The Black Rose* (1950), about a disinherited Saxon noble (Tyrone Power) in Mongolia, and *Prince Valiant* (1954), a stylish Arthurian saga featuring a splendid climactic sword fight between Robert Wagner and James Mason. His distinguished series of westerns included *Rawhide* (1951) and a series of John Wayne vehicles: *North to Alaska* (1960), *The Sons of Katie Elder* (1965), and *True Grit* (1969), in which Wayne's portrayal of the cantankerous, one-eyed Rooster Cogburn won him an Oscar. Affectionate portraits of homespun Americana included *The Shepherd of the Hills* (1941) and *Home in Indiana* (1944).

To his reputation for expertise in these three genres, Hathaway added a skill in making documentary-style thrillers, beginning with *The House on 92nd Street* (1945). This "March of Time"-like story was taken from the case files of the FBI and chronicled the prewar infiltration of a spy ring of fifth columnists. Shot on location, it spawned numerous imitators, including Hathaway's own *13 Rue Madeleine* (1946), a story of the operations of the OSS during the war; *Call Northside 777,* a superior noir about a cynical newspaperman (James Stewart) who endeavors to overturn the wrongful conviction of an accused murderer; and *Fourteen Hours* (1951), a fact-based account of a suicide attempt by a man on a ledge high above New York City. Related to these pictures are several notable crime noirs, especially *Kiss of Death* (1947), whose nominal star, Victor Mature, was overshadowed by Richard Widmark's spectacularly over-the-top performance as a giggling, psychotic killer. The naturalism of these pictures—including the use of location photography, handheld 16-mm cameras, and natural sound recording—was nothing short of a revolution in postwar filmmaking, and placed Hathaway on a par with other practi-

tioners of the noir style, like Jules Dassin and Anthony Mann.

Hathaway was famous for his willingness to take on virtually any kind of project in the offing. On the whole, however, he preferred his noirish documentaries. "Those documentaries are my favorites," he said with characteristic practicality; "it's the genre I like best. Most people seem to prefer my westerns, but I'm not so fond of them. They're so damn difficult. There's no proscenium arch; you're outside and you've got to create your own. You can't have a man backing in from the sidelines and saying 'Stick 'em up' when you could have seen him coming for twelve miles. Just getting people in and out of scenes is hard and frustrating." Critic and historian Andrew Sarris was rather dismissive of him in his book *The American Cinema* (1968): "Hathaway's charm consists chiefly of minor virtues, particularly a sense of humor, uncorrupted by major pretensions, but this charm is also a limiting factor. The professional detractors of [JOHN] FORD and [HOWARD WINCHESTER] HAWKS almost invariably attempt to palm off Hathaway as a reasonable facsimile, but such a comparison is patently absurd." Historian Scott Eyman is more generous, observing that Hathaway was one of the most dependable, versatile craftsman in Hollywood. He was for 20th Century-Fox what RAOUL WALSH had been for Warner Bros., "the hardnosed professional who would take on a troublesome story or an obnoxious actor and, one way or another, turn out a watchable, if not always galvanic, film. In return, they would be occasionally favored with a first-rate script and sober actors."

Much of Hathaway's success undoubtedly derived from his solid professional relationship with his boss at Fox, Darryl F. Zanuck. "In the 20 years I worked for Darryl, I never turned down one script he handed me," he recalled. "I made pictures. Some dogs, yes, but a lot of good ones too. When I went into the hospital for a cancer operation in 1950, [Zanuck] gave me a script to work on while I recuperated, which not too many people did after cancer operations back then. But Darryl was right about both the script and my recovery; he held up the film [*The Desert Fox*] until I could do it." Hathaway died in Los Angeles on February 11, 1985.

Other Films   *The Witching Hour* (1934); *Now and Forever* (1934); *Go West, Young Man* (1936); *Souls at Sea* (1937); *Spawn of the North* (1938); *The Real Glory* (1939); *Johnny Apollo* (1940); *Brigham Young—Frontiersman* (1940); *Diplomatic Courier* (1952); *Niagara* (1953); *White Witch Doctor* (1953); *Legend of the Lost* (1957); *From Hell to Texas* (1958); *Seven Thieves* (1960); *Nevada Smith* (1966); *The Last Safari* (1967); *Five Card Stud* (1968); *Raid on Rommel* (1971); *Shootout* (1971); *Hang-Up* (1973).

References   Eyman, Scott, "'I made movies . . .': An Interview with Henry Hathaway," *Take One,* September–October 1974: 6–12; Sarris, Andrew, *The American Cinema* (New York: E. P. Dutton, 1968); Scheuer, Phillip K., "Henry Hathaway," in *Directors in Action,* ed. Bob Thomas (New York: Bobbs-Merrill, 1973).

—J.C.T.

Hawks, Howard Winchester (1896–1977)

According to critic Andrew Sarris, Howard Hawks has been one of the least known and least appreciated giants in American cinema. Reluctant to discuss his films as anything other than practical working assignments, and remaining within the Hollywood establishment throughout his life, he seems on the face of it a poor candidate for true auteur status. Historian Gerald Mast has referred to him as an "invisible" man who made films less idiosyncratic and stylized than his peers, like FRANK CAPRA, JOHN FORD, and ALFRED HITCHCOCK: "The seeming artlessness and ordinariness [of his films] not only tends to make their creator invisible but also makes it exceedingly difficult to evaluate them according to the existing standards, terms, and values for discussing films." Yet, in the eight silent and 32 sound features he directed between 1923 and 1970, there are consistent stylistic and thematic elements that demand close consideration.

He was born on May 30, 1896, into a prosperous business family in Goshen, Indiana. The eldest of three sons, he was something of a daredevil and preferred racing cars to studying in school. After a stint at Cornell, where he majored in mechanical engineering (but where he really studied gambling and drinking), he went to work as a prop man at Paramount in 1916. He flew in the Army Air Corps during World War I and returned to Hollywood, to direct his first feature, *The Road to Glory,* in 1926. Fiercely independent from the very beginning, Hawks refused to attach himself to any studio or type of film for very long and managed to produce many of his own pictures.

In his 40-year career, his best films were made for those companies that gave him the greatest freedom and control. He wrote, or supervised the writing of, every one of his films. His mania for control and his slow shooting pace were maddening to one and all. In his personal life he had three unsuccessful marriages, to Athole Shearer, Nancy Raye ("Slim") Gross, and Dee Hartford; and few lasting friends, excepting fellow director Victor Fleming and cameraman Gregg Toland. His true identity seems to have always been linked to his work, to his passion for films. His versatility and range were legendary. *Scarface* (1932), financed by Howard Hughes and starring Paul Muni as an Italian gangster modeled after Al Capone, stands out as the grittiest and bloodiest of the early 1930s crime cycle. Hawks would top it later with *The Big Sleep* (1946), a classic crime noir with a plot so convoluted even the screenwriter, William Faulkner, could not figure it out. *Twentieth Century* (1934), *Bringing Up Baby* (1938), and *His Girl Friday* (1940) are keystone films in the genre of the screwball comedy. Here, Hawks's penchant for nonstop verbal pyrotechnics, overlapping dialogue, and sexually suggestive banter reaches its apotheosis. Indeed, the sexual politics of *His Girl Friday's* subtext—a female "Hildy Johnson" (Rosalind Russell) replaced the male role that had been in the original Broadway stage play and thus became

Howard Hawks (right) (Author's collection)

a sexual and professional foil for Cary Grant's "Walter Burns"—hilarious as they are, in actuality function as a clever and probing examination and revision of conventional gender identity. Conversely, in *I Was A Male War Bride* transsexuality works in the opposite direction, when Cary Grant spends much of the film in drag as a WAC.

Indeed, Hawks's treatment of women particularly and gender issues in general is a key element in his films. Paradoxically enough—for Hawks has been rightly accused of being a notorious sexist in his private life—Hawks frequently portrayed women positively in nontraditional roles: "He is one of the few classic Hollywood directors," notes

historian Jean-Pierre Coursodon, "whose films are not based on the assumption that a woman's place is in the home and her happiness lies in caring for a family." However, this sometimes meant that his heroines had to be caricatured in order to claim center stage, as was the case with the two heroines in *Gentlemen Prefer Blondes,* who, says Coursodon, "are an interesting example of hyperfemaleness breaking through the sex barrier and coming full circle, back to a kind of masculinity." In other words, the more women are accepted on men's terms, the more "manly" they seem to become, as was the case with the character played by Paula Prentiss in an underrated Hawksian comedy, *Man's*

Favorite Sport (1963). So powerful are these women at times, that they have to assume dominant positions over their men, whose behavior has been more like that of little boys than of mature males. One thinks of Joanne Dru and Jean Arthur intervening in the squabbling between the male rivals in their lives in, respectively, *Red River* (1948) and *Only Angels Have Wings* (1939). Coursodon speculates that these themes point toward Hawks's denial of femininity itself, "to ultimately erase sex distinction in favor of a system in which the sexes are interchangeable." Hawks characteristically dismisses such speculations as mere twaddle. "I haven't thought too much about the [women's liberation] movement," he said in a 1971 interview, "mostly because the people who seem to be doing most of the talking are so unattractive that I don't think it's fun. The kind of women that I use are just honest. The men I like are not very talkative, so the woman has to do a little about the thing. . . . That happens to be the kind of woman that I like—I don't see why they have to sit around and wash dishes."

All of this notwithstanding, Hawks also delivered solid action pictures about men in physical and psychological crisis, particularly in his highly personal aviation pictures, including *The Dawn Patrol* (1930), *Ceiling Zero* (1936), *Only Angels Have Wings* (1939), and *Air Force* (1943). Whereas in his comedies the men are plagued by failure, humiliation, and frustration, they are virile and self-assured in the dramas. They are, moreover, obsessed with "getting the job done" in a professional manner, whether it is shark fishing, flying the mail, bagging wild animals, conducting a bombing run, driving the cattle, racing a race car, or putting out oil fires. For Hawks the highest human emotion is the camaraderie of the exclusive, self-sufficient, all-male group, and it is necessary to pass a test of ability and courage to win admittance. "Professionals are the only people I'm interested in," says Hawks. "Amateurs I'm not interested in. I'm interested in the guys who are good. I hate losers, and the ones

who are not good are bound to be losers. So I just don't pay any attention to them." While this is a rather confining agenda, marginal characters, especially women, can always be counted on to provide a measure of moral and emotional reorientation. *Only Angels* gave Cary Grant one of his best roles, casting him against romantic type as a hard-boiled airmail pilot. *Air Force* chronicled the odyssey of a B-17 bomber crew as it struggles to get into the war after the bombing of Pearl Harbor. As effective as the cast members are, including John Garfield and Harry Carey, Sr., it is the airplane that emerges as the real "star" of the film.

Of all Hawks's genre pictures, however, the westerns, particularly the later ones, pose special problems for critics and viewers. Frequently they tend toward a stylization verging on caricature and self-parody. While the aforementioned *Red River* (1948) pits trail boss Dunson (John Wayne) against Matthew Garth (Montgomery Clift) during a drive to get cattle to market, its denouement depends more heavily on sorting out a Freudian love triangle than anything else. Late westerns like *Rio Bravo* (1959), *El Dorado* (1966), and *Rio Lobo* (1970) are relatively static and stagebound, their male and female characters acting out their roles on a chessboard of formulaic schemas. They seem, at once, both anti-westerns and meta-westerns. In all of these genres and in all of these films, Hawks's visual style is obscured by what critic Manny Farber describes as an "undemonstrative camera" and a pacing that is a "straight-ahead motion." He never uses flashbacks, pretentious crane shots, odd camera angles, or decorative cutting. The talking may at times be nonstop, but, as Farber notes, there is little attention to profound themes; rather, a "poetic sense of action" emerges from strutting braggarts, boyishly cynical dialogue, and melodramatic situations. "I don't analyze any of these things," said Hawks. "I've found that if I think a thing is funny, the audience thinks it's funny. If I think it's exciting, the audience thinks so. If I like a girl, the audience likes her. If I like a man, the audience likes him. So I don't worry. I just go ahead and make a movie." Howard Hawks died on December 26, 1977, of complications sustained from a head injury.

Other Films *A Girl in Every Port* (1928); *The Criminal Code* (1931); *Tiger Shark* (1933); *To Have and Have Not* (1944); *The Big Sky* (1952); *Monkey Business* (1952); *Hatari!* (1962).

References Coursodon, Jean-Pierre, *American Directors,* vol. 2 (New York: McGraw-Hill, 1983); Goodwin, Michael, and Naomi Wise, "An Interview with Howard Hawks," *Take One* 3, no. 8 (November–December 1971): 19–25; Mast, Gerald, *Howard Hawks, Storyteller* (New York: Oxford University Press, 1982).

—J.C.T.

Hepworth, Cecil (1874–1953)

Cecil Hepworth was an important participant in the birth and development of the British motion picture industry. If pride of place must go to ROBERT WILLIAM PAUL as the "Father of the British Film," Hepworth lagged not far behind. Indeed, he came to stand at the forefront of the industry until the outbreak of World War I. He was the son of a noted lantern-slide lecturer, and he worked for a while designing and selling projector lamps. In 1898 he set up his first major film studio at Walton-on-Thames. Within the next five years he worked as a producer on short actualities and story films in the manner of GEORGES MÉLIÈS and Paul. His six-minute chase film, *Rescued by Rover* (directed by Lewin Fitzhamon), was such a spectacular success at home and abroad that, like the American story film, *The Great Train Robbery,* made two years earlier, it spawned numerous imitations and helped establish the story film as the preeminent form of film entertainment of the day. "I have never in my life before or since witnessed such intense enthusiasm as these short, crude films evoked in audiences who saw films for the first time," he recalled in his autobiography, *Came the Dawn* (1951).

His handbook on film, *Animated Photography,* was one of the earliest published works on the new medium. He experimented with synchronized sound as early as 1910, when he patented a system called Vivaphone. In 1914 he returned to directing and worked with a stock company of actors trained entirely in the cinema, including Alma Taylor, Chrissie White, Violet Hopson, and Stewart Rome. These films were mostly literary or theatrical adaptations, but despite their exquisite photography they reveal little of the penchant for experiment in story structure and editing seen in his earliest films. *Annie Laurie* (1916) and *Boundary House* (1918), for example, are formulaic and static. However, they do benefit from his tendency to eschew the studio and shoot scenes in natural locations. "I would never work indoors if I could possibly get into the open air," he said. "It was always in the back of my mind from the very beginning that I was to make English Pictures, with all the English countryside for background and with English atmosphere and English idiom throughout." He declared bankruptcy in 1924 and after 1927 made no more films. His remaining years were spent directing short advertising films and trailers for National Screen Service. He died in 1953.

Other Films *Falsely Accused* (1905); *Oliver Twist* (1912); *David Copperfield* (1913); *Alf's Button* (1919); *Comin' Through the Rye* (1922).

References Armes, Roy, *A Critical History of British Cinema* (New York: Oxford University Press, 1978); Hepworth, Cecil, *Came the Dawn: Memories of a Film Pioneer* (New York: 1951).

—J.C.T.

Heckerling, Amy (1954–)

Amy Heckerling was born on May 7, 1954, in the Bronx, New York City, and raised there and in Queens. After high school at the Manhattan School of Art and Design, Heckerling earned her undergraduate degree from New York University. She then became a directing fellow at the American Film

Institute in Los Angeles, where she made the half-hour film *Getting It Over With,* about a 19-year-old girl who wants to lose her virginity by the time she is 20. This early effort secured Heckerling an agent and led to her first feature-film assignment, 1982's *Fast Times At Ridgemont High.*

Reviled or dismissed by many critics at the time as just another teen exploitation film, *Fast Times* is now widely seen as a groundbreaking, even radical film for its funny yet painfully candid portrayal of teen life as well as its consistently thoughtful expression of adolescent female points of view in a genre usually dominated by male points of view. *Fast Times* was also the film debut or first major role for many actors in its extraordinary cast, including Sean Penn, Judge Reinhold, Jennifer Jason Leigh, Phoebe Cates, Eric Stoltz, Forrest Whitaker, and an underage Nicholas Cage (credited under his real name, Nicholas Coppola). The film was one of the first commercially successful mainstream Hollywood films to be directed by a woman; many years and several video releases later, it has only grown in popularity.

The success of *Fast Times* brought Heckerling many copycat scripts, but instead of repeating herself she made *Johnny Dangerously* (1984), an affectionate pastiche of 1930s gangster movies and an homage to her favorite screen actor, Jimmy Cagney. Starring Michael Keaton, then a relative newcomer, the film was ambitious but uneven, and it was not successful. Seeking to restore her bankability, Heckerling then agreed to direct 1985's *National Lampoon's European Vacation.* Though most fans think this effort the weakest of the *Vacation* series, and Heckerling herself has expressed displeasure with the result, the film did good business and restored her Hollywood luster.

Her most resounding success, however, came with a film inspired by her own pregnancy and giving birth: *Look Who's Talking* (1989). This story—of an abandoned mother (Kirstie Alley), a sassy baby who's talking even from *before* his conception (Bruce Willis, though only the film viewer

can hear him), and a heartthrob who provides aid and solace to the mother (John Travolta in a performance that revitalized his career)—grossed nearly $300 million worldwide and was just as popular overseas as in the United States. The artistically disappointing sequel, *Look Who's Talking Too* (1990), was rushed into production while Heckerling was undergoing a divorce and other difficult times in her life; it nevertheless did respectable business.

Not until 1995, however, did Heckerling achieve both commercial and immediate critical success, winning that year's National Society of Film Critics' best screenplay award for her film *Clueless.* This adaptation of Jane Austen's *Emma* launched Alicia Silverstone's career and secured Heckerling's reputation as not only a gifted writer/director but also one of the most interesting and refreshing talents in Hollywood. Although 2000's *Loser* opened to mixed reviews and flopped at the box office, Heckerling remains a forceful and innovative presence in Hollywood. Extraordinary with actors; masterful with pace, music, montage, and tone; the queen of the sight gag, Heckerling combines the sass of an independent filmmaker with the commercial instincts born of her long love affair with the movies.

Other Films   As producer: *A Night At the Roxbury* (1997). As executive producer: *Molly* (1998).

References   Cole, Janis, and Holly Dale, *Calling the Shots: Profiles of Women Filmmakers* (Kingston, Ontario: Quarry Press, 1993); Singer, Michael, *A Cut Above: 50 Film Directors Talk About Their Craft* (Los Angeles: Lone Eagle, 1998).

—W.G.C.

Henson, Jim   (1936–1990)   Before his untimely death at 53, Jim Henson devised the beloved fantasy characters known as the Muppets and brought them to a generation of grateful children. James Maury Henson was born September 24, 1936, in Greenville, Mississippi, the son of Paul, a biologist for the U.S. Department of Agriculture, and Betty Henson. He spent his earliest years in Leland, Mississippi, until a change in his father's work prompted the family to move to Hyattsville, Maryland. Henson went on to graduate from Northwestern High School in Hyattsville in 1954. At that time, Henson, who was enchanted by the magic of television and film, began appearing on WTOP's *Junior Good Morning Show,* performing as a puppeteer. At the time, he saw puppets only as a means to break into film, never realizing he was on the way to creating an entire empire of children's entertainment.

While studying at the University of Maryland (he received his degree in 1959), he met Jane Nebel, who would become his partner in broadcasting and life. (They married in 1959; although they later separated, they remained married until his death.) In 1955, the pair began making *Sam and Friends* (which ran for the next six years) for WRC-TV in Washington, D.C. Among the Muppets (Henson's newly coined term for his puppet creations) in the cast of this show was one Kermit the Frog, Henson's alter ego, who would eventually vault to stardom as a popular-culture icon along the lines of Mickey Mouse or Bugs Bunny. Henson and his Muppets began making appearances on late-night programs and national specials hosted by the likes of Jack Paar, Ed Sullivan, and Steve Allen, and they became popular in commercials.

In 1963, Henson began his partnership with Frank Oz, his longtime friend and collaborator. The next year, the Muppets increased their national exposure when Rowlf the Dog (voiced by Henson) became a regular on *The Jimmy Dean Show.* Henson continued his own efforts at creative expression, however, as he continued to view the Muppets as a means to an end. His short film *Time Piece* (1965) reveals his experimental and artistic side; it was nominated for an Academy Award for best short film. He followed this experimental piece with *Youth '68* (1968), a psychedelic/impressionistic documentary on the youth

culture of the late 1960s, and *The Cube* (1969), a surreal, black-and-white avant garde drama about a man's own psychological prison; both were broadcast by NBC. For several years in the late 1960s, Henson and his chief writer Jerry Juhl attempted to complete the "Cyclia Project," an experimental nightclub using a variety of constantly changing images to create a visual world. Plans were for multiple projectors and screens, including one method of projecting images onto dry ice, but the project was eventually dropped as other, more feasible plans became possible.

In 1969, Jim Henson teamed with the Children's Television Workshop to create *Sesame Street,* a PBS program designed as an aid to Head Start in teaching preschool children their numbers and letters. A variety of film and advertising techniques were used with segments, as well as songs and animation sequences; but the program really came to life with the addition of a cast of Henson's Muppets, including his own characters Kermit, Ernie, and Guy Smiley. Although he was initially reluctant to include his creations on the program—for fear he would be typecast as merely a children's performer—Henson's creative force shaped and defined the series, and throughout the 1970s he did establish himself as his generation's Walt Disney, with his Muppet characters becoming universally recognized icons. Along with STEVEN SPIELBERG and GEORGE LUCAS, Henson helped create the popular culture for a new generation, through the characters' continued guest appearances and specials. Despite their popularity, Henson struggled to sell a series to American networks, but only Lord Lew Grade in England was interested, and *The Muppet Show* premiered in 1976 and ran for five successful seasons as an international hit.

The Muppets continued their international success with their feature debut in *The Muppet Movie* (1979), a whimsical view of a Muppet quest for Hollywood success; Kermit's ballad "The Rainbow Connection" earned Henson an Academy Award nomination for best song. Henson, who had directed television episodes and specials, made his big-screen directorial debut in 1981 with *The Great Muppet Caper,* for which he claimed his second best-song nomination for the love ballad "The First Time It Happens." The following year, he codirected *The Dark Crystal* with FRANK OZ. The ambitious fantasy was a critical success, as Henson created an entire world and characters through sophisticated puppetry utilizing animatronic and remote-controlled technology to create lifelike creatures and beings. Following this film, Henson created the Creature Shop, a London-based company that specialized in this advanced form of technical puppetry.

In 1983 he premiered the cable series *Fraggle Rock* (which ran for five seasons), an international series based on themes of diversity and understanding. Henson's storytelling functioned on multiple levels, and he pursued his desire to produce sophisticated fantasy stories with his next directorial effort, *Labyrinth* (1986)—produced by George Lucas from a story by Henson and Terry Jones and using Creature Shop creations—as well as the films he produced through the Creature Shop, such as *Return to Oz* (1985) and *The Witches* (1990). In the late 1980s, alongside several Muppet specials, Henson produced *The Storyteller* (1987–89)—an anthology series of fables and myths brought to life through a combination of puppetry and live action—and *The Jim Henson Hour* (1989), a series combining new Muppet stories with imaginative fantasies.

Henson discussed merging his company with Disney, but the deal fell through when he refused to sell the rights to *Sesame Street* (keeping its profits with Public Broadcasting). Shortly after these negotiations fell through, Henson visited Ahoskie, N.C., to see his mother for Mother's Day. Feeling ill, he returned to his New York home, and on May 16, 1990, he died from a bacterial strain of pneumonia. In the decade that has followed, his son Brian has succeeded him as head of Jim Henson Production, and both the Muppets and the Creature Shop have continued creating new, original productions in both puppetry and fantasy filmmaking.

Other Films   *The Muppets Take Manhattan* (1984); *Sesame Street Presents Follow That Bird* (1986).

References   Finch, Christopher, *Of Muppets & Men: The Making of The Muppet Show* (New York: Muppet Press/Alfred Knopf, 1981); Finch, Christopher, *Jim Henson: The Works—The Art, the Magic, the Imagination* (New York: Random House, 1993); Borgenicht, David, *Sesame Street Unpaved: Scripts, Stories, Secrets, and Songs* (New York: Hyperion, 1998).

—H.H.D.

Herzog, Werner (1942–   ) Werner Herzog is one of the original auteurs of *Das neue Kino,* the German "New Wave" that emerged during the 1970s. His strange, disturbing, and enigmatic films are not easily categorized; and perhaps that is part of their appeal. The images that dominate his films are at once mesmerizing and "sublime" but also distorted and perverse. Fantastic locales, fanatical characters, and idiosyncratic stories and incidents find safe haven in the Herzog universe.

Herzog was born Werner Stipetic on September 5, 1942, and spent his childhood in Bavaria with his divorced mother. He began writing scripts as a teenager while attending the Classical Gymnasium in Munich and stole a 35-mm camera to shoot his early films. Educated at the University of Munich, Herzog worked for German television and, for a time, as a welder in a steel factory for the U.S. National Aeronautics and Space Administration.

In 1966 he founded his own production company, Werner Herzog Filmproduktion. Herzog's first feature film, *Signs of Life* (*Lebenszeichen* [1967]), details the detention in a Greek island fortress of a German soldier who gradually grows from alienated prisoner to aggressive fighter. An almost mystical identification with landscapes—both native and exotic in his later films—becomes prominent in images and themes in Herzog's work. *Signs of Life* received much acclaim, both for its themes of alienation and aggression and for its almost documentary style, with the camera objectively recording the events (a style that would permeate his subsequent work). *Signs of Life* won the *Bundesfilmpreis* and the Silver Bear Award at the Berlin Film Festival.

Aguirre, the Wrath of God (*Aguirre, der Zorn Göttes* [1972]), considered by some to be his best film, depicts the life of a 16th-century conquistador intent on conquering the mythical Incan kingdom of El Dorado. The natural images of the Amazonian jungle are at once majestic and intimidating, dwarfing the characters as they traverse the terrain. Nature, for Herzog, is both seductive and potentially destructive. In *Aguirre,* Herzog visualizes nature as an antagonistic force that eventually destroys the person who intrudes or invades—the colonizer. It is a stunning film visually, and the presence of Klaus Kinski (Herzog's most dependable actor) as the obsessed and finally insane Aguirre, makes the film's themes of possession, madness, and colonialization even starker.

Kinski did his best work for Herzog. His astonishing presence also dominates *Nosferatu—Phantom der Nacht* (aka *Nosferatu, the Vampire* [1979]), Herzog's meticulous remake of and tribute to the classic silent film that F. W. MURNAU loosely adapted from Bram Stoker's *Dracula* in 1922; *Woyzeck* (1980), adapted from the fragmented play Georg Büchner wrote in 1936 about a soldier driven insane by "scientific" experimentations forced upon him by the military; and *Fitzcarraldo* (1981), in which Kinski played a mad Irishman obsessed with the desire to bring grand opera (and an opera house) to the interior of Brazil and Peru. Kinski had a particular talent for portraying Herzog's obsessed and afflicted central characters. Several of Herzog's best films are built upon the actor's considerable and eccentric skills. Herzog would later pay tribute to Kinski and their volatile relationship in the documentary, *My Best Fiend: Klaus Kinski* (1999).

Herzog himself has been appropriately characterized as a monomaniacal, maddening autocrat. Still, it cannot be denied that his temperament and style drive films like *The Mystery of Kaspar Hauser* (aka *Jeder für sich und Gott gegen alle* [1974]) and *Stroszek* (1978), both of which demonstrate sympathy for displaced and alienated characters and a pessimistic view of modern civilization. This is especially evident in *Stroszek,* in which Herzog's mysterious actor, identified as "Bruno S.," transplanted from a brutal existence in Germany to a godforsaken American landscape in Wisconsin, falls into a depression and finally commits suicide on a ski lift. For the film *Heart of Glass* (*Herz aus Glas* [1976]), Herzog had the actors hypnotized in the hope of portraying "people on the screen as we have never seen them before." Herzog believes that "film is not the art of scholars, but of illiterates."

Herzog's films are full of disparate characters: misfits, fanatics, dwarfs, megalomaniacs, rebels, and heretics. His two favorite, most frequently used actors, Kinski and Bruno S., have been compared to the grotesque, expressionistic characters of German silent film. Bruno S. is like a blank slate: the viewer has to interpret the actor's ambiguous blankness. Klaus Kinski, on the other hand, goes to the other extreme, projecting a hyperkinetic energy that reflects the director's own craziness and obsessions. While using these actors to depict his own dreamlike, adventurous self-realization and ideas, Herzog's films reflect the director's exaggerated and distorted vision. They also show moments of the sublime, whether it be in the Andes Mountains (*Aguirre*) or in the Wisconsin wheatfields (*Stroszek*).

Herzog's presentation and style are both romantic and realistic, coupling a childlike wonder at life with the ugly, disturbed nature of humankind. A continual theme in Herzog's work is that of aggressive colonialization and exploitation, with *Aguirre, Fitzcarraldo,* and *Where the Green Ants Dream* (*Wo die grünen Ameisen träumen* [1984]), which depicts the destruction by mining engineers of the land of Australia's aborigines. Herzog's films challenge viewers into reorienting themselves away from traditional movie styles, just as his actors must do when they enter his world.

Over his career, Herzog has made numerous documentaries, features he considers just as important as his narrative films. These documentaries often deconstruct the genre by using innovative filmic techniques. Beginning as early as 1970 with *Fata Morgana,* and more recently with *Wodaabe: Shepherds of the Sun* (*Wodaabe–Die Hirten der Sonne* [1988]), Herzog has unobtrusively observed people in their normal surroundings, performing normal rituals and behavior. They are a far cry from the intense, emotionally scarred characters of his narrative films. Still, the powerful images carry the subject's message, without relying upon fictional characters. (Herzog himself proved a fascinating subject in Les Blank's *Burden of Dreams* [1982], a documentary about Herzog and the making of *Fitzcarraldo.*) His films are paradoxical: they are at once disarming in their pessimism, but one often feels immense pleasure and awe derived from Herzog's eccentric but passionate, hauntingly beautiful, astonishing, and astounding images. The worlds of his films are haunting and passionate and intensely personal: "You must understand I am not a philosopher," Herzog has said. "I am not an intellectual. I make films to rid myself of them, like ridding myself of a nightmare. There seem to be many broken people in my films, and much cruelty. But there is also a dignity which transcends the suffering."

Other Films *Even Dwarfs Started Small* (*Auch Zwerge haben klein angefangen* [1970]); *Handicapped Future* (*Behinderte Zukunft* [1970]); *Land of Silence and Darkness* (*Land des Schweigens und der Dunkelheit* [1971]); *The Great Ecstasy of the Sculptor Steiner* (*Die grosse Ekstase des Bildschnitzers Steiner* [1974]); *How Much Wood Does a Woodchuck Chuck* (1976); *Ballad of the Little Soldier* (*Ballad vom kleinen Soldaten* [1984]); *Gasherbaum–The Dark Glow of the Mountains* (*Gasherbaum–Der leuchtende Berg*

[1984]); *Cobra Verde* (1987); *It Isn't Easy Being God* (*Es ist nicht leicht ein Gott zu sein* [1989]); *Echoes from a Somber Kingdom* (*Echos aus einem dustern Reich* [1990]); *Scream of Stone* (*Schrie aus Stein* [1991]); *Jag Mandir* (aka *The Eccentric Private Theatre of the Maharajah of Udaipur* [1991]); *Lessons of Darkness* (*Lektionen in Finsternis* [1992]); *Bells from the Deep* (*Glodcken aus der Tiefe* [1993]); *The Transformation of the World into Music* (*Die Verwaandlung der Welt in Musik* [1994]).

References Atkinson, Michael, "The Wanderings of Werner Herzog," *Film Comment* 36 (2000): 16; Basoli, A. G., "The Wrath of Klaus Kinski: An Interview with Werner Herzog," *Cineaste* 24 (1999): 32; Corrigan, Timothy, ed., *The Films of Werner Herzog* (New York: Methuen, 1986); *Images at the Horizon: A Workshop with Werner Herzog Conducted by Roger Ebert* (Chicago: Facets Multimedia, 1979); Ott, Frederick W., *The Great German Films* (Secaucus, N.J.: Citadel Press, 1986); Overbey, David L., "Every Man for Himself," *Sight and Sound* 2 (1975): 73–75.

—W.V. and J.M.W.

Hill, George Roy (1921–)

Hill was born in Minneapolis, Minnesota, on December 20, 1921. He attended Yale University, where he studied music (B.A., 1943) and then served as a marine pilot in World War II (1943–45). After the war he attended Trinity College, Dublin, earning a B. Litt. degree in 1949. In Dublin he also began acting on the stage. Following further combat duty in the Korean conflict, he moved to New York and resumed acting. In the 1950s he began directing for television, receiving an Emmy for *A Night to Remember* in 1954, and later for the New York stage.

Hill did uncredited directing work on *The Jagged Edge* (1955), but his first credited directing assignments were for plays he had directed on Broadway—Tennessee Williams's *Period of Adjustment* (1962) and Lillian Hellman's *Toys in the Attic* (1963). His third film, *The World of Henry Orient* (1964), is based on a novel by Nora Johnson, daughter of Nunnally Johnson. It tells the modest story of two young girls who fantasize innocently about pianist Orient (Peter Sellers) and follow him around New York as he attempts to seduce a married woman and fails to rehearse for his concerts. Though flatly photographed, the film is a charming period piece; romantic fantasy is innocent, same-sex bonding is unsalacious, and New York is perfectly safe for 14-year-old girls. It displays Hill's strong feel for telling a good story directly and resourcefully and his concern for film music; the score is one of four Elmer Bernstein did for Hill.

Hill went on to a major studio assignment, *Hawaii* (1966), with Julie Andrews, Max von Sydow, a cast of thousands, and another Bernstein score; then *Thoroughly Modern Millie* (1967), also with Andrews. *Millie* began as a small musical; producer Ross Hunter had wanted to film *The Boyfriend,* which had brought Andrews to Broadway, but couldn't get the rights, so he wrote his own script. Having Andrews in a musical enticed Universal to pump the project up to road-show status; the result was a bloated film (with music by Bernstein and André Previn, among others).

Hill next directed the central film of his career, *Butch Cassidy and the Sundance Kid* (1969), based on William Goldman's original screenplay. Despite nearly universal poor reviews, the film took off because audiences loved the charm of its main characters, played by Paul Newman and Robert Redford, its wit, and its emotional range. It was nominated for six Oscars and won four (cinematography, Conrad Hall; best original score, Bert Bacharach; best song, "Raindrops Keep Falling on My Head," Bert Bacharach and Hal David; and best original screenplay, William Goldman). *Butch Cassidy* combines the death-of-the-West motif with archaic romanticism about its outlaw heroes. The freeze-frame at the end, in which Butch and Sundance pass through death into legend, is a striking cinematic rendering of the film's complex attitude toward its subject matter. Both Goldman and Hill were drawn to the story because the historical figures on whom it is based sensibly fled the West for Bolivia instead of stubbornly hanging on, only to die in a mindlessly heroic last stand. The film celebrates their anti-heroic practicality, then translates them into legend by letting them stumble into the heroic last stand they had fled. It made Redford a star and inscribed its characters in popular American history; Butch and Sundance are now as central to our vision of the western outlaw as are Billy the Kid and Jesse James. *Butch Cassidy* is also notable for its use of music, nearly always a strength in Hill's work. Instead of program scoring to underline action and guide audience response, it offers three musical interludes. One features the hit song "Raindrops Keep Falling on My Head"; another introduced the Swingle Singers to popular culture.

Hill next made an unsuccessful adaptation of Kurt Vonnegut's *Slaughterhouse-Five* (1972), with music by Glenn Gould, then took the assignment of directing Newman and Redford in another male-bonding narrative, *The Sting* (1973). A caper film set during the depression, *The Sting* is richly decorated, carefully photographed, and deeply entertaining. It earned a great deal of money and seven Oscars (best music, best art direction, best costume design, best editing, best screenplay, best picture, and best director). The score by Marvin Hamlisch returned Scott Joplin to popular culture.

The Great Waldo Pepper (1975), based on a story by Hill, offers Redford as a pilot who just missed aerial combat in World War I and has had to resort to barnstorming and exhibition flying to nurture his dreams of heroism; in an impromptu quasi-battle with a real German ace now reduced to stunt flying in Hollywood, Pepper proves to himself that he could have met the challenge he longed to face. Redford's filmic heroism in the photography of the aerial combat satisfies us, but probably not Waldo Pepper. This time the music is by Henry Mancini.

The comedic *Slap Shot* (1977) has Newman as the coach of a struggling semipro hockey team who grudgingly uses new players specializing in violence to boost ticket sales; it is another story about changing measures of male stature. In *A Litte Romance* (1979), Hill effectively tells the story of first love between a very young French boy and an equally young American girl; Laurence Olivier plays an elderly con artist who joins them on a picaresque journey to Venice so they can kiss under the Bridge of Sighs. It is a modest, measured film, completely sure in its handling of both comedy and sentiment. It won an Oscar for Georges Delerue's original score.

The World According to Garp (1982) is a big-budget adaptation of John Irving's very popular novel, which offered Robin Williams his first dramatic role. *The Little Drummer Girl* (1984) finds both Diane Keaton and Hill unequal to John Le Carré's complex, moody tale of espionage. *Funny Farm* (1988) gives Chevy Chase a decent role as a sportswriter retiring to New England to write his big novel; it is a slack film with sporadic comic moments and more music by Elmer Bernstein.

Because he started directing films relatively late, at the age of 40, Hill's career was comparatively brief. All his films are marked by careful attention to telling the story clearly and giving the principal characters room to develop fully. He is the only director in the pre-Spielberg/Lucas era to have two films on the list of top ten moneymakers. His 12 films won 13 Oscars; at least one of them, *Butch Cassidy,* is central to American film in the century's last half; and three others, *The Sting, Waldo Pepper,* and *A Little Romance,* are durable works.

References Shores, Edward, *George Roy Hill* (Boston: Twayne, 1983); Horton, Andrew, *The Films of George Roy Hill* (New York: Columbia University Press, 1984); Goldman, William, *Adventures in the Screen Trade* (New York: Warner Books, 1983).

—W.K.

Hill, Walter (1942–) Born on January 10, 1942, in Long Beach, California, Walter Hill grew to become a member of the so-called movie-brat generation of filmmakers who came to prominence in the 1970s. However, unlike most of his generation, Hill seems to have deliberately set out to become a genre director along the lines of ANTHONY MANN and DON SIEGEL. Like those filmmakers, Hill's filmography is largely composed of westerns, gritty crime films, and action adventures.

After graduating from Michigan State University and working a series of odd jobs, Hill got his start in the film industry as a screenwriter. Perhaps his most famous screenplay from this time is *The Getaway* (1972), which was directed by the legendary SAM PECKINPAH. In 1975, Hill made his

Walter Hill (Universal)

directorial debut with *Hard Times* (or *The Street-fighter*), a depression-era story about bare-knuckle boxing. Hill's next film, *The Driver* (1978), featured Ryan O'Neal as a man (known only as "the Driver") hired by criminals to pilot their getaway cars. The film was an updated film noir and featured several exciting chase sequences.

Hill's first major success, however, came the next year with *The Warriors* (1979), a dark and disturbing depiction of war between New York City street gangs. The film did well at the box office and has attained cult status in the 20 years since its release. The following year Hill released his first western, *The Long Riders* (1980), a retelling of the Jesse James legend. Hill cast the film's several sets of outlaw brothers (the James, Youngers, and Fords) with pairs of real-life brothers such as James and Stacey Keach, David and Keith Carradine, and Randy and Dennis Quaid. The film also marked the first pairing of Hill and composer Ry Cooder, who would go on to score a number of Hill's films. Hill's next film, *Southern Comfort* (1981), was a box-office disappointment. The film was about a squad of Louisiana National Guardsmen on maneuvers who get lost in the bayou where they are picked off one by one by the local Cajuns. On the surface the film is tense and exciting, but it should really be viewed as Hill's metaphor for the U.S. involvement in Vietnam.

Perhaps spurred on by that film's failure, Hill next turned to a more conventional style of filmmaking with 1982's *48 Hours.* This cop thriller/buddy picture teamed slovenly cop Nick Nolte with a slick prison inmate played by the young Eddie Murphy, who together attempt to thwart the murderous plans of two escaped convicts. The film was a huge hit and launched the relatively little-known TV comedian Murphy into the ranks of A-list movie stars. Hill used the cachet of *48 Hours*'s success to bankroll what may be his strangest film to date, 1984's *Streets of Fire.* This rock-and-roll fantasy reached back to *The Warriors* for its gang-warfare plotline, but the dominance of its musical

numbers, and the bizarre retro/futuristic setting, proved too weird for most film viewers, and the film did little box office. To recover, Hill tried to recapture the magic of *48 Hours* by teaming with comedian Richard Pryor for a mainstream, comic remake of *Brewster's Millions* (1985). The result was an intermittently funny but largely forgettable film. Hill's next film, another musical, was 1986's *Crossroads,* which featured Ralph Macchio as a young guitar prodigy and Joe Seneca as the aged blues master who takes the kid under his wing. A valiant failure, the film did little to restore Walter Hill's box-office clout. Hill returned to his roots for his next work, 1987's *Extreme Prejudice,* a tougher-than-leather modern-day western starring Nick Nolte as a driven cop and Powers Booth (both of them Hill vets) as the drug lord he vows to bring down. In 1988, Hill again tried to find success with *Red Heat,* a cop thriller/buddy picture, by teaming Arnold Schwarzenegger as a by-the-book Soviet policeman, with a slovenly Jim Belushi as the Chicago cop forced to help Schwarzenegger stop an international drug lord. A moderate success, the film allowed Hill to return to stranger, more-personal fare with 1989's *Johnny Handsome,* a taut crime thriller about a deformed criminal's quest for revenge. Again, the film did poorly at the box office.

At the same time, Eddie Murphy's career seemed to be heading into a slump after the failure of his directorial debut, *Harlem Nights.* Murphy and Hill thus reteamed with Nolte for *Another 48 Hours.* Even more far-fetched (though not as entertaining) as the original, the film did not achieve the kind of breakthrough success as its predecessor. Hill followed *Another 48 Hours* with the gritty-but-flawed crime drama *Trespass* (1992). Based on a screenplay by ROBERT L. ZEMECKIS and Bob Gale, the film depicts a pitched battle between two white firefighters and an African-American street gang for a fortune in gold stashed in an abandoned East St. Louis factory. Hill next returned to the western for his two most interesting works in the 1990s. The first, 1993's *Geronimo: An American Legend*—starring Gene Hackman, Robert Duvall, Jason Patric, Matt Damon, and Wes Studi (in the title role)—was an entertaining epic in the John Ford mold. 1995's *Wild Bill,* on the other hand, was a kind of anti-western depicting the legendary lawman (ably played by Jeff Bridges) as an opium smoker and killer of cripples. In 1996 Hill released *Last Man Standing,* a remake of AKIRA KUROSAWA's *Yojimbo* (1961). Bruce Willis starred as the remorseless killer playing one gang against another in a nearly deserted small town. The film was a box-office failure, and this perhaps explains why Hill took four years to return to feature filmmaking.

In 1999 Hill began work on the science fiction thriller *Supernova* (2000); however, unhappy with studio-mandated cuts, Hill had his name removed from the film, which is now credited to Thomas Lee, a pseudonym. Despite his box-office troubles as a director, Hill has found some measure of success as a producer with both the *Alien* series and HBO's *Tales From the Crypt* television show. Still, one hopes that the *Supernova* disaster has not burned Hill out on feature films. Good, unpretentious genre directors are too scarce for the loss of a Walter Hill to be taken lightly.

References Andrew, Geoff, *The Film Handbook* (Boston: G. K. Hall, 1989); Hardy, Phil, ed., *The Overlook Film Encyclopedia: The Western* (Woodstock, N.Y.: Overlook Press, 1991); Monaco, James, ed., *The Encyclopedia of Film* (New York: Perigee Books, 1991).

—F.A.H.

Hitchcock, Alfred (1899–1980) Although he worked in a wide range of genres, from straight drama to musicals, Alfred Hitchcock is known above all else for the genre that practically bears his shape—with which, indeed, his very shape, in its famous silhouetted form, is identified—the Hitchcockian suspense thriller. The genre is typically characterized by inventive plotting rich with red herrings (Hitchcock has come to be identified with the "MacGuffin"); and by stories invoking the struggle of common men against greater forces (Cary Grant ducking beneath the swooping plane in *North by Northwest*), subversively witty dialogue (the delightful repartee between Robert Donat and Madeleine Carroll in *The 39 Steps*), distinctive and often tricky technical facility (the long takes in *Rope*), the experiment in 3-D filming (*Dial M for Murder*), hallucinatory imagery (the distorting effects in *Spellbound* and *Vertigo*), the psychopathological case study (*Strangers on a Train* and *Psycho*), subtexts concerning the voyeuristic experience of cinema spectatorship (the explicit theme in *Rear Window*), and of course the cameo appearance of the director himself (first seen in the 1926 *The Lodger*). Over the course of his long career, Hitchcock successfully managed the transition from silent film to sound (his early part-talkie, *Blackmail* [1929]), exists in both silent and sound versions); and with equal success he adapted to the new medium of television with the run of *Alfred Hitchcock Presents* from 1955 to 1962.

Yet, it is almost accidental that Hitchcock came to filmmaking at all. Born on August 13, 1899, in East London, Hitchcock studied under the Jesuits at Saint Ignatius College. His engineering studies were short-lived, since after the death of his father in 1914, he was forced into wage labor at Henley's Telegraph and Cable Company in 1915. When hired by the newly established London branch of Lasky's Famous Players in 1920, his aptitude for art led to a job designing and lettering title-cards. The opportunities in the fluid early film industry were rapidly taken advantage of by Hitchcock, who served in any available capacity—designing titles, writing scripts, editing—before finally being offered his first directing job at Gainsborough Studios with *Number Thirteen* (1922). More significant was his next film, *The Lodger* (1926), an atmospheric thriller about the hunt for a Jack the Ripper–like figure, which featured the first complete explication of the Hitchcockian theme of misplaced guilt and suspicion. According to

Alfred Hitchcock

FRANÇOIS TRUFFAUT, it was "the first true Hitch-cock." As commentator Thomas R. Tietze notes, "transference of another's guilt becomes a pervasive psychological concern in nearly all of his subsequent films." In his first sound feature, *Blackmail* (1929), one of the most sophisticated early talkies of the period, sound cues were employed as an integral part of the developing suspense. His first 17 features are, in the opinion of historian Maurice Yacowar in his invaluable *Hitchcock's British Films,* "a remarkably fruitful area of study for anyone interested in Hitchcock, in British films, or in aesthetics in general. For Hitchcock was from the outset a brilliant experimenter in cinematic expression."

Although Hitchcock would continue to work in a wide range of film genres in the 1930s, ranging from an adaptation of Sean O'Casey's *Juno and*

the *Paycock* (1930) to the musical bio-pic of Johann Strauss, Jr., *Waltzes from Vienna* (1933), his most memorable work in the decade came in the half-dozen suspense thrillers he developed. These included *Murder!* (1930), a rare instance of a straight whodunit from Hitchcock's hand; *The Man Who Knew Too Much* (1934), a classic study of a family that finds itself trapped in a densely layered plot of intrigue; *The 39 Steps* (1935), a delightful mix of romance comedy and suspense thriller, which employed the British music hall as its central locus of events and intrigue; the spy yarn *Secret Agent* (1936), based on Somerset Maugham's novel *Ashenden; Sabotage* (1936), based on Joseph Conrad's *Secret Agent,* about anarchist conspiracies in London; and *The Lady Vanishes* (1938), rightly regarded by historian Maurice Yacowar as "the high point in Hitchcock's British period." Over the course of this remarkable body of work, Hitchcock steadily improved in his mastery over the medium, evident above all else in the increased control of atmospherics, dialogue, and suspenseful turns of plot.

Hitchcock was lured to Hollywood by David Selznick in 1939 to direct the romantic thriller *Rebecca* (1940), beginning a fascinating, but troubled relationship between the two men. Excepting for a brief time span in Britain to produce war propaganda, *Bon Voyage* and *Aventure Malgache,* Hitchcock would henceforward be a Hollywood director. And, although Hitchcock was still not quite a one-genre director—*Mr. and Mrs. Smith* (1941) is straight comedy and *Lifeboat* (1943) amounts to a philosophical meditation on people under the stress of war and survival—he increasingly hewed to the suspense-thriller genre. During the early war years Hitchcock stoked the cause of anti-Nazism with suspense plots rooted in the European conflict, like *Foreign Correspondent* (1940) and *Saboteur* (1942). The use in the latter film of a climactic chase atop the Statue of Liberty prefigures the fantastic chases of the later films, like the pursuit atop Mount Rushmore in *North by*

Northwest. Other works of the period, such as *Suspicion* (1941) and the classic proto-noir, *Shadow of a Doubt* (1943), are more concerned with pathological characters and situations involving imperiled women than with politics.

Perhaps the richest period of film production for Hitchcock came in the postwar years, beginning with *Spellbound* (1945) and concluding with *The Birds* (1963) and *Marnie* (1964). These 18 films include many of his most widely acknowledged masterworks. In *Notorious,* characterized by Donald Spoto as "the artistic rendition of an inner life that might have exploded if denied expression," Hitchcock transmuted his personal grief over his mother's death into romantic suspense. The relatively neglected *Rope* not only experiments with fashioning a film out of a seeming single long take, but also explores Nietzschean ideas of the superman's transcending of conventional morality. A remarkable experiment, the stagebound drama dispenses with traditional suspense entirely since the audience knows the identity of the killers from the story's opening dialogue. A similar preoccupation with criminal pathology—played out against a series of set-piece scenes in a train, a tennis court, and an amusement park—informs the Hitchcock classic *Strangers on a Train* (1951). After adapting the stage thriller *Dial M for Murder* to the screen in 1954, Hitchcock directed his quintessential statement about the essentially voyeuristic implications of spectatorship and the film medium, *Rear Window.* James Stewart portrayed a disabled photographer whose curious gaze, aided by his telephoto lenses, reveal the circumstances of a murder in the apartment across the court from his second-story window. Ever fascinated by technical challenges, *Rear Window* required most of the action to be seen from the fixed vantage point of Stewart's window, a frame that functioned, in effect, like a stage proscenium, or the boundaries of a camera's viewfinder.

The remake of *The Man Who Knew Too Much* (1955) may or may not be better than Hitchcock's own original, but it provides an interesting variation on the theme, casting Doris Day as the woman whose song, "Que sera, sera," proves to be a vital element in the solving of a kidnaping plot. *The Trouble with Harry* (1955) is a rather atypical black comedy with a distinctly macabre edge.

Vertigo (1958) and *Psycho* (1960) are justly considered Hitchcock's most complex masterpieces. *Vertigo* has been described by Robin Wood in his seminal book as the "nearest to perfection" of all his films, "a perfect organism, each character, each sequence, each image, illuminating every other." Its high drama operates first in the depth of its understanding of the characters' obsessions and in its manipulations of the viewer's own voyeuristic tendencies. Based on *D'Entre des morts* (1954), by Pierre Boileau and Thomas Narcejac, the story concerns a man's obsessive attempts to transform a young woman into the simulacrum of his dead girl friend. Its voyeurism ideally suited Hitchcock, and it may be regarded as the middle third of a voyeuristic "trilogy," bracketed by *North by Northwest* and *Psycho.* As commentators like Donald Spoto and John Russell Taylor darkly suggest, *Vertigo* is about Hitchcock himself who, like Roger in the novel and Scottie (James Stewart) in the film, continually "made over" his leading ladies— Madeleine Carroll, Grace Kelly, Vera Miles, Kim Novak, Tippi Hedren—into his archetype of the icy, ethereal blonde, dictating their hair color, their clothing style, their deportment. "*Vertigo* in that respect," writes Taylor, "is alarmingly close to allegorized autobiography, a record of Hitch's obsessive pursuit of an ideal quite as much as a literal tale of love lost and found again."

Psycho (1960), shot on a shoestring in chilling black-and-white, blended the Grand Guignol theatrics of the Robert Bloch novel with a stunning psychological probe into the criminally disordered mind of the psychotic Norman Bates (Anthony Perkins). Its horrors, notes Robin Wood, "belong to the age that has witnessed on the one hand the discoveries of Freudian psychology and on the other the Nazi concentration camps." Significantly, its most celebrated sequence, the shower murder of Janet Leigh, is played out in a sterile, aseptic environment rather than a dark and dank dungeon. "When murder is committed in a gleamingly sanitary motel bathroom during a cleansing shower," notes critic Andrew Sarris, "the incursion of evil into our well-laundered existence becomes intolerable. We may laugh nervously or snort disgustedly, but we shall never be quite so complacent again." At the same time, notes Carol J. Clover in her classic study of the modern horror film, *Men, Women, and Chainsaws, Psycho* is "the appointed ancestor of the slasher film," with the now-familiar elements of a psychotic killer who is the product of a sick family, a victim who is a beautiful, sexually active woman, and a slaying that is particularly brutal and is registered from the victim's point of view. The film's reception was little short of sensational. "No amount of optimism or carefully orchestrated hucksterism could have prepared anyone—least of all Alfred Hitchcock—for the firestorm the film was creating," writes commentator Stephen Rebello in his analysis of the film. "Certainly no one could have predicted how powerfully *Psycho* tapped into the American subconscious. Faintings. Walk outs. Repeat visits. Boycotts. Angry phone calls and letters. Talk of banning the film rang from church pulpits and psychiatrists' offices. Never before had any director so worked the emotions of the audience like stops on an organ console."

If, as *Psycho*'s promotion justly proclaimed, we can never feel safe in the shower again after seeing it, *The Birds* (1963) will make anyone think twice before getting a pet parrot. But seriously, the fact that the invasion by the birds has no rational explanation is the very point of the film and the very stuff of Hitchcock's universe, according to Robin Wood. "This seems to me the very function of the birds," writes Wood. "They are a concrete embodiment of the arbitrary and unpredictable, of whatever makes human life and human relation-

ships precarious, a reminder of fragility and instability that cannot be ignored or evaded and, beyond that, of the possibility that life is meaningless and absurd." *North by Northwest* (1959), on the other hand, brings Hitchcock back to the familiar, by contrast cozy, territories of endangerment, chase, and intrigue.

Meanwhile, beginning on the night of November 13, 1955, Hitchcock began introducing what would become 365 segments of his weekly half-hour television series, 20 episodes of which he directed himself. "In selecting the stories for my television shows," he later recalled, "I tried to make them as meaty as the sponsor and the network would stand for, and to offset any tendency toward the macabre with humor." In his essay on Hitchcock's television work, Gene D. Phillips point out that Hitchcock "consistently elected to direct teleplays that closely paralleled the situations and themes associated with his theatrical films, and often cast actors in these short movies whom he also used in his features." Hence, continues Phillips, "these TV films deserve analysis as part of the Hitchcock canon, especially since the series remains in permanent syndication." For example, the episode entitled "One More Mile to Go" (1955), contends Phillips, prefigures in its situation of a corpse concealed in a car trunk incidents in the later *Psycho.* Indeed, as Phillips demonstrates, the stripped-down techniques of television production provided the model for the making of *Psycho.* "*Psycho* was an experiment in this sense," Hitchcock said; "I asked myself if I could make a feature film under the same conditions as a television show." Moreover, several of the best of these television episodes were derived from master storytellers of the grim and ghastly, like John Collier ("Back for Christmas") and Roald Dahl ("The Landlady" and "Lamb to the Slaughter").

Hitchcock's later years were less productive, and critical opinion on the late work more divided. The 1960s saw his return to the genre of political thriller he had deserted after World War II; but neither *Torn Curtain* (1966) nor *Topaz* (1969) works the territory quite as successfully as his earlier work had. And while *Frenzy* marks a return not only to strong form but also to earlier themes (with a Ripper-esque killer loose in the streets of London), Hitchcock's final film, *Family Plot* (1976), has found few advocates. Still, after a career of over 60 films, a final fall from form can be forgiven the master. That we still designate the best suspenseful thrillers that make their way to the screen as "Hitchcockian" is surely testimony to his enduring impact on the suspense film genre. In summing up his work, filmmakers ERIC ROHMER and CLAUDE CHABROL stated: "Hitchcock is one of the greatest *inventors of form* in the entire history of the cinema. Perhaps only [F.W.] MURNAU and [SERGEI] EISENSTEIN can sustain comparison with him when it comes to form. . . . An entire moral universe has been elaborated on the basis of this form and by its very rigor. In Hitchcock's work form does not embellish content, it creates it."

Other Films *The Pleasure Garden* (1925); *The Mountain Eagle* (1926); *Downhill* (1927); *Easy Virtue* (1927); *The Ring* (1927); *The Farmer's Wife* (1928); *Champagne* (1928); *The Manxman* (1929); *Juno and the Paycock* (1930); *The Skin Game* (1931); *Rich and Strange* (1932); *Number Seventeen* (1932); *Jamaica Inn* (1939); *The Paradine Case* (1947); *I Confess* (1953); *The Wrong Man* (1956); *Marnie* (1964).

References Auiler, Dan, *"Vertigo," the Making of a Hitchcock Classic* (New York: St. Martin's Press, 1998); Clover, Carol J., *Men, Women and Chainsaws* (Princeton: Princeton University Press, 1992); Leff, Leonard J., *Hitchcock & Selznick* (New York: Weidenfeld and Nicolson, 1987); Phillips, Gene D., "Hitchcock's Forgotten Films: The Twenty Teleplays," *Journal of Popular Film and Television* 10, no. 2 (Summer 1982): 73–76; Rebello, Stephen, *Alfred Hitchcock and the Making of "Psycho"* (New York: Dembner Books, 1990); Rohmer, Eric, and Claude Chabrol, *Hitchcock: The First Forty-Four Films* (New York: Frederick Ungar, 1979); Spoto, Donald, *The Dark Side of Genius: The Life of Alfred Hitchcock* (Boston: Little, Brown, 1983); Truffaut, François, *Hitchcock* (New York: Simon and Schuster, 1966); Wood, Robin, *Hitchcock's Films* (New York: A. S. Barnes, 1965); Yacowar, Maurice, *Hitchcock's British Films* (Hamden, Conn.: Archon Books, 1977).

—T. Prasch and J.C.T.

Holland, Agnieszka (1948–) Agnieszka Holland learned her filmmaking techniques and her politics together in Czechoslovakia during the brief Prague Spring of the late 1960s, when Alexander Dubček sought to create "socialism with a human face" by relaxing censorship and encouraging a more open exchange of ideas in cinema and other arts; and she was still in Prague when Russian tanks put an end to the experiment. She came of age as a director at the height of the Polish "New Wave" of the 1970s, when filmmakers in Poland, under the leadership and tutelage of ANDRZEJ WAJDA, the postwar master of Polish cinema, explored issues of moral dissent within a communist regime while testing the limits of censorship. These formative experiences shaped Holland as a director and writer, making her a filmmaker unusually attuned to the interface between the personal and political, deeply aware of the ambiguities of political positions, and strongly inclined toward the darkly ironic, characteristics she has carried over to her Hollywood career during the past decade.

Holland was born in Warsaw on November 28, 1948, to a divided family: her mother a Catholic, her father a Jew (and a Communist Party official). He died when she was 13, in mysterious circumstances; police reports claim that he leapt to his death from a window during an interrogation. Barred from Polish schools, she was accepted into a Czech film school at the age of 17; there, she was trained in filmmaking by such figures as MILOŠ FORMAN and married Czech director Laco Adamik, while continuing her political education in the streets. Arrested in the wake of the Soviet invasion, she returned to Poland in 1971. Her first dozen screenplays were rejected by Polish censors, but Wajda invited her to join his Film Unit X. She worked as assistant director with Krzystof Zanussi, contributed to the screenplays of Wajda's works, and began to direct her own material.

By the mid-1970s, Holland's own films were gaining release and, like other Polish directors in the decade that would climax with the emergence of Solidarity, she increasingly challenged the restrictions imposed by state censorship. In films like *Screen Test* (1977) and *Provincial Actors* (1980), she employed self-referential tales of actors and filmmakers to illuminate the spaces available in Poland in the 1970s for both political critique and personal development. In works like *Sunday Children* (1977) and *Lonely Woman* (1981), she explored the more personal dimensions of life under communist bureaucracies, with a pronounced feminist slant. She also tried her hand at political thrillers in *Le Complot* (1973) and *Fever* (1981).

The imposition of martial law put an end to such experiments. It also forced Holland into exile: she was in Paris when martial law was declared and was not allowed to return home (her husband and daughter were forced to stay in Poland). In the 1980s, Holland was thus forced to remake herself abroad. She did so by writing scripts for Poles also working in exile—including Wajda's *Danton* (1982), *A Love in Germany* (1983), *The Possessed* (1988), and *Korczak* (1990), and KRZYSZTOF KIESLOWSKI's *Blue* (1993)—and by developing projects with Western European production companies, most notably *Bitter Harvest* (1985), *To Kill a Priest* (1988), *Europa, Europa* (1990), and *Olivier, Olivier* (1992).

Holland's films in the decade after being forced into exile continued to reflect her political commitments (*To Kill a Priest,* for example, dramatizes the assassination of a Polish Catholic priest by communist authorities) and her interest in the personal, especially the familial (as in her exploration of the meaning of family and identity in *Olivier, Olivier*). But it is the trio of works that focus on the Holocaust—her own *Bitter Harvest*

and *Europa, Europa,* and her screenplay for Wajda's *Korczak*—that best reveal the rich depth of her engagement with politics, history, and personal experience. *Bitter Harvest* tells the complex tale of the relationship between a Polish peasant and the Jewish woman he hides from the Germans; *Korczak* explores the real history of the doctor who ran the Jewish orphanage in the Warsaw ghetto; and, most famously, *Europa, Europa,* also drawn from a real biography, tells the tale of Solly Perel, a Jewish boy who survives the war by constantly shifting identities—loyal young communist while in Soviet-occupied Poland, equally loyal Hitler-jugend when the Nazis invade, and Jewish again only when war's end made it safe to be one. In each of these films, striking stories provide the foreground, but the background is equally illuminating: in contrast to the firmly etched black-and-white of standard depictions of Nazism, Holland offers a range of shades of gray, of equivocation and compromise. Her films have been criticized as a result; *Shoah* director Claude Lanzmann absurdly denounced *Korczak* as "revisionist" when it was shown at Cannes, and all three films have been condemned by those who prefer moral certainties to Holland's ambiguities. But each richly evokes the far more complex realities of wartime Europe.

Beginning in 1993, Holland has worked within the Hollywood system, with mixed results. Her films remain complex explorations of the personal, often with interesting political overtones, but they lack the decisive vision of her work in the 1980s, and none has been greeted with the wide acclaim of *Europa, Europa*. In *Secret Garden* (1993), she brought dark psychological and class subtexts to the popular children's tale. In *Total Eclipse,* she dramatized the bleak, obsessional homosexual alliance between French poets Verlaine and Rimbaud. *Washington Square,* Holland's contribution to the brief 1990s boom of Hollywood adaptations of Henry James, is both more sinister and more ironic than competing versions. And *Third Miracle* (1999) explores issues of skepticism and faith, measured against human frailties, in a tale of the possible making of an American saint.

Even in minor work, however, Holland continues to keep her dark edge. In *Golden Dreams,* the short she was commissioned to make for Disneyland's new California theme park, she not only celebrates immigrant successes, but insists as well on noting such darker historical facts as Japanese internment during World War II, the abuse of Chinese railroad workers, and the dustbowl migrants of the depression era.

Other Films *Hrich boha* (1970); *Wieczor u Absona* (1975); *Pictures from Life* (1975); *Cos za cos* (1977); *Les Cartes postales de Paris* (1982); *Kultura* (1985); *Largo desolato* (1990); *Fallen Angels,* TV series (1993).

References "Woman of Iron," *Vogue,* February 1993; Todorov, Tzvetan, "Parisian Themes: The Wajda Problem," *Salmagundi* 92 (Fall 1991): 29–35.

—T. Prasch

Hu, King (1931–1997)

King Hu was born as Hu Chin-ch'uan on April 29, 1931, near Beijing in the adjoining county of Yung-Nien, and was educated at the capitol's National Art Institute. During a 1949 visit to Hong Kong, he found himself unable to return home when the communist forces under Mao Zedong defeated Chiang Kaishek. Since the borders were closed, he had to earn a precarious living performing several occupations such as tutor, proofreader, and graphic artist. He also worked briefly for the Voice of America. However, he was hired as an art director by a Hong Kong studio after his painting of a movie poster came to their attention.

During his apprentice years in the Hong Kong film industry, King Hu worked as an actor and art designer for Longma, Great Wall, and the Shaw Brothers companies before beginning his career as a film director. Before acting as a guerrilla leader in his first film as director, *Sons of the Good Earth* (1964), King Hu functioned as executive director on *The Story of Sue Sen* (1962) and associate director on *Eternal Love* (1963). *Sons of the Good Earth*

was a World War II drama dealing with the struggle of the Chinese against the Japanese invaders. Although this was competently shot in CinemaScope, a practice he developed during his career, the film attracted little attention since it easily fit the format of one of Hong Kong cinema's traditional genres in the 1960s.

It was his next film, *Come Drink with Me* (1965), that first saw the emergence of his distinctive talent. Featuring former Shanghai dancer Cheng Pei-pei in the role of female swordswoman Golden Swallow, this Shaw Brothers production was the first of his famous "inn" trilogy, the others being *Dragon Gate Inn* (1966) and *The Fate of Lee Khan* (1972). As well as injecting humor and drama into the martial-arts genre, King Hu brought other artistic innovations into Hong Kong cinema. The "inn" trilogy was so-named not just because certain scenes occurred in that environment but also due to the director's use of suspense and movement in certain sequences very much in the manner of the strategy used in a chess game (or Chinese checkers). This strategy became explicit in one famous scene in *The Valiant Ones* (1975), when the outnumbered Ming Dynasty heroes plot their future strategy against their Japanese opponents by using a Chinese checkers board to convey information relayed by one of their men in the musical accompaniment of a flute. King Hu choreographed his films very much in the performance style of Beijing Opera, and his close association with revered martial-arts director Han Yingjie (known to Western audiences as the title character in Bruce Lee's *The Big Boss*) in *Come Drink With Me, Dragon Gate Inn,* and *A Touch of Zen* (1969) brought the type of fighting sequences characteristic of most Hong Kong–genre film to the sophisticated level of a ballet performance.

After leaving Shaw Brothers, King Hu moved to Taiwan where he directed most of his major works. *Dragon Gate Inn* was his greatest success in Southeast Asia, eclipsing *The Sound of Music* in box-office revenue. Set in the Ming dynasty

(1368–1644), the film dealt with a group of Han patriots attempting to protect the surviving children of an assassinated official from death at the hands of an evil eunuch played by Bai Ying. Starring actress Shangguan Lingfen and Shi Jun as the chief patriots, it also featured Han Yingjin and Xu Feng, who would appear in other Hu films before becoming a well-known producer of works such as *Farewell My Concubine*.

The Ming dynasty was the director's favorite historical period both because of his interest in the type of calligraphy he often used in his films as well as the fact that he felt that the era echoed the turbulent conditions of his own century. King Hu also claimed that he made *Dragon Gate Inn* as a protest against the James Bond films. The Ming Dynasty's secret service also had its license to kill (and torture!).

A Touch of Zen took some three years to film. Based on a well-known short story by Pu Songling, it became the only Hong Kong–Taiwanese film to gain acclaim at the Cannes Film Festival and win an award for technical superiority. Starring Hu Feng, Shi Jun, Bai Ying, and Han Yingie, it featured the director's first collaboration with the great character actor Roy Chiao. Despite his Christian beliefs and his activities as a missionary in America, Chiao played the role of the chief Buddhist monk to perfection in the same manner as he would play noble Chinese officials in Hu's other works. Sammo Hung also played a minor role and assisted in the martial-arts direction. The film is one of the greatest artistic achievements in world cinema. But despite acclaim by *Cahiers du cinéma* and theatrical release in Paris and London, it has never been seen to the extent it deserves.

Hu's next film, *The Fate of Lee Khan,* was set in the closing years of the Mongol rulership over China prior to the Ming dynasty. In addition to Roy Chiao, Zu Feng, Bai Ying, and Han Yingjie in key roles, it also featured martial-arts heroines Angela Mao Ying and Helen Ma, as well as veteran actress Li Li Hua. Utilizing Hu's checkers motifs

and choreography superbly, the film contained a stunning performance by Xu Feng as Lee Khan's dangerous sister, as well as Tian Feng in the title role. After directing *The Valiant Ones* in Taiwan, Hu then directed *Raining in the Mountain* and *Legend of the Mountain* in 1979. These two works were his swan song as director, since the industry had changed and passed him by.

After directing his only contemporary film, *The Juvenizer* (1981), and his Tang dynasty chamber drama *All the King's Men* (1982), he found it difficult to find work. Despite reverence by a new generation such as TSUI HARK and Ann Hui, he left *Swordsman* (1990) following a violent argument with the former. *Painted Skin* (1992) with Joey Wang and Sammo Hung is a poor example of his work. From the 1960s, Hu always relished directing his project about Chinese laborers on the great American railroad. Sadly, he died in Taiwan from a botched operation, at a moment when it looked as if he would finally realize his dream.

Reference Kar, Law, ed., *Transcending The Times: King Hu and Eileen Chang,* Urban Council of Hong Kong: The 22nd Hong Kong International Film Festival.
—T.W.

Hui, Ann

Hui, Ann (1948–)   Hui On-wah was born in Manchuria in 1948 and moved with her family to Hong Kong in 1952. She received a Catholic high school education and graduated from Hong Kong University majoring in English and comparative literature. After working on a master's degree about Alain Robbe-Grillet, she studied for two years at the prestigious London Film School before returning to Hong Kong in 1975. She worked for a short period as assistant to the great Chinese director KING HU before beginning work for Hong Kong's TVB television station. During this period, working at TVB was equivalent to an apprenticeship at ROGER CORMAN's New World studios, since Hui and many of her contemporaries, like TSUI HARK and RINGO LAM, gained the valuable experience that would help their future careers as directors. Hui made some 26 documentaries at TVB before moving to the film department of the Independent Commission Against Corruption. She made six hour-long dramas, although some were never aired due to their controversial material concerning police corruption.

In 1979 she directed her first film, *The Secret,* which was an experimental narrative merging several popular Hong Kong genres such as the thriller and the ghost story. She followed this with *The Spooky Bunch* (1980), featuring veteran Hong Kong film actress Josephine Siao Fong-fong, with whom she would collaborate on *Summer Snow* 15 years later. The film superbly mixed the genres of Cantonese opera, ghost stories, and comedy. Hui then directed *The Story of Woo Viet* (1981), a film dealing with the exploitation of Vietnamese Chinese refugees. It featured Chow Yun-fat in his first major serious role. But *Boat People* (1982) brought her international attention, despite its questionable representation of post–1975 Vietnam.

Despite Hui's interest in political themes, she has never claimed to be a political director but more one interested in the situation of Chinese women, both past and present. The theme of exile is a strong motif in her work, whether physical or symbolic, as seen in her 1990 quasi-autobiographical film *Song of the Exile.* Maggie Cheung's Hueyin struggles throughout the film to reconcile her dual national identities. She is the child of a Chinese father and Japanese mother. Like several of her 1990s works, the film frequently uses voiceovers and flashbacks to contrast an individual's understanding of the past with the necessity of negotiating her role in the present.

Hui has also adapted two narratives by the Shanghai writer Eileen Chang (Zhang Ailing), whose work depicts a particular form of female subjectivity. In 1984 she directed Chow Yun-fat in one of Chang's most well-known stories, *Love in a Fallen City,* and the versatile Cantonese actress-singer Anita Mui in *Eighteen Springs* (1997).

Although suffering a career setback during the early 1990s, Ann Hui directed *Xiatian de xue* (*Summer Snow* or *Woman, Forty*) in 1994, which won many awards at the Taiwan Golden Horse and Hong Kong film festivals. Featuring Josephine Siao Fong-fong and King Hu veteran actor Roy Chiao, the film sympathetically deals with the plight of a resilient Hong Kong woman whose father-in-law contracts Alzheimer's disease. Both leading characters are alienated from each other in terms of history, gender, and personal background. But the film shows these two diverse characters coming closer and, indirectly, reaffirming family ties strained in an increasingly complex society. On the strength of this film, both Hui and Josephine Siao became two of the final Hong Kong citizens to gain an MBE from Queen Elizabeth before the 1997 reunification with the mainland. Josephine Siao then retired from films to become a child psychologist.

Hui's next film, *Ah Kam: The Story of a Stuntwoman* (1996), was less successful due to budget problems and the injuries suffered by its star Michelle Yeoh on the set. But her following films, *As Time Goes By* (1997) and *Ordinary Heroes* (1997), saw her return to form, dealing with the issues of history and personal relationships that appear in many of her best films.

Other Films *Romance of the Book and the Sword* (1987); *Princess Fragrance* (1987); *Starry Is the Night* (1988); *Zodiac Killers* (1991); *My American Grandson* (1991).

References Erens, Patricia Brett, "The Film Work of Ann Hui," *The Cinema of Hong Kong,* eds. Poshek Fu and David Desser (New York: Cambridge University Press, 2000); Williams, Tony, "Border Crossing Melodrama: Song of the Exile," *Jump Cut* 42 (1988): 94–100.
—T.W.

Huston, John (1906–1987)   Born on August 5, 1906, in Nevada, Missouri, to Rhea Gore and Walter Huston, John Marcellus Huston began his show business career on stage in Dallas, Texas, as "Yankee Doodle Dandy" at the age of three.

Huston attended Lincoln Heights High School in Los Angeles from 1921 to 1922 and dropped out to become an art student at the Smith School of Art and Art Student's League. In 1924 John Huston left Los Angeles for New York where he began a professional acting career at the Provincetown Playhouse Theatre. His debut as a professional actor was in a 1925 production of *The Triumph of the Egg.* In 1926 Huston went to Mexico following a mastoid operation. There he received an honorary commission in the Mexican cavalry. He married Dorothy Jeanne Harvey in 1926 and settled in Malibu, California, to pursue a career as a writer. After a brief publishing career in New York he received an offer to become a contract writer for Goldwyn Studios in 1930. This began Huston's screenwriting career in the commercial cinema.

After six months at Goldwyn, with no writing assignments, Huston was hired by Universal Studios where he was a contract writer from 1931 to 1933. Some of the films that Huston served on as a screenwriter include *A House Divided, Law and Order,* and *Murders in the Rue Morgue.* Following a stay in Great Britain where he was employed by Gaumont-British, Huston returned to the United States and appeared in the WPA Theatre production of *The Lonely Man* in Chicago. Huston became a contract writer for Warner Bros. from 1938 to 1941. Among the films Huston wrote at Warners were *Jezebel, The Amazing Dr. Clitterhouse, Juarez, Dr. Ehrlich's Magic Bullet,* and *High Sierra.* His scripts for both *Dr. Ehrlich's Magic Bullet* and *High Sierra* received Oscar nominations and provided Huston with the opportunity to direct a feature film as a result of a clause in his contract. The film Huston chose was Dashiell Hammett's *The Maltese Falcon,* which had been filmed twice before at Warner's. The film featured Humphrey Bogart, the star of *High Sierra* and a Warners contract actor of long standing. After another screenwriting assignment, *Sergeant York,* Huston directed *Across the Pacific* and *In This Our Life,* both 1942, before entering the military service following Pearl Harbor. John Huston was commissioned as a lieutenant in the Signal Corps, which enlisted a number of Hollywood directors to record the war's progress. Huston made three outstanding wartime documentaries: *Report from the Aleutians* (1943), *The Battle of San Pietro* (1942–43), and *Let There Be Light* (1946). The latter film concerned psychologically disabled veterans and their attempts to adjust to civilian life. The film was suppressed by the military and not shown publicly until 1980.

Following his military service, Huston contributed to the screen adaptation of Ernest Hemingway's *The Killers* (1946), produced by Mark Hellinger and directed by ROBERT SIODMAK. In November 1946, Huston directed a stage production of Jean-Paul Sartre's *No Exit,* translated by Paul Bowles, at the Biltmore Theatre in New York. Huston's next film, *The Treasure of the Sierra Madre* (1948), is considered by many to be one of his finest achievements as a director. The film featured Humphrey Bogart and Huston's father, Walter Huston, who received an Academy Award for best supporting actor. John Huston received an Oscar for best screenplay and best director, thus marking the first time a father and son were nominated—and won—for the same film. Huston's screenplay was adapted from the novel by B. Traven. Huston's next film, *Key Largo* (1948), based on the verse drama by Maxwell Anderson, was his last film for Warner Bros.

Huston and producer Sam Spiegel formed their own production company, Horizon Pictures, the first production of which was *We Were Strangers* (1949), with John Garfield and Jennifer Jones. In 1947, Huston with director WILLIAM WYLER and screenwriter Phillip Dunne formed the short-lived Committee for the First Amendment in protest of the treatment of the Hollywood Ten by the House Un-American Activities Committee (HUAC). In 1950 Huston directed *The Asphalt Jungle,* the progenitor of the heist film, and the end of his film-noir period. Huston received Oscar nominations for both direction and screenplay for the film. Huston's next film, *The Red Badge of Courage* (1951), was based on the story by Stephen Crane and starred Audie Murphy. The film received critical, if not box-office, success. The next and final film for the short-lived Horizons Pictures company was *The African Queen* (1951). The film was shot in the Congo under adverse conditions and starred Humphrey Bogart and Katherine Hepburn. The film's screenplay, an adaptation of the novel by C. S. Forester, was written by James Agee and John Huston. The film was both a box-office and critical success and gave Humphrey Bogart his only Academy Award as best actor. Throughout the 1950s Huston undertook projects that were filmed in various countries and based on literary source material—a staple of his screen work. These films include *Moby Dick* (1956), *The Roots of Heaven* (1958), and *The Misfits* (1961).

In the 1960s Huston supplemented his directorial duties by acting in a number of films. Beginning with *The Cardinal* (1963), for which he received an Academy Award nomination for best supporting actor, Huston's subsequent acting career included such films as *Candy* (1968), *Myra Breckenridge* (1970), *Battle for the Planet of the Apes* (1973), and most prominently, *Chinatown* (1974). Among Huston's most critically acclaimed films as a director in the 1960s and 1970s are: *Night of the Iguana* (1964), *Fat City* (1972), *The Man Who Would Be King* (1975), and *Wise Blood* (1979). After a fiasco film version of the Broadway musical *Annie* (1982), which earned Huston a nomination for Worst Director from the Razzie Awards, the director returned to critical acclaim with *Under the Volcano* (1984) and *Prizzi's Honor* (1985). Huston received an Academy Award nomination for best director for *Prizzi's Honor,* an adaptation of a Richard Condon crime novel. In 1983 Huston was awarded the American Film Institute's Lifetime Achievement award. And in 1985 the Director's Guild of America presented Huston with its most prestigious award, the David Wark Griffith

Award for Career Achievement. In 1986 Huston, in ill health, began work on what was to be his final film, an adaptation of James Joyce's short story *The Dead.* The film was written by his son, Tony Huston, and starred Huston's daughter, Angelica. Huston entered Charlton Memorial Hospital in Fall River, Massachusetts, on July 28, 1987. Huston died on August 28, 1987, in Middletown, Rhode Island, at the age of 81.

Other Films As screenwriter: *Dark Waters* (1944); *The Stranger* (1946); *Three Strangers* (1946). As director: *Beat the Devil* (1954); *Heaven Knows, Mr. Allison* (1957); *The Barbarian and the Geisha* (1958); *The Unforgiven* (1960); *Freud* (1962); *The List of Adrian Messenger* (1963); *Reflections in a Golden Eye* (1967); *Casino Royale* (1967); *Sinful Davey* (1969); *The Kremlin Letter* (1970); *The Life and Times of Judge Roy Bean* (1970); *The Mackintosh Man* (1973); *Independence* (1976); *Love and Bullets* (1979); *Victory* (1981).

References Cohen, Allen, and Harry Lawton, *John Huston: A Guide to References and Resources* (New York: G. K. Hall, 1997); Grobel, Lawrence, *The Hustons* (New York: Scribner's, 1990); Huston, John, *An Open Book* (New York: Knopf, 1980); Studlar, Gaylyn, and David Desser, eds., *Reflections in a Male Eye: John Huston and the American Experience* (Washington, D.C.: Smithsonian Institution Press, 1992).

—R. W.

Hytner, Nicholas (1956–) British director Nicholas Hytner was educated at Cambridge University before working his way up from associate director of the Royal Exchange Theatre in Manchester to the Royal Shakespeare Company, overseeing the transfers from Stratford-upon-Avon to London's Barbicon Center of *Measure for Measure* and *The Tempest* (1989). His West End theater debut was his production of *The Scarlet Pimpernel,* starring David Sinden, which transferred from Chichester to London in 1985. His greatest theatrical success was the epic musical *Miss Saigon,* written by Richard Maltby, Jr., with Alain Boublil and Claude-Michel Schönberg in the vein of

Madame Butterfly, but involving a Vietnamese bar-girl who conceives a child after having an affair with an American marine in 1975, the year of the American evacuation of Saigon. Dramatized spectacularly on stage with an airborne helicopter, *Miss Saigon* opened at the Theatre Royal, Drury Lane, in 1989. As associate director of Britain's Royal National Theatre, Hytner's productions included Alan Bennett's *The Madness of King George III* (which was later adapted to the screen as *The Madness of King George,* Hytner's debut as film director), Alan Bennett's stage adaptation of *The Wind in the Willows,* and Martin McDonagh's *The Cripple of Inishmaan.* Other West End triumphs included *The Importance of Being Earnest,* with Maggie Smith, and his National Theatre production of *Carousel,* which made a very successful transfer to New York's Lincoln Center Theatre, where it won five Tony Awards, including best director.

Hytner's feature film debut, *The Madness of King George* (1994), successfully transformed to the screen the political dilemma of a pathetic George III, trying to hold on to his throne while suffering from a debilitating disease that affected his mind. Empowered by rave reviews and enthusiastic word-of-mouth, the film was able to cross over from the art-house circuit to become a mainstream hit that earned four Academy Award nominations. Helen Mirren won the best actress award at the Cannes Film Festival in 1995 for her portrayal of Queen Charlotte and was also nominated for an Academy Award. Other Oscar nominations went to Nigel Hawthorne, who played King George, for best actor, and to Alan Bennett for best adapted screenplay. The film won an Oscar for best art direction. This success was then followed by Hytner's film adaptation of Arthur Miller's classic, *The Crucible* (1996), a tremendous success, shaped for the screen by Miller himself. The film earned nominations for Golden Globe Awards for best supporting actor for Paul Scofield's chilling portrayal of Judge Danforth and for Joan Allen's sensitive and dignified portrayal of Elizabeth Proctor, unjustly accused of witchcraft. Joan Allen was also nominated for the best supporting actress Academy Award, and Arthur Miller was nominated for best adapted screenplay. Later films fell short of this level of success. *The Object of My Affection* (1998), a romantic comedy adapted from Stephen McCarthy's 1987 novel by the Pulitzer Prize-winning playwright Wendy Wasserstein, was a moderate commercial success (over $29 million), but not a critical success. His next film, *Center Stage* (2000), was even less successful and considered a disappointment. Hytner's best work, then, was done in collaboration with supremely gifted playwrights, and his special talent involved intelligent stage-to-screen adaptations.

References Wolf, Matt, "On Stage: The British Field—A New Line Up," *New York Times,* August 27, 1989, sec. 2, pp. 7, 27; Wolf, Matt, "No Thorns in Hytner's Hollywood," *The* (London) *Times,* January 21, 1997, p. 34.

—J.M.W.

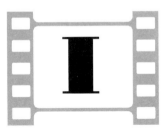

Ichikawa, Kon (1915–) Born in the city of Ise, in Mie Prefecture, on November 20, 1915, Japanese director Kon Ichikawa was educated at the Osaka Commercial School and began his career as a cartoonist in the animation department of the J. O. Studios in 1933. He also won first prize in a story-writing contest sponsored by a newspaper, *Asahi Weekly,* and went on to write a screenplay for a film that was to have been directed by Mikio Naruse. His first directing credit was a puppet film entitled *A Girl of Dojo Temple* (1946) that was banned by the American Occupation forces because Ichikawa had not obtained official permission to make the film. In 1948 Ichikawa was promoted to director and went on to make a series of melodramas, beginning with *A Flower Blooms.* Ichikawa worked for Shin Toho, Nikkatsu, and, after 1956, primarily for Daiei. In 1948 he married screenwriter Natto Wada, who wrote many of his film scripts.

His breakthrough picture, set during what the Japanese call the Pacific War (World War II), was *The Harp of Burma* (1956), adapted from the novel by Michio Takeyama, surely one of the most effective antiwar films ever made, about Private Mizushima (Shoji Yasui), a gentle soldier who has mastered the harp, converts to Buddhism, and

devotes his life to burying the Japanese war dead. The story is about defeat, isolation, and, ultimately, spiritual regeneration, as Private Mizushima leaves his unit to persuade an isolated garrison into surrendering. He fails in this attempt and is knocked unconscious by artillery fire. Rescued by a passing Buddhist monk, Mizushima disguises himself as a Burmese Buddhist monk, and then gradually assumes the monk's calling. At first he intends to rejoin his company, but he becomes obsessed by the need to bury the Japanese bodies he finds strewn across the countryside. His colleagues worry about what may have happened to him, but they sense that he may have survived when they hear the strains of his distinctive harp-playing at night. The film won the San Giorgio Prize at the 1956 Venice Film festival as a film that best demonstrates "men's capacity to live with one another."

A second antiwar film was to follow, *Fires on the Plain* (1959), a brutally graphic depiction of the horrors of war involving cannibalism. Set during the final days of the Japanese occupation of the Philippines, a Japanese army unit is surrounded and isolated, deprived of all food and supplies, but determined to resist as long as possible and to die with dignity for the Imperial cause. In desperation, they are finally forced to feed upon the bodies of their own fallen comrades. Informed by Ichikawa's antitraditional view of human corruption, this film was as ghastly and realistic in its portrayal as his earlier film was gentle and "poetic." "War is an extreme situation which can change the nature of man," Ichikawa told Joan Mellen. "For this reason, I consider it to be the greatest sin."

Considered an idiosyncratic filmmaker with a fine sense of visual texture and a taste for black humor and obsessed characters, Ichikawa was most often interested in spiritually abnormal behavior resulting from the social environment of his characters. This tendency is found in *Odd Obsession* (1959), Ichikawa's adaptation of Junichiro Tanizaki's novel, *Kagi* (The key [1959]), a cynical and perverse black comedy of family intrigue, sexual indulgence, and murder involving a man going through a midlife crisis and his awful wife and daughters. *Conflagration* (1958), adapted from Yukio Mishima's *Temple of the Golden Pavilion,* tells the story of a young fanatic who burns down a beautiful historic temple in Kyoto in a purification ritual because he is appalled by the corruption he perceives in the world in which he lives. Identifying Ichikawa's recurring themes as "the loss of value of the individual in our modern world and outsiders who struggle to escape—not to change or accept," critic John Allyn claimed, "It is for these subjects and the satirical black comedies that Ichikawa will be most remembered. But," he added, "even the darkest subject matter is relieved by humor and beauty."

Other Films *365 Nights* (1948); *Human Patterns* [and] *Endless Passion* (both 1949); *Sanshiro of Ginza, The Hot Marshland, Pursuit at Dawn* (all 1950); *Nightshade Flower, The Lover, The Man without Nationality, Stolen Love, Bungawan Solo, Wedding March* (all 1951); *Mr. Lucky, Young People, The Woman Who Touched Legs, This Way—That Way* (all 1952); *Mr. Pu, The Blue Revolution, The Youth of Heiji Senigata, The Lover* (all 1953); *All of Myself, A Billionaire, Twelve Chapters about Women* (all 1954); *Ghost Story of Youth* [and] *The Heart* (1955); *Punishment Room* [and]

Bridge of Japan (1956); *The Crowded Train, The Pit, The Men of Tohoku* (all 1957); *Money and Three Bad Men* (1958); *Goodbye—Good Day* [and] *Police and Small Gangsters* (1959); *A Ginza Veteran, Bonchi, A Woman's Testament, Her Brother* (all 1960); *Ten Dark Women* (1961); *The Outcast* [and] *Being Two Isn't Easy* (1962); *An Actor's Revenge* [and] *Alone on the Pacific* (1963); *Money Talks* (1964); *Tokyo Olympiad* (1965); *The Tale of Genji* (1966); *Topo Gigio e sei Ladri* (Italy [1967]); *Tournament* (documentary [1968]); *Kyoto* (documentary [1969]); *To Love Again* (1972); *The Wanderers* [and] *Visions of Eight* (both 1973); *I Am a Cat* (1975); *Between Women and Wives* [co-directed, and] *The Inugami Family* (both 1976); *The Devil's Bouncing Ball Song* (1977); *Queen Bee* [and] *Island of Horrors* (both 1978); *The Phoenix* [and] *House of Hanging* (both 1979); *Koto* (aka *Ancient City* [1980]); *Kofuku* (aka *Lonely Hearts* [1982]); *Sasame Yuki* (aka *The Makioka Sisters* [1983]); *The Actress* [and] *Princess from the Moon* (1987); *Tenkawa Densetsu Dsydijin Jiken* (1991); *Fusa* (1993); *47 Ronin* (1994).

References Allyn, John, *Kon Ichikawa: A Guide to References and Resources* (Boston: G.K. Hall, 1985); Mellen, Joan, *Voices from the Japanese Cinema* (New York: Liveright, 1975); Svensson, Arne, *Japan* (New York: A. S. Barnes, 1971).

—J.M.W.

Ince, Thomas Harper (1882–1924) Known more as a producer than a director, Thomas Ince exerted a pioneering influence in the rise of the American studio system and in the development of efficient methods of film production. He was born on November 6, 1882, in Newport, Rhode Island, the second of three sons to a family of entertainers. While still a boy, he appeared in numerous stage productions, both on the road and on Broadway. At age 28, he shifted his sights to the newly developing motion picture industry and worked as an actor and director in films for the Biograph Company and the Independent Motion Picture Company. Among the many short films he directed at this time were several Mary Pickford vehicles. Relocating to the New York Motion Picture Company in Los Angeles in 1911, he quickly grew dissatisfied at his assignments to direct routine westerns ("They ride uphill on Tuesday and downhill on Thursday," he complained). Accordingly, in 1912 he hired the entire Miller Bros. 101 Ranch Wild West show and utilized their cowboys, Indians, horses, buffaloes, teepees, and covered wagons in his films. Anxious to expand the traditional one-reel length of films, Ince, with the assistance of the redoubtable cinematographer Ray C. Smallwood, shot a two-reel deluxe western, *War on the Plains,* that was praised for its historical accuracy and "startling realism." "The history—the true history—of early life in the Wildest West is being written on the film," praised one critic of the day. "The impression that it all leaves is that here we have looked upon a presentation of western life that is real and that is true to life."

By the end of 1912, Ince had produced under the imprimatur of "101 Bison Pictures" two dozen more two-reelers and three additional three-reelers—at a time when rival filmmaker D. W. Griffith was still restricted, with rare exceptions, to one-reelers—including *Custer's Last Fight* (1913). Contributing in large part to the success and the scenic values of these films was the 18,000 acres of diversified scenery along the Pacific that Ince had leased. He erected a stage for interior shooting, built village sets along the cliffs and mountain passes, and proceeded to establish the studio conglomerate that became known as "Inceville." With scenario editor Richard Spencer, he worked out a detailed method of preparing shooting scripts to maximize production efficiency, and he personally trained a staff of directors and writers to carry out his plans. Props, costumes, extras, and locations were all worked out well in advance of each production, and Ince himself insisted on maintaining editing control on all films shot at Inceville, even those he did not direct himself. Aware by late 1913 that westerns were falling out of public favor, he shifted his priorities to stories of immigrant life (*The Italian* [1914] is a remarkably tough and real-

istic example) and American history (*The Battle of Gettysburg* [1913] was hailed as an unprecedented large-scale epic). Among the many actors who made their names in Ince productions in the next few years were William S. Hart and Charles Ray.

In 1915 Ince turned his back on Inceville and built a new studio in the area soon to be known as Culver City, where he formed one "angle" of the Triangle Film Corporation, along with Mack Sennett and DAVID WARK GRIFFITH. It was for Triangle that he supervised a number of significant productions, including *D'Artagnan* (1916) and *The Coward* (1916), and his most important film, *Civilization* (1916), a pacifist allegory in support of the international policy of President Woodrow Wilson. The jury is still out as to the extent of Ince's personal involvement in the direction of the film. After quarreling with his partners, Ince began releasing through Paramount-Artcraft and, later, through Metro and First National.

Before he could finish a western called *The Last Frontier,* legend has it that Ince died under mysterious circumstances on the night of November 19, 1924. While aboard William Randolph Hearst's yacht, he was stricken with a mysterious malady. Among the many rumors that circulated thereafter was that he had been murdered by Hearst out of jealousy over a presumed affair with Hearst's protégée, Marion Davies. This story, typical as it is of so many Hollywood scandals, has nonetheless no bearing in fact. In truth, Ince suffered a heart attack and died soon thereafter of natural causes. "Ince was an energetic and efficient director," writes KEVIN BROWNLOW, "[and] proved a figure of heroic proportions in the development of the motion picture."

Other Films *The Indian Massacre* (1911); *The Crisis* (1911); *The Battle of the Red Men* (1912); *The Law of the West* (1912); *With Lee in Virginia* (1913); *Days of '49* (1913).

References Brownlow, Kevin, *The War, the West, and the Wilderness* (New York: Alfred A. Knopf, 1979); Pratt, George C., "'See Mr. Ince . . .,'" in *"Image"* on the

Art and Evolution of the Film, ed. Marshall Deutelbaum (New York: Dover, 1979), 85–95.

—J.C.T.

Ingram, Rex (1893–1950) One of the supreme visual stylists of the American silent film, Rex Ingram also launched the careers of Rudolph Valentino and Ramon Navarro. He was born Reginald Ingram Montgomery Hitchcock in Dublin, Ireland, on January 15 or 18, 1893, to the Reverend Francis Ryan Montgomery Hitchcock, a clergyman in the Church of England. Growing up in several parishes in rural Ireland, he acquired from his parents a love of the dramatic arts; and while still a boy he revealed talents as a writer and as a graphic artist. Restless and a bit of a loner, Reginald sailed to America in 1909, where he took on work as a clerk in the New Haven freight yards and enjoyed spare-time attendance at the Yale School of Fine Arts. A fascination with cinema led to a job as a writer and (as "Rex Hitchcock") a bit-part actor for the Edison Company.

He wrote and directed his first film in 1916 for Carl Laemmle's Universal-Bluebird Photoplay company. *The Great Problem* was a social drama about a woman's struggles with her criminal past. This and subsequent pictures, like *Black Orchids* (1916) and *The Reward of the Faithless* (1917), revealed his penchant for melodramatic action against exotic locales. He interrupted his budding career for a stint in the Royal Canadian Air Force as a flyer, but he had to return to work after suffering wounds in a plane crash. Now known as "Rex Ingram," his breakthrough came after joining Metro Pictures, where he directed *The Four Horsemen of the Apocalypse* (1921), based on the popular novel by Vicente Blasco Ibanez, and starring the then-relatively unknown Rudolph Valentino as Julio Desnoyers, a wealthy Argentinian nobleman. Also starring in the film was Alice Terry, whom Ingram had married the year before and who would appear in most of his later films. Ingram's preoccupation with set design, costumes, props, and camera setups would become legendary in Hollywood, rivaled only by the singular obsessions of Erich von Stroheim. The film, with its wartime atmosphere and its erotic tango sequence, was an international hit and pulled Metro out of its financial doldrums. Hollywood's new "golden boy," the handsome, cultured Ingram next made *The Conquering Power* (1921), adapted from Balzac's novel, *Eugenie Grandet.* Again, Valentino was in the cast, this time as a city cousin who falls in love with the daughter of the miserly Pere Grandet. Two swashbuckling romances followed, *The Prisoner of Zenda* (1922) and *Scaramouche* (1923). The latter, a story of a French nobleman who disguises himself as a commedia dell'arte player during the Revolution, was greatly admired for its convincing period detail and handling of crowd scenes. Increasingly dissatisfied with Hollywood, yet possessing enormous clout as an artist, Ingram took his Rex Ingram Studios production company to Nice in 1925, where he entertained royalty and made pictures like *Mare Nostrum* (1925), an espionage drama adapted from another novel by Ibanez; a horror drama, *The Magician* (1926), a fantasy adapted from Somerset Maugham's novel about a Satanist; *The Garden of Allah* (1927), about a Trappist monk who breaks his vows when he falls in love with an English girl; and *Baroud* (1930), Ingram's only talkie, a story of Foreign Legionnaires in the Atlas Mountains of North Africa. Retired from filmmaking, he spent the next few years researching Arab life and living in cities like Cairo and Alexandria. He returned to Hollywood in 1936 and spent his last years writing and sculpting. He died of heart disease on July 22, 1950.

Despite criticism that his narrative pace was occasionally sluggish and his melodramatic tendencies excessive, Ingram is generally regarded as one of the silent screen's supreme poetic craftsmen, ranking with other pictorialists like DAVID WARK GRIFFITH, Maurice Tourneur, and JOSEF VON STERNBERG. "Ingram's art was essentially that of the painter," writes William K. Everson. "His films were rather stiff, formal, and unexciting dramatically, but photographically they were superbly lit and composed, and used color tones to breath-taking pictorial effect." To the end, despite studio interference, Ingram stubbornly insisted on gaining full control over each picture: "My sympathies are all with those directors who stand or fall on their own merits," Ingram said; "I have too often seen a good picture, and the career of a promising director, ruined by so-called *supervision*."

Other Films *Broken Fetters* (1916); *His Robe of Honor* (1918); *Under Crimson Skies* (1920); *Shore Acres* (1920); *Turn to the Right* (1921); *Where the Pavement Ends* (1922); *The Arab* (1924); *The Three Passions* (1929).

References Brownlow, Kevin, *The Parade's Gone By* (New York: Alfred A. Knopf, 1968); Everson, William K., *American Silent Film* (New York: Oxford University Press, 1978); O'Leary, Liam, *Rex Ingram, Master of the Silent Cinema* (Dublin: Academy Press, 1980).

—J.C.T.

James Ivory (Warner Bros.)

Ivory, James (1928–) With his partners, producer Ismail Merchant and writer Ruth Prawer Jhabvala, James Ivory has directed a notable series of "prestige" historical dramas and literary adaptations. Ivory was born on June 7, 1928, in Berkeley, California, into an upper-middle-class Irish-American family. He majored in fine arts at the University of Oregon and furthered his study in France. His first taste of "show business" came in working for Special Services with the Second Armored Division in Germany during the Korean War. "I learned basic lessons in the Army which proved very useful later on in filmmaking," he writes, "like. . . . how essential good advertising is; and, most important, accepting useful suggestions from all sorts of unlikely people without letting one's ego come into it. A film director should have no ego, or perhaps I should say he must be above ego, or outside it." Back in America he enrolled in the Film Department at USC, where he made his first film, *Venice: Theme and Variations* (1957), a 28-minute color documentary.

In 1960 he met a young Indian student, Ismael Noormohamed Abdul Rehman Merchant— Ismail Merchant—with whom he made a film called *The Householder,* about the coming of age of an ingenuous Indian youth named Prem in a Bengali village. The picture was to prove highly significant to the team, because it was based on a novel by Ruth Prawer Jhabvala, a Polish-German writer educated in Britain and married to an Indian. Her work on the film adaptation led to her subsequent involvement in all the Merchant-Ivory pictures. Their second feature, *Shakespeare Wallah!* (1965)— the term "wallah" in Hindustani means a small-time operator—set the standard that was to prevail in their subsequent efforts, i.e., juxtaposing a romantic tale against the contexts of class upheaval and cultural change. It chronicled the adventures of a small Shakespearean troupe of English players touring post-independence India. This modern India, culturally speaking, is a changing world more interested in the current novelty of Hollywood-style musical films than in its own literary traditions. The disasters that befall the Buckingham Players thus exemplify the schisms opening up between worlds old and new, between classical and popular entertainment. "One is always conscious of [the Buckinghams] as being constrained by their theatrical calling," notes historian Patrice Sorace, "which has lost popularity to Indian films that represent the new, indigenous Indian culture." The eminent filmmaker, Satyajit Ray, composed the score.

Although *Shakespeare Wallah!* was warmly received, four more years passed before Ivory directed his next feature, *Bombay Talkie* (1970), about a Western journalist (Jennifer Kendal) who becomes infatuated with a young Indian movie star (Shashi Kapoor). A variety of films followed: *Roseland* (1977) consisted of three vignettes about the denizens of the fabled Roseland dance hall in New York City. *The Europeans* (1979) was Ivory's first Henry James–based film, a delicate comedy of manners occasioned by the arrival of a brother and sister, reared abroad, in the rural precincts of Boston in the mid-1840s. Another Jamesian adaptation was *The Bostonians* (1984), a re-creation of the cultural and social milieu of Boston in the 1870s. *Quartet* was an adaptation of Jean Rhys's autobiographical novel, an evocation of 1920s Paris. *Heat and Dust,* from Jhabvala's 1975 novel, juxtaposed a modern and a flashback narrative in its depiction of life in colonial India. Another tale of India was *The Deceivers* (1988), an action-filled drama of the clash between English spies and the deadly Thugee cult in the early 19th century. Two E. M. Forster adaptations rounded out the 1980s. *Room with a View* (1986) was based on Forster's 1907 novel about a series of complications arising from the interactions between a well-brought-up English girl (Helena Bonham-Carter) and two free-thinking English gentlemen (Denholm Elliott and Julian Sands) she meets in Italy. Critic Richard Schickel wrote that the "formality of James Ivory's style suits [the book] admirably, counterpointing and controlling the theatrical overplaying he encourages." It won three

Oscars, including screenplay, art direction, and costume design. The second Forster adaptation was his autobiographical *Maurice* (1987), a story of homosexual love. Scripted by Ivory himself, it was photographed in the authentic locations of Cambridge and Pendersleigh, and its depiction of the relationship between Maurice (James Wilby) and the gamekeeper Alec (Rupert Graves) was depicted with dignity and reserve. "One of the virtues of the film," writes Long, "is its precision—its quiet, steady revelation of the oppressive formality in Edwardian society that keeps people apart, and the step-by-step inevitability of Maurice and Alec's desperation."

The decade of the 1990s saw the flowering of Merchant-Ivory with some of their finest films, all drawn from respectable literary sources and offering finely observed social commentaries and richly textured period re-creations. *Mr. and Mrs. Bridge* (1990) brought the Merchant-Ivory-Jhabvala team to Kansas City, Missouri, to film Evan Connell's classic novels, *Mrs. Bridge* and *Mr. Bridge,* about a driven businessman and his repressed wife. The setting of the Midwest in the 1930s—the first time a Merchant-Ivory film was set in America's heartland—particularly appealed to Ivory, who declared that it was the only film he made "about my own childhood and adolescence." Paul Newman and Joanne Woodward played the eponymous couple.

Howard's End (1992) was another Forster adaptation, a tale chronicling the intersections among three families who represent very different aspects of English class and culture at the turn of the century—the Schlegels are artists and intellectuals; the Wilcoxes are grasping businessmen; and the Basts are lowly, downtrodden souls at the edge of society. At the heart of this richly textured film are exemplary performances by Emma Thompson as Margaret Schlegel, the rightful heir of Howard's End, and Anthony Hopkins as the cruel, insensitive Mr. Wilcox.

The Remains of the Day (1993) reunites Anthony Hopkins and Emma Thompson in a drama of near-misses and might-have-beens that transpires in two time frames, the 1950s and the 1930s. A bittersweet, frustrated romance between two people in service to the Darlington Estate in England (Hopkins and Thompson) frames the larger context of the debate between isolationists and interventionists concerning England's role in the oncoming war. In both personal and public contexts, the rigid conventions of class and tradition struggle against new sensibilities emerging after the war.

Jefferson in Paris (1995) transpires in Paris in the 1780s. Jefferson (Nick Nolte) and his daughter arrive in a Paris that is already seething with angry citizens threatening revolution against the monarchy of Louis XVI and Marie Antoinette. As the minister plenipotentiary to the French court, Jefferson is immediately challenged by the Marquis de Lafayette for representing America as a democracy while slavery still persists there. During his courtly duties, consigning his daughter to a convent, and dallying with the delectable Maria Cosway (Greta Scacchi), Jefferson faces revolt from within his own house when his black slave, James Hemmings, begins demanding his own freedom. Moreover, Jefferson finds himself in the grip of a powerfully erotic attraction to James's sister, Sally. The faults and virtues of the Merchant-Ivory style are everywhere in evidence: On the debit side is a pace that is maddeningly deliberate and a narrative structure—alternating between the words of Jefferson's letters and the latter-day testimony of an alleged descendent of a Jefferson-Hemmings union—that seems unnecessarily convoluted. Its controversial (at the time) take on the Jefferson-Hemmings affair is so discreetly muted that it ultimately effaces itself. However, the real glory of the film lies in its ravishing visuals, as if Pre-Raphaelite painter Edward Burne-Jones had gone back a century to record life in late-18th-century Paris. "Paris is every day enlarging and beautifying," wrote Jefferson in one of his letters; and the entire film seems to share the sentiment. In addition to dwelling lovingly on locations like the Palais de la Légion d'Honneur, the Tuilleries, Les Halles Park, and the gardens of the Forest of Marly, there is a visit to one of Marie Antoinette's courtly pageants, a peek over the shoulder of painter John Trumbull at his easel, and a reserved seat at a performance of Sacchini's opera, *Dardanus.*

Ivory and his colleagues Merchant and Jhabvala show no sign of slackening their pace. Recent films include *Surviving Picasso* (1996), with Anthony Hopkins portraying the famous artist in his middle years; *A Soldier's Daughter Never Cries* (1998), with Kris Kristofferson in the role of an alcoholic novelist patterned after James Jones; and *The Golden Bowl* (2000), adapted from Henry James's late novel about the complications that ensue after the marriage between an impoverished Italian prince (Jeremy Northam) and an American heiress (Kate Beckinsale).

Ivory's sensitivity and impeccable visual taste are everywhere in evidence in his films. "It is often said that Ivory's films have his personal stamp on them," writes biographer Robert Emmet Long, "—a way of speaking, perhaps, of personal qualities that enter into them: sophistication, tolerant affection, sharp wit, a feeling for place.... Reviewers sometimes grouse that . . . the pacing of his movies is too slow, but his way is to be careful and probing as he creates texture and verisimilitude. He can't be hurried."

Other Films *The Delhi Way* (1964); *The Guru* (1969); *Adventures of a Brown Man in Search of Civilization* (1971); *Savages* (1972); *Autobiography of a Princess* (1975); *Hullabaloo Over Georgie and Bonnie's Pictures* (1978); *Jane Austen in Manhattan* (1980).

Reference Long, Robert Emmet, *The Films of Merchant Ivory* (New York: Citadel Press, 1993).

—J.C.T.

Iwerks, Ubbe ("Ub") Ert (1901–1971)

Although Ub Iwerks is best known for his innovative work for Walt Disney, he enjoyed a brief stint as a cartoon producer and director in the 1930s.

Because of his modest demeanor and aversion to the spotlight, he remained behind the scenes for most of his life, venerated by his colleagues in the profession, but mostly unknown to the general public. He was born in Kansas City, Missouri, on March 24, 1901, the son of a Dutch immigrant and inventor. Interested in the mechanics of animation since an early age, he was just 18 when he met fellow teenager WALTER ELIAS DISNEY while working at the Kansas City Film Ad Company (later known as United Film Ad). In 1922 he and Walt quit their jobs and formed their own company, Laugh-O-Gram. Although they worked hard and produced a series of animated advertisements for Kansas City theaters, several fairy-tale cartoons (including *Puss in Boots, Jack and the Beanstalk,* and *Cinderella*), and a cartoon/live-action short, *Alice's Wonderland,* the first in a series of "Alice in Cartoonland" shorts, the business went bankrupt. Iwerks returned to Film Ad and Disney departed for greener pastures in Los Angeles.

Iwerks received a summons from Walt in 1923 to join him in L.A. and work with him and Walt's older brother Roy in their newly formed studio venture. A much more talented artist and graphic designer than Walt, Ubbe (called "Ub" for short) soon found himself the primary creative force behind Disney's animated projects in the 1920s. These included more of the "Alice" series and a new series about "Oswald the Lucky Rabbit." When many of Disney's key artists were lured away from him in 1927 by Universal contract producer Charles Mintz, Ub loyally remained; and soon thereafter he visualized and drew the immortal Mickey Mouse. The first three Mouse cartoons, which Ub drew in their entirety—*Plane Crazy, Gallopin' Gaucho,* and *Steamboat Willie*— were a sensation; and soon Ub was up to his own … er … ears in work. Without question, it was Ub who was primarily responsible for the "look" and the early development of the Mouse, as well as the spectacular technical gains of the innovative, first series of Silly Symphonies.

Acknowledged as the best animator in the business by now, the 28-year-old Iwerks broke away from Disney in 1930 to start his own studio and create a character of his own, Flip the Frog. The first Flip cartoon was *Fiddlesticks,* a two-color Technicolor film in which the frog appeared as a semi-human character, with large eyes, a bow tie, and clothing. MGM distributed the series as its first cartoon venture. The Flip series had a unique energy, as Flip's universe seemed completely anthropomorphized; and Flip himself, as historian Leonard Maltin reports, "was happy, loose-limbed, and engagingly 'cartoony,' the chief inhabitant of an animated world that bore little relationship to reality." Ub hired many future animation greats as members of his team, including Grim Natwick, Shamus Culhane, Frank Tashlin, composer Carl Stalling (a fellow former Kansas Citian), and a promising youngster named CHARLES MARTIN ("CHUCK") JONES. Among the 37 Flip cartoons, many reveal promising gag situations: In *Movie Mad,* Flip crashes a Hollywood studio; in *The Cuckoo Murder Case* he satirizes the detective-story fad; and in *Funny Face* Flip experiments with plastic surgery. Even less known than the Flip series at this time were two more Iwerks cartoon series: "Willie Whopper," about a tall-tale-spinning little boy; and "Comicolor Cartoons," a series of fairy tales that featured a new two-color process called Cinecolor.

As dazzling as these cartoons were in a technical sense, their storylines, according to Maltin, were weak—Ub "lacked Disney's story sense and comic know-how"—and MGM withdrew from its releasing partnership. After 1936 Ub found himself without a company; and after three years of desultory work, found himself back with Disney. Although the friendly relations between the two boyhood pals had noticeably cooled by then, Ub remained with Disney the rest of his life, happy no longer to be an animating director but content to be a supervisor of special effects. Among his many award-winning technical innovations were the development of the Disney Multiplane Camera (a concept he had introduced several years before in his own cartoons) and several processes for the blending of matte shots and live action as seen, most notably, in *Song of the South* (1946) and *Mary Poppins* (1965); he also received the Kalmus Award and two Oscars.

Ub Iwerks died in 1971. His granddaughter, Leslie, produced a documentary on his life in 1998, *The Hand Behind the Mouse.*

References Crafton, Donald, *Before Mickey* (Cambridge, Mass.: MIT Press, 1982); Maltin, Leonard, *Of Mice and Magic: A History of American Animated Cartoons* (New York: New American Library, 1980); Merritt, Russell, and J. B. Kaufman, *Walt in Wonderland: The Silent Films of Walt Disney* (Baltimore: Johns Hopkins University Press, 1993).

—J.C.T.

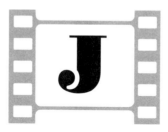

Jarman, Derek (1942–1994) Derek Jarman was a major figure in British avant-garde filmmaking during the 1970s and 1980s. His films display a painterly, richly textured, violent, mytho-poetic homoeroticism often compared to the work of underground filmmaker Kenneth Anger. A highly personal and political filmmaker, Jarman rejected the national tradition of British social realism in favor of a visually elegant style and experimental narrative forms, arguing that, in film, the relationship to image and sound is closer to poetry than it is to prose. Because of his dedication to gay art and politics, Jarman is often considered to be the "father figure" of the "New Queer Cinema" of the 1970s and 1980s.

Jarman was born in Northwood, London, on January 31, 1942. He developed an early interest in the visual arts, taking training that would lead to becoming a successful designer of theatrical sets and costumes for opera and ballet, work he continued throughout life. While working as a set designer on KEN RUSSELL's films *The Devils* (1971) and *Savage Messiah* (1972), Jarman became interested in making his own films and produced a series of short Super-8 films. In 1976 he wrote and codirected his first feature-length film, *Sebas-*

tiane, a euphorically sadomasochistic depiction of the life of the martyred saint.

Jarman's 1978 feature *Jubilee* is a punk fantasy depicting England's future. Queen Elizabeth I is transported by her astrologer to see for herself the current state of British society, where she finds only destruction and chaos. Queen Elizabeth II is dead, and Buckingham Palace has been turned into a recording studio. The cast of the film is made up of punked-out characters played by the likes of punk musician Adam Ant and Little Nell (of *Rocky Horror* fame). The score includes a punk version of "Rule Britannia" and music by Adam and the Ants, Siouxsie and the Banshees, and Brian Eno. *Jubilee* was quickly embraced as a seminal text for the British punk movement of the 1970s. Jarman followed up with a dizzying revisioning of Shakespeare's *The Tempest* (1979). For the next several years, Jarman returned to the world of opera and dance while continuing to make short experimental films and authoring in 1984 the first of several books, a biography/aesthetic manifesto titled *Dancing Ledge.*

Jarman returned to feature filmmaking in 1986 with *Caravaggio,* one of his most impressive and popular films. The highly stylized biopic stars

Nigel Terry as the famed artist and Tilda Swinton as one of his lovers. It was the first of a number of Jarman films featuring Terry and Swinton, who became closely identified with Jarman. *Caravaggio* depicts the conflicts between the artist's need for financial patronage, his deeply felt religious beliefs, and his homosexuality. A postmodern rendering of 16th-century art history, the film is rife with anachronisms, such as typewriters and motorbikes, AIDS activists, and Annie Lennox crooning Cole Porter, while at the same time re-creating exacting facsimiles of some of Caravaggio's best-known works. The postmodern style of the film invites the viewer to read the film as an essay on creativity. Jarman suggests that the power of Caravaggio's work, particularly his vision of the martyrdom of St. Sebastian, welled up from the complex interaction of the aesthetic inspiration and sexual stimulation the artist derived from the affair he had with the ruggedly handsome, if dangerously violent, street thug he used as a model.

During the late 1980s, Jarman's filmmaking became increasingly impressionistic, often incorporating footage from the personal Super-8 film "diaries" he continued to make throughout his life. The most-notable examples are *Angelic Conversation* (1985), *The Last of England* (1987), and *War Requiem* (1988). In *War Requiem,* Jarman employed the World War I poems of Wilfred Owen, set to the music of Benjamin Britten, in service to a film essay on the waste of past wars, comparing them to the modern ravages of AIDS. *The Angelic Conversation* drops all narrative form, with the only dialogue being Judi Dench's offscreen reading of 12 Shakespearean sonnets while the screen is filled with stop-action photography. It was reportedly Jarman's favorite film. He called it "extraordinary, with an almost archaic quality. The film is aces." Harlan Kennedy in *Film Comment* concurred, noting that "Jarman uses Shakespeare's sonnets as a way to make British culture leap out to join the imagery of Dante and Michelangelo, [JEAN] COCTEAU and Kenneth Anger."

Jarman returned to the postmodern biopic with *Edward II* (1991), a lush, sensuous, "rewriting" of the Christopher Marlowe play about the downfall of Britain's gay monarch. In the film, Jarman not only rewrites Marlowe's play, but also English history, to make Marlowe's play a denouncement of contemporary homophobia, and Edward II a mythic gay political hero. Jarman's *Wittgenstein* (1993) continued to challenge audiences with an eccentric "biography" of the philosopher.

Jarman's later films, particularly those made in the 1990s, were deeply inflected by Jarman's status as a "person with AIDS." After testing positive for the AIDS virus in 1986, he devoted increasing amounts of his remaining time to merging his political role as a gay and AIDS activist to his work as an artist. AIDS plays a major role in *Blue* (1993), Jarman's last and most unconventional film, which displayed a cobalt-blue screen for 76 minutes. By 1993 AIDS-related causes had left Jarman blind. In *Blue,* inspired by the conceptual art of Yves Klein, Jarman shares with his audience the filmmaker's sightless world while discussing his now nearly lost battle with AIDS. According to Raymond Murray, Jarman said of the film, "It's a hospital diary. . . . We've packed it with reminiscences and stories and things to do with the color blue. It makes a jolly good signing off film." Jarman died of complications due to AIDS at the age of 52, in February 1994. The art world had lost one of its most dedicated and visionary rebels.

Other Films   "Louise" segment of the compilation opera film *Aria* (1988); *The Garden* (1990); *Glitterbug* (1994).

References   Jarman, Derek, *Dancing Ledge* (Woodstock, Ga.: Overlook Press, 1993); Murray, Raymond, "Derek Jarman," in *Images in the Dark: An Encyclopedia of Gay and Lesbian Film and Video* (Middlesex, U.K.: Plume, 1996), pp. 72–75; O'Pray, Michael, *Derek Jarman: Dreams of England* (London: British Film Institute, 1996); Pecke, Tony, *Derek Jarman* (Woodstock, Ga.: Overlook Press, 2000); Rendall, Simon, *Derek Jarman: Today and Tomorrow* (London: Art Books International, 2000).

—T.P.

Jarmusch, Jim (1953–) The films of Jim Jarmusch are lyrical reflections of his mind's eye. His love of music acts as a major influence in all of his work. He believes that his films are, as he puts it, "somehow more related to poetry as a form than to prose." He was born in Akron, Ohio, on January 22, 1953. He lived in Akron until 1970, when he enrolled in the School of Journalism at Northwestern University. He soon transferred to Columbia University in New York, in 1971, where he majored in English and American literature. During his last semester of school, Jarmusch traveled to Paris, where he spent a great deal of his time exploring the film archives of the Cinématheque Française. His interest in film influenced his writing and led Jarmusch to apply to New York University's graduate department of film where, despite his inexperience with the medium, he was admitted.

Jarmusch has been influenced by a variety of filmmakers, such as Charles Laughton, Imamura, and SAMUEL FULLER; and NICHOLAS RAY, WIM WENDERS, Amos Poe, and Chris Sievernich all influenced and encouraged Jarmusch to make films. His first project was an 80-minute film called *Permanent Vacation* (1979). Two years later, Jarmusch began working on the script for *Stranger Than Paradise,* a short black-and-white film he shot in just one weekend in February 1982. After winning the International Critics prize at the Rotterdam Film Festival in 1983, Jarmusch traveled to Europe looking for some financial backing for the feature-length version of the film. Aspiring film producer Otto Grokenberger gave Jarmusch what he needed and the filming resumed. In 1985, *Stranger Than Paradise* was awarded the Camera d'Or at the Cannes Film Festival and best picture of the year from America's National Society of Film Critics.

Stranger Than Paradise was an underground independent film that gained mainstream attention. The film features John Lurie (of the music group the Lounge Lizards), Richard Edson, and Estzer Balint. The story is in three parts. It begins when Willie, a young Hungarian immigrant who lives in a shabby New York City apartment, is visited by his teenaged cousin, Eva, newly arrived from Budapest on her way to Cleveland. Part two begins when Willie and his friend, Eddie, drive to Cleveland to visit Eva. After a desultory visit, the three head south to Florida. Boredom follows them to the Sunshine State, where once again they fall into a stifling malaise. Rather than containing plotted scenes with dramatic climaxes, *Stranger Than Paradise* is made of vignettes of the mundane lives of the trio of characters. Each vignette is captured in an uncut shot. "The viewer is allowed to choose what he wants to look at in a shot," says Jarmusch, "just as he would pick out and concentrate on a character or a situation in a staged play." In his study of the film, Richard Linnet claims that Willie and Eddie as a team are "a comic marriage in the great tradition of hilariously subversive screen couples. John Lurie's self-centered, petulant, sometimes pathetic Willie is to Oliver Hardy and Ralph Kramden what Richard Edson's simple, passive, and endearing Eddie is to Stan Laurel and Ed Norton. The closest similarity is perhaps to Samuel Beckett's Vladimir and Estragon."

The next film Jarmusch created was *Down by Law* (1986). For this black-and-white feature-length film, Jarmusch teamed up John Lurie, Tom Waits (singer and songwriter), and Roberto Benigni (a well-known Italian actor who had not yet been discovered in the United States, and who began learning English on the set). Jarmusch wrote the script with these three men in mind. The characters grew from collaborative work between each actor and Jarmusch. During *Down by Law*, Jarmusch worked closely with cinematographer Robby Müller to enhance the symbolic use of light throughout the film. The lighting and the score (composed by Lurie) amplify the movie's fluidity and set each scene's mood.

In 1989, *Mystery Train* became the first color film that Jarmusch directed. *Mystery Train* consists of three separate stories, all of which take place in the Arcade Hotel in Memphis, Tennessee. Each story occurs at the same time as the other two. Each is seen in its entirety from the perspective that it is the only story. All eight of the characters are connected by the sound of the train, the location, and the gunshots on the soundtrack at the end of each scene. With *Mystery Train,* Jarmusch again creates something that mainstream Hollywood typically would not produce. The multiple story lines weave in and out of each other in arresting ways. As in *Stranger Than Paradise,* the camera remains stationary and the characters walk in and out of the frame during each scene. The use of silence and sparse dialogue affirm that Jarmusch likes "the spaces that happen between things . . . sometimes that's more meaningful than the dialogue itself." Jarmusch has also written and directed the feature films *Night on Earth, Dead Man,* and the trilogy of short films *Coffee and Cigarettes.* He worked on a concert film and documentary of Neil Young and his band Crazy Horse, entitled *Year of the Horse.*

Ghost Dog: Way of the Samurai (2000) deserves special mention. One of his most visually and spiritually satisfying films, it concerns a mysterious loner (Forrest Whitaker), known only as "Ghost Dog," who lives in solitude in a rooftop tarpaper shack and who carries out his assassination assignments with ruthless but quiet dispatch. When his employers, petty mobsters, turn on him, based on a misunderstanding, Ghost Dog wreaks his revenge by massacring the gang, sparing only the leader. In the end, Ghost Dog faces his boss in the street and is shot dead. Like its central character, the film is one long, gentle deadpan take on life and death. It is also an elegy on the turning of seasons, the end of times for professionals like Ghost Dog. Indeed, one of his monologues is concerned with the sense of an age coming to a close—not just for him, but for the code of professionalism that once prevailed amongst the samurai.

Jim Jarmusch has a disarming way of balancing the mystical with the mundane, of investing spiritual issues with an ordinary vernacular. Unpredictable and always wholly idiosyncratic, he stands in the forefront of today's independent film artists.

References Colbath, Thomas, and Steven Blush, "Jim Jarmusch Interview," *Seconds Magazine* 37 (1996); Linnett, Richard, "As American As You Are: Jim Jarmusch and 'Stranger than Paradise,'" *Cineaste* 14, no. 1 (1985): 26–28.

—M.V.

Jennings, Humphrey Sinkler (1907–1950)

Humphrey Jennings will always be remembered as the poetic voice of the wartime English documentary film. He was born in 1907 in Walberswick, on the Suffolk coast. He was educated at Perse School and Pembroke College, Cambridge, where he took his degree in 1934. Immediately upon leaving university he took a job at the General Post Office Film Unit as scenic designer and editor. The coming war brought Jennings the urgency and drama he needed to come into full flower as a filmmaker. He never felt the urge to use his films to harangue or educate his viewers. Rather, he preferred to illuminate human behavior through vignettes and representative anecdotes. For these reasons, perhaps, he never won the wholehearted support of his chief, JOHN GRIERSON, who preached that films should support leftist political ideals.

Listen to Britain (1942) eschews the expected melodrama and shrill propaganda of wartime combat and delivers instead an impressionistic mosaic of a London citizenry quietly going about its business—until the viewer realizes that unsettling implications of a country at war are intruding subtly into the imagery. A second look at the offices and buildings reveals thousands of protective sandbags. The shadows under the trees conceal tanks. The picture frames in the National Gallery are empty. The audience for a lunchtime piano recital by Dame Myra Hess is comprised mostly of uniformed soldiers. An acoustic weave of fragments of narration, snatches of dialogue, items from a news broadcast, songs (ranging from ditties sung by women at the factory lathes to music-hall tunes and a choral rendition of "Rule Britannia") coalesces into a collective "voice of a nation."

Jennings's feature-length masterpiece, *Fires Were Started* (1943), documented one day in the life of the Auxiliary Fire Service during the air raids on London. The action is seen through the eyes of a new recruit, Barrett. Dialogue consists mostly of the small talk of firemen while waiting for the alarm call. In the climactic fire scene, a man is killed in a scene as graphically dramatic as anything by FRITZ LANG or ALFRED HITCHCOCK. Yet, as historian David Thomson points out, there are no phony histrionics or plot contrivances to mar the drama: "This fire is arbitrary, inevitable, and in its way radiant. . . . There is equally little reason to recollect it as the work of wicked Germans. The fire is, rather, the life these men expect. It needs to be extinguished, but the men would not have purpose or fellowship without fire. This is the kind of crisis, or 'disaster,' that gave people the best years of their lives." Jennings provides no commentary, just a tapestry weave of actions, conversations, phone calls, maps, and chalkboards.

A Diary for Timothy (1945) is Jennings's most ambitious and poetically complex film. More than any other film it relies on narration (written by E. M. Forster and voiced by Michael Redgrave). In this case the "voice" is a "diary" written for and addressed to one "Timothy James Jenkins," a baby born late in the war. It is a voice of assurance, and it is a voice of warning. The war is almost over, yet a potential Armageddon lies ahead for the next generation. A symbolic dissolve shows the baby emerging from the flames of war. Jennings was only 38 years old when the war ended. Yet, he never recovered his purity and intensity of vision. "Good films could only be made in times of disaster," he confessed.

In 1950, while preparing a film for a series called *The Changing Face of Europe,* he died as a result of a fall from a cliff on the Greek island of Paros. In the opinion of historian Jack C. Ellis, Jennings's great gift was to provide a note of self-reflection in times of crisis. His films brought quiet reassurance to a country surrounded by the chaos of war. "In rising to this particular occasion," notes Ellis, "Jennings became one of the few British filmmakers whose work might be called poetic. He is also one of a small international company of film artists whose propaganda for the state resulted in lasting works of art."

Other Films *London Can Take It* (1940); *Heart of Britain* (1941); *A Defeated People* (1946); *Dim Little Island* (1949); *Family Portrait* (1950).

References Thomson, David, "A Sight for Sore Eyes," *Film Comment,* March–April 1993: 54–59; Ellis, Jack C., *The Documentary Idea* (Englewood Cliffs, N.J.: Prentice-Hall, 1989).

—J.C.T.

Jewison, Norman (1926–) Canadian filmmaker Norman Jewison was born on July 21, 1926, in Toronto, Ontario. Early on he studied piano and music theory at the Royal Conservatory. Jewison later staged and performed in dramas and musical comedies at the Malvern Collegiate Institute, and made his professional debut in a minstrel show, which he also directed and cowrote. His education was interrupted by service in World War II with the Royal Canadian Navy. Discharged in 1949, he enrolled at the University of Toronto, eventually earning a bachelor's degree in general arts. He spent his summers tending bar, waiting on tables, and producing shows at the Banff Springs Hotel.

After college Jewison took what acting assignments he could find on stage and in radio for the Canadian Broadcasting Corporation and eventually served a two-year work-study internship with the BBC, London. Returning to Canada, he wrote, directed, and produced for seven years

Norman Jewison (Monarchy Enterprises B.V. and Regency Entertainment; photo by Suzanne Hanover)

before being lured to America in 1958 to direct for such CBS television shows as *Your Hit Parade* and *The Andy Williams Show.* He went on to earn three Emmy Awards after directing television specials with Judy Garland, Frank Sinatra, Danny Kaye, and Harry Belafonte.

Jewison's Hollywood career started modestly in 1962 with the Tony Curtis picture, *Forty Pounds of Trouble.* As a contract director for Universal, Jewison made *The Thrill of It All* (1963), *Send Me No Flowers* (1964), and *The Art of Love* (1965), the first two starring Doris Day. He then went to MGM as an independent filmmaker for *The Cincinnati Kid* (1965), which he also cowrote, a critical and box-office success with an all-star cast that included Steve McQueen, Edward G. Robinson, Ann-Mar-

garet, Karl Malden, and Tuesday Weld. He would work again with Steve McQueen in *The Thomas Crown Affair* (1968), a signature film during his early career. Jewison directed successful pictures in several genres, including thrillers, political satire (*The Russians Are Coming! The Russians Are Coming!* [1966]), romantic comedy (*Moonstruck* [1988]), and, especially, such musicals as the rock opera *Jesus Christ Superstar* (1973) and *Fiddler on the Roof* (1971), a blockbuster hit that was especially praised by *New Yorker* critic Pauline Kael.

Though he knew how to entertain, Jewison will be best remembered for his more serious pictures that probed the legal system (*. . . And Justice for All* [1979]), the labor movement (*F.I.S.T.* [1978]), and, especially, race relations in the American South. *In the Heat of the Night,* for example, made at the peak of the Civil Rights movement in America, won five Academy Awards, including best picture of 1967. The film was later cloned into a popular television series. In 1984, moreover, Jewison worked with playwright Charles Fuller to direct *A Soldier's Story,* adapted from Fuller's 1982 Pulitzer Prize–winning drama, *A Soldier's Play,* a tragedy disguised as a murder mystery involving the death of an African-American sergeant on an army base in Louisiana in 1944. The cast was predominantly black and featured Howard E. Rollins, Jr., as the military lawyer, Captain Davenport, investigating the case, and talented actors from the original Negro Ensemble production, including Larry Riley, Denzel Washington in one of his very first movie roles, and Adolph Caesar, who played the murder victim. The film earned three Academy Award nominations, including best picture, but it was especially important for demonstrating that there was a possible "crossover" audience from the dominant white majority that would support what might once have been considered a "race" movie. Made on a budget of $6 million, the film earned $30 million for Columbia Pictures.

Another play adaptation, *Agnes of God* (1985), starring Jane Fonda, Meg Tilly, and Anne Bancroft, was less successful than *A Soldier's Story,* but John Pielmeier's 1979 play about a novitiate nun (Tilly) who becomes pregnant under mysterious circumstances was simply not as powerful as Charles Fuller's tragedy. Even so, Anne Bancroft, as the play's mother superior, and Meg Tilly, as the novitiate nun, both got best-supporting-actress Oscar nominations. *Other People's Money* (1991) was also adapted for Jewison by Alvin Sargent from Jerry Sterner's satirical play about corporate greed and a successful financial takeover, starring Danny DeVito as the caricatured, ruthless tycoon Lawrence Garfield, also known as "Larry the Liquidator."

One of Jewison's best films was adapted from Bobbi Ann Mason's novel *In Country* in 1989, featuring Emily Lloyd and Bruce Willis in one of his very best, serious movie roles as a traumatized Vietnam veteran. Despite this critical success with Mason's novel, Jewison, who began his career as an actor, has been considered an actor's director who has often demonstrated a particular talent for adapting plays. *A Soldier's Story* was a marvel of cinematic construction, and *Agnes of God* also got Academy Award attention.

Jewison's career has also been sustained by well-made but less-serious entertainments as well. *Moonstruck,* for example, was an engaging romantic comedy, set in New York's Little Italy, scripted by Off-Broadway playwright John Patrick Shanley, and starring Cher and Nicolas Cage as an offbeat, eccentric couple. A box-office success, *Moonstruck* earned an Oscar nomination for best picture of 1988, while Cher and Olympia Dukakis won Oscars for best actress and best supporting actress, and Shanley won the Oscar for best original screenplay. In addition to the many Oscar nominations his pictures have enjoyed, Jewison was also honored in Ottawa by being appointed an officer of the Order of Canada in 1982, Canada's highest civilian decoration. In 1986, Jewison founded the Canadian Center for Advanced Film Studies, following the model of the American Film Institute, to assist the career development of aspiring young filmmakers in his native country.

Other Films   *Gaily, Gaily* (1969); *Rollerball* (1975); *Best Friends* (1982); *Only You* (1994); *Bogus* (1996).

References   Singer, Michael, *A Cut Above: 50 Film Directors Talk about Their Craft* (Los Angeles: Lone Eagle, 1998); Welsh, Jim, "A Soldier's Story: A Paradigm for Justice," in *Columbia Pictures: Portrait of a Studio,* ed. Bernard F. Dick (Lexington: University Press of Kentucky, 1992).

—J.M.W.

Johnson, Martin (1884–1937) and **Osa** (1894–1953)   Photographers, explorers, naturalists, authors, and entrepreneurs, Martin and Osa Johnson captured and presented tens of thousands of images in their 21 films, 18 books, hundreds of magazine articles, and numerous vaudeville and lecture presentations across America. How these natives of southeast Kansas—Martin grew up in Independence and Osa Leighty in nearby Chanute—came to become celebrated world travelers and ethnographic filmmakers is a fascinating story. Indeed, the Kansas prairie might seem an unlikely stimulus for risk-taking, but in 1906 the 22-year-old Martin, armed with some experience as an itinerant photographer, left Independence to travel the South Seas with Jack London in the sea voyage of the *Snark.* "I want to see things and places other people don't," wrote Martin to London, seeking a position as mate for the voyage. "But if you think you could not use me, I hope to run across you in some part of the world." Upon his return to Independence, he presented a travelogue of his adventures, which attracted the admiration of the equally adventurous 16-year-old Osa.

Something of a tomboy, Osa also harbored dreams of being a movie actress. She joined Martin's act and sang songs during his lecture. They eloped in 1910 and began their 27 years of adventure and exploration together, documenting their trips to the New Hebrides in the South Seas, Borneo, and Kenya in theatrical documentaries like *Among the Cannibal Isles of the South Pacific* (1918), *Simba* (1928), and *Congorilla* (1932). The Johnsons's efforts on behalf of animal preservation, night photography, aerial photography, and camera safaris have influenced later generations of naturalists and documentarians.

In spite of their far-flung travels, the Johnsons remained rooted to the Midwest. For instance, upon arriving in Africa during one of their global jaunts, they planted Kansas sunflowers on the mountain slopes. Despite the highly romanticized tenor of their films, there is a compelling mixture of bravado and hucksterism, as well as a sense of ongoing restlessness. Certainly they were not above embroidering their pictures with dubious claims. For example, the "cannibal feast" depicted in *Jungle Adventure* (1921) was probably a banquet of a different order entirely, but there was enough doubt about the issue for them to rationalize their claim. From their Nairobi home they were able to manipulate the behavior of captured gorillas in controlled conditions. And Osa's on-camera presence with natives would sometimes smack of a patronizing attitude. Nonetheless, it was not fiction that they supped with headhunters, incurred tropical diseases, mounted epic safaris across veldt and jungle, and survived long dry and wet seasons. "I want to take a picture of Africa that will be different," wrote Martin in comparing his work with rival showman Jack Buck. "It will be the whole story of a country, its people and its animals, slowly unrolling against a background of magnificent scenery. . . . It will show the animals, not hunted and afraid, but natural and unaware, untroubled by man."

After Martin's death in a plane crash on January 12, 1937, Osa published the autobiographical (but mostly ghost-written) *I Married Adventure* (1940). She died in 1953 of a heart attack in her Park Avenue apartment. The Martin and Osa Johnson Safari Museum in Chanute, Kansas, houses the Johnsons's maps, native artifacts, personal memorabilia, and dozens of films (which can be viewed in a 30-seat theater). For more information, call the Safari Museum at 316-431-2730.

Other Films *Jungle Adventure* (1921); *Trailing Wild African Animals* (1923); *Baboona* (1935).

References Froehlich, Conrad, "Martin and Osa Johnson: Adventuring Filmmakers," *Classic Images* 229 (July 1994): 26, 28, 56; Imperato, Pascal and Eleanor, *They Married Adventure: The Wandering Lives of Martin and Osa Johnson* (New Brunswick, N.J.: Rutgers University Press, 1992); Johnson, Osa, *I Married Adventure* (New York: Kodansha America, 1997; reprint).

—J.C.T.

Jones, Charles Martin ("Chuck")

(1912–) With his wry grin, tousled hair, and trim bow tie, Chuck Jones has personified the sophisticated wit and childlike energy of the American cartoon. During his peak years with Warner Bros., he directed more than 200 cartoons, many of which are regarded as masterpieces of the form. He was born in Spokane, Washington, on September 21, 1912. He received his art training at age 15 at Chouinard Art Institute in Los Angeles and his training as an animator with Ub Iwerks and Walter Lantz. In the mid-1930s he came to the home of "Looney Tunes" and "Merrie Melodies," the Leon Schlesinger Studio (dubbed "Termite Terrace" in honor of the non human critters who inhabited the place), to work as an assistant for Tex Avery. After two years with Avery, Jones took over his own unit. "When I first started animating, it never occurred to me that I'd be a director," recalls Jones. "I was so delighted to animate. . . . But once I got the feeling of direction and being a director, I never wanted to do anything else and I still don't want to do anything else."

As a director, it was his responsibility to supervise six-minute cartoons under severe budgetary and time restrictions. He oversaw the conceptualizing, the writing, the key drawings, the storyboards, and the timing of a picture before it was sent to the animators. He tended to choose subjects that were less weird and abrasive than those of, say, TEX AVERY. Many featured small, quiet characters negotiating a rather forbidding environment. For example, his very first cartoon was *The Night Watchman* (1938), which was about a kitten who took his father's place as night watchman in a kitchen. Other examples include *Dog Gone Modern,* where two puppies are trapped in a "House of the Future"; and *Curious Puppy,* about a dog that accidentally throws a switch that activates an amusement park. Jones's first original character, Sniffles the Mouse, likewise struggles to survive in an oversized world of humans. *Old Glory* was a real departure for Jones and for the studio: Porky Pig learns the true meaning of the Pledge of Allegiance from Uncle Sam in the studio's first completely serious cartoon. Jones inherited the established Warners characters, of course, and in 1940 his *Elmer's Candid Camera* teamed up Bugs Bunny with Elmer Fudd. Meanwhile, he began experimenting with the assistance of layout/background artists John McGrew, Bernyce Polifka, and Eugene Fleury. In the surreal *Inki and the Lion* (1943), a youthful cannibal named Inki is confronted at unlikely moments by an exasperating mynah-bird character who hops through the scenes to the strains of Mendelssohn's "Fingal's Cave Overture."

The period from 1946 to 1956, when Warner Bros. bought out the Schlesinger Studio, saw Jones in full stride. His chief collaborators were writer Michael Maltese, animators Ken Harris and Ben Washam, layout artist Maurice Noble, voiceman Mel Blanc, composer Carl Stalling, and background artist Philip De Guard. As historian Leonard Maltin notes, Jones loved to explore his characters. "He refined his grasp of comic nuance to the point where he could get a laugh just by having a character wriggle his eyebrow." He loved to pit Bugs Bunny against Daffy Duck in the early 1950s in cartoons like *Rabbit Fire* and *Duck! Rabbit! Duck!* Jones quickly made Bugs over into his

Chuck Jones (Author's collection)

own conception. "A wild hare was not for me," he says; "what I needed was a character with the spicy, somewhat erudite introspection of a Professor Higgins, who, when nettled or threatened, would respond with the swagger of D'Artagnan as played by Errol Flynn, with the articulate quick-wittedness of Dorothy Parker—in other words, the Rabbit of My Dreams."

In 1953 he and Michael Maltese created one of the true masterpieces of the field, *Duck Amuck,* a tasty piece of meta-cinema, in which Daffy battles an unseen animator who arbitrarily changes the background scenery, alters Daffy's form and voice, and with a pencil eraser threatens to annihilate him altogether. When the defeated and baffled Daffy finally begs to know who is responsible for these outrages, the camera pulls back to reveal Bugs Bunny at the drawing board. "The cartoon stands as an almost clinical study of the decon-struction of a text," notes commentator Louis Black, "in the way it presents a whole at the beginning and then dismembers every facet of the cartoon, only to put them together at the end." Meanwhile, other classics included the Jones "deconstruction" of Wagnerian opera in *What's Opera Doc?,* his spoof of science fiction serials in *Duck Dodgers in the 24½ Century* (1953), and the immortal *One Froggy Evening* (1955), with Michigan J. Frog's reiterated refrains of "Hello, My Baby." New characters leaped from Jones's drawing board: "Pepe LePew" was an aggressively amorous French skunk; Road Runner (*Accelerati Incredibus*) and Wile E. Coyote (*Carnivorous Vulgaris*) debuted in *Fast and Furry-ous* (1948). Speed and gravity were the major forces on display here, and most of the gags grow out of them.

After Warner Bros. closed down the animation unit in 1962, Jones moved to MGM, where he directed more than 30 "Tom and Jerry" cartoons. He also continued to keep the Warner Bros. cartoon stars alive with a series of television specials, including a feature, *The Bugs Bunny-Road Runner Movie* (1979), which blended new footage with old cartoons. Other television specials included *How the Grinch Stole Christmas* (1967) and *Rikki-Tikki-Tavi* (1975). His one feature-length venture was *The Phantom Tollbooth* in 1971. He has won three Academy Awards, for *So Much, So Little* (1949), *For Scentimental Reasons* (1949), and *The Dot and the Line* (1965).

Other Films *Good Night Elmer* (1940); *The Scarlet Pumpernickel* (1950); *The Rabbit of Seville* (1950); *Lumber Jack Rabbit* (1955), in 3-D; *To Hare Is Human* (1957).

References Jones, Chuck, *Chuck Amuck: The Life and Times of an Animated Cartoonist* (New York: Avon, 1989); Kenner, Hugh, *Chuck Jones: A Flurry of Drawings* (Berkeley: University of California Press, 1994); Maltin, Leonard, *Of Mice and Magic: A History of American Animated Cartoons* (New York: New American Library, 1980).

—J.C.T.

Jonze, Spike (1969–) Prior to the release of his first feature film in 1999, Spike Jonze had created quite a name for himself in the world of TV commercials and music videos. He's done spots for such big-name corporations as Sprite, Coca-Cola, Snapple, Nike, and Levi's. He's directed numerous music videos that are as memorable as any of his full-length features, such as the Beastie Boys's "Sabotage," Weezer's "Buddy Holly," and Fatboy Slim's "Praise You." Then came Jonze's chance to make his full-length debut with *Being John Malkovich.*

The film, about the discovery of a portal that leads into the mind of John Malkovich and the scandal and get-rich-quick scheme that follow, is as genuinely quirky as much of Jonze's other video works, yet it carries with it a much heavier meaning. *Being John Malkovich* not only earned Jonze an Oscar nomination for best director, but also won him several awards. Among them are the Independent Spirit Award for best first feature, the New York Film Critics' Circle Award for best first film, and the Deauville Film Festival Critics' Award and Grand Special Prize. All together, Jonze won an impressive 11 out of 19 awards for his work on the film.

Not so long ago, however, most of Jonze's filming experience was with the shooting of skateboarding videos. In fact, his career began when he was offered a job writing and shooting photos for a BMX magazine straight out of high school. The offer sent him straight to Los Angeles rather than to college. It was his love for the camera that afforded him the job offer after freelancing for the magazine while still in high school. It was a way for Jonze to combine his love for skateboarding and BMX with a creative outlet. It would also lead to his first break in the music video business— shooting skate footage for Sonic Youth's video "100%" in 1992.

In 1992 Jonze also began working for Satellite, a subdivision of Propaganda Films Commercial and Music Video Division (Goldrich). Once at

Satellite, Jonze began establishing himself as a director, becoming one of the most sought-after music video directors by big-name alternative artists including REM, Bjork, the Breeders, and Ween. Soon, Jonze's handiwork became commonplace on MTV's *The Buzz Bin* and *120 Minutes.*

Part of Jonze's appeal is his sense of offbeat artistry. His quirkiness comes across in his work as deliriously goofy as well as dangerously artistic. In a 1999 review in *Film Comment,* Chris Chang describes Jonze's craft as projecting "an unmistakable love for the visually illogical." Who else but an artist such as Jonze could successfully combine karaoke with a near-death emergency room patient in order to hawk jeans? Or how about his business-as-usual from a runner's point-of-view ad for Nike that portrayed joggers on the first day of the Millennium oblivious to the fact that the apocalypse had begun the night before? "No matter what happens in the world, a runner will run," Jonze states.

Indeed, Jonze prefers his work to speak for itself, leading one journalist to describe him as being "too cool for small talk." As far as personal information is concerned, Jonze doesn't offer too much of himself. He was born Adam Spiegel, and he grew up in Bethesda, Maryland. In 1999 he married Sofia Coppola (director of *The Virgin Suicides* and daughter of Francis Ford Coppola). When labeled as the heir-apparent to the Spiegel catalog fortune, he either abruptly changes the subject or rejects the claim as a silly rumor. In fact, Jonze won't explain his changing of his name. In a *Newsweek* article from October 1999, Karen Schoemer describes Jonze's interview approach as "an adaptation of the standard adolescent way of dealing with a prying parent. He doesn't say much which makes you wonder what kind of wildly eccentric thoughts and ideas he's hiding."

Despite his big-screen success, Jonze has not lost his love for working on the small screen. Around the same time he began earning numerous award nominations for *Being John Malkovich,*

Jonze made the decision to stay with Satellite, extending his contract with the company for three years in February 2000. Of his decision to continue at Satellite, Jonze said, "Music videos and commercials are really fun because you have an idea and then you can write it, prep it, shoot it, edit it, and get the whole thing done in a month." Jonze also joined the advisory board for Atom-Films.com in Fall 2000, signing a two-year deal.

As if all his directing endeavors were not enough, Jonze can be seen on-screen as well. He began acting in 1993 with a bit part as a teenage drug customer in ALLISON ANDERS's *Mi Vida Loca (My Crazy Life).* Jonze had two more small parts: in *The Game* (1997) as an EMT and in *Being John Malkovich* as Derek Mantini's assistant for the Emily Dickinson puppet. His first costarring role came alongside Mark Wahlberg and George Clooney in 1999's *Three Kings* as Private Conrad Vig. Jonze also worked as a producer on the MTV series *Jackass,* on a 15-minute campaign film for Al Gore, and in the 2001 film *Human Nature.*

For a man just barely into his thirties, Jonze seems to be enjoying a huge amount of success in an often-finicky profession. He's currently working on his second feature film *Adaptation,* based on Susan Orleans's novel *The Orchid Thief.*

References Chang, Chris, "Head Wide Open," *Film Comment,* September 1999; Healy, Mark, "Being Spike Jonze," *Harper's Bazaar* 3456 (November 1999), pp. 146–147; Nashawaty, Chris, "Spike Jonze," *Entertainment Weekly* 266 (March 17, 1995), pp. 33–34; Schoemer, Karen, "Being Spike Jonze," *Newsweek* 134, no. 16 (October 18, 1999), pp. 74–75.

—L.H.

Jordan, Neil (1950–)

Neil Jordan has become one of Ireland's most recognizable and respected filmmakers. His best films have a distinctive Irish feel to them, and encompass themes of alienation, freedom, politics, and love in various settings in Ireland and the United Kingdom. His work is highly stylized, often evoking strange or unusual images while maintaining sensitive, realistic character portraits.

Neil Jordan was born in Sligo, Ireland, on February 25, 1950, and grew up in Dublin, where he later studied history and literature at University College. Jordan began writing from an early age and, while working in fringe theater, published a collection of stories, *Night in Tunisia,* in 1976. He began writing for Irish television and the BBC and published a novel, *The Past,* in 1980 before directing his first film, *Angel* (1982). The film explores an individual who becomes inadvertently embroiled in violence.

Dealing with lost innocence and moral ambiguity, themes that recur in Jordan's work, *Angel* was one of the more auspicious film debuts sponsored by Channel 4 in Britain, a new media operation that also produced many other now-critically acclaimed filmmakers during the early 1980s. Jordan's foray into films was unexpected but surely welcomed. "The novel, as a form, seemed to me overloaded with history," Jordan has explained. "Narratively, there were more interesting things you could do in the cinema. And I also found that I was writing myself into a corner because my prose and fiction were so visual they were almost like blueprints for movies."

His next film, *The Company of Wolves* (1984), depicts a mixed nightmare world of fairy tale, horror, and psychoanalysis. Based on the Little Red Riding Hood story, the film has two distinct worlds of fantasy and reality that merge by the movie's end. It is a magical, stylistic film, embellished with nuanced terror and symbolic imagery. The movie won Jordan best film and best director awards from the London Critics Circle. Jordan's subsequent film, *Mona Lisa* (1986), garnered him international notice after it won best picture at Cannes. This was also a film about the loss of innocence, morality, and corruption, and deals with the social conflicts between the lower and upper classes. Of that film, Jordan said, "If I have a Point of View, it probably emerges more in [*Mona Lisa*]

than in anything else I have done." It presents directly, often with biting humor, the unattractive world of prostitution and drug addiction, but also offers decent, emotional characters in search of understanding and redemption.

After making two American-financed films during the late 1980s, Jordan returned to Ireland to make *The Miracle* (1991), a darkly sensuous coming-of-age drama that takes an unexpected turn that surprises the audience. It was his next film, however, with its own unnerving and unsuspecting twist, that earned Jordan his most acclaim. *The Crying Game* (1992) won Jordan an Oscar for best screenplay. It is at once a tightly wound political drama, an action-thriller, and a love story. The plot twist became one of the most talked-about in recent screen history, which led the film to have both massive critical, media, and commercial success. It starts as a political drama, with an Irish Republican Army militant who kidnaps a British soldier and who later sets out to find the soldier's girlfriend, facing only obstacles and surprises once he does. All of the characters are unique and somewhat mysterious, imperfect yet impassioned.

Jordan's next project, an adaptation of Anne Rice's *Interview with the Vampire* (1994), was a glossy, expensive, Hollywood-backed film that was stereotyped and tedious, but still did marginally well became of the star power of Tom Cruise, Brad Pitt, and Antonio Banderas. A much better film was to follow, *Michael Collins* (1997), an historical portrait of the Easter Rebellion of 1916 and the establishment of the Irish Republic in 1922. Collins (Liam Neeson) and his Irish Free State forces battle De Valera (Alan Rickman), both of whom have different notions about how to gain freedom for Ireland during the civil war. It is a complex political history that, as the introductory titles suggest, conveys all the "triumph, terror, and tragedy of the period."

Another striking film was to follow, *The Butcher Boy* (1998), based on a 1993 novel by Patrick McCabe, one of the screen's most disturbing portraits of psychotic paranoia and mental disintegration. Set in 1962 during the Cuban missile crisis, what begins as a sort of Irish "Peck's Bad Boy" (Eammon Owens as "Francie Brady") lurches inexorably toward a darkly Gothic horror story, a sort of "Erin-go-boo!" The boy's descent into homicidal mania unleashes a slipstream of images, both real and fantastic, with the borderline in between growing ever more blurred. For example, when Francie plays cowboys, the idyllic green valley surrounding them erupts into a roiling atomic mushroom cloud (later Francie hallucinates that the entire village is littered with charred pigs' heads). And there's the terrifying moment when Francie, armed with butcher's tools, bursts into a woman's house and savagely slaughters her (later burying her body beneath a pile of garbage). A final confirmation of the boy's madness is his encounter with Sinead O'Connor, portrayed as the Madonna.

In Dreams (1998) is a horror film that is a cross between *Nightmare on Elm Street* and *Don't Look Now,* a triumph of dazzling visuals over trite subject matter. Annette Benning portrays Claire Cooper, whose violent nightmares—horrifying images of drowning children, red apples, and cryptic graffiti—are precognitions of the kidnapping of her child. These images, she claims, are telepathic transmissions from the kidnapper (Robert Downey, Jr.). The film's highlight is a performance by children of a fairy pageant. In a style that is pure Jordan, the boys and girls flit about in the twilight wood, wearing their fairy wings and intoning their rhymes. The disappearance of Claire's little girl is implied by the sight of her abandoned wings, caught on a bush, a poignant emblem of lost childhood and innocence.

Jordan's next film, an adaptation of Graham Greene's celebrated 1951 novel *The End of the Affair* (1999), is set during the London blitz. It was not only a subtle probe into the quirks of love and jealousy but also an existential examination of the enduring nature of love and the bewildering workings of God. Dominating the film is one of Jordan's most striking images, a bomb blast that becomes an epiphany for the character of Sara (Julianne Moore), an adulterous woman who is thereby transformed into a saintly presence who performs miracles. Because of its complex tangle of flashbacks and differing points of view, it might be considered the *Citizen Kane* of wartime melodramas.

Reflecting on his work, Jordan has said: "I like to choose characters who are surrounded by a life that seems understandable and who slowly find themselves in situations where everything has changed, where no rules exist and where emotions and realities are brought into play that they are not prepared for." Along with Peter Weir, Jordan is perhaps our finest poet of apocalypse.

Other Film   *We're No Angels* (1989).

References   Gould, Lois, "Neil Jordan Interview," *New York Times Magazine,* Jan. 9, 1944, p. 22; McSwiney, "Trying to Take the Gun Out of Irish Politics: an Interview with Neil Jordan." *Cineaste* 22 (1996): 20–24; Rogers, Lori, *Feminine Nation: Performance, Gender, and Resistance in the Works of John McGahern and Neil Jordan* (Lanham, Md.: University Press of America, 1998).

—W.V. and J.C.T.

Kasdan, Lawrence (1949–) Lawrence Kasdan was born on January 14, 1949, in Miami Beach, Florida. He was raised in West Virginia and earned a master's degree in education at the University of Michigan. Discarding his ambitions to become an English teacher, Kasdan soon found himself copywriting TV commercials and, in his spare time, writing screenplays. After receiving numerous rejection notices, Kasdan's script *The Bodyguard* was optioned by Warner Bros. in 1977. His screenplay *Continental Divide* was read by STEVEN SPIELBERG, who asked Kasdan if he would be interested in writing a script for a proposed adventure film "about a guy who has a whip and a leather jacket and he's named after my dog, Indiana."

Kasdan's big breakthrough came in 1980 with *The Empire Strikes Back.* Screenwriter Leigh Brackett had died after completing a first draft of the script, and Kasdan, who had finished writing the screenplay to the aforementioned *Raiders of the Lost Ark,* was asked by GEORGE LUCAS to take up writing the *Star Wars* sequel. Following the success of both *The Empire Strikes Back* (1980) and *Raiders of the Lost Ark* (1981), Kasdan received his first directing credit with *Body Heat* (1981)—for which he also wrote the screenplay—a noirish erotic

drama starring newcomers William Hurt and Kathleen Turner. The film was a steamy update of *Double Indemnity* refitted for a 1980s audience. Kasdan wrote the screenplay for the third installment in the *Star Wars* trilogy, *Return of the Jedi* (1983). The same year he directed *The Big Chill,* a story of "forty-something" angst that boasted a talented ensemble cast including Glenn Close, William Hurt, Tom Berenger, Kevin Kline, and Jeff Goldblum. Similar in many ways to John Sayles's

Lawrence Kasdan, director of *Body Heat* (The Ladd Company)

Lawrence Kasdan (right) directing Kevin Kline (left) and Steve Martin in *Grand Canyon* (Twentieth Century-Fox)

Return of the Secaucus Seven (1980), it chronicled the bittersweet weekend reunion of friends who were survivors of the radical youth movement of the 1960s. *Silverado* (1985) was Kasdan's paean to the western genre. "It was all our favorite things from westerns put together," Kasdan said. "And it is a kind of metaphor for the filmmaking process . . . in that it's about strangers with particular skills who come together on a journey and who use their skills to help each other get through a difficult passage, which is what true filmmaking is about. And it's very much about westerns."

In 1988 Kasdan directed *The Accidental Tourist,* based on the novel by Anne Tyler. The story of a travel-guide author who hates traveling, fears the love of the dog-trainer Muriel, and tries, in general, to "slip through life unchanged" seemed

unlikely material for a film, but Kasdan characteristically defended the effort as a movie that permits close scrutiny of the characters: "[It] takes you closer to things [and] doesn't allow you to avoid anything at all." The film starred William Hurt and Geena Davis and was nominated for best picture at the 1989 Academy Awards. Davis received an Academy Award for best supporting actress. This was followed by what many consider Kasdan's best and most personal film, *Grand Canyon* (1991). It picks up on a group similar to *The Big Chill,* now entering middle age. The connections among them are even more tenuous. Kevin Kline is the central character, an immigration lawyer. When he is saved from a gang of attackers by a black tow-truck driver, Simon (Danny Glover), a series of changes mysteriously enter his life and the lives of others around him, including his wife (Mary McDonnell) and his friend Davis (Steve Martin), a producer of schlock-shock films. "The canyon of the title," explains critic James Kaplan, "—which stands both for the place itself and the chasm in this country between the haves and have-nots— could just as well refer to the abyss of sentimental pretentiousness over which Kasdan walks a tightrope. Occasionally he wobbles, but who else could stay up so long?" The film was nominated for an Academy Award for best original screenplay and in addition received the Golden Bear Award at the Berlin International Film Festival. In 1992 Kasdan finally produced his earlier screenplay, *The Bodyguard,* with Kevin Costner and Whitney Houston. The director returned to the western genre with the epic-length *Wyatt Earp* (1994), starring Kevin Costner. Kasdan wrote the screenplay in addition to serving as the film's director and producer. In 1999 Kasdan directed *Mumford,* the tale of a small-town psychologist.

Foregrounding characters and minimizing the directorial presence is Kasdan's personal goal as a filmmaker. "I do believe in an art that hides itself," he says, "one where there may be enormous craft and thought but which . . . eventually disappears, seamless."

Other Films As director: *I Love You To Death* (1990); *French Kiss* (1995). As producer: *T.A.G. the Assassination Game* (1982); *Cross My Heart* (1987); *Jumpin' at the Boneyard* (1992).

References Tibbetts, John C., "Hurt, Turner, and Director Kasdan Chat about Anti-Cinema Appeal of 'Accidental Tourist,'" *Christian Science Monitor,* March 28, 1980, 10–11; Kaplan, James, "Their Generation," *Entertainment Weekly,* February 14, 1992, pp. 31–33.

—R.W.

Kaufman, Philip (1936–) Writer-director Philip Kaufman was born in 1936, grew up on the North Side of Chicago, and was educated at the University of Chicago, where, as an aspiring novelist, he met Anaïs Nin in 1962, a meeting that eventually led to his film *Henry and June* (1990), nearly 30 years later. In 1963 he turned his unfinished novel into his first film, the comedy *Goldstein,* made on a shoestring budget and starring players from Chicago's "Second City" group. The picture won the Prix de la Nouvelle Critique at the 1964 Cannes Film Festival. In 1965 he wrote and directed *Fearless Frank,* a satire starring Jon Voight in his film debut, which led two years later to a contract with Universal Studios. Other early films included *The Great Northfield Minnesota Raid* (1971), a screwball western starring Robert Duvall and Cliff Robertson, and *The White Dawn* (1973). After moving to San Francisco in 1977, Kaufman made a striking remake of the Don Siegel classic *Invasion of the Body Snatchers* that carried that 1950s paranoia of the original to another level, and stood

Philip Kaufman (The Ladd Company/Warner Bros.)

as a worthy remake in comparison to Siegel's adaptation of Jack Finney's novel. *The Wanderers,* his adaptation of Richard Price's gang novel, followed in 1979. His screenwriting credits include *The Outlaw Josey Wales* (1976) for Clint Eastwood and the original story for *Raiders of the Lost Ark* (1981) for George Lucas.

Kaufman's breakthrough picture was his brilliant and deviously satiric adaptation of Tom Wolfe's astronaut epic, *The Right Stuff* (1983), which received eight Academy Award nominations, including best picture, and won four Oscars. He earned Writers Guild and Directors Guild Award nominations for *The Right Stuff* and Writers Guild and Academy Award nominations for his adaptation of Czech writer Milan Kundera's novel, set during the turmoil of 1968s' Prague Spring, *The Unbearable Lightness of Being* (1988), which Kaufman directed and coscripted with Jean-Claude Carrière. Thereafter he won the international Orson Welles Award for best filmmaker of 1989.

Set in 1931–32, his film *Henry and June* (1990) was adapted from the diaries of Anaïs Nin and the autobiographical novels of Henry Miller (played by Fred Ward, with Uma Thurman as his wife June and Spanish actress Maria de Medeiros as Anaïs Nin). The director's wife, Rose Kaufman, cowrote the screenplay with him. Because of its sexual content, the film tested the limits of the MPAA rating system, and was originally rated X but eventually given the first NC-17 rating in motion picture history. Besides having met Anaïs Nin in Chicago, Kaufman had gone to Big Sur in 1960 to meet Henry Miller, the author of *Tropic of Cancer* and *Tropic of Capricorn,* two books that helped rewrite censorship laws in America, so it is appropriate that Kaufman's film treating Henry Miller's life managed to change the rating system of the Motion Picture Association of America. Regardless, the film was not a box-office success.

Kaufman had better success with his adaptation of Michael Crichton's Japan-bashing novel *Rising Sun* (1993), starring Sean Connery and Wesley Snipes, though Kaufman and Crichton were at odds about how the treatment should be handled. Kaufman's treatment made essential changes in the plot and characters, not the least of which was making the Wesley Snipes character an African American, and Crichton was outraged. Although this politically correct treatment changed the original story considerably, the damaged discourse did not seem to hurt the film's popularity.

Kaufman has always functioned best as a Hollywood maverick willing to push the envelope. His most recent film is *Quills* (2000), a picture made in England in which an Australian (Geoffrey Rush) plays the notorious Marquis de Sade, described by Kaufman's friend David Thomson as "wickedly funny, impious, [and] blasphemous," but also "mischievous, subversive, and liberating," arguably Kaufman's "best work yet." Thomson described this de Sade as "one more of Kaufman's outsider heroes, dangerous to themselves and alarming to society." In a *New York Times* piece written, perhaps, to hype the forthcoming film, Thomson referred to Kaufman as a "forgotten" filmmaker, but he has proved himself many times over as a gifted adaptor and an unquestionably talented director. He certainly caught the satiric tone of *The Right Stuff* far better than Brian De Palma was able to do in his later adaptation of Wolfe's *Bonfire of the Vanities* (1990). Though De Palma is the more famous director, Kaufman had "the right stuff."

References   Mitchell, Sean, "Strangers in a Strange Land," *Premiere* 6, no. 2 (August 1993), pp. 58–63, 111; Rafferty, Terrence, "Duplicity," *New Yorker,* October 8, 1990, pp. 98–101; Thomson, David, "A Filmmaker Both Promising and Forgotten at 64," *New York Times,* September 10, 2000, sec. II, pp. 63, 73.

—J.M.W.

Kazan, Elia (1909–)   Elia Kazan successfully straddled the worlds of American theater and film in a career that brought many important playwrights and novelists to the screen. Born Elia

Kazanjoglou (an Anatolian Greek) in Constantinople (now Istanbul), Turkey, on September 7, 1909, Kazan moved with his family to New York in 1913, where his father sold rugs for a living. Kazan attended the Mayfair School and New Rochelle High School in New York. Upon completion of an undergraduate education at Williams College (1930) and drama study at Yale School of Drama (1930–32), Kazan became a member of the left-wing Group Theatre as both an actor and assistant manager. While a member of the Group Theatre, Kazan worked under such directors as Harold Clurman, Cheryl Crawford, and Lee Strasberg. Kazan began directing plays in 1938 and became one of the leading directors on Broadway throughout the 1940s. He directed the premiere productions of Thornton Wilder's *Skin of Our Teeth,* Tennessee Williams's *A Streetcar Named Desire* and *Cat on a Hot Tin Roof,* and Arthur Miller's *Death of a Salesman,* among others. Always the consummate actors' director, Kazan later recalled, "I worked like a maniac. . . . I took the Stanislavski training with utmost seriousness. . . . I thought of the roles mostly psychologically . . . [analyzing] the main drive of a character, and from the main drive there were stems, the 'beats' that would build up the whole part."

Such success caught the attention of Hollywood and producer Darryl F. Zanuck at 20th Century-Fox. Kazan had already had considerable experience in films. He had appeared in Ralph Steiner's documentary short, *Pie in the Sky* (1934), and had directed two documentary films, about Tennessee miners, *The People of the Cumberland* (1937), and food rationing, the U.S. Department of Agriculture's *It's Up to You* (1941). As an actor he had also gained favorable notices in two films directed by Anatole Litvak, *City for Conquest* (1940) and *Blues in the Night* (1941). But now he turned his energies toward directing theatrical feature films, debuting in 1945 with *A Tree Grows in Brooklyn,* adapted from Betty Smith's autobiographical novel about a poor girl growing up in New York. Subsequent critically and commercially successful films included another literary adaptation, *A Sea of Grass,* about the 19th-century struggle for possession of grasslands by farmers and cattle ranchers; *Gentleman's Agreement* (1947), an indictment of anti-Semitism in postwar America, which received eight Academy Award nominations (winning for best director, best picture, and best supporting actress for Celeste Holm); *Boomerang!* (1947), a police procedural drama about a man wrongfully accused of murder; *Pinky* (1949), a light-skinned black woman who passes for white; and *Panic in the Streets* (1950), a documentary-style drama about a fugitive murderer infected with bubonic plague.

In 1951 Kazan brought his famous production of Tennessee Williams's *A Streetcar Named Desire* to the screen, with Marlon Brando recreating his stage role. In 1952, while filming *Viva Zapata!* based on a screenplay by John Steinbeck and also starring Brando, Kazan was called before HUAC (House Un-American Activities Committee) regarding his involvement with the Communist Party and the Group Theatre. Although Kazan had been a member of the Communist Party in the mid-1930s, he denied that the Group Theatre was a front for communist activity and refused to supply the committee with names of other communists. Later, when 20th Century-Fox president Spyros P. Skouras informed him that he faced the possibility of being blacklisted if he did not cooperate with HUAC, Kazan once again testified and this time supplied them with the names of friends and associates who were suspected communists. Among the names Kazan gave the committee were Clifford Odets, Lee and Paula Strasberg, Lillian Hellman, Joseph Bromberg, and John Garfield. Kazan was maligned by many in New York and Hollywood for "selling out" to save his Fox contract. Arthur Miller, who was one of Kazan's closest friends, spoke out against him in a letter to the *New York Post.* To this day Kazan continues to justify his belief that in postwar

America the communists posed a real threat and in Russia repressed artistic activities.

In the 1950s and early 1960s Kazan directed a succession of some of his finest films. *On the Waterfront* was based on a script by Budd Schulberg, which in turn had drawn from a series of magazine articles by Malcolm Johnson about mob control of the New York area docks. It was filmed on location in Hoboken, New Jersey, and starred Marlon Brando and Eva Marie Saint. *On the Waterfront* won seven Oscars, including best picture, best director, best actor, and best cinematography (Boris Kaufman). Many consider the film as Kazan's justification of his HUAC testimony, citing the similarities between Terry Malloy's testimony before the crime committee with his own. Kazan's next film was *East of Eden,* starring James Dean and based on the last third of the novel by John Steinbeck. A retelling of the Cain and Abel story set in California's Salinas Valley at the turn of the century, it was a critical and commercial success, netting Kazan another Oscar nomination for best director. Working again from a Tennessee Williams play, Kazan directed *Baby Doll* in 1956, drawing heavily from the Actors Studio for his cast. The story of two men competing for the affections of "baby doll" Carroll Baker earned more censorial attacks than critical praise. In 1957 Kazan directed *A Face in the Crowd,* based on a script by Budd Schulberg, a scathing attack on the power of television and the cult of media celebrity, starring Andy Griffith as country yokel "Lonesome Rhodes," discovered by a reporter (Patricia Neal). Kazan's association with playwright William Inge resulted in *Splendor in the Grass,* based on Inge's Oscar-winning original screenplay about frustrated adolescent sex in a small midwestern town in the 1920s. *America, America* (1963) was based on Kazan's novel about the life of his Greek uncle and his immigration to the United States at the turn of the century.

Kazan's final film as a director was *The Last Tycoon* (1976), based on the unfinished novel by F.

Scott Fitzgerald and adapted by playwright Harold Pinter. Kazan's autobiography, *A Life,* was published by Alfred Knopf in 1988. In 1998 Kazan was again in the spotlight and a center of controversy—aroused by his selection to receive the Academy of Motion Picture Arts and Sciences' Lifetime Achievement Award. Many continued to harbor resentment over Kazan's actions of 50 years earlier, claiming that the careers he ruined by naming names should deny him any further recognition. Nonetheless, the televised ceremony prevailed. In assessing Kazan's career, historian Lloyd Michaels noted that "during a decade and a half [1950–1965] of anxiety, gimmickry, and entropy in Hollywood, Kazan remained one of the few American directors who continued to believe in the cinema as a medium for artistic expression and who brought forth films that consistently reflected his own creative vision."

Other Films *Man on a Tightrope* (1953); *Wild River* (1960); *The Arrangement* (1969); *The Visitors* (1972).

References Kazan, Elia, *A Life* (New York: Knopf, 1988); Michaels, Lloyd, *Elia Kazan: A Guide to References and Resources* (Boston: G. K. Hall, 1985); Pauly, Thomas H., *Elia Kazan and American Culture* (Philadelphia: Temple University Press, 1983); Smith, Wendy, *Real Life Drama: The Group Theatre and America, 1931–1940* (New York: Knopf, 1990); Young, Jeff, *Kazan: The Master Director Discusses His Films* (New York: Newmarket Press, 1999).

—R.W.

Keaton, Buster (1895–1966) Comedian, acrobat, film director, and producer, Buster Keaton deserves a place in the pantheon of America's greatest comic geniuses. He was literally a child of storm. He claimed that Kansas tornadoes blew him into the world, christened him, and flung him onto the stage and screen. When his mother was eight months pregnant, a cyclone tore down the Keatons' medicine-show tent. A little later, on the night of his birth, October 4, 1895, in the tiny farming town of Piqua, Kansas, a twister almost leveled the town. Three years later, during another tour of the state, his parents left him in a boarding house during their performance—and a howling vortex sucked him out of a second-story window, sailed him over trees and houses, and deposited him safely in the middle of the street three blocks away. The toddler just blinked (the first of many deadpan reactions to life's catastrophes). Thereafter, his mother decided he would be safer on the stage with his family than left to the whims of the South Wind.

But little Joseph Frank Keaton merely traded one disaster for another. As the newest member of the "Three Keatons," the roughest vaudeville act in show business, he found himself subjected to slapstick routines where he was kicked, pummeled, and hurled about the stage by his father, Joe Keaton. Aptly dubbed "Buster" by magician Harry Houdini, a member of the Keaton troupe—the story may be apocryphal—the rubber-limbed child grew up to become a vaudeville headliner, renowned for his hair-raising falls. By age 21, after a stint in the army, he was on his own in Hollywood, serving a kind of apprenticeship with another Kansan, the redoubtable Roscoe "Fatty" Arbuckle. By 1920 he had his own production company, and during the next decade made 30 shorts and features, most of them regarded today as classics of the American cinema.

His amazing acrobatics—falls from trains (*Sherlock, Jr.* [1924]), dives from waterfalls (*Our Hospitality* [1923]), and tumbles down mountainsides (*The Paleface* [1922], *Seven Chances* [1925])—rival the stunts of the great Douglas Fairbanks, Sr. His impeccable period re-creations—the Old South in *Our Hospitality* (1923); the Civil War in *The General* (1926)—and his keen-edged social satires (*Seven Chances* [1925]) beat the more prestigious DAVID WARK GRIFFITH and ERNST LUBITSCH at their own game. His intricate, inventive gag trajectories (*Neighbors* [1920], *Cops* [1922], *The Navigator* [1924]) surpass anything by Harold Lloyd. And his penchant for bizarre, dreamlike situations

Buster Keaton (Author's collection)

(*The Playhouse* [1921], *Sherlock, Jr.*) are as peculiar as anything out of the contemporary French avant-garde.

While it is undeniably true Buster was funny, audiences during his peak years in the 1920s relegated him to third place as a box-office draw, well behind CHARLES CHAPLIN and Harold Lloyd. Even his masterpiece, *The General,* commonly cited in critics' polls as one of the 10 greatest films ever made, was originally dismissed by some critics as "a mild Civil War comedy" and rejected by audiences (it lost more money than any of his other films). Keaton's decline in the 1930s was as abrupt as one of his pratfalls. He lost his independent status when he left United Artists for MGM in 1928. Although his first MGM pictures made money (*The Cameraman* [1928], *Spite Marriage* [1929], *Parlor, Bedroom, and Bath* [1932]), his personal life was collapsing and he sank deep into alcoholism. By the mid-1930s he was down and out, estranged from the studio, and capable only of a string of cheap comedies that were but pale ghosts of his work a decade earlier.

The climb back was slow and painful. The upturn began with a successful marriage in 1940 to Eleanor Norris, a young dancer who would remain devoted to him during their 26 years of marriage. His alcoholism back under control, he returned to MGM as a writer and gag man for Red Skelton and Lucille Ball. Then, in rapid succession, came an adulatory tribute to him by the esteemed critic/writer James Agee for *Life* magazine in 1949; a successful stint in live television in the early 1950s; a movie biography, *The Buster Keaton Story* (1957); and memorable cameo roles in films like *Limelight* (1953) and *Around the World in 80 Days* (1956). A major revival of his films got under way in the early 1960s. And before his death from cancer on February 1, 1966, he was abashed but pleased to find himself the darling of the intelligentsia and the college crowd and secure in his status as a comic artist.

Like his screen personae, the real Buster had proven to be a tough and resilient fellow. "What I expected was hard knocks," he said in his autobiography, *My Wonderful World of Slapstick* (1957). "I always expected to have to work hard. Maybe harder than other people because of my lack of education. And when the knocks came, I felt it was no surprise. I had always known life was like that, full of uppercuts for the deserving and undeserving alike." Indeed, despite the hazards and exotic imagery, Buster remained ever the prairie pragmatist, the *bricoleur* (handyman) of the south forty. In every one of his films he took a moment to stand his ground and assess the situation. The pose is familiar: a small figure in flat porkpie hat and baggy pants leaning forward slightly against the wind, eyes shaded with the palm of his hand, his gaze mutely surveying the far horizon. Every crisis—a cattle stampede in *Go West* (1925), a runaway ocean liner in *The Navigator,* a stolen loco-motive in *The General,* a deranged house in *The Haunted House* (1921), a cyclone in *Steamboat Bill, Jr.* (1928), a newsreel camera with a mind of its own in *The Cameraman*—was both a confrontation and a negotiation. "He is an explorer," wrote critic Walter Kerr in his indispensable *The Silent Clowns* (1975), one of the most insightful analyses on Keaton extant. "He explores the universe exactly as he explores film: with a view to measuring the immeasurable before he enters it, so that he will know how to behave when he is there." In 1995 the film preservationist David Shepard released through Kino International, of New York City, a generous package of all the surviving post-Arbuckle shorts and silent features for the edification of a new and admiring generation of viewers. And finally, at this writing, Keaton and his world of silent comedy are the subject of annual "Keaton Festivals" in the town of Iola, Kansas, near his birthplace. Held during the last weekend of September, the festivals are a mix of humanities scholars, film historians, Hollywood celebrities, Keaton family members, and enthusiasts who attend screenings, symposia, discussions, dinners, and late-night parties. Keaton as a Kansan is always a prime topic. Is it not true that the flattest and most prosaic of landscapes may contain the wildest visions? And did not Keaton, the most silent of clowns—whose "deadly horizontal" hat (the term is Agee's) was such a perfect symbol for the level prairie—constantly confront the highest precipices, steepest descents, and most improbable of catastrophes? Keaton said it simply: "I used to daydream an awful lot in pictures; I could get carried away and visualize all the fairylands in the world."

Other Films *One Week* (1920); *The Saphead* (1920); *The Three Ages* (1923); *Battling Butler* (1926); *What, No Beer?* (1933); *Le Roi des Champs-Elysees* (1935).

References Keaton, Buster, *My Wonderful World of Slapstick* (Garden City: Doubleday, 1960); Kerr, Walter, *The Silent Clowns* (New York: Alfred A. Knopf, 1975); Tibbetts, John C., "The Whole Show: The Restored

Films of Buster Keaton," *Literature/Film Quarterly* 23, no. 4 (1995): 230–242.

—J.C.T.

Kelly, Gene (1912–1996)

Eugene Curran Kelly was born on August 23, 1912, in Pittsburgh, Pennsylvania, and educated at the Sacred Heart School, Peabody High School, Penn State, and the University of Pittsburgh. His passion for dancing led to playing the vaudeville circuit with his brother, and getting some of his first stage roles. In 1940 he played the lead in the stage musical *Pal Joey* and met STANLEY DONEN. In 1942 after making his movie debut in *For Me and My Gal,* a BUSBY BERKELEY musical with Judy Garland, he worked as a contract player for MGM from 1944 to 1947. In 1950 he made his directing debut by codirecting *On the Town* with Stanley Donen, a musical that revolutionized the genre by shooting on real locations in New York City. "When I got out of the Navy after World War II," he told Michael Singer, "I wrote a little storyline idea and showed it to Stanley Donen, and we sold it to MGM." Getting the studio to agree to the location filming, however, was not easily done. *On the Town* was a defining picture both for Manhattan and for Gene Kelly.

Although known mainly as an actor and dancer, Kelly was also a gifted choreographer and choreographed several films for other directors, most notably Vincente Minnelli's *The Pirate* (1948), *An American in Paris* (1951), and *Brigadoon* (1954). He worked with Donen on what is probably his most famous film, *Singin' in the Rain* (1952), and it was his idea to add to the lyric, "I'm singin' *and dancin'* in the rain." Kelly went on to direct *It's Always Fair Weather* (1955) and *Invitation to the Dance* (1956), which won the Grand Prize at the Berlin Film Festival. In 1958 Kelly directed *Flower Drum Song* on Broadway and *Tunnel of Love* in Hollywood. After he retired from dancing at the age of 46, Kelly continued to direct: *Gigot* (1962), *A Guide for the Married*

Man (1967), *Hello, Dolly!* (1969), and *The Cheyenne Social Club* (1970). He also continued working as an actor, most notably hosting *That's Entertainment* (1974) and its 1976 sequel, *That's Entertainment, Part II.* One of his last films was also one of his most magical, *Xanadu* (1980). As early as 1951 the Motion Picture Academy recognized his versatility as "an actor, singer, director, and dancer" with an Honorary Oscar. In 1980 Kelly won the Cecil B. DeMille Career Prize, followed by the Kennedy Center's Life Achievement Award in 1982 and the American Film Institute Award in 1985.

References Silverman, Stephen, *Dancing on the Ceiling: Stanley Donen and His Movies* (New York: Knopf, 1996); Singer, Michael, *A Cut Above: 50 Film Directors Talk about Their Craft* (Los Angeles: Lone Eagle, 1998); Yudkoff, Alvin, *Gene Kelly: A Life of Dance and Dreams* (New York: Back Stage Books, 1999).

—J.M.W.

Kiarostami, Abbas (1940–)

In the words of commentator Godfrey Cheshire, Iranian filmmaker Abbas Kiarostami "is the most important filmmaker to appear on the world stage in the Nineties." His career parallels the time line of contemporary Iranian cinema—beginning with the New Wave of the late sixties, maturing in the seventies, and flowering with renewed brilliance in the nineties (when the film medium as an artistic enterprise was particularly venerated). A native of Iran's capital city, Tehran, Abbas Kiarostami was born on June 22, 1940. In 1958 he won a painting competition and then left his home to study graphic design at the Faculty of Fine Arts of Tehran University. Throughout the 1960s, he worked as a designer and illustrator, gaining a reputation especially for his poster designs and illustrations for children's books, but venturing also in film and television through the design of commercials and credit sequences. He cites an early viewing of FEDERICO FELLINI's *La Dolce Vita* as a prime impetus in his interest in film.

The Iranian New Wave ignited in the late sixties after the spectacular success of a groundbreaking film, Dariush Mehrjui's *The Cow.* The intellectual climate of the new movement was defined by a rejection of the violence and spectacle that characterized older Iranian films, in imitation of Indian imports. Instead, filmmakers returned to national culture and to the realities of working-class Iranians, following the cinematic path of Italian neorealism. Kiarostami took part in this resurgence of his country's cinema, through the creation of a film department at his place of work, the Institute for the Intellectual Development of Children and Young Adults. He has worked at this center ever since, and in his long career has made more than 14 short and medium-length films and six feature films.

Kiarostami's fame in the West came, however, only in the early 1990s with the success in the international festival circuit of his third feature-length film, *Where Is My Friend's Home* (1987). It is the story of a small child who finds out that he has swapped with a classmate the notebook he needs to do a homework assignment. Against his mother's advice, he sets out to find his friend's house in a neighboring town. The storyline of the movie was suggested by an experience of Kiarostami's own son, "within the allegorical structure of a mystical tale," in Miriam Rosen's words.

His next film was *And Life Goes On* (1992), inspired by a real event in the aftermath of the 1991 earthquake that devastated Iran. In it a fictional film director (who is supposed to have made *Where . . .*) sets out in a quest to find whether the child protagonist of his former film is still alive after the earthquake. With his young son Puya, he travels by car to the city of Rudbar, into the region where the quake hit the worst. They have a series of brief encounters with peasants around the town of Koker, whom they help in different ways. The director finds a baby alone in the woods and gives it to his mother as she arrives. He helps a woman load a gas cylinder and offers a ride to a man who

had worked in his previous film. Later, Puya goes exploring and finds a woman who lost a son in the disaster and who reproaches God for his death. Puya reminds her that God did not allow Abraham to sacrifice Isaac. As they continue driving, they find a boy, Mohammed, who also had worked in the film. They go with him to a place where some survivors are trying to install an aerial antenna to watch the Argentina-Brazil World Cup soccer match. The father does not understand the villagers' frantic efforts to watch the game, while his son sympathizes with them. As the film draws to an end, the focus on finding the boy is gradually lost, replaced by the images of life slowly resurging amidst the ruins. As Kiarostami has said, "Finally, I felt that perhaps it was more important to help the survivors who bore no recognizable faces, but were making every effort to start a new life for themselves under very difficult conditions and in the midst of an environment of natural beauty that was going on with its old ways as if nothing had happened. Such is life, it seemed to tell them, go on, seize the day."

Just as *And Life Goes On* had been inspired in the events surrounding the making of *Where Is My Friend's Home,* Kiarostami's next film also sprang up from the shooting of *And Life Goes On.* This final entry in his "Koker trilogy" (so named after the town where the three movies take place) is entitled *Through the Olive Trees* (1994). This movie, which film theorist Laura Mulvey cites as a proof that cinema can "still be surprising, beautiful and cerebral," concerns the efforts of a poor, illiterate young man to marry a woman against the opposition of her family and the force of village tradition. By "sheer luck," they are cast opposite each other as actors in *And Life Goes On.* Throughout the movie, the viewers accompany the young man's persistent efforts to glean even a word from the woman, who does not even condescend to talk with him. As Mulvey writes, ". . . Kiarostami's film seemed to have more in common with the avant-garde than with art cinema, while his way of storytelling, shooting and dealing with cinematic reality touched on ideas familiar to film theory but defying any expected aesthetic and analytic framework. My sense of intellectual and aesthetic uncertainty was followed by a feeling of intense curiosity."

Kiarostami's next feature as a director was his most celebrated film, *A Taste of Cherry*. The story follows the attempts by a middle-aged man to recruit a helper among the unemployed day workers gathered in the outskirts of Tehran. He drives through the city, stopping here and there to approach the men, who clearly are appalled by his proposal. We soon learn that the man is under a terrible predicament and wants to commit suicide by taking sleeping pills. He needs a man who will go the next morning to the little tree that he has selected to mark his grave and bury him. Three men are the main targets of his effort: a young soldier, a student of Islamic theology, and an old man. Each of them tries to give him a reason not to kill himself. Kiarostami's strategy was to never show the actor playing the driver and to show the passengers in a two-shot, except in the case of the third passenger. In fact, for most of the film, Kiarostami himself occupied the driver's seat, with his camera and microphone ready to capture the interlocutor's thoughts on why life is worth living.

Critics in the West were enthusiastic. Richard Corliss in *Time* magazine proclaimed it simply "The Best Film of The Year." And Stephen Holden in the *New York Times* wrote that "Mr. Kiarostami, like no other filmmaker, has a vision of human scale that is simultaneously epic and precisely minuscule." Indeed, the celebrated Japanese filmmaker AKIRA KUROSAWA praised Kiarostami as a rightful successor of SATYAJIT RAY, as a filmmaker with the ability to touch everyone, regardless of nationality, with stories about the human condition. "When Satyajit Ray died," said Kurosawa, "I became quite depressed, but after watching Kiarostami's films, I thought God had found the right person to take his place."

Identity is precisely the subject of another of Kiarostami's better-known films. *Close-up* (1989) started when Kiarostami saw a newspaper account of a real-life situation indirectly involving his fellow filmmaker Mohsen Makhmalbaf. A young man, Hossain Sabzian, had been accused of fraud and was going to trial. Earlier, Sabzian had impersonated Makhmalbaf and gotten some money from a family whom he persuaded to appear in a film he was supposedly making. Kiarostami took his cameras to the court and obtained the judge's approval to film all the involved parties, including the testimony of the accused, who explained, in pathetic tones, how Makhmalbaf was his hero and how he was tempted to initiate the charade when a woman confused him, a poor nobody, with the director while he was busy reading a film book on a bus. The woman was a member of the family who was accusing him of fraud. The movie, highly self-referential, was a dazzling example of Kiarostami's style and thematic concerns, mixing reality with fiction and providing a chance to reflect on the importance of cinephilia in Iran as well as on the role of filmmakers as bearers of an ethical as well as aesthetical mission.

The director's latest film to reach the West is *The Wind Will Carry Us.* In this film, Behzad, a television journalist, arrives at a remote village with the intention of filming the funeral of a 100-year-old woman, wherein the women of the town are supposed to scratch and scar their faces in mourning. As he arrives, however, it turns out that the woman is still ailing, and he has to wait in town for her imminent death. The city slicker, wielding a mobile phone and accompanied by a crew (which is unseen, but talked about throughout the picture), concocts a story about a buried treasure and enlists the help of a local boy to be his informer and main liaison with the villagers. Whenever he receives a phone call, he must drive to the top of a hill at the cemetery to be able to talk with the city. In one of these calls, he learns that by waiting for the woman's burial he is missing the funeral of one of his own relatives in the city. While he impatiently awaits the woman's death, Behzad also meets a worker who is digging a hole for some "telecommunications" purpose and the young fiancée of the man, whom he tries in vain to entice with flirtations. The title of the film is inspired by a line from an erotic poem by Foroogh Farrokhzaad (1935–67), a poet much revered in Iran.

For critic Jonathan Rosenbaum, "The particular ethics of *The Wind Will Carry Us* consist largely of Kiarostami reflecting on his own practice as a 'media person' exploiting poor people: Behzad may be the closest thing in Kiarostami's work to a critical self-portrait, at least since the hero in his highly uncharacteristic 1977 feature *Report*." As Rosenbaum also notes, the director here follows his concern of contrasting city to village and the power of the middle-class protagonists of his films in contrast with the working-class peasants who often become their employees, a theme that runs through the Koker trilogy as well as—in reverse—*Close-up* and finally *The Wind Will Carry Us.*

One of Kiarostami's most notable features is the complex blending of fiction and documentary. Casting nonprofessional actors, often children, Kiarostami departs from rigid distinctions between fact and fiction. His production strategies resemble those of postwar Italian films, but, as he explained to Pat Aufderheide, this is more due to circumstantial factors than to imitation: "Of course, I began watching movies by watching Italian neorealism, and I do feel a kinship with that work. But it's more a question of congruence of taste than it is a decision to follow their example." And he adds: "I think the most important and obvious reason why there is a similarity is the similarity between the present situation of Iran and of postwar Italy. Italy then was under the pressure of the postwar situation, and we have similar circumstances. Another similarity that may provoke parallels is that I don't adapt from literature or

mythology. I get my stories from daily life, like they did. I also don't have big, expensive sets and elaborate production values and special effects. My films are low budget."

The filmmaker's work has been subjected, however, to more overtly political readings. One of them is by Hamid Dabashi, an Iranian-born sociologist who works at Columbia University. He posits two historical paradigmatic discourses in Iranian literary culture, those of theocentricity and homocentricity. He situates Kiarostami within that dialectic on the side of homocentricity, following a long tradition of Persian poets, as opposed to prophets. For Dabashi, Kiarostami's cinema "puts forward a radically subversive reading of a culture of inhibition brutally institutionalized by a theocratic revolution." Furthermore, "If Kiarostami is successful in holding our attention constant for a while and thus teaching us to see differently—he has endured so far for some twenty-five years, through an imperial dictatorship, via a gut-wrenching revolution, in the thaws of an Islamic theocracy—he will map out the principal contours of a post-metaphysical mode of being in which no ideology, no absolutist claim to truth, no metanarrative of salvation, ever will monopolize the definition of our 'identity.'"

Lately, Kiarostami has adopted the latest technologies for his cinematic work. The filmmaker's latest film, still unreleased at the writing, is a documentary on AIDS in Africa. And he is planning to shoot his next project in digital video. In a review of French filmmaker Agnès Varda's *The Gleaners and I,* Rosenbaum wrote: "One obvious thing that digital video does is place people on both sides of the camera on something that more nearly resembles an equal footing. A 35-millimeter camera creates something like apartheid between filmmakers and their typical subjects, fictional or nonfictional—because between them stand an entire industry, an ideology, and a great deal of money and equipment. This is the subject of many of Abbas Kiarostami's major features, including

Homework, Close-up, Life and Nothing More, Through the Olive Trees, and *The Wind Will Carry Us;* he recently shifted to DV in part because he wanted to achieve something closer to equality with whom and what he shoots."

Other Films *Bread and Alley* (short film, 1970); *The Traveler* (Kiarostami's first feature, 1972); *The Report* (1977); *Case No. 1 Case No. 2* (1979).

References Afshari, Reza, "An Essay on Scholarship, Human Rights, and State Legitimacy: The Case of the Islamic Republic of Iran," *Human Rights Quarterly* 18, no. 3 (1996): 544–593; Aufderheide, Pat, "Real Life Is More Important Than Cinema, An Interview with Abbas Kiarostami," *Cineaste* 21, no. 3 (1995): 31–33; Cheshire, Geoffrey, "Abbas Kiarostami, A Cinema of Questions," *Film Comment* 32, no. 4 (July–August 1996): 34–42; Dabashi, Hamid, "Re-Reading Reality: Kiarostami's *Through the Olive Trees* and the Cultural Politics of a Post-Revolutionary Aesthetics," *Critical Studies: Iran and Middle East* 63, no. 79 (1995); Mulvey, Laura, "Kiarostami's Uncertainty Principle," *Sight and Sound* 8, no. 6 (June 1998): 24–27; Rosen, Miriam, "The Camera of Art: An Interview with Abbas Kiarostami," *Cineaste* 19, nos. 2–3 (1993): 38–40; Rosenbaum, Jonathan, "Precious Leftovers, *The Gleaners and I,*" *Chicago Reader,* May 11, 2001.

—F.A.

Kidron, Beeban (1961–)

Born and raised in London, Beeban Kidron became a prize-winning photographer before she was a teenager and later worked as an assistant to the legendary photographer Eve Arnold. She enrolled in the National Film School with the ambition of becoming a cinematographer and worked on several films as camera operator before turning to directing. Her very first film was an award-winning documentary *Carry Greenham Home,* about the women's peace camp at Greenham Common. This film won the Golden Hugo Award at the Chicago Film Festival in 1983 and was later shown at the Berlin Film Festival of 1984. Later work included *The Global Gamble* (1986), a documentary on the deregulation of the City of London.

Her first feature film, *Vroom,* made for British Screen and Film 4 International, became the centerpiece of the 1988 London Film Festival. Her short fiction film *Alex* won the award for best short in 1990 at the Los Angeles Women's Film Festival. Other films made for British television during the late 1980s included: *Itch, At First Sight,* and *Eve Arnold, A Portrait,* most of them focusing on women or on unconventional sexual situations. Kidron gained critical attention internationally with her 1990 award-winning BBC television drama *Oranges Are Not the Only Fruit,* based on Jeanette Winterson's novel about a young woman struggling to come of age in the midst of religious, parental, and sexual repression. Its awards included a BAFTA Award for best series as well as the FIPA d'Argent Award at Cannes in 1991 and the Prix Italia. Another significant breakthrough was *Antonia and Jane* (1990), a BBC/Miramax feature dealing with a long friendship between two women, Antonia (Saskia Reeves) and Jane (Imelda Staunton), first seen in the United States at the 1990 Telluride Film Festival.

Kidron's Hollywood debut was the 20th Century-Fox feature *Used People* (1992), adapted by playwright Todd Graff from his 1989 off-Broadway stage production, *The Grandma Plays,* and starring Shirley MacLaine, Jessica Tandy, Sylvia Sydney, and Kathy Bates. The film is a comedy about a middle-aged American Jewish woman courted by an Italian (Marcello Mastroianni). This was followed by Kidron's 1993 documentary, *Hookers, Hustlers, Pimps and Their Johns.* Also in 1993 she directed *Great Moments in Aviation*—starring Vanessa Redgrave, Rakie Ayola, John Hurt, and Jonathan Pryce—the story of a West Indian woman who goes to England in the 1950s intending to become a great aviator. Kidron then returned to Hollywood to make *To Wong Foo, Thanks for Everything, Julie Newmar,* starring John Leguizamo, Patrick Swayze, and Wesley Snipes as homosexual cross-dressers who find themselves stranded in a dusty little town in the American Midwest. Reviewers regarded this picture as a sanitized attempt to cash in on the success of Australian Stephan Elliot's camp drag-queen comedy, *The Adventures of Priscilla, Queen of the Desert* (1994).

Her next film was a greater critical success, *Swept from the Sea* (1997), adapted by writer Tim Willocks from the Joseph Conrad short story "Amy Foster" (published in 1901), and released under the title *Amy Foster* in Britain. It tells the story of a young adventurer from Eastern Europe, Yanko Gooral (Vincent Perez), destined to be misunderstood, stranded along the English coast after his boat capsizes, "rejected for his differences, and doomed to a tragic death," as Willocks described him. He is befriended by an English doctor named James Kennedy (Ian McKellen, who narrates the film) and, of course, by Amy Foster (Rachel Weisz), whom he marries. The adaptation moves Conrad's setting from the dreary Kentish coastline to the lovely cliffs and seascapes of Cornwall. Amy is portrayed as a self-reliant, attractive, and sympathetic child of nature who returns to her dying husband to share with him a moment of transcendental love. Though true to the framework of the story, the film is a radical transformation of the Conrad text.

References Holden, Stephen, "Ukrainian Patient," *New York Times,* January 23, 1998, p. B10; Watson, Wallace S., "Misogyny and Homoerotic Hints Feminized and Romanticized: Conrad's 'Amy Foster' and Swept from the Sea," *Literature/Film Quarterly* 29, no. 3 (2001): 179–195; Willocks, Tim, *Swept from the Sea: The Shooting Script* (New York: Newmarket Press, 1997).

—J.M.W. and W.S.W

Kieślowski, Krzysztof (1941–1996)

Krzysztof Kieślowski was one of the most distinguished directors to emerge from Poland during the late 1970s. Master of both documentary and narrative film, Kieślowski established himself as a master technician and storyteller, evoking unusual images and thoughtful character studies in his work. His reputation spread among film circles by virtue of his provocative, personal vision, though he was never a major commercial success. Yet, with his talent and drive, he produced over 20 documentaries and 10 features, as well as shorts and films for television, which garnered him much critical praise.

Krzysztof Kieślowski was born on June 27, 1941, in Warsaw. He graduated from the prestigious Lódź Film School in 1969, where other noted Polish filmmakers—ANDRZEJ WAJDA, ROMAN POLANSKI, Skolimowski, Zanussi—also graduated. In his early documentaries he was, as Annette Insdorf suggests, "painfully aware of the discrepancies between screen images and the daily life of most Polish people; he turned his quietly inquisitive camera to a real—if bleak—world." Kieślowski emphasizes the reality of the society he documents: the working class, the economic structure of institutions, and the relationship between individuals and institutions. *From the City of Lodz* (1969), *I Was a Soldier* (1970), *Factory* (1970), and *Before the Rally* (1971) evince themes of workers at odds with the government and the general state of affairs in Polish life. For example, *From the City of Lodz* is a portrait of the town, and the town's unique eccentricities, shown in all of its deprivation—ruins, hovels, and foul sanitation practices. *Before the Rally* shows two Polish race car drivers as they prepare for the Monte Carlo rally. Their failure to finish the race may be construed as an allegory of Poland's economic and individual shortcomings. Other early documentaries include *Worker's '71* (1972), a film about a worker's strike, and *Hospital* (1976), which documents a group of surgeons on a 32-hour shift. Kieślowski mostly satirizes the bureaucracy in these films, shedding light on the injustices suffered by many individuals.

Kieślowski has said that shooting documentaries enabled him to film "a reality that is rich, magnificent, incommensurable, where nothing is repeated, where one cannot redo a take. Reality—

and this is not a paradox—is the point of departure for the document. One merely has to believe totally in the dramaturgy of reality." According to Insdorf, Kieślowski "gradually [grew] into an artist by learning his craft, observing the world closely, and later developing a personal vision."

Indeed, Kieślowski's great subject, the plight of individuals in a constrictive society, is most clearly manifested in his narrative features. They retain the somber, if not pessimistic view of the world Kieślowski had clearly seen while making his documentaries. His first full-length feature, *The Scar* (1976), is a story about a man put in charge of the construction of a new chemical factory. Though his intentions are admirable, the townspeople are more concerned with their immediately tangible needs, and do not see the long-term benefits of a new factory. Growing more disillusioned, the man gives up the post. The film initiates themes that dominate Kieślowski's later work: disillusionment, conflict between individuals, and moral ambiguity. *Camera Buff* (1979) was a critical success and helped Kieślowski's reputation grow outside of Poland and Europe. It is an allegorical tale about a man who, after buying an 8-mm camera, begins to record his life and surroundings. Filming at work, the man faces censorship charges, which have extreme ramifications; as a result of his time spent filming, his wife, disillusioned with their marriage, leaves him. The complex images in the film are poignant, satiric commentaries on film sense and personal meaning in a cruel, harsh environment. Essentially, the protagonist loses his job, wife, and child because of his passion for the camera. The film is "about a character," Kieślowski said, where "humor is a manifestation of my sympathy, of sympathy for human miseries that can be funny." This idea—sympathy for human miseries—is found in *Blind Chance* (1981), where there are three different outcomes to the protagonist's life, stemming from a seemingly banal incident at the beginning of the film; and in *No End* (1984), where the daily lives of people are affected by a ghost.

Kieślowski's *Decalogue* (1988) is often recognized as his greatest achievement. The *Decalogue* is a series of 10 short films, made for television, based on the Ten Commandments. Two of these, *A Short Film about Killing* (1988) and *A Short Film about Love* (1988) were extended and released as features. *A Short Film about Killing* received the Grand Jury Prize at the Cannes Film Festival. The *Decalogue* brought Kieślowski international attention. "*Decalogue* is an attempt to narrate ten stories about ten or twenty individuals," he has said, "who—caught in a struggle precisely because of these and not other circumstances, circumstances which are fictitious but which could occur in every life—suddenly realize that they're going round and round in circles, that they're not achieving what they want." The universality of the themes presented in the *Decalogue* enabled viewers to locate their own beliefs and understandings of morality, law, religion, and politics. Insdorf notes, "Rather than asking us to be like-minded, the *Decalogue* provokes contemplation of how the spirit of the commandments might still be applicable to our daily lives."

The Double Life of Veronique (1991), a story about a young woman who has a double and thus leads a parallel life, brought Kieślowski more recognition as a world-class filmmaker. Lead actress Irene Jacob won the best actress award at the Cannes Film Festival. The film allows viewers to reflect on the ties that bind people to outside forces, forces we are unable to contain. Kieślowski's final three films form his *Three Colors* trilogy: *Blue* (1993), *White* (1993), and *Red* (1994). *Blue* won best film at the Venice Film Festival and lead actress Juliette Binoche won best actress. The films are loosely based on the concepts of liberty, equality, and fraternity, which are recurring themes in all three films. All three films are visually stunning, with bright, distinct colors juxtaposed with darker hues and shadows, and are characterized by individuals who seek meaning and existence in a world where things often seem futile and people distant or cruel. Kieślowski said, "All the three films are about people who have some sort of intuition or sensibility, who have gut feelings." In all three films, the characters, whether faced with tragedy or compassion, forge their own decisions and conclusions based on their needs or initial impulses. The protagonists, like so many in Kieślowski's work, struggle with the ambiguous relationship between reason and feeling. In the end, these films invoke similar feelings in audiences, which is why they are so compelling and appealing.

Kieślowski died of a heart attack in 1996. He was a self-admitted pessimist, and many of his films depict a decidedly somber picture of the world. However, his characters are also noble, inquisitive, and often admirable. Insdorf states that Kieślowski deals with "chance, faith, and self-delusion" in his films, and deals with them in a variety of ways and through an array of themes. Kieślowski's cinema is enriching, for his documentaries of real people and his complex characterizations in his features show true sides of human nature. In both documentary and narrative film, Kieślowski was a master, and his films provide rich, enjoyable, and arresting depictions of individuals very familiar to all audiences.

Other Films *The Calm* (1976); *I Don't Know* (1977); *A Short Working Day* (1981).

References Insdorf, Annette, *Double Lives, Second Chances* (New York: Miramax Books, 1999); Stok, Danusia, *Kieślowski on Kieślowski* (London: Faber and Faber, 1993).

—W.V.

King, Henry (1886–1982)

King, Henry (1886–1982) A consummate craftsman and director of great versatility, Henry King's long career spanned almost a half century. Despite a handful of acknowledged masterpieces, however, he still awaits auteur status. Never a maverick, he worked comfortably within the Hollywood studio system. As historian William K. Everson has noted, "For directors of the past to be rediscovered by contemporary critics, they usually have to have been off-beat, ahead of their time, or even abysmally bad but at the same time interesting in a bizarre way. But King fits into none of these categories. Far from being ahead of his time, he was exactly *of* his time." Which, of course, is precisely why he is of great interest.

He was born on June 24, 1886, near Christianburg, Virginia. When he was four years old, the family moved to Lafayette, where he went to high school. His interest in theatrical activities led to a job with the Empire Stock Company, a touring repertory company. His barnstorming days continued with a stint in the Jolly American Tramp Show, with which he traveled across the United States. Engaged by the Lubin West Coast Company, he came to Los Angeles to appear as an actor in the movies. He quickly advanced to an apprenticeship in directing under the supervision of Thomas Ince in 1916 with his first feature, *Little Mary Sunshine*. After a series of purportedly lackluster programmers, he made *Tol'able David* in 1921. This acknowledged classic reveals some of the traits that would distinguish his more mature efforts. The rural story, of a young man (Richard Barthelmess) forced by dire circumstances to prove himself a man, is sensitive to landscape and is a tribute to the virtues of the family unit. Pudovkin praised its editing strategies in his book *On Film Technique*. "There was a great deal of me in *Tol'able David*," King recalled. "It was made just eighty miles from where I was born. I knew the people. I knew what the boy's desires were. His experiences were things I had known as a child. Every motion picture that you make has something of yourself in it, something you've learned, something in the back of your mind."

Other notable films in the silent period include a Lillian Gish vehicle, *The White Sister* (1923), the first and still the best version of *Stella Dallas* (1925), and a western that brought Gary Cooper to the screen, *The Winning of Barbara Worth* (1927). The best of his early talkies, *Over the Hill* (1929), returns to the simplicities and virtues of rural family life.

This unaffected idealism of the American scene reappears in King's best work of the 1930s and 1940s, when he began to work exclusively for Fox and Darryl F. Zanuck in pictures like *State Fair* (1933), starring Will Rogers; *In Old Chicago* (1938), a spectacular re-creation of the Great Chicago Fire; *Alexander's Ragtime Band* (1938), a thinly disguised biopic of songwriter Irving Berlin; and *Margie* (1943), a loving evocation of a schoolgirl's life in the 1920s. Differing in conception and scope were a western, *Jesse James* (1939); an overblown political epic, *Wilson* (a dismal failure at the box office in 1944); and several swashbucklers that featured Tyrone Power (*The Black Swan* [1942], *Captain from Castile* [1948]). Two psychological thrillers from this period are *Twelve O'Clock High* and *The Gunfighter* (both 1950). Both feature Gregory Peck as a heroic figure beset by the challenges of age, circumstances, and mental turmoil. Action is downplayed in favor of a meditation on a character in crisis. King's last nine films were shot in the CinemaScope wide-screen process. *The Sun Also Rises* and *The Snows of Kilimanjaro* were adaptations of Ernest Hemingway; *Carousel* (1957), based on the Rodgers and Hammerstein musical play, and *Love Is a Many-Splendored Thing* (1955) are unabashed romantic essays on love's labors lost; and *I'd Climb the Highest Mountain* (1951) marks a return to King's favorite themes and settings of ordinary country life.

Before his death in 1982, King's work began to enjoy a renewed interest through retrospectives and critical reassessment. He remained active to a ripe old age, passing a pilot's physical and renewing a flying license at age 94. To the end, he remained matter-of-fact about his work, refusing to indulge in speculations about its "artistic" pretentions. "I just like to tell stories," he said. "Making a motion picture is the greatest fun I've had in my life. You can work yourself completely to death and enjoy every minute of it." To this day, however, as critic Andrew Sarris has noted, King's work is "a subject for further research."

Other Films *Romola* (1925); *She Goes to War* (1929); *Stanley and Livingstone* (1939); *The Song of Bernadette* (1943); *King of the Khyber Rifles* (1953); *The Bravados* (1958).

References Gillam, Barry, "Henry King," in *American Directors*, ed. Jean-Pierre Coursodon, vol. 1 (New York: McGraw Hill, 1983), pp. 187–194; Thompson, Frank, ed., *Henry King, Director: From Silents to 'Scope* (Los Angeles: Directors Guild of America, 1995).

—J.C.T.

Korda, Alexander (1893–1956)

Director of a handful of movie masterpieces, a producer/studio mogul responsible for many dozens more, and a true man of the world, Alexander Korda possessed an artistry that extended well past his more than a hundred films and into a colorful lifestyle that was his greatest achievement. He was outsized in many ways, in his private and public passions, in his extravagance, in his ambitions, in his failures as well as his achievements, and in his ability to win the undying loyalty of his associates. "He pressed a button and the greatest story tellers of the world went to work to turn out plots and scenarios," writes biographer Paul Tabori, "a man who lifted one finger and a herd of elephants or a pride of lions were caged for his pleasure. To his countless associates he was a charmer with a foreign accent and a wonderful command of invective; to his actors, directors, technicians he was something of a father-figure—as, indeed, he often called them 'my children.'"

He was born Sandor Laszlo Kellner on September 16, 1893, in the tiny Hungarian village of Pusztaturpaszto, the son of a farm bailiff. He was 13 years old when his father died and the family relocated to Budapest. Living in grinding poverty, he attended school and in his after hours wrote articles for a liberal daily newspaper. He adopted the surname Korda, from a journalistic term, "sursum corda" (meaning, "lift up your hearts"). He left school before graduating and, driven by the wanderlust that would afflict him for the rest of his life, departed for Paris to pursue a writing career. That did not work out, but he returned to Hungary aflame with a new enthusiasm, motion pictures.

He entered films working as a title writer for Pictograph Films, Budapest. His first directorial effort was *The Duped Journalist,* in 1915, followed by six more productions. Three years later he formed his own production unit, Corvin Films, in a northeastern suburb of Budapest. His first wife, Maria Corda, appeared in several of his films and would be featured in other subsequent productions. Although by this time he had become the leading film producer in Hungary, and had publicly declared his undying enthusiasm for the future of Hungarian film production, he had to flee the country after the Great War, when the Hungarian Soviet Republic was overthrown by Admiral Horthy's anti-Semitic and anti-liberal White Army.

He went to Vienna in 1919 and a few years later formed Korda-Films in Berlin. Ever on the move, he came to Hollywood and First National Pictures in 1927 to make *The Private Life of Helen of Troy,* starring his wife as Helen. Its sly wit and historical anachronisms would mark many of his later pictures; and its success earned him a series of features starring the actress Billie Dove. But the Hollywood personal and professional lifestyle irritated him. "I found working in Hollywood rather difficult," he said later. "They talk too much shop. Shop, shop, shop, from daybreak to sunset and on to daybreak again. There are very few people out there who are possessed of any general culture."

He left Hollywood in 1930, disgruntled at the experience, and, after directing three films in France, including the classic *Marius* (1931), went to London, where, as the founder of London Films and the builder of Denham Studios, he directed one of the most phenomenally popular British films of the day, *The Private Life of Henry VIII* (1932). While it is not true that it was the first British film to win international acclaim, it unde-

niably put Korda and his cast—including Charles Laughton, Merle Oberon (who would become his second wife), Binnie Barnes, and Robert Donat—on the cinematic map. The film was a highly romanticized version of the life of England's King Henry VIII that skipped over the political and religious ramifications of his reign and concentrated on his marital status, beginning on the day of Anne Boleyn's execution (the first wife, Catherine of Aragon, is not considered because, as an opening title explains, she was too respectable) and depicting the succession of wives thereafter. This was a king seen as a man rather than the other way around—history seen from bottom to top, as gossip, through the keyhole, as it were. Aside from the films he directed—*The Private Life of Don Juan* (1934), starring his old friend Douglas Fairbanks, Sr., in his last picture; *Rembrandt* (1936), with Charles Laughton in the title role; *That Hamilton Woman* (1941), pairing LAURENCE OLIVIER and Vivien Leigh as Admiral Nelson and his mistress Emma Hamilton—he supervised many others, including: *Catherine the Great* (1934); *The Scarlet Pimpernel* (1934), a story of the French Revolution with Leslie Howard; *The Drum* (1936), a justification of English imperialism in India; *The Four Feathers* (1938), a saga of English colonialism in the Sudan; *The Thief of Bagdad* (1940), an Oriental phantasmagoria starring Sabu; *The Fallen Idol* (1949), based on the short novel by Graham Greene; and *The Third Man* (1949), based on another Greene script. After losing control of the Denham Studios in 1938, he relocated to Hollywood during the first two years of World War II to make *That Hamilton Woman* (for which he was knighted in 1942), occasionally returning to London on several projects.

That Hamilton Woman was not just a piece of patriotic puffery about the romance between Lord Nelson and Lady Emma Hamilton. Korda had been empowered by Winston Churchill himself to use this film to promote the British cause against Germany and to sway the isolationist American

Congress and press toward an interventionist stance. Thus, the characters of Nelson and Napoleon, the antagonists of the film, would in actuality be "stand-ins" for Winston Churchilll and Adolf Hitler. Indeed, the film's pro-British sentiments provoked the Foreign Relations Committee to order Korda to appear and justify his film. The bombing of Pearl Harbor, however, ended all that. Meanwhile, the film ran afoul of the Hollywood Production Code for other reasons, namely, it seemed to condone the adultery between Nelson and Hamilton. It was released only after Korda inserted some dialogue in which Nelson was made to admit the wrongness of his action.

After the war he reorganized London Films and founded the British Film Academy (now the British Academy of Film and Television Arts). Mention should be made that collaborating with him throughout his career were his two talented brothers, Zoltan, who also directed, and Vincent, who was an art director. Whether he directed or produced, all of his films are noteworthy for distinctive moments and affecting scenes—Laughton's card-playing banter with his prospective wife, Anne of Cleves (Elsa Lanchester), in *Private Life of Henry VIII;* Don Juan's (Douglas Fairbanks) confrontation on a theater stage with the actor impersonating him in *The Private Life of Don Juan;* Laughton again, as the aging Rembrandt surveying his wrinkled face in a cracked mirror, declaiming to himself, "Vanity, vanity; all is vanity. . . .''; Sabu's tussle with the giant spider in *The Thief of Bagdad;* Lady Hamilton's (Vivien Leigh) eager politicking with the queen of Naples on behalf of her lover, Admiral Nelson (Laurence Olivier); Orson Welles as Harry Lime emerging from the dark doorway in *The Third Man.*

Alexander Korda died of a heart attack in London on January 23, 1956. Reportedly, he was once asked who could be his successor after his death. "I don't know," he replied with a smile. "You see—I don't grow on trees." Biographer Tabori concludes that "films were his life and his obsession." Beneath

his flamboyant lifestyle and undeniable artistry, moreover, was a solid understanding of the sheer *craft* of the medium: "He became one of the greatest technicians of the cinema and had every detail of its very complicated techniques at his fingertips; in set design or camera angles, problems of sound recording or make-up he could speak with equal authority."

Other Films *Man of Gold* (1918); *A Modern Dubarry* (1926); *The Stolen Bride* (1927); *Her Private Life* (1929); *Perfect Strangers* (1945); *An Ideal Husband* (1947).

References Kulik, Karol, *Korda: The Man Who Could Work Miracles* (New Rochelle, N.Y.: Arlington House Publishers, 1975); Slide, Anthony, *Fifty Classic British Films, 1932–1982* (New York: Dover, 1985); Tabori, Paul, *Alexander Korda: A Biography* (New York: Living Books, 1966).

—J.C.T.

Koster, Henry (1905–1988) Henry Koster was Hollywood's chief purveyor of sweet-natured whimsy; his signature style was every bit as effective as the "[ERNST] LUBITSCH touch" and, in terms of box office, a lot more profitable. The charming films he made with Deanna Durbin between 1936 and 1941 were so popular with audiences that Koster and Durbin have been credited with saving Universal from bankruptcy. And Koster's whimsical "touch" brought a special kind of vibrancy to all kinds of films, from musicals (*My Blue Heaven* [1950]) to dramas (*A Man Called Peter* [1955]) to comedies (*Harvey* [1950]) to epics (*The Robe* [1953]).

He was born Hermann Kosterlitz in Berlin on May 1, 1905. His father was a salesman of women's underwear and his mother was a musician who occasionally accompanied silent films on the piano. Young Hermann won a scholarship to the Academy of Arts at age 15 and studied drawing and painting. It was here that he began to get experience in filmmaking, too, working on "trick" advertising films that were shown in movie theatres. In addition to drawing newspaper illustrations, he also found work as a newsreel cameraman and film editor and, in 1924, began writing screenplays.

After serving briefly as an assistant director to Erich Engel, Hermann began directing on his own with *Das Abenteuer der Thea Roland* (1932) and a few other features. He might have become a major German director except that his first successes occurred at about the same time that Adolf Hitler was rising to power. Hermann, a Jew, saw the writing on the wall and escaped to Paris in 1933.

Producer Joe Pasternak had met Hermann in Berlin and had seen promise in the young man. So Hermann contacted Pasternak from Paris and reintroduced himself; soon the two were working together in Budapest. But the film they were planning was never made. Pasternak was summoned back to the United States by his bosses at Universal. He informed them that he would return only if he could bring Hermann with him.

In Hollywood, Pasternak changed Hermann's name to Henry Koster (Hermann didn't want to change the monogram on his shirts) and put him to work directing 14-year-old Deanna Durbin in her feature film debut, *Three Smart Girls* (1936). Durbin had become popular on the radio with her surprisingly mature soprano voice but she had no acting experience. Koster coached her through the role, line by line, gesture by gesture. In the process, he not only helped her mature as an actress, but also created for her a character that would be her stock in trade for the greater part of her film career—a sweet teenage girl who is nonetheless rather willful and sassy.

Durbin and Koster followed up their success with four more films: *100 Men and a Girl* (1937) costarring Adolphe Menjou and Leopold Stokowski; *Three Smart Girls Grow Up* (1939), *First Love* (1939)—in which Durbin received her first screen kiss, from young Robert Stack, and the event was reported in newspapers around the world—and *It Started With Eve* (1941), costarring

Charles Laughton and Robert Cummings. Each of them was wildly popular and each was filled with the kind of effortless charm for which Koster was already well known to moviegoers.

Unlike most contract directors of the era, some of whom directed four or five features a year, Koster worked more sparingly, rarely directing more than one film a year. His was a specialized talent that did not easily lend itself to genre films or programmers. And the elements that he brought to his work were not easily duplicated by other Hollywood filmmakers. *The Bishop's Wife* (1947) is a beautiful blend of whimsy, comedy, and romance, but it is laced with a sense of gravity and longing that give it real emotional weight. The story of Dudley, an angel (Cary Grant) who comes down to Earth to give aid to a beleaguered bishop (David Niven) and his wife (Loretta Young), is at once a warm Christmas parable and a clear-eyed meditation on spiritual and emotional obligation. Dudley is not simply a magical creature, but a complex being who can feel love, anger, and loneliness. Loretta Young and Koster made another religious-themed Christmas film two years later, *Come to the Stable* (1949). While it lacks the supernatural elements of *The Bishop's Wife,* its story of faith and sacrifice is just as magical in its way, and just as warm.

Even Koster's biographical films are like no others: *Stars and Stripes Forever* (1952), the story of John Philip Sousa (played by Clifton Webb), and *A Man Called Peter* (1955), the story of minister Peter Marshall (played by Richard Todd), are blithely unconcerned with conventional ideas of plot; Koster simply meanders through these two lives, seeking out important moments that define character, but leaving out the invented suspense or melodrama that so many other filmmakers would have found impossible to avoid. Even *The Robe* (1953), the first film released in CinemaScope (the first film *produced* in CinemaScope was JEAN NEGULESCO's *How to Marry a Millionaire* [1953]), is far more thoughtful than the average biblical epic. In

Koster's hands, it is a story about individuals, not casts of thousands.

While Koster's last films—including *Mr. Hobbs Takes a Vacation* (1963) and *Dear Brigitte* (1965)— are not quite on a par with a gentle masterpiece like *Harvey* (with whom they share a star, James Stewart), neither are they the dismal last gasps typical of so many other long Hollywood careers. Only 61 when he retired, Koster was still at the peak of his powers, still capable of filling each frame with the understated charm that seemed to come so naturally to him. But, having no interest in television, and seeing that the tone of Hollywood was moving away from the kind of films he loved to make, Koster quit the business and lived out his days happily painting and drawing, coming full circle in his artistic life.

The films he left behind retain the "Koster touch" that made, and continue to make, them so enjoyable. In a world where movies are most often defined by bombast and crudity, Koster's gentle, subtle, witty, delightful films remain an oasis of warmth and humor and genuine emotion.

Other Films *The Rage of Paris* (1938); *Spring Parade* (1940); *Music For Millions* (1944); *The Luck of the Irish* (1948); *The Inspector General* (1949); *No Highway in the Sky* (1951); *My Cousin Rachel* (1953); *Flower Drum Song* (1961); *The Singing Nun* (1966).

References Atkins, Irene Kahn, *Henry Koster: A Directors Guild of America Oral History* (Metuchen, N.J.: Scarecrow Press, 1987); Koster, Bob, "Henry Koster Biography," in The Internet Movie Database [online].

—F.T.

Kozintsev, Grigori (1905–1973)

The career of Grigori Kozintsev was shaped by the artistic and theatrical experimentalism and turmoil of the Soviet Revolution, which took place as he was growing up. Consequently, his work has been overshadowed by the achievements of Sergei Eisenstein, Vsevolod Pudovkin, and the other great Soviet pioneers of the 1920s. Indeed, his most famous films, adaptations of Shakespeare and

Cervantes, would not be made until after the death of Joseph Stalin in 1953. Not many of his films were easily available in the United States during the Cold War, when the cinema studies movement was just getting underway. A breakthrough for Kozintsev came in 1971 when his great adaptation of *King Lear* was featured at the World Shakespeare Congress held in Vancouver, Canada, with Kozintsev attending to introduce his film to other Shakespeareans.

A Ukrainian by nationality, Kozintsev was born in Kiev on March 22, 1905. By the time he was 12, the Bolsheviks had seized power. Before turning to theatre and film during the 1920s, Kozintsev studied art under the modernist painter Alexandra Exter. He found employment as a scene painter at the Lenin Theatre (formerly the Solutzovsky Theatre) in Kiev, where he formed a friendship with another artist, Sergei Yutkevitch, who would also go on to direct films, and with Leonid Trauberg, with whom he collaborated on his first several films, starting with *The Adventures of Oktyabrina* in 1924, and including their trilogy, which won the Stalin Prize in 1941: *The Youth of Maxim* (1935), *The Return of Maxim* (1937), and *The Vyborg Side* (1939). In 1921 they had founded the experimental Factory of the Eccentric Actor (FEKS), which carried over from theater to film and influenced the style of their later work. By 1947 their partnership ended, with Trauberg turning to screenwriting as Kozintsev continued to direct.

During the last phase of his career, Kozintsev created his most famous adaptations, starting with the classic Cervantes novel *Don Quixote* (1957), adapted by Yevgeni Schwartz, followed by Kozintsev's own adaptations of *Hamlet* (1963) and *King Lear* (1971), both films based on the Russian translations of Boris Pasternak. These latter are among the very best adaptations of Shakespeare ever filmed, a little old-fashioned, perhaps, in their interpretations of the plays, but beautifully realized and wonderfully acted by Innokenti Smoktunovski as Hamlet and Yuri Yarvet, whose native language was Estonian rather than Russian, as an unforgettable King Lear. Kozintsev died in Leningrad on May 11, 1973, finally recognized in the West as a major talent.

References Kozintsev, Grigori, *King Lear: The Space of Tragedy* (Berkeley: University of California Press, 1977); Kozintsev, G., *Shakespeare: Time and Conscience* (New York: Hill & Wang, 1966); Leaming, Barbara, *Grigori Kozintsev* (Boston: Twayne, 1980).

—J.M.W.

Kramer, Stanley (1913–2001) Stanley Earl Kramer was born in New York on September 29, 1913. He attended DeWitt Clinton High School in New York City and also went to New York University where he received a B.S. in business administration in 1933. He became an apprentice writer at 20th Century studios in 1934 and then a senior editor at Fox in 1938. From 1939 to 1940 Kramer was a staff writer for Columbia and Republic studios. Kramer joined MGM in 1942 as an associate producer. Following his military service in the Army Signal Corps, 1943–45, where he was involved in the making of training films, he formed his own production company, Screen Plays, Inc., in 1947 with Herbert Baker and Carl Foreman.

Kramer was one of the first independent producers to emerge in post-war American cinema. Kramer's work during this period was particularly attentive to social issues. This is evidenced in such films as *Champion* (1949), *Home of the Brave* (1949), *The Men* (1950), *The Sniper* (1952), *The Member of the Wedding* (1952), and *The Juggler* (1953). In 1951 Kramer was forced, because of economic reasons, to bring his production company under the Columbia studios wing. *The Caine Mutiny* (1954) was the only film from this brief tenure that was a commercial success. The arrangement was terminated in 1954.

In the late 1950s Kramer returned to independent production as well as directing. His first film as

a director was *Not As A Stranger* (1955), a routine medical drama starring Robert Mitchum and Olivia de Havilland. This was followed by *The Pride and the Passion* (1957), an action drama of the Napoleonic War based on a novel by C. S. Forester and filmed in VistaVision. With these two productions out of the way, Kramer began a series of films, for which he is most noted, concerning social issues. *The Defiant Ones* (1958) examined racism and bigotry in the South and starred Tony Curtis and Sidney Poitier as escaped convicts who are chained together throughout most of their flight. The film received an Oscar nomination for best picture and best director. Kramer followed this film with *On the Beach* (1959), based on the bestselling novel by Nevil Shute. This grim drama is set in Australia after a nuclear war has destroyed life on the rest of the globe; the survivors await the inevitable radioactivity, which will eventually reach them. Kramer then made two courtroom dramas that are among the best in the genre. *Inherit the Wind* (1960), based on the play by Lawrence and Lee, was Kramer's first collaboration with actor Spencer Tracy. The film dramatized the events surrounding the Scopes Trial. *Judgment at Nuremberg* (1961) also starred Spencer Tracy and an all-star cast including Burt Lancaster, Maximilian Schell, Judy Garland, and Marlene Dietrich. The film concerned the Nuremberg war-crime trials following World War II. This film earned Kramer two Oscar nominations for best picture and best director.

In 1963 Stanley Kramer directed the widescreen comedy epic *It's A Mad, Mad, Mad, Mad World,* which featured an all-star cast of comedians in an affectionate tribute to slapstick comedy. The film was made in Cinerama and received the full road-show treatment. Unfortunately the film did not do well at the box office, primarily because of the proximity of its release date and the Kennedy assassination. Kramer's next production was a film adaptation of Katherine Anne Porter's novel *Ship of Fools* (1965). Although the film was a box-office disappointment for the director, who felt that he had both overproduced and overdirected it, the motion picture won Oscars for best cinematography (Ernest Laszlo) and art direction. This was also Vivien Leigh's final film. *Guess Who's Coming to Dinner* (1967) marked Kramer's return to "social consciousness" cinema. The film, which dealt with interracial marriage, starred Spencer Tracy (in his last screen role), Katharine Hepburn, and Sidney Poitier. The film received numerous Oscar nominations, including best picture and best director. During the 1970s Stanley Kramer's output was a bit sporadic. Among his best features during this period were *Bless the Beasts and Children* (1971), *Oklahoma Crude* (1973), and his final film, *The Runner Stumbles* (1979).

In 1991 Kramer received the Producers Guild of America David O. Selznick Lifetime Achievement Award. And in 1962 he was the recipient of the Academy of Motion Picture Arts and Sciences Irving G. Thalberg Memorial Award. According to Bill Nichols, "Kramer's films continue a long-standing Hollywood tradition of marrying topical issues to dramatic forms, a tradition in which we find many of Hollywood's more openly progressive films."

Other Films As producer only: *Champion* (1949); *Cyrano De Bergerac* (1950); *Death of a Salesman* (1951); *The Sniper* (1952); *My Six Convicts* (1952); *The Happy Time* (1952); *Four Poster* (1952); *Eight Iron Men* (1952); *High Noon* (1952); *The 5,000 Fingers of Dr. T* (1953); *The Wild One* (1954). As director: *The Secret of Santa Vittoria* (1969); *R.P.M.* (1970); *The Domino Principle* (1977).

References Kramer, Stanley, *A Mad, Mad, Mad, Mad World: A Life in Hollywood* (New York: Harcourt, Brace, 1997); Nichols, Bill, "Stanley Kramer," in *International Dictionary of Films & Filmmaking,* vol. 2: Directors, ed. Laurie Collier Hillstrom (New York: St. James Press, 1997); Spoto, Donald, *Stanley Kramer, Filmmaker* (New York: Putnam, 1978).

—R.W.

Kubrick, Stanley (1928–1999)   In a career that spanned 40 years—but included a mere baker's dozen of feature films, released in ever slower sequence as his tendencies toward reclusiveness and extended development of projects became more pronounced—Stanley Kubrick established a distinctive but divided reputation as a director, famous for controversy and unpredictability as much as for meticulous professionalism and technical innovation; and for producing works that have consistently divided critics as well as broader audiences. Kubrick famously got memorable performances from his best actors (think of Peter Sellers in *Dr. Strangelove* [1964] or Jack Nicholson in *The Shining* [1980]), but he also provoked actors with demanding and often lengthy shooting schedules and multiple retakes of even minor scenes. The Kubrick films *2001: A Space Odyssey* (1968) and *The Shining* essentially claimed for the big-budget cinematic mainstream the previously pulpish genres of science fiction and popular horror; but he was equally at home adapting relatively obscure literary works like William Makepeace Thackeray's *Barry Lyndon* (1975) or Arthur Schnitzler's *Traumnovelle* (the source for *Eyes Wide Shut* [1999]), working in established genres like the war film (*Paths of Glory* [1957] and *Full Metal Jacket* [1987]), or inventing entirely new categories of film (as he did most notably in the nuclear war comedy *Dr. Strangelove*).

The range of genres across which Kubrick worked makes his body of films difficult to categorize, although some basic common ground can be found. On a thematic level, all Kubrick's films feature a dark, sometimes even malevolent skepticism about human nature (but essentially male human nature; none of Kubrick's work shows much of an effort to understand women's psyches). In structural terms, many of his works involve highly divided plots (most obvious, perhaps, in *Full Metal Jacket,* but characteristic of other Kubrick films as well). On a technical level, they are marked by striking visual compositions (especially favoring a haunting symmetry), fluid camera movements (often employing newly developed technologies), and memorable use of musical scores.

Kubrick was born on July 26, 1928, in the Bronx, to a family of Romanian heritage. Critic Anthony Lane finds it highly significant that his father gave the young boy a still camera and taught him to play chess, "an inspired, if slightly ominous, combination." Kubrick, like Nabokov, continues Lane, "would later be hailed as the grand master of aesthetic strategy—or, if you prefer, as the Bobby Fischer of cinema, the hermit wonk who used his players like pawns and trapped his harried audiences in check." When Kubrick was 17, he got a job at *Look* magazine and continued in the position for four years before resuming his education. But in a very real sense, this *was* his education, as he noted to interviewer Alexander Walker: "Four and a half years of working for *Look* magazine, traveling all over America, seeing how things worked and the way people behaved, gave me some useful insights plus important experience in photography." He also cites MAX OPHULS's films, Stanislavsky's acting methods, and VSEVELOD ILLARIONOVICH PUDOVKIN's *Film Technique* as seminal influences on his camera strategies and directing and editing practices. After fashioning a trio of short documentaries, beginning with the self-financed *Day of the Fight* (1951), Kubrick plunged into feature films with *Fear and Desire* (1953), a war film about four soldiers lost behind enemy lines in an unnamed war. He followed this up with *Killer's Kiss* (1955), a boxing picture shot in New York City locations. He all but disowns the picture: "The only distinction I would claim for it is that, to the best of my belief, no one at the time had ever made a feature film in such amateur circumstances and then obtained world-wide distribution for it." More interesting was the noirish *The Killing* (1956), a racetrack heist tale enlivened by Sterling Hayden's portrayal of a just-paroled con man and the script assistance of novelist Jim Thompson. It was also the first film on which Kubrick was proud to have his name.

It is with *Paths of Glory* (1957), however, that Kubrick comes into his own. Again working with Thompson on the script, and with Kirk Douglas as his leading actor, Kubrick fashions a devastating critique of military hierarchies and class systems amid a brutal portrait of the trench warfare of World War I. *Paths* is divided between battle action, which re-creates much of the horror of the trenches, and a court-martial of three soldiers accused of refusing to follow orders, chosen to be made examples for the rest of the fighting forces. The battle sequences feature aggressively filmed dramatic action reinforced by the sounds of war, while the court-martial proceeds in relative silence, framed by the ironic elegance of a French chateau. If the horrors of war provide the story's background, its narrative focuses even more decisively on the French high command's class-based indifference to the plight of the common soldier.

Douglas would land Kubrick his next directing job, taking over the troubled shooting of *Spartacus* (1960) from director ANTHONY MANN. The epic account of a Roman gladiator who led a slave revolt remains a classic among the era's many historical reenactments of the Roman past, but Kubrick's inability to exert control over the studio's final cut cemented his disenchantment with the Hollywood studio system. After this, he moved to the semirural region of Hertfordshire, just outside London, and would for the rest of his career direct at an ocean and a continent's distance from Hollywood. It is true, declared British critic Alexander Walker in 1971, that Kubrick's seclusion in the English countryside assured him a quiet place "where time, energy, inspiration, confidence cannot be eroded by too much contact with the world"; however, continues Walker, it was also a location where he "finds it easy and attractive to keep in contact with the international film scene, and, indeed, with the larger world, from wherever he happens to be."

His distrust of studio systems would be further reinforced by the difficulties surrounding his adaptation of Vladimir Nabokov's controversial novel *Lolita* (1962). Kubrick can be said, in response to the constraints of the time, to have found a way to substitute Humbert's ironic subjectivity (relying heavily on James Mason's insightful portrayal) for the more open sensuality the novel would seem to have demanded, but the resulting film was still controversial and suffered at the hands of the Hollywood censors. "I wasn't able to give any weight at all to the erotic aspect of Humbert's relationship with Lolita in the film," Kubrick told interviewer Gene D. Phillips, "and because I could only hint at the true nature of his attraction to Lolita, it was assumed too quickly by filmgoers that Humbert was in love with her. In the novel this comes as a discovery at the end, when Lolita is no longer a nymphet but a pregnant housewife; and it's this encounter, and the sudden realization of his love for her, that is one of the most poignant elements of the story." Still, many critics, including Pauline Kael, liked the results. "The surprise of *Lolita* is how enjoyable it is; it's the first new American comedy since those great days in the forties when Preston Sturges created comedy with verbal slapstick. *Lolita* is black slapstick and at times it's so far out that you gasp as you laugh."

If *Paths of Glory* established Kubrick as a director, his next project, *Dr. Strangelove, or How I Learned to Stop Worrying and Love the Bomb* (1964), loosely based on Peter George's novel, *Red Alert,* secured his independence. A wild, dark comedy about nuclear holocaust, the film employs a talented cast (most notably including Peter Sellers, in a range of roles, and George C. Scott) to create a menagerie of human grotesques responsible for carrying out the nightmare scenario of accidental nuclear destruction. Starkly outrageous in its portrait of out-of-control militarism, in its linkage of nuclear policy and Nazism, and in its celebratory rendition of the destruction of humanity, the film hardly seemed an obvious candidate for popular success in the duck-and-cover age of Cold War nuclear fears, but Kubrick's bleak slapstick hit a receptive nerve. "My idea of doing it as a nightmare comedy came in the early weeks of working on the screenplay," Kubrick told interviewer Phillips. "I found that in trying to put meat on the bones and to imagine the scenes fully, one had to keep leaving things out of it which were either absurd or paradoxical in order to keep it from being funny; and these things seem to be close to the heart of the scenes in question."

After four full years, *2001* appeared, based on Arthur C. Clarke's "The Sentinel," and marked a striking shift in tone, pace, and theme. About man's exploration of space, but also about intelligent life beyond Earth (and the possibility that that life has guided human development), with sideplots about violence as a principle underpinning human evolution, and the capabilities of artificial intelligence, and featuring the memorable psychedelic rollercoaster ride of its concluding segment, the film is a masterpiece of metaphysical mystery, working more through evocation than deliberate narrative. Regarding the celebrated opening sequence, where an ape discovers digital dexterity, Kubrick told interviewer Phillips: "Somebody said that man is the missing link between primitive apes and civilized human beings. You might say that the idea is inherent in the story of *2001* too. We are semicivilized, capable of cooperation and affection but needing some sort of transfiguration into a higher form of life." The film also involved Kubrick in extensive technical research, ensuring insofar as possible both the accuracy of his futurist vision and the technical means to bring it to the screen.

Kubrick followed *2001* with an adaptation of Anthony Burgess's 1962 novel, *Clockwork Orange*. Released in 1971, the film was a darkly dystopian nightmare vision of youth culture gone utterly awry, a portrait of an ultraviolent British future dominated by hedonist gangs inclined toward excess. Coming in the wake of a series of increasingly violent Hollywood releases (this was the era of SAM PECKINPAH's most active filmmaking, for example), its controversy was enhanced because the film's tone appeared deeply ambiguous, seemingly celebrating as much as condemning the dark violence of its vision, mixing brutality and slapstick, layering comic-book images into its most violent scenes, and offering a final "redemption" that plunged its hero back into the realm of gangster excess. Above all, the film was a kind of "dance of death." "It was necessary to find a way of stylizing the violence, just as Burgess does by his writing style," Kubrick explained to critic Andrew Bailey. "The ironic counterpoint of the music was certainly one of the ways of achieving this . . . and in a very broad sense, you could say that the violence is turned into dance, although, of course, it is in no way any kind of formal dance. But in cinematic terms, I should say that movement and music must inevitably be related to dance, just as the rotating space station and the docking Orion spaceship in *2001* moved to the 'Blue Danube.'" In 1974, disturbed about accounts of violent acts attributed to screenings of the film, he ordered it pulled from circulation in Britain, although it remained in release elsewhere.

In no subsequent film has Kubrick as successfully conveyed his vision or attained such solid commercial and critical acclaim. It is less a matter of lost control of craft—he continued to pioneer new film techniques, to bring actors to masterful exertions, and to produce films of elegant technical mastery, although continuity flaws, a mark of his method, became increasingly apparent—than of a faltering unity of vision, perhaps exacerbated by an increasing obsessiveness (evident in the slowing pace of releases and the multiplying tales of multiple takes). After *Clockwork Orange* (and several failed projects), Kubrick shifted gears again with *Barry Lyndon,* a slow-paced, narrative-heavy period piece set in the 18th century. The vision of humanity offered in its leisurely tour through battlefields and drawing rooms of the era is every bit as dark as that in his earlier work, although the restraint of the period style and the elegance of the settings somewhat ameliorate the pessimism of the tale. *The Shining* (1980) transforms Stephen King's pulp novel into a richly envisioned but distinctly interior meditation on insanity, spiced with the occultism and cathartic bursts of violence the genre demands. Kubrick contributed to the Vietnam genre of the later 1980s with *Full Metal Jacket* (1987), but the bitter antiwar drama suffers from a starkly split narrative, and its distanced detachment compares poorly with *Platoon*'s more vital grunt's-eye view of the war, which it had the misfortune to follow in release. Kubrick's last film, *Eyes Wide Shut* (1999), a dreamy, dark allegory about eroticism and human desire (and quite strikingly of desire rather than fulfillment), released shortly after the director's death, received a decidedly mixed reception, divided between those who celebrated its brilliance and those who found its allusive ambiguities merely irritating.

In a career highlighted by long development and work on multiple projects, Kubrick is almost as famous for films that were never made as for those he finished. Particularly noteworthy among these is *One-Eyed Jacks,* a project with Marlon Brando that had faltered by 1961, and an epic picture about Napoleon, envisioned by Kubrick in the late 1960s (and alluded to in both *Clockwork Orange*'s musical choices and *Barry Lyndon*'s emblematic final scene). Another long-term project, *A.I.* (for artificial intelligence), has been taken over by STEVEN SPIELBERG and is slated for release in summer 2001. Kubrick's undoubted genius tends to obscure an essential emptiness in his films, declares critic Anthony Lane: "He wanted to make everything new—the plushest costume drama ever, the most baroque science fiction, the war to end all wars—but, for all his erudition, he rarely paused to ponder what might lie in the bedrock of the old, or the ordinary, or the much loved." Kubrick died on March 7, 1999.

Other Films *Flying Padre* (1951); *The Seafarers* (1952).

References   Kagan, Norman, *The Cinema of Stanley Kubrick* (New York: Holt, Rinehart and Winston, 1972); Lane, Anthony, "The Last Emperior: How Stanley Kubrick Called the World to Order," *The New Yorker,* March 22, 1999, pp. 120–123; LoBrutto, Vincent, *Stanley Kubrick: A Biography* (New York: Donald I. Fine, 1997); Nelson, Thomas Allen, *Kubrick: Inside a Film Artist's Maze* (Bloomington: Indiana University Press, 1982); Phillips, Gene D., *Stanley Kubrick: A Film Odyssey* (New York: Popular Library, 1975); Raphael, Frederick, *Eyes Wide Open: A Memoir of Stanley Kubrick* (New York: Ballantine Books, 1999).

—T. Prasch

Kuleshov, Lev Vladimirovich (1899–1970)

One of the prime architects of Soviet film in the 1920s, Lev Kuleshov numbered SERGEI EISENSTEIN, VSEVELOD ILLARIONOVICH PUDOVKIN, and ALEXANDER PETROVICH DOVZHENKO among his students. A teacher and theoretician, as well as a filmmaker, he laid the groundwork for modern montage practices. He was born on January 1, 1899, in Tambov, near Moscow. Because of his early interests in art and mechanics, he enrolled in Moscow's School of Fine Arts at age 15 to study painting. Two years later he apprenticed to Yevgeni Bauer, one of the most respected filmmakers in pre-Revolution Russia. Inspired also by the work of the Americans EDWIN S. PORTER and DAVID WARK GRIFFITH, he regarded the film medium as a plastic art with great potential for restructuring the images of the physical world. In 1918 he published the first of his major writings, "The Tasks of the Artist in Cinema," in which he combined Meyerhold's theories of acting and biomechanics with the more pragmatic concerns of American editing strategies.

After releasing his first film, *The Project of Engineer Prite* (1918), he formed his own workshop as part of the newly established State Film School in Moscow. His pupils included Eisenstein and Pudovkin. Due to the shortage of equipment, props, and film stock, he and his students had to devise what he called "educational etudes"—scenarios and short playlets—and stage them before an unloaded camera. Editing exercises were conducted with "found" footage from newsreels and commercial films.

One experiment, the famous "Mozhukin Experiment," intercut shots of the rather impassive face of the great Soviet actor, Mozhukin, with images of objects like a knife, a child's coffin, and a crying baby. Each juxtaposition of face and image aroused different interpretations among the viewers. This was the famous "Kuleshov Effect," arising from the calculated linkage of the individual shots. "If you have an idea-phrase," wrote Kuleshov, "a particle of the story, a link in the whole dramatic chain, then that idea is to be expressed and accumulated from shot-ciphers, just like bricks." Other experiments included "creative anatomy" (the editing together of body parts of different actors to contribute to a "composite" anatomy); and "creative geography" (the intercutting of different locations to form a "composite" scene, or "artificial landscape"). In short, notes biographer Ronald Levaco, "he sought to demonstrate that physical space and 'real' time could be made virtually subordinate to montage."

In 1920 Kuleshov and his students made the two-reel *On the Red Front,* a combination newsreel and reenacted drama about the Russo-Polish War. With Pudovkin, he made *The Extraordinary Adventures of Mr. West in the Land of the Bolsheviks* (1924), which satirized Western misconceptions about the Soviet state, as seen through the eyes of an American, Mr. West. *By the Law* (1926), generally considered his best film, was distributed by the newly organized distributing company called Sovkino. It was based on Jack London's story of the Alaskan wilderness, "The Unexpected." Not shown in English-speaking countries until the late 1930s, the low-budget film was a tale of murder and retribution with a gesturally stylized acting style not unlike that seen in German expressionist films. Three people, joined together by their complicity in a murder, are isolated from civilization by winter storms and spring floods. According to historian Jay Leyda, the film's absence of conventional devices (no hero, no villain, no variety of locale, no parallel action) "surprised and attracted advance-guard film-goers, much as the early Thomas Ince–William Hart films had excited perceptive Parisians." Above all, continues Leyda, "its physiological tension was unique on European screens." Few films better exemplify the application of biomechanics to montage cinema, wherein the almost mathematical precision of every gesture and movement is codified to represent emotions and idea-states. "Kuleshov taught his workshop that the hands, arms and legs are the most expressive parts of the film actor's body," explains Leyda, "and we can observe that their movements create as much of the film's tension as does the facial expression." The interpretive "performance" of an actor is erased in favor of the collective impression emerging from the juxtaposition of pieces of film. In 1929 he wrote one of the seminal documents in film theory, *A Grammar of Film Art*. He had to wait three years before tackling a synchronized-sound film, *Horizon* (1932), about a Russian Jew's disillusionment with America and his subsequent immigration to Russia.

Increasingly, however, Kuleshov came under attack for his alleged "formalism," which ran afoul of the Soviet-mandated "First Five-Year Plan." He was attacked specifically for his statements that the structuring of cinematic material—montage—overrode the significance of the narrative or dramatic events to be expressed. Officially branded a "formalist" by Stalinist critics in 1935, he nonetheless was able to continue writing and teaching. His later books included *The Rehearsal Method in Cinema* and *The Practice of Film Direction* (1935). In 1967 he was "rehabilitated" and received the Order of Lenin. He died on March 29, 1970.

Other Films *The Death Ray* (1925); *Your Aquaintance* (1927); *The Gay Canary* (1929); *The Great Buldis* (1930); *Siberiaki* (1940).

References Birkos, Alexander S., *Soviet Cinema: Directors and Films* (Hamden, Conn.: Archon Books, 1976); Leyda, Jay, *Kino: A History of the Russian and Soviet Film* (London: George Allen & Unwin, 1960); Levaco, Ron, ed. and tr., *Kuleshov on Film: Writings of Lev Kuleshov* (Berkeley: University of California Press, 1974).
—J.C.T.

Kurosawa, Akira (1910–1998) Long regarded as Japan's most famous film director, Akira Kurosawa has successfully breached the gulf between Western and Eastern cinema. He was born in Tokyo on March 23, 1910, the youngest of eight children, to Isamu and Shima Kurosawa, of the Samurai class. Displaying an early interest in art, he was allowed to attend a private art school while still a teenager. Aspiring to become a commercial artist, he studied at the Doshusha School of Western Painting in 1927 and attended the Tokyo Academy of Fine Arts. He worked as a painter and illustrator with the Japan Proletariat Artists' Group before deciding on a career in film, when, in 1936, he began working as an assistant director at Toho Film Studios and eventually met the actor Toshiro Mifune, who would play a prominent part in many subsequent Kurosawa films, during the shooting of *Drunken Angel* (1947). He directed his first film, *Sugata Sanshiro (Judo Saga* [1943]) at the age of 33.

Kurosawa directed 10 more films during the 1940s, but it was his film *Rashomon,* released in 1950, that gained international attention when it won the 1951 Golden Lion Award from the Venice Film Festival and later won the Oscar for best foreign film in 1952. Influenced by such foreign directors as JOHN FORD and WILLIAM WYLER, and inspired by Western literary classics and popular culture, Kurosawa made well-plotted, character-driven films that crossed over cultural divides and were easily accessible to foreign viewers.

A number of remarkably successful films followed throughout the late 1940s and beyond, confirming Kurosawa's status as a world-class filmmaker.

Especially famous for his samurai films, Kurosawa also directed many literary adaptations, including *The Idiot* (*Hakuchi* [1951]), adapted from Dostoyevski's novel; *The Lower Depths* (*Donzoko* [1957]), based on Maxim Gorky's play; his celebrated *Throne of Blood* (*Kumonosu-jo* [1957], aka *The Castle of the Spider's Web*), loosely adapted from Shakespeare's *Macbeth;* and contemporary dramas, such as the detective thrillers *Stray Dog* (*Nora inu* [1949]) and *High and Low* (*Tengoku to jigoku* [1963]); social-problem films, like *I Live in Fear* (*Ikimono no kiroku* [1955], aka *Record of a Living Being*), treating the post-Hiroshima "fear" of nuclear devastation, and *Red Beard* (*Akahige* [1965]), which treats problems in bringing modern medicine to tradition-bound Japan; and intensely moving character-driven dramas, particularly *To Live* (*Ikiru* [1952]), one of the screen's most poignant depictions of an elderly man facing death. It is worth noting here that in his last film, *Madadayo* (*No, Not Yet* [1993]), Kurosawa returned to the theme of a life well lived in telling the story of a retired professor. Quite apart from their subject matter and acting, these and other films display Kurosawa's genius for wide-screen formats, composition in depth, and the employment of deep-focus shots.

Of course, Kurosawa's fame for many viewers resides in his *jidai-geki* films, or period costume films, such as *Shichinin no samurai* (*The Seven Samurai* [1954]), *Yojimbo* (*The Bodyguard* [1960]), and *Sanjuro* (1962), described as "the thinking man's *Yojimbo,*" which attracted his largest following abroad. Audiences admired these films for their visual beauty and spectacular action scenes, which combined long tracking shots, slow-motion sequences, and fast-paced editing. For the monumental battle sequences of *The Seven Samurai,* which he knew would be impossible to match-cut in the way he envisioned them, Kurosawa used three cameras running simultaneously: "I put the 'A' camera in the most orthodox positions, used the 'B' camera for quick, decisive shots, and the 'C'

camera as a kind of guerrilla unit," Kurosawa explained. He would continue to make use of this shooting technique throughout his career: "With multiple moving cameras," Kurosawa pointed out, "the actor has no time to figure out which one is shooting him."

In all of his films, Kurosawa delighted in framing his characters against vast backdrops of sky—not merely for the beauty of the shot, but to contrast the scope of man's endeavors with the enormity of the world around him, a technique especially evident in *Ran* (*Chaos* [1985]), his wonderfully visual and colorful transformation of Shakespeare's *King Lear*. His films were particularly admired in the West for their humanistic values; they unfailingly emphasize the dignity of the individual, deeply rooted in the Japanese samurai code of behavior, which extols working for the good of others and the subordination of selfish desires.

Since Kurosawa's films possessed universal appeal, European and American filmmakers openly imitated them. *Shichinin no samurai* and *Yojimbo,* for example, inspired two popular and influential westerns: *The Magnificent Seven* (1960) and *Per un pugno di dollari* (1964), released as *A Fistful of Dollars* in America in 1967. Even the American science fiction classic *Star Wars* (1977) was, in part, an imitation of *Kakushi toride no san akunin* (*The Hidden Fortress* [1958]).

During the 1960s Kurosawa's reputation began a steady decline from the pinnacle of success he had achieved in the late 1950s. In Japan, he was criticized for being too "western" and his choice of such writers as Shakespeare, Dostoyevsky, and Dashiell Hammett was viewed with suspicion. Some critics began to regard his work as outdated and overly melodramatic. In 1971, Kurosawa attempted suicide.

It is a further tribute to Akira Kurosawa that his recovery from the depths of the depression that had led to his suicide attempt was to result in the achievement of a new level of success that surpassed even his previous one. In 1975, he found

Akira Kurosawa

Chicago Tribune but "also of the culture of Kurosawa's youth and young manhood, a meditation, like the films of his longtime model, John Ford, on a vanished past."

More popular internationally than in his native Japan, Kurosawa was courted many times by the Hollywood establishment. And although he was contracted to codirect a binational production of *Tora! Tora! Tora!* (1970), he left the project over a controversy with the producers and never came to Hollywood. In 1990, the Motion Picture Academy presented Kurosawa with an Honorary Award for cinematic accomplishments that have inspired, delighted, enriched, and entertained worldwide audiences and influenced filmmakers throughout the world. Two years later Kurosawa received the D. W. Griffith Award from the Directors Guild of America.

On Sunday, the 6th of September, 1998, the director was felled by a stroke at the age of 88. The world mourned his loss, and the Japanese government awarded him the People's Honor Award, a national prize given for high cultural achievement.

Kurosawa's experimental *Rashomon* is demonstrative of that achievement and deserves special attention. Kurosawa combined two short stories by Akutagawa: "In a Grove," which provides the basis for the main story, and "Rashomon," which constitutes the frame of the main narrative. The film's title refers to the Rajomon gate in Kyoto, a main gate to the outer precincts of an ancient capital. Essentially, the central action involves a murder and the presumed rape of a young princess, the details of which are continually contradicted by the differing accounts given by the participants and witnesses. It not only opened the floodgates of Japanese cinema to the West, but also its treatment of the theme of the subjective relativity of truth has never been surpassed, although director MARTIN RITT took a crack at it when he directed a loose adaptation, *The Outrage* (1964). "Human beings are unable to be honest with themselves about themselves," writes Kurosawa. "They cannot

regained respect with *Dersu Urzala,* a film made in the USSR. *Kagemusha* (*The Shadow Warrior*), his tale of a man who serves as a "double" for a dead feudal lord, won the Golden Palm from Cannes in 1980. In 1985, his version of *King Lear,* titled *Ran,* was released and later received an Oscar nomination for best director in 1986. Kurosawa's other films of this period include *Akira Kurosawa's Dreams* (1990), *Hachigatsu no Kyoshikyoku* (*Rhapsody in August* [1991]), and *Madadayo* (*No, Not Yet* [1993]). The latter film, set in Tokyo during World War II and the postwar era, was a portrait not only of a teacher, Michael Wilmington wrote in the talk about themselves without embellishing. . . . Egoism is a sin the human being carries with him from birth; it is the most difficult to redeem." Interestingly, Joseph Anderson and Donald Richie point out that this theme "is essentially un-Japanese," running "contrary to the prevailing philosophy of Japanese" filmmakers. Thus, even within his own culture, Kurosawa was a completely original talent. He has left a legacy of over 30 films that future generations may continue to enjoy.

"I don't really like talking about my films," Kurosawa once said. "Everything I want to say is in the film itself; for me to say anything more is, as the proverb goes, like 'drawing legs on a picture of a snake.'" However, Kurosawa's autobiographical essay, *Something Like an Autobiography,* published in 1982, contains many interesting insights into the man and his work.

Other Films   *Men Who Tread on the Tiger's Tail* (*Tora no o wo fumu otokotachi* [1945]); *No Regrets for Our Youth* (*Waga seishun ni kuinashi*) and *Those Who Make Tomorrow* (*Asu o tsukuru hitobito* [both 1946]); *Drunken Angel* (*Yoidore tenshi* [1948]); *The Bad Sleep Well* (*Warui yatsu hodo yoku nemuru* [1960]); *Dodes'ka-den* (1970).

References   Anderson, Joseph L., and Donald Richie, *The Japanese Film: Art and Industry* (Princeton, N.J.: Princeton University Press, 1982); Ficarra, Carmen, "The Director's Heart: Akira Kurosawa, 1910–1998," *MovieMaker Magazine* 31 (December 1998); Kurosawa, Akira, *Something Like an Autobiography* (New York: Knopf, 1982); Prince, Stephen, *The Warrior's Camera: The Cinema of Akira Kurosawa* (Princeton, N.J.: Princeton University Press, 1991); Richie, Donald, *The Films of Akira Kurosawa* (Berkeley: University of California Press, 1969); Sato, Tadao, *Currents in Japanese Cinema* (Tokyo: Kodansha Intl., 1987).

—D.K.

Kusturica, Emir (1955–)   Emir Kusturica

has alternately been called an auteur, iconoclast, dreamer, and politico. His films reflect his idiosyncratic personality, having been called both humanistic and surrealistic. Still, Kusturica is generally regarded as an adventurous, daring, and visionary filmmaker whose works are universally lauded even when they induce impassioned criticism.

Kusturica was born on November 24, 1955, in Sarajevo and later studied directing at the Prague Film School. His experiences growing up in Yugoslavia help shape his films, which are grounded very much to his homeland. Kusturica started his career with a couple of television movies before his first theatrical release, *Do You Remember Dolly Bell?* (1981), gained him international notice, winning the Golden Lion award at the Venice Film Festival. The film presents a recurring theme in his subsequent works: growing up, a rite of passage, and initiation into adulthood. Of his themes, Kusturica has said, "I like simple people, natural people, emotional people, people who are ready to sacrifice or who you are ready to sacrifice. Intellectuals don't mean anything to me." Kusturica doesn't consider himself an artist, insisting "I am a craftsman. I was always starting with my wishes to do something about human beings and about the position of outsiders in every kind of society." These people interact to create vignettes applicable to various other people and cultures. Though *Dolly Bell* is a coming-of-age comedy, the film is also political, taking subtle jabs at communism.

Kusturica's next film, *When Father Was Away on Business* (1985), is also a coming-of-age story with slight political overtones. The film was enthusiastically received, earning best picture at Cannes and receiving an Oscar nomination for best foreign film. The story is seen through the eyes of a six-year-old boy, whose father has been sent away into exile for three years. Set in the early 1950s after Tito's split with Stalin, the film details the young boy's maturation through familial and political strife.

Time of the Gypsies (1988) is another coming-of-age story but deals more explicitly with the fascinating lives of gypsies. In telling the story of a young gypsy boy who becomes involved in the criminal lifestyle, Kusturica dots his film with an odd and colorful assortment of characters who are strange, comic, and magical (similar to characters in all his films), which is why Kusturica has often been compared with Fellini. Still, it is a unique and personal film with emotionally charged individuals searching for a place in society and the world. The film earned Kusturica a best director award at Cannes, and in 1989 he was awarded the Roberto Rossellini Prize for lifetime achievement in film—at age 34.

After teaching at Columbia University for a couple of years—and failing to make a Hollywood movie—Kusturica returned to Yugoslavia, found his country in turmoil, and made *Underground* (1995), his most ambitious and overtly political film. The movie is a wild, surreal phantasmagoria of sights and sounds spanning 50 years of Yugoslav history, from World War II postwar reconstruction and the corruption of Tito's regime to the Balkan wars of the early 1990s. The film centers upon the friendship between two Serb-speaking gangsters, who are, by turns, revolutionaries, guerrillas, and black-marketeers. The film was highly praised, winning best picture at Cannes, but also criticized by many for its pro-Serbian sympathies. (Kusturica is Bosnian.) Generally, critics thought Kusturica should have documented the Serbian atrocities against his countrymen. One critic went so far as to call him "Karadzic's Riefenstahl." Kusturica discussed and defended *Underground* as a lament for his country, concerning a war in which all sides are culpable. For the film's style, he cites Orwell,

Kafka, Tarkovsky, and Leone. "I was attacked for what I was fighting against in my movie," Kusturica said, "which is the final, ultimate craziness that exists today. I was attacked for bringing propaganda into a movie that is fundamentally against propaganda." As a result of the constant attacks, Kusturica announced his retirement from filmmaking. That retirement was not permanent: Kusturica returned to another story of gypsy life with *White Cat, Black Cat* (1998).

Kusturica has a definitive style that makes his films comic, strange, and dramatic representations of human activity. Often politically charged but still highly personal, the films express notions of desire, hope, escape, and resurrection. "I put a lot of experience in my movies," Kusturica says. "If you have people in a scene just exchanging information, it's nothing. But if you put people in the context of changing energies, emotions, that's the thing. That's meaning." Indeed, it is the human element that makes Kusturica's films universal. With only a few movies to his name, Emir Kusturica has established himself as the most important Balkan filmmaker today.

Other Film *Arizona Dream* (1993).

References Dieckmann, Katherine, "When Kusturica Was Away on Business," *Film Comment* 35 (1997): 44–49; Pachasa, Arlene, "Kusturica," *American Film* 15 (1990): 40–42; Wrathall, John, "Gypsy Time," *Sight and Sound* 12 (1999): 10–13; Yarovskaya, Marianna, "Underground," *Film Quarterly* 51 (1997): 50–54.

—W. V.